Voice and Gender

and other contemporary issues in professional voice and speech training

presented by the Voice and Speech Review

The official Journal of the Voice and Speech Trainers Association

Voice and Speech Review Editorial Staff

Mandy Rees, Editor-in-Chief
  California State University, Bakersfield

Ethics, Standards and Practices
Barry Kur, Associate Editor
  The Pennsylvania State University

Heightened Speech, Verse and Scansion
David Carey, Associate Editor
  Royal Academy of Dramatic Art
Rena Cook, Associate Editor
  University of Oklahoma

Pedagogy and Coaching
Paul Meier, Associate Editor
  University of Kansas

Private Studio Practice
Jack Horton, Associate Editor
  Presenter's Studio

Pronunciation, Phonetics, Linguistics, Dialect/Accent Studies
Lynn Watson, Associate Editor
  University of Maryland—Baltimore County

Reviews and Sources
Karen Ryker, Associate Editor
  University of Connecticut

Singing
Wendy DeLeo LeBorgne, Associate Editor
  Blaine Block Institute for Voice Analysis and Rehabilitation

Vocal Production, Voice Related Movement Studies
Marth Munro, Associate Editor
  Tshwane University of Technology

Voice and Speech Science, Vocal Health
Ronald C. Scherer, Associate Editor
  Bowling Green State University

Special Topic—Voice and Gender
Michael J. Barnes, Guest Associate Editor
  Wayne State University

Production Editor
Julia Guichard
  Miami University

Assistant Production Editor—Photo Processing
Eric Armstrong
  York University

Founding Editor-in-Chief
Rocco Dal Vera
  University of Cincinnati

Cover artwork: graphic assistance provided by
Marilyn Stone.

Citation Information

Title: Voice and Gender and other
contemporary issues in professional voice
and speech training presented by the Voice
and Speech Review
Editor: Rees, Mandy
Date: 2007
ISBN: 978-0-9773876-1-8

Publisher: Voice and Speech Trainers
Association, Incorporated, Cincinnati, OH
Description: The official journal of the Voice
and Speech Trainers Association containing
articles on a wide variety of issues in professional voice and speech use and training, many
centered on the issues of voice and gender as
they relate to training actors and working with
clients. 410 pages, 8.5" x 11", 100+ b&w photos,
paperback.

Correspondence

US Mail, Shipping
Mandy Rees
Theatre Department
California State University, Bakersfield
9 MUS
9001 Stockdale Highway
Bakersfield, CA 93311-1022

Telephone:
(661) 654-2240, ms
(661) 654-6901, fax

Email:
mrees@csub.edu

The Voice and Speech Review is an official publication of the Voice and Speech Trainers
Association (VASTA), Inc.

VASTA is a non-profit organization and also
a focus group of the Association for Theatre
in Higher Education (ATHE).

From the Editor

A person's voice and speech conveys a remarkable amount of information. This is no news, of course, to voice and speech trainers. Emotion, personality, age, education, health, where a person was raised and resides...these are among the myriad of things we learn from listening closely. Also reflected in a voice is gender, and gender and the issues surrounding it compose the central topic explored within these pages.

What are our expectations regarding how a female voice should sound? What makes a male voice male? What characteristics are unique to each? What vocal issues does each gender face? When a performer must play a role outside his/her gender, what does this require? How does sexual identity affect the voice? How can a vocal trainer assist transgendered individuals in their vocal transition?

I remember encountering the Roy Hart techniques for the first time, about fifteen years ago in a VASTA sponsored summer workshop in North Carolina. Imagine being given not only permission but also encouragement to explore pitches outside your normal range. I traveled down the piano keys to the "masculine" notes and left behind my conception of what my female voice should sound like. From gravelly low moans to squeaky high pops, we were challenged to make all kinds of sounds, both the grotesque and the sublime. Often the sounds seemed to come from somewhere outside the person, or perhaps because the sounds did not match the person I was seeing, I had trouble marrying the two. We accessed vocal/emotional power and vulnerability through our explorations, and left with more open minds about where our voices could go.

Societal expectations, especially those surrounding gender and sexual identity, can cause us to limit our vocal palette. This in turn limits our ability to express ourselves. Our job as vocal trainers is to help performers and private clients embrace and expand their vocal capabilities by giving them the confidence and tools to do so. I hope the articles to follow will provide some inspiration in this task.

On a personal note, I want to acknowledge what a privilege it has been serving as editor of this publication. It has allowed me to work with and learn from exceptional people from around the globe. I am happy to welcome Rena Cook into this position and wish for her an equally enriching experience.

Voice and Gender

Contents

5

Contents (continued)

Voice and Gender

Cover Articles

VASTA Mission Statement

VASTA is poised to become an exciting international organization and is actively planting seeds for global networking, other cultural involvement and resource-sharing.
Our mission is to:

Practice and encourage the highest standards of voice and speech use and artistry in all professional arenas.

Serve the needs of voice and speech teachers and students in training and practice.

Promote the concept that the art of the voice and speech specialist is integral to the successful teaching of acting and to the development of all professional voice users.

Encourage and facilitate opportunities for ongoing education and the exchanging of knowledge and information among professionals in the field.

VASTA is all about:

Vision
Artistry
Standards of conduct
Training enhancement and
Advocacy for our profession.

The Voice and Speech Review accepts several types of submissions. While one of our primary missions is to publish peer-reviewed scholarship, we are also interested in presenting letters to the editor, opinion pieces, essays, interviews, reviews, poetry and other forms of writing. Material may be submitted to:
Rena Cook
Associate Professor
University of Oklahoma
School of Drama
Norman, OK 73019
renacook@ou.edu

vasta.org - The VASTA Website

Visit www.vasta.org, the VASTA website. The site includes: News & Updates, Resources, Communication and Publications, Professional Index, and Website Details. Any **VASTA** member may list contact information, resume, and teaching philosophy in the Professional Index. The site also includes information on conferences and workshops, links to voice and speech related websites, the Mentoring Program, the Newsletter Archive, and organization Bylaws.

VASTA Publications

Available Online at www.vasta.org:
• *Guidelines for the Preparation of Voice and Speech Teachers*
• *Promotion, Tenure and Hiring Resources*
  — *Typical Job Responsibilities*
  — *Evaluation Guidelines*
  — *Recommended Models for Evaluating Teaching, Creative and Service Activities*
  — *Are You On the Promotion and Tenure Track?*
  — *Documentation*
  — *Suggestions on the Creation of a Teaching Dossier*
  — *Some Questions to Consider Before Accepting a Tenure Track Position*
• *VASTA Professional Index*
• *How to Use a Vocal Coach*
• Online Newsletter Archive
• *VASTA Bylaws*
• Internet Resources for Voice and Speech Professionals
• Conference Information
• VASTA Online Bibliography

VASTA Voice - eNewsletter,
published 5 times a year.
Members — free
Individual Subscription $10.00
Institutional Subscription $20.00

Voice and Speech Review,
published bi-annually
Members — free
Individual Subscription $35.00
Institutional Subscription $35.00

To order any of the above materials consult the VASTA website at:www.vasta.org

We are grateful to the following experts for their close and careful reviews of material submitted to the Journal:
Barbara Acker
Claudia Anderson
Mary Baird
Michael J. Barnes
Cynthia Barrett
Pamela Haig Bartley
Mark Brotherton
Kate Burke
David Carey
Linda Cartwright
Pam Christian
Mel Churcher
Marie-Heleen Coetzee
Susan Conover
Rena Cook
Rocco Dal Vera
Robert Davis
John Franceschina
Carol Freidenberg
Kate Foy
Emily Groenewald
Roger Gross
Daydrie Hague
Laura Hitt
Jack Horton
Nancy Houfek
Phil Hubbard
Mary Irwin
Jim Johnson
Gillyanne Kayes
Dudley Knight
Nancy Krebs
Barry Kur
Wendy DeLeo LeBorgne
Judi Lehrhaupt
Karina Lemmer
Christine Mallinson
Paul Meier
Liz Mills
Wendy Mortimer
Allan Munro
Marth Munro
Richard Nichols
Bonnie Raphael
Ruth Rootberg
Karen Ryker
Steven Satta
Ron Scherer
Robert A. Sloane
Ros Steen
Phil Timberlake
Lesley-Ann Timlick
Judylee Vivier
Lynn Watson
Jill Zager

Editorial *by Phil Thompson*

I attended my first VASTA conference in 1996 and I can clearly recall an impassioned discussion among the membership on the need for VASTA to publish a juried journal. It was a tantalizing idea, that we could articulate the principles of our profession and the fine points of our practice in a forum that would be taken seriously. Still, the organization was only 10 years old and there was no strong tradition of publication in the discipline: it would be a huge undertaking.

What I hadn't bargained on was the force of will generated by the combined energy and intelligence of our members. Joining the board as secretary, I witnessed some of the efforts that went into creating the journal. I saw the departments laid out and editors chosen. Reporting to the board Rocco Dal Vera, our founding editor, reminded us regularly that the journal was more aptly called a "serialized monograph." I should have know that something astounding was on its way. Still I was unprepared to have this massive tome dropped in my hand, and I'm sure, with the present volume in your hand you'll agree that there is more here than we ordinarily expect from a journal.

The editorial plan of *The Voice and Speech Review*, a central, organizing theme but with numerous articles covering ideas outside of that theme, seems a perfect match for our organization. I learned as secretary that we are a group that loves "big conversations." We're unafraid of tackling difficult issues and we don't mind discussing several topics at once. In short, we like to talk.

I'm certain you'll find much that's compelling in the cover topic of "Voice and Gender." It's a topic of considerable personal interest to VASTA members, certainly. Our membership is 75% female and 25% male and the dynamics of gender are made more conspicuous to those of us working in academia where the gender ratio of our home institutions may well be the reverse. But the idea of gender is, of course, broader than "male" and "female." Gender intersects with the work of the voice and speech trainer in numerous ways because voice and gender are inextricably tied to identity. Whether theorizing about the ways we construct our own identity or training student actors to represent a range of identities vocally, we are surrounded by these issues. The articles in this edition bring us a wealth of perspectives and tools for the task. Outside of the cover topic you will find articles that touch on language and identity, the notion of self, even voice and the soul. And, of course, there are articles aplenty that depart entirely from these themes.

Please enjoy our big conversation and I hope that next time you will be moved to add your voice.

❦

9

Editorial *by Michael J. Barnes*

From the Guest Editor

When I was asked to be the Guest Associate Editor for the *Voice and Speech Review* as it tackled subjects of the voice's relation to gender and sexual identities, I was thrilled to help VASTA explore subjects that have fascinated me for years.

In 1995, I decided I wanted to present a workshop at the San Francisco ATHE conference called "Vocalizing Gender." The coordinator at the time mentioned to me that Bonnie Raphael was also interested in exploring these ideas, so I ended up leading a workshop that included Bonnie, Carol Freidenberg, and Ivan Midderigh. In the workshop we discussed cross-gender casting, approaching voice training with the gay or lesbian acting student, voice training for the transgendered client, and expanding vocal ranges beyond preconceived ideas of male and female. This is the point that kicked off my explorations into these studies and caused me to notice my colleagues' interest as well.

Over the past 12 years, I have grown more and more proud of my VASTA colleagues in their growing interest toward approaching these issues in their own special ways. I believe all of us who teach voice recognize how it is the ultimate reflection of one's emotional soul and identity. Thus, it makes perfect sense that we recognize how important the role of the voice is in mirroring a person or character's gender and sexual identity.

The authors who contribute to this journal each bring their own experiences of exploring these expressions of the voice. The included articles cover a wide cross-section of topics that I believe everyone will learn from. Articles move from explorations of actors' discoveries in cross-gender characterization across a wide spectrum to encompass ideas of empowering one's own understanding of sex, gender, and sexuality through his or her voice; and finally land on topics of understanding and assisting the transgendered client to find his or her true voice.

As I watched an episode of 20/20 a few weeks ago, where Barbara Walters was highlighting three families with transgendered children, I realized that our VASTA membership has been leading the way toward understanding the sex/sexuality/gender relationship as it pertains toward vocal expression. Looking through the theatre's mirror to life, we truly are an enlightened group of people. The articles contained within the pages of this issue will help to further illuminate this pathway for all of us. ❦

Michael J. Barnes is Voice and Speech Specialist at Wayne State University and the Hilberry Theatre company. Theatres for which he has coached include Utah Shakespearean Festival, Shakespeare Santa Cruz, Arena Stage, Denver Center Theatre Company, Wilma Theatre, Pearl Theatre, and Colorado Shakespeare Festival. He coaches for television and has acted professionally in regional theatre. In addition, he served as the dialect coach for the feature films *Convicted* and *Broken Bridges*. He has an MFA from The National Theatre Conservatory, BFA from the University of Oklahoma, and is a Certified Associate Teacher of Fitzmaurice Voicework. He has taught at University of Miami, Temple University, the University of Delaware and the University of Central Oklahoma. He assists with the instruction of Fitzmaurice Voicework National Training Workshops.

Pedagogy and Coaching *Paul Meier, Associate Editor*

Editorial Column *by Paul Meier, Associate Editor*

This is my final issue as an associate editor before I give the reins into the capable hands of Jeff Morrison, whose fine article, *Voices of the Cold War*, is one among the seventeen that grace this section of the journal. It has been an honor to have edited this section since the inaugural issue in 2001, but under the press of other commitments, I will step down after this issue.

The reader will find wonderful variety here: more than a third of the articles explore the cover theme of gender, while other topics include ritualized lamentation, voice pedagogy east and west, the use of technology in the teaching of voice, the difficulty the actors face in practicing on their own, using both reason and intuition in teaching Shakespeare, the decline of heightened text on the curricula of British drama schools, and coaching a multi-racial cast in South Africa.

Happy reading!

Paul Meier is Head of Voice and a Professor in the Theatre and Film Department at the University of Kansas. He is Founder and Director of IDEA (International Dialects of English Archive) at www.ku.edu/~idea. He is the author of *Accents and Dialects for Stage and Screen*, and *Dialects of the British Isles*, available with accompanying CDs from Paul Meier Dialect Services at www.paulmeier.com. His "show-specific" dialect CDs are leased world-wide, while he has coached a dozen feature films in the last decade, including Ang Lee's *Ride With The Devil*, and Paul Cox's *Molokai: The Story of Father Damien*.

Applying Theories of Learning Styles and Modalities in the Exploration of Shakespearean Text

Kathy Maes is the Interim Dean, College of Arts and Media, University of Colorado-Denver. Kathy served as dialect coach for four productions for the Royal Shakespeare Company and co-dialect coach with Joan Washington on the Royal National Theatre's Olivier Award-winning production of Arthur Miller's *American Clock*. Kathy has coached such notable actors as Ralph Fiennes, Brenda Blethyn, Sir John Wood, and Pierce Brosnan. In summer 2003, Kathy served as vocal/dialect coach for Sir Peter Hall Company's in London and Bath, England. She served as Head of Voice at the Denver Center Theatre Company prior to coming to UCD in 1992.

To encapsulate the premise of the theories of Learning Styles and Modalities I presented in my first three articles in *The Voice and Speech Review*, all students absorb information to be learned in either a **sensory-intuitive-experiential** way or in an **analytical-reasoning-logical** way, and then process the information taken in by actively using it, or reflectively observing or thinking about it. Further, the information being processed is finally learned through the use of verbal/mental repetition or by actively using the information in a repeated, connected and/or meaningful way.

In summary, there are four basic learning styles preferred by all learners outlined by Bernice McCarthy in her book *The 4MAT System*. **Innovative Learners** take in the information in a concrete manner (observe the reality) and process the learning reflectively (generalize on what they observe); **Analytical Learners** absorb the information in a more abstract way (start with an idea) and process the learning reflectively (generalize on what they observe); **Common Sense Learners** assimilate the information more abstractly (start with an idea) and then experiment with the learning (try things out for themselves); and **Dynamic Learners** prefer to receive the information in a concrete manner (observe the reality) and then experiment with the learning (try things out for themselves). Additionally, learners also have a preference as to what senses they utilize the most in taking in the learning or the experience: visual, aural, or kinesthetic. Good teaching incorporates the use of a variety of experiences and methods that encourages learning across all styles and modalities, providing a "way in" for all learners. By approaching learning in this way, students in turn become more adaptive, creative and effective learners because they have enhanced their ability to learn in a variety of ways and situations.

For actors, Shakespeare's language can present a difficult learning challenge. It is rare that you find an acting student who has a clear approach to unlocking the wonder and mystery of Shakespearean language. It is vitally important that the actor clearly understands what the character is saying in order for the actor to comprehend what it is the character wants. Without this clear understanding, determining acting objectives and actions becomes virtually impossible.

As vocal coaches, we know that one of the best tools we have to aid actors in understanding the complexity of Shakespeare's language is found through the use of scansion. By discovering where Shakespeare has placed the stressed beats in the line will isolate the stressed words in the line, which creates a "Shakespearean Telegram" as it were. This can be found by isolating all the one-syllable words that are stressed beats in the line:

- / - / - / - / - /	
But, soft! What light through yonder window breaks?	**Soft light breaks.**
- / - / - / - /	
It is the east, and Juliet is the sun!	**Is east, is sun.**
- / - / - / - / - /	
Arise fair sun and kill the envious moon,	**Sun kill moon,**
- / - / - / - / - /	
Who is already sick and pale with grief	**Is sick, pale grief**
- / - / - / - / - /	
That thou her maid are more fair than she.	**Thou maid more fair she.**

Pedagogy and Coaching
Applying Theories of Learning Styles and Modalities in the Exploration of Shakespearean Text
by Kathryn G. Maes (continued)

Whenever I teach IPA, I never cease to be amazed at how many students have trouble determining which syllable is stressed in a word. I have developed a way of sensitizing their aural inability of determining stress through a kinesthetic method of reinforcement through beating on the floor or desk as they say the word. I have them alternate the beat on each syllable in the word, and they quickly discover through experimentation which is the "correct" beat and, therefore, where the stressed beat is found in the word. Once that breakthrough is made, they quickly develop the ability to "hear" the stress without having to use the beating technique.

The following is a teaching lesson plan for an initial session for a group of acting students learning scansion for the first time across the four Learning Styles and the three Modalities. The plan is designed to help the students: 1) develop an awareness of a stressed versus an unstressed beat, 2) develop an understanding of the four two-beat feet used by Shakespeare in his iambic pentameter line, and 3) develop the skill of determining what possible feet might be used within a given selection (the actor may have to make a choice as to which of the possible feet to use based on a character or acting choice).

I have discovered in teaching scansion that almost all students benefit from starting with the Concrete Approach which requires that they first learn to "hear" the stressed versus the unstressed beats in a highly kinesthetic way, which is strongly supported by the aural modality (i.e., simultaneously "hearing" the beat and then exploring it in a kinesthetic way). All students participate in all activities regardless of their particular Learning Style and Modality preference. At some point in the session, all Learning Styles and modalities are addressed and explored, creating a "hook" for all learners.

Introductory Session for Student Actors Learning Scansion

Goal of the Session: To develop an awareness of: 1) a stressed versus the unstressed beat, 2) the four two-beat feet used in Shakespeare's Iambic Pentameter, and 3) the possible two-beat feet that could be used in a given selection.

I. Taking in the Material: Discovering the difference between a stressed and an unstressed poetic beat and delineating the four possibilities of a two-beat foot.
  A. Concrete Approach—observe the reality (accommodates Innovative and Dynamic Learners):
    1. Have the students sit on the floor and listen to a variety of two syllable words (either live or recorded)—**accommodates Aural Modalities.** As the words are spoken, have them beat out the rhythm of the word with the same hand (either right or left)—**accommodates Kinesthetic Modalities.** This helps them feel the two beats contained

in the word (not necessarily to determine the stressed versus the unstressed beat).
    2. Once they have felt the two beats in the word, the next step is to help them determine which syllable in the word receives the strongest stress. Repeat the list of two syllable words, and as you say them, do each word two ways: first use the correct stress on the word (e.g., "before"—[bɪˈfɔər]); then the incorrect stress (e.g., [ˈbiːfɔər]). By using the right hand beat for the strong stress and the left hand beat for the weak or unstressed beat, have the students beat on the floor left, right for the first pronunciation; then right, left for the second pronunciation—**accommodates both Aural and Kinesthetic Modalities.**

  B. Abstract Approach—start with an idea (accommodates Analytical and Common Sense Learners)
    1. Create a list of two-beat feet words both iambic (unstressed-stressed [- /] e.g., "before") and trochaic (stressed-unstressed [/ -] e.g., "people"). Give each student a copy of the list and have them mark the beat on their own. The stressed beat is marked with a straight line [/] and the unstressed beat is marked with a dash [-]. Demonstrate an example: ("before"— [- /] "people"— [/ -])—**accommodates both Visual and Kinesthetic Modalities.**
    2. Ask the class what two additional combinations might exist that use stressed and an unstressed beats. Give some examples (e.g., "ice cream" [/ /], versus "to the" [- -]). Have the class break into small groups to create a list of words of two syllables or two-word two-beat phrases that present how the stressed and unstressed beats are used in various combinations (e.g. "until" [- /]; "table" [/ -]; "true minds" [/ /]; "of a" [- -]).

II. Processing the Material: Applying the use of the four two-beat feet possibilities in the Shakespearean text
  A. Using the Material Reflectively—generalize on what they observe (accommodates Innovative and Analytical Learners
    1. Pass out a short selection from Shakespeare, hopefully one that contains the use of all four two-beat feet. Work through the selection, and allow students to present all possible feet, according to the rules of scansion (see "A Shakespearean Scansion Key Ring" included in the previous issue). For example, do not accept an unnatural stress on a given word ("Nature" can't be pronounced [neɪˈtʃɝ]). They may use any of the techniques used in the sessions (e.g., beating on the floor to discover the beats, etc.)—**accommodates the Aural, Visual and Kinesthetic Modalities.**

```
  -   /  -  /  -  /  -  /  -  /
Thou, Nature, art my goddess; to thy law
  -  /  - -  /   /      /   -   -   /
My services are bound. Wherefore should I
  /   -  -   /   -  /  -   -   -  /
Stand in the plague of custom, and permit
  -   - -  /  -  /  -   -   -  /   -
The curiosity of nations to deprive me.... (or possibly)


  /    /  -  /  -  /   -   -  /  /
Thou, Nature, art my goddess; to thy law
 /  /  - -  /   /       /    -  /  /
My services are bound. Wherefore should I
  /   -   -   /   -  /  -   /   -  /
Stand in the plague of custom, and permit
  -   - -/-/  -  /  -   /  -  /   -
The curiosity of nations to deprive me....
```
                    (*King Lear*, Act 1: Scene 2, lines 1-4)

These are only two of the many possibilities you will see. At this point it is not critical if they have included too many beats in the line, as they have not been introduced to the concept of elision, or any of the rules of scansion for that matter. Those concepts will be introduced and explored in future sessions. The focus is solely on developing the understanding of the possible two-beat feet at this time.

B. Using the Material Experimentally—try things out for themselves (accommodates Common Sense and Dynamic Learners)

1. Give students each a four-line verse from Shakespeare and have them work individually on the selection, discovering as many possibilities as they can regarding the use of the two-beat feet in the selection.

2. Ask them to do one final version that represents to them the best use of the possible two-beat feet. Have each of them read their selection aloud. Have a discussion with the group around the following issues:

    a. Were any of the words mispronounced because the wrong syllable was stressed?

    b. Were certain readings of the selections more effective than others? If so, why?

It is extremely important that the students first experience the rhythm of the feet and develop a strong kinesthetic sensitivity to the line before they can move to the next level in the scansion process. They must discover that the two-beat feet are the building blocks of the line's rhythm, and the culminating rhythm of the speech provides the backbone for clarity of meaning and emotion upon which character is built and acting choices are made. The absence of this connected

internal rhythm will make the speech seem "disembodied," confusing and difficult to understand, offering no help in delineating character and action. On the other hand, once the actors have discovered the connected pulse and rhythm contained in the line (whether it is a regular or irregular beat), this will free them to explore the full range of emotions and objectives of the characters in a highly kinesthetic and unforgettable way. Scansion is the key to the demystification and discovery of the power found in the "heartbeat" of Shakespeare's language. Applying the theories of Learning Styles and Modalities provide the pathway for the learning to take place.

❧

Bibliography
McCarthy, Bernice. *The 4MAT System: Teaching to Learning Styles with Right/Left Mode Technique.* Barrington, IL: Excel, Inc., 1987.

Column *by Robert Barton*

Many "Right" Ways: Honoring Diverse Teaching Methods and Learning Modes

Gender Phone Speak

It is estimated that women use an average of 22,000 words each day while men average 8,000. This contrast is supported by empirical research I have done regarding messages left for my twenty-year old son on our answering machine. Here is a typical female friend's recording: "Hi Drew. This Celina. How's it going? I was wondering if you might like to hang out sometime this week. Late afternoons are good for me, pretty much every day. But some evenings work too. What about you? So give me a call and we'll figure something out, OK? Talk to you soon. Bye!" Here is a typical male friend: "Drew, it's Alex. Call me."

A second common contrast in these recordings is that the young woman, almost without exception uses what I call a "baby voice," high pitched, hesitant, and constantly upward inflecting. The young man often uses what I call a "non-voice," low, rapid, virtually uninflected. What would the subtext behind these choices be? The first might be "I am trying to come across as harmless, vulnerable, and nice. I don't want any of my vocal choices to imply that I am remotely stuck-up, pushy or mean." The second potential subtext might be "I am trying to seem matter-of-fact, mature, and cool or at least not sound like a geek."

My initial reaction was amazement at how retro all this seems. Haven't we come much farther along in our thinking than to fall into such flagrant sexual stereotypes? But the statistics and the voice machine do not lie. Something is going on here.

If these callers were non-theatre folk (or, as we call them in our house, "civilians") the contrast would not surprise me so much. But nearly all these friends were actively involved in theatre in high school and are now majoring in it in college. All have training. I have been present in the audience and heard most of them use voice and speech in powerful, rooted, and varied ways. I have heard the women speak with authority in roles like Electra and Lady Macbeth. I have heard the men speak parts such as Romeo and Cyrano with emotional availability and music. They are, for better or worse, making a choice to sound a certain way on voicemail.

I doubt these choices permeate all encounters, but may pop up when there is a disconnect of some kind. The fact that the person called does not answer and that someone else may hear this message first causes a shift in delivery. Unfortunately, these same choices may be made when meeting a total stranger, particularly someone in a power position who may be potentially intimidating, particularly one who may or may not cast you.

When we examine voice/speech and gender, the desire to use many words or few, which apparently is quite different for most men and women, is a noteworthy variable. And when actors do not have a designated character to play, it is important to examine how they choose to characterize themselves. I am certain that all these young women did not have a meeting where they made a group choice regarding "phone speak" and am even more certain that the men did not meet or vote. Something in our culture influences a sameness in this context. I would suggest that our actor training and specifically our voice

Robert is professor emeritus and continues to teach acting at the University of Oregon. He is the author of the widely used texts *Acting: Onstage and Off, Style for Actors,* and (with Rocco Dal Vera) *Voice: Onstage and Off* as well as numerous articles. He is the recipient of the ATHE's Best Book Award as well as ACTF's Outstanding Acting Coach award. He has acted professionally in most of the plays of Shakespeare and has directed half of them. His new texts *Theatre in Your Life* and *Life Themes* will be published next year.

and speech classes would benefit from examining gender tendencies, conditioning, and areas of unfortunate conformity.
We should not stop with helping actors to fulfill characters as
written, but also provide mentoring in how they choose to
present themselves in social encounters, including phone calls.

Most college Acting 1 students do not arrive with a full range
of secondary theatre experience and training. If the tendencies
noted above are this common among young experienced
actors, they are even more likely to be firmly embedded with
those who are not, and may bleed over into scripted role-play-
ing rather than simply social interaction. Since I write books
with titles ending in phrases such as "Onstage and Off" or "In
Your Life," I must admit to a bias regarding actor training that
goes beyond theatre to helping one learn to act one's life better. Many of our students will not pursue professional careers,
but practically all of them will wish to be effective on the
phone, in basic interactions with strangers, in getting job
interviews and then interviewing successfully. Those that do
pursue acting careers will often need to master these encounters before even getting a chance to audition.

Actors need to relax and be more truly themselves in
interview/audition settings as well as "cold calls" where
judgment and fear of rejection can influence us to come across
the exact opposite. Of course, by "more truly themselves" I
mean on a good day when we are relatively full of the joy of
life and believe we have what it takes. Some days, we feel so
unlike that, that we may need to role play, but this should be
a role we are always ready to play, not one that requires excessive effort. Many young actors do not understand how important it is to carry the old admonition "It's show time!" into
contexts beyond opening night. Actor training can focus on
helping us achieve this state. When we speak on the phone
and perhaps even more so to a machine, we need to get into
our voice a sense of the genuine, complex, interesting person
we are. Actors and others who do so will be miles ahead of
those who do not.

So a part of each actor's self-analysis should be understanding
the circumstances under which he or she tends to revert to
gender stereotype, lack of disclosure, and overly conformist
choices. I suggest that students will benefit significantly by
being asked to answer these questions:

—How do my vocal choices differ when I act a role from
when I am myself?
—What are my life circumstances in which I take on certain
habits that tend to limit the depth and range of the impression I am making?

—What do I sound like on the phone? Is this impression in
any way deceptive?
—How does this impression differ depending on whether I
am speaking to a machine, a stranger or someone known
to me?
—How do these choices alter in other direct encounters, particularly when I am speaking with someone for the first time?
—Do I fall into any gender cliché behavior? If so, under what
circumstances and what exactly is that behavior?
—What do I want my basic vocal characterization to be like?
How far is this from the choices I now make?

Many actors will be clueless about themselves and draw blanks
for these questions, so will need to ask friends and fellow
actors to observe them. Teacher feedback, while valuable, is
likely to be limited to classroom context, so those who have
hung out with said subject in various outside activities, need
to step up. Classmates could be assigned to be responsible for
researching and providing this information to each other, possibly even imitating or demonstrating what they have
observed. Perhaps women and men in class can identify and
act out what they have observed as the more stereotypical
behavior of the opposite sex among classmates. Each actor
should be encouraged to focus on the vocal lives of his or her
public persona as part of the performance process.

Going back to the tendency for men and women to choose to
use widely differing numbers of words, it may be that with
relatively inexperienced performers some organic learning is
needed to help break through stingy word tendency. A young
contemporary male actor tackling his first Shakespearean
monolog, probably a character for whom abundant and eloquent use of language is essential, may need to learn first and
foremost what it is like to need to speak at that level. A young
woman playing Greek tragedy may need to organically comprehend powerful impulses that overcome any tendency
toward self-conscious girlish digression and qualification in
favor of direct confrontation. Some boys may need to learn to
want to use many words. Some girls may need to learn to
want to take no prisoners. The character analysis process and
use of the "magic if" is to recognize when the vocal tendencies
of the character are far different from our own and then to
embrace their tendencies organically as if they were our own.

In some acting programs, an attempt at political correctness
leads to a refusal to acknowledge any significant differences in
behavior patterns between sexes. I would suggest we will serve
our students far better by acknowledging these differences can-
didly, encouraging self-analysis, and then working to head
these differences off at the pass.

Peer Reviewed Article *by Leigh Wilson Smiley*

Cowboy Resonance in America

This article explores how an American myth, in particular the myth of the cowboy, resonates in the voices of many of the young American men I have trained in Conservatory and actor training programs. I will discuss two specific models of the cowboy iconography affecting the development of young men's voices. One is the silent individualist model—the man who rides into the sunset to a life of lonely hardship. The second model is that of the heroic conqueror of the frontier—the Charles Bronson, Lee Marvin, "tough it out" and "stay the course" tight-jawed model. These iconic characters have a powerful and distinct resonance in young men's voices today. Specifically, the cowboy resonance is characterized by a marked lack of expressivity in the voice, a severely limited vocal range, a lack of movement of the front of the face and articulator muscles, and a gruff voice that lives in the back of the throat, expressed either as a mere mumble or as a vocal attack.

How does the American cowboy image impact the vocal training of young men who are learning to become actors and vocally expressive artists? Voice experts work with the premise that there are hundreds of environmental, physical, psychological, spiritual, and cultural forces that influence the development of an individual's voice. In this field we are intimately aware of how environment and image affect the physiognomy, breath and vocal choices of our students. These factors often manifest in habits and systems of survival that limit the actor's expressive instrument. Image affects thought, thought affects breath, and breath affects voice. Cultural and gender images, even images that are not current in the conscious mind, do influence the unconscious mind and thereby the voice.

People acquire (and sometimes reject) the vocal habits and characteristics of the family, culture, peer group, region and environment from which they emerge. Usually, the voice reflects socially accepted, gender-based stereotypes and mirrors cultural expectations of what men and women "should" sound like. For American men, this can mean pushing the voice down into a chest resonance that may not be a natural vocal placement for their individual instrument. For American women it can mean tightening the vocal apparatus to acquire a higher, lighter resonance and tone. Numerous books about voice and about the psychology of girls and boys have examined these particular frequencies and the social advantages and disadvantages they produce for men and women. How we speak, resonance, accent, physical and vocal presence affect how we are perceived and progress through social and work environments. To be vocally different from the predominant icon of maleness or femaleness in any culture is to stand out from the crowd. When we are in the process of discovering and defining who we are in adolescence (just as hormones kick in and voice changes occur) it is a rare choice to stand out and be different. Most young people seek community and acceptance. My observation is that the standard icon of manliness, the cowboy, becomes a hook for young men that influences their sound and becomes a significant hurdle in the initial training of these young men for the theatre.

In youth we look to role models to create who we will be and to mirror back to us who we would like to become. Being able to freely express one's self is a process of knowing and trusting who we are. We hear and absorb other voices, and refract the voices we hear through our own instrument. If lucky, we listen to and are heard by people who are like us and who become our

Leigh Wilson Smiley is an Assistant Professor in the Department of Theatre's Performance Program at the Univ. of Maryland. Leigh has voice/dialect/text coached and consulted at John F. Kennedy Center for the Performing Arts, The Folger Shakespeare Theatre, Arena Stage, People's Light and Theatre, Walnut Street Theatre, Olney Theatre, Philadelphia Shakespeare Festival, Shakespeare & Company, Comprehensive Language Center, Inc., and The Corporate Theatre (London). She has taught at Emerson College, NYU Experimental Theatre Wing, Fordham Lincoln Center, Univ. of Pennsylvania, Univ. of the Arts and the Linklater Studio. In 2006 she was a guest teacher in Aberstwyth, Wales at the internationally acclaimed *Giving Voice* Festival. In 2007 Leigh will be voice and text coaching at the Folger Shakespeare and Off-Broadway at the Micheal Weller Theatre.

role models. What happens though, if we are not hearing ourselves reflected in the culture? If verbal story and theatre (nowadays mostly film, television and print ads) mirror to us our own nature, what does the American male hear and see? Is he in fact getting a distorted image of masculinity thrust back at him and how does this affect his voice? The Marlboro man ad campaign (cowboy on a horse) is the most successful image in American marketing history. It whispers into the ears of many a young man. In observing the concept of male identity, the author Susan Faludi states that:

> …the internal qualities once said to embody manhood—sure footedness, inner strength, confidence of purpose—are merchandised back to men to enhance their manliness. The more productive aspects of manhood, such as building or cultivating or contributing to a society, could not establish a foothold on the shiny flat surface of a commercial culture looking-glass before which men could only act out a crude semblance of masculinity (Faludi 1999, 543).

Herb Goldberg suggests:

> It is very much in style today to urge men to feel. However this urging is partially reminiscent of taunting a crippled man to run…It is unlikely that a mere act of will on his part can unlock the hurricane of repressed feelings within him. Today's man is the product of massive, defensive operations against feelings…He controls himself by denying himself (Goldberg 1976, 68-69).

Roger Horrocks states:

> This is the cryptic message of masculinity: don't accept who you are. Conceal your weakness, your tears, your fear of death, your love for others. Conceal your impotence. Conceal your potency (Horrocks 1994, 25).

All three of these authors, specialists in gender studies, are describing the qualities that define the American cowboy.

The leading authorities in the training of the voice for the actor, (Kristin Linklater, Cicely Berry, Patsy Rodenberg, and Catherine Fitzmaurice) are women, and VASTA members are predominantly women. Does this reality have an effect on young men's voices? I am aware that my students, on a conscious or unconscious level will, to a certain degree, try to emulate my sound. Given this fact, how profoundly does teacher gender imbalance affect young male trainees' voices and does having a vocally expressive male voice teacher change the cowboy dynamic in the young male student's voices? In addition, most young men do not encounter a male teacher in their early schooling until junior high and high school. The

NEA website <*http://www.nea.org/teachershortage/03malefactsheet.html*> states:

> According to NEA research, just 24.9 percent of the nation's 3 million teachers are men. And over the last two decades, the ratio of males to females in teaching has steadily declined. The number of male teachers now stands at a 40-year low. The percentage of male teachers in elementary schools has fallen regularly since 1981—that year, it reached an all-time high of 18 percent. **Today, a scant 9 percent of elementary school teachers are men** (bolding mine). Likewise, the percentage of males in secondary schools has fluctuated over the years, but now stands at its lowest level (35 percent).

Combined with the above figures is the fact that at least 50% of marriages end in divorce, and the children, for the most part, go to live with their mothers. Therefore, many young men are not even growing up with adult male resonance in their house. I imagine these factors have an enormous impact on boys' voices.

The cowboy archetype is absorbed into American culture through childhood play, the fashion industry, the growing popularity of Country music, and contemporary movies such as Tommy Lee Jones' *Three Burials*, Ang Lee's *Brokeback Mountain*, Kevin Costner's *Dances with Wolves*, and Clint Eastwood's *Unforgiven*. Politically, the current President of the United States, George W. Bush, aligns himself with the power of the cowboy icon through his use of language and his Texas accent. Regarding terrorists he talks of "smoking out" the baddies and states that they "can run but they can't hide." The cowboy image propagates nationalism and more subtly, it embodies the concept of the male power-broker in our society. Predominant in media, advertisement, fashion, literature and children's play, how could this mythic image not affect how our young men live in their bodies, how they breathe and how they speak? As David Coleman points out in Fashion section of the *New York Times* on March 13, 2005:

> The cowboy is the guy version of blonde…It's a classic icon of manliness. All guys relate to it…It's been romanced forever. I wasn't thinking of some real cowboy out there, but that imaginary image I have of how we expect him to be. You know, the cowboy is in our heads.

Classically, the American cowboy is a mythical figure that embodies and ennobles the positive characteristics of silent sacrifice, quiet courage and unarticulated bravery. When things get bad, they are men of action not words, they pull a punch (or a gun), they suffer, or they ride away, alone, into the sunset. The media images of the cowboy are too numerous to list, but may primarily be exemplified by both fictional and real characters such as the Lone Ranger, General Macarthur,

John Wayne, Lee Marvin, Montgomery Clift, James Dean, and Clint Eastwood. Our current fascination with the American cowboy takes a new turn in Ang Lee's film *Brokeback Mountain* when two cattle wranglers fall in love and sustain, over many years, a long distance relationship that is culturally taboo. But again, they sacrifice and silence their true selves in order to appear heterosexual. In Sergio Leone's *The Good, the Bad and the Ugly*, hardly any dialogue exists at all. Emotion, action, and thought are expressed through eyes and facial twitches—not through voice and words. Charles Bronson, Lee Marvin, Custer, and MacArthur represent the heroic conqueror cowboy model of the cowboy icon. In George W. Bush we have a gun-toting President with a western twang who adopts this powerful archetypal image. For a voice teacher in the theatre, these characteristics, when emulated by young men searching for identity, become habitual limits in expression that may take years to release.

The Birth of Pleasure by Carol Gilligan (one of America's most distinguished writers and teachers in the field of psychology and gender studies) shares case studies of fathers watching and discussing how their sons acquire the "walls" of silence around their feelings and the tough-boy vocal veneer. A palpable sorrow tinges these fathers' stories, as does the question of what the choices of expression are for their sons. These fathers discuss their fear that their sons will be ostracized for their openly emotional voices, and conversely, that in covering their real voices the sons' spirits will be squashed by a culture that expects and embraces the tough-guy model of manhood.

The stability and confidence of American manhood has shifted with the fluctuations of the patriarchal cultural and social systems in which they exist. Stereotypically, American men have been trained to express the rational, and are inarticulate in expressing feelings, as throughout history this has been considered a feminine trait and therefore undesirable. Historically acceptable communicative behavior for young men was the art of rhetoric (attacking or defending a position or thesis). This formal study of oral discourse was used as a means of persuasion and finding "truth." Renowned linguist Walter J. Ong called it "rational level of ceremonial combat" (Borisoff & Merrill 1985, 12). Rhetoric follows the masculine model of being direct, confrontational, logical, and forceful. The men who grew up in America in the 1930s and 1940s had a significantly different social construct in which to develop their vocal selves from the men who grew up in the 1960s and 1970s when the feminist revolution was at a new peak and men were being influenced by this movement. The men who are coming of age now, when "metro-sexual" exemplifies the urban cool male, and cowboy fashion is once again in the magazines and stores—who do they emulate? Who are influences and role models? How do the men in power today

speak? How do they learn to express themselves verbally in this world? Ultimately, for the young actor, how does he find his own voice so he can develop and use it as an artist.

I have found male students in the 14 to 22 year range to be especially inexpressive, using about three notes in the scale, very low frequency and limited use of breath and articulatory muscles. The iconographic, stoic and silent cowboy figures played by Heath Ledger in *Brokeback Mountain* and Tommy Lee Jones in *Three Burials* demonstrate this limited expressive vocal range. Nigel Andrews, film critic for the *Financial Times* asserts about the power of images in his article "The Cowboy Rides Again" (published on December 2, 2005) that "iconic myths":

>…look at us and say: 'We are indestructible. Like humanity, we are riddled with guilt, paradox and complication. But you cannot make us go away. If you try we will come back in another form. But that original form, however ghostly, will always be there: for heads to scratch over its contradictions, for scholars and moralists to probe its defects, for human beings to respond to what was once—and at some level always will be—honest, resonant, idealistic.'

Young men entering actor-training programs are in the middle of discovering who they are as speakers and as men. It is not surprising, therefore, given the strength of the iconic myth of the cowboy, that they frequently enter training with severely curtailed vocal range and limited expressive ability reflecting the cowboy resonance. Not only do I find that the front of the face and articulation muscles have frozen from lack of use (try saying "how dare you" using no lip or face muscle, and then say it again, really using these muscles and you will get a feel for the difference between muscles that pick up impulse and those that don't), but also the emotional range of the voice has atrophied from lack of use. Cowboys do not cry—this is a given, if not spoken fact (big boys don't cry). Their anger is expressed physically through the tight jaw, the fist or the gun. Their fear is not expressed but courageously conquered. Tenderness is reserved for necessary moments of "weakness" around a loved one. Very little feeling is reflected in the face or in the voice of the cowboy. This stoicism of silent feeling, this non-expressiveness, is understood in the genre to define maleness. So where does this leave young men who are entering a field where they will be rewarded for their ability to vocally express and for their very range of expression?

Given the choices of icons and the predominance of the cowboy image, I think many of the challenges American men have in expressing themselves today have to do with an ambiguity about how to express oneself in a culture that clings to a stereotypical style of gender expression. Though other male role models exist in the culture, in the forms of fathers, teachers, brothers, and/or mythical figures from literature or film, young men are treading an unknown path into grown-up territory and searching for the voices that will lead them there. We all seek voices, real or mythical, to emulate. What these voices say and how they say it become the iconic sounds we will emulate.

At a certain stage of maturation, young men become profoundly affected by their peers as well. They frequently find it is not cool to be vocally or physically expressive and to demonstrate feelings of being upset, sad, or angry or even joyful. As Carol Gilligan, states:

> I have seen this wall going up in young boys when their faces no longer register their emotions or let only a few emotions show through, when they steady their voice and adjust its pitch to a few notes that carry the image of themselves they want to project (strong, tough, invulnerable) (Gilligan 2003, 179).

In the United States, young men who follow their muse into the theatre arts are embracing a devalued component of society (the expressive and emotionally-connected voice). It requires a stoic and/or courageous cowboy to enter into the expressive art of theatre! The difficulty for young male students lies in allowing their voices to *reveal* the way they feel and the nuances of their thoughts. It is much more socially acceptable to *describe* what they feel in a neutral tone. When large feeling comes up in text, or as in impulse happens in the actor's body, I often see a strong, physical and muscular clamping-down or tightening in the body; the breathing muscles become taut and held, the actor's head and eyes drop or pull back, and the head is shaken from side to side. In this shaking of the head, I see the actor's body saying "no" to whatever expression of thought/feeling is alive in and emerging from the body. A stiff mask of a smile shows up on his face, and silence ensues. When a large expression releases, it is accompanied by large vocal strain and effort. Neither of these examples works for the actor in that they do not express the pure connection between body, mind, breath and vocal expression and do not directly communicate the state of the character, unless the character, of course, is vocally repressed. Nonetheless, the character can be as limited as the text demands but the actor must strive to work from a place of no limits.

One of my students calls the above behavior his "wall." Expressive feeling—be it anger, sorrow or any mixture of what are often mislabeled as "negative feelings," have been to him so taboo, so frightening in their power and consequence, that he has not allowed himself to give them voice without hurting

his throat by speaking without breath and straining and grinding the vocal musculature. Another young man is unable to release large feeling at all in the context of acting work. He speaks in a breathy voice, his articulation is weak, his physical gesture, posture and vocal/physical energy are those of someone who is placid, non-threatening, and not present. He is a large man of color who yearns to be perceived as sensitive and not as a societal threat. That part of him that is vocally free and expressive has been buried under many layers of protection and is gradually being unearthed. I have another student who was terrified to allow the vocal energy of his thought and feeling out on text because his anger, in the past, had been labeled as "psychotic episodes" for which he'd been medicated. In the lab and through vocal practice he discovered that what had previously been labeled as psychotic was in fact a huge release and with this release came significantly expanded range of expression in his voice. Through his discoveries he is able to express feeling on his voice, is frequently cast in large expressive roles, and speaks and breathes without the old fear of losing control. The cowboy recedes.

So, how do we honor the power of the icon and at the same time open the potential voices of the performers affected by this image? For voice teachers, the answer lies, in part, in overcoming the cultural influence of the cowboy. To be a successful actor, one's voice must carry the subtleties and nuances of thought and feeling. The process of finding the channels for the expression of the whole self requires these young men unlearn many social influences and reclaim their young primary-impulse self. Vocal coaches teach within parameters that ostensibly work for their students in opening range and expression. In my own teaching, this has been accomplished through consistent practice, guided and focused awareness, and a healthy sense of imaginative play. Kristin Linklater's progression of tools, in particular, allow the actor to work from a container of physical awareness, to breath awareness, to sound, amplification, specific resonators, breath and voice power and range to articulation exercises. The very specificity of thought which her tools demand provides a structure through which the actor can safely explore and discover the range, subtlety and power of his own voice as well as the influences that have limited it. I strongly encourage the consistent, daily practice of vocal and physical tools, awareness of self, moment-to-moment shifts in states of being, awareness of habitual physical and mental impulses, and, most fruitfully, a healthy sense of non-judgment and humor. Marrying the inner, whole-body expressive five-year-old, with the mature, rational self allows a huge range of expression to emerge. This marriage usually occurs only with practice, discipline and a very strong desire to communicate. Ultimately, awareness is all. When one is aware of how one speaks and how it is perceived by others, then choice can step in. The desire to be understood, the desire to communicate translates to practice and awareness and can break the young actor from the bonds of stereotypical models of expression into a seemingly limitless range of vocal expressivity and role possibilities.

The American cowboy image really is one of the mind. It is through the acts of voice and speech, articulating one's thoughts and feelings, that we gain the power to affect other people's thoughts and feelings. Finding ways to empower men to find healthy, free and expressive voices potentially opens up a new definition of American masculinity.

Bibliography:

Borisoff, Deborah, and Merrill, Lisa. *The Power to Communicate: Gender Differences as Barriers*. Illinois: Waveland Press, 1985.

Faludi, Susan. *Stiffed: The Betrayal of the Modern Man*. London: Chatto and Windus, 1999.

Gilligan, Carol. *The Birth of Pleasure, A New Map of Love*. New York: Vintage Books, 2003.

Goldberg, Herb. *The Hazards of Being Male: Surviving the Myth of Masculine Privilege*. New York: Nash, 1976.

Horrocks, Roger, *Masculinity in Crisis: Myths, Fantasies and Realities*. New York: St. Martins Press, Inc., 1994.

Essay *by John Kenneth DeBoer*

Getting the Gay Out: Addressing Sexual Identity in the Voice Classroom

John Kenneth DeBoer is a third year Master of Fine Arts Candidate at Virginia Commonwealth University studying with Janet Rodgers. During his time in Richmond he has coached several productions and taught various courses, including the cross-disciplinary performance course which will be the subject of his thesis, "Camp: Ridiculous Theatre as Serious Drama". A life-long native of South Bend, Indiana and the University of Notre Dame, he elected to attend Indiana University and Bloomington where he received his Bachelor of Arts in Theatre and Drama with a minor in Speech and Hearing Sciences in 2004.

My first assignment as a graduate student in the Theatre Pedagogy program at Virginia Commonwealth University was assistant vocal coach to Janet Rodgers. The play was *Wait Until Dark* by Frederick Knott and a diverse group of student actors with varying backgrounds and levels of experience was cast in the thriller about a blind woman who defends herself against a gang of conmen pursuing a hidden stash of drugs. The villainous Harry Roat—originally played by Robert Duvall in the 1966 Broadway production[1]—was portrayed by a young African-American actor, while the role of Gloria—traditionally played by a child actress of 9 or 10 years—was reinvented by a deaf adult actress as a mentally-challenged adult. While both of these choices were notable, the casting of a gay male actor as the suave and presumably heterosexual conman, Mike Talman, sparked my pedagogical interest the most.

When I learned of this actor's sexual orientation I found myself critiquing his vocal performance in terms of that information, as well as traditional voice and speech elements. Was I participating in some hegemonic process that labels Gay, Lesbian, Bisexual, and Transgender [GLBT] individuals as divergent? As a gay vocal coach, I try to be diplomatic when someone makes a crack that a person's voice is "too gay." However, in this case, my bias stemmed from the fact that, in the beginning, this gay actor's performance was not nearly gay enough. He used little of the pitch variety often associated with the gay male voice, his resonance seemed to be pressed unnaturally low in his chest, and his physicality was stiff and uncomfortable. This approach certainly avoids the stereotypical flamboyant voice common on television shows such as *Will and Grace* and *Queer Eye for the Straight Guy*. The problem with this tactic is that its result is a cold, rigid, and uninteresting Mike Talman, which is not how he is written in the text. So while flamboyance may not be appropriate, neither is a complete absence of vocal variety. Either the actor had made a poor choice or some deeper block was impeding his performance.

With this in mind, I asked Janet if I could address these concerns with the student one-on-one. Away from the other actors, I asked him the usual questions.
- Who is your character?
- What is he trying to accomplish?
- What vocal tactics could he use to succeed?
His answers to my queries were thoughtful, precise, and supported by the text. It was apparent that the vocal quirks had nothing to do with his intellectual acting process, and they certainly were not present in his voice during the casual chatter of rehearsal breaks. So making my own tactical shift, I began insinuating there might be something he was trying to suppress in his performance. Before I could devise an appropriate way to confront what I believed to be the real issue, he looked me straight in the eye and said, "So you basically want me to *get the gay out?*"

Yes, I wanted him to set "the gay" free instead of using his voice to suppress his sexuality. His vocal tactics up to that point were only serving to smother his character with preconceptions. He was so concerned with performing masculinity and heterosexuality that neither character choice was represented in any meaningful way. The actor and his character are never mutually exclusive, and suppression of the actor's identity leaves little opportunity for the character's identity to develop.

Many facets of an actor's personal identity can manifest themselves in the voice. Culture, race, nationality, class, faith, gender, and sexuality are all part of the palette from which an actor can paint performance identities. Even though this student had chosen to play Mike Talman as a very masculine heterosexual, his performance was enriched when he finally "got the gay out" as he so eloquently put it. His original process was intrinsically flawed. By focusing on the suppression of his own identity, he caused himself unnecessary physical and psychological vocal tension. This psychological tension is akin to the actor who sucks in his stomach to feign the appearance of a flat abdomen at the expense of personal comfort and physical versatility. When I made the student aware that the vocal manifestations of his sexual identity were applicable to his character regardless of whether or not they both desired men, he was able manipulate his sexuality in the same manner an actor controls the other aspects of identity to create a performance.

So, when I refer to *sexual identity*, I am speaking of how a person identifies his or her own sexual orientation in terms of its relation to the dominant standard of heterosexuality—the colloquial nomenclatures gay, straight, lesbian, and bisexual, work well to define sexual identity. Sexual identity is one part the all-encompassing notion of *personal identity*. All facets of identity can then be manifested physically in the voice and body. Physical and vocal manifestations of identity are performances, so manifestations of sexual identity are an individual's *sexual performances*. Sexual performances go hand-in-hand with *gender performances* in that an individual can act traditionally masculine or feminine, but not necessarily with any regard to the genitalia they possess. The adjectives butch, femme, lipstick, bull-dyke, and straight-acting are all examples of gay sexual performances.

For the theatre, an actor creates a *performance identity* which is fashioned to the role being performed using facets of their own personal identity as the foundation. In order to create a multitude of successful performance identities, students must be freed from the notion that one particular identity has more intrinsic worth than another—for instance, masculine behavior does not have more theatrical worth than feminine behavior and vice versa. However the more ignorant the student remains of such possibilities, the greater the likelihood they might make a choice similar to the student actor in *Wait Until Dark*.

Theatre training programs can serve as a forum to introduce students to the diverse spectrum of personal identities, and specifically sexual identities. By identifying these manifestations, the student can then filter them out and create a neutral identity on which to build the performance identity of his or

her character. Ideally this deconstruction and reconstruction process will help the student actor to develop fluid and adaptable performance identities and create characters that are more than an exercise in imitation.

Exploring identity in a voice and speech classroom can correlate with the development of sexual identity in young adults. In *Working with Lesbian, Gay, Bisexual, and Transgender College Students: A Handbook for Faculty and Administrators*, Patricia Sullivan outlines fives stages through which students progress as they become aware of differences in sexual identity: *naiveté, acceptance, resistance, redefinition*, and *internalization*. It can be assumed that most students will come to the voice and speech classroom already aware of their own sexual identity and the fact that not all people share it. This is what Sullivan would call the *resistance stage*. The student actor portraying Mike Talman in *Wait Until Dark* needed to "get the gay out" in order to break free of the resistance stage. He had come to terms with his sexual identity as it related to his personal identity, but resisted integrating it with his performance identity. He appeared so concerned that audiences identify his character as straight, that he was not honoring the textual versatility of Mike Talman's words. This form of resistance is the reverse of the student who acknowledges a regionalism, but refuses to learn how to reduce it for performances.

An effective performance should illuminate the character's identity rather than function as a means to hide the actor's. In this pursuit, the student must learn to identify the manifestations of sexual identity in order to observe objectively how they affect possible performance identities. Pamela R. Hendrick writes, "When we learn how much of gender behavior is learned performance, we come to know more about ourselves in ways that further our capabilities, and we learn more about others in ways that can increase our social understanding."[2] It is not uncommon for young men to limit pitch variety and speak in short direct sentences that end in a step down in pitch. Young women are more apt to use a broad variety of pitches, long hyperbolic sentences and "often tend to use the modal 'would,' 'should,' 'could,' 'can,' 'may,' 'might,' thereby turning a command into a more polite request."[3] Some gay men take on these feminine behaviors and, according to Rudolf P. Gaudio, under certain conditions elongate consonants such as /l/, /sp/, and /sk/—although these conclusions were reached through sampling the speech of both gay and straight males reading a piece of text in what they felt was a stereotypical gay voice.[4]

Students aware of the voice and speech patterns that convey sexual identity might fear they will be stereotyped professionally with a particular performance identity. The first step actors must take in pursuit of a neutral and fluid performance identity is to break down the intricacies of their sexual identity. The actor playing Mike Talman was continually told in rehearsal to honor the question marks in his text. He constantly ran over interrogative statements as if they were declarative. His concern with presenting a stereotypically *butch* pitch range caused him to delete even appropriate variations in pitch. To correct this, first I had to make him aware this was an exaggeration of masculine vocal qualities. In the classroom, I find that students who struggle to separate their personal identities from their performance identities are the same students who cannot vocally honor a question mark.

Up to this point I have focused on a student who needed to "get the gay out." However, there are also those students who impose their personal identity on every performance identity. This sort of rigidity does not apply only to gay students or manifestations of sexual identity, but to every facet of identity that might affect vocal performance. For instance, some gay men have flamboyant vocal qualities that hinder the development of a fluid performance identity. Flamboyant derives its meaning from the middle French word, *flambé* or *to flame*. While this term has often been used primarily to describe gay male sexual identity, I believe its meaning can be expanded to encompass all facets of personal identity. If something is *flaming*, it burns brightly and is overtly perceivable. Are there not heterosexual identities which might be considered flamboyant in terms of this definition? If you have ever been to a fraternity party you might say yes.

There are many examples of flamboyant heterosexuality manifested in the voice and body that are linked to sexual identity performance. Like a peacock showing its feathers, males and females, regardless of which sex they desire, will perform in order to attract a mate. So because of this, actors are often asked to portray flamboyant heterosexual identities in theatre and film. Remember the boys from *Animal House*, the young ladies from *Clueless*, or Stiffler from the *American Pie* films? Consider most characters from Christopher Durang's *Betty's Summer Vacation*. With each character, an actor must choose how they will perform their sexual identity. If the character is to be flamboyant, the choices will be more extreme. The character Stiffler from *American Pie*, as played by heterosexual actor Sean William Scott, prepares to phonate by flexing every muscle in his overly-trained body, placing resonance as far back in his throat as his glottis will allow, until breath explodes from his chest to proclaim the all-purpose declarative, explicative, and interrogative word, "dude." In fact, the only non-traditional aspect of his heterosexual flamboyancy is his fabulous use of pitch variety. Flamboyant performance is present in all different aspects of identity, and students must

be taught to use it as a precision instrument rather than a paint roller.

Gay students in the resistance stage often manifest sexual identity with a certain degree of *camp* defensiveness, which shares the passive, hyperbolic qualities of stereotypical feminine voicing, but adds a dismissive tone towards other identities. While valued for its humor, camp can be trying if overplayed. In the classroom boundaries must be laid out for when camp is appropriate and when it is not. Susan Sontag writes, "One must distinguish between naïve and deliberate camp. Pure camp is always naïve. Camp which knows itself to be camp ("camping") is usually less satisfying."[5] So according to Sontag, deliberate camping is a form of sexual performance that must be used efficiently if it is to be effective.

For instance, two colleagues and I spent a day working on voice and movement with a first year acting class while their instructor was out of town. We led them through an exercise that David Leong teaches to the movement graduate students at VCU. In the exercise, students were paired off and given an active verb to perform. One actor performed the action to their partner and the partner had to react appropriately. The catch: no specific words were to be used, only vowel sounds could be phonated, and all movements had to be abstract. As it is usually quite difficult to get novice actors to turn off their brains, most pairs had difficultly "living in the moment." The desire to impress the instructor often impedes successful completion of the exercise. The students were focused on getting it right the first time, as if they were auditioning for something, rather than learning about the process. A few of the male students resorted to imitations of their favorite *Mortal Kombat* moves when the phonation became particularly aggressive. This was amusing, but resulted in a loss of focus from both the participants and spectators, and my colleagues and I had to intervene.[6]

One pair of students—an openly gay, white male and an African-American female whose sexual identity was unknown to me—had an especially difficult time adapting to this new experience. They were instructed to envy each other, and at first they honored the terms of the exercise. However, as time wore on and they began to grow uncomfortable with the lack of structure which text and circumstances provide, their reactions devolved into gay and African-American camp. The male student exclaimed "oh—it's on"[7] and proceeded to mime the removal of large earrings, a wig, and high-heels. His partner followed his lead and the exercise became a very campy, stereotypical, and unsuccessful catfight parody. The actors knew they were camping and hoped their referential humor would mask their inability to maintain neutral and open performance identities. When the process failed them, they instinctively used camp as a last resort. They hid behind the *flame* of flamboyant performance.

Bradley Boney identifies the development of these camp defense mechanisms as symbolic of a gay (or any non-dominant demographic) transition-period where individuals shift from being oppressed for a divergent identity into what he calls *queer-affirmative-subjectivity*. For gay, lesbian, bisexual, and transgendered (GLBT) individuals this could almost be described as *homosexism*, which identifies GLBT sexual identity performance as superior to the norm. The opposite of would be *heterosexism*, which identifies straight sexual identity performance as superior. Either subjectivity is detrimental to performance, resulting in the same stifled characterization exhibited by the actor from *Wait Until Dark*, or the affected camp stereotyping that took place during the aforementioned exercise.[8]

Pamela R. Hendrick suggests that students be allowed to explore different forms of gender performance in order to expand vocal and physical versatility. The next logical step would be to include the varied forms of sexual performance in the exploration, since gender alone does not dictate the performative tactics individuals use to attract a mate. Prior to beginning the exercise the students would be required to take stock of their everyday gender and sexual performances. Something as simple as a journal entry describing the performative forms their gender and sexual identities take would allow the instructor to evaluate the student's level of personal awareness.

Once the self-evaluations were completed, focus of the discussion would then shift to how society in general perceives gender and sexual representation. On this topic Bradley Boney writes,

> *Maleness* derives its value and *effeminacy* its non-value, from established differentials in the fields across which they are defined, primarily gender (masculine/feminine) and sexuality (heterosexual/homosexual). *Maleness* appropriates *masculine* and *heterosexual*, the privileged positions of those binaries that consequently infuse it with value and power.[9]

An understanding of the societal worth imposed on different gender identities and its impact on sexual identity and performance is a valuable acting tool. However, instructors should approach this material with caution and neutrality, placing no more emphasis on any aspect of identity performance. After this discussion, students should attempt to explore methods of sexual vocal performance different from their own. These can be improvised or taken from the vast number of plays, which deal with sexuality. They do not all

have to be subjectively affirmative and positive portrayals. Uncomfortable sexual identities such as the characters in *Unidentified Human Remains* are perfectly valid and important for students to explore.

If the instructor does not present a well-balanced overview of all sexual vocal identities, some students might be woefully unprepared to make strong identity choices. In young male actors this lack of preparation often results in what I call the *winsome-male-voice*. This soft, reassuring, almost breathy voice is used most often when I see a young actor working with a female partner. During auditions for a production of *Medea* at VCU, I observed this voice many times in young men who appeared to distrust the value of their own masculinity, afraid to appear insensitive, or even misogynistic. During call-backs, instead of using direct and declarative intonation towards Medea—who at the time was read by the female director—actors reading for the roles of Jason, Kreon, Aegeus, the tutor, and the servant, all approached the text with a passive, almost sympathetic tone, as if to show the director how sensitive they were. This was unfortunate, because as the director understood the text, Medea was not an innocent and knew that none of the male characters would treat her as such.

In fact the only actor to successfully deliver a cold reading of Aegeus—in my opinion—was a young gay man who is often hounded for his campy performance identity. His success is linked to his adaptation of his own identity to the needs of the text. The other actors seemed to believe that creating this sensitive male sexual identity to interact with the female characters was the most desirable choice. However, this performance of sexuality—masculine, presumably heterosexual male—was inconsistent with the text. One of *Medea*'s key themes is the inevitable failure of the dominant society—earthly humans, which could be read as male—to peacefully assimilate the unnatural other—Medea, both supernatural and female. The conflict between two dominants disrupts the establishment, and if the tragedy is to succeed, this must be evident in the male performances. The director implied that the actors reading for the male roles should play the dominant male, speak with the voice established in the text, and disregard modern societal pressure to respect the feminine—although not in so many words.[10] When this advice was heeded not only were the performances more pleasing to those watching the callbacks, but also the text and intentions were more comprehensible.

As I continued to work on this production of *Medea*, a young gay actor cast in the role of the tutor was having problems similar to the young man who earlier coined the phrase, "get the gay out." This student was constantly going off of his support and voicing at about fifty-percent of what I knew him to be capable. He was not necessarily trying to sound masculine, but simply seemed afraid to make any decision regarding his character's identity. I knew this student had an excellent voice because he was also in my third-year dialects section. He excelled in private coaching sessions where we reviewed the basics of phonation and resonance. All of the skills for a quality performance were in place, but when the time came to perform in the context of a scene, all of the work we had done disappeared. One session became so frustrating that I finally outright told him to "get the gay out." This young man had been out of the closet to his friends and family for close to a year. I could not understand why he would need to suppress his sexual identity to such an extreme degree during a classical Greek production playing a character that Kenneth McLeish had translated—in my opinion—to be quite campy.

I finally asked the student, "When in your life did you decide this is how you needed to speak?" He admitted to me he had made specific vocal choices while in the closet which were now a part of his everyday life. During the course of our conversation I realized that the closet metaphor is intrinsically flawed. Growing up in rural southern Virginia, this student had spent close to two decades creating an identity based on suppression and misdirection. Public acknowledgment of sexual identity is not nearly as simple as opening up a door and stepping out. My student had merely knocked a brick loose from the masonry he had built around himself, and the foundation of his years of denial would take much longer to chip away. The focus of my work with him on *Medea* was no longer merely a physical training regimen; it had become an exploration of his ever-evolving identity.[11]

We started by looking at the text and specifically the tutor's first line in the translation:

> Well, Nurse? My lady's trusty slave.
> What brings you out here? A public place!
> What wrongs are you muttering this time?
> Did Medea ask to be left alone?[12]

Initially he delivered this line with varied levels of tentativeness or worse, apathy towards the material. We examined why these questions are important to the verse, and why the tutor would go so far as to mention that the nurse is Medea's "trusty" slave during a simple greeting. I asked the student when in his own life he would use such an adjective. We discussed the vocal tactics he could adapt from his life to the character's verse lines to make them resonate within his voice. All of these questions helped the student understand how his vocal identity could be utilized to create this performance identity and why he as an actor was chosen to do it.[13]

The students with whom I have discussed issues of performance identity were usually under the assumption that one gender and sexual identity was superior to another, or believed that those around them assumed as much. While the experience of certain identities might be uncomfortable to students for various reasons, it must be understood that some plays will require their performance. If students can begin to approach the identities of their characters as archetypes rather than stereotypes, they will be empowered enough to fully commit to a specific vocal performance. As society's perceptions of masculinity and femininity are constantly changing, any rubric developed to encompass the typical performative vocal qualities will be obsolete before researchers can commit a theory to paper. Fortunately theatre lives in a place out-of-time where studious actors can use their own identities to create a wealth of characters representing a wide variety of identities. Part of the professional educator's charge is to assist students in the development of appropriate "current and future self images."[14] Voice and speech professionals need to be just as diligent when dealing with the vocal needs of a student's gender and sexual identity as they are with dialect and articulation. Without guidance, students unable to find vocal and physical versatility will remain trapped forever within a single performance identity. By fostering an environment where students feel free to explore identity and even "get the gay out," educators can impart valuable tools for creating strong and versatile vocal performances.

❧

Endnotes
1. Internet Broadway Database, *Wait Until Dark*.
2. Hendrick, "Two Opposite Animals," 115.
3. Hendrick, "Two Opposite Animals," 119.
4. Crist, "Duration of Onset Consonants."
5. Sontag, "Notes on 'Camp.'", 58.
6. THEA 114
7. THEA 114
8. Boney, "The Lavender Brick Road," 36-39.
9. Boney, "The Lavender Brick Road," 39.
10. *Medea*, Auditions, callbacks, and rehearsals.
11. *Medea*, Auditions, callbacks, and rehearsals.
12. McLeish, *Medea*, 2.
13. *Medea*, Auditions, Callbacks, Rehearsals.
14. Taylor, et al, "Addressing the Career Needs," 127.

Bibliography
Besner, Hilda F., and Charlotte J. Spungin. *Gay and Lesbian Students: Understanding Their Needs*. Washington: Taylor & Francis, 1995.
Birden, Susan. *Rethinking Sexual Identity in Education*. Lanham: Rowman and Littlefield Publishers, Inc., 2005.
Boney, Bradley. "The Lavender Brick Road: Paul Bonin-Rodriguez and the Sissy Bo(d)y." *Theatre Journal* 48.1 (1996): 35-57.
Crist, Sean. "Duration and onset of gay male stereotyped speech." *U. Penn Papers in Linguistics* 4.3 (1997): 53-70.

Engelken, Laura C. "Making Meaning: Providing Tools for an Integrated Identity." *Working With Lesbian, Gay, Bisexual, and Transgender College Students*. Ed. Ronni L. Sanlo. Westport: Greenwood Press 1998, 23-30.

Hendrick, Pamela R. "Two Opposite Animals? Voice, Text, and Gender on Stage." *Theatre Topics* 8.2 (1998): 113-125.

Hauser, Karen. "Wait Until Dark (1966)." *Internet Broadway Database*. © 2001-2005. The League of American Theatres and Producers, Inc. (06 May 2006) <http://www.ibdb.com/production.asp?ID=3128>.

Kiesling, Scott F. "Dude." *American Speech* 15.3 (2003): 281-305.

Medea, Auditions, Callbacks, Rehearsals, Virginia Commonwealth University, (April-October, 2006).

Meier, Paul. Email Correspondence. (April 2, 2006).

Roughgarden, Joan . "Evolution and the Embodiment of Gender." *GLQ: A Journal of Lesbian and Gay Studies* 10.2 (2004): 287-291.

Sanlo, Ronni, ed. *Working With Lesbian, Gay, Bisexual, and Transgender College Students*. Westport: Greenwood, Press (1998).

Sullivan, Patricia. "Sexual Identity Development: The Importance of Target or Dominant." *Working With Lesbian, Gay, Bisexual, and Transgender College Students*. Ed. Ronni L. Sanlo. Westport: Greenwood Press (1998): 3-12.

Taylor, Simone Himbeault, Kerin McQuaid Borland, and Sharon D. Vaughters. "Addressing the Career Needs of Lesbian, Gay, Bisexual, and Transgender Students." *Working With Lesbian, Gay, Bisexual, and Transgender College Students*. Ed. Ronni L. Sanlo. Westwood: Greenwood Press, (1998). 123-134.

THEA 114, Acting 1. Classroom Observation, Virginia Commonwealth University, (March 31, 2006).

Wait Until Dark, private coaching sessions with a student actor at Virginia Commonwealth University (2005).

Essay *by Lisa Anne Porter*

Gender and Voice: The Profound Worth of Drag

Lisa Anne Porter is a designated Linklater voice instructor, an acting/voice/dialect/text professor at Syracuse University and a professional actress and director. She has taught master classes in voice/text at the American Conservatory Theatre, Shakespeare & Company, the Tepper Center, Naropa University, California Shakespeare Festival, Berkeley Repertory Theatre and the Academy of Art University. She has performed with numerous repertory companies and Shakespeare festivals throughout the country and is a member of the Los Angeles Women's Shakespeare Company. She has a BA in Theatre and American Studies from Wesleyan University and an MFA from the American Conservatory Theatre.

My journey as an actress, a teacher, a woman, and a human being has been intrinsically linked to my evolving sense of my voice as form—a physical instrument, and as content—my dialogue with myself and my world. This journey has been rooted in a desire to know how to be a woman; what is it to have a woman's voice and to be able to recreate women onstage that are recognizable to other women. Ironically, by challenging my sense of self by crossing gender on stage, I discovered aspects of myself that I had only thought were natural to men. By giving free voice to these seemingly foreign parts, I came to own them as you can own all parts of your vocal range. And I realized that regardless of how or why I existed as half of myself, I was the only one who could take away the limitations and choose to more freely step into a fuller human and female body and voice. Doing this cross-gender work led me to incorporate what I had experienced empirically on and off stage into my voice and text teaching and to expand it to include both my female and male students. It has become a staple in my understanding of voice and my teaching of it.

I believe the story begins when at age five I first stepped onto a stage, lip syncing and sashaying in an au courant calico peasant dress to *Secondhand Rose* by Barbara Streisand because I wanted to express my relationship to my evolving female body and my growing sense of diva, my expression of supreme and generous self-worth. I embodied Martha Graham's entreaty,

> There is a vitality, a life-force, an energy, a quickening that is translated through you into action and because there is only one of you in all of time, this expression is unique. And if you block it, it will never exist through any other medium and be lost
> (Graham www.womenshistory.about.com).

The response of the audience was overwhelmingly positive and I was on my way. Now if I had been a boy it would have been the death knell for society's view of my machismo and the beginning of a fabulous career in girl drag. Years later, I stepped out on a stage in Los Angeles in full boy drag—a black leather motorcycle jacket, black pants, Doc Martens, black leather gloves, a blond ponytail down my back, complete with rapier and dagger as Laertes in an all female production of *Hamlet*. Both moments stand out as deeply pleasurable, generous and full. The period in between however was a journey of hide and go seek.

From the ages of five to eleven, my play involved lots of dress-up and exaggerated forms of the femme fatale, the damsel in distress, the queen, the witch; and my free, full voice explored a wide range of expression. I gave equal time to breaking free from any stereotype and spent hours sprinting down alleyways and through woods, climbing over fences, up trees, onto roofs, jumping over hedges and off rocks into lakes all with complete vocal and physical abandon. I recall with pure joy the experience of being as fast and as strong as any of my pals regardless of gender. Both of my choices of play were full and deeply pleasurable and I felt three dimensional.

Then somewhere in my eleventh year, it all changed and I became a classic case as described by Lyn Mikel Brown and Carol Gilligan in *Meeting at the Crossroads*. They write,

> For over a century the edge of adolescence has been identified as a time of heightened psychological risk for girls. Girls at this time have been

29

observed to lose their vitality, their resilience, their immunity to depression, their sense of themselves and their character…Our journey into this hitherto uncharted territory in women's psychology this land between childhood and adolescence-has been guided by girl's voices (Brown 1992, 2).

The reasons involved in my development included all the typical pressures put upon young girls in the late 1970s and 80s, and those particular to my highly dysfunctional and sometimes abusive family life. I continued to need to act on stage, but gone was the girl warrior and all my performances became a revolving door of female archetypes. My voice became breathy and the ending upward inflection of the question mark became a continual pattern. I became obsessed with my weight and having flat abs and had no sense of my body below the belly button. My tactics became indirect, my breathing shallow, and life ceased to hold much of the pleasure that it had once had. I continued to act throughout my teens and into college. There I started to be able to share the underbelly of this hyper-female archetype—an aching vulnerability, a receiver and responder to others. My voice expressed this part of myself honestly; it just did not venture to express anything else.

With graduate school, age and the growing confidence that perhaps my perceptions of the world were true, that earlier *warrior* voice and body began to bubble through. I applied to graduate schools with an essay on how Lucy in *You're a Good Man, Charlie Brown* hearkened me back to the little girl doing Streisand and led me to realize my inner ambitions—to wear a red dress, stand up on a chair, fully present in body and voice and be *Queen*. The American Conservatory Theatre took the risk and I spent two years integrating that freedom, confidence, pleasure, and range back into my body and voice. When I graduated, I was breathing a little more deeply but out in the professional world, I just did not know what to do with that mighty SHE that I had rediscovered. There seemed to be no roles for her unless I funneled her through limited text and she emerged as one note. I moved to Los Angeles and became truly despondent. I was that earlier little girl, trying to figure out what female dress-up I was supposed to wear in order to please. If I pleased, then I would be cast and possibly given permission to have *a voice*, however restricted that voice would be.

Then one day, I saw an open-call general audition notice for an all-female production of *Hamlet* by the Los Angeles Women's Shakespeare Company. I went. I clearly remember walking down the aisle of this theatre on Sunset Boulevard, hopping up onto the stage, feeling my feet on the ground underneath me, the breath dropping in, a forward energy in my body and Lady Percy's first lines erupted out of me. I finished and then this voice came out of the black—this full, generous female voice that climbed naturally up and down octaves as she spoke, complementing me on the work, offering adjustments, and asking me when I could come back and read for Claudius. The voice belonged to Lisa Wolpe, the artistic director of the company, who has been instrumental in my development as an actress, a person, and a teacher. I joined the company and began the work of putting myself in a man's shoes; not imitating one by speaking low, grabbing my crotch and swaggering but really imagining the "what if I had been born a man and in these given circumstances." Natsuko Ohama and Fran Bennett led me through voice warm-ups, Tony Simotes taught me to fight with rapier and dagger and Lisa Wolpe taught me to move and speak with a directness of purpose that was full of emotion yet forward in thought and action. And so I found myself entering the stage as Laertes, fully present, the diva and the vulnerable child and everything in between. For the first time in so many years, I felt three-dimensional and deeply human. Ironically, by playing a man, something unlocked and I began to allow myself to feel and speak more fully as myself, a woman.

I continued to work with the company, began playing male and female roles in numerous Shakespeare productions, met many fabulous voice teachers and in turn decided to designate with Kristin Linklater whose voice-work had been at the core of my transformation. I started teaching at Syracuse University, encountering many young women who reminded me of myself at their age. I took them through the progression and into text and they began to breathe and feel and speak, but I was noticing that there was often this plaintive note of the victim in their voices, the question mark would reoccur and they would back off the action of the thought and their connection to breath midway through the line. We were also working with antithesis at the time so I assigned them all the Richard/Anne scenes from *Richard III*, with women playing both parts. In the beginning, they struggled a bit with the part of Richard. They would muscle the sound forward with their jaw or tongue, and often drop into some one-dimensional characterization of an "evil man" that they assumed was very much "the other." But we stuck with it, always coming back to their physical connection with the ground, their spine and the impulse for thought and action coming with the breath connection at their center. They would find it, and boldly head into the scene. Something surprising and impolite in the world of female mores would occur; they would back off, giggle, and frequently apologize. And we would go back into it again. After a week or two, they stopped apologizing and started to dip into what we termed their "inner Richard." And they would end the scene with this look of wicked pleasure, having actually physically and vocally pursued something they desired fully, using a myriad of tactics that always lead them forward into and through the line of text. And there they would be waiting to see what Anne would do or say so that they could respond. It was immensely satisfying to watch.

The next step was to switch back to playing the women. So the actresses playing Anne and Richard switched parts. At first, the actress switching from Richard to Anne would get very frustrated and upset because she did not like how it felt to play Anne. She often felt limited physically and vocally which was a great thing to discover. So we examined what the actress was specifically doing, searching for when she was placing limitations upon the character and therefore her breath capacity and her vocal and physical range. We found those moments when Anne could be direct and most important when perhaps the character and the actress might surprise herself. In the end, the exercise gave each of the women a vocal, physical, emotional, and intellectual experience of themselves that challenged what they had previously thought. It had been a pleasurable experience because they had felt empowered and unapologetic. Therefore these students wanted to do it again and the exercise became a touchstone we could refer to throughout the year as we explored other characters and texts.

Because the work was helping the young women in the class to strengthen and develop their voices, finding dimension and pleasure in the work, I thought I would explore the same avenue with the men. So again we took the Richard/Anne scene and also the Richard/Elizabeth scene from *Richard III* and had the scene partners learn both parts. This time the pairings were male/female. We started with the traditional casting of the scene and worked through all of the thoughts, actions and the very intimate dance of antithesis in both scenes. The actors became clear in their thought and action but the work tended to be predictable and a bit general. Their voices were limited to a few honest notes. In my opinion, they were limited in some fashion by their own concept of their gender. Then the students switched roles and all bets were off. It was exciting and raw. There were these wonderful moments where they surprised themselves. I remember clearly one scene ending with the woman playing Richard leaning/crawling over the man playing Anne. Both were breathing and focused and had no idea what was going to happen next. It had been a moment-to-moment "Well, you say and do THAT. I will…say and do THIS. And what are you going to do now? Oh no, you DIDN'T!" Their voices had traveled octaves. For the man playing Anne, it had been a real exploration of what it feels like to be truly vulnerable and without the assumption of power. His voice had soared into places in his range he may not have known since he was age five. For the woman playing Richard, it had been scary and exciting to experience herself

powerful in the presence of someone bigger than herself. Her voice has dipped deeply into her chest and directly forward through her mouth and sinuses with a column of breath underneath her at all times. The students witnessing the work were engaged and inspired. I remember one young woman turning to the man playing Anne and remarking that she learned so much from watching him in the scene because there was a physicality and a directness that she had not thought possible for the character of Anne. But it had worked.

We immediately switched back, man as Richard, woman as Anne, and suddenly the scene had layers and surprises. The students were able to break free from their limited ideas of what the character and they as the actor "should" do. They started to really feel what it is like to want something and pursue it through another person in a dance that invites change and transformation. They experienced what it was like to have the free act of their speaking be the instrument of change and satisfaction. Again the audience learned as much as the actors and the students all remarked on how the work was breaking down the limitations that they had placed on their characters and the scene. Everyone was remarking they were hearing one another in a new light. Everyone was eager to cross gender and find out what they might be capable of and where their voices might go.

As I describe this work, I do not mean to describe it a continuously successful progression of satisfaction. The process was very difficult and frustrating at times. I remember one instance when Richard/Elizabeth had switched and the man playing Elizabeth kept forgetting his/her lines. At first, I became suspicious of whether he had done his work and actually knew his lines. He kept saying that he did. So we would reach this moment when his mind would go blank and he would check in to see if he was breathing. I would ask him what Richard had just said and where in turn his thought was going. And he kept saying he did not know. So someone would feed him the line and finally he burst out, "That doesn't make sense. She doesn't make sense. Why would I say that? I feel like a failure because it makes no sense." And we realized that Elizabeth's thought patterns/tactics were very foreign to him. And the work became a real opportunity to explore a very alien set of given circumstances. Something about her character as a mother and a woman in that court determined her tactics. To the women in the class, her motives and more so, her tactics made sense. But to this young actor from Kansas, Elizabeth was doing things that were not direct in their methods. He felt he was backing off from his intentions. It was fascinating to me. He wanted to quit but we kept working on it for a week or two and finally he was able to do the scene with out losing his thought. Several times, he just stood there as Elizabeth, breathing, not knowing what came next while Richard repeated the cue line. All of a sudden, the forgotten line would drop into him because he discovered how it followed from Richard's cue line. In the end, Elizabeth's thoughts and changing impulses became his and he, the actor, began to discover aspects of himself in her words. He and his scene partner became so focused and excited by the work that one day I had them switch characters mid-scene. They flipped back to him playing Richard and she playing Elizabeth, and once again the scene soared with all of the audience rapt, excited, and not knowing what was going to happen next. Their voices were supported by breath, full of nuance and expressing a tension free range of thought and feeling. I believe that this experience deeply changed this actor's work and shifted him into a real experience of himself in reaction rather than his habit of pure action. All of his work became three-dimensional and every part became an investigation of who he might be in the given circumstances. His throat opened up, the back of his tongue relaxed and his voice traveled out of a strained place in the middle of his range and began to freely dip low into his chest and high into his sinuses. These shifts happened because that's where his thought and feeling lived in a particular moment.

This cross-gender work has taken different forms and I have expanded the texts I use from that original exploration of scenes from *Richard III*. Classes have seen two men doing scenes between Beatrice and De Flores in *The Changeling*, three men doing the three queen scenes from *Richard III*, three women doing clown scenes from *The Tempest*, and a man and a woman switching roles in *The Duchess of Malfi*. I pick the material according to the actors, their vocal limitations, and where they may learn from boldly going. The students often want to cross gender and come to me with a character they are interested in exploring. Throughout the work, we continually come back the breath and the voice, the impulse from the center, the wide open channel of the throat, and the ease of the jaw and tongue. The students witnessing, those working, and I are always looking for the unnecessary vocal effort that is being added. The actor/student is made aware of the unnecessary vocal tension, exercises are employed to remove that tension and the work is repeated until a freer expression can be found. The cross-gender work is not a magic wand; we break it down so that everyone understands what is physically happening, and so the students can become empowered to lead themselves. They notice their physical and vocal habits and the limitations with regards to gender that they place upon the character that perhaps are not part of the given circumstances of the scene. They learn how to get rid of their habits and make choices that are rooted in the words of the character. The work leads them toward a full, free expression of their ever-expanding sense of their own humanity. One

hopes that it will be a humanity that embraces the complexities of their own gender, carries empathy for the other gender after having walked in their shoes, and most important, that it will be a humanity that is expressed freely through their bodies and voices.

Bibliography

Brown, Lyn Mikel & Carol Gilligan. *Meeting at the Crossroads*. New York: Ballantine Books, 1992.

Martha Graham. <http://womenshistory.about.com/cs/quotes/a/qu_graham_m.htm> (28 November 2006).

Essay *by Erica Tobolski*

Opposite Gender Monologue: Expanding Vocal Range

Erica Tobolski oversees the voice component of the professional actor-training program at the University of South Carolina. She coaches voice and dialects for professional theatres, including the Utah Shakespearean Festival and Charlotte Repertory Theatre and was dialect consultant for an Edinburgh Fringe Festival production and for the radio play *Merry Go Round* on NPR. She presents her work nationally and internationally, maintains a private voice practice and regularly performs in theatre and voice-over work. Her article on broadcast journalists appeared in the 2003 *Voice and Speech Review.* Professor Tobolski presently serves as a Board Member of the University/Resident Theatre Association.

"I need to sound like a man when I'm playing Shui Ta." This was the opening line into my most recent foray into coaching an actor to sound like the gender opposite to his or her own. The production was Bertolt Brecht's *The Good Person of Setzuan* and I was coaching a first-year graduate student who had not yet had the benefit of working on the Opposite Gender Monologue, a project I assign in the second year of their training at the University of South Carolina. We embarked on a crash course in vocal dynamics and ultimately she successfully created the voices of female Shen Te as well as her male alter-ego, Shui Ta.

My previous experiences in this line of work began with a private client in transition from male to female. "Joe" at the time he contacted me, was about to embark on the arduous journey taken by transgender individuals. He needed to develop a female voice to match his image as he transitioned to "Joanna." Could I help? I admitted I had never worked specifically in this area, but if he was willing to experiment with me, I was interested in the challenge. I believe I learned as much from Joe/Joanna as he did from me. He began to understand how his voice worked and its level of flexibility; I gained insight into both the potential of the human voice and how it is shaped by cultural expectations. It affirmed my belief that gender and the social roles associated with gender can be equally comfortable and restrictive, depending on the circumstance and situation. A question that resurfaced for me was this: when we change the way we speak, other's perceptions of us shift; is there an accompanying shift in our own thinking about ourselves? My ensuing work would indicate this is true.

Not long after this experience, I saw a need in the graduate training program for further work on stretching vocal range, particularly in regard to pitch inflection and general pitch range. Though this is an enormous generalization, the male actors tended to use volume as their primary emphasis of operative words whereas the female actors used pitch inflection. Partly out of physiology and reinforced through socialization, the men stayed within the lower notes of their range and the women used primarily higher notes. In actuality, the general male and female pitch ranges differ by less than an octave, with average frequency of 120 Hz and 225 Hz respectively (with middle C at 261.6 Hz), as cited in *The Articulate Voice* by Lynn K. Wells. Recalling the challenge of work done in the private studio with my transgender client, I came up with the following idea: have the actors work on a monologue written for the opposite gender. The result addressed the goal of extending range; it also led to an unexpected discovery of how vocal choices are based in psychology.

To begin the unit on Opposite Gender, we discuss what is perceived as masculine and feminine stereotypes in our culture as it applies to voice. We distinguish the difference between voice (resonance, vocal quality and inherent pitch range), linguistics/vocabulary and paralinguistics (volume, pitch inflection, rate/duration and articulation) and to what extent these aspects can be shifted. Pitch range, as previously stated, is determined in part by the physical difference between males and females, though there is a great deal of overlap in potential range. And there are the exceptions to the rule: in class discussions, students often cite Bea Arthur as a woman with a particularly low pitch range (see old episodes of *Golden Girls*) and Gilbert Gottfried (*Saturday Night Live* comedian and the voice of the duck on AFLAC commercials) with a pitch range higher than expected for men. Physiologically, the length and thickness of the folds are greater in men than for women, resulting in a difference in resonance and vocal quality. Altering the vocal quality can be affected in both sexes by re-learning to use the voice, specifically by how much contact of the vocal folds is made during phonation. Essentially, my work with Joe/Joanna focused on re-directing resonance to the head vs. the chest.[1] While vocal quality is not the objective of my gender work with actors, attempting to change resonance and quality brings a new awareness and understanding of how to work with the voice. Rather than the ability to "pass" as one gender or the other, the focus in this class remains increased expressiveness.

Much work has been written on gender schema and the influence on vocabulary, grammar and sentence structure. In her book *The Right to Speak*, Patsy Rodenburg describes these differences as applied to voice and body. Through research, discussion and the work itself, I've identified the following qualities: in conversation, women tend to request rather than state, invite discussion and compromise, discuss emotions and are expected to be submissive; men, on the other had, tend to state rather than request, clarify positions and actions, affirm beliefs rather than emotions and are expected to be assertive. Because these *broad* gender roles lead to word choice, actors are encouraged to choose text that reinforces male and female stereotypes.

Examples are invaluable. There are a number of films that feature crossover roles, some for comedic effect, some not. I show clips as part of the discussion and research; among these are:

Female to Male:
- *Victor/Victoria* (Julie Andrews plays a female playing a male who is a female impersonator)
- *Shakespeare in Love* (Gwyneth Paltrow playing Romeo on stage)
- *Boys Don't Cry* (Hilary Swank as Brandon Teena)
- *Fires in the Mirror* and *Twilight: Los Angeles* (Anna Deavere Smith in numerous roles in her filmed plays)

Male to Female:
- *Stage Beauty* (Billy Crudup plays female roles on stage)
- *Tootsie* (Dustin Hoffman as Michael Dorsey/Dorothy Michaels)
- *The Crying Game* (Jaye Davidson as Dil)
- *Mrs. Doubtfire* (Robin Williams as Daniel Hillard/Mrs. Euphegenia Doubtfire)

Throughout, I re-emphasize that we are dealing in generalities and that taken to an extreme, we find a stereotype. Ensuing discussions lead students to recognize their own prejudices and opinions about what our culture considers acceptable behavior in regard to gender roles. I find it useful to address the stereotype and both the positive and negative associations therein in order to diffuse any potential resistance to what may be seen as a risky proposition.

Once we've identified overall patterns, it's time to get down to specific skills. The greatest area for change, and the focus of the assignment, is dynamic

1. The transgender individual moving from female to male may opt for testosterone hormone treatments, which permanently change the structure of the vocal folds, increasing low-end resonance. Conversely, female hormones do not affect the already developed male voice. My work with Joe/Joanna focused on vocal usage because of the negative impact of female hormones on the voice.

range. These vocal variables are the markers of feminine and masculine speech, and include pitch inflection, volume, rate/duration and level of articulation. Below is a chart that identifies general tendencies, based on personal observation and the work of Melanie Anne Phillips, Patsy Rodenburg and Kate Bornstein.

VOCAL VARIABLE	MALE	FEMALE
Volume—overall	Louder	Softer
Volume to emphasize key words	Yes, nearly exclusively	Yes, to some extent
Pitch—overall range	Lower; staying within a smaller range	Higher; moving through a variety of pitches
Pitch—inflection to emphasize key words	Used rarely	Used extensively
Rate (number of words per minute)	Not gender-specific	Not gender-specific
Duration (length of individual sounds/words; use of pauses)	Words/sounds of shorter duration; pause at end of ends of sentences	Words/sounds of longer duration (often to accommodate a pitch inflection); pause in middle of sentences
Level of articulation in vowels and consonants	Less articulation	More articulation

Students are led through several exercises to increase access to the "opposite" set of vocal variables. To extend pitch range, they find their highest and lowest pitches that can be spoken comfortably, then work in those areas in order to strengthen them. Men are instructed to stop short of the falsetto range and to feel greater resonance and vibrations in the head and mask of the face. Women are directed to feel a greater resonance in the chest and pharyngeal areas but to avoid pushing and vocal "fry." Patsy Rodenburg's exercise of intoning into speaking as applied to range[2] is particularly useful for both sexes in order to find support and placement in pitch ranges that may be habitually unfamiliar.

Volume to punctuate operative words is used universally. However, the use of volume as an overall tendency is not. If a female student generally speaks at a quiet level or de-voices through a breathy quality, suddenly finding power in volume can be startling or exhilarating. Similarly, a male actor who habitually speaks with a high volume may discover that doing the opposite evokes a sense of ease and/or powerlessness. There are as many reactions as there are individuals.

Pitch inflection is perhaps the most difficult to change for both sexes. Executing upward, or rising, inflection for the men seems as hard as suppressing those pitch changes for the women. These patterns, at one point consciously chosen by the individual, become ingrained to the point of non-awareness; habit replaces choice. Sensitivity to nuances in pitch needs to

2. Patsy Rodenburg, *The Actor Speaks* (Great Britain: Methuen Drama, 1997), pp. 100-101.

35

be cultivated. Practice with moving from one pitch to another on a syllable or word can shade the text to reveal a variety of feelings or beliefs. The acceptability of revealing emotion depends on many factors—status, occupation, situation—however, we operate under cultural expectations. Melanie Anne Phillips, a transsexual female who has how-to CDs and DVDs of her steps to creating a female voice, cites an example of her experience in the workplace in her article "How to Develop a Female Voice" found on her website <http://heart-corps.com/journeys/>. When she returned to her occupation as a camera operator as a woman rather than a man, she discovered she had to *sound* like a woman in order to be successful. Her colleagues simply didn't respond to a person who looked feminine but gave orders rather than invited input. In this case, Ms. Phillips discovered that both linguistics and paralinguistics must match the gender presented.

After a series of exercises in class, students go off on their own, working their monologues from a Stanislavsky-based approach in order to understand the character's motivations, actions and given circumstances. They then begin to layer in vocal choices as appropriate to character and within gender stereotypes. Class time is devoted to side-coaching, guiding them through the process. I coach them first individually, giving notes and suggestions for further exploration. Then they team with a partner who gives them additional feedback. This also gives the partner a chance to learn through observation. After further work on their own, they present their work to the entire class and the final presentation is recorded in audio format. Students complete a Vocal Profile, a checklist I devised for students to identify vocal characteristics such as patterns in breath, pitch, and articulation. Other areas in the profile include phrasing, level of emotional expressiveness and descriptive adjectives or phrases that illustrate the voice. A paper outlining the process and discoveries focuses on the following questions:

• How did you come up with your choices—what part did imagination/cultural norms/text play and how did they interact with each other?
• How did your physical life affect the voice?
• How did this voice compare to your own—similarities/differences?

Regardless of overall patterns, both genders benefit from further work with vocal variables, particularly in regard to training for heightened text. I found the project to be extremely successful in extending vocal options and expanding students' awareness and usage of their own voice. A female student remarked in her process paper:

Finding Moon's [character from Jane Martin's play *Middle-Aged White Guys*] pitch was the most challenging aspect of the assignment, because I am physiologically limited in the depths of my pitch range. I explored how low-pitched I could go while maintaining a healthy level of variation and audibility. On the days that I was most tired and vocally at ease, I found the most freedom to explore my low pitches and chest resonance. On days when I was working hard and using my voice a lot, I felt like there was a cap on how low I was able to go on that day. The challenge was allowing my vibrations to resonate and not tense up despite my frustration.

An unintended discovery, and one that I find to be as or more valuable than simply developing the technique, has to do with the bridge between acting and voice. Students found they had to think differently in order to execute vocal choices truthfully. Here is what a male student had to say:

While I did not develop a detailed physical characterization, one physical adjustment that proved useful was to smile. This is interesting for a couple of reasons. First, if women are conditioned to be softer and less direct, then it makes sense that things said with conviction might need to be softened with smiles in order for them to be acceptable. Adding the smile helped me to express Zephyr's [character from *Idols of the King* by Ronnie Claire Edwards] deep concern for Elvis' twin brother and strong opinions about his mama in a way that felt passionate and feminine at the same time.

This quote speaks to one of the most important aspects of voice for the actor: to reveal the character's inner life through the outward manifestation of the voice.

In the most recent foray into the Opposite Gender Monologue project came an unexpected twist. I happened to run into my former client at a theatrical production; she proudly showed me her new driver's license. She was now officially Joanna and was living and working full-time as a woman. That week, the students were presenting their monologues and I invited her to come and watch, provided the students were comfortable with an outside observer. Joanna joined us for the presentation of monologues and, at the end of the discussion, shared her story with us. Her ability to transform her voice reinforced my beliefs that the human voice is far more flexible than we normally require of it.

The work with Joanna as well as with performance students indicates that the Opposite Gender Monologue project produced the desired results: a significant increase in the actor's available dynamic range. Actors in particular need to expand their range in order to meet the unexpected demands of roles they encounter, especially those that require a drastic change such as that of Shui Ta/ Shen Te in *The Good Person of Setzuan*. The ability to base choices on a perspective other than the actor's own is where this work offers a unique insight into, and articulation of, human behavior.

Works Cited

Rodenburg, Patsy. *The Right to Speak*. New York: Routledge, 1992.
Rodenburg, Patsy. *The Actor Speaks*. Great Britain: Methuen Drama, 1997.
Wells, Lynn K. *The Articulate Voice*. 4th ed. Boston: Pearson Education Group, 2004.
Bornstein, Kate. *My Gender Workbook*. New York: Routledge, 1998.
Phillips, Melanie Anne. "How to Develop a Female Voice." *http://heartcorps.com/journeys/*

Films Cited

Victor/Victoria, directed by Blake Edwards (MGM, 1982).
Shakespeare in Love, directed by John Madden (Miramax Films, 1998).
Boys Don't Cry, directed by Kimberly Peirce (Fox Searchlight Pictures, 1999).
Fires in the Mirror, directed by George C. Wolfe (American Playhouse, 1993).
Twilight: Los Angeles, directed by Marc Levin (Offline Releasing, 2000).
Stage Beauty, directed by Richard Eyre (Lions Gate Films, 2004).
Tootsie, directed by Sydney Pollack (Columbia Pictures, 1992).
The Crying Game, directed by Neil Jordan (Miramax Films, 1992).
Mrs. Doubtfire, directed by Chris Columbus (20th Century Fox, 1993).

Essay *by Rinda Frye*

Gender Voice: Coaching *Act a Lady* at the Humana Festival

Last spring I was voice and dialect coach for Jordan Harrison's new play *Act a Lady*, a production in the Humana Festival at Actors Theatre of Louisville. Harrison is one of the up-and-coming young playwrights on the American theater scene and in *Act a Lady* (the third of his plays to be performed at the Humana Festival) he explores gender roles, cross-dressing and meta-theatre.

Originally commissioned by the Commonweal Theatre Company, *Act a Lady* was to be about some aspect of the history of the small town of Lanesboro, Minnesota (population 800). Harrison was inspired by museum photographs of "a curious Midwestern custom from the 1920s and '30s: the presentation of elegant full-scale weddings in which every 'part'— including brides, brides-maids, and flower girls—was played by men." In Harrison's words,

> The most striking thing about these pictures: These men had put a great deal of effort and care into portraying women. They were not lampooning women. When I asked people in town about it, it started me thinking about the innocence at the time. I don't think a bunch of guys in a small town thought they would crash through gender boundaries (Huyck 2006).

He wondered, "What was it like to come back from the farm and dress up in women's clothes? What would it be like to be queer in a small town and have your swish suddenly celebrated? How did this affect their lives?" (Kleiman 2006, 45)

Act a Lady is about the denizens of a small Prohibition-era town in the Midwest who put on a play about the French Revolution in which the all-female cast is played by men in drag. Not only do we see how the gender-bending shifts their self-images, especially when the characters in the play-within-the-play take on a life of their own offstage, but in the second half of the play, the women in the cast also appear in drag as the offstage male char-acters from the first act. This allows the men (as their female personas from the French Revolution melodrama) to have philosophical conversations with themselves (played by the women in drag). As one character (Casper, played by a woman), says to his alter ego (Greta, played by Casper from the first act), "But if you're Greta—and I'm here—and you're there…then who am I?" and Greta answers, "That is the eternal question, Monsieur Casper" (Act 1).

The gender-bending doesn't end there. One of the French characters from the play-within-the-play (the Countess de Rocquefort played by True, the roman-tic hero of the town) finds she must disguise herself as a boy to escape the Revolution. Thus, in true Elizabethan fashion, we have a man disguised as a woman who is in turn disguised as a boy.

Harrison also portrays gender behavior as a performance in everyday life. When Casper's evident crush on True makes the latter uncomfortable, True teaches him how to "act a man." He gives Casper a picture of Mary Pickford, advises him to gaze at it nightly, wolf whistle, and declare "look at those stems" and then "you'll be fine" (Act 1). Casper tries, but with little success. Later, when the play-within-the-play is shut down by the Ladies' Temperance Society, Zina, the director, teaches Lorna, the romantic heroine, how to flirt with the sheriff so the show can open. Dorothy, who has been watching this, asks, "Can a lady act a lady?" and Zina answers, "It's something you learn,

Rinda Frye is an associate professor at the University of Louisville where she teaches stage speech and acting for the MFA program, directs and coaches acting and voice. She frequently coaches for Actors Theatre of Louisville and has coached for the Kentucky Shakespeare Festival and Music Theater of Louisville. She has acted at the Kentucky Center for the Arts and the Kentucky Shakespeare Festival, and in a short film, "Star Spangled Eyes." She was co-founder and past artistic director of the Utah Shakespeare Players, Inc. in SLC, Utah. She holds a PhD from the University of Oregon and is the author of *William Poel's Hamlets: The Director as Critic*. She is currently writing a book on stage dialects for the multi-cultural classroom.

like anything else. Did you come out of the crib batting your eyelashes?" Dorothy declares, "I never bat my eyelashes" (Act II).

The shifting of genders seems to open minds to new ways of seeing the world, and it is sexy, too. As True and Lorna fall in love, they shift stereotypical sexual roles. When they first kiss, True is in drag for rehearsals. They giggle at the absurdity of this, as if there's "two of Lorna . . . but I'm [True] still around to watch." As Lorna takes the lead, touching him, True wonders, "Think this'll make us go twisted?" She replies hopefully, "Maybe" (Act I).

Dialect and voice work

My job then was a daunting but exciting one—to help the actors find believable male and female voices, with strong contrasts between their two personae, and appropriate class differentiations, while mastering a regional American accent (along with European accents for some), and while contrasting everyday speech with the elevated diction of good, albeit melodramatic, 1920s theatre. Oh, yes, and they had to be able to act, too.

I began discussions with the director, Anne Kaufman, late in January. Fortunately, Annie is both clear about her own ideas and open to hearing the ideas of others. Her flexibility and the highly talented, good-natured cast made this more of a collaboration than some of my previous dialect coaching assignments. For instance, although the play had been inspired by a town in Minnesota, Annie and Jordan preferred to set it more generically in the Midwest. This gave me more leeway in terms of place and that meant I could tailor those decisions to the needs of the specific characters. We reasoned that while some of the characters had spent their entire lives in one little town, others had ventured further into the world, and their speech could reasonably have been affected by those experiences. For the "real life" voices, I spent some time with the wonderful IDEA (International Dialects of English Archive) website <http://www.ukans.edu/~idea/index2.html> and the NPR website <http://www.npr.org/>. I found excellent samples of both male and female voices from Kansas and Missouri that seemed to fit each of the characters in the town.

Annie and I agreed that we didn't want to distance the audience from the play-within-the-play characters by imitating too closely a period style of speech. This was particularly important because the stage characters all step out of the play and into the world of the small town where they effect changes in their alter egos. We wanted the audience to identify with those changes. I searched for a heightened theatrical sound that resembled the acting style of the 1920s without being too

antiquated for modern tastes. Fortunately, I also happened to be directing Douglas Carter Beane's *As Bees in Honey Drown*, in which the central character has created herself from a composite of great female film stars, so I already had samples of Rosalind Russell and Coral Brown in *Auntie Mame*, and Tallulah Bankhead in *Lifeboat*. I added to that a sample of Judith Anderson in *Rebecca* that I found through Google <www.google.com>. Here were strongly theatrical female stage voices with masculine/androgynous edges, all from the 1940s and '50s, that seemed a little old-fashioned to the modern ear, but without the sing-song vocal patterns of actors from even earlier periods. Then, even though I didn't want to imitate the acting styles of the 1920s, I thought it would help the actors to hear classical performers from that period, just to hear how good stage acting would have sounded. I found a sample of Ben Greet playing the Duke in *As You Like It* in 1912, one of Forbes-Robertson playing Hamlet, and one of Sir John Gielgud playing Jacques in 1930—all available, at that time, on the web. (Sadly, these web sites have since disappeared, as too many web sites do.)

The first read-through is always exciting: seeing the design presentations, meeting and listening to the actors read—and thinking about what each brings to his or her respective roles. I always present my samples after the first reading and teach the basics of the dialects, handing out my printed materials with my analyses of sound substitutions and melody. This first rehearsal was like others, except two cast members were missing because of unpredictable February weather in Louisville. A sudden snowstorm had canceled their flights. I was particularly disappointed because one of the missing was Zina, the "foreign," free-spirited, trousers-wearing director of the play-within-the-play. The actress was originally from England, and I wondered how well she would manage the Midwestern dialect since, as her alter ego, she would be playing Casper in the second act. Still, those present seemed excited about the samples and the implications for their characters. True loved the trilled "r" from the early 20th Century samples and decided to incorporate it, sparingly, but with great gusto into the Countess de Roquefort.

Time issues

One exciting aspect of working in the Humana Festival is that there are six or more plays in rehearsal at about the same time. Each has a rehearsal room with a set that physically correlates to the actual set (even as that is being changed, often on a daily basis), with props, sound effects, and costume pieces almost from the second rehearsal on. But, with so much happening in one producing organization, scheduling is often difficult. We have just over three weeks to mount a new show, and with rehearsal needs, script changes, and costume appointments, often the vocal work is fit in on a catch-as-catch-can basis.

Usually, after the first presentation and group coaching, I leave the actors alone for a few days to work on their own before private coaching. In this case, because the director was also worried about how Zina would manage an American dialect, they scheduled me for a session with her within a couple of days of her arrival. I remember we were both a little nervous. I tried to relax her a bit; she wanted to get down to business immediately. Within an hour or so, we were both greatly relieved. The actress had a fairly good ear, mimicked well, and had come prepared with her tape recorder to tape the coaching session. (I usually digitally record each session for the actors, but was impressed that she had planned ahead and brought her own recorder.) We worked through all of her Casper lines, drilling and playing with substitutions, intonation, melody, and intentions until we found a satisfactory Midwestern accent.

After this initial session, though, scheduling time with the actors became more and more difficult. I like to watch a rehearsal with several actors working so I can hear how they actually sound in the play, not just in a room alone with me. Unfortunately, rehearsal schedules shifted, people would forget I was only available mornings, technical meetings were scheduled during the times I was available, or costume fittings conflicted. Desperate after almost a week, I just dropped into a rehearsal unannounced one morning and was able to hear almost everyone for at least half an hour. Offstage, the actors practically mobbed me, begging for private sessions. I wound up coaching in the hallway as actors came free—working for ten or fifteen minute shifts with each.

Then, in a sudden flurry, I was wanted for coaching sessions almost every morning. I lost precious time searching for samples for a "foreign" dialect for Zina. I tried Marlene Dietrich but the director didn't want a German sound. I found some Ingrid Bergman and searched for Greta Garbo or Hedy Lamarr, but in the end Annie chose to go with what the actress was doing in rehearsal: something vaguely Eastern European, perhaps Russian with a little French thrown in. Suddenly we realized that the character Valentino (played by Miles who also played Lady Romula), who had only a one-page scene, would need a "Mediterranean" accent. I brought in Italian samples, only to discover they had decided instead on Spanish during the morning's rehearsal. We quickly switched; I found some samples to back up my memory of Spanish and the actor playing Miles added an amusing Castillian lisp to cap it off. Finally, I had private appointments with each actor, but by that point, after almost ten days of rehearsals, they had begun to set certain vocal patterns without me.

Passive dialects

Douglas Honorof points out that most people "know when an accent is true, even when we have never used it before" because "we all have a great deal of very specific passive knowledge of accents we have heard but in which we have never spoken…We don't have to be dead to play dead…because we can draw on our own memories of rest in life" (Honorof 2003, 107). Unfortunately, the flip side of this truism is that as actors, we usually rely on our own life experiences, and with accent/dialect work, we often turn to a familiar accent that "feels right" for the character even if it isn't quite the right accent for the play.

This was particularly problematic with the Midwestern dialect for *Act a Lady*. After all, the Midwest is in the center of the United States and because of various migration patterns through that area, it shares certain sound patterns with dialects further west, south, north and east. Left to their own devices for too long, the actors had shifted the Midwest in all directions. Miles was a convincing Midwesterner until his native non-rhotic Boston accent revealed itself. Zina had worked hard on all of the substitutions and melodic changes for Casper; but her own British dialect, which I had thought was "RP," was actually closer to Estuary so that cardinal vowel 2 [e] always began with a schwa [ə]. This tiny detail always grated on my ears; it became the "tell" that revealed an otherwise adept American accent to be foreign. True, like a real movie cowboy hero, had gone west; I estimated him to be somewhere near Wyoming. *Brokeback Mountain* was playing at the time and I think this unconsciously had facilitated his journey. But most problematic were Dorothy and Lorna who hailed respectively from Texas and Virginia. Both had gone home to the south and their use of Cardinal vowel 4 [a] for the diphthong [aɪ] had spread infectiously throughout the cast.

Many hours and much ink were expended trying to move them back to the Midwest. The southern patterns in the speech of Dorothy and Lorna seemed key to shifting the rest of the cast. In a long session with Dorothy we carefully worked our way out of Texas to Kansas, only to slip back south again and again. She understood the specifics of the problem, but kept falling into old vocal patterns that she had worked hard to break in her own speech when she first became an actress. Although she was classically trained, she had frequently been cast as a Southern country woman, similar in type to this character. That and the similarities of Midwestern speech to Southern kept pulling her back to the familiar. As we discussed this, she lamented that our production of *Lady* wasn't set in Minnesota, as it had been originally conceived. After all, she said, she could do a good Minnesota. On a hunch, I asked her to demonstrate and indeed, she was right. Then I asked her to do the speech again in the Minnesota accent, but to drop the characteristic [ɔ] for [o] sound. Suddenly Dorothy was back in Kansas and she seemed to be able to sustain it, at least for longer periods of time.

As I worked with Lorna, I realized that her Southern exposure was less integral to her speech than was Dorothy's. She had relatives from the South and had spent time there, but had not lived there for extended periods of time. She was using a cute little character voice for the role I assumed she'd chosen because it sounded right for a 1930's heroine—not unlike Betty Boop. I wondered if her southern [a] for [aɪ] stemmed from tensing her tongue to produce that voice. When I raised this, I discovered that tongue tension had been a sore issue with her all through her training. She thought she'd changed this to please her teachers, and was dismayed to find the tension was still there.

Gender Voice
I suggested to Lorna that tongue tension wasn't such a big issue as she feared. Except for the single [a] vowel, which she could easily change, her character voice was a fine choice for Lorna, both in terms of the period and a certain "girliness" that it brought to the role. But, it interfered with her portrayal of True. I pointed out she was playing True in the same register as Lorna, even though the male True had dropped his voice quite low in his chest to contrast with his female character, Rocquefort. This seemed particularly odd since she had worked carefully to develop a masculine physicality. I wondered if the tongue tension was connected to the use of her upper register for True. We then worked to open her lower register while releasing the tongue. Not only did this help to move Lorna out of the South, but it opened a whole new range of emotional expression for her as True. One of the oddities of the gender bending in the play is that her female persona allowed a far more limited emotional range than the male role.

Overall, I spent far less time with the cast working on gender voice issues than with dialect work. Partly, this stemmed from the limitations of the rehearsal schedule. But to a greater extent this came from the style of play itself. Harrison's notes on the male cross-dressing insist that:

> in the play within-the-play scenes, the drag should be devoted, meticulous, 'well-acted' (from a certain late 19th century school of melodrama), ridiculous when necessary, but always dignified. It is the ideal performance the Midwesterners would give, not the actual one (Act 1).

But men in drag, as characters in a play, can rely on the heightened theatricality to carry their work because the drag is

experienced by the audience as a metatheatrical device. Each man in the cast worked scrupulously to achieve Harrison's wishes, but speaking in falsetto with period diction and movement was sufficient to achieve their aims. They didn't need much coaching for this. True talks about this phenomenon backstage during rehearsals:

> Back in the merchant marines, I remember a fella who put two coconuts on his chest and called that a lady. Entered himself in the cadet talent show, strummed on a banjo missing a string and sang "Under the mango tree...

> He didn't look pretty, no, far from, with a big mouth drawn on like the south sea natives, it weren't half pretty. But I remember everybody leaned forward in their chairs, like they watched it sorta different because of how he looked. Guess it had the interest of something uncommon. Like a magnet—it's hard to explain. He put on those two coconuts and suddenly everyone with their eyes bigger than if he were a hundred-percent lady swishing in that grass skirt (Act 1).

The women needed more attention because their task was more difficult, but they were less successful than the men in drag. The women had to imitate actual male voices the audience would have already heard on the stage, in a register lower than most women can reach. Both Miles and True understandably shifted their male voices deep into their registers to contrast with the falsetto they used for the women they would play. Lorna could never achieve True's bass tones; and although Dorothy, who sang in the show, often hit notes that were as low as Miles's voice, for some reason she couldn't manage to do this when playing Miles. Since Casper's role was that of a closeted gay man, he spoke in his own tenor. Zina, then, didn't face as difficult a vocal task (though, ironically, she had the deepest voice of all the women). But because of quick changes, she had to under-dress costumes. So her Casper seemed a bit bulky and therefore more "feminine" than her male counterpart.

I suspect that in general, theater lends itself more easily to the female impersonation than male. Men in female drag seem more authentic on the stage than women in male drag, an oddity the play also acknowledges. As Zina, who wears pants in life, declares:

> The first time I attempted a prestigious drag spectacle, I put ladies on stage beside the boys. Ladies in trousers, boys in skirts. I thought: why should the boys be the only ones to escape what's expected of them every day?

> Right away I learned: People are not so quick to laugh as they are when a man puts on a dress. Trousers speak louder

off stage: the woman who wants to fight beside her
husband in battle; the woman who wants the world to
read her words, jut as they read a man's words; the woman
who wants a life in the Theater.

The stage is for skirts. Pants are a power in real life
(Act II).

Works Cited

Harrison, Jordan. *Act a Lady*, unpublished manuscript. New York:
Playscripts, Inc., 2006.

Honorof, Douglas. "Reference Vowels and Lexical Sets in Accent
Acquisition." *Film, broadcast & e-Media Coaching presented by the Voice
and Speech Review.* Rocco Dal Vera, ed. Cincinnati, OH: Voice and
Speech Trainers Association, 2003, 107.

Huyck, Ed. "Jordan Harrison: Living the Airport Terminal Life",
Backstage.com The Actors Resource, April 03, 2006. *http://www.
backstage.com/bso/news_reviews/midwest/article_display.jsp?vnu_
content_id=1002276531*

Kleiman. Jaime. "Jordan Harrison: Nothing's Impossible." *American
Theatre*, March 2006, 45.

Essay *by Linda Wise*

Voice and Soul—The Alfred Wolfsohn/Roy Hart Legacy

Born in Kenya, Linda Wise trained at the Royal Scottish Academy of Music and Drama before joining the avant-garde and studying with Roy Hart from 1969 until his death. Founding member of the Roy Hart Centre. *Moby Dick* by the RHT won the French Jean Vilar prize under her direction and she played Nedda in the OBIE winning production *Pagliacci*. In 1985 she joined Enrique Pardo and Pantheatre <www.pantheatre.com> as an actress and later as co-director. In 2007 she has directed at the Tisch School of Arts and a project based on *The Seagull* in Norway. She teaches extensively throughout Europe, South America and Australia. Passsionately concerned with a vision of the voice that engages the widest possible perspective on each person's individuality she incorporates into her practice a range of vocal approaches from Roy Hart's extended range techniques to bel canto.

1. Noah Pikes, *Dark Voices—the Genesis of Roy Hart Theatre*, (New Orleans: Spring Journal Inc.), 2004—the most researched book on the Wolfsohn/Hart legacy that is currently available.

2. Alfred Wolfsohn, *Orpheus, oder der weg su einer Maske*, English translation Marita Gunther, circa 1938.

3. Sheila Braggins, *Alfred Wolfsohn: The Diary of Events 1896–1962*, Roy Hart Theatre Archives.

The voice: a war stricken heritage

Without war Alfred Wolfsohn might have become another man. He was only 18 when he was conscripted to the front line in 1914, and what has been called his "descent into hell."[1]

> We are in a foreign country. Here in this foreign country are trenches, trenches are everywhere. I am living in these trenches. Every now and then the darkness of the night is lit up very light—strange stars made by man. Shells burst right and left.
>
> I throw myself to the ground, my hands are clawing the earth. Often someone next to me is hit. Each time I am astonished that I have been spared!
>
> Barrage all around me. The guns from which it is coming are manned by four or five Frenchmen. I don't know where they come from, I don't know who they are. They don't even know they can easily kill me. It's no good shouting: Jean Baptiste—Maurice—Pierre—I have done you no wrong, what do you want from me?
>
> I keep crawling.
>
> The hours pass. The fire is getting stronger and my peril greater. I pray to God but He doesn't hear me. From somewhere I hear a voice shouting. 'Comrade! Comrade!' I close my eyes, shaking with terror, thinking: how can a human voice utter such a sound, a voice in extremis.

> The year was 1917, we were entrenched somewhere at the front, we did not know where; under heavy bombardment. At long last came the relay. Heavy rain had turned the trenches into swamps of mud and in a short while I became trapped in it. I called for my comrades to help but no one heard and soon I was quite alone. Hour after hour, inch by inch I crawled back. After a while I heard a voice nearby moaning incessantly:

> Help, Help. I fought a terrible struggle with myself: should I try to crawl to him or not. I did not do it. After an agony of more than twenty hours I reached a reserve dugout. I do not remember what happened after that except that I learnt later that I had been hit and buried by a grenade and that I awoke the next morning in the cellar of a house in St Quentin, amongst a heap of corpses.[2]

Alfred Wolfsohn emerged from these war years suffering from shell-shock, post trauma syndrome and plagued by aural hallucinations. One voice in particular echoed through his mind with an ever-increasing sense of guilt—the soldier he had failed to help. In spite of psychiatric help nothing would stop the cacophony of screaming and groaning soldiers. We do not know the exact chronology of events that led Wolfsohn to want to sing but according to Sheila Braggins, one of the few remaining pupils of Wolfsohn, the desire was born during a journey to Italy after the war.[3] He began to work with singing teachers and voice specialists—one worked in the line of primal screams, another worked with music and "vocalises"—but his voice did not improve and his symptoms remained. Whilst in hospital he had begun to read some of Freud's writings and was convinced that if he were able to re-find and release the emotion of the sounds of those voices in himself he would cure his symptoms. He began to create what could be called his own "vocal exorcism," studying literature, philosophy, ancient myths, the scriptures, psychology—anything to do with the human being—in an attempt to understand "the mystery behind the human voice."[4] He began to work with other singers—often singers who had problems—adopting the same approach as he had used for himself:

It was not their voice that was suffering but their **soul**.

The seeds of the idea that the voice is an audible vision of the soul were sown.

A passionate lover of opera, Wolfsohn developed his method from a very musical basis, using the piano as a support for his vocalises and exercises. He began to imagine in his inner ear a voice that could sing all the parts of *The Magic Flute*—male and female.

For a Jew, life in Berlin became too dangerous and in 1938 Wolfsohn fled to Britain. He was interned as an "enemy alien" but later volunteered for the Pioneer Corps which had a company for "aliens and other undesirables"—around 1942 he was invalided out of the army and the following year was given permission by the Home Office to give singing lessons. By this time he was reading Jung and the language of psychoanalysis filtered into the singing studio—animus and anima/ consciousness/psyche/shadow/projection. These concepts helped to articulate his idea that "the voice is the muscle of the soul," and gave another vocabulary to relate the evolution and revelation of the voice to the singer. The link between voice and soul was not new since as early as 1839 Longfellow wrote in Hyperion:

O how wonder is the human voice!
It is indeed the organ of the soul.

What **was** new was the recognition that psyche plays an indissoluble role in the revelation of the voice in all its full register—from Bel Canto to Hell Canto.[5]

The group of students grew, and many artists, philosophers, scientists came to visit the studio, now known as the Alfred Wolfsohn Research Centre. Alfred Wolfsohn died of tuberculosis in 1962. Written on his tomb in Golders Green are Nietzsche's words:

"Lerne singen, O seele."
(Learn to sing—O my soul!)

He has been named "the Prophet of Song"[6] but for me it is essential to see singing, the singer, and the song as a metaphor in order to begin to understand Wolfsohn's work. He wrote:

Let me underline that when I speak of singing I do not see it only as an artistic exercise but as a possibility and a means to know oneself and to transform this knowledge into conscious life.

It is not important to speak about where he was born, where he lived and how he died all that matters are his IDEAS.[7]

Not without some trepidation he was fully aware that his ideas would be developed and changed—and he was also aware that Roy Hart, of all his pupils, would be the one who would have the widest impact.

4. Knut Hamsun, *Mysteries*, (New York: Carroll & Graf Publishers), 1990.

5. Nick Hobbs, lecture on Captain Beefheart—Pantheatre, Paris 2004.

6. Paul Newham, *The Prophet of Song: The Life and Work of Alfred Wolfsohn*, (London: Tiger's Eye Press), 1997.

7. Braggins, *Alfred Wolfsohn: The Diary of Events 1896–1962*.

From war wounds to guru

Roy Hart certainly took Wolfsohn's ideas and developed them into an empirical societal living experience. He had abandoned a promising career in the theatre to dedicate himself completely to Wolfsohn's work. A gifted actor with a strong natural voice, a leader with a lot of charisma, he was also driven by a passion to come to terms with what appeared to him to be contradictions in himself. Unlike Wolfsohn, he was not a prolific writer and the few pieces of writing that remain under his name were mostly written by his wife, Dorothy Hart. His early diaries reveal a sensitive, gifted but very lonely student. It is not surprising therefore that the one area where he shone—theatre—should become the basis of his philosophy, and that a great part of his life's work was an attempt to bridge the separation between the artist and his private life. Life or Theatre—Wolfsohn's ideas, and we find them as well in the paintings of Charlotte Salomon.[8]

During the period from Wolfsohn's death in 1962 to the creation of the Roy Hart Theatre in 1969, there was a definite shift in the structure of the work from the intense one to one teacher/pupil relationship to a more collective "group" experience guided by Roy Hart. The "singing lesson"[9] was always present but expanded to group rehearsals, discussions, meetings, and public presentations. More and more people were attracted to the studio and though Roy Hart would say that he never sought to be the leader of this group it is obvious in retrospect that there was little place for a collective leadership. This too was a movement of the times—it was the sixties—people everywhere were looking for masters and for an alternative in living. Subtly, the language and the philosophy behind the work on the voice began to change:

> Most of these people were not naturally gregarious or prone to follow a leader: yet they chose to subject themselves to each other and (as some at first thought) to me, but in fact both they and I are subject to the creative research we do—to the *principle* of the *eight octave voice*. We find that any normal human voice, male or female, usually reckoned to have a range from two to two and a half octaves, may be extended, with training to six or more octaves, gaining in expressiveness and emotional content in the process. This cultural-philosophical system of voice training is an empirical lay activity. To my mind its most interesting aspect is the emergence of genuine family relationships and of a growing social awareness among those who adhere to the work.[10]

To subject oneself to the principle of the "8 octave voice" was also to subject oneself to what became known within the hermetic circle as the "idea." Like many groups at that time there was a strong hierarchical circle towards the centre, but Roy Hart was very consistent and he never excluded anyone who wished to work with him—so long as it was on his terms:

> I was interested in the relationship between the actor and his personal life. I became concerned with the relationship between the voice and the personality. I could not develop an attribute so specifically human as the human voice without studying life itself—deeply. Singing as we practice it is literally the redemption of the body. The capacity to 'hold' the voice in identification with the body makes biological reality of the concept 'I am.' Because I had learned to hold myself in sound I found I was able to hold others as a leader in concentration. Concentration is the summoning of the whole body in one effort: True concentration is prayer. It is because we

8. *Life? Or Theatre? A play with music,* the title that Charlotte Salomon (1917 – 1943) gave to the approximately 780 paintings in which she fictionalised her own life. Jewish Historical Museum.

9. The "one to one" lesson—teacher/pupil that Alfred Wolfsohn practised.

10. *How A Voice gave me a Conscience,* 1967—paper delivered by Roy Hart at the 7th International Congress of Psychotherapy in Wiesbaden.

explore every human impulse and raise it to the level of conscious artistic expression that our work contains the seed of its evolution.

This paper ends with a quotation from Nietzsche:
And this secret spake life herself to me. 'Behold,' said she, 'I am that which must ever surpass itself…'

In 1956 the Science correspondent for the Observer had written:
Mr Wolfsohn does not regard the voice as a delicate plant to be carefully cultivated, but rather as a potential athlete in need of strict but thorough strenuous training. He uses a kind of assault course technique and the voice certainly seems to be capable of putting up an astonishing performance.

Likewise, Roy Hart's work took on a hugely striving heroic dimension and physical effort and sweating engagement forged the bodies and sounds of his followers, but engagement was not limited to the singing studio, it was required 24 hours a day. In one of his frequent demonstrations he describes his work as a:
Biological education of the personality.

The different members of my community attack with the utmost effort of body and will the different centres of energy—a form of shock treatment for the cells.

I had to educate my voice to produce at will a great variety of timbres and nuances that relate to immediate experience rather than an acted simulation of experience. My life's work has been to give bodily expression to the totality of myself. This means bringing an enormous unconscious territory into consciousness. I have often referred to my art as 'conscious schizophrenia.'[11]

11. Roy Hart, *The Objective Voice*, a paper given at the 7th International Congress of Psychodrama in Tokyo, April 1972 (unpublished).

Roy Hart was a virtuoso of the voice but ironically for someone who was so gifted at holding his group together, he was unable to hold the artistic relationships he created with some of the most famous contemporary artists of the time. He would break relations over moral and financial issues, which he described as questions of integrity:
It is my attitude to my art that is more revolutionary than the particular sounds that fellow artists find they can copy or embellish.

I believe that what I do with my voice is the point of balance between machine and mysticism. Stockhausen, Henze and Maxwell-Davies all had an immediate, unconscious strong response to my voice: they felt a tremendous something speak to them, but I know that none of them really grasped the significance of that something. They have not the psychological experience to do so.

Roy Hart Theatre 1968 - 1989[12]
In 1969 I was an aspiring actress studying at the Royal Scottish Academy of Drama. I received an invitation to the Roy Hart Theatre's performance of *The Bacchae* at the Roundhouse, in London. Fate had it that I was performing in the same play at the same time. My personal experience with

12. For full accounts of the creation of the Roy Hart Theatre see Noah Pikes, *Dark Voices—the Genesis of Roy Hart Theatre*; Marian Hampton and Barbara Acker (eds.) *The Vocal Vision—views on voice* (New York: Applause Books), 1997; and Roy Hart Theatre Archives, < http://www.roy-hart.com>

The Bacchae had been one of my most interesting theatre experiences but two events blurred the pleasure I had from the performance. The first was that my director had a nervous breakdown, ostensibly because of the material of the play, and the second was that I had been sent by the director of the Academy to see a voice therapist. According to the staff of the academy I had severe voice problems, which manifested themselves during the performance. I was vexed because I had heard during this production sounds that had never fallen from my mouth and had also experienced a sense of wild depth that seemed to me in complete accord with the contents of the play—I was after all playing a deranged follower of Dionysus who leads her colleagues to murder with the tearing apart of Pentheus. The well placed voice seemed to me to have no place here—and neither had it perturbed my director—on the contrary he had encouraged me to go as far as I was able in the direction of releasing energy. But now he was being cared for in a psychiatric hospital. I attended my first appointment with the voice therapist. She placed a bone prop in my mouth and asked me to say AHH. With my arrogant youthful convictions I felt she understood nothing—and I took the plane down to London.

I had no pre-conceptions and could never have anticipated what awaited me. I walked into a studio hidden in the recesses of a Sports Club in Hampstead and discovered an amorphous mass of groping beings making a polyphony of all the sounds that were causing my "severe voice problems." The impact was enormous—here were 15 to 20 bodies deeply engaged in emitting all the sounds that had been forbidden to me. I understood what I had intuited—that: there is a difference between a broken sound and a broken voice. Two days later I resolved this voice research would be the subject of my university thesis, and I changed the entire orientation of my career.

Voice and Soul
The concept of singing has evolved enormously over the last 30 years. There has been an explosion of scientific, spiritual, psychological and ethnological research in voice. When I began to study with Roy Hart we were considered "voice freaks." The sounds we discovered or uncovered have gradually entered into the world and are no longer shocking…and thanks to many advances we are able to know much more about the physiology—and what is actually happening to the vocal folds and the larynx when we emit certain sounds.

Now 30 years since Roy Hart's death I find it helpful to work with the idea that there is a place, a geography for the voice determined by the anatomy of each individual: his or her lungs, larynx, diaphragm, vocal folds, palate etc. I like the precision of anatomy and very often use this in my work, as I might encourage students to work with techniques like Feldenkrais and Alexander, but still with all this knowledge I often hear: "I do not know where my voice is."

Somewhere the connection with me/my voice has not found its inner imaginative space. I have an image of *La Bocca della Verità* in Rome. The open mouth that defies one to place one's hand inside, and which will reveal whether or not you are being/speaking/manifesting the truth. Why do we attribute all that pours forth from an open mouth to have a capacity for revelation? It is as if by wanting to expose the voice to the light of consciousness we seem to expose the most dark, the most deep, the most hidden, and by implication the most authentic, the most true, the most sacred. What or where is this place of revelation where the invisible becomes voice? This place where impalpable air becomes tangible sound. Could not this be called a search for soul?

I co-direct with Enrique Pardo a company called Pantheatre, named after the mythical figure of the Greek God Pan. Shortly before putting an end to his life, Socrates is supposed to have addressed a prayer to Pan, the famous Socratic prayer, which goes: "Beloved Pan and all ye other Gods who haunt this place, give me beauty in the inner soul so that inner and outer man can be at one."

What did Socrates mean by "soul"? He used the word *psyche*. The connotations and prestige of the word vary enormously with the times, and the places. In the last 50 years or so in the Anglo-Saxon world "soul" has become a best seller—look at soul music and the explosion of books titled with soul. The philosophical and cultural references with which I feel closest, and which have most influenced my own use of the term, are associated with the re-visioning of psychology undertaken by James Hillman in his work and writings.[13]

13. For the references of James Hillman books and articles see: <http://www.mythosandlogos.com/Hillman.html>

James Hillman was director of studies of the C.G. Jung Institute in Zurich in the early 1970s, where, together with a circle of collaborators, he founded the Post-Jungian current of thought known as archetypal psychology named after Jung's notion of archetype. Hillman elaborated an extraordinary opus around the notion of soul, using both the Greek mythologies of Psyche and the Latin concept of *Anima* in his commentaries and in the links he makes with Platonic and Neo-Platonic philosophies.

There are three aspects in Hillman's phenomenology of soul that are of particular importance here:

First is his work on the *personification of soul* found in *Anima, the Anatomy of a Personified Notion.* For Hillman, soul is personified in the figure of Psyche, especially as she appears in the myth of Psyche and Eros.

Second is his differentiation between *soul* and *spirit* exposed in his essay "Peaks and Vales." Spirit aspires to sublime upward moves away from materiality; it seeks the pure and rarefied air of peaks, the "high" of detachment. Soul, or Psyche, is drawn to descend into the vales of worldly experience—it is attracted by the downward deep entanglements with Eros: the experience, the tears and pleasures of connection (from Hillman's *The Myth of Analysis*).

Third, archetypal psychology links soul-psyche with *imagination*—perhaps in this context the most important. Images come from soul. Soul is the crucible where experience becomes matter, releases emotions that "matter," connect, "have meaning," and can be transformed into images, or, in this context, I would say "sound images."

The Roman word for soul/sense of soul—is *anima*. One could speak of *anima* as that which animates; in other words a soulful voice is one which is animated by the singer and which animates the listener. I often ask myself can one be objective about the voice; when your "soul" is moved can I be sure that mine will be too? Alfred Wolfsohn asked the same question…and Roy Hart implied an answer by writing of his work under the title: *The Objective Voice.*

There is no doubt that for Wolfsohn and Hart singing included a transcendental dimension based on a physical, lyrical, athletic, muscular "going beyond" one's possibilities…and my education was in this mindscape. As I have said it was a truly heroic proposition built in their time, but when I met James Hillman in 1980 I discovered a perspective that made sense to me and which has probably influenced more deeply the philosophy of my work today than the notions of "eight octave living" and "consciousness" that were Roy Hart's philosophical concerns.[14] In many ways, it seems to me that Roy Hart was closer to the teachings of Gurdjieff.[15]

"The Voice is the Muscle of the Soul"

If you are what you sing, if your soulful dimension, or definition of your personality as soulful can be measured by your voice, then what you cannot voice could be named as unrealised soulful potential. The notion of an eight-octave voice is an allegorical formulation of this ideal. Within such a mindscape, the voice, and singing, become a vocation, a spiritual journey, an initiation.

But sometimes one's soul needs to let go of heroic strivings…

Psyche in the Singing Studio
Little whimpers of being, not making.

One day I was waiting for a new student, a singer with one of the most reputed madrigal choirs in Paris. I found standing on my doorstep a little man with glasses and a briefcase. I thought he was a member of the Jehovah's Witness and was about to say that I did not have the time to speak with him when he thrust out his hand and announced his name: my new student. He came in, took off his coat, folded it neatly on his knees and sat bolt upright on the sofa. We talked for a while and then I invited him to work. He removed his shoes, placing them neatly next to his briefcase from which he removed a little brown notebook. He asked if he could take notes. I answered that normally I discouraged people from taking notes whilst they were working but if he felt he needed to he should. He nodded and placed his notebook in his pocket. We began to explore some sounds which he seemed to hold for inspection and then would transfer to his notebook. Once transcribed the note and book returned to his pocket. I was fascinated by the precision of his inquiry. His voice was very melodious, almost liturgical in its purity. As we moved into the higher ranges the notebook sometimes did not return to his pocket, and then the whimper happened. A tiny little choke of sound where his voice shifted off the note. His face creased. Puckering into a look of total disbelief, and an indecipherable expression like a child who has just tasted something he has never eaten and cannot yet decide if it is good or bad…then a full, complete smile spread from his face to his toes. The little upright man let go and collapsed onto the sofa, falling back into the cushions.

"I think I needed a place for that little voice to speak," he said. He paused and then wrote vigorously in his little book. I could not follow his

14. See "Roy Hart speaks": interviews with José Monleon published in *Primer Acto* no.130, Madrid, March 1971, published in English as *Let there be Consciousness Tonight and Forever.* (But the phrase "Let there be consciousness tonight…" was not part of the interview; it was a telegram that Roy sent at the time from Madrid to the RHT in Belsize Lane. The telegram was used as the front cover of the English translation to these interviews.)

15. See George Gurdjieff: *Meetings with Remarkable Men*, and P.D. Ouspensky: *In Search of the Miraculous: fragments of an unknown teaching.*

imaginative note-taking but I continued to work with his voice. He continued to take notes. Sometimes less, sometimes more. Until suddenly one day the note-book disappeared. Was he as Jung says "letting the little voices speak?"

Mnemosyne

Sara came to work with me first in her late forties—a delightfully vivacious woman with a passion for the theatre. She had the kind of timbre in her voice that held the traces and scars of life. It was not broken and yet sounded with minute slides and breaks of continuity—a voice brimming with undefined emotion. It was not surprising, therefore, that at a certain moment tears began to flow. What was surprising was the fact that these tears, leading to sobs, would always return on a specific note—the E above Middle C. Not a semitone up or semitone down. It was impossible for her to sound on this note without emotion taking over. In order to be able to continue working I would find strategies to avoid the note until one day I decided that I would sing it instead of leading her with the piano. For the first time she was able to sing the note at the same time as allowing her tears to flow. She was no longer overwhelmed. Over time and months the passage became easier and she could sing the note like any other. It emerged in our talks after the work that her daughter had been a pianist and had died at the age of 18 in very violent circumstances. Was it possible that this terrible memory was held into the vibrations of this one specific note? Was it the timbre of the piano? Was it all of this, a conjunction of psyche and soma—the resonating note specific to her physiology, personality and voice typology?

Emotion is a subject of considerable controversy when it comes to singing. Some teachers refuse to acknowledge that there is the need to work with it and will talk of the voice as an instrument separate from the person. The capacity to feel, to express and to transmit clearly what one feels is an art, and this art as expressed in being able to let go of emotion, is one of the major reasons people give for wanting to work on their voice. Being able to feel, and to express one's feelings was a large part of Roy Hart's training, and until I came to this work I had no idea of what feeling one's voice could mean or indeed that the feeling of one's voice or one's feelings can also direct a way of working.

Sound Breaks

There is often emotion where registers change. It is in these areas that the voice may begin to wobble, to lose its centre and a sense of vulnerability may often follow because the singer is no longer able to sense the space, or feel the affirmation that comes when the voice is clear and strong. When we sing in a more classical mode this vulnerable space would not be the space into which we would go for we are seeking a stable,

homogeneity in the voice. But literally, and metaphorically, there are bridge areas, vulnerable passages, changes of mode. Where there is confidence we can move right into them and explore their imaginative landscapes.

There is a huge fear of allowing the sound to break particularly for a singer who has trained for many years to avoid breaks. If the singer can relax and accept a break the sense of instability can give way to a sense of pleasure at the freedom of moving between spaces. Fear leaves as familiarity with a constantly moving centre becomes a pleasure, and an art, as we can hear in the yodel of Bavaria, or the songs of Siberia, North Africa etc. The problem lies with the fact that when the voice leaves its central axis the person begins to feel lost, unstable and unable to find security in the infinity of changing viewpoints. The most simple glissandi may generate this sense of instability.

Boundaries

Recently a highly sensitive and intelligent psychoanalyst came to work with me because his clients had difficulty in hearing him. He has a naturally musical voice and a gift for improvising melody, but he is touchingly shy and can never sing towards me. Most often he will turn and look out of the window. He struggled for weeks with a total blockage in the face of being able to let his voice slide or sigh. Finally he explained to me that for him what was so intimidating was allowing himself to let go into a place with no boundaries. For him boundaries are essential in his work with psychotic patients.

Very often trained singers are unable to slide between the notes and the physical and psychological changes of mode or register pose problems. For one very gifted classical singer whom I shall call Marie, an extended glissandi was so destabilising she ended in tears—she lost her musical reference points and so could no longer channel her voice. This is the other extreme where boundaries chain us psychologically and imaginatively. Marie was a musicologist. She had perfect pitch and a beautiful voice. A gifted musician who played the violin and the piano. She watched tetanised as young inexperienced beginners found their own music and improvised freely whilst she was blocked by her gift to hear the notes. She could not work without naming the notes in her mind whilst she was singing; DO SI Re Mi bemol etc. She needed to shift her music from her ear to the sensations and vibrations of her body. Engaged with her physical body she let the centre of her concentration shift but was still moving in the waters of extreme vulnerability like a newborn foal taking its first steps. For someone with her experience it takes a lot of courage to move into such areas of vulnerability and…failure…but something was pushing her to seek change.

Masters and Mentors

They say that behind every great singer is a great singing teacher. Il Maestro, the guiding mentor is part of the mythical landscape of voice teaching. The relationship between pupil and teacher can be fraught with complexes, and transference and counter-transference—as one colleague wittily said: "The note is played on the piano but chained to the note is the master!"

When we allow singing considerations to move beyond technique into the realm of psyche/soul the implications of personal relationships become more complex. Alfred Wolfsohn and Roy Hart moved deeply into personal and erotic engagement with their pupils—both men and women. I am not saying that the engagement was always literalised but the model of teaching was one in which boundaries were often crossed. The interaction between Eros and Psyche—which James Hillman considers to be the central "Myth of Analysis"—pervaded the singing work.

Descent to the underworld

Recently I have followed the journey of a woman who had a beautiful singing voice. She lived through the process of losing a much longed for baby. Her constant hospital visits for treatment transformed into the nightmare of discovering that she had lymph cancer. She fought for her life and continued to sing all through her chemotherapy treatment. Side effect followed side effect like enforced early menopause and losing her hair, and…"losing" her voice. I have never experienced such dramatic changes in a voice. From never having been comfortable below middle C, her voice literally plunged to the depths. She could only groan on the deepest of bass sounds. Her vocal folds were undamaged by the treatment but when she regained some voice we had to work with an emotional vibrato that destabilised everything except her very deepest notes. Her voice seemed to tremble with a voiced fear that made her husband ask her not to sing. I tried not to think of recovery but of coming to terms with another way of being, another way that she might sing. There were days when I am sure we both despaired. She found her path. Five years later she is singing as she never sang before—trusting her intuition, her body and knowing that she has changed profoundly in order to become someone, and to sing in a way she had never imagined.

Gender questions

A high-ranking business executive was sent to me by one of his childhood friends. He had great difficulty in sounding the lower ranges of his voice. It seemed to cause a lot of pain, whilst the higher ranges and particularly the more archetypal feminine sounds gave him a great sense of pleasure and elation—almost euphoric. One day a beautiful soprano sound emerged in his voice and for the first time one could say he sang "in tune." The sound prompted him to tell me the dream he had had the night before of a rather kitsch blue Madonna that you might find in a baroque South American church. For him she was the voice that sang "in tune." She was melodic and warm, and sensual. In his next lesson his voice dropped easily to comfortable warm deep tones in the lower range. The journey of this man has been quite moving. The contract between us was unusual. The chauffeur would wait downstairs, the mobile phone would be left on, and his impeccably pressed suit would remain buttoned and belted until he could bear it no longer. His voice was tight and small and one could say that it had become a cultural social front, product of his "persona," the required voice imposed by the required character held in between almost invisible lips. In spite of his powerful position he had no inner sensation of his size and on the opposite scale the tiny letting go of a sigh became a huge trauma—a letting go of the brilliant high-achiever for a moment. After six months of work he would arrive telephoneless, chauffeur-less and dressed in a T-shirt. His mother no longer recognised his voice on the phone. Over this year of work he was also in therapy recovering from a suicidal depression. This year of metamorphosis lead him to uncover, affirm and come out with his homosexuality.

I revolt at any facile diagnosis that the higher registers of a man's voice reflect his femininity and vice versa but I observe the impact of sounds that go beyond a person's social voice. One male student I had literally blushed each time his voice entered into more archetypal female sounds. At these times I think: "Tread carefully for you tread on dreams."

These sounds, as indeed do all sounds, come with images with which the singer needs to come to terms if he is to stay with them. We all have sounds that we cannot accept easily and often it is a deep work of letting go into the imagination to allow ourselves to enter certain audible images.

Loss of Soul

Alfred Wolfsohn felt that he had lost his soul during the First World War. There are times that one is confronted with the sense that the soul has left the singer. Last summer I worked with an opera singer. She was born with a naturally beautiful voice. She had been "discovered" by her teachers and from the age of 13 was trained to stardom. As she told me—years of work and discipline in which a clearly natural gift was developed into an astonishing voice. At 25 she had a breakdown and lost all sense of direction and the clarity of the path constructed for her over the past 18 years. I met her when she was already in therapy—a therapy that had restored her self-confidence and an idea of who she was, but a therapy that had not restored her wish to sing. She came to my classes with great trepidation. She did indeed have an amazing voice—full generous, supple, expressive and with a very clear technique. She knew what she was doing—but it is true—there was no joy. I felt that I could make all kinds of propositions she would follow like a good soldier and it would mean nothing. After a week of work we were beginning to know each other and I began to introduce her to a exercise I use in which the singer takes a journey, trying as far as he or she is able, to follow the path that his or her voice wants to take. Gail, as I shall call her, began the work as conscientiously as she always did and it was clear that everything in her body and voice was seeking to excavate down—and that everything in her training was seeking to elevate her voice. She worked patiently and very slowly until her body began to relax and she found the channels she was searching for. Of course, her emotion was great, not manifested with tears. I can only describe it as if her whole body was "blushing," as if in this slow descent she was bringing to the surface the blood of a hidden passion. When we advanced further to work on her music she sang with such beauty that she suddenly stopped in the middle of her song: "I am singing from my soul"—that so familiar but unfamiliar place.

The Roy Hart Theatre Diaspora

Roy Hart was often asked if he would write a book about his work. He would turn to those around him and say: "You are my book."

When he died there were over 40 members of the Roy Hart Theatre. Approximately 20 of them are still working in the domain of the arts, and the voice work has been experienced by thousands of students all over the world. It was slow in coming but gradually there was a recognition that one cannot hold a work like this into a status quo—it is a living moving process—and in my view it is right and necessary that each person who studied with Wolfsohn and Hart can only develop his or her own work in relation to this experience. A few days before his death Roy Hart asked me to replace him in a press conference in Austria. A request from Roy at that time was more like an order, particularly to someone as young as I was. He wanted me to go to the conference and to announce, "I am Roy Hart." I refused, at the time out of modesty, but in fact it was a decisive moment. I was not Roy Hart and neither did I aspire to be him.

I am sure that if you asked each person who had worked with Roy Hart about his or her current work and philosophy, the replies would be very different. So where is the "book," the connections that link us to the "master." I would call it an attitude to the voice. One that takes into account and respects the psyche of the "singer."

We are working in the fields that lie between science and faith: the space where imagination lies—where we become something else because we have learned to suspend our disbelief.

The fear of the imagination and opening into unimagined possibility is great, and as Alfred Wolfsohn would quote: "God curses us by making our dreams come true."

Essay *by Paul Meier*

Paul Meier is Head of Voice and a Professor in the Theatre and Film Department at the University of Kansas. He is Founder and Director of IDEA (International Dialects of English Archive) at www.ku.edu/~idea. He is the author of *Accents and Dialects for Stage and Screen*, and *Dialects of the British Isles*, available with accompanying CDs from Paul Meier Dialect Services at www.paulmeier.com. His "show-specific" dialect CDs are leased worldwide, while he has coached a dozen feature films in the last decade, including Ang Lee's *Ride With The Devil*, and Paul Cox's *Molokai: The Story of Father Damien*.

A review of some of the leading programs for training voice trainers

Some years ago, Janet Rodgers, during her tenure as president of VASTA, suggested to me that bringing together the leading figures in the field of voice pedagogy would make an excellent article for the Pedagogy and Coaching section of the *Voice and Speech Review*. We often consider how we train our students and clients; we also want to consider how we train our future voice teachers. What follows are brief descriptions of some of the leading voice trainer programs, in each case submitted by a representative of the school or organization.

The schools, systems, or organizations represented are as follows:
1. Fitzmaurice Voicework certification program, Catherine Fitzmaurice, director
2. Northwestern University, Linda Gates, director
3. York University, David Smukler, director
4. Lessac Training and Research Institute, Inc., Arthur Lessac, director
5. National Institute of Dramatic Art, Bill Pepper, director
6. Freeing the Natural Voice: Teacher Training with Kristin Linklater, Kristin Linklater, director
7. Virginia Commonwealth University, Janet Rodgers, director
8. University of California, Dudley Knight, director emeritus; Phil Thompson, director.
9. University of Alberta, Betty Moulton, director.

The people on the list all directly train trainers. In other words, they work explicitly with schools or systems that certify, matriculate, or grant degrees to our future teachers of voice. One key program not represented in this article is London's Central School of Speech and Drama, under the direction of Joe Windley. Information about their one-year postgraduate course in voice pedagogy can be found at their website:
<http://www.cssd.ac.uk/courses/postgraduate/pg_voice.htm>

Voice specialists for the theatre receive their training from and are influenced by a great many sources not represented on the list. We acknowledge that by inviting submissions only from those who explicitly train trainers, we have excluded many important figures.

Fitzmaurice Voicework Certification Program
Catherine Fitzmaurice
The approach to voice teaching that is now called Fitzmaurice Voicework developed from my training in voice teaching at the Central School of Speech and Drama in London, which I followed with my own explorations into somatic systems of residual muscle tension release and access into unrestricted autonomic breathing response. My interests as a teacher lie in the aesthetics, psychology, and healing potential of the voice.

As I state in my article "Breathing is Meaning" in the book *The Vocal Vision* (Applause Books, 1997): "In searching for models beyond my own empirical experience and my observation of students and actors, the modern and ancient somatic training systems of Bioenergetics, yoga, and shiatsu have been most influential. In experimenting with these exercises myself and on others I explored means to most directly affect breathing and vocal sound, and the adaptations of these systems that I use with actors have over the years resulted in a series of exercises and interventions that I call Destructuring." I have also studied, and incorporate adaptations of, several energy healing modalities.

In the early nineteen-nineties I was approached by several voice teachers who had worked closely with me in preceding years. These were all teachers who were using my approach to voice teaching in their own practice, within both university training programs and in professional coaching. They asked me to begin teaching a coordinated set of workshops with the intention of making this work available to more voice professionals around the country. In 1995, I began offering five-day training sessions, with these teachers as my associates, to colleagues around the country, focusing primarily on my Destructuring/Restructuring work, and later on its application to text and to singing.

By 1998, there had developed a strong demand from those newer teachers who had already had some experience using my work in studio and coaching environments, to provide a more intensive, long-term, and individually-focused training that might lead to their certification by me as Associate Teachers of Fitzmaurice Voicework. These certification programs began in 1998 as a single, multi-week set of training sessions, taught by me and those teachers that I named at that time "Master Teachers" of my approach: they currently teach at the University of Southern California (Paul Backer), American Repertory Theatre/Harvard University's Institute for Advanced Theatre Training (Nancy Houfek), and Temple University (Donna Snow and Lynne Innerst). Dudley Knight and Joan Melton have since retired, respectively, from the University of California at Irvine and California State University at Fullerton. Since 2002, I have expanded the certification program so that it now takes place over a two-year period; it consists of two intensive four-and-a-half-week periods of work, during the same month in consecutive years. There are now, after five programs, about one hundred associates and two new Master Teachers, Philip Thompson at the University of California at Irvine and Saul Kotzubei, working privately in Los Angeles. Their names are on my website at <*www.fitzmauricevoice.com*>.

All the teachers whom I admit into the certification program have already spent some period of time training in—and teaching with—the Fitzmaurice Voicework approach. This is a requirement. Some of these certification candidates come from the many MFA acting programs that base their vocal training on this approach. Others have studied extensively with some of the certified Master or Associate Teachers of the work.

Some candidates have attended two or more of the five-day workshops.

Some of the candidates who seek intensive training in Fitzmaurice Voicework have also had extensive experience using other major training pedagogies, or have come from a background as trained singers, professional actors, professional dancers, or as speech pathologists. I welcome the enrichment that such varied experiences bring to these certification groups. While Fitzmaurice Voicework does differ substantially from the other voice training approaches, I have always considered it to be an inclusive process, not an exclusive one.

My aim in training teachers is to provide an environment in which each individual teacher is able to experience the work deeply and knowingly. The purpose is not to have the teacher simply learn a set of exercises or physical actions; rather, it is to enable the teacher to fully embody the work, to represent it in their own speaking performance, and to so thoroughly understand it that they can carry their training into their own concepts and practice in unique, individual ways that can go beyond the regimen of the certification sessions themselves. This is one reason why I have increased the amount of time that I spend observing and critiquing the practice teaching sessions and also the performances of the certification candidates. It is also why I do not guarantee certification as an Associate teacher at the end of the formal certification program: not infrequently, I will ask a teacher (and often it is a very skilled teacher) to reexamine or deepen his or her understanding of some aspect of the work by working individually with me or with one of the Master Teachers, or by exploring the work more thoroughly in their own teaching, before I grant certification.

The overall arc of the now nine-week certification program in its current form is a natural progression from basic principles to performance and teaching. In the certification program I am joined in the instruction by most of the certified Master Teachers of the work, by selected Associate Teachers, and by guest artists and lecturers. It is very important to me that the participants in the program experience the work through the voices of many teachers who have found their own unique ways of utilizing this approach in their own teaching.

The first week of the program focuses on an overview of vocal function and health. The second week focuses on the so-called "Destructuring" work, a set of physical positions and exercises designed to release rapidly the deeply-seated residual muscle tensions that inhibit free, open, and responsive breathing. The third week brings the participants from destructuring to the interrelated dynamic of "Restructuring," in which the participant explores the deliberate and intentional use of the breathing muscles, as is necessary when speaking, in a natural and physiologically sound manner as the speaker moves into full phonation. The final week of instruction in the first year brings the destructuring process and the restructuring process together in language use and movement.

The second year begins with a specific focus on shaping the responsive flow of breath/voice into a variety of speech actions in a non-prescriptive, but very active, manner. Here the participants focus largely on the very useful work of my colleague, Dudley Knight. In the second week the participants explore taking the destructuring/restructuring work into singing. The third week of year two is an intensive exploration of text, taking the participants into performance of voice/movement pieces they have devised. The final week is devoted to practice teaching by each participant, with observation and critique by me and several of the Master Teachers of the work.

The essentials of the certification training, since its inception in 1998, have remained the same. The specifics of the training have undergone a more or less constant evolution and revision. I welcome—in fact I expect—feedback from the participants about every aspect of their experience during the training process. I regard the nine weeks of certification training to be a process of mutual learning and growth.

I also find that as the certification program has progressed, and as more teachers of Fitzmaurice Voicework are working with young actors in MFA training programs around the country (and in conservatories abroad), as well as with undergraduates and young and seasoned actors in professional situations, the nature of the five-day workshops has evolved also. Ten years ago most of our workshops were introductory, providing a way for teachers to experience Fitzmaurice Voicework for the first time. Then we began adding workshops that were focused more specifically on singing or on classical text. Today, many young teachers have already experienced the basics of Fitzmaurice Voicework outside of the five-day workshop setting; many of the Associate Teachers are now offering introductory Fitzmaurice workshops of their own. So we are able to offer more five-day workshops nationwide that are specifically focused on one aspect of the work. These focused workshops have also proven useful for Associate Teachers, or aspiring Associate Teachers, to deepen their experience in a chosen area.

For the last forty years, it seems that the dominant model for "training the trainers" in voice and speech in America has been based on a kind of "craft guild" system, where prospective teachers study with persons who have developed—or are

primary exponents of—a few major teaching approaches. Whether this is indeed the best way for voice teachers to be trained as we move into a new millennium is a reasonable subject for debate, but while it is still the model I make every attempt to see that the certified trainers who are teaching Fitzmaurice Voicework to aspiring and practicing professionals have a sense of "owning" their intensive training in this approach, of letting it interact fruitfully with their own artistic sensibilities, so that each "trained trainer" remains a unique intellect and spirit.

Northwestern University
Newly Proposed International MA in Theatre Voice
Linda Gates, Head of Voice

In 1992, when I arrived at Northwestern University's Department of Theatre as Head of Voice, there was already a mandate to create an MA in Theatre Voice. My goal was to develop a training program that was international, focused on the needs of performers, that did not adhere to one "system," but rather reflected the best practices of many approaches.

Training for theatre voice and speech teachers in America has never been systematic. Most voice and speech teachers—and I include myself here—have initially either received their theatre voice training as actors in university drama schools where they study voice and speech as part of the acting curriculum, or they apprentice themselves to a "Master Teacher" whose work constitutes a system. The result is often confusing for theatre educators who have to select teachers for their programs defined by categories such as "designated Linklater teacher," "Skinner/Berry/Rodenburg influence," "Associated Teacher of Fitzmaurice Voicework," or "Lessac Certified Trainer" with little or no information as to what defines these systems, their effectiveness, how they are different from each other or how proficient the candidate is in teaching them. It is also confusing for students, who often face conflicting theories and vocal practices if they move from one institution to another.

As an acting student, I studied voice and speech at Carnegie Mellon University (then Carnegie Tech) with Edith Skinner, and then, by chance, with Edith's own teacher, Margaret Prendergast McLean, who had come out of retirement in her 80s to fill in for Edith's assistant who had become ill. I also studied singing with a private teacher in the music department. After leaving Carnegie, I studied in New York with Alice Hermes, another voice teacher who had studied, like Edith and Margaret Prendergast McLean, with William Tilley at Columbia University. I then joined the acting company of The Actors Workshop in San Francisco, where, to my surprise, I found myself teaching company members voice and speech because there was no voice coach in the company.

A few years later, I was asked to teach at New York University School of the Arts as an assistant to Nora Dunfee, Master Teacher of Speech. Kristin Linklater was Master Teacher of Voice. Ted Hoffman, who was then Head of the program, hoped that the assistants to both Nora, in Speech, and Kristin, in Voice, would eventually be able to bridge the gap between the two approaches. He assigned us, the young assistants of each Master Teacher, to work with both teachers for a year. I was thus very fortunate to work with Kristin Linklater who introduced me to an entirely new way of teaching voice. After two years at NYU, I went to teach at Columbia University School of the Arts with Robert Neff Williams—now on the Juilliard faculty, whose approach was quite different from that of Kristin or Nora. Two years later I left to teach at the Yale School of Drama, working with Marjorie Phillips, who had been trained at the Central School of Speech in England—and whose work on voice and breathing was again different from anything I had experienced before. Returning to New York University—now the Tisch School of the Arts—in the 1980s, I again taught with Nora Dunfee and several Linklater-trained teachers and began to study singing with V. William Reed. I also began attending the yearly symposium "Care of the Professional Voice" sponsored by The Voice Foundation at The Juilliard School which opened up the exciting and new-to-me world of voice science. I then went on to teach at the Central School of Speech and Drama in London, replacing one of their voice teachers, who was on leave. There I worked with Jane Cowell, Julia Wilson-Dixon and George Hall, discovering yet another approach to voice and speech work which involved the integration of the singing voice for all acting students. During the time I was teaching in these different schools, I also did professional vocal coaching on and off-Broadway and in regional theatre. In other words, my experience was of a broad range of vocal approaches and experiences which profoundly influenced they way I teach and led me to develop a graduate MA in Theatre Voice at Northwestern University Department of Theatre in partnership with the Central School of Speech and Drama in London.

Founded in 1906 by Elsie Fogerty, a legendary teacher of dramatic voice and diction who taught Laurence Olivier, John Gielgud and Peggy Ashcroft among other great stars of the British stage, Central School of Speech and Drama proposed to offer an entirely new form of training for young actors and other students. The choice of name—the Central School— highlighted the School's commitment to a broad range of training systems for vocal and dramatic performance. While teaching there, I became acquainted with the Voice Course which trained voice teachers for the theatre. I even did some teaching on the course, which is how I got to know of it and in later years to set up our partnership. Due to the wide range of influences in my own approach to voice teaching, I was impressed by the interdisciplinary nature and wide scope of the Voice Course at Central. At that time David Carey was Head of the Voice Course and working together, we developed an International MA in Theatre Voice at Northwestern and Central School. Since 1999 we have graduated five students who are now teaching voice in theatre departments at Indiana University, University of Illinois at Urbana Champaign, The Dalton School in New York and DePaul University.

Due to structural changes at both Northwestern University and the Central School we are currently reviewing our MA in Theatre Voice and developing plans to create a new program that will draw on the inter-disciplinary offerings of our recently renamed School of Communication (formerly the School of Speech) which consists of five departments: Theatre; Performance Studies; Radio, TV, Film; Communication Sciences and Disorders; and Communication Studies in conjunction with supporting courses in the School of Music and Weinberg College of Arts and Sciences. Students will then go to London for a term in which they will take courses and work with theatre faculty at a British conservatory. The goal is to restructure the curriculum to reflect the strengths of a major research university, serve the needs of a text-based Department of Theatre and Performance Studies, and draw on the curriculum of a British theatre conservatory to train voice and speech teachers who exemplify the best practices of both countries.

The following are some of the course offerings that are being considered in the different schools at Northwestern. Students will begin their graduate work at Northwestern and then go to England for a term at a British conservatory. They will then return to Northwestern for practice teaching and an internship with a professional Chicago theatre.

The School of Communication at Northwestern has a multifaceted series of departments that, while separate entities, can link together to support a strong professional training program in theatre voice and speech.

The Department of Theatre at Northwestern supports a strong undergraduate acting program. There are four core voice courses that support that program and its curriculum.

All freshman acting students take *Voice for Performance*, which focuses on relaxation, body alignment, individual vocal analysis, breathing, vocal placement and resonance, study of English speech sounds through use of the International Phonetic Alphabet, and culminates in a final project in which the students perform on stage an individual poem of their choice, and a group poem. In the final weeks of training, Joseph Mills, the Head of Dance, comes into the class and helps the students connect physical movement to the text.

This is the class that the MA in Theatre voice candidate will teach under the supervision of the Head of Voice.

The second class in the core curriculum is *Training the Actor's Voice* which builds on the voice work in *Voice for Performance* through the use of Shakespeare's text. Students review the IPA speech sounds, continue work with the piano to increase range and begin group work on a set speech, work through and perform individual sonnets of Shakespeare, then work on partnered scenes and monologues. Their final exam is a performance on stage of the individual sonnets, scenes, and monologues.

The third class of the core curriculum is *Advanced Voice Styles* which continues the work of heightened text through the exploration of the language of comedy. The work includes Moliere, Restoration Comedy, Oscar Wilde, Bernard Shaw, Noel Coward, and Tom Stoppard.

The final class in the series is *Dialects for the Stage*. Using the IPA, recordings of native speakers and dramatic text written in dialect, students study British, American and European dialects and perform each of them throughout the class.

Movement for the Theatre explores movement/body awareness through improvisational techniques using time, space, weight and effort as the instrument of expression.

Musical Theatre Techniques is taught in conjunction with the Music Theatre program, which is shared jointly with the Department of Theatre and the School of Music. MA candidates with a strong musical theatre background may pursue more intensive work in this area under the direction of Dominic Missimi, the Head of the Music Theatre Program.

Other Department of Theatre classes that are included in the curriculum are *Story Telling 1, 2* which explore ancient traditions and the current renaissance of storytelling with strategies for selecting, preparing and sharing stories in performance.

Candidates will also have individual voice coaching and graduate seminars to support their work in each of these classes.

The Department of Performance Studies is a separate and unique department whose classes are open to both Theatre and Performance Studies students. The courses explore an inter-disciplinary range of literary, cultural, and personal texts in performance. The department has particular strengths in the study of literature through solo performance, the ensemble adaptation and staging of poetic narrative, and non fictional texts, intercultural performance and performance art. Some of

the many Performance Studies classes which would support the MA in Theatre Voice are: *Analysis and Performance of Literature, Performing Modern and Contemporary Poetry, Presentation Aesthetics, Studies in Performance.* (Taught under the supervision of Frank Galati [now retired], Mary Zimmerman, Paul Edwards, and the Performance Studies faculty.)

The Department of Communication Sciences and Disorders specializes in basic science and research in communication and its disorders. It will provide the scientific underpinning for the MA in Voice candidate through the following courses: *Anatomy and Physiology of the Vocal Mechanism, Phonetics.* Currently all our entering Freshman receive a complete vocal screening through CSD with follow up vocal therapy as necessary at their clinic.

Weinberg College of Arts And Sciences offers a liberal arts education that combines broad exposure to the insights and methods of the principal academic disciplines. Among the wide range of courses that support the MA in Theatre Voice are included: Classics, Literature, Languages, Drama and Linguistics.

The School of Music has a strong connection with the Department of Theatre through the joint Musical Theatre Program. Course offerings include: *Keyboard Skills*, which gives the MA Candidate training in rudiments of piano and accompaniment; and *Private Singing*, which gives the candidate an understanding of the singing voice in addition to the speaking voice.

Although we are still in the process of restructuring the MA in Theatre Voice, our thinking about the role of the candidate within the Theatre Department and in the Acting curriculum is inclusive and hands-on. Because of the need for mentoring and close communication between students and faculty we envision a small cohort of only one or two students a year. Students would work closely with the acting faculty and be an integral part of the acting classes. As the voice curriculum supports the work of the acting classes, the voice candidate would function as a vocal coach for the students in that class with his or her work supervised by both the acting teacher and the Head of Voice. The candidate would also work closely with the MFA in Directing candidates on their productions.

At present the role of the UK conservatory in the curriculum has not been determined. A great deal depends on whether we decide to create an MA or an MFA. Our thinking is that after the candidates take the core curriculum in voice at Northwestern the first year, they would then go to a UK conservatory for advanced work in text and vocal coaching, returning to Northwestern for practice teaching, coaching and a professional theatre internship at a Chicago theatre.

York University
Graduate Programme in Theatre
Graduate Diploma in Voice Teaching
David Smukler

The Program
York University's Graduate Program in Theatre began training voice specialists on an informal basis when the Graduate Program was established in 1980. The university senate gave permission to officially grant a Graduate Diploma in Voice Teaching as of 1994 acknowledging the commitment of those MFA Acting and Directing students who undertake extensive additional training in Voice and Voice Teaching during their two year MFA program. This is the Concurrent Voice Teacher Diploma. In 2001, a one-year Stand Alone Voice Teacher Diploma was added. The program has been designed and conducted primarily by David Smukler (a Designated Linkater Teacher) who was one of the first teachers trained by Kristin Linklater. In 2003, he was joined by Eric Armstrong. The alumni are teaching in conservatories, colleges and universities across Canada, the United States and abroad.

Voice Teacher Candidates are expected to have professional acting experience and/or teaching experience subsequent to their Bachelor's degree or equivalent. Candidates must also have other advanced training, for example from Canada's National Voice Intensive, Shakespeare & Co, Equity Showcase Theatre, or other professional voice training programmes. The Stand Alone Voice Teacher Graduate Diploma is to aid those candidates who have already completed an MFA in Acting or Directing and wish to acquire the additional training and certification. The Stand Alone Diploma is also offered to those with advanced degrees (MA or PhD) who come from related fields (phonetics, speech pathology, linguistics, mass communications) and intend to apply voice and performance skills to business and mass communications. All Stand Alone Diploma candidates are expected to have some advanced performance training or professional performance experience, and/or teaching experience.

The Objectives
The overall objective of the Voice Teacher Diploma is to train voice specialists who will have the breadth of skills to teach the full spectrum of voice and to work as a member of an acting-movement-voice team. They must have an understanding of performance as well as teaching. We expect the voice specialist to have a strong aesthetic and philosophical grounding from which they can develop their own voice and speech work and their teaching skills. Additionally, they need

a basis on which to explore other methods and styles of voice training. The core of the training is the Linklater approach.

Although the focus of the program is designed to help prepare teachers for college and university-level studio teaching positions, a number of the alumni have successful careers as freelance coaches in business, film and television.

Unique Elements of the York Program
It is important to note that the York University is the only school in Canada that offers an MFA in Acting and that the age range in the program is often 23 to 53 with the average age usually in the early thirties. Most of the graduate students come with a professional theatre background or teaching experience. In special circumstances, experienced, mature performers without an undergraduate degree are accepted.

The structure of the course at York University has evolved through the extraordinary team-work of the acting, movement and voice faculty, where all three are working in a emotion-rooted, body-centered approach to naturalistic acting which provides the student actor with a strong, flexible core from which they can easily move around various forms of classical and contemporary theatre and the world of the camera.

Course of Study
Voice teachers in the two-year concurrent Voice Teacher Diploma program take the full course of study in the acting stream (acting, movement, voice, text, research seminar), to which are added the specific voice teacher activities. These extra requirements are the equivalent of three full graduate courses, spread over the five semesters of the MFA programme. The one-year Stand Alone Voice Teacher Diploma candidates focus solely on Voice Teacher activities. Because there is always a small number of candidates each year, they can be guided on an individual basis.

In addition to their actor assignments, Concurrent Voice Teacher Diploma candidates usually coach between two and three productions each year. The Stand Alone candidates coach three or four productions during their year. The coaching assignments include the range of Western theatre repertoire from modern naturalism to Shakespeare.

The voice teacher training focus includes an understanding and application of the philosophy and practice of the Iris Warren/Kristin Linklater approach to voice training including the teaching of a classical voice warm-up. We hope to train a teacher who has a rich body-centered, actor-focused palate of resources. The study of anatomy and physiology is a cornerstone of our work. We examine how the study applies to voice use, and how various philosophies of body and voice training

(Roy Hart, yoga, etc.) look at the psycho-somatic interplay and the potential realizations in voice work.

In response to the needs of acting for both the stage and camera, we include the study of phonetics (the International Phonetic Alphabet) and the problems of teaching diction for contemporary theatre and film as well as investigating the study of dialects as a total cultural, socio-economic, linguistic event. In the multi-cultural theatre and film world they need the tools for coaching speakers of a wide range of voices and languages, speech and dialects.

The senior faculty is continually engaged in the observation and analysis of the teacher trainees—in their teaching in the studio, their production coaching, and in leading their warm-ups for classes and rehearsal rooms for both the graduate and undergraduate conservatories.

Through their activities at the National Voice Intensive, Equity Showcase Theatre as well as sessions at York University, the Diploma students observe, assist and are mentored by senior voice faculty, giving them the opportunity to witness a broad range of teaching techniques and approaches. The candidates all have the opportunity to teach introductory Voice and Speech classes and frequently, second level Voice and Speech classes, Speech Improvement classes, and Shakespeare acting classes, with continual supervision by the senior voice faculty.

Through the Voice Teacher Seminars they have an opportunity to develop familiarity with other approaches to voice teacher training (physical, musical, speech and language approaches) and literature in the associate fields: Voice Science, Voice Therapy (medical, holistic and theatrical models), and Speech and Language (historical perspective, contemporary developments, current practices in language and speech education).

When possible, we attempt to provide an overview of styles and methods of voice training for the singer (pop, classical Eurocentric, Asian, African and Indigenous North American forms).

The Voice Teacher Diploma candidate is expected to attend (on a national or international level) a voice intensive, a training programme, or a conference where they present a paper, to observe and assist master teachers. They prepare a major voice-training research project which may be presented in oral or in written form. Frequently, other opportunities for additional observation of teaching arise (for example at the Stratford

Festival, the Shaw Festival, York University, Equity Showcase Theatre, or at Canada's National Voice Intensive).

There is also importance given to training the teachers in the development of spoken language skills, in improvisation as well as text study. This includes: the study of poetic forms, an in-depth exploration of Shakespeare's sonnets, Elizabethan rhetoric and poetic devices, Shakespeare's text, the First Folio (and how to examine period publications). As well, other specific periods and styles of writing and performing are explored such as Greek, 17th and 18th Century, Restoration, the Romantics, Caribbean, 19th Century American, and contemporary writing styles.

In summary: the Voice Teacher training at York University is a hands-on approach where the training is conducted through seminars and participation in studio classes as students, assistants, or practice teachers. Observation of master teachers, teaching and coaching assignments, research projects, individual guidance and a major research project/paper enhance the learning experience.

The Lessac Voice, Speech & Body Work
Crystal Robbins

The Lessac Voice, Speech and Body Work is so named because of the contributions, wisdom, and innovative research of founder and creator, Arthur Lessac, a living legend in voice work at the age of 97. Arthur's approach to voice work is unique in that he draws upon his experience as speech therapist, voice and dialect coach, opera singer, actor/director/ movement artist, and his especially keen take on behavioral vocal research. Notable influences on the early development of his work were German singer Lilli Lehman and Bernard Kwartin—engineer, cantor, and singing teacher. The Lessac Work evolved out of Arthur's professional studios in NYC in the 1930s, '40s, '50s where the problem-solving capabilities of his work became highly respected. As word of the success of this particularly gentle style of voice and body work spread in the '60s and '70s, colleges and universities across the country and abroad began to take up the work. Such champions of his work included Sue Ann Park at The Goodman School of Drama in Chicago and SUNY Binghamton, and Paul Baker at The Dallas Theatre Center and Trinity University, among many others. The work at SUNY Binghamton, where Lessac was mandated to overhaul the entire acting program, led to the development of a one-year Lessac Certification program. Participants from that program (VASTA member Barry Kur, for example) are still today teaching the work and are highly respected in the vocal arts. Further requests for training encouraged an organized approach to the Lessac Summer Intensive Workshop. These workshops used to run a full eight weeks and are still a requirement for Certification. Today, workshops exist that meet many needs: from weekend to one-week to the now four-week Intensive. The workshops serve not only those seeking Lessac Certification, but also actors, dancers, singers, teachers, speech therapists/pathologists, and those seeking personal creative human development.

Lessac's *Body Wisdom* (the accompanying body book to *The Use and Training of the Human Voice*) followed the voice text and, indeed, eventually led to a new edition of the voice text, as his research developed. For those unfamiliar with the specifics, The Lessac voice work maintains that tone can be felt and perceived within the body as a musical entity. The same kind of artistry used in feeling instrumentality in, say, a cello or violin (the perceivable vibrations and placement and skill, the ease and beauty and radiance), can be understood as ways to enjoy and build the voice we have. Drawing on the rich, easy, unencumbered tones we experience in childhood, along with the freedom in our bodies at that age, the Lessac work re-acquaints us with that freedom we all hold within. When the body is aware of its inherent body energy qualities (NRG in Lessac's books) and how to use them, the voice can begin to respond and relate to those NRG states. It is not over-stating it to say that the entirety of the voice work is grounded in the body, and that the body work is drawn entirely from behavior. The disconnect between awareness of the body and voice led to the development of a practical, useful, and gen-uinely perceivable series of "experiments" or "explorations" with the body (Lessac teachers eschew the words "practice" or "exercise" and prefer the more creative, open-ended goals of "exploring" or "experimenting") that then foster a sensibility of the body and voice as mutually beneficial parts of the body-whole that require cooperation and harmony to be of creative and healthful use.

From the lyrical and musical consonants to the music of the voice in tone (which seamlessly organizes low and full concen-trated tones, including how to effortlessly use "belt" and all singing tones) to the diversity and variety of the vowels aided by the practicality of structure which just so happens to satisfy an "American Standard" of speech that is not imitative but healthfully optimal; Lessac Voice, Speech and Body Work is useful, easy and good for the body.

The Lessac Training and Research Institute offers voice train-ers the opportunity to be designated as Lessac Practitioners or Lessac Certified Trainers. One must complete study in two Lessac Intensive workshops and successfully complete an oral examination to be designated a Practitioner. At that point, a teacher may apply for Certification Candidacy, where the trainer will be assigned a mentor who provides guidance throughout the Certification process. Final Certification is granted upon a subsequent written examination, application

of the work, and assessments of teaching as observed by Master Teachers.

Today there are Certified Trainers in the work across the globe. The work is being taught in Brazil, China, South Africa, Australia, Germany, Belgium and England; and even more than that credit the contributions of Lessac's particular influence to their own vocal discoveries and innovations with-in their fields. The Lessac Institute has seen an incredible growth of applicants for Certification in the past five years and has Certified 20 new teachers since then, including two new Master Teachers. Currently, there are approximately 45 Lessac Certified and Master Teachers, with another dozen in the certification process. This rejuvenation of interest in the work surely lies in the renewed awareness of the body/voice connec-tion as more occidental and oriental wisdoms infiltrate our physical and mental workouts and processing. Lessac work has often been compared to the wisdoms of tai-chi, yoga, and Pilates; although undoubtedly the heart of the work lies in the human heart of the master himself, Arthur Lessac. It is a rich gift indeed that we have him with us to learn from and grow with, for he teaches by example that there is still more to learn, more bridges to gap, more freedom to be found and more NRG qualities to discover.

National Institute of Dramatic Art (NIDA)
Graduate Diploma in Voice Studies
The Graduate Diploma of Dramatic Art in Voice Studies is a one-year, full-time course.
Aim
The Voice Studies course is designed to provide specialized study in voice teaching, text interpretation, communication skills, English as a Second Language, voice pathology, corpo-rate needs and accent and dialect. It is designed for people with suitable educational and professional experience in the voice and communication areas.

The course aims to train teachers of voice and speech to deal with the heightened use of voice and language required by var-ious dramatic styles; the needs of communicators in every area of society including those whose native language may not be English; and the needs of teachers, young people, actors, media presenters, public speakers and the corporate sector.

Approach
The purpose of voice teaching is to assist all human facul-ties—body, intellect and emotion—to interact harmoniously and support each other in the development of accurate and colorful vocal communication.

The course encourages a close interaction between theory and practice. Mornings are devoted to formal classes conducted by

NIDA staff and guest lecturers, and to voice classes with students of the Acting Course. During the afternoons and some evenings, students are assigned to productions in the NIDA Production Program, where they learn to apply theory to practice.

Towards the end of the course, each student is expected, under supervision, to assume responsibility for some Acting Course voice classes. Students work with NIDA voice teachers coaching student actors during the rehearsal process. At an appropriate time during the year, they are normally seconded to other teaching institutions, to production companies or to organizations which deal with communication skills.

All students are expected to develop a special interest in one aspect of voice work, which culminates in a major research paper and an oral examination conducted by a specialist in the field.

Subjects are Voice Theory, Practical Voice, Phonetics and Linguistics, Accents and Dialects, Text Interpretation, Movement, Communication and Teaching Skills, Corporate Voice, Voice with Children, History of Theatre and Professional Development.

Admission Requirements
Enrolment in the Voice Studies Course is limited as all work is carried out in small groups and there is a great deal of individual instruction.
Applicants seeking admission usually must:
• Have reached the age of 20 before the commencement of the course
• Hold a degree or diploma from a tertiary arts course, or have appropriate professional experience in theatre, film, television, radio or education
• Show at an interview authority, tact and artistic sensitivity and the ability to work with other people
• Be in excellent health
• Be fluent in the English language, both written and spoken, and demonstrate knowledge of literature at the graduate level
• Demonstrate a good speaking voice and the ability to critically evaluate other voices
• Show evidence of a serious commitment to a career in voice teaching.

The primary criterion for admission to the Voice Studies Course is evidence of the applicant's ability and potential to make a career as a voice teacher in the arts entertainment industry or educational fields.

Masters Degree in Voice Studies
The Masters Degree in Voice Studies is a one-year full-time course.

Aim
The aim of the course is to assist students to master the skills required of a professional voice teacher. This involves an in-depth knowledge of the discipline, advanced teaching skills and experience of the process of working creatively with actors and directors in theatre, film and television.

Approach
The course consists of three components:
1. practical work which involves teaching voice classes; voice work on play productions; and dramatic presentations focusing on heightened speech
2. a research thesis requiring an in-depth study of voice and speech in the industry or in education
3. a secondment to a theatre, film or television production or to an appropriate educational institution for experience in the field

Admission Requirements
The course is primarily designed for people who hold the NIDA Graduate Diploma in Voice Studies.

However, it is also open to people who have a primary degree in theatre studies, a basic knowledge of voice and some experience of voice teaching.

Freeing the Natural Voice
Teacher Training with Kristin Linklater
Kristin Linklater
Andrea Haring has assisted Kristin Linklater in the training of teachers since about 1990 and is the Coordinator of the Linklater Teacher Training. Our training process was developed out of a desire to make sure our teachers were thoroughly trained and out of a need to distinguish to the theater and academic worlds which teachers were legitimately "Linklater Designated."

For the Linklater teacher-training an important distinction should be made between "student" and "teacher trainee." We only accept those candidates who can demonstrate considerable experiential background in theatre performance and teaching. Our teacher-trainees are usually between 25 and 50 years old. We do not "seek" candidates—they seek us. Kristin Linklater is, in a sense, a reluctant teacher trainer. Consequently, those who apply to train with her and Andrea Haring must have an ardent interest, need and determination to pursue their studies. Those who are ultimately included in the final intensive program that teaches HOW to teach are noted for their own individual creativity, maturity, generosity of spirit, openness and curiosity. Although a sense of humor seems to us essential for a teacher, it can't be said to be an initial requirement; of course, it usually develops in the course of the training.

The training process for a Designated Linklater Teacher takes three to four years and costs may eventually add up to as much as $20,000. Some of our teachers have been able to coordinate their training with a Masters program such as the Gallatin program at NYU or a similar one at Antioch. A trainee is taught on several levels: personal connection to the work and their own voice, observing a senior teacher who mentors them, observing Kristin Linklater teach, participating in one-day teacher training workshops with the trainee group, and, if accepted, going through an intensive five-week teacher-training workshop led by Kristin Linklater. To be accepted as a trainee the person must have had some exposure already to the work—preferably through a two- or three-year training at a University with a designated Linklater Teacher or at the month-long workshop at Shakespeare & Company (in Lenox, Mass.). Depending on where the trainee lives he/she is assigned to the nearest senior Linklater teacher to go through the vocal progression very specifically in one-on-one sessions. This takes about a year. In the beginning the most important thing is to do the work personally in order to find vocal freedom and to embody the wide range of exercises fully. Trainees are required to observe senior teachers teaching and to talk with them about issues that come up in the classroom. Thereafter they may be invited to observe Kristin Linklater teach at Columbia University's Graduate School of the Arts. At this time trainees will be invited to attend teacher-training one-day workshops with Andrea Haring in NYC where they discuss and experience the theory and practice of the progression of exercises and talk about the philosophy behind the work. In these workshops Andrea works with the prospective teachers, individually and as a group. These trainees are required to become familiar with complementary techniques such as Alexander, Feldenkrais, Singing (especially Roy Hart technique), IPA and Louis Colaianni's Joy of Phonetics work. A trainee must learn the rudiments of playing the piano (enough to execute scales and arpeggios), take an anatomy class—preferably experiential anatomy—and seek out Acting classes if he or she has not previously trained as an actor. Trainees are encouraged to perform as often as possible so that the work is always brought back to the artistry of theater and responsibility to the text. At this point the trainee is also encouraged to practice-teach the work to students.

The final step in the teacher-training process is the five-week Designation Workshop. In order to be accepted, the trainee auditions for Kristin Linklater, Andrea Haring and other senior teachers. In the audition he/she teaches a section of the warm-up to the other teachers, performs a Shakespeare speech or sonnet, sings and is interviewed. Those accepted go on to the five-week workshop. Between 14 and 16 people are accepted. As the preliminary process is time-consuming, and the selection process rigorous, the Designation Workshops only take place every three to five years. Thus far there have been five Designation Workshops including one in Germany. The Designation Workshop is an intensive experience that takes place out in the countryside and involves living together, eating together and participating in teacher-training six to eight hours a day, six days a week. Kristin and Andrea observe the candidates teaching each other and teaching a practice group of new students. They get detailed feedback on the accuracy with which the work is taught and on their teaching qualities. Issues that come up encompass: Do you know WHY you are teaching each exercise? Can you explain how it connects to the acting process in terms of integrating intellect and emotion with body and voice? Are you present in yourself when you teach? Are you really taking the group in? Are you listening to your students with empathy? Are your diagnostic abilities accurate both in what a particular actor needs to be vocally free as well as creatively expressive? Kristin conducts master classes in each aspect of the work and there is always a guest movement teacher for one or two week's residency. Most evenings are spent discussing the art of teaching, singing together, and speaking poetry. At the end of the workshop there is a ceremony with Designation certificates awarded to the successful teachers and a celebration dinner where the new teachers meet the established ones and are welcomed into the community of Linklater teachers.

Virginia Commonwealth University
Janet B. Rodgers

Virginia Commonwealth University, in Richmond, VA, offers an MFA in Theatre Pedagogy with emphases in Voice and Speech, Movement, Directing, Acting and Design as well as a newly-created combination Voice and Speech/Movement emphasis. Janet B. Rodgers is the Head of Voice and Speech Training. Dr. Aaron Anderson teaches both voice and speech and movement. Professor Rodgers describes her approach to voice and speech training as "Infinite Voice Training." It is based on her experiences with voice and speech training in Eastern Europe, the British Isles and the USA and honors the many approaches to voice and speech training as practiced today. Its progression is described in the article, "Spheres of Voice and Speech Training" included in this publication.

The program in Voice and Speech is two to three years depending upon the background of the candidate. Graduate students in Voice and Speech will take three years of graduate voice and speech classes that cover Dialects, Shakespeare and Text, Vocal Extremes and one other special topic (i.e.

Archetypes and the Voice, Great Speeches etc.) During each semester, the graduate Voice and Speech students will participate in private tutorials in which they will address their own special vocal needs as well as meet as a small group to discuss pedagogy issues. During the first year, students co-coach mainstage shows while second and third-year students work on their own under faculty supervision. Depending upon the graduate students' past experience, they are assigned to teach a sophomore level voice and speech class (basic work in vocal production and resonance) during the fall semester, followed by IPA as a tool for ear training and dialect acquisition during the spring semester. Also during the second semester, graduate students will teach kinesthetic vocal adjustments with applications to character voices. During the first or second year, again depending upon experience, students will observe, as teaching assistants, junior level classes in dialects during the first semester, and Shakespeare and Text during the spring semester. Occasionally graduate students will be assigned to teach one of these classes during their final year of study.

Besides classes in Voice and Speech, graduate students are required to take twelve credits of graduate level Theatre History/ Dramatic Literature and Theory. They take three credits of pedagogy, taught by Dr. Noreen Barnes, Director of Graduate Studies as well as discuss pedagogical issues in all of their respective areas of study. In the pedagogy class, they create a syllabus and teach in front of graduate student colleagues. During the pedagogy course, department chair, David Leong, assists with resume writing and the business of teaching. In addition to these classes, graduate students in voice and speech are encouraged to take movement and directing classes as well as to dialect and vocal coach, when they are ready, in theatre companies in the Richmond area. During their years of studies, graduate students are frequently critiqued by the full-time faculty who observe them in the classroom.

We encourage our graduate students to get involved with VASTA, ATHE (Association for Theatre in Higher Education), and SETC (Southeastern Theatre Conference) as well as VTA (Virginia Theatre Association). In addition, the graduate students have created an organization called the GOGS, a well-run and highly respected part of our graduate student life. The GOGS coach undergraduate students on monologue preparation, teach workshops for our undergraduate population and serve as a resource for disseminating information. We encourage our graduate students to teach workshops outside of our department whenever possible. This provides important experiences in preparation for the expectations of university teaching. In the classroom, teachers address the work from an artistic point of view but also from a teaching point of view.

Graduate students in Voice and Speech are also encouraged to participate in workshops with other master teachers. Frequently they have already done this before entering our program but we realize that working with master teachers, both in the USA and abroad, is part of an on-going life-art building experience.

Theatre VCU's Voice and Speech program honors the work of all teachers who have taught voice and speech through the ages and from various angles, yet subscribes to no one pedagogical "system." Students become familiar with all of the current books on the subject of Voice and Speech and are encouraged to create their own ways of working and to find their own teaching methodology. They are required to observe the entire teaching faculty in the classroom and have the opportunities to work with high profile guest artists who visit the department for one week to two month residencies. At VCU's Medical College of Virginia, Voice and Speech students are encouraged to observe otolaryngologist Dr. Lawrence DiNardo, who studied with Dr. Robert Sataloff, as one familiar with the needs of the professional voice user. They are also encouraged to observe Dr. Michael King who specializes in speech pathology. They are encouraged to accompany students to appointments with these doctors when problems are being addressed.

No program can expect to give every student everything they will need in order to teach for the rest of their lives, but what we do give to our students are the tools so that each student can find his/her voice in the classroom and profession.

University of California, Irvine
Dudley Knight (Professor Emeritus)[1]

I find myself—and "find" is the operative word—training trainers in several contexts, none of which are forms I ever intended to serve as complete curricula in any sense. The contexts are three, and deserve brief mention.

Context number one might be described as training by association: in 1995 at UCIrvine I co-produced the first five-day workshop to present the voice pedagogy of Catherine Fitzmaurice specifically to practicing voice faculty.[2] Since then, as more and more teachers have found Fitzmaurice's work to be of great value to them and to their students, I have continued as an active and enthusiastic participant in the teaching of what have now come to be full teacher certification programs in Fitzmaurice Voicework. In these programs I have had the honor of working—in an ancillary capacity—with a large number of brilliantly talented faculty who are now teaching in theatre programs all over the country

Context number two might be termed pre-training training, and to me it is an important part of the process. While it is crucial to train committed voice professionals in effective pedagogies on an advanced level, it is also necessary first to create environments within which aspiring young theatre professionals may decide that they want to concentrate on voice and speech teaching as a career. The MFA Acting Program at UCIrvine is just that: a demanding training program for professional actors. But it is also one that has always valued its voice and speech program as a central part of acting training. Although most of our MFA actors go on to successful professional acting careers, I have noted that over the years we have produced a substantial number of persons who have gone into voice and speech teaching as an academic (or sometimes freelance or corporate) career. Many of them have gone to take advanced work through the Fitzmaurice Voicework Teacher Certification; some have not. I believe that I and my faculty associates[3] in the voice and speech program at UCIrvine have been successful over the years in establishing within our students' artistic awareness a sense of the centrality of voice and speech skills in the acting process, as a way of gaining access to the deepest roots of their creative spirit and a way to potentiate their abilities to communicate richly with others. That central awareness of the extraordinary utility of voice and speech skills often sparks an appetite within students to continue the learning process after the structured environment of a training program has been left behind. In the voice and speech program at UCIrvine—especially as it has evolved over the years—we take care to provide our MFA students with an intensive experience in all aspects of voice and speech work. We are working with graduate students and we treat them as graduate students. At the same time that they are being introduced to the experiential delights of Fitzmaurice Destructuring work, they are also receiving an in-depth introduction to vocal anatomy and physiology. This has regularly included direct-observation analysis through videoendoscopy of all entering MFA students, as well as acoustic analysis on some of the Kay Elemetrics Computerized Speech Lab programs as well as standard audio recording and video analysis of performance selections. Thus our students come to understand, early in their training, some of the ways in which objective assessment through voice science techniques can give them powerful information without blocking their own personal experiential awareness. The ongoing development of this dynamic dialogue between objective and subjective awareness—often bifurcated in voice training programs—is a distinguishing, though certainly not unique, feature of the training at UCIrvine.

As in many voice programs, the instructional focus throughout the three years of study moves progressively into more and more focus on specific vocal/acting issues, including extreme vocal use, voice acting and voiceover techniques, and meeting the challenges of complex texts. We also devote one academic quarter in the third year to the exploration of pedagogies in voice training other than Fitzmaurice Voicework, the approach that forms the foundation of our training. Finally, selected graduate actors have the opportunity, in their third year, to teach sections of the undergraduate voice/speech course on both a beginning and intermediate level.

Speech is taught as a separate curricular arc from voice at UCI, but of course its work becomes more integrated with the voice arc as the training progresses. The speech program at UCI is the area in which I and my colleagues, especially Philip Thompson, have tried to establish an approach to training that makes a unique contribution to the field. Over the years, as we explored the theoretical and practical implications of letting go of the older, highly prescriptive and restrictive approach to speech training for actors, we realized that the implications of this departure from the pedagogical fold were far-reaching and profound. This realization has been an ongoing, "unfolding" (in both senses of the word) process, and therefore the speech program at UCIrvine has been in a constant state of evolution for the past fifteen years or so. It is only in the last five years or so that our work has strongly coalesced into a thoroughly unified approach. To a large extent, it is the generations of talented graduate actors at UCIrvine who have succeeded in pushing me to go even further in my redefinition of speech standards and to an intensive exploration of how one might effectively realize these altered—and, in my view, more demanding—standards in day-to-day instructional terms.

The result of the UCIrvine speech program is that graduate actors (at least, those who have been paying attention!) emerge from it with a great freedom of articulation and a huge variety of phonation possibilities. Further, they have gained powerful analytical skills in discerning, and then physically replicating, subtle changes in articulatory shaping of sound. In the course of acquiring these skills that allow them to move easily into and out of vocal and dialect characterizations, they gain a very thorough knowledge of narrow IPA phonetic transcription for descriptive purposes. It is not surprising, then, that some of our graduates wish to carry these explorations on, after graduation, into a teaching environment.

This brings me finally to Context Three, the series of intensive speech training workshops that Philip Thompson and I have been teaching for faculty colleagues around the country. We have structured these in two parts, each lasting three days, with the first three-day part sometimes taught as a separable workshop. These first three days are devoted to a completely physical exploration of articulation possibilities. We announce it as being free of phonetic transcription—which is true—but it is also true that participants, by the end of the three days, have physically produced all of the sounds of the IPA—that is, all the sounds of the world's languages—and have learned to codify them in terms of physical action, without ever having transcribed any of them, at least in this workshop. We have also provided an introduction to the Detail Model, which is a flexible model of detailed speech actions based solely on criteria of intelligibility in differing speech environments. There is a gradation of activity in each speech action: less or more activity might be appropriate in each speech environment, ranging from an intimate conversation to a tirade in an outdoor theatre. The Detail Model, in our view, provides a more useful and flexible prescriptive model than the older prescriptive pattern, especially since the articulatory actions of the Detail Model, once internalized, can be applied as needed to any accent or vocal characterization.

The second three days of our workshop concentrates on using the current formulation of IPA phonetic transcription as a descriptive and analytical tool in speech and accent work. We work on analyzing connected speech. We explore the "physical posture" of the articulators in accents and in vocal characterization. Over the years we have discovered—to our pleasure and slight surprise—that once the ground-work is laid for phonetic acquisition by students through aware physical embodiment of the sounds of the world's languages, the final step of codifying this into phonetic symbols is very easy for students to master. In our UCI training curriculum phonetic symbols are introduced at that point when our students are already feeling the *need* to communicate their perceptions in written form. So even in our actor training program we find that it takes only a few weeks for the students to learn and use the entire IPA, not to mention the additional symbols and diacritic modifications. In a much more compressed way, with a highly knowledgeable and motivated group of teaching colleagues, we can accomplish the same thing in less than a day.

At present, the Speechwork training for teachers exists in this three-day or six-day format. Professor Thompson's and my goal is to make the essentials of the approach available to colleagues in a readily accessible form. If the demand develops, we may consider ongoing workshops for those teachers who wish to explore some of the more advanced work, especially some of Philip Thompson's innovations in using computer-manipulated sound samples to teach accents. As the Speechwork approach continues its progress in being adopted in more professional training programs, we may expand the nature of the training.

So while I do indeed "train trainers," the contexts in which I do so do not constitute, as of this writing, a complete curriculum that leads to "certification" or "designation" or a formal advanced degree. As our field continues to develop, I am sure that our training modalities will continue to evolve as well.

Footnotes
1. Dudley Knight retired from Irvine in 2005. His curriculum, largely unchanged, is continued by Philip Thompson and Cynthia Bassham.
2. This is not to suggest that this was by any means the first workshop taught by Catherine Fitzmaurice; only that it was the first one using the five-day structure that she continues to employ in much of her teaching today.
3. Joan Melton, Lynn Watson, Debora Cahn, and Philip Thompson.

University of Alberta, Edmonton, Canada
Betty Moulton, Director

The new MFA in Theatre Voice Pedagogy at the Department of Drama in the University of Alberta (inaugural year, 2006), is an exciting addition to this dynamic department. The program will bring together all the elements of training needed by the voice teacher in the context of the theatre, and will also provide practice in coaching for public speaking. Aspects studied include knowledge of healthy and responsive physical choices that affect voice and speech production, elements of voice that are extended for theatrical expression and a strong understanding of how text interpretation feeds the acting moment. The two years will provide a comprehensive base for a wide-ranging career. Avenues for this profession are in the theatre world but also in the business world for personal presentation skills.

As this program is just beginning, I have many hopes in place and much experience to come. The curriculum will certainly spring from current texts on voice and speech pedagogy; the expertise my colleague and I have gleaned from the experiences we have had over the years teaching, coaching, and learning in many workshops, symposia and intensive periods of study with master teachers; and also from the shared experience of all my VASTA colleagues in the form of publications written over the years. But the program will also clearly evolve and be influenced by the strengths and interests the students bring with them. The questions and discoveries so far in the Voice pedagogy seminars this fall term have been truly inspirational. As we all know, when we teach, we have the opportunity in turn, to learn a great deal.

The philosophical and psychological underpinnings of this wonderful profession are both clear and cloudy, straight forward yet infinitely complex as well. When you consider the layers that are contained in every moment a teacher spends with an actor, two years seems to be inadequate to impart enough knowledge and experience to launch someone on this life long road of discovery. My plan and wish is that the time will be well spent learning more about the theatre in classes, reading the philosophies and practices of the major theater voice master teachers, viewing, participating and assisting David and me in our roles of theatre voice teachers and coaches, in collaborating with other theatre professionals on productions, in having experience in translating theatre voice coaching skills for professional voice users in business and education, and in connecting with medical professionals who provide care and therapy for vocal problems throughout society. All this will give a solid foundation from which to continue the exploration into human communication in all its forms.

When I devised the program, I felt it would be rightfully placed in the Department of Drama. It is an ideal setting: a theatre department where we strive for authentic communication that is charged with the highs and lows of human intellect, emotion and personal achievement. All aspects of the cry of the human heart are the business of theatre and any training to help an individual communicate in any situation, real or imagined must allow and encourage this. The "vocal athletes" in theatre require rigorous, in-depth and carefully constructed training to promote the full blossoming of their communication powers. The basis for authenticity and power is built in an excellent actor training program and this is where the voice teacher needs to be tested for the ability to enter into the relationship with the actor who agrees to go to those human places of risk with integrity, honesty, fearlessness, intent, and power. The voice teacher must go with them to help guide the journey and needs to understand the challenges this poses for the actor. Collaboration is the hallmark of the journey to seek out the expression that will touch and move the audience, so the teacher employs the means together with the actor that encourage and strengthen that journey, and both need to be engaged on a very deep level.

MFA Theatre Voice Pedagogy Program Highlights
The two year program offers a wide variety of opportunity to participate in all aspects of a theatre practitioner's training, to study voice, speech and text work in a full context for performance. MFA Theatre Voice students benefit from superb facilities and interaction with all programs currently run in the Department.

There are opportunities for:
• Participation and observation of voice classes in the BFA professional actor training program.
• Coaching and teaching both supervised and unsupervised in the BA drama program, the BFA acting and for MFA directing projects.
• Shared classes and projects with MFA directors, designers and MA drama candidates.
• Teaching and coaching for any production in the department.

The core courses in Theatre Voice Pedagogy and Vocal Coaching are supplemented by graduate seminars in the department including Dramaturgy and courses on directing which bring candidates in direct contact with specialists in those two disciplines to explore the role of the vocal coach in the production process.

The thesis will consist of the preparation and execution of a major vocal coaching assignment for either Studio Theatre, the Department of Drama's resident theatre company, or an outside professional production. It will include written research, documentation and analysis considering a combination of dialect, complex and heightened language, special physical challenges to vocal size or characterization, singing and choral speech. The thesis will be followed by an oral defense.

A wide variety of forums and people with various purposes in studying voice will round out the learning situations in which the MFA students are engaged.

The two students train with me, Professor Betty Moulton, and my colleague, Professor David Ley. Both of us have extensive professional resumes in acting, teaching and coaching in professional theatre companies and training schools, and also in presentation skill coaching for business and education. We both maintain close connections with various international theatres and centres for the study of voice. I have been teaching in actor training schools in the US and Canada for over twenty years, David for over ten. I have been the voice, speech and text coach for the Colorado Shakespeare Festival for ten seasons and David has had the same position on a team of voice coaches at the Stratford Festival for eight seasons. These two festivals have provided us the opportunity to work with a very large contingent of actors who come from a breadth of professional theatre experience and represent a large cross-section of training from programs across North America The skills we have developed in coaching such a diverse group will be an important addition to the perspective we can provide the MFA Voice students.

I am particularly excited by the unique connection the program has to the Speech Pathology and Audiology department at the University. The students take a Speech/Language Pathology course in speech science, which gives a strong anatomy and physiology base for their work with actors and other public speakers. This access will put them in touch with the latest advances in voice and speech science, vocal hygiene and health issues. I expect there will be great opportunities for cooperation on research projects between the disciplines. This will also build professional connections for the future as the two professions assist "professional voice users" throughout their careers.

The Department of Drama has been training students in all aspects of theatre for over 50 years. As a result, there is a continuing and extremely strong connection to a rich professional theatre community. Per capita, there are more theatre organizations and theatrical performances each year in Edmonton than anywhere else in Canada. As many of the key players at all levels are U of A grads, there are many opportunities for coaching and teaching in the profession, and for forging relationships for the future.

Ideal Applicants to the Program

Applicants come with an Undergraduate degree in theatre, with a strong emphasis on acting and/or directing. Teaching and coaching build skills that allow the transmitting of information within the discipline chosen. The time in the MFA is spent exploring the art itself but also teaching methods that are effective in the theatrical context. Breadth of background in the theatre provides the base for this exploration.

They must possess a strong understanding of and proven ability in handling complex and heightened language in the theatrical context. Actors in training are always being challenged by a wide variety of texts to stretch the range of their intellectual, emotional and creative soul in expression. A strong background in text analysis of various styles is necessary to support the new voice, speech and text teacher when he or she coaches the acting moment in whatever style is required.

Professional performance experience in the theatre is also an important asset so that the MFA student understands the process from the inside. A good voice teacher is always in the moment of working on self, as he or she works with an actor. The physical empathy necessary to guide the actor into new intellectual, emotional and physical knowledge is a major aspect of the work.

Conclusion

I want to document quickly my path to heading up this training program, and in doing so, to thank all those who have influenced me to pursue this complex and hugely rewarding profession. All of their lessons are in this new MFA program. My journey began with my first "drama teacher and director," Mrs. Petrie, through my studies with Mrs. Aymong at the Royal Conservatory of Music in Toronto in Speech Arts and Drama as I grew up; continued through my theatre studies at Queen's University into the profession of acting. As my interest in the voice teaching aspect of the theatre slowly grew to surpass my desire to be an actor full time, I learned from many master teachers who touched me deeply along the way in voice, speech, interpretation, movement, dance, acting and singing. For the past 30 years I have been attending these

workshops and courses and conferences and as many teachers of my generation, this is how I learned my craft. Also, so much knowledge and inspiration for me has come along this journey from my VASTA colleagues, because of their dedication to the encouragement of human communication that is joyous and free.

It is my humble desire to promote the continued devotion to the depths and thrills of human communication through teaching those who will teach: those who desire similar freedom in their own expression.

Contact Information

Fitzmaurice Voicework certification program, Catherine Fitzmaurice, director:
http://www.fitzmauricevoice.com/index.html
cfvoice@hotmail.com

Northwestern University, Linda Gates, director:
http://www.communication.northwestern.edu/
lhg984@northwestern.edu

York University, David Smukler, director:
dsmukler@yorku.ca

Lessac Training and Research Institute, Inc., Arthur Lessac, director:
www.lessacinstitute.com

National Institute of Dramatic Art, Bill Pepper, director:
http://www.nida.unsw.edu.au/fulltime_courses/courses/voice_studies/default.html
b_pepper@nida.unsw.edu.au

Freeing the Natural Voice: Teacher Training with Kristin Linklater, Kristin Linklater, director:
http://www.kristinlinklater.com
http://www.linklater.de/
kl@kristinlinklater.com

Virginia Commonwealth University, Janet Rodgers, director:
jrodgers@vcu.edu

University of California, Dudley Knight, director emeritus; Phil, Thompson, director
pthompso@uci.edu

University of Alberta, Betty Moulton, director
emoulton@ualberta.ca
http://www.uofaweb.ualberta.ca/drama/

Essay *by Janet B. Rodgers*

Spheres of Voice and Speech Training

A pedagogical tool to help the Voice and Speech Trainer describe the many layers of his/her work.

How do we Voice and Speech Trainers clearly describe to our students what we do and where we plan to take them on their voice and speech journeys?

In the fall and winter of 2004, I was a Fulbright Scholar in Romania. During my months of teaching and observing at Lucian Blaga University and the Radu Stanca National Theatre in Sibiu as well as Babes Bolyai University in Cluj Napoca, I kept asking myself how I could quickly and easily explain what I do—in a universal language that was clear and direct. How could I lay out a map of the voice and speech journey as I undertook it with my students?

One cold December day, as I was sitting in my small Transylvanian kitchen eating a bowl of corn flakes, the inspiration came to me in the form of a graphic design on the back of a corn flakes box that came from the Czech Republic. Using concentric circles of three different colors and picturing the various foods in each circle, the graphic described: 1. Foods that were *perfect* to eat (fruits, vegetables, and whole grains). These were depicted in a green inner circle; 2. *Not bad* foods (milk, cheese, olives, fish) which were depicted in pale orange ring around the pale green circle; and 3. Foods to *be careful* of (sausages, creamy sweets, chocolate, french fries) which were pictured in an outer pale yellow ring. Underneath the descriptions, in seven languages, were the written descriptions of the essences of each ring.

Suddenly my months of thinking about how to describe the many spheres of voice and speech training came together in a single image. I hastened to the stationery store, purchased a set of colored pencils and a protractor and set about drawing my ideas. They flowed forth in a series of concentric circles, which followed the colors of the rainbow. Around the center circle of black I drew ½ inch circles and colored them first red, then orange followed by yellow, green, blue, indigo, violet and, finally, white. Each of the circles represented a focus or aspect (or even level) of voice and speech training. Black represented the beginnings of training with **Body Awareness** of centering and aligning of the body from which all work emanates. Red represented **Breath**, and was followed by the orange concentric circle that represented **Sound**. This was followed by a yellow concentric circle that represented the **Dynamics** of sound, followed by a green circle representing **Expansion** of sound. Then came a transition into articulated or spoken sound; a blue circle for **Diction**; indigo for **Dialects**; a violet circle for **Elevated Texts** and finally, a white circle for what I consider to be the most advanced levels of voice and speech training—explorations of **Archetypes** (based on the work of Frankie Armstrong), **Chakras** and **Alba Emoting** (based on the work of Suzanna Bloch).

During the previous summer I had taken a course in which I had explored the eastern Chakra Systems and had discovered that each chakra has not only a corresponding color (that follows the order of colors of the rainbow) but also that each chakra has a particular phoneme and a musical pitch associated with it. I included each of these elements in my schematic. The following is how each chakra essence, in my model, loosely corresponds with each element and level of voice and speech training.

Janet B. Rodgers, Past President of VASTA, is Head of Performance and Voice and Speech Training for VCU's Department of Theatre. She has taught at The Boston Conservatory of Music and was principal actress with Boston Shakespeare Company and The Lyric Stage. She has dialect coached over 100 plays for Theatre VCU as well as for Theatre Virginia, The Barkdale and others. She has taught in Serbia, Romania (where she was a Fulbright Scholar), Switzerland and Great Britain. Past President of VASTA, her book, *The Complete Voice & Speech Workout*, was written in conjunction with 50 VASTA members. Her current research has taken her to Serbia to work with the DAH Theatre. She is collaborating with Frankie Armstrong on a book about archetypes and performance.

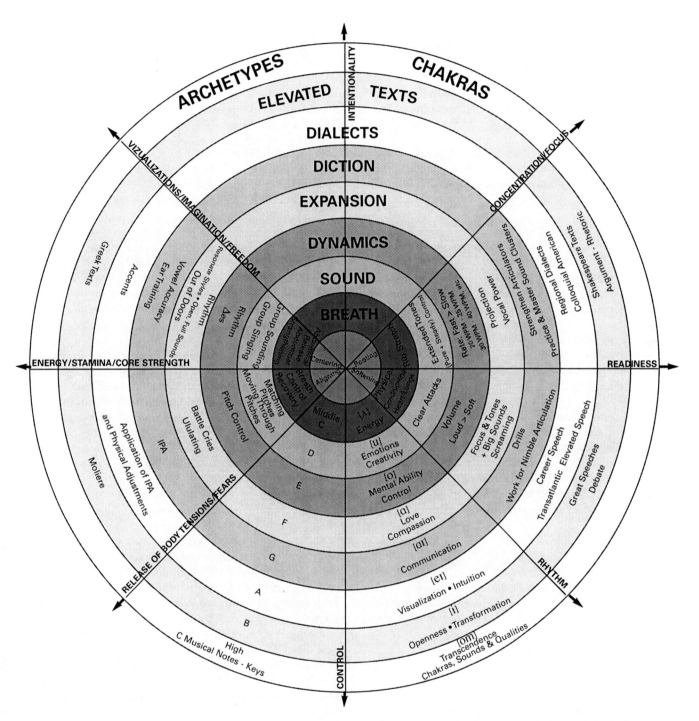

Accompanying my schematic is a verbal description of what each level of work includes (see next page). (A full-color version may be found on-line at <*http://www.vcu.edu/arts/JanetRodgers*>)

Black Circle: **Body Awareness**: rooting, centering, aligning, and softening of tensions-especially in jaw and back of neck

Red Circle: **Breath**: Development of abdominal strength (core strength), centered breath, physical conditioning of heart and lungs, rhythm of breath, extension and breath control

Orange Circle: **Sounds**: Extended sound, clear tone free of attacks, breathiness or tension (restriction), group singing and sounding, practice in matching pitches, control of breath/sound

Yellow Circle: **Dynamics of Sound**: Rate changes, pitch changes, rhythm control, volume changes

Green Circle: **Expansion of Voice**: Projection, focusing of big sounds, screaming, ululating, resonance explorations, character voices, open, full sounds in big spaces

Blue Circle: **Diction**: Strengthening and making nimble muscles needed for clean, strong articulation of sound, consonant/vowel accuracy, ear training, psycho-physical explorations

Indigo Circle: **Accent and Dialect Study**: foreign accents, regional dialects, career speech (general American dialect), transatlantic dialect

Violet Circle: **Elevated Texts**: Shakespeare, Greeks, Moliere, Great Public Speeches: Work out of doors and in big spaces; study of the art of debate, argument, and rhetoric

White Circle: **Archetype Work, Chakra Explorations and Alba Emoting Breath work**

Also included in my schematic are eight radiant lines emanating from the center circle. These lines represent elements that, I believe, absolutely must be present in all acting and training work. These include:
1. Concentration/Focus
2. A State of Readiness
3. A sense of Rhythm
4. Control
5. Freedom from body tensions and fears
6. Energy/Stamina
7. Imagination/Ability to Visualize
8. Ability to play with Intentionality

Once I had clarified my overview of voice and speech training on paper, I began to challenge myself with some very difficult pedagogical questions.

1. What exercises/explorations do we do in the classroom to bring each student into and through each circle (level) of training?
2. How do we measure learning of skills?

In addition, I began to clarify a very strong teaching philosophy (no doubt influenced by my experiences in Romania) that included my belief that students need to enter into all of their training from a neutral place; ideally all dressed in neutral (ideally black), loosely fitting clothes (t-shirt tucked in, sweat pants), sans jewelry, "body art," piercings, watches and logos.

I believe that movement, rhythm, energy, focus, and clear intentionality must be included in all voice and speech work and that practice, repetition, and application are the keys to bringing about change in the student actor. Since my return from Romania, our department has enforced a very strict dress code for our performance classes that reflects the above demands.

My teaching has changed dramatically since my return from the Fulbright experience. The **Spheres of Voice and Speech Training** schematic provides me with a daily reminder of my roadmap. I begin each class with a statement of intentionality, followed by a clear hit on a Tibetan chime during which time each person present in the classroom listens, breathes, and when they can no longer hear the resounding resonance of sound takes a large breath, exhales, and enters into the work at hand.

In August of 2006 I presented my visual schematic at the VASTA conference in Chicago and received some very valuable feedback from my beloved VASTA colleagues. It was felt that the schematic needs to be more pliable and I couldn't agree more. Imagine, if you will, an inhaling and exhaling amoeba-shaped organism made up of our rainbow concentric circles. This moving image reminds us that we always, in our training, must come back to center, breath, and sound, even as we move into the more advanced spheres of training. We learn and return. We learn about our breath and always return to it. We learn about our voice. We expand our dynamics and diction while always returning to our source; our bodies, our breath, our voice…not unlike our yearly return to the sea for renewal.

Peer Reviewed Article *by Jeff Morrison*

Voices of the Cold War

Jeff Morrison teaches Voice and Speech at Marymount Manhattan College in New York City and the American Repertory Theatre's Institute for Advanced Theatre Training at Harvard University. He has also taught at San Diego State University, the Moscow Art Theatre, the Old Globe School in San Diego, Tufts University, and the University of Northern Iowa. Morrison received his BA in Theatre and Folklore from the University of Pennsylvania; his MFA (Acting) from University of Wisconsin-Madison; and is a Certified Associate Teacher of Fitzmaurice Voicework. He has coached voice, text, and dialects in New York, Boston, Los Angeles, and San Diego.

Shortly after the end of World War II, the US and USSR entered into a contest of ideologies, the Cold War, that dominated political discourse, foreign and domestic policy, and cultural products of the globe for almost 50 years, creating stereotypes, influencing thought, and affecting art. With trade and exchanges between the US and the former USSR now blossoming, we are still discovering the Cold War's influence on what we grew up thinking and feeling—not just about the threat of the "Red Menace," but about the purpose and meaning of our life in America, freedom of self-expression, and hidden ideologies and invisible assumptions regarding the right way to live.

During the Cold War, certain artists rose above the pernicious influences of McCarthyism in this country and the restriction of self-expression that characterized the Soviet regime. Because these artists were persecuted in both countries (Solzhenitzyn in the USSR, for example, and blacklisted artists in the US during the McCarthy era), there is a myth that artists from both sides were united in their pursuit of a universal truth, and that therefore these artists—and by extension all of us—were the same. While great artists were able to resist persistent ideas that either side was "right" in the global conflict, deeply ingrained cultural attitudes regarding the meaning of human existence still colored artistic products on both sides of the divide. What these great artists had in common was their loyalty to the higher ideal of self-expression. What they expressed, however, was inevitably a product of their identities, and their identities were inseparable from their cultural environment—artists in the US and Russia *were* different.

Observing difference, confronting it, and understanding it offer the greatest opportunities for learning. Seventy-plus years of institutionalized difference, in spite of the fact that theatre practitioners in both countries claim the same Russian "father," Stanislavksy, has affected how artists in these two different cultures create theater, conceive of truth and human nature—and teach voice. Voice training is concerned, ultimately, with connecting the actor's utterance to some kind of truth using the voice as a medium, so that ideally, even the actor's smallest sound communicates something meaningful about being human. It should come as no surprise that this question—what is the nature and meaning of human existence—would have different answers in these different places. But this question is influenced by ideologies so deeply ingrained in our daily discourse that they disappear; surprisingly, this invisible history has a profound effect on how we train our students to use their voices, to think about voice, to find their voices in themselves, and to create vocal art.

THE PROJECT

This paper is concerned with the differences (and similarities) in voice training in the theatrical traditions of Russia and America, the invisible history implicit in those trainings, and what we can learn from the differences. My interest in Russian voicework grew out of many years' association with the American Repertory Theatre (ART), where I teach voice and speech during the summers, and with the Moscow Art Theatre (MXAT). Because the ART's acting and movement curriculum shares faculty with the MXAT School, I have been able to observe numerous acting classes taught by Russian faculty. I have also visited and taught at the MXAT School on several occasions, for two weeks to three months at a time. I have witnessed how the

Russian approach to acting differs from our own, how it inspires American acting students, and the remarkable results it achieves in imaginative accessibility and physical awareness.

The historical record shows exchanges between Russian and American theatre practitioners dating back to the 1920s. These collaborations ultimately gave rise to one of the most significant developments in American actor training, now known as the Method. However, exposure of this kind has been limited to acting and movement techniques, with few recorded visits of Western voice teachers to theatre schools in Moscow, and even fewer that went the other way (as I learned during various interviews and conversations in the US and in Russia, Kristin Linklater likely made the first post-*perestroika* visit to the MXAT in 1989, and returned in 1991; Catherine Fitzmaurice taught American students at the MXAT and showed her work to Marina Brusnikina in 2001; Cicely Berry visited GITIS during the late 1980s or early 1990s; and it's likely that a Roy Hart member visited Moscow during the Soviet regime. In the other direction, Anna Petrova studied with Kristin Linklater at the 1990 Shakespeare and Co. Winter Intensive, and returned a few years later with Victor Markhashev and several other Russian teachers). There seem to be two major reasons for this puzzling lack of international contact: one, a belief that the sounds of each language are so different that these two traditions would have nothing to say to each other, and two, a belief, true of each tradition, that its teachers have discovered a fundamental truth about the human voice, naturally leading teachers in each tradition to focus their exploration on that perceived truth. In other words, proponents of each tradition believe theirs is right, and that the other system has serious flaws. This leads to limited thinking, and I have a young man's fascination with poking holes in limitations of that sort. I believe each tradition has something to offer the other precisely because we are different and don't agree on all points.

THE BIG IDEA: CULTURAL EXCHANGE

I secured funding from the Trust for Mutual Understanding for a bilateral teaching exchange to explore these issues. Three voice trainers from the MXAT School came to San Diego State University (SDSU) from February 4-11, 2006, which was followed by a similar visit by an American group to Moscow from October 7-14, 2006. We discovered many similarities in pedagogical goals: both groups want audible performers with expressive resonances, a reflexive inhale rather than a postured or labored one, and a lack of tension in the jaw and neck. We also found substantial differences, which manifested in the observable effects of different exercises taught in different styles, the Russian teachers' expectations of students' abilities, and non-discursive speech signifiers like tone of voice. One of the most notable differences we observed was a goal-oriented discipline and classicism that parallels American perceptions of

Russian ballet and gymnastics. We also saw a significant difference in how we teach breathing. The pervasive nature of these differences, observed in both San Diego and Moscow, reinforced the notion that culture plays a significant role in vocal pedagogy. The exchange became an oral history laboratory for dissecting cultural assumptions that influence vocal pedagogy.

However, it is important to point out the limited scope of this exchange. The teachers spent only five days in each city, with one to four sessions of one to two hours per day. Such a small data sample, with the added difficulties of translating technical language, makes only theoretical statements possible about the complete trajectory of training programs in the US or in Russia, and makes the hypotheses of this paper necessarily intuitive or intellectual. Nevertheless, it became evident after only ten days that the Russians have a way of training voice based on their understanding of the human personality—a way that is particularly Russian, and perhaps still a bit Soviet, influenced by seventy years of cultural conditioning, that focuses on the body in a materialist way, not necessarily taking into account the feelings of the person in that body. The American way seems to indulge and privilege the individual.

As it developed, this project took on characteristics of folklore or oral history research, in which anecdote, interview, and observation hold more significance than previous scholarly work. This is appropriate to our discipline, I believe, since voice teachers as a group tend to rely on oral tradition more than many other artists. In trying to relate the nature of the experience as well as some nuggets of practical information, I realized I had a daunting amount of material, and I had to make some decisions about what to include. Therefore, throughout this paper I have described the Russian work in much more detail than the American work. This is intentional. Any readers interested in pursuing the American voice methodologies mentioned in this paper, namely Linklater, Fitzmaurice, Roy Hart, and Jan Gist's work, will find those easier to learn about than the Russian work. I have also omitted descriptions of some of the daily work in cases of repetition or where the description was not germane to the argument of the paper. Many of the direct quotes are extracted from the video footage shot on each day of each residency; in those cases, I have cited the speaker in text, and the date of the quote can be determined from the section heading. I also shot numerous fixed-camera interviews; where those interviews have been quoted, there is an in-text citation that refers to the bibliography. Finally, we used translators for both residencies: Russian faculty and students at SDSU, and professional translators provided by the MXAT in Moscow. All remarks made by Russian voice teachers (except Natalya Kovaleva, who gave her interview in English) are translated from the Russian.

LABORATORY, PART 1: SAN DIEGO

The participants in the American phase of the project besides myself included Marina Brusnikina, Head of Voice, MXAT School; Aleksandra Nicolaeva and Victor Markhashev, Professors of Voice, MXAT School; Catherine Fitzmaurice, Professor of Theatre, University of Delaware; Jan Gist, Associate Professor of Dramatic Arts, University of San Diego/Old Globe Theatre; Anne Harley, Associate Professor of Music, UNC Charlotte; and Ursula Meyer, Senior Lecturer in Theatre, UC San Diego/LaJolla Playhouse. The exchange began on Monday morning, February 6, 2006.

February 6, 2006: First Impressions.

Catherine Fitzmaurice was the first presenter; she led a beginner De- and Re-structuring class for my students with the Russians observing. I decided that, in the interest of creating goodwill, the exchange should begin with teachers observing instead of being students. I hoped to build trust and curiosity through mutual observation so that by the end of the week the teachers would ask to participate. I felt that asking the Russians to tremor right away would have been too intimidating.

Following Catherine's presentation, we observed the first demonstration of Russian instruction. Marina Brusnikina showed some basic vibration and resonance work. The work began on "sigh-of-relief" sounds, with very little relaxation. Marina's teaching style used a lot of images, similes and metaphors: relaxation phrases like "a comfortable feeling"; phrases for sound such as "sounds like when you wake up," "cry, whine, make happy sounds," and "drink in the sound, like when you're drinking milk." The students were instructed to roll onto their bellies and "pay attention to how you're breathing, what's happening on the in and out." Next: "feel the back rise as the breath comes in, and have the back fall when the breath comes out." Teachers came around to each student to actually push the ribcage towards the floor on the exhale, the first indicator that the Russians have a different way of doing things, and something that would surface again and again in observations and interviews in San Diego and in Moscow. As Anne Harley put it near the end of the exchange in Moscow:

> [There] seems to be a sort of an undifferentiated space in their pedagogy about breathing in that they are not very specific about the abdominal muscles, and they're not very specific about the movement of the ribs during the inhale and during the exhale. It seems to be pretty much left up to the individual actor as to whether or not those parts of the body move in a way that I feel is most efficient for singing or for acting. They tend to have a lot of rib squeeze, and for singing. I really feel that on the exhale the

ribs come out and float down rather than squeeze in and push extra air against the vocal folds. That causes a lot of fatigue and I don't know if the Russians are even aware of that. It doesn't seem to come up in any of the teaching we have seen so far (2006).

What we saw on this first day appeared to be direct encouragement to squeeze the ribs; other work in the following days reinforced this initial impression. However, in listening to the Russian teachers (and in listening to their students later in Moscow), it didn't seem to affect stamina or vocal health. In fact, there is something powerful about the sound: Catherine Fitzmaurice said of Marina's work which she saw in Moscow in 2001:

> They were lying on the wooden floor, and making sound, and feeling it come back into their body, and the sound was wonderful—they made a lot of very strong sound…There was a lovely classical facility—they made good noise (2006).

When asked to add sound, it was described "like you're throwing a tantrum, like you have a fever," the class was asked to find a single note, and then sat up and began to move vibration to different parts of the body by using the hands on the face to pull sound out, going back-to-back with partners, and other physical actions. Although the work was clearly effective, creating strong results and pleasing the students, our first exposure to Russian techniques nevertheless evoked Cold War stereotypes: muscular movement and vibrant sound taught through rigorous methods, but with little attention to the details of personality and vocal health that are some of the hallmarks of American voice work.

February 7, 2006: Action and Imagination.

The second day began with a presentation from Jan Gist, who covered release of jaw and neck tension, rib opening, moving sound forward and out, and a resonance exercise that the Russians loved so much they asked her to repeat it in Moscow eight months later. The exercise, conducted while standing, began by finding "optimum pitch," extending the pitch on an easy tone, then exploring resonance forward, back, up, down, and all around the head and torso by "pulling" the sound there with the hands.

Victor Markhashev began the Russian class on this day. He had a large group of students, mostly inexperienced freshman. He began with a simple exercise, "this is actually a support exercise," he said: rolling an /r/ and pulsing the sound from the belly—the belly pushing *out* with the exhalation—another indicator that Russian instruction regarding breath movement is much less specific than in some American traditions, and it runs counter to what some of us in the US would call "correct." Victor proceeded to demonstrate an exercise for a *reflexive inhale*: flicking the hand at someone across the circle as if you are challenging that person to a duel, the student exhales on /t/—"he flicks the /t/ and already without any effort there is an inhale." The purpose of the exercise was to have an active exhalation and to then let the breathing reflex bring air in with no thought. There was no specific instruction with regard to the movement of the abdominal muscles or the ribs.

Victor and Marina continued with articulation exercises. Victor showed a sequence with nonsense syllables: /knukt/ /knokt/ /knakt/ /knehkt/ /knikt/; he continued the same vowel sequence using increasingly difficult consonant clusters (/rr/ represents /r/ trill): /vrrluvrrl/, /tupurruchu/, /lumunirrui/, and so on. The students found this, while fun, almost impossibly difficult and were amazed at the facility and speed of the Russian teachers—another characteristic (marvelous technical ability with speech) that we were to see again.

Marina continued with a sequence of exercises for physicalizing the consonants using prescribed hand gestures. This was among the most interesting things we saw during the San Diego week, perhaps because it was a concrete series, easy to learn and separate from a structured arc of long-term development. She said, "each consonant has a life of its own, and the work with the hands represents the action of the consonant. You must find the life in each one and how they feel different." The students performed the sounds and gestures standing in a circle, following a rhythm set by the teacher. The hand gestures covered most sounds used in English, not always differentiating between voiced and unvoiced consonants, but always accentuating possibilities of rhythm and effort inherent in the various consonant sounds—for example, both /p/ and /b/ used the fingertips coming together and apart in the same way, but /v/ pressed the heels of the hands forward in space, while /f/ flicked the fingertips in a "shooing" motion. Marina encouraged active pursuit of images and how they affected the embodiment of the movement, allowing for significant variation in the rhythm and effort motivated by the imagination: She described /m/ as "water flowing down your face," using the hands to smooth down the cheeks, but she also used images like "a fog of /m/ under your hands," inviting a different sound.

The marriage of image, action, and sound in these series brought a boost of energy and pleasure into the room—not the elusive kinesthetic pleasure so often hard for students to discover, but a simple playfulness. I have adapted the consonant gesture sequence for English speech. Students learn something about oral posture; they also laugh, dance, and have a terrific time. It changes their attitude about speech, and

because they feel excited, it permits greater detail in my explanations of technical details, which I can do as I run the sequence. Anne Harley has also adapted this work for singing, saying, "[It's] the kind of thing that opera singers need all the time, and they don't get nearly enough training in that because we're so vowel-centric in the musical world. I've used it already in my teaching and I will continue to use it" (2006).

That afternoon, the group traveled to the University of San Diego to observe a graduate-level Shakespeare and text class taught by Jan Gist: walking with the text, turning on punctuation, and playing with inflection by keeping the text moving physically using partners. This is material many American teachers would find familiar. The Russian teachers felt the same way—they decided they didn't need translators for this class because they "understood absolutely everything" because it was "the same work they did at home." We clarified that they didn't necessarily have the same exercises, but they did have the same concerns with forward movement and energy in text delivery, and they tried to solve the problem in similar ways; this discovery foreshadowed one of the major successes of the Moscow residency in October.

February 8, 2006: How Nice Is Too Nice?
The third day began with breath support work from Aleksandra Nikolaeva. This was very energetic, muscular activity, quite different from most American work. After a very brief relaxation, she instructed the students to begin single and double leg lifts and leg drops, exhaling on /f/ with the leg drop. The movements were abrupt and muscular. She continued in this vein with arm movements, bicycling and scissoring the legs, standing up and running in place with high knee lifts, all on rhythmic pulses of /f/ with the sound coordinating with the action. Students were sweaty by the time they were finished. Aleksandra, a sweet, reticent woman, became very stern during this sequence, barking out instructions and shouting "Stop!" with sharp claps of the hands. Phrases describing the work included instructions such as "The most important thing is to jerk your arms up," and "do it *hard*, just drop." The Americans identified this energetic and muscular approach as a hallmark of Russian voicework:

> There's a kind of muscular urgency and dynamic and even roughness, I would say, in the Russian approach, and the Americans, I would say there's a gentler, softer, kinder, more patient, internally connecting approach (Gist 2006).

> The Russian [work] seems to be more product-centered, more result-centered, resonance-centered, articulator-centered…And there seems to be a pattern of brute repetition, that if you do something enough times, that gradually you become better at it…There's a sort of athletic, Olympic quality to their training that I don't see in the American training (Harley 2006).

Marina continued with more resonator work. She asked the students, lying prone, to imagine they were "underwater, everything is beautiful, you are breathing through a small straw, breathing out all the air. It takes time to send the breath out all the way up through the water; once you breathe out, hold your breath until you feel like inhaling." The instructions continued: "the exhale is pretty long, then there is a pause, then the inhale is fast." Marina used many images, and this one may be familiar to anyone who has experience with Linklater: "There is an ice ceiling over you and you want to melt that ceiling, so the exhale should be warm…Add sound to that exhale, "haa" sound, like you're breathing fire." In terms of connecting the resonator work to the previous breath work: "Make sure your sound isn't trembling on the exhale, and that depends on the accuracy of the exhale, it's steady." She then moved to open vowels "to fill the room…the building…the whole university…and all of San Diego."

Victor finished this class with some breathing exercises, "very old" ones: the "gymnastics of Lubanov." He told the students: "The stereotype of widening the ribcage" evens out sound, prolongs exhalation, and practices "location" of all the consonants in the alphabet, or diction. The exercise itself was similar to Linklater's "rib umbrella" sequence: the students were instructed to raise the elbows with hands and fingers resting on the chest and collarbones, with slight arch in the back, "very confident in your stance," then sound on /bulu//vulu//gulu//dulu//zhulu/. The exercise was a bit confusing for the students because, while familiar to them because of work in my classes, it was different in a way the translator could not articulate.

Here, another issue began to surface: translation. Much of our instruction is based not only on the meaning of the words themselves, but on their intonation and inflection. Additionally, in cases where Russian exercises were so similar to work that we know in America, it was often hard to tell whether or not the goal of the exercise from the other tradition was the same. Marina's instruction to "hold your breath" after the exhale may have been the result of this dynamic. Either the concepts are different, or the translator did not understand the implication of "holding" the breath within the context of voice work.

In contrast to the "Olympic" Russian work of the morning, Ursula Meyer's work in the afternoon seemed soft and indulgent. A Designated Linklater teacher, Ursula took the students through warm-up material familiar to many Americans: a sound and movement "name game" with "what you're feeling right now," and a "mill and seethe" exercise in which the students worked "with the body of the creature of how you're

feeling." She also worked with "sigh of relief" and "the productive hum." For the sigh of relief, she used language like "Sigh, and it's important to find something you are relieved about, and let that be the impulse for the sigh"; "feel the need for a new breath, and have a sigh—but all voice work is about growing and expanding, driving to the end of the thought, so you want to think of the energy going forward…we want to sigh without deflating." She described the productive hum in terms of how we "amplify the touch of sound…amplify or *resound* it. That's a lot of what being moved is, feeling the vibrations of another person, so if we can vibrate the audience and each other, the theatre will provoke and challenge and move us." She then demonstrated several wrong ways and a right way for productive hum, asked students to imitate and feel and introduced the open channel with the ingressive /k/. After this, she worked up into head and mask resonance with participants standing in a circle and bathing one person at time in the center with "good vibrations."

Observing Ursula's class I was struck by how kind, soft, indirect, and inclusive her language was compared to what we witnessed in the Russian classes; she spent a lot of time and energy grounding the exercises in the students' immediate, personal feelings about themselves or about the work and making sure everyone felt safe and "okay" about the activities. This seems to be a hallmark of American methods, part of what Kristin Linklater calls the "humanistic, psychophysical, 'use yourself' approach," which is opposite to the "other style of teaching that manages to avoid the personal, emotional problems altogether…the school that says 'leave your personal life behind you when you come into the classroom'" (Linklater 1997, 6-7). The Russians don't concern themselves as much with the issue of personal emotion, and adhere more to the "other style." We saw more of this during the rest of the week, and much more in Moscow the following October. Interestingly, the observing American teachers found this approach refreshing, citing "rigor and vigor" (in the words of Ursula Meyer) as one of the most valuable things they would take away from the exchange.

February 9, 2006: Virtuoso.
Marina showed us an articulation sequence on Thursday that further demonstrated her extreme technical ability with consonants, and again, while hilariously fun for my students, was impossible for them to execute at the speed she required. She began with a familiar warm-up, and then dove into a long and intricate series of tongue twisters. She did many variations on combinations of /d/, /t/, and /rr/, combining them in alternating groups. Some nonsense words were familiar: /mommola/ /bobbola/ /dobbola/. Some were not and included difficult Russian consonant clusters and pure vowels: /ptki/, /ptke/,

/ptka/, /ptko/. She also required the students to execute difficult group rhythms with the tongue twisters, doing overlapping canons with slight variations from cycle to cycle, creating multi-rhythmic series with different groups of students in different time signatures, and dividing the students into parts and requiring them to sing the tongue twisters on major and minor chords.

It's difficult to get a sense of these exercises from notes alone, because on paper, Marina's work seems similar to American work, and even uses some of the same nonsense syllables. However, the manner in which she conducted these exercises showed a marked difference from the American norm. She required speed and precision (that she performed with ease) far exceeding even the American voice teachers' abilities. There was also the added difficulty of the work with group rhythm, which required extreme concentration, listening to others while executing a difficult solo task at the same time. We saw this characteristic of the Russian approach every day during both halves of the exchange: focus directed outside of the self onto maintaining a rhythm, listening to others, and working with the sound of others, not just the sound of the self.

February 10, 2006: Friends.
The final day of work for the San Diego week included an open exchange of ideas and exercises for teachers, with no students present. The afternoon session was a round-robin exercise session and discussion of the issues we had covered in sessions during the week: jaw and neck tension, breath, resonance, and text—basic voice teacher concerns, regardless of tradition. I planned to initiate in-depth discussion of difference as a way of promoting change on both sides; however, I discovered I had to wait. Because the Russians were trying their best to be good guests and the Americans to be good hosts, discussion tended to minimize conflict and accentuate similarities. Participants were reluctant to critique or question the essential value of the exercises they had seen. We collectively concurred we were faced with the same problems and we all generously agreed that we approached our tasks with only slightly different exercises. Marina Brusnikina stated the exchange provided "more evidence all schools are the same. The differences are not great. From your perspective we may have a lot to offer, but from ours it all appears to be the same thing." She acknowledged that "through the translator it's hard for students to respond to the words of the teachers," and so the result may not be what they demand of their own students, but she "realized we're all on the same path nevertheless." The Americans' single lasting impression of the Russian work took the form of an enthusiastic endorsement of the "rigor and vigor." Or as Jan Gist said, "The main thing I'll take back is the muscle…and [the number of] repeats over and over again. I think I go more gently…from thing to thing

to thing, but there was more muscle and power, and more repeats for longer periods. But it was still free—it had muscle and freedom and generosity."

The tone and content of this discussion suggested that while we had made significant progress establishing cross-cultural communication and trust, we had only scratched the surface of the potential this collaboration holds for the growth of American and Russian pedagogical traditions. Because of the necessity of creating bonds of friendship, the kind of critical examination of self and other so crucial to growth simply couldn't happen in this first exchange. But even if we couldn't yet discuss differences with our new Russian colleagues, a number of concrete issues were illuminated.

CONCLUSIONS, LABORATORY, PART 1
After five days, two basic things seemed clear: Americans spend a lot more time and energy on breath and relaxation, and we are much more concerned with release and "feeling good." The Russians seem to enforce a remarkable discipline of muscularity and repetition that results in virtuosic skill.

In their enthusiasm for this Russian discipline, the American participants expressed an implied frustration of their own need to be so attentive to the emotional needs of their students. Teachers seemed to suggest that when nurturing crosses the line into coddling, the work slows down, and it is occasionally exasperating. The Russians certainly didn't coddle our students. Anne-Charlotte Harvey, Professor of Theatre at SDSU, said, "American students do not like repetition—to repeat…is anathema…I've seen how difficult it is for the students to do what you want them to do because they don't have the skill, but [also] the satisfaction they experience when they do do it."

The other major difference had to do with the pedagogy of breath. Most American techniques invest significant time in breathwork and coordinate theory and practice to connect breath, impulse, and sound to acting. Because of this, American voice teachers prefer a particular easy, free, and released sound that indicates spontaneity or truthfulness. This is different from the sound the Russians seem to prefer; to our ears, the Russian sound is "pressed." Catherine Fitzmaurice describes this, based on her experience in Moscow and with a MXAT actress who attended one of her certifications:

> They're using sound as this kind of long continuous ribbon which is chopped up into words by the articulators…The voice itself is not so free or buoyant that you can really hear the creation and expression of a thought. I think the reason for this is that what I'm hearing in the voices is that they're pressed…if they are supported from the abdomen, it's with the entire abdomen, not with the isolation that I teach of the transverse, so that there is more muscle to it,

and I think that there is also the engagement of the inner intercostals, which squeezes the lungs so that you get this kind of pressed forceful sound—which is a good sound, it carries, and it's a strong sound, but it's an unvarying sound (2006).

Jan Gist made similar observations:

You don't see them move when they breathe. There's not a lot of movement, in fact it seems like they're pressing down, and I'm always telling my students don't squeeze the breath out, because that, in my students, causes tension in the throat, jaw—everything tenses and limits everything with squeezing. But they seem to be finding an empowerment of squeeze in all sorts of places and still get sound forward and out (2006).

I can't imagine the Russians would have agreed with our assessment at the end of the first week, and I had no clear idea what they really thought of our work. I had no doubt, however, that they liked us. Because this exchange had created such trust and collegial relationships among this group, I hoped the stage had been set for a deeper critique of the two teaching models in Moscow.

LABORATORY, PART II: MOSCOW

The participants in the Russian phase of the project included me, Jan Gist and Anne Harley; additionally, Grace Zandarski, Lecturer, Yale School of Drama and faculty at The Actor's Center, NYC, and Kelly Mizell, Lecturer in Theatre, UNC Charlotte, made the trip. Both Grace and Kelly, like me, had taught voice for the ART during its three-month Moscow residency. I also brought Tim Powell, a Hollywood director and television producer, now Assistant Professor, Film and Television, SDSU, to record professional quality archival video and fixed-camera interviews. Organized on the Russian end by Marina Brusnikina, with the support of the Dean of the MXAT School, Anatoly Smeliansky, most of the sessions took place in a small studio theatre on the first floor of the American Studio of the MXAT School, with the participant teachers and students on stage. Voice teachers and students (sometimes as many as 40) joined us from all around the city to sit in the audience and observe. This arrangement, in addition to professional translators, gave everything a performative feel, very different from the casual atmosphere of San Diego.

October 9, 2006: Tools.

On the first day, we observed a work-demonstration with Professor Ignatova, a speech pathologist who works with MXAT School students who have problems with "jaws that are too heavy, lips that are…too weak, cheeks that are too heavy or lack muscular strength, which are problematic." Marina

Brusnikina described the need for this work: "This is a common problem these days—they come to school and they can't open their mouth. The boys all need to be brave and silent…I don't know why, but almost everybody has an immobile upper lip. It's a very big problem for us, so our school pays great attention to bring them back to normal shape."

Professor Ignatova demonstrated a series of interventions to correct these problems in Pasha, a Russian student with a slight underbite. She massaged deeply into the joint capsule of the mandible with fingers and metal tools with rounded ends, working in steps to open the joint as far as it would go, massaging the entire time. The massage was meant to "give them the sensation of opening so that they can start working on their own." Unable to restrain ourselves, we all jumped up on the stage to get a closer look—this was unlike anything we had seen before. The mere idea of approaching students' problems in this way was very stimulating, as described by Kelly Mizell:

I know I can help some of my students who have very specific needs—sometimes even myself, whenever my /s/ gets a little weak—and the main idea behind it of exercising muscle in certain ways so that then it begins to work the way you need it to work…This is very important…The understanding of the idea behind it can help me then figure out what I need to figure out for any given problem a student might have (2006).

Professor Ignatova also massaged the cheek muscles, the cheekbones where the cheek muscles attach, the lip muscles, the tongue root inside the arch of the mandible, and, using the metal probes, reached inside his mouth to massage his tongue and even his soft palate. She discussed muscle, nerve, and reflex: "There's this little hole under the chin, and if I

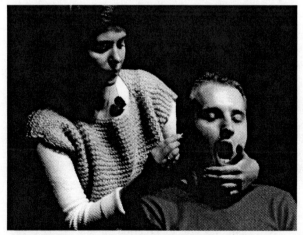

Professor Ignatova working on Pasha's jaw. Photo by Tim Powell.

massage it, the base of the tongue releases…it's a spot where the nervous endings come together, so when I massage this little spot, the signals go up the nerves to the base of his tongue."

This demonstration introduced several themes we were to see repeated during the week. Direct intervention and somewhat rough touch (by our standards) seemed to be the norm, indicating a somewhat mechanistic approach to vocal problems. Telling students they had problems or they did not have "normal" function, and so needed to be "fixed," was also normal; in fact, Professor Ignatova referred to Pasha within his hearing as "a pretty bad case."

October 10, 2006: Mystery.
On Tuesday morning we observed demonstrations from the faculty of the Shchukin School also called the Vakhtangov School. Elena Laskova led the first session and showed "the very basic, the very beginning" work for first-year students. She said "the actor is not just a talking head, it is a sounding body—like the violin is not just strings, it is also the body of the violin." The breath work in this demonstration was very similar to the work Aleksandra Nikolaeva showed in San Diego, very muscular, repetitive, in unison with the rest of the class, and following a count. Description of breath movement was similarly imprecise: "Try to send the breath to the lower part of your lungs." The consonant work was reminiscent of the hand sign series we had learned from Marina Brusnikina. The rest of her work presented a mystery: Anne Harley, based on her many years of teaching material she learned from Richard Armstrong at Banff and in other workshops over a concentrated period of five years, recognized the series Elena Laskova demonstrated as basic material from the Roy Hart Theatre. Numerous elements, including warming the hands, breathing into a partner's joints, the relaxation on the floor for breath, the "yawn and stretch," easy, released resonance, and the adaptation of the consonant sign language into a sound and movement game were all either identical or remarkably close to Richard Armstrong's material.

This occurrence brought up another interesting topic: What is the provenance of our exercises? While Professor Laskova had no knowledge that her exercises were related to the Roy Hart material, since she works as an actor at a theatre long known for being experimental and hosting international guests, it's likely that a Roy Hart member visited this theatre in Moscow to teach and gave the work to someone who gave it to Professor Laskova—or did it go the other way? Intellectual property rights to exercises hold little significance for voice teachers, it seems, because we recognize the importance of oral traditions in our work. We would see other echoes of familiar

work transformed by Russian instructional philosophy during the rest of our stay, prompting me to wonder what aspects of our exercises appealed to them and why—and what this revealed about Russian pedagogy.

Natalya Kovaleva led the second session from Shchukin, in which she worked with meter and intonation in poetry. She referred to the iamb with the familiar adage as "the most natural [rhythm], because it is the rhythm of the heart." She played with elements of scansion familiar to many of us: iamb, trochee, pyrrhic, spondee, anapest, dactyl, and amphibrach; but she did it in a way that was both technical and physically active. The students began by intoning full lines of dactyls, anapests, and amphibrachs on nonsense syllables while standing in place and moving the hands in coordination with stressed and unstressed syllables. The work got more and more intricate, finishing with each student setting up a pattern dictated by the teacher that included a trick (a hard caesura, or difficult combinations of feet), clapping the hands towards the ceiling for the stressed beat, and down towards the floor for the unstressed, all speaking in unison on the rhythm. They chose very difficult sound clusters: /vgitis/, /mstism/, /mxitm/, /shika/ and so on. She also had them waltz on text, following the rhythm of the dance (dactyls) in the text they were delivering as they danced.

I'd never seen such direct and, in some ways, dry work on rhythm before. I don't know if it would work with American students. It was difficult to imagine how to adapt this work to our own circumstances, particularly since the Russian students themselves were clearly having difficulty with it—"it's not easy, but gradually they can implant this resonance in their body and in their brain." I was nevertheless captivated, perhaps because the result was undeniable. Professor Kovaleva had two advanced students deliver some Russian poetry; even though I couldn't understand a word, I was impressed by the rhythmic sophistication of their delivery, particularly considering their young age. It was remarkable work, showing a rare depth of emotional connection to the rhythm and sound of Russian speech.

Tuesday was the American debut for the Russian faculty. I led an alignment sequence using material adapted from Alexander, Feldenkrais, Klein Technique and Contact Improvisation. Kelly Mizell showed a simple exercise for neck release in which students lean against a wall, suspending the weight of the body between the feet and the occipital point. Staying in that position for at least three minutes creates a tremendous sensation of lightness and ease in the head after coming off the wall. This exercise was very popular with the Russians, and they began using it in their classrooms before we even left.

The students responded to the instruction with discipline and highly focused attention—another common thread, and an aspect many American teachers commented on: "I'm really impressed with the...Russian students. I would love to have that kind of gung ho, I'm-ready-no-matter-what energy [in my classroom]" (Gist 2006). The Russian observers were curious about how long we spend on alignment—"How long before you get to the actual sound? Do you work with text?" they asked. They were confused about why I had done so little with sound. They also had questions about American curricula and how much time we spend with students, the variety of types of instruction, and class size. Evidently, the circumstances many American teachers desire (a four-year arc with students who all want to be actors), but which few actually enjoy, are obtained everywhere in Moscow and possibly everywhere in the country, even at the less prestigious schools. They were half-amazed, half-horrified when we described our educational system.

October 11, 2006: Action and Imagination Redux.

Kelly Mizell led off on Wednesday with an introduction to Destructuring from Fitzmaurice Voicework. She led a group of Russian students through some basic relaxation and into one simple tremoring position. This delicate work was successful, as it was when Catherine presented her work herself in 2001: "They're very good students...they're trained to listen...and take it on, really commit themselves to it, so there was no problem in their attitude or behavior or the way they did it, and they all...tremored somewhat" (2006). One student, as the tremoring started to shake his body, tremored out the Russian word for excellent, *otlichna*, drawing a laugh from the whole room: "*ooootliiiiichnaaa!*" Kelly and I finished by demonstrating the entire Destructuring sequence for the attendees.

Grace Zandarski took over and taught a Restructuring series that excited the students. She finished by working with a few students individually in front of the entire assemblage:

I took a risk that day, because not knowing their training, it was hard to gauge whether or not it was going to be successful. But in the end it paid off and the first young man...he got it almost immediately. He felt my hands around his ribs, and they shifted and changed; he was also able to drop his effort out his upper chest and let things flow...I could also see when we were doing Destructuring earlier that his ribs were moving, and that his abdomen was moving without overly extending itself or pushing, so I thought he was a good risk candidate...and he was thrilled, you could see that his eyes lit up when he had this little [head] voice that played through the space...But what was particularly thrilling was that the girl who was to

the right of him...grabbed my hands, put them around her ribs, and said 'me, now do me, do me.' She was intent on not leaving the stage without having an experience, because she had seen something change in her classmates, so she wanted to have some change for herself (2006).

After the demonstration Victor Markhashev pulled me aside and told me the students were asking for more—they wanted "more shaking." The teachers were curious about whether the tremoring led to trance and why the amplitude of tremors was smaller in students than teachers, which led Grace Zandarski into a discussion of individuality and involuntary sound:

Most of my students don't get as big as what you saw here. Because I never demonstrate; I let them find it. So they find their own rather than trying to find a certain look. [And their own sounds as well?] Yes, absolutely, because if you try to make a certain sound, the body learns nothing. And eventually the smaller sounds of the body come out. The vulnerable sounds, the parts that we never touch, that we never hear.

In response to "what the shaking was," I said, "the shake is about a reflex in the muscle—so you can use your mind to suppress the reflex, or you can learn to allow your mind to let go. When the thinking lets go, the body lets go...we use a voluntary action to trigger an involuntary response." The word "reflex" seemed to be a key. Once the word was translated, I saw heads began to nod around the room. Only a few teachers were interested in the notion of an individual sound. The idea of reflex, however, appeared to be a familiar concept to everyone.

That afternoon, we saw a class at GITIS, now called RATI, the oldest theatre school in Moscow, and the one Stanislavky attended. The beginner class, taught by Svetlana Zemlakova, again showed us new material. The entire class was conducted with the students sitting on stools. Svetlana told us they "make sure that their feet are flat on the ground so that they feel the muscles a little bit more sharply in their upper body, so that they end up sitting on the correct muscles, on their sit muscles. And in that sense the absence of their legs is an obstacle that they have to overcome." Grace Zandarski said of this sequence:

I love that they sat on stools as opposed to sitting on chairs, and that's something that really impresses me about these students is that...they have a sense of spine. They have a sense of their tailbone, and that movement up to the top of the head; there's a real flow (2006).

Svetlana's intricate class showed less repetition and more variety than other classes we had seen up until this point. The whole class was conducted in partners or as a group; there was no individual work at all. It demonstrated for the first time somatic work that seemed familiar. However, it was conducted with a pretty rough touch, vigorously pulling the head off up the neck; the passive joint release (partners cradling and jiggling the head, shoulders, and arms) was similarly rough. The partner resonance work, with hands resting on specific areas of the body where the students sent vibration, was very active and required the partner to do as much work as the sounder, vigorously pressing the sounder's body. They also did a series of activities involving physically tense and free positions in various configurations with partners, sounding sometimes during the tense moment, and sometimes during the soft moment. A notable aspect of the class was work with squishy, hollow balls: They sounded into them, squeezed them between various body parts while sounding, and used them for massage. We saw some expected elements: consonants with hand motions, no relaxation, and no specific instruction regarding breathing patterns. One new thing was a connection between voice, action, and imagination from the first exercise—every piece of the class required active participation from the students. None of the exercises permitted a passive or receptive state, and the students were vibrantly energized by the end. Svetlana is known for this partnering work; for her, the voice is always action, connection, and communication. This class reinforced external focus on *doing* with the voice as another strong element of Russian vocal pedagogy.

Svetlana Zemlakova's students work with rubber balls. Photo by Tim Powell.

Two other elements from earlier in the exchange resurfaced on this day: exercise provenance and translation. We saw some familiar somatic elements I assumed had found their way into the Russian classroom via Western visitors. If that was the case, it was also clear that these principles had been adapted to fit different preferences. But in fact, it's impossible to tell where they came from. Many Americans freely adapt and improvise in the classroom, solving problems by departing from original exercises, and develop new exercises by doing so. These almost-familiar exercises in Svetlana's class suggest a similar dynamic at work; the differences in execution yield clues to Russian pedagogical principles, reinforcing once again what Linklater refers to as the "other way."

As the students were working with head and neck release, rolling and pulling on the hair at the back of the head, the translator kept saying, "Let the head be free. Let the neck be

free." Because of what I saw as roughness in the work, I asked the translator if that's what the word he was using actually meant, and he said, "No, it means something like 'loose and active.'" This may be splitting hairs; perhaps "loose and active" is close enough to "free" to make the difference merely semantic, but the episode made me realize the importance of considering the cultural context of words across languages. Word choice and quality of delivery can sometimes mean the difference between a student's success and failure in an exercise, so if we place so much emphasis on words like "allow" and "free," and if in Russian those words have slightly different connotative meanings, what does that signify for the results of pedagogy? This is a very large issue, one that requires a high degree of frankness, openness and trust to discuss. We hadn't reached that stage yet in the exchange, but I hoped to by the end of the week.

October 12, 2006: Folklore.

The morning began with observation of the "folklore" class, a large group-singing class that focused on traditional music from Russia taught by three teachers. The sound was incredibly vibrant and unbelievably loud. We listened to songs for about 20 minutes; some they knew and some they were learning in an oral style—no sheet music, all call and response. Everything was a cappella. The singing took on a life of its own after awhile, many students clearly having a great time, smiling and dancing spontaneously. The group moved into soundscape improvisation: the whole class knelt with foreheads on the floor, and created a forest soundscape that transformed into an improvised song. Their improvisation was fearless, precise, and uncannily lifelike, had seamless transitions, and demonstrated a high degree of listening to the other—focus on the voice outside the body appeared again as an important element.

After the singing, the teachers spoke about how the "ancient Russian music" helped them discover the difference between ensemble and choir: "[They] are different because in a choir, you can't step out, you have to follow the chord the way it's written; in ensemble singing, at least in Russian ensemble singing, there…have to be variations, and each person has to think of his or her own little improvisation within the phrase of a very simple melody, maybe two or three notes…they have to feel it themselves, and ideally they don't have to be told when to sing apart and when in unison." They described their breathing model as "the Oriental breathing technique, that breathes down very low, and they have a very long exhale…and for the inhale they just release their muscles. And we don't do anything in the chest. So the body inhales as much as it needs." They teach this breathing technique in one or two classes separate from the singing class, using techniques similar to yoga cleansing breath or vacuuming the lungs. They also turn the tailbone under on the exhalation, and train the sound using images of "calling to someone across the street; it's very important to get their attention." As these teachers worked with our group, they kept clenching their fists by the lower abdomen, indicating what we interpreted as active movement in those muscles. Even though the breathing technique was similar to ours, offering us a possibility to succeed in learning this particular resonance, no matter how hard we tried, their effortless resonance in this "scream" had overtones and richness that ours lacked.

This emphasis on externals, action, and the prescriptive instruction towards a particular resonance further reinforced the sense that we were seeing an outside-in, mechanistic or materialist approach to the voice. However, with this group for the first time we saw breathwork similar to our own. It was unclear what relationship this breathing technique bore to what our theatrical colleagues taught, but the emphasis on activating the abdominal muscles on the exhale, and a reflexive inhale connected to "need," resonated with parts of more than one American breathing pedagogy.

After the folklore class, we had a session with Anna Petrova, the reigning matriarch of Russian voicework, with the status, in Russia, of the most prominent teachers in the US. Both Catherine Fitzmaurice and Kristin Linklater have met Anna Petrova, and it was through her that Kristin's work first made it to the newly created Russian Federation in 1989:

> I got a very official invitation from Anna Petrova from the voice part of the actor's union to come…She set up a

Anna Petrova discusses Russian voicework. Photo by Tim Powell.

week…six sessions of about an hour…with 60 voice teachers from all over Russia. I was going to the theater every evening and hearing these…*glorious* voices, and each morning I'd come in feeling more and more depressed and diminished and useless, redundant…till one day I came in and I was really in a state…I got up and I said 'I've been going to the theatre and hearing all these wonderful voices, and you all obviously know so much about voice and you don't need me, I don't know what I'm doing here…' I was really in a state, you know, and from the back, Anna Petrova's voice came out and she said, 'Madame Linklater, we have brought you here all the way from the United States of America, people have come here, they have left their students, they have left their families, they have come from the Caucasus, they have come from Siberia, to hear you teach…so teach!' So I taught (2006).

Anna Petrova began her talk in a much less intimidating way by saying "I think that all our profession is about asking questions. We ask ourselves, and the older we are, the more we ask ourselves. When we are young, it seems that everything is clear, but with people of my age—I've worked here for 50 years—I have only questions." The questions she proceeded to ask us over the next hour were surprisingly simple ones. She diplomatically stated she had worked with Kristin Linklater

A Russian student performs material from *Medea*. Photo by Tim Powell.

out what is working well…but I don't necessarily say 'you're doing that wrong.' I think they hear a lot of that here, and they rise to the occasion in an interesting way…without shutting themselves down. My experience at home is that if you tell a student to work on something, they obsess on it so much that it becomes a very big problem…what I'm very curious about is this pedagogical point of view—expressing 'you have a problem with this'—and Anna Petrova was saying it to the two students that she brought in; both were 'problem students,' and yet they didn't seem to have 'problem hang-ups'—they had overcome [them] (Zandarski 2006).

and said "we accept very much what you…have done, because freedom is the basis of everything, but right now I am interested only in this zone: [gesturing to the jaw] the throat, everything we don't see, everything we can't guide directly. All my pedagogical problems have something to do with this zone." Working with two "problem students," she spent most of the hour working this area, starting by discussing head-neck relationship. Her hands-on work with the students was direct and a little rough. She placed the students face down on tables and began manipulating the head and neck in the sagittal plane, then she had them stand, and with a hand on the jaw, moved their heads back and up—similar to Linklater's "top jaw" exercise. She also showed an interesting exercise using the tip of the tongue to lick the roof of the mouth while sounding to discover the place, by recognizing the change in tone, where the soft palate lifts and the tongue root drops.

She discussed a wide range of topics, from the changing standards of Russian speech to the role of voice and speech in politics. She exhibited a voracious curiosity, wide-ranging interests, and a determination to follow those interests toward making a difference. Historically, Anna Petrova was one of the few people brave enough to challenge the system in the early 1970s—a courageous thing to do during the height of the Cold War—and again in the early 1990s after working with Kristin Linklater in the US and in Russia. Her interactions with students were notable because she took no interest in their feelings or personal comfort and was, as mentioned above, a bit rough with them. The students remained cheerful and focused. Teachers from both countries commented on this difference between Russian and American classroom behavior:

It seems to me that these teachers are much more specific at pointing out what is wrong than [I am]; I tend to point

The American students get offended more easily than Russian students do. Russian students don't get offended. For example, if I see a Russian student in my class who is opening his mouth the wrong way, and I can go up and jokingly show him where his jaw is opening, and the Russian student won't get offended, but the American might. But this is part of the fun. (Markhashev 2006).

October 13, 2006: *Medea.*

The final day began with a demonstration of advanced voice-work from Marina Brusnikina's class. This was a virtuosic demonstration of material they had developed to exercise principles of their training. In her words, "The work divides into two parts: technical speech [resonance and articulation] and work with text—meaning. The task is to make students flexible and capable with the production of sounds, and to prepare them to make sounds freely in a wide variety of rich tones and with flexibility on the stage" (2006). The students engaged in a thorough and richly voiced warm-up, and then presented material from *Medea*: solo and paired sound scores and stylized ensemble work, which we would call postmodern in this country, with non-naturalistic movement accompanying the text. In retrospect, it is easy to identify in this presentation the various elements we had been exposed to over the week, but at the time, none of us were conscious of this. The material nevertheless demonstrated incredible facility with the material we had been shown—rhythm, resonance, clear articulation, the "shout" from singing class, and partner and group work. The overall impression was of tremendous power, presence, and technical ability harnessed to emotional intensity. It was well-rehearsed, with seamless transitions from one vocal action to another, and no self-consciousness on the part of the students.

The afternoon was devoted to another round-robin discussion including most of the observers and many of the Russian presenters from the week. This discussion ranged widely over many topics, and while it did not live up to my hopes of a frank and open discussion about perceived strengths and weaknesses in each others' teaching methods, it covered some very interesting ground, opened up new areas of inquiry, and "cracked the nut" on the question of difference, preparing the way for more fruitful collaborations in the future.

Examining the video record, it appears that during this discussion the participants were concretizing many of the ideas printed in this paper. But in the moment of speaking, most of us were still in a state of shock, trying to process the enormous amounts of information we had received. Even so, the same themes surfaced again and again. I spoke about the fearless Russian students:

Your students have so much energy and so little fear. And…I don't know why, but our students are different, judging themselves, judging the material, judging the teacher: 'Is it good? Is it right?…Is this voice exercise going to make me famous?' [laughter] But I see the energy the Russian students have and the energy they get from all of your exercises, and it's making me think very hard.

Anne Harley addressed imagination and action:

These exercises that include action and intention with the sound…are so important. I have…young students, and it takes a long time for the voice to get to a place where they feel that their sound is a reflection of themselves. Because the voice is so close to the self, when that is not an accurate reflection of what's going on inside, it's very humiliating and painful. So I'm really happy to find these exercises that exemplify the expressive qualities of the sound and [don't] judge the aesthetic quality of the sound.

When Jan Gist addressed the issue of "muscle" and the roughness we had seen by describing the goal of American bodywork, saying "the point is to melt the inside, not to push on the outside, so that the upper layer can soften and lengthen, so that the inside can open up," one of the Russian teachers replied by saying that "when you knead the muscles strongly, afterward they are a lot better. This is a principle of massage, contrast of tension and release, so to have a bigger release, you need bigger tension," in essence defending why they used rough massage. This response indicates that this was not an area where we were achieving any new understanding—we could not understand why they were so rough, and they did not recognize that we were trying to offer another way. Nor were we willing to consider any validity in their approach to massage.

However, when we started discussing text, the entire group became excited. Jan Gist showed her version of the familiar "what" game in which a speaker and a listener work together, with the listener inserting the word "what?" whenever the action, image, or thought is unclear. Elena Laskova of the Shchukin School shared a similar exercise where the partners stood back to back, feeling the sound with the body, rather than actively listening with the eyes. At this point I was asked to get up and do the exercise with her, using the Russian word for what, *shto*, when it was unclear. The audience of watching teachers was rapt, and after that everyone seemed to relax.

We began discussing forward movement of text, another common problem, and Jan shared another exercise for finding rising inflections: a speaker and listener walking together, with the speaker "taking the friend along" with word energy and inflection. If the speaker uses a downward inflection at a place that is not a full stop in the text, the listener stops walking. Anna Petrova showed a similar exercise with a scarf as connective tissue between the two people. Jan and Anna did these exercises together to much laughter and applause. The discussion of inflection proceeded into the differences between Russian and American intonation patterns, and Marina attempted to explain "intonations of development" in which a question can be asked with a rising or falling tone, because the important element is to develop the last syllable, stressed or unstressed, into something that carries the intention past the end of the line. Anna Petrova said this has something to do with using the sound itself (as opposed to the word) as an action, and focusing on the reaction, saying "this [sound] is what maintains my intonation, not me but what I'm getting from the other person, what I'm expecting to get." While this language makes sense in the context of acting pedagogy and its connection to voice, it was clear there was a technical or aesthetic issue important to the Russians in this idea that we did not understand.

Grace Zandarksi attempted to use Destructuring to find a non-discursive, intuitive connection between breath and text by putting a young teacher against the wall to tremor and feel the breath sensation drop into her pelvic floor, and allow a spontaneous breath movement. This seemed to confuse many of the Russian teachers. I attempted to clarify by saying that one way of working with text is breaking up the idea according to the logical thought; another way is to let the natural, purely physiological movement of breathing in dictate, in the moment, the rhythm of speech—a fundamental idea from Fitzmaurice voicework that Catherine describes:

There is a step beyond tremoring into this release of managed breathing which is…not the only reason to tremor, but for me is the crucial reason to tremor—is to allow the breath to be spontaneous so that it's responding to the need for oxygen, and it's responding to the need to get rid of carbon dioxide, moment to moment, which means that the breath pattern can change moment to moment…so that there is a much more individual and spontaneous effect, if you like, to the reading of lines, so it sounds like they're being thought and made up rather than they're being delivered (2006).

The Russians were trying to understand, but something about what Grace and I were saying simply wasn't translating. Finally Anna Petrova said it may not work for Russians; they may need an adjustment for their own culture "because your school is based on Freud—there are a lot of taboos [in Russia] against this zone in general [referring to the pelvic region]; you can do whatever you want but you never talk about it." This mention of Freud, and its apparent opposition to "reflex," confirmed something I had already begun to suspect as a fundamental difference between our school and the Russian school.

CONCLUSIONS: WHAT'S DIFFERENT? WHY?
The observations of these two five-day residencies suggest almost comically stereotypical conclusions: the Americans talked about feelings, the Russians embodied a "just do it" philosophy. Stereotypical or not, there seems to be some truth in this assertion. The comments of the American teachers that most deeply revealed their beliefs about voice during the discussion on the final day focused on the individual, "inner connection," the self, "melting on the inside" and so on. We interpreted exercises for imagination and action in terms of how they help fix the problem of performers whose voices don't accurately reflect "what's going on inside," a problem requiring attention because "it's very humiliating and painful." Russian comments tended to focus on action outside the self, the ensemble, physical metaphors, and tasks. The big surprise of the exchange was that the place where our two philosophies overlap is text work. In direct contradiction to early assumptions, text work, the place where internal and external meet, does cross language and culture.

As Anna Petrova suggested, one of the primary guiding principles of American voicework is deeply rooted in social and cultural aspects of American psychology. This ideology finds concrete expression in what Linklater describes as the difference between "natural" and "habitual": we all exhibit unconscious behavior created through repeated and therefore habituated responses to physical and emotional stimuli. Unfortunately, this habituation seldom leads to efficient ways of moving, breathing, talking, or thinking—instead it leads to chronic tension, restricted modes of thought, and repressed emotions: "Certain neuromuscular programming has developed habits of mind and muscle that cuts us off from the instinctual

connection between *emotion* [emphasis added] and breath" (Linklater 1976, 12). These tensions have a negative effect on the voice, and therefore, one of the primary tasks of the voice teacher is to *release* these tensions so that new, more efficient or advantageous behaviors arise in their place.

Release is of paramount importance in Western voice training. The word signifies more than mechanistic reprogramming of nerve and muscle: it means encouraging students to "get out of their own way" and "allow" the voice to express directly from their state of being. This idea is central to most of the major English-speaking teachers: Catherine Fitzmaurice refers to "the unconscious response of the diaphragm to a need for oxygen," and the "physical and emotional aspects" of her work and the "resulting growth of the personality" (1997, 248-9). Kristin Linklater describes Iris Warren's contributions to voicework in terms of "adding psychological understanding to physiological knowledge," "unblocking the emotions," and shifting exercises from "external physical controls to internal, psychological ones" (1976, 2-3). She further describes her approach to her own work in terms of "emotional energy and resonating response," and the conditioning that squelches the "animal instinct level of emotional response to stimulus, deep within the unconscious mind" (10-11). Like Catherine Fitzmaurice, Linklater describes a "psycho-physical" process, working on the body and mind at the same time (19). Patsy Rodenburg describes the "natural personality" that "has been masked by one or a series of alien habits" and suggests "we have to release sound naturally in order to release ourselves" (1993, 22, 26). She also discusses the imposition of habits not just by the repetition of physical movement, but also by emotional stressors like divorce, a "blow to self-esteem," or an "experience of violence" (28). Cicely Berry describes the voice as "the most intricate mixture of what you hear, how you hear it, and how you unconsciously choose to use it in light of your personality and experience" (1973, 7). She also lists personality as one of the four elements that conditions anyone's voice, saying "it is in the light of your own self that you…unconsciously form your own voice…it is your emotional reaction to your family and environment…your own individual need to communicate, and your ease and unease in doing so, which are the contributory factors that make you evolve your own completely personal voice and speech" (8).

AMERICAN PSYCHOLOGY OF VOICE
Our ideas about ourselves as teachers and learners are implicit in the vocabulary we choose to describe our own work: Not only phrases like "psycho-physical," but also "psychological," "emotional," "unconscious," "personality," and "self." Freud plays a role in this insofar as we have, as a culture, embraced his idea that our behavior is controlled in part by hidden motivations, and uncovering them offers the possibility of

self-knowledge; in Western voicework, that self-knowledge correlates to a highly valued expression of truthfulness in vocal sound.

Although therapeutic elements in voicework rightfully stimulate ongoing discussion in the discipline, I don't think any American voice teacher would deny there is a psychological and occasionally therapeutic dimension to our daily classroom work. Kristin Linklater suggests we must embrace the risks and rewards of deep personal work: "The actors whom we train must be able to conjure up their own psychological monsters...tame them, and train them to leap through hoops of fiery texts" (1997, 4). Voice teachers need to be prepared for the situation when in a simple relaxation exercise "student belly muscles let go so that breath can enter a body fully for the first time in years, and the student begins to cry uncontrollably" (5). The notion that "a character...is rooted in truthfulness because rooted in me" makes us "inevitable inhabitants of therapeutic territory" (4, 5).

Fitzmaurice Voicework acknowledges a direct connection to Wilhelm Reich, a one-time student of Freud. Reich incorporated somatic elements into his therapeutic work, believing the body was the site of emotional memory, and emphasized self-determination of the individual (Fitzmaurice 2006). Certainly Fitzmaurice teachers must be prepared for emotional releases of joy, grief, rage, and fear—while emotional catharsis is not the point of Fitzmaurice release work, such release is common. Release and its connection to the empowerment of the individual is a central idea in Fitzmaurice's work:

> My project is to find the individual in the text delivery in the way the person breathes; it's to allow that individual to be empowered and to be a co-creator so that they're not just a channel for the writer, they're a co-creator of the moment. And certainly in America, actors like that are very popular—Jack Nicholson, John Malkovich—these actors that seize the play and make it their own are what we admire. I'm not sure that would be so in Russia. I think they'd consider...that they weren't supporting the play, that they were just going off on a narcissistic rant. But...I don't think that the tremor work...leads to narcissism; it leads to self-empowerment, which is a different thing, and it...leads to a communication which is more subtle (Fitzmaurice 2006).

Linklater further suggests we are "privileged" to "have been relieved enough of our survival needs to be free to focus on internal survival and something which has come to be called 'human growth'" (1997,10). Clearly, we voice teachers see ourselves as something more than mere instructors. Many of us feel our work is an avocation that necessarily incorporates

some therapeutic elements. Jan Gist sums this up most clearly:
> We are a generous, visionary group of healers; I think we're...the shamans of the theatre. We are the mental health, the physical health, we are the connection between the script, the audience, the actor, the director; we look out for all those parts...No matter the differences of language and culture and system...I think all of us voice teachers in both countries long for beauty and form, humanity, insight...How do we join up in giving each other what we can to heal and help the world? (2006)

Given this cultural context that correlates personal and vocal exploration, it becomes clear why some of the Russian techniques seem impersonal and mechanical to us.

RUSSIAN PSYCHOLOGY OF VOICE

Because the Russians have a different set of assumptions motivating their pedagogy does not mean those assumptions have nothing to do with psychology. Voice teachers navigate the murky territory of self and its connection to expression—but there is more than one way to define the self. Our way focuses on consciousness (and its correlate, the unconscious), how it forms physical and emotional habit, and the connective tissue between the two. As suggested above, this paradigm shows influences of Freud's individual psychology. Russians have been working under another paradigm for over 70 years, and only since 1979 have Freudian ideas like the unconscious been permitted as part of official discourse (Chertok 1981, 575).

Ironically, the subversive spirit that gripped Russia before and during the revolution found Freud's ideas stimulating (Kozulin 1984, 85). The unconscious was an important part of Russian psychological discourse as early as 1903, and was mentioned as an important aspect of otherwise materialist theories of emotion (Miller 1998, 22). But this all changed in 1929, when Stalin came to power. His regime demanded "all 'bourgeois' schools be repudiated so that a uniquely Soviet psychology might emerge" (Joravsky 1987, 190). By 1931, every theory in the USSR had to agree with, support, or justify the principles of Marxist materialism. Not located in biological organs, with no empirically provable scientific evidence that they existed, Freudian concepts, especially the idea of the unconscious, were considered "mythical, atavistic, archaic, and...'a grandiose attempt to give people an incorrect conception of human behavior, to cloud people's understanding'" (Brozek and Slobin 1972, 52). Furthermore, Freud himself was highly critical of Communism, believing "efforts to eliminate class distinctions were bound to fail" and (presciently) that "Communism would inevitably yield to psychic reality: the inexorable needs for authority, hierarchy and violence" (Hoffman 1987, 263). His ideas were banned.

Instead, Soviet psychology began to focus on what Americans called behaviorism, an approach to psychology grounded in the idea that understanding internal mental states, the focus of Freudian individual psychology, was not necessary to the understanding of behavior, and behavior could be studied and understood on its own terms. Soviet behaviorist psychology, called, tellingly, *reflexology*, "gave license to theorizing that connected the nerves to the psyche and even to the social nature of human beings" (Joravsky 1989, 273, 271). In other words, truth about human behavior could only be found in what was measurable, which was, in this case, biological function. Imagination was either discouraged or focused on the state. Kristin Linklater relates a story from her experience when Anna Petrova came to the US to the Shakespeare and Company winter intensive in 1990:

> I remember working with her one day, sitting in a chair, and getting her to close her eyes and turn her (and this is easy to us, a perfectly ordinary thing)…attention inwards. 'Let your attention go into your breathing.' And then working on the text: 'What is it you picture? What's your imagination?' And she opened her eyes and said 'I don't understand.' So I said, 'It's your inner imagination.' She said, 'I don't understand.' I said, 'It's the ability to tap into yourself and your own personal imaginative life.' And at that point we had a long conversation, and she explained that up until then, up until *glasnost, perestroika,* the move away from Communism, all their work was being done…for the country, for the state. So all your imagination, all of the exercises…were to do with imagining 'out there,' and imagining with the other person and the interaction and [all] that…It was ideologically not possible to pursue your own personal imaginative life, because that didn't belong…She could remember that all her working life in the theater, everything [she] did was created in order to serve the greater good of the state…There is no personal…emotion. 'My emotion is there for the play'…and it does not have what in this country we would say is the essential connection to your personal emotion, which then is transformed into the character emotion (2006).

Natalya Kovaleva of the Shchukin School remembers Soviet times:

> We had the only system for all schools, for all teachers, and we taught the same…For example, when I was a student, I hated speech lessons, because it was [all] about muscles. I didn't know anything about muscles. Nothing about my imagination, nothing about my body, because [the] body was a forbidden topic… All I heard in my lessons was 'work with these muscles, work with these muscles,' that's all. And nothing about imagination. And I think this is a poor way for actors, because all our profession is about

imagination, we live in [an] imaginary world, and [through] little exercises step by step, we can learn this process, how to get in our images, how to get in this imaginary world. This, I think, was missed in our work in former times (2006).

Anna Petrova states: "Things in the last 50 years have changed a lot…a long time ago we had a totalitarian system, and of course the theater was part of it, and the pedagogical process was under it as well so we had just one system for everyone. All alternative systems did not have a right to exist" (2006).

As she herself observed, our voicework is grounded in the very "alternative system" which was banned in the USSR until 1979. Little wonder some of our cherished assumptions make no sense to them.

WHAT WE HAVE TO LEARN

These two psychologies—one inward-looking, individual, and allowing for hidden motivation of behavior, the other rational, empirical and "scientific," mechanistic and focused on action—had profound effects on the theatre in the US and in Russia, and on voicework. As a result, our traditions are different: there is a major thread that runs through voice work in the West which is based on an understanding of the self as *individual*, and focuses on a personal connection to dramatic utterance. The Russians work under a paradigm—which, though it may be shifting, still dominates—that makes elements other than the individual the primary focus: other people, tasks that move focus outside of the self, and technical mastery.

The strongest aspects of Russian vocal pedagogy emphasize these active, task-oriented exercises and conceptualize the vocal training of the actor as the learning of a craft or the adding of skills. The American school excels when it conceptualizes the vocal training of the actor as the refining of an instrument and emphasizes the removal of barriers in the self as the path to experiencing human reflexes and their vocal correlates in a performing context. Those elements of American techniques that do exemplify a mechanical approach (Restructuring, for example) do so to ultimately access inner connection; conversely, elements of Russian training that would seem to have the most direct connection to American work (emphasis on the imagination) are focused on external tasks, and remain true to materialist principles. This creates certain characteristics in the actors trained in these methods: The Russians (from an American point of view) have a "pressed" sound which interferes with the kind of spontaneity and truthfulness we crave in our actors; the Americans (from a Russian point of view, and in the implicit opinions of some Americans) are occasionally self-indulgent and overly concerned with their own feelings, sometimes at the expense of what the play requires. Both methodologies claim to be pursuing the same goals, both acting traditions are rooted in the work of the same man, Konstantin Stanislavsky, but both voice traditions have focused on certain culturally determined preferences, at the expense of other possibilities.

Soviet artists were not permitted a personal imaginative life. The result is a legacy of passionate practitioners inspired by a materialist model that understood action and emotion as reflexive responses to external stimuli. This historical emphasis on the physical, at the expense of the imagination, as well as suspicion of the experience of deep release in the body, may explain why Fitzmaurice Voicework, elements of Linklater technique—any voicework that addresses individual psychology—are so challenging for the Russians. Ironically inspired by the same Stanislavskian ideas as the Russians, American actors before and during the Cold War were journeying inward, mining the connections between imagination and ideas of self absorbed from Freud's individual psychology and its offshoots. Voicework followed suit, and in another irony, methodologies now considered mainstream were in fact conceived in reaction to materialist attitudes to voice training from the British tradition. This reaction created a preference in this country for work that opens the voice by opening the self, and may explain why Americans are so suspicious of materialist philosophies that privilege function and action over inner connection.

Examining the differences between these two traditions brings out what is "otherwise too familiar to be noticed" (Joravsky 1987, 189), the radically different ideologies that have so strongly affected vocal pedagogy in these two milieus. What is considered obvious or common sense is not (to borrow some terminology from our discipline) necessarily *natural*; it may be *habitual*. This project demonstrated that while Americans perceived problems with Russian pedagogy ("pressed" sound; little willingness to explore the inner self), they also found much to admire ("muscularity," discipline, and engagement with action and imagination). This is not to say discipline and imagination are not present in American work, but because they receive greater emphasis in the Russian tradition, they evidently understand practical things about these elements that we do not. Exploring these differences offers all of us the greatest opportunities for growth. We would be foolish to ignore their expertise, just as they would be foolish to ignore ours.

Bibliography:

Bauer, Raymond A. *The New Man in Soviet Psychology.* Cambridge, MA: Harvard University Press, 1968.

Berry, Cicely. *Voice and the Actor.* New York: Macmillan Publishing Company, 1973.

Brusnikina, Marina. Interview by author. Trans. Natalya Fedorova. Video recording. Moscow, Russia, October 13, 2006.

Brozek, Joseph and Dan I. Slobin, eds. *Psychology in the USSR: An Historical Perspective.* White Plains, NY: International Arts and Sciences Press, 1972.

Caplan, Eric. *Mind Games: American Culture and the Birth of Psychotherapy.* Berkeley: University of California Press, 1998.

Carnicke, Sharon M. *Stanislavsky in Focus.* London: Harwood Academic Publishers, 2003.

Chertok, Leon. "Reinstatement of the concept of the unconscious in the Soviet Union." *American Journal of Psychiatry* 1981; 138: 575-583.

Gist, Jan. Interview by author. Video recording. Moscow, Russia, October 13, 2006.

Fitzmaurice, Catherine. "Breathing is Meaning." In *The Vocal Vision: Views on Voice by 24 Leading Teachers, Coaches, and Directors.* Edited by Marion Hampton and Barbara Acker, 247-252. New York: Applause Books, 1997.

Fitzmaurice, Catherine. Interview by author. Sound recording. New York, NY, November 20, 2006.

Harley, Anne. Interview by author. Video recording. Moscow, Russia, October 12, 2006.

Hoffman, Louise E. "The Ideological Significance of Freud's Social Thought." In *Psychology in Twentieth-Century Thought and Society.* Edited by Mitchell G. Ash and William R. Woodward, 253-269. Cambridge: Cambridge University Press, 1987.

Joravsky, David. "L. S. Vygotskii: the Muffled Deity of Soviet Psychology." In *Psychology in Twentieth-Century Thought and Society.* Edited by Mitchell G. Ash and William R. Woodward, 189-211. Cambridge: Cambridge University Press, 1987.

Joravsky, David. *Russian Psychology: A Critical History.* Cambridge, MA: Basil Blackwell, 1989.

Kozulin, Alex. *Psychology in Utopia: Toward a Social History of Soviet Psychology.* Cambridge, MA: MIT Press, 1984.

Kovaleva, Natalya. Interview by author. Video recording. Moscow, Russia, Oct 12, 2006.

Linklater, Kristin. *Freeing the Natural Voice.* New York: Drama Book Publishers, 1976.

Linklater, Kristin. "Thoughts on Theatre, Therapy and the Art of Voice." In *The Vocal Vision: Views on Voice by 24 Leading Teachers, Coaches, and Directors.* Edited by Marian Hampton and Barbara Acker, 3-12. New York: Applause Books, 1997.

Linklater, Kristin. Interview by author. Sound recording. New York, NY, November 17, 2006.

Markhashev, Victor. Interview by author. Trans. Natalya Fedorova. Video recording. Moscow, Russia, October 13, 2006.

Miller, Martin A. *Freud and the Bolsheviks: Psychoanalysis in Imperial Russia and the Soviet Union.* New Haven, CT: Yale University Press, 1998.

Mizell, Kelly. Interview by author. Video recording. Moscow, Russia, October 13, 2006.

Petrova, Anna. Interview by author. Trans. Natalya Fedorova. Video recording. Moscow, Russia, October 12, 2006.

Rodenburg, Patsy. *The Right to Speak.* London: Routledge, 1993.

Stanislavsky, Konstintin and Burnet M. Hobgood (trans.) "Stanislavsky's Preface to 'An Actor Prepares.'" *Theatre Journal,* Vol. 43, No. 2 (May, 1991), pp. 229-232.

Zandarski, Grace. Interview by author. Video recording. Moscow, Russia, October 13, 2006.

Essay *by Lyn Darnley*

Starting With the Words:
A UK Perspective on Voice Training for Classical Performance

I recently participated in an ATHE symposium on producing Shakespeare in the academies. Amongst other issues, there was a general concern among the panel and the audience about the difficulty that young student actors have with the language. The role of the training institutions in the preparation of young actors for classical theatre is powerful and they do an excellent job within a limited and pressured period.

I believe the academy rehearsal process provides the most appropriate and effective opportunity for teaching the fundamental language skills necessary for performing Shakespeare and all classical texts, and once these skills are established they can be built upon in subsequent rehearsal processes, throughout an acting career. I believe this work should begin in the classroom and transfer to the rehearsal room, where it should develop organically alongside character and motivation.

Three-year conservatory courses provide the most traditional route to a career in theatre in the United Kingdom and each institution has its own philosophy. Places at the conservatories are difficult to secure, with many students auditioning for every place.

An increasingly popular route for students to train for theatre is through the universities, which offer varying levels of practical and theoretical content in their drama programmes. Students are able to join highly active and often well-funded theatre societies where they develop their skills in their own time through performance, regardless of the subjects they are studying. Oxford and Cambridge do not offer courses in drama training but have extremely successful drama societies, which produce some notable performers. Students choosing the university route often go on to do specialised conservatory training after graduating. There are one and two-year specialist courses available at some of the drama schools. These courses are very expensive for students who have already completed three years of undergraduate training, and so a number of young actors work their way into the profession through the National Youth Theatre, the Edinburgh Festival, Pub Theatres, profit share ventures and Theatre in Education companies.

With such a diversity of training possibilities there are currently no guarantees that actors will enter the profession with, what could be described as, a sound method of approaching Shakespearean or classical language.

Is There a Language Issue?

The training that young actors undergo is generally detailed and comprehensive but, by necessity, much time is spent on acting methodology and preparing them for the areas of work that offer the greatest employment. Most training includes some work on Elizabethan texts but young actors working in classical theatre often feel there is much more for them to explore. With every generation we move further from the era that produced these plays. Our living language is evolving, and in order to keep the plays accessible to audiences, actors must first be confident of accessing the language for themselves. The loss of an oral culture and of verbal storytelling must inevitably have an effect on the language skills of young people. Unless young actors are allowed to forge a relationship with classic language they will never know the joys of it and are unlikely to pursue a career in classic theatre.

Lyn Darnley is the Head of Voice and Artist Development with the Royal Shakespeare Company where she has worked since 1992. Formerly Head of Voice at the Rose Bruford College of Speech and Drama in London, she has an MPhil from the University of Birmingham's Shakespeare Institute. With Stephanie Martin she is co-author of *The Teaching Voice* (Whurr, 1996) and *The Voice Source Book* (Winslow Press, 1992). She has been an external examiner on many courses including the Voice Course MA at Central School of Speech and Drama. Her work has taken her to the USA, the Far East, France and Africa, Australia and New Zealand.

At the RSC I work with a team of Voice and Text teachers to help actors—newly-graduated and experienced—break down the barriers that can result from being faced with language that often feels archaic and non-naturalistic. Many actors return to the stage after years of working in film and television and want to reawaken their relationship with language that can be epic, lyrical, rhetorical, and narrative, all within one text. Unless actors begin to develop a love and joy of words early on in their training, it is possible that they will never be given the roles that will allow them to be truly excited by the challenge that Shakespeare's language offers. If we do not have the actors who want to work with classical texts simply because they love the feel of the words in their mouths and the power of the words to move both actor and audience, we will lose an essential part of the plays that goes beyond the story and touches us with the very sound and rhythm of the language.

No matter how visually and physically effective a production is, unless it also addresses the language it will be missing the layers and textures and contemporary echoes of the text.

Many critics believe we are developing actors without the skills to speak the text. Comparisons are made between generations of actors, and their fashions and style of delivery are documented by scholars who study Shakespeare as performance. The profession itself is concerned by the loss of language skills and this can be seen in the number of day courses available through the Actors' Centres and by the development of professional "in house" training in Shakespeare companies and other theatres. The RSC is one of the theatre companies investing in continual professional development.

Artist Development
The RSC has a history of ensemble and of training, and is strengthening its commitment to the ensemble ethos by embracing the belief that the company that trains its ensemble invests in the future, and that an actor's training never ends. It also recognises there is a broader curriculum in the drama schools and other training establishments than there was twenty years ago and thus less detailed work on the language of Shakespeare and the other classic writers is possible for students. The RSC is currently forging closer relationships with the drama academies by hosting a student festival in the Swan Theatre as part of the 2006 Complete Works Festival. It is also offering young directors' and new writers' workshops in epic and heightened language.

Peter Hall established the RSC in 1960 and provided work on text from the beginning. In 1970 Trevor Nunn brought Voice Director Cicely Berry to the RSC and she developed what is

often seen as an RSC approach to voice and verse in which she reveals the text by freeing it physically. She still works regularly with the actors, offering them her insight and wealth of experience. Since 2004, Michael Boyd's core ensemble has been offered continuing training in fundamental skills such as verse and text, voice, rhetoric, movement, and music. Although all aspects of performance are included in the training, the prime focus is still on the skills required for the speaking of classical language. Consequently all actors work together, regardless of age and experience, resulting in the cross-fertilization of accumulated experience with new ideas and energy. The concept of an RSC Academy for young graduates was successfully piloted in 2001 but rejected in favour of the production-linked professional ensemble-training model. The need to balance tradition with new ideas is essential, and the ensemble approach embraced by the RSC is committed to experimental projects as well as holding onto what is traditionally valuable, while challenging the concept of a lost *Golden Age* of verse speaking sometimes referred to by critics. The programme includes invited practitioners from other companies and cultural traditions. The ensembles are offered regular classes from John Barton (verse), Cicely Berry (verse), members of the Voice Team, Associate Artists and Directors, teachers of rhetoric and those directors currently working with the ensemble. Visiting teachers have included Sir Peter Hall, Patrick Tucker, Lev Dodin, Janet Suzman, Clare Asqith, Rob Clare, Ralph Williams (University of Michigan) and Peter Gill. Lecturers from universities speak on the language and the academic issues relating to the plays. Jonathan Bate and Carol Rutter from Warwick University offer regular lectures to all members of the company including administration staff. The Company has recently offered free text workshops for the profession and student actors, conducted by John Barton. These were master classes with actors from the company and visiting actors including Ian McKellen, Timothy West, Jane Lapotaire, and Ian Richardson. The audience and actors benefited not only from seeing John Barton work, but also from the discussion and the suggestions made by very experienced actors.

Many young actors accept a contract at the RSC because they know they will be supported in their desire to extend their knowledge and practical work on classic text. They know the understudy system will offer them opportunities to work on larger roles while gaining experience playing smaller ones. They have the advantage of help from young directors and verse and voice coaches. A Stratford contract is seen by many young actors as an opportunity to refresh and build on their verse and prose techniques.

The Role of the Academies
Academies usually include at least one Shakespeare and often

another classical text in the three-year curriculum, and also work on classic monologues and audition speeches. This means they are in a position to introduce essential language skills alongside the other training, so that when they come to work on the plays they are able to use the language as a way into the psychology, and so marry both the language and the psychological approach. The fear that using the language as the starting point works against acting methods is unfounded. "Actioning" could be described as a language exercise. All productions can benefit from work on the physical dynamics and of the language. Murray Cox in his books *Shakespeare as Prompter* (Jessica Kingsley, 1994) and *Mutative Metaphors in Psychotherapy: The Aeolian Mode* (Cox and Theilgaard, Tavistock Publications, 1987) illustrates the indivisible link between language and the sub-conscious. For this reason focusing on language can benefit any rehearsal room regardless of the period of the text. Cicely Berry, who pioneered a physical approach to language, developed her work in the rehearsal room. The work sits comfortably alongside acting and supports the work of directors.

The Need

Language skills were the core area of training in UK drama conservatories until the 1970s and remain a high priority in some schools. There is clearly a need for specific text training for classical theatre because the demands are very different from those needed for television, the medium from which most graduates earn a living. Some teachers working in conservatories say there is increasing pressure from some course directors to move away from using verse when teaching voice because they feel it is inappropriate for the contemporary actor. Many teachers disagree with this because contemporary text also embodies rhythm and language dynamics shared with classical text. Training in language can only benefit an actor and complement the delivery of the most naturalistic language.

The RSC is not the only Shakespeare theatre instituting artist development programmes. Stratford, Ontario has developed an excellent and effective professional conservatory. The Oregon Shakespeare Festival employs voice and text coaches. The Globe has a Master of Voice and The National Theatre has a Voice Department started by Patsy Rodenburg now led by Jeanette Nelson, which addresses both Voice and Language. There is now a far greater use of voice and text coaches in the commercial theatre. There are also a number of post-graduate courses developing in the UK created for the specific study of the performance of classical theatre. The move towards post-graduate and professional training clearly illustrates that a gap exists.

I suggest the following factors have contributed to the displacement of language at the centre of actor training:

The Loss of the Oral Culture

We are rapidly losing touch with our oral cultures. With every generation we move further away from the culture that produced these texts. We no longer memorise long tracts or entertain each other with verse or stories. Even the language used in churches and the modern versions of the bible have moved us away from the language, formality, and structures of the King James version. Television and film do our storytelling for us through visual, not verbal, images. Fewer of us listen to the radio. Gone are the family drawing room entertainments that fostered the speaking of heightened texts in Victorian actors. Public poetry speaking is not fashionable, although the popularity of rap offers an opportunity for developing specific skills. We mistrust the structured language of politicians because we can often see the techniques of persuasion at work: they often develop the craft but not the art.

Shakespeare in the Classroom

Most people first encounter Shakespeare and the classics in the classroom. In the primary and high school system, although the language of the text is studied literally in order to reveal the narrative, there is little time dedicated to the way in which the language and poetry of these plays work to affect and move audience and actor, or the multi-layering that results from the fusion of rhythm, sound and structure. Even in theatre studies or drama classes at A Level or university level, where the plays are studied as performance, it is directorial concept and interpretation that is of prime interest. The plays were written for performance and should be spoken when studied because their power is in the way that the words affect the audience. The study of classic dramatic text as literature rather than performance robs young people of the opportunity to "feel" what changes when we connect muscle and sound, and allow the rhythms of language to take over from rational thought.

Fewer Repertory Opportunities

The "rep" system did at least expose young actors to a rapid turnover of a variety of *word-based* texts which exercised their language skills. It is also true that a larger percentage of actors earned their living through theatre and not television or film than is now the case. If we want to maintain the skills of speaking classical texts in a way that places the language at the centre, we have to prepare students and actors more thoroughly as the opportunities for work-based development are fewer.

Fewer Opportunities to Play Shakespeare

Unfortunately, the opportunities for any actor to perform in classical plays are limited because of the large casts and costs involved in staging them. Opportunities for young women to acquire skills simply through performing the smaller number of Shakespearean roles for women are now extremely limited and yet many directors and voice and verse coaches are female, so it is essential that they are offered equal opportunities to learn the skills they will pass on later in their career.

Shakespeare on Film
The filming of the classics has made them easily accessible, and Shakespeare's plays have reached thousands through this medium. Many students are studying Shakespeare as film and enjoying the plays that way. That the demands on the actor and audience are different cannot be denied. In film the verbal image is backed up by a visual one. On stage the actor is usually responsible for the creation of that image. It may be that many directors believe the way forward is to dispense with the problematic language and tell the story in a visual way, to put clarity of narrative as the prime objective and not to challenge the actor or audience through the words. If so, the psychological and motivational work done by the actor is incomplete. Shakespeare's insight into the connection between language and psychology was profound, and he made language the starting point for character.

Young actors can feel very vulnerable when asked to "trust the language" and they cannot do so unless they have had the prior preparation and adequate time to build up a relationship with the words and rhythms.

Are There Specific Skills to Teach?
Although most British drama schools require applicants to speak a piece of classic text at audition and the success of their attempt often determines whether or not they are accepted, the percentage of the training that is concerned with classical theatre is small. The common belief is that the loss of the repertory system has led to a lowering of the standard of classical theatre because young actors no longer go straight from training into these companies and learn their craft by being exposed to a number of classical productions on a regular basis. In fact, "rep" actors played a host of different genres, not all of which were challenging in terms of classical text.

They presented an opportunity for young actors to play a variety of classical roles, to hear the delivery of experienced actors and emulate a style of delivery. This does not mean that what was passed on was in any way definitive. It is just as possible for poor skills to be passed down, and fashion always plays a part in determining style. We know that the ever-growing size of auditoria in London led to a declamatory style that amplified scale and emotion but did nothing for the quality of language speaking. The old wax recordings often sound sung rather than spoken. There is a danger that in holding on to traditions we fail to reject what is truly outdated. The aim must be to take forward what is essential and excellent and feed it into a style appropriate to the period.

What Skill and Experience is Essential for the Undergraduate Embarking on a Heightened Text?
Above all the young actor should develop a physical connection with words. This requires regular work with words that connects breath and muscle to vibration. It calls for allowing the language to affect the body and therefore the character. Eventually the breath, sound and vibration create the emotion so that it does not need to be "added on." Very important is exposure to a variety of different styles of language. Student actors should speak the language out loud, moving to release the sound and finding the language for themselves so that the words cease to be lodged in the head and become connected with the breath and muscle, resulting in developing a relationship with the sound, vibration, rhythm and energy of the language rather than seeking the literal meaning. This is what is meant by embodying the "physicality of the language."

Of course actors must develop craft, and this embodies specific skills. Technical skill does develop naturally when this fundamental work comes first but it takes time and repetition to develop ownership of language and too often the technique it expected to develop before this connection is made.

Some of the essential technical skills needed by young actors approaching Shakespeare or the classics are:
- Sufficient breath to phrase long and complex thoughts
- A connection of the breath to voice and verbal muscularity
- The dexterity of articulation to convey the energy and precision of ideas through language
- A connection with syllabic value, which because of the rhythms of Shakespeare are significant. In the vernacular, syllables are collapsed and contracted
- A feeling for the importance of the *unstressed* beat as well as the stressed beat; otherwise the language cannot "trip along"
- Recognition of the neutral vowels and weak forms in the language. Without a sense of these in the body, the teaching of the iambic pentameter becomes an academic exercise
- An appreciation of the power and impact of muscular diction and the relationship between muscle and audibility
- The ability to think on the line and on the word and to keep the words alive through to the end of the thought
- The ability to recognise the main or principal clause in an extended sentence and to be capable of keeping the thought alive while negotiating the subordinate clauses

- Understanding of the need to take an audience through the long, meandering thoughts. Often the thoughts are broken up in an attempt to find clarity and they lose their meaning, scale and sensuality
- The ability to connect with the rhythms of verse and prose in order to allow the non-verbal aspects of language to emerge through the rhythm
- An ease and familiarity with words and their textures and an enjoyment of the fabric and texture of words, beyond their literal meaning
- The ability to use heightened language in a simple and meaningful way that supports a compound sense of "truth" rather than compromises it.

Words: The Starting Point

Starting a programme of language development as soon as training begins allows for early exposure to ways of making the sometimes difficult transition from "head bound" words on the page to the essential, physical, muscularly spontaneous words that live at the heart of the play. This fundamental work can then be revisited and developed with every new production whether classic or contemporary. Once a connection with the words is made the plays can be what they were intended to be: language led. Too many young actors still feel that in order to speak Shakespeare they need to conform to a standardised accent. This brings with it a notion that "good speaking" is about carefully articulated speech and southern English vowels.

Ideally the work of the voice class should be as closely linked to the work of the rehearsal room as the acting class is.

The voice class traditionally focused on text and language, but many of the newer systems of voice focus on the freeing of the voice without channelling the freedom through the language. This physical but non-verbal voice work is often linked to a psychological approach rather than a theatrical one. There are obvious benefits to any actor developing a voice that is free. Losing the close relationship between voice-work and speech and language work has increased the division between voice and words; reversing the situation and re-instating the language link is one sure way of increasing verbal skills. Forging a connection with muscular sound and language dynamics can be developed in the voice class so that the voice is developed with communication in mind. This helps the students to stop listening to themselves and reclaim the relationship between sound and meaning that we are fast losing. It also allows the development of breath stamina and muscularity that is so essential for Shakespeare. The "investment" we make in the sound of language takes us beyond the literal meaning into the multi-faceted layers of words that compound the meaning through rhythm, assonance, dissonance and alliteration which often combine to affect and resonate with the words around them and in so doing move both the speaker and the audience.

The poetry of language is revealed when words are explored physically and without a pre-conceived notion of their literal meaning. The sound of words embodies energy and music that is often lost through familiarity of the accepted literal meaning of the word. When young actors allow themselves to be led by the words instead of forcing the language into a generalised meaning, they rediscover the intrinsic dynamics, energy, onomatopoeia and music within it, and this brings language to life. Examples of exercises in this work are readily available in the books of Cicely Berry. She developed her work through many years working with actors and directors at the RSC including working with Peter Brook, whom she acknowledges as an important influence. Her focus on freeing the voice *through the language* makes it ideal work when producing Shakespeare. Her methods are also very useful in the training of directors. The books *The Actor and the Text*, (Virgin, 2000) and *Text in Action*, (Virgin, 2000) offer clear guidance to student actors and directors. Voice coaches are often familiar with this work and that of Linklater and Rodenburg.

Generalised Speaking

Young actors are often accused of approaching the text with "generalised" rather than specific thought. Some of the qualities that result from this are:

- Overstressing in an attempt to be clear; using stress as the only way of emphasising and ignoring all the other options open to an actor such as poising and phrasing; giving one idea more space and time in a line; using the vowel and consonant dynamics of the word to give it more energy.
- Using an emotion to show the importance of the idea rather than letting the language do it. This results in the audience receiving one literal message rather than the multi-layered combination of literal meaning, sound and rhythm and juxtaposition of the words that create the poetry.
- "Explaining" the language rather than allowing it to "speak." This irons out subtlety and "tells" the audience what to think.
- Shouting in order to give words importance and scale. Rather than drawing the audience in, shouting results in alienating it.
- Actors who are inexperienced in delivering classical text often turn verse into prose.

It takes confidence to allow the language to speak for itself and that confidence comes only with experience and practice.

Searching for Clues in the Text

The text offers direction and young actors can learn to look for help by observing its shape and structure. The invaluable observance of changes from prose to verse, half lines, capital letters, alliteration, repetition, mono and multi-syllabic lines, image and metaphor and antithesis can inform the student on possible ways to play the text. These clues also allow the argument to become clear and accessible. It is also empowering for the student to know that there are areas of research that are so practical and applicable to their performance. The writings of Hall, Barton, Berry, Linklater, and Tucker offer clear guidance in this area. Young actors often panic about the "rules." They hear different opinions about end-stopping, run-on lines, shared lines, caesura, metrical pauses, feminine endings etc. Just knowing there are no rules—just guidelines and options—can be helpful.

The Voice Coach in Rehearsal

Greater dialogue between directors and voice coaches creates an opportunity for more work on the text in a physical rather than an analytic way. The role of the voice coach in classical theatre is growing. The development of the role is indicative of the need. When there is dialogue between the director and the voice coach and they have a shared objective, the student or actor can be properly supported and the director need not feel compromised by the involvement of an "outsider."

Language Work with Student Directors and Writers

If student directors are able to work with and alongside voice coaches and can learn to trust that exploration of the text will not usurp their directorial authority, the chances of changing the culture will improve as the relationship between voice coach and director strengthens and it become evident that the voice coach can support the director in his or her vision.

Ideally directors should have the same practical language training that actors undergo. All directing programmes should include practical language classes. They need to develop the same connection with the language they ask of their actors. If they work on the language themselves they will have a clearer idea of what to ask of the actor. This work is done in addition to the necessary research and text analysis—not instead of it. Many writers begin as actors. Any training they have received will benefit their writing.

Verse Speaking

Speaking classical verse and prose aloud from the start of training allows that experience to develop. When students need to analyse, analysis should arise out of the speaking of the language rather than before it. The experience begins with the words and the meaning reveals itself, not the other way round. A feeling for rhythm can only be taught so far, through clapping, singing, moving and percussion. The verse speaker needs to "feel" the rhythms and speaking poetry is the best way to develop the ability to do so. Exposure to language and verse can be done in groups and chorally. The additional pay-off is that such work develops group dynamic and improves listening skills as well as speaking skills. Voice coaches need to challenge any suggestion that we should abandon the teaching of verse. If anything, we need to balance the loss of an oral culture with more poetry, both classic and contemporary. Verse and language teaching can only benefit an actor, not just in the delivery of classical theatre but in all theatre whether it is classical, contemporary, physical or visual.

Leading Shakespearean actress Harriet Walter gives a clear summary of the goal the academies could aim for, in a quote from her book, *Other People's Shoes: Thoughts on Acting* in which she draws on her experience of playing Shakespeare.

If, [however] I follow Shakespeare's score, I will find words that jolt the ear just when it has been most lulled. I will find images so unexpected that they force the imagination beyond the bounds of logic and comfortable reason. I will find rhythms which work at such a subliminal level that all I have to do is follow them and they will move the audience far more than I could do by emoting sighs and tears. All this because Shakespeare the poet knew a thing or two about making plays.[1]

❦

1. Walter, Harriet. *Other People's Shoes: Thoughts on Acting.* London: Nick Hern Books, 1999 (reprinted in 2005), 164.

To Tech or Not to Tech:
Revising an Undergraduate Voice & Speech Course

To Tech or Not to Tech: That is the Question!

It seems to be the cry across university and college campuses everywhere—technology, technology, TECHNOLOGY! When my new dean announced a technology initiative for the School of Fine Arts, my first response was resistance. After all, I'm trying to get my theatre students to live in present time and space, to listen with their whole selves, to connect to and express human experience. What use did I have for technology beyond the ability to record sound samples, burn CDs for my students, and use the web to find dialect resources? And I discovered I am not alone in my resistance. Many faculty are concerned about the amount of time required to integrate technology into their teaching. They cite concerns about the payoff in terms of improved teaching and/or recognition of their work in the tenure and promotion process, as well as a lack of adequate tech support and training (Swain 2005). Poole and Bates suggest, "The additional workload that most instructors perceive to be an inevitable consequence of using technology for teaching is perhaps the most serious barrier to its use" (17). They also identify another barrier to the use of technology as "its potential threat to the power and control of teachers" (18). Many faculty perceive technology as the latest gimmick that is, at best, a waste of time and at worst, replacement of the teacher by a machine.

Elaine Garofoli and Jim Woodell in their article "Faculty Development and the Diffusion of Innovations" suggest:

> What's needed is an examination of the source of the resistance. Why would some faculty be so skeptical when others have achieved great success and discovered new ways to increase learning outcomes? Why would faculty resist tools that can help them simplify their work? The answer is not all believe in the inherent ability of technology to achieve these outcomes. They have to be convinced before they will integrate technology into their teaching (1).

I certainly was skeptical that any technological tool could be significantly helpful in a studio course where the work is inherently about face-to-face interaction. However, faced with pressure from the administration to engage with technology, and deeply committed to the pursuit of best teaching practices, I was willing to ask some questions: what if technology could innovate and improve student learning? What—if anything—was to be gained in the voice and speech classroom by introducing technology? I decided that *to tech* was worth an experiment.

Pedagogical Framework

To support my experiment, I joined a faculty learning community to improve teaching. With almost a decade of university teaching experience under my belt, I was mildly surprised to discover that skill in my discipline did not automatically translate into a deep understanding of effective pedagogy to promote student learning. Many of us who teach in higher education are not well versed in pedagogical methods; we know what works by trial and error or by following the examples of our own teachers. In her excellent new book, *Blueprint for Learning*, Laurie Richlin suggests[1]:

> …although many professors have deep concern for their students' learning, most have no way of grasping the complex problems of teaching and learning. Nor should they know how to improve learning: In almost

Julia Guichard is an Assistant Professor at Miami University in Oxford, Ohio where she teaches acting, voice, speech, script analysis and Alexander Technique. Julia holds a BFA in Acting from the Goodman School at DePaul University and an MFA in Acting from Penn State. She is a certified teacher of the Alexander Technique, holding certificates from The Performance School and Alexander Technique International. Julia has served as the Production Editor for 3 issues of the *Voice & Speech Review* and has published in *Theatre Topics*.

1. I highly recommend Richlin's book. It takes you through a step-by-step process for designing, implementing and assessing a course to maximize student learning. The book uses minimal jargon and relates ideas in accessible, easy to follow language.

all cases no one has ever taught them anything about the subject (ix).

While acknowledging I already had some success in the classroom, I was inspired by the notion that I could consistently improve on my teaching year after year by engaging in scholarly teaching; that is, by designing courses that are informed by the existing scholarship of teaching and learning, and by continuously assessing the effectiveness of my pedagogy in achieving student learning outcomes. Richlin continues:

> College instructors usually make their teaching decisions implicitly—and oftentimes in the midst of a live classroom situation. Although I believe most professors make good professional decisions on course activities, methods and assessment, if those decisions are not clarified, they cannot be evaluated and improved (4).

This systematic approach to course design appealed to me. As a certified teacher of the Alexander Technique, I am well aware of the power of conscious, rather than habitual behavior. We, as educators, are encountering students with an increasingly diverse set of needs and goals, training them for a rapidly changing work and social environment. Our teaching must constantly adapt to changes in our departmental cultures, institutional expectations, and student needs. And one of the central issues in both higher education and the "real world" is technology:

> Learning is too critical a human endeavor to allow us the luxury of remaining in traditional comfort zones. Advances in technology demand that we adjust or be left behind. Scrutinizing the science and the art of human learning causes us to shift our perspective (Bennet & McGee 2005, 28).

Participation in a faculty learning community required me to develop a teaching project. I chose to focus on the implementation and assessment of technology in the introductory voice and speech course. After teaching the course for several years, I was not completely satisfied with the voice work in departmental productions. I was noticing many students did not warm-up their voices adequately for rehearsal or performance; most could not be consistently heard or understood in the performance space; many had unhealthy vocal hygiene habits; and unless they were working with dialect, most gave no attention to consciously developing vocal choices for a specific character. These are all issues I had addressed with students in the voice and speech classroom, but they were clearly not carrying the information and skills forward into production as well as I had hoped. I could see ample opportunities for improving the course's outcomes, but would implementing technology afford me any help in doing so?

I set out to investigate the potential for technology in the course. As I looked at various technologies available to me, I quickly became entranced with the *bling* of sexy gadgets and cool software. It was overwhelming—the endless possibilities of technology. Should I podcast? Use learning objects? Use web-based inquiry? However, I soon realized that technology is not a topic—it is a tool. And as with any tool, I needed to have a teaching problem or goal to address in order to use that tool appropriately.

I needed a clear and specific method for determining the most effective approach in helping my students to understand and, most important, apply vocal skill in their performances beyond the classroom. In her excellent text, *Teaching for Understanding with Technology*, Martha Stone Wiske suggests approaching course design through a set of goals, much like those an actor uses in building a role:

> Goals for a particular lesson are coherently connected to larger goals for a longer curriculum unit; unit goals, in turn, clearly connect to even larger term-long or year-long goals. The Teaching for Understanding project referred to such overarching goals as 'throughlines' because they serve like an actor's throughline to shape and focus a whole strand of performances. A clear and coherent, nested set of goals helps both students and teachers focus on the core purposes of every aspect of the learning process (Wiske et al 2005, 7)

To develop my throughline, I began by reviewing the existing syllabus for the course in order to understand exactly what the course structure was already doing to help students learn and apply skills. I reviewed student evaluations of the course for the prior three semesters. I also interviewed my two undergraduate teaching associates, each of whom had taken the course in a previous semester. Together, we examined each project and component of the course in terms of: 1) implied or stated goal; 2) content (knowledge or skill set); 3) opportunity for practice or demonstration of knowledge or skill set; and 4) overall value to the student. I discovered a common thread: the students felt that although the course was valuable and they learned a lot, they didn't feel able to apply the information and skills to performance work outside of class. Where was the disconnect in the carryover of skill from classroom to outside performance work? Perhaps the students were having difficulty applying voice work outside of class because they weren't learning to self-direct their own learning in class. What if I shifted the objective for the course to something like: "to develop student self-directed vocal skills for application in performance work"? Then I could design a throughline for the course that would lead student actors toward self-sufficient behavior. This may seem obvious. After all, I thought I had been pursuing this objective of student self-sufficiency all along. But the evidence clearly demonstrated that my teaching methods were falling short of the goal. With a clear objective in place, I could now design/adapt all assignments and projects in the course by assessing their value in moving students along the throughline of action toward that objective. An added benefit of thinking about learning in terms of throughline is that it makes the process active, much like a character's journey through a play is active:

> Statements of goals usually include action verbs like *appreciate*, *analyze*, and *explain* rather than more passive phrasings such as *know that*, *list*, or *correctly use* (Wiske et al 2005, 7).

I began to design assignments that would challenge students to work independently both in and out of the classroom, to think critically about their own learning styles, to apply familiar concepts in new ways and to take responsibility for their own learning.

Choosing and Implementing Technology

So, surely it would be possible to facilitate this throughline without the use of technology, right? We're back to the original question: to tech or not to tech. My use of technology was driven primarily by a desire to formally extend student learning outside of the classroom. On a purely practical note, I also wanted to free up as much time as possible in class for face-to-face interactions. There is never enough class time to work with students! To this end, I then asked, "what functions might technology effectively serve?"

Poole and Bates provide an excellent framework for the selection and use of technology in their text, *Effective Teaching with Technology*. They suggest a systematic approach using something they call the "Sections Model," a set of questions that can guide instructors making decisions about technology in a course (78-105). This model addresses:

S	Student demographics, access and learning styles
E	Ease of use and reliability
C	Costs
T	Teaching and learning
I	Interactivity
O	Organizational issues
N	Novelty
S	Speed

(Poole and Bates 2003, 79-80)

Keeping these criteria in mind, I came up with three broad categories for employing technology: disseminate information, practice skills, and lecture/demonstration. I will describe the specific tasks for each category and the ways in which technology was utilized to facilitate those tasks.

Disseminate Information

This is perhaps the easiest function to address; many instructors are familiar with using technology to provide information. Most, if not all, universities now employ a Content Management System (CMS) such as Blackboard or WebCT to deliver course specific material to students. Before this current attempt to revise the voice & speech course, I had already experimented with using Blackboard to post announcements, communicate to students via email, provide links to web resources, post grades and course documents such as handouts and syllabi. In the past, this had primarily been a back-up task for me. If students lost a document, they could pull it off the web. I could remind them of an announcement made in class on the site. But now, I created a more deliberate flow of information electronically. While I used to burn the first 3-5 minutes of a 50-minute class for class business, all informational tasks were shifted out of the classroom. All announcements were posted on Blackboard exclusively and students were expected to check the site daily. Instead of presenting assignments in class, I now posted assignment instructions on Blackboard; it takes much less class time to clarify an assignment in class than to introduce it. Students' written assignments were submitted via Blackboard rather than being collected in class, saving a few more minutes. All of these relatively minor savings paid major dividends, allowing me to commit the first 5-10 minutes of each and every class to warm-ups. In previous incarnations of the class, I had often sacrificed warm-ups in the second half of the semester, as I needed the time to cover other material. In the revised version of the class, what started out as a timesaving device had other, unexpected, benefits. After the first few weeks, students discovered if they didn't check Blackboard, they missed important information and were not prepared for class. This immediately began to foster a sense of responsibility in them for their own learning. Also, the class site became a rich source of related materials: websites, articles, audio samples. And because students now had to visit the site regularly for vital class information, I discovered they were more likely to browse and use the resources I provided for them. And perhaps most significant of all, eliminating all the class business at the start of class changed the entire climate of the classroom. Students began to walk in the door and get immediately to work, warming up independently to get ready for the day's task.

Practice Skills

Directly related to my teaching objective—to develop student self-directed vocal skills for application in performance work—I wanted to create structured opportunities for students to practice classroom skills outside of class. For example, I wanted students to not only learn, but also apply effective methods for warming up their voices. I had always taught vocal warm-ups in voice class, but students still did not demonstrate effective warm-ups in situations outside of class. They articulated a variety of reasons for this: "I can't remember them well"; "I don't have time"; "I don't think I need them"; "They're boring"; and "I forgot." So, in addition to making sure to reinforce warm-ups by devoting the first 5-10 minutes of *every* class for the duration of the semester to a vocal warm-up, I developed a *warm-up CD* assignment. I recorded a digital sound file for each individual warm-up exercise that I had introduced in class.[2] These files were then uploaded onto Blackboard. Students were asked to create two different real-life scenarios that would require a vocal warm-up, then choose the most appropriate exercises for each scenario to create two different warm-ups (one 5 minutes long; one 15-20 minutes long). Finally, they had to edit the sound files for the exercises together, underscoring with music of their choice, creating a single track for each warm-up scenario that could be loaded onto an mp3 player or burned onto a CD for use in rehearsals, daily vocal work-outs, auditions or performances. This assignment moves beyond a simple repetition of warm-up exercises, requiring students to assess a problem, develop a strategy and apply a solution. *Old* technology such as tape recorders isn't flexible enough to do this project easily. New, easily available and easy-to-use technology (digital audio recorders and editing software) made this assignment possible.

Less complex opportunities to encourage student skill practice are readily available on the web. Online *learning objects* are often excellent tools that engage students in a virtual learning environment.[3] While there is much debate about the definition of a learning object, Wiley defines it as "any digital resource that can be reused to support learning" (7). An example of an existing learning object that I incorporated into my voice and speech course is the interactive IPA chart developed by Paul Meier and Eric Armstrong. This is an excellent site that provides audio samples of each symbol in the IPA.[4] My students found it invaluable for practicing listening and transcription skills. While many excellent resources exist on the web (and can be found on the VASTA home page under "Internet Resources"), the trick can be integrating them into the course work actively. Students need to be asked to use the resources to help them solve a problem or move them toward a goal.

Lecture/Demonstration
In the previous two categories, the costs in both time and money to implement technology were manageable. Not so with this third category. The most challenging work of this course revision, by far, was the creation of two learning objects to address specific course content and to engage students outside the classroom. The key to creating effective learning objects is twofold: first, define specific goals for the object (what should students be able to do when they are finished?) and second, give the object interactivity (in other words, give the student something to *do* so that she will learn actively). In her fascinating book, *Computers as Theatre*, Brenda Laurel applies dramatic theory to the problem of designing computer/human interfaces. She proposes that much like theatre, computer graphical interface design aims at "creating representations of worlds that are like reality only different" (10). Within this representation, the potential power of computer technology lies in its capacity to "represent action in which humans could participate" (1). She continues, "Designing human-computer experiences isn't about building a better desktop. It's about creating imaginary worlds that have a special relationship to

2. I am indebted to Eric Armstrong for inspiring this assignment. He recorded himself talking through a vocal warm-up for his students, and then created a podcast so they could use it outside of class.

3. Online databases such as MERLOT (Multimedia Educational Resource for Learning and Online Teaching) are an excellent source of free, accessible, peer-reviewed learning objects. Access to MERLOT is at <www.merlot.org>.

4. Meier and Armstrong's excellent IPA site can be accessed on the web at <www.yorku.ca/earmstro/ipa/index.html> or <www.paulmeier.com/ipa/charts.html>.

reality-worlds in which we can extend, amplify, and enrich our own capacities to think, feel, and act" (33).

As I thought about content I might move online, I looked for material that had potential to come alive in one of these "imaginary worlds." I also wanted to be sure the content could be delivered digitally without losing (or ideally, even improving) the quality of teaching and learning. The first object I created was a *Cosmo* magazine style quiz on vocal health and hygiene. This was a very easy object to create, consisting of a series of questions about behaviors that impact vocal health. After completing the quiz, students get a score that provides feedback in several categories (hydration, vocal misuse/abuse, environmental irritants) and suggests possible methods for improving vocal hygiene. This relatively simple first try gave me the confidence to try something more complex. It also connected me to instructional technology staff at my university and taught me how to use the available resources for technology support.

The second, and far more complex, learning object is the Voice Recipe Online. This object replaced one of the few true lecture/demonstrations I use in class, covering material from Robert Barton and Rocco Dal Vera's text, *Voice Onstage and Off.* The Voice Recipe is one method for analyzing a voice based on nine parameters or *ingredients* of a voice such as tempo, pitch, quality, etc. (238-55). This particular subject had the potential to succeed as a learning object when measured by the Sections Model:
- **Students**—the Voice Recipe Learning Object (VRLO) would be accessible 24 hours a day for the entire semester, allowing students to learn at their own pace, revisit the material at any time, and could be designed to accommodate a wide variety of learning styles.
- **Ease of use and reliability**—proven technology is readily available to create and deliver the VRLO.
- **Cost**—due to its connection with an existing, popular textbook, the VRLO would have high potential for reusability in a variety of contexts, justifying the expense of creating it.
- **Teaching and learning**—the VRLO could both provide content and develop skills that could be used as a foundation for classroom projects.
- **Interactivity**—perhaps the most valuable potential for the VRLO was the possibility for fun: we could engage student interest through the use of audio files and graphics to present the material, then have them *do* something to demonstrate their knowledge in an interactive game.[5]
- **Organizational Issues**—the VRLO would not have been possible without the support of my university's Instructional Technologies staff. They provided all the programming and graphic design expertise to realize the project. A great deal of support for this project was present on all levels: the dean's office, faculty development services, and the chair of the theatre department.
- **Novelty**—while not employing cutting edge technology, the VRLO was original and innovative.
- **Speed**—This was a difficult issue. It takes enormous amounts of time to develop a complex learning object. Work on the VRLO began in August 2005 and was just barely finished in time for implementation in January 2006.

5. "Most theories of learning suggest that for learning to be effective it needs to be active...It is not enough merely to listen, view or read; learners have to do something with the learning material" (Poole and Bates, 98-99). This concept is instinctive to voice and speech teachers, but we may not immediately understand how to transfer the concept to digital materials.

My co-author, Rocco Dal Vera, and I designed the VRLO with two parts. Part I introduces the components of the voice recipe and provides numerous audio samples so that students can learn basic concepts and practice listening skills (lecture/demonstration).

Part II challenges learners to test their knowledge by analyzing the voices of "celebrity chefs," famous characters from television and film (application of concepts). Playing the celebrity chef game is randomized, so learners can return to the site again and again, drawing different voices and ingredients each time.[6]

Screen Shot of introductory page to the Voice Recipe Online. Artwork and programming by Advanced Learning Technologies, Miami University

After learning and practicing the voice recipe online, students were asked to record and analyze their own voices, then to creatively present their individual recipes in class. This exercise helps students to think specifically about their own voices, the first step in enabling them to make conscious vocal choices for characters. The major advantage to introducing the voice recipe through a learning object proved to be the opportunity for each student to learn at his or her own pace, returning to the site as many times as necessary to understand difficult concepts. In a traditional lecture/demonstration, students learn at the pace set by the instructor. In addition, the wealth of carefully constructed audio samples on the site provides a more complete and detailed presentation of the material than the limits of a 50-minute classroom experience can afford. The time in class can be more effectively used to play with the concepts that were introduced and practiced online.

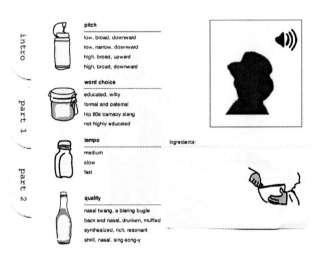

Screen Shot of the Celebrity Chef game in Part II. Artwork and programming by Advanced Learning Technologies, Miami University

6. The Voice Recipe Online can be accessed at <http://www.academic.muohio.edu/the233/voice_recipe/> or through MERLOT at <www.merlot.org> (arts/theatre listing).

7. A proposal for the study entitled "Study of Pedagogy in a Performance Classroom" was approved by the Institutional Review Board for Human Subjects Research at my university. Surveys were anonymous; students chose code names to protect their identity. Interviews were conducted and recorded by the undergraduate associates for the class, then transcribed by a professional who removed all identifying markers on the transcripts.

Assessment

In order to assess learning outcomes for the course, students were asked to participate voluntarily in a semester-long study.[7] At the semester's start, each participant completed a survey that addressed perception of his or her own voice. Each student participating also then completed an identical survey at the end of the course, four months later, in order to provide a method for measuring change in student self-perception. In addition, students provided feedback throughout the semester on specific assignments (Voice Recipe, *Cosmo* Quiz, Warm-up CD) to determine how well technology was working to facilitate student learning. Finally, students were invited to give short interviews after the final exam was finished to give them a chance to respond in more detail to their experience in the course. Out of the 14 students registered for the course, 10 chose to participate in the study. I have broken down assessment data into two categories: student learning outcomes and effectiveness of technology.

Learning Outcomes

The following tables illustrate the change in student self-perception regarding five learning outcomes for the course.

Q1: How would you describe the health of your voice?

	Very healthy	Mostly healthy	Not healthy
January, 2006	10%	70%	20%
May, 2006	30%	70%	0%

40% reported improved vocal health; 50% no change; 10% less health

Q2: How would you respond to the following statement: "I know how to effectively warm-up my voice for rehearsal."

	Strongly agree	Agree	Disagree	Strongly Disagree
January, 2006	0%	60%	30%	10%
May, 2006	70%	30%	0%	0%

70% reported improved skill; 30% no change

Q3: How would you respond to the following statement: "I am confident in my ability to make vocal choices for a character in a production."

	Extremely	Confident	Unsure	Never think about it
January, 2006	0%	20%	70%	10%
May, 2006	50%	40%	10%	0%

90% reported increased confidence; 10% no change

Q4: How do you feel about your voice?

	Love it	Like it	Dislike it	Hate it
January, 2006	0%	40%	60%	0%
May, 2006	10%	70%	20%	0%

50% reported increased comfort with their voices; 50% no change

Q5: How confident are you in your audition skills?

	Very confident	Confident	Unsure	Lost
January, 2006	10%	30%	60%	0%
May, 2006	30%	50%	20%	0%

60% reported increased confidence; 30% no change; 10% decreased confidence

Of particular interest are questions 2, 3, and 5 since these specifically relate to my original objective for the class: to develop student self-directed vocal skills for application in performance work. The data clearly shows improvement for a large majority of the students, sometimes dramatically. For example, while only 20% (two students) reported confidence in making vocal choices in a production at the start of the semester, 90% (9 students) felt confident or extremely confident in that area by the end of the course. Confidence about audition skills also increased significantly for 60% of students. Most impressive of all, an overwhelming 100% of students reported that by the end of the course they could warm-up their voices effectively.

In addition to citing improved skills, students also reported a change in perceptions about their voices. By the end of the semester, 50% of students liked their voices more than they had at the start of the course. There was also significant changes in how students described their voices: "Prometheus" went from "irregular, rough, raw" to "advancing, progressing, better"; "M13 Voice" went from "loud, sometimes forced, fluid" to "full, warm, versatile."

These student perceptions are supported by my observations and by those of my two undergraduate associates. One associate observed:

> I was impressed with the quality of work I observed throughout the semester. The level of work was significantly higher [than in previous semesters] and showed a high level of understanding. Students seemed pleased with what they had learned and confident in important areas like warm-ups and vocal choices.

The other wrote:

> The students really got a lot out of the course. The bridging techniques are starting to work! The techniques to be used in the future are now much more emphasized. Much of what seemed to be busy work has been eliminated.

All three of us were impressed with the students' skill when applied to audition-ready monologues in the final exam. Also, most of the students in the course went on to use their "voice" monologues in the Fall 2006 round of departmental production auditions. When I sat in on auditions, students from the course had clearly continued to work on their voice monologues over the summer break, demonstrating their improved confidence in carryover of voice work to situations outside of class. Anecdotally, I have observed more consistent use of warm-up exercises in rehearsals for departmental productions. And two students from the course have reported using their warm-up CDs: one for professional auditions, and the other to teach warm-ups to the cast of a production he was directing. A variety of evidence, both self-reported and observed, suggests an affirmative shift occurred for students both in their perception of skills acquired and also in their ability to apply those skills outside of class. While the small size of the test group prevents the drawing of definitive conclusions, the results of the study are encouraging.

Use of Technology

Overall, the selection and implementation of technology in the course was successful. The online management of information through Blackboard was effective and efficient, freeing up valuable class time for student learning. And although the initial set up of projects such as the warm-up CD and the online learning objects required the investment of significant time, energy and money, all of that is now in place and can be reused in my future courses and by other instructors.

Students were generally positive about the use of technology in the course. In interviews they seemed most positively affected by the online learning objects:

> …oh, the online learning really helped me through the whole [final] monologue process too…the voice recipe was probably the most influential…just because I went back to it every time reviewing what every ingredient was and taking it into account when trying to write out my own voice recipe for my character (Student A).

> I liked the technology a lot. I thought the different games…the voice recipe stuff was really helpful. And the online IPA made it a lot easier. Like if I forgot something I could just click on it and hear what it sounded like (Student B).

> I think the technology for the most part was beneficial. Especially the IPA alphabet online… that was really great. And the voice recipe online was really good too. It's the…I think it's the audio examples that we listened to…those are really helpful (Student C).

Specifically, the data from the Voice Recipe Online survey was encouraging. Students made multiple visits to the site, spending an average total of 90 minutes with it during the initial assignment period, double the time they would have spent with the material in the traditional classroom lecture/demonstration. From the interview comments, it is clear that some students spent even more time revisiting the site later in the semester. When asked "How well did this site prepare you for the in-class voice recipe assignment?" they responded: Very well (75%), Adequately (12.5%), Not very well (12.5%).[8] On a scale of 1-10, the students rated the Voice Recipe Online for clarity (9.3), ease of navigation (9.6), content (9.25), fun (8.9), value (9.4), and overall effectiveness (9.5). Classroom presentations of the students' personal voice recipes demonstrated better understanding of the material than in previous years when the material was taught inside the classroom. Recipes were more specific. For example, students did not describe their own voices as having "average pitch" or "normal speed," instead using terminology such as "median pitch, broad range, upward inflection" and "variable tempo in the rhythm of a march."

In addition to improved specificity, the in-class student voice recipe presentations were enormously creative. A sample of the formats used include: a child's storybook, an interior room design, a puppet show, and a breaking-news broadcast describing the search for an escaped voice, complete with reports from the field. And even though I had decided not to grade their presentations, the students spent a great deal of time and energy on them. At least, in part, this enthusiasm might be linked to the students' engagement with the Voice Recipe Learning Object.

The *Cosmo* quiz on vocal health and hygiene and the warm-up CD assignment met with more mixed success. Although students enjoyed the *Cosmo* quiz, it did not effectively replace the classroom experience for them. I think that I misjudged the real activity of that particular day in class, thinking it was all about lecture. Students needed the opportunity to discuss the issues of vocal health and hygiene, not just identify them. Perhaps an online discussion

8. The student who chose "not very well" made a point of noting that s/he enjoyed the site, but preferred to learn from the textbook. This comment reinforces the need to address different learning styles when delivering course content.

forum following the quiz would solve the problem. The warm-up CD, while clearly valuable to some students, caused problems for other students who did not already possess the necessary technical skill to record and edit sound files. Their perception of the value of the assignment was affected by their frustration with learning and implementing new technologies. In the future, providing students with structured tutorials to learn and practice software such as GarageBand or Audacity[9] prior to beginning the project might decrease their anxiety and improve the cost/benefit ratio for students.

9. The web abounds with free or inexpensive software for editing sound files. For example, Audacity is a program that runs on both Mac and PC and can be downloaded free off the web. I use GarageBand (for Mac), which comes as part of an affordable software package called iLife. A little investigation and experimentation will help you determine the best software for your needs.

Conclusion

The key for the effective use of technology is rooted in best teaching practices. At the end of the day, good pedagogy is good pedagogy, whether it involves traditional lecture, collaborative learning, textbooks or the Internet. Now when I'm dissatisfied with student progress I ask myself, "what are my teaching goals and learning outcomes, and what is the best technique or tool to accomplish those goals?" While I still believe that technology cannot and should not replace most of what goes on in a voice and speech classroom, I am now one of the converted. Used appropriately, technology can increase student learning, connect classroom learning to "real world" application, and free up valuable class time for the experiences that demand instructor/student interaction. So, "to tech or not to tech?" Yes…and yes. Both have their place in the 21st century voice classroom.

Works Cited
Barton, Robert, and Rocco Dal Vera. *Voice Onstage and Off*. Fort Worth: Harcourt Brace, 1995.
Bates, Tony, and Gary Poole. *Effective Teaching with Technology in Higher Education*. San Francisco: Jossey-Bass, 2003.
Bennett, Kathy, and Patricia McGee. "Transformative power of the learning object debate." *Open Learning* 20:1 (2005): 15-30.
Garofoli, Elaine and Jim Woodell. "Faculty Development and the Diffusion of Innovations." *Campus Technology. http://syllabus.com/article.asp?id=7093* (accessed 12 September 2006)
Laurel, Brenda. *Computers as Theatre*. Reading, MA: Addison-Wesley, 1991.
Swain, Colleen. *Technology in Teacher Education: Faculty Visions and Decision Making. http://web.uoregon.edu/ISTE/uploads/NECC2005/KEY_6447637/Swain_SwainNECC2005_R P.pdf#search=%22faculty%20resistance%20technology%20study%22.* (accessed 12 September 2006).
Wiley, David. "Connecting learning objects to instructional design theory: a definition, a metaphor, and a taxonomy." *The instructional use of learning objects*. Ed. David Wiley. *www.reusability.org/read/chapters/wiley.doc* (accessed 21 September 2005).
Wiske, Martha Stone, and Kristi Rennebohm Franz and Lisa Breit. *Teaching for Understanding with Technology*. San Francisco: Jossey-Bass, 2005.

Peer Reviewed Article *by Anne Schilling*

An Introduction to Coaching Ritualized Lamentation

Nurse:
O woe! O woeful, woeful, woeful day.
Most lamentable day. Most woeful day
That ever, ever I did yet behold.
O day, O day, O day, O hateful day.
Never was seen so black a day as this.
O woeful day, O woeful day.

Anne Schilling, Assistant Professor, Voice and Speech, California State, Long Beach. Taught at Cincinnati College-Conservatory of Music, Ohio University, and in the UK at Guildford College and Guildford School of Acting, in addition to coaching privately while living in London. Works as a professional actor in a variety of theatres from Seattle to New York, particularly with Shakespeare companies. MA in Voice Studies, Central School of Speech and Drama and performance certificate, Circle in the Square Theatre School in New York. Lamentation has been the focus of her research and workshops for a number of years.

Six years ago during rehearsals of *Romeo and Juliet*, in the margin of my script, I penciled in a title for the section of the play containing the above excerpt. I called it "O Woeful Day," because rehearsing Act IV, scene v was downright painful—and not in a way that served the scene. I was playing the role of the presumed-dead Juliet and thus was not faced with the gargantuan task of having to participate in the three-page wailing. Instead, I would lie there listening to an endless string of complaints from the skilled and competent actors who represented Juliet's friends and relatives, as they tried to deliver this emotionally-charged and challenging text. Even the director admitted defeat after valiantly trying to meet the vocal, physical and emotional demands of "O Woeful Day," and she grumbled about the lack of constructive suggestions on how to deal with it.

I knew we were not the first theatrical group to struggle with the difficulties of lamenting. As an audience member, I often noticed when actors vocally grieved onstage over a character's death I frequently felt disconnected from the tragedy, especially when the wailing was combined with passages of text. I began doubting that emotional outcries in historical plays could ever feel authentic to a contemporary audience. However, what none of us knew during "O Woeful Day" was this scene represents a lamentation ritual, not simply impromptu howling and screaming, and vocalizing text like the Nurse's passage above, has deep historical roots and specific, identifiable elements. Had we known this, perhaps we would have been more capable and less fearful of delivering it.

An actor's basic objective for any production is to create and convey an authentic and intelligible performance. A fundamental element necessary to achieve that goal is for the actor to gain an understanding of what it is the text is asking her/him to communicate. Thus, when that text has a ritual attached to it, as in the case of a lament, recognizing and comprehending the inherent elements of that ritual should enable the actors to produce a more fully-informed performance. Ultimately then, they will be better equipped to imbue meaning into a ritualized form of lamentation and rise to the vocal demands required of such performances. This way, actors would have a greater probability of reaching any and all audiences, no matter how "contemporary." I now believe that when assisting actors with lamentation scenarios, the job of the Vocal Coach is to educate actors about the ceremony and to provide suggestions informed by the history of those who lamented long before our time.

The aim of this article is to offer some details about traditional lamentation rituals and to provide the Vocal Coach with a basic direction and possibilities to consider when coaching actors on ritualized lamenting. The goal when presenting such options to actors is to encourage them to develop engaged, passionate—and informed—lamentation performances through the exploration of specific choices and actions. We shall look first at some of the elements specific to traditional lamentation, examining the ritual through the familiar acting questions of: what is it?; who performs it?; when is it performed?; where is it performed?; and how is it performed? Once those circumstances have been established, the article concludes with suggestions for the Vocal Coach about how to bring the historical particulars of ritualized lamenting onto the stage.

A CONDENSED HISTORY OF RITUALIZED LAMENTATION
What Types of Lamentation Rituals Will Serve as Focus for this Article?

Though ritualized lamentation is practiced in a number of countries worldwide—including China, New Guinea, India, the Middle East and Africa—the following information focuses on traditional Irish and ancient Greek cultures. A Western actor will tend to encounter lamentation most frequently within Irish and Greek plays, primarily because of the proportionally higher rate of production these plays have within Western societies. Obviously, the shows most often produced directly affect the work and information that the Vocal Coach must be prepared to relay. Thus, the cultures of ancient Greece and traditional Ireland seem particularly relevant for this investigation. Furthermore, within an examination of these two cultures, the Vocal Coach might discover some universal aspects of lamentation that could prove useful when assisting with any type of theatrical mourning scenario.

What is Keening and Vocalized Lamenting?

> This grief of the keen is no personal complaint for the death of one woman over eighty years, but seems to contain the whole passionate rage that lurks somewhere in every native of the island. In this cry of pain the inner consciousness of the people seems to lay itself bare for an instant, and to reveal the mood of beings who feel their isolation in the face of a universe that wars on them with winds and seas.[1]

J. M. Synge articulates what is arguably at the heart of lamentation in this description of the "keening" he witnessed during a burial in the Aran Islands of Ireland. The need to vocalize the overwhelming effect death has on the living reaches beyond recitations and explanations about grief and loss. Through laments people find ways to sing, sob, scream, wail, and even laugh out their sentiments, providing words with incredibly powerful emotional support. And, as exemplified in Synge's excerpt, it is an experience intended to be shared by the whole community.

"Keen" derives from the Irish "caoin," the stem of "caoinim" which means "I wail." It is often denoted as a high-pitched moaning. Keening refers to the repetitive inarticulate wails which traditionally accompany textual laments.[2] Like the Irish, Greek lamenting incorporates the same kinds of fully-released yet incoherent vocal sobs and moans. Sometimes translators and/or adaptors of Greek plays will even use the Irish term "keening" in their English stage directions to define the actions and/or sounds desired for a scene utilizing the act of vocalized lamenting. However, ritualized grieving is not comprised solely of inarticulate crying. In conjunction with those wails, actors are usually responsible for delivering poetic text—the actual lament—that is vital to the ceremony of lamentation.

1. Synge 1907, 52.

2. From Betty Cahill's article "Vocal Expression in Oral Traditions and Theatrical Performance with particular reference to the 'Caoineadh'" for University College Dublin's Irish Theatre Forum found at <www.ucd.ie/irthfrm/issue4.htm#bcahill>.

What are Laments?

Basically, the cultures of traditional Ireland and ancient Greece claimed that the ability to release the complex emotions surrounding an event like death was more easily attained by channeling those emotions through the structure of a lament. A complete account of what a lament represents and entails would require an extremely detailed, lengthy report. For the purposes of clarity, brevity and simplicity, the following condensed information highlights certain aspects of laments that distinguish them from other textual passages. It is divided into the origin, lifespan, purpose, content, structure and delivery of laments and ritualized lamentation. The analysis aims to provide the Vocal Coach with several details about laments that may prove valuable in the rehearsal room.

Origin of Laments and Ritualized Lamentation

Laments and lamentation rituals passed originally by word-of-mouth from generation to generation. Since it depended on oral conveyance, no one can pinpoint exactly when lamentation originated. In her groundbreaking book, *The Ritual Lament in Greek Tradition*, Margaret Alexiou alleges that traditional laments probably occurred long before the second millennium BC when the Greek language was documented, "since the lament is among the oldest recorded types of song."[3] Many researchers affirm Homer was first to record its use within ancient Greek society, possibly dating ritualized lamentation to before 700 BC.[4] In Ireland recorded dates are even harder to deduce. In his book, *Irish Wake Amusements*, Seán Ó Súilleabháin declares that "[t]here is clear evidence to show that female keeners were active in Ireland over a thousand years ago."[5] The famous book of Irish folklore, *Dindshenchas*, estimated to be over a thousand years old, contains a poem that documents the rite of ceremonial weeping and helps validate Ó Súilleabháin's declaration that "there is clear evidence."[6] But as in Greece, keening was presumably being practiced long before its documentation.

Lifespan of Ritualized Lamentation and the Use of Laments

In both Greece and Ireland, lamentation rituals withstood changes in politics and religion that repeatedly threatened to demolish the ceremonies altogether. The contents of *Dindshenchas* refer to assemblies of people and ritualized ceremonies that can easily be construed as pagan practices, an idea that contributed to the demise of ritualistic keening in Ireland. In Ireland, bans on keening started happening particularly in the seventeenth century due to its being considered pagan practice by the Catholic Church.[7] In Greece, legislation against group-oriented, ritualized lamentation possibly began in late sixth-century BC. Theories regarding its decline often highlight the fact that women dominated the vocalized portion of the lamentation ceremony and therefore posed as a potential threat to a growing patriarchal society.[8] For theatrical purposes, it may be worth noting that over time, in many areas, public grieving was replaced by the eulogy. It presented a tighter, more emotionally-bereft structure usually delivered by one individual praising the dead, similar to what is customary in today's funerals. But the ritualized version of lamentation, present within countless classical plays, would refer to the emotionally rich and unrestrained grieving expected within Irish and Greek traditional societies. And though the practice of lamentation rituals was severely impaired by restrictive laws placed upon it over the years, the practical function public grieving served for the community guarded against its complete demise.

3. Alexiou 2002, xv.

4. In his introduction to *The Odyssey*, Bernard Knox cites references to Homer in Aristotle's *Poetics* as well as other ancient text fragments—even a vase painting—to support his argument for the 700 BC figure. He claims that "back beyond about 700 BC we cannot go" (Homer 1996:xi-xiii).

5. Ó Súilleabháin 1997, 144.

6. Macalister 1931, 157 & 161.

7. Ó Súilleabháin 1997, 138-40.

8. Women were basically in charge of traditional lamenting. Their behavior during these ceremonies often was considered noisy, unrestrained and emotional. More important, the lament offered them a powerful means by which they could speak their minds—which might include their political opinions—and therefore possibly sway the minds and hearts of the grieving society (Holst-Warhaft 1995:3,26-7,102).

9. Alexiou 2002, 44.

10. Havelock 1968, 118.

11. Synge 1904, 75-7.

Purpose of Laments

Margaret Alexiou explains the "true purpose of ritual lamentation" as being "a collective tribute to the dead from the whole community."[9] Traditional Irish and ancient Greek laments functioned to maintain a delicate balance of honouring and appeasing the dead while allowing people to express wide-ranging, conflicting emotions. They facilitated the cathartic release obtainable through the act of coming to terms with the grief that accompanies loss.[10]

Lamentation rituals strove to create a mediating tie between life and death, and the powerful aura mourners generated was intended to penetrate the entire community. The following passage from J.M. Synge's *Riders to the Sea*, exemplifies an Irish community's response to the death of Maurya's son, and their automatic execution of the ritual which accompanies it:

> [She pauses again with her hand stretched out towards the door. It opens softly and old women begin to come in, crossing themselves on the threshold, and kneeling down in front of the stage with red petticoats over their heads.]
>
> MAURYA: [half in a dream, to Cathleen]. Is it Patch or Michael, or what is it at all?
>
> CATHLEEN: Michael is after being found in the far north, and when he is found there how could he be here in this place?
>
> MAURYA: There does be a power of young men floating round in the sea, and what way would they know if it was Michael they had, or another man like him, for when a man is nine days in the sea, and the wind blowing, it's hard set his own mother would be to say what man was in it.
>
> CATHLEEN: It's Michael, God spare him, for they're after sending us a bit of his clothes from the far north.
>
> [She reaches out and hands Maurya the clothes that belonged to Michael. Maurya stands up slowly and takes them in her hands. Nora looks out.]
>
> NORA: They're carrying a thing among them, and there's water dripping out of it and leaving a track by the big stones.
>
> CATHLEEN: [in a whisper to the women who have come in]. Is it Bartley it is?
>
> ONE OF THE WOMEN: It is, surely, God rest his soul.
>
> [Two younger women come in and pull out the table. Then men carry in the body of Bartley, laid on a plank, with a bit of a sail over it, and lay it on the table.]
>
> CATHLEEN: [to the women, as they are doing so]. What way was he drowned?
>
> ONE OF THE WOMEN: The gray pony knocked him over into the sea, and he was washed out where there is a great surf on the white rocks.
>
> [Maurya has gone over and knelt down at the head of the table. The women are keening softly and swaying themselves with a slow movement. Cathleen and Nora kneel at the other end of the table. The men kneel near the door.][11]

This scene mirrors aspects of the keening J. M. Synge witnessed in the Aran Islands. It illustrates several fundamental elements found in lamentation rituals, some of which are outlined in the content and delivery sections later in this article. However, in reference to the purpose of laments and their rituals, especially noteworthy is the community's response to Maurya's loss. They pour into the house and, rather than offering Maurya condolences then leaving, they begin the process of grieving with her, letting her know that *she is not alone.*

The lament could also function as a channel between life and death. It was thought that mourners could exceed the boundaries of corporeal reality through a lament, which *permitted them to communicate directly with the dead.* This often happened in the form of a one-sided dialogue. An observer might have described it as watching someone (the primary lamenter) who seemed possessed. The idea was that the spirit of the dead could "enter" the body of the living and thus communicate with the lamenter through the lament. It gave the opportunity for the deceased individual to deliver her/his last words, which could range from comforting mourners to requesting the rectification of something that happened while (s)he was alive.[12] This type of vocal interaction eventually invited the entire lamenting group to respond to the "deceased person" through their communal wailing. Ultimately, it bonded not only those directly linked to the corpse, but united the whole grieving community.

Some researchers claim that ritualized lamentation was ultimately fueled by fear and that a major purpose for the ritual was to *satisfy the dead*. In both ancient Greek and traditional Irish cultures, it was not just the personal realization of one's own mortality but also a terror of the Underworld's tangible existence that helped prompt these elaborate funeral rituals. They allowed the living an opportunity to show respect, sympathy and honour for the dead in the physical presence of the corpse, thereby granting a final occasion for contact between the two levels of "existence."[13]

Finally, the *emotional release through vocalization* was arguably one of the most important intentions behind ritualized lamentation. The lament provided the means for an immediate vocal and physical response to the loss. James D'Angelo, in his book *Healing with the Voice*, defines keening as a "Natural Sound": a sound produced with the purpose of release to purge the body of "impurities that fester within, not allowing us to vibrate."[14] He adds that "vibrations of emotion" function almost medicinally by "shaking loose rigid patterns both in body and psyche."[15] Lamentation rituals supplied a transition level between the excessive emotional responses provoked by death and the final acceptance of physically losing someone dearly loved. Consequently, they helped alleviate some of the overwhelmingly difficult effects of grief. Roy Hart advocated that catharsis is accomplished through community support, personal expression and emotional release, which collectively exemplify the key components of lamentation rituals.[16]

Textual Content of Laments

The content of laments reflected configurations passed down through history and consisted of a number of specific details. Laments frequently began by stating a particular *time period* and proceeded by naming *main characters* and *geographical settings*. Firmly establishing the precise time and place of death gave the event a certain realism that kept the deceased alive in mourners' memories.[17] Another common device was *contrasting the past and the present.* For example, the mourner might have depicted life before the person died and juxtaposed that image with the current, tragic state of life in his/her absence. The act of *praising the individual* and *recalling the person's life journey* kept the dead tangibly present in the world of the living and made stock lament structures more personal.[18]

12. Holst-Warhaft 1995, 1-3.

13. For example, Ó Súilleabháin (1997) explains that the Irish wake traditionally focused entirely on showing the dead, not the relatives, goodwill and sympathy in order to deter any future ghostly hauntings from the deceased individual (171).

14. D'Angelo 2001, 62.

15. Ibid., 62-3.

16. Pikes 1999, 6.

17. Alexiou 2002, 59.

18. Holst-Warhaft 1995, 35.

19. Alexiou 2002, 75-6. *The Lament for Art O'Leary* is an example of an Irish lament that calls for revenge. Look for Frank O'Connor's wonderful translation of it.

20. Pound and Fleming, Trans. of Sophokles' *Elektra*, 1987, 50-2.

In addition to stating facts and recalling memories about the deceased, laments were as famous for expressing rage and a desire for retribution through the text as they were for emoting grief and humility. In the presence of a strong support group, the *public declaration of reproach or need for revenge* released the mourners' pain from the confines of her/his body and addressed the anger that often accompanies grief. Accusations may have targeted the deceased, cursed the state (for going to war), accused God (for taking the person), or condemned a third party thought responsible for the death.[19] Vengeful statements promoting retribution appeared repeatedly in laments and historically proved powerful enough at times to kindle fury within an entire community, which sometimes led to violent action.

The following text excerpt from Ezra Pound and Rudd Fleming's version of Sophokles' *Elektra,* exemplifies how the content of a lament can be personalized in order to imbue special meaning into the lament's delivery. By vocalizing the specific circumstances of the death, the mourner was more likely to be able to express a full spectrum of uninhibited emotions. (S)he was allowed to wail her/his personal story and her/his relationship to the deceased through the lament, and experience the wide range of feelings roused by the loss. Doing so enabled individuals to release stifled grief, confusion, and anger in order to begin the process of healing.

ELEKTRA'S KEENING:
All that is left me
my hope was Orestes
dust is returned me
in my hands nothing, dust that is all of him,
flower that went forth.

Would I had died then
ere stealing thee from the slaughter
died both together
lain with our father.

Far from th[y] homeland
died far in exile
no hand was near thee
to soothe thy passing
corpse unanointed
fire consumed thee
all now is nothing
strangers have brought thee
small in this urn here
sorrow upon me
fruitless my caring.

I as mother and sister both
thy nurse also ere thou hadst thy growth
this was my past
and swept away with thee
ever to me
thy summons came.

All in a day
and is no more.

Dead Agamemnon, dead now my brother,
I am dead also, the great wind in passing
bears us together.
Mirth for our foemen.

(anger now stronger than grief, for a moment: spoken)

And that bitch of a mother is laughing
and they haven't sent back even the shape of him,
but a ghost that can't do its job.

Ajnn, ajnn.

Thou the avenger, no more avenging
born to misfortune, ashes avail not
shadows avail not.
Ahi, Ahi
bodiless
brother that art not.

(spoken)

The spirits love me no longer.
You kept sending messages
secretly, you would take vengeance.

(sings)

Thy death, my dying
dread road thou goest
brother, my slayer

(singing into the urn)

Oimoi! Oimoi!

Take me in with you
I now am nothing, make place beside thee
naught into naught, zero to zero
to enter beside thee
our fortune equal
death endeth pain.[20]

Again, as with the *Riders to the Sea* excerpt, several common aspects of ritualized lamentation are represented in this passage. However, the fundamental point is that laments were constructed to communicate specific information through an assortment of emotions. Notice that Elektra names the main characters of her lament, establishes the place of Orestes' death, describes her relationship to him in both the past and present, and expresses her sadness for his death and her anger towards Klytemnestra ("mother"). These were all typical, identifiable elements frequently found within traditional laments. And if, for example, Elektra's rage established enough evidence that Orestes' death demanded vengeance, a lament of this type could have ignited a community into retributive action. Laments did not spring from a pool of generalized grief. They demanded attention from the community and blessings from the dead, and were anything but passive.

Structure of Laments

The structures of ancient Greek and traditional Irish laments generally followed similar patterns. In the case of the improvised lament, a mourner drew from a handful of stock phrases, varying in form and intent, to satisfactorily meet the needs of each situation. In states of heightened grief, these preexistent structures facilitated the transformation of basic weeping into a focused emotional response.[21] Lamentation structures respected some syntactical rules which endowed the text with the skeleton that gave the lament its shape. The following list offers particular structural elements evident in many laments, but performances could and would differ and, as with any other art form, no two laments were exactly alike.

A question often instigated laments, such as, "How can I express in words how I feel about this person?" It suggested a certain humility that purposefully lowered the speaker's status and raised that of the deceased.[22] The frequent use of *metaphor* and *indirect allusions* permitted the lamenter to personalize stock phrases, added poetic eloquence and avoided any superstitious anxieties a particular individual (or character) might have about directly addressing the dead. Laments often incorporated *singing and/or music*, performed *a cappella* or with the inclusion of musical instruments.[23] Both Irish and Greek laments used literary techniques, such as *antithesis, antiphony, repetition,* and *refrain* to provide laments with drama, excitement and emotional builds that produced a *cathartic conclusion. Stichomythic dialogue* (dialogue, usually associated with classical Greek drama, delivered by two actors in single alternate lines) created heightened tension within scenes and sometimes may even have provided a "medium of expression for...dialogue between living and dead."[24]

The following is an example of a dialogue between Andromache and Hecabe (Hecuba), with the inclusion of the Chorus, from P. Vellacott's translation of Euripides' *The Women of Troy.* Notice the use of call and response, the repetition of phrases and words, the sharing of lines, the direct address to the dead, and the energy these elements infuse into the dialogue.

> [ANDROMACHE approaches, drawn in a chariot by
> Greek soldiers. She holds ASTYANAX on her lap]
> CHORUS:
> Hecabe, see! Andromache is coming,
> Drawn in a Greek chariot, beating her breast;
> And Hector's son Astyanax is with her.

21. Holst-Warhaft 1995, 34.

22. Alexiou 2002, 162.

23. Alexiou (2002) offers a list of possible musical performance options from ancient Greece (that arguably transfer to forms in traditional Irish) that follow: "with a soloist, accompanied by chorus only in the refrain; with a chorus alone; with one or more soloists and a chorus, singing antiphonally; and finally, in the form of an imagined dialogue between living and dead" (131).

24. Ibid., 137.

25. Vellacott P., Trans. of Euripides' *Women of Troy* 1973, 108-9.

26. Holst-Warhaft 1995, 101.

27. Crossley-Holland 1982, BBC Radio 4.

28. D'Angelo 2001, 70.

Where are they taking you, sad Andromache,
And beside you Hector's sword and armour of bronze,
And other spoils of Troy, which Achilles' son
Shall dedicate in distant temples of Thessaly?
ANDROMACHE:
The Achaeans are carrying home their property.
HECABE:
O Zeus, have pity!
ANDROMACHE:
That prayer is mine by right—
HECABE:
O Zeus!
ANDROMACHE:
—bought with my husband's blood, my tears.
HECABE:
Children!—
ANDROMACHE:
No more your children: all that is ended.
HECABE:
Once we were happy, and Troy—all that is ended.
ANDROMACHE:
Ended.
HECABE:
My noble children!
ANDROMACHE:
They are gone.
HECABE:
Gone; and my home, my lovely city—
ANDROMACHE:
Gone!
HECABE:
Now smoke and ashes!
ANDROMACHE:
Hector, my own husband —
HECABE:
Hector is with the dead. Hector, my son!
My daughter!
ANDROMACHE:
Hector, when will you come to help me?
HECABE:
Priam, aged king of my princely sons,
Priam, fallen a sport for you enemies,
Soothe my head on the pillow of death!
ANDROMACHE:
All the love we have lost!
HECABE:
The grief we have gained!
ANDROMACHE:
All that we knew, destroyed!
HECABE:
All anguish doubled![25]

This brief exchange encourages Hecabe and Andromache to build in their grief together. Also, observe how even within the structural boundaries of a traditional lamentation scenario such as this, the actors are still free to make choices about the intentions within the lines and their emotional journeys.

Delivery of Laments
The framework of the ritual assisted lamenters by providing a controlled environment, like a trapeze artist's safety net. Knowing there was a structural "net" allowed mourners to risk springing spontaneously from one emotion to the next. When mourners engaged in heightened states of emotion, the ritualistic nature of lamenting assured them that they need not worry about doing psychological damage to themselves (because while improvising, they knew they could return to the structure at any time). They also did not fear being criticized by the community (because it had been established as a communal event). As alluded to in "Textual Content of Laments," lamenting women easily *switched abruptly between different modes of behavior* with no sense of incongruity, from tears to rage to laughter. A sense of exploring one's "inner-opposite" through lamentation emerged from this paradoxical conduct.[26] It permitted mourners to delve into and submit themselves to emotions they may have never expressed in their everyday lives.

Lamenters may have conveyed those emotions through *soft, wailing tones* before suddenly swinging into *cries of anger and pain. Impromptu screams* and *howls* occurred at any time to help frighten dead spirits.[27] *Sobs, sighs* and sudden *audible ingressive breaths* evolved into vocal releases such as *groaning. Reiterating wails and cries, repeating lines and phrases, howling and grunting* like wild dogs, *cooing* like birds, and *calling, chiding, blaming, and pleading directly to the dead*, all allowed for a full-bodied release through uninhibited and wide-ranging vocalizations. The combined effect of allowing these extensive emotional expressions to flow freely was like pulling a plug that released accumulated emotional and physical pressure, which naturally diffused feelings of frustration, anger and grief.[28]

Physical actions such as *self-mutilation, tearing at the hair and face* and *beating of fists upon the breast and upper chest* reflected an inclination for mourners to risk venturing into unfamiliar emotional territory in order to reach a new level of "being" or consciousness. In traditional Ireland, a common illustration of a keening woman depicted her as howling and pulling at her disheveled hair and sporting torn or tousled clothing and bare feet. It signified what the average observer might consider madness (ancient Greece had a similar representation of the lamenting woman). This may have stemmed from an idea that the funeral represented a transitional state[29] that let living individuals explore behavior opposite of what was culturally acceptable.[30] Textual passages in plays often describe women as *raising their arms in the air* and *rhythmically swaying or rocking their bodies*. In the previous excerpt from *The Women of Troy*, the Chorus depicts Andromache as "beating her breast" when she is wheeled out by the Greeks. In *Riders to the Sea*, the keening women are described as "swaying themselves with a slow movement."

Ultimately, Holst-Warhaft claims that a truly great lament, one that is respected and remembered, depends on the lamenter's ability to transfer her personal grief into a larger comment or "communal reflection on death."[31] This means that a "great lament" went deeper than the simple recitation of learned text; it invited the mourner and all those around her/him to embrace the full experience—mind, body, voice and spirit—of lamenting. Both the Irish and the Greeks advocated passionate lamenting that summoned the dead, fellow lamenters and all of society to listen.

Who Performs Laments?

Kinswomen

Researchers seem to agree that within the vast range of practicing cultures, performers of ritualized laments are usually women, especially relatives and close friends. Such was the case, for the most part, in traditional Ireland and ancient Greece. Current theories for this range from the claim that women feel grief more deeply to the suggestion that women experience a more direct understanding of death because of the physical relationship established when they wash and dress the corpse.[32] Holst-Warhaft quotes lamentation researcher, Steven Feld, as stating that women dominated lamentation because of their ability to "turn weeping into a controlled, often contemplative lament."[33] During his research, he observed that the ability to transform tears of grief into articulated ideas and actions seemed to be a unique ability exclusive to women. Whatever the reason, the fact remains that women were usually in charge of dealing with the corpse and responsible for enforcing many of the necessary funereal customs, including the lamentation ritual.

It is worth noting, however, that especially when dealing with dramatic literature, keening is (and was) not always strictly a female privilege. In traditional Ireland both men and women could be found participating in the keening, though the women primarily authored laments and were more likely to perform ritualized lamenting in groups.[34] Particularly onstage, men are not exempt from performing long, passionate laments. There are countless examples of men lamenting in classical Greek plays. Though the Chorus might offer some vocal support, many male laments are solo performances. The following excerpt from Sir Richard Claverhouse Jebb's translation of Sophocles' *Antigone* is an example of a man's lament. Creon wails for the death of Haemon and Eurydice on his own. The Chorus and Messenger are present and offer details about the deaths, but they do not appear to participate in Creon's grieving. Notice that though this translation is not in verse format, it still upholds the elements of a traditional lament.

> CREON: Oh Hades, all-receiving, whom no sacrifice can appease. Have you no mercy for me? You herald of bitter evil tidings, what word are you uttering? Alas, I was already as dead, and you have smitten me anew!

29. The funeral symbolizing a transitional state meant that people were allowed to express the full spectrum of emotions that a person undergoes in response to death. In detailed studies on the psychological affects of death, Elisabeth Kübler-Ross (1969) offers lists of specific stages that humans experience when dealing with death, spanning from feelings of extreme anger to those of numbness and/or denial. Consequently, I believe the extreme range of physical and emotional choices available in lamentation may provide actors with an incredible array of vocal possibilities.

30. Holst-Warhaft 1995, 27-8.

31. Ibid.,71.

32. Women were in charge of preparing and laying out the corpse in both Ireland and Greece.

33. Holst-Warhaft 1995, 20.

34. Ó Súilleabháin 1997, 130-1.

What are you saying, my son? What is this new message that you bring—
woe, woe is me!—of a wife's doom, of slaughter heaped on slaughter?
CHORUS: You can behold; it is no longer hidden within.
(The corpse of EURYDICE is revealed.)
CREON: Ah me, yonder I behold a new, a second woe! What destiny, ah
what, can yet await me? I have but now raised my son in my arms, and
there again I see a corpse before me! Alas, alas, unhappy mother! Alas,
my child!
MESSENGER: There, at the altar, self-stabbed with a keen knife, she
suffered her darkening eyes to close, when she had wailed for the noble
fate of Megareus who died before, and then for his fate who lies there, and
when, with her last breath, she had invoked evil fortunes upon you, the
slayer of her sons.
CREON: Woe, woe! I thrill with dread. Is there none to strike me to the
heart with two-edged sword? O miserable that I am, and steeped in
miserable anguish!
MESSENGER: Yes, both this son's doom, and that other's, were laid to
your charge by her whose corpse you see.
CREON: And what was the manner of the violent deed by which she
passed away?
MESSENGER: Her own hand struck her to the heart, when she had
learned her son's sorely lamented fate.
CREON: Ah me, this guilt can never be fixed on any other of mortal
kind, for my acquittal! I, even I, was your slayer, wretched that I am—I
own the truth. Lead me away, O my servants, lead me hence with all
speed, whose life is but death![35]

Professional Mourners

Though rarely mentioned in theatrical texts, in traditional Ireland and ancient
Greece, hired mourners became an imperative for any funeral. The origin possibly stemmed from a family's insecurity about their own keening abilities, so
professionals were paid with money, food and/or drink to deliver a high
quality performance—"the louder the better."[36] Historically, paid mourners
met many necessary requirements in lamenting, not the least of which was
their superior knowledge of what tradition required when someone in the
community died. They frequently relied on thinking about a personal experience to conjure grief, after asking permission from the family to do so,
believing that this added more concentrated sincerity to the lament.[37] In
antiquity, before the emergence of eulogies, and aside from the aforementioned male lamenting in Greek tragedies, laments rarely promoted exclusively
solo performances. They generated a sense of the collective, and professional
mourners possessed the expertise to create that desired aura.[38]

When Are Laments Performed?

The timing of vocal lamentation was vital. In both traditional Ireland
and ancient Greece, tradition insisted that the dead should not be
keened/lamented until the soul officially left the body, because weeping prior
to its departure was a bad omen.[39] Once it was established that the person
had died, the first round of wailing took place. Ritualized lamenting for both
the Irish and the Greeks tended to occur three specific times during the
funeral ritual: at the wake; during the funeral procession; and at the tomb.
The first collective wail notified the rest of the community that the death had

35. Sir Jebb, Trans. of Sophocles' *Antigone* 1967,
146-7.

36. "The more a dead person was mourned, even in
such an unreal way, the better it was. Keening was
an intrinsic part of both the wake and the funeral
and, like so many other practices associated with
death, was discontinued only with great reluctance"
(Ó Súilleabháin 1997, 137).

37. Alexiou 2002, 41.

38. Ibid., 134.

39. In Ireland the belief followed that the soul needed
to pass peacefully by the Devil's dogs, which would
awaken if the keening started too early (Ó
Súilleabháin 1997, 130). In Greece there was a fear
that premature lamenting might frighten the angels
and spirits who accompanied the soul into death,
thus leaving the soul to be escorted by a worse fate
(Alexiou 2002, 38).

occurred and that the wake was about to begin.[40] After that important initial cry, group lamenting could happen again at any time from sunrise to sunset during the wake. When a group keened, mourners took turns lamenting, passing the position of primary lamenter from person to person and replacing each other when individuals grew tired or hoarse.[41] Ritualized lamenting happened twice on the final day: while the body was carried from house to tomb in ritualistic procession, and then lastly at the gravesite when the coffin was in the grave.[42]

Where Does Lamentation Occur?

As mentioned in the previous section, ritualized vocal lamenting happened at the wake, on the road to the graveyard and at the tomb. However, in terms of the location where the body was actually laid out and keened, in ancient Greece, festivals and funerals were open to everyone. Greek lamenting occurred in public and probably outdoors in front of, and for the benefit of, the entire community.[43] Traditional Irish wakes differed from those Greek, open-air occasions in that large contingencies of relatives, friends and neighbors packed into the house of the deceased.[44] In both cultures, lamentation took place where people felt it was essential to announce the passing of someone in the community, and where they received support and encouragement from other community members in response to this tragedy.

Performance Details of Each Ritual
The Irish Wake

Though now a wake tends to last only one night, traditionally in Ireland wakes could last two to three days, depending on the time of death.[45] During the wake, the body was laid out and surrounded by lit candles. Ó Súilleabháin refers to Eugene O'Curry's description of a traditional Irish lament ritual that included professional mourners to explain the act of vocalized lamenting. At least four hired keeners (in addition to family who sat or stood near or around the bier), situated themselves at the head, feet and sides of the body. The head mourner began with a note or partial cry which the mourner at the foot then joined with another note of equal length. The two side mourners entered the dirge, called the "caoineadh," by singing a long or double part, in which the family could participate, especially with the chorus or refrain at the end of stanzas.[46] The term "caoineadh" differs from "keening" in that it signifies the articulate and text-oriented elegy delivered within the lamentation ceremony. In Synge's account of the Aran Island burial, he depicts how each woman took a turn in leading the recitative (the caoineadh) while the others supplied accompaniment through intoned inarticulate sobs, all the while swaying and rocking.[47] Again, by taking turns and passing the dirge around, mourners could take breaks and refresh themselves between bouts of vocalization, and thereby keep the lament going for an indefinite amount of time.

The Greek Próthesis

The "próthesis" is the Greek term for the laying-out of the body. It formally commenced at sunrise with the ritual breaking of clay vessels to frighten evil spirits that might force the deceased's soul to Hell.[48] The mourners surrounded the body (again, four seemed to be the magic number) and the chief mourner positioned herself at the head of the corpse, often clasping it with both hands. The others tried to touch the corpse's hand with their own

40. Wood-Martin 1892, 346.

41. Fewer 2001, 16.

42. Alexiou 2002, 6-7.

43. Holst-Warhaft 1995, 104.

44. Ó Súilleabháin 1997, 130.

45. Before midnight meant a two night wake, whereas if the person died after midnight the wake spanned over three nights (Dorian 2000, 311).

46. Ó Súilleabháin 1997, 136.

47. Synge 1907, 50-1.

48. Alexiou 2002, 27.

right hands stretched over him/her. "Most frequently both hands are raised above the head, sometimes beating the head [their own] and visibly pulling at their loosened hair."[49] A kinswoman commenced the lament and quickly received support from the rest of the group who wailed in chorus. At some point, the chief mourner took over by stretching her right hand over the body and grasping the hand of a mourner to her left indicating the dirge be passed to her. The silent hand stretching seemed to act as a cue and allowed the group to pass the lament back and forth throughout the day.[50] Like the Irish, this way they could take breaks and trade off lamenting responsibilities in order to keep the dirge going for as long as necessary.

PUTTING THE HISTORY ONTO THE STAGE

Collective grieving can reach us through any language because of our instinctive human ability to comprehend vocal expressions of deep sorrow without having to understand actual words. In Greek texts, many translations incorporate Greek cries, such as "Ahi Ahi" or "Oimoi, Oimoi," as exemplified in the Elektra excerpt, because the sounds inherent in the ancient language exceed the aural boundaries that an English translation may place upon those exclamations. Nancy Houfek's article, "Oedipus' Aiee's: Using Ancient Greek on the American Stage," recounts her experience learning and then teaching ancient Greek to actors rehearsing *Oedipus* for Harvard University's American Repertory Theatre. She explains how once the actors ascertained how to embrace the sounds and language structure of ancient Greek, "Everyone in the rehearsal hall could sense how visceral and dynamic this ancient language could be."[51] She goes on to note that, "This language seemed to provide more emotional depth than either English translation."[52] The prevalence of vowels in configurations foreign to the English ear can invite the audience to instinctually, rather than cognitively, respond to the primal roots of language and communication inherent within the sounds of lamenting.

However, a modern audience's ability to respond to foreign sounds is obviously not limited to ancient Greek. When performing Shakespeare, the Vocal Coach can encourage actors to relish in the extendable "O's" and "Ah's" that tend to be littered through scenes focused on lamenting. The famous Linklater saying that vowels tend to carry "the emotional component" of text helps explain why those open vowels are vital to lamenting, whether they be in Greek, Gaelic or English.[53]

We have the vocal capacity to elevate the meaning beneath words, through words, in our efforts to communicate personal pain and search for comfort from those around us. The communal nature of ceremonious lamentation teaches us that a strong connection exists between humans in states of grief. That need to connect is why the ritual appears on our theatre stages. By providing some of the history and major characteristics which identify historical laments and ritualized lamentation, my aspiration is that a vocal coach, director and/or actor may be able to approach lamentation with at least a more informed understanding of it. Armed with that knowledge, hopefully actors will be more willing to trust themselves and the text and reach for those connections (with each other and with the audience) vital to the act of keening. The following list addresses ways actors and vocal coaches can tackle each aspect of lamentation described in the history portion of the article.

49. Ibid., 6.

50. Ibid., 40.

51. Houfek 2005, 176-7.

52. Ibid., 177.

53. Linklater 1992, 15.

In Reference to: What are Laments?
The Origin and Background
• Actors need to understand the world they are presenting onstage, which includes societal ethics and religious belief systems within a culture. The Vocal Coach's brief explanation of the history and context of lamentation may help inform acting decisions/choices.

• By relaying how ritualized lamentation changed over time, the Vocal Coach may help actors make an important mental shift. Our view of grieving at a funeral in today's society, where restraint and silent tears represent strength and merit admiration, is very different from how a community mourned in traditional Ireland and ancient Greece. We now know that lamenting used to promote noisy, emotional, unrestrained expressions of grief. Classical texts which include a lament or group lamenting demand that actors participate in the ritual with the same understanding and passion as those who performed them long ago.

The Purpose
• When bringing lamentation to the stage, it is important to remember that, traditionally, ritualized lamenting attempted to unite the community through vocalizing their shared grief. By providing background information on how mourners used to work together to support each other vocally and emotionally, the Vocal Coach may encourage actors to engage with one another in a similar manner. It enables an ensemble of actors to work from a shared frame of reference onstage, and, as a result, live within the same onstage world. It furnishes them with an environment they can all agree upon and trust. This not only fulfills the communal function of a traditional lamentation ritual, it hopefully strengthens the actors' abilities to listen and respond to each other overall. Onstage, actors become the mourners and audiences are the community, invited to participate in experiencing and contemplating the universal tragedies that occur in human life.

• Another purpose for the lament was to provide a channel that connected the living and the dead. It was thought that the deceased person could actually communicate with mourners through the lament. If this approach is incorporated into an onstage lamentation ritual, the Vocal Coach might suggest that only one actor from the group emulate the deceased character onstage for clarity purposes. The Vocal Coach could encourage the actor to experiment with integrating common vocal tones or physical gestures that the "deceased" character used when "living," to explore embodying the other individual. The other actors/mourners could support and respond to this through their vocalizations. Again, for the whole ensemble it means

that lamenting can be performed as a supportive group effort, working together to communicate something specific through vocal interactions.

The Textual Content
• First and foremost, the Vocal Coach can help actors and directors spot the textual elements that characterize laments and help determine whether or not a selection of text might be suitable for ritualized lamenting. Please refer to the history section on content for a list of content details.

• Once it is established that the text is a lament, the Vocal Coach can assist the actor by helping her/him analyze the emotional journey the character might be experiencing through the text. For example, in the case of the Elektra insert, Elektra seemingly vacillates between feelings of grief and anger, in addition to any number of other emotional states the actor might wish to explore in rehearsal. The Vocal Coach and actor can determine these fluctuations by examining Elektra's language choices. For instance, is she praising the individual or calling for revenge or both? Also, as in this case, the stage directions might offer additional help directing the actor's emotional journey.

The Structure
• In addition to mining the text for content clues, the Vocal Coach may assist actors by helping them highlight the various structural elements within the text as well. By scoring the text in this way, the actor will be more aware of the emotional and textual builds woven into the piece's framework by the author, and consequently be more able to convey them. The Vocal Coach could refer to the structural features of a lament as "textual guides" for the actor, revealing specific places an actor may choose to express her/his most intense emotional peaks, rather than allowing the performance to remain on one extreme level. Not only will this help turn a generalized scene about grief into a specific, motive-driven event onstage, it will hopefully avoid the possibility of the actor doing excessive damage to the voice and keep her/him (and consequently, the audience) engaged with the text. Please refer to the history section on structure for structural details often used in laments.

The Delivery
• An essential objective of lamentation is for both participant and observer to reach catharsis through the primitive, instinctive connection established between people sharing states of grief. The Vocal Coach may urge actors to strive for those connections and steer them away from falling into states of private emotional indulgence when performing vocal lamentation. This way we all share in the ritual—actor and audience alike.

• The Vocal Coach can help urge actors to explore their full vocal range within a variety of vowel sounds while making clean, swift shifts between emotional states, such as grief and anger (as mentioned briefly as something to consider when analyzing textual content). In his article, "The Voice in Heightened Affective States," Rocco Dal Vera warns that actors often stay in one emotion for too long, inhibiting the unpredictable and often irrational changes possible in a character's emotional life. Often the reality is that when dealing with circumstances that are highly emotional, a person's emotions "will swing wildly without an externally observable logic, and without warning."[54] The Vocal Coach may encourage actors to be bold with their vocal and physical choices and risk surprising themselves by swiftly shifting from one emotional state to another. An actor may find it challenging, but by delving into the opposite of an emotion to which the actor habitually gravitates, (s)he might unlock the very thing that could help her/him embrace the essence of the lament and lamenting.

• There are many vocal and physical options an actor can choose to incorporate into the delivery. Please refer to the history section on the delivery of laments for specific suggestions.

In Reference to: Who Performs Laments?

As stated earlier, women tend to dominate the world of ritualized lamentation, but that does not exclude men from lamenting—especially when it comes to the stage. The Vocal Coach may need to try different tactics when working with either men or women. A way to approach both sexes is to ask the actor to start from an emotional state (s)he feels comfortable expressing, a state which often differs between men and women. The most important task will be to urge the actor (woman or man) to work from a pure state of that emotion, devoid of other emotional entanglements, before (s)he progresses into an exploration of another, possibly more unfamiliar, emotion. Many of the details listed in the sections on content, structure and delivery of laments may be recognized and incorporated for both genders according to what works best for the individual actor and her/his character's development.

In Reference to: When Are Laments Performed?

As a general rule, when asked to identify when a lament is happening in a play, the Vocal Coach should rely more on recognizing the structure and content of the play's text, rather than on the timeline of the play. A playwright may need to take "creative license" with the timing of the play, mostly so that the show stays within a reasonable running time. It means (s)he may choose to incorporate ritualized lamenting at a time when it would not have been traditionally performed. Also, the inconsistencies and errors that can happen in the process of translating from one language to another make the dependability of stage directions and "realistic" timing specificity somewhat unreliable. Again, the Vocal Coach should look for clues in the text to determine if a passage is an actual lament or not rather than relying on when it occurs in the play.

In Reference to: Where Does Lamentation Occur?

Similar to the previous section, the historical guidelines for where laments were performed may or may not prove useful to each given play. Because the playwright must work within a confined area that must be visible to an entire audience, maintaining a level of accuracy to the historical "truths" about where laments were performed could be tricky. In general, the Vocal Coach should aim to recognize and accept where the text asks the actors to lament.

Final Suggestion

The Vocal Coach should aim to be adaptable and consider the director's judgments, the overarching artistic conceptualization of the entire play, and the actors' individual abilities when deciding how to proceed with instruction.

Admittedly, the information I have provided does not constitute all the aspects of lamentation in ancient Greek and traditional Irish cultures that could appear onstage. Continued research will inevitably reveal further effective ways of expressing the spectrum of vocal possibilities accessible through lamentation. However, in a theatrical setting, perhaps the Vocal Coach, working in conjunction with directors and actors, will be able to reach deeper into the core of lamentation onstage by examining and exploring the limited number of elements outlined in this article.

I continue to return to that infamous *Romeo and Juliet* "O Woeful Day" scene to this day. When I read it, I contemplate the fantastic potential embodied within those vowels, words, phrases, and sentences.

> NURSE:
> ...My lord! My lady!
> LADY CAP.:
> What noise is here?
> NURSE:
> O lamentable day!
> LADY CAP.:
> O me, O me! My child, my only life.
> Revive, look up, or I will die with thee.
> Help, help! Call help!
> (enter Capulet)

CAP.:
For shame, bring Juliet forth, her lord is come.
NURSE:
She's dead, deceas'd! She's dead! Alack the day!
LADY CAP.:
Alack the day! She's dead, she's dead, she's dead!
CAP.:
Ha! Let me see her. Out alas. She's cold,
Her blood is settled and her joints are stiff.
Life and these lips have long been separated.
Death lies on her like an untimely frost
Upon the sweetest flower of all the field.
NURSE:
O lamentable day!
LADY CAP.:
O woeful time!
CAP.:
Death, that hath ta'en her hence to make me wail
Ties up my tongue and will not let me speak.
FRI. L.:
Come, is the bride ready to go to church?
CAP.:
Ready to go, but never to return.
O son, the night before thy wedding day
Hath Death lain with thy wife. There she lies,
Flower as she was, deflowered by him.
Death is my son-in-law, Death is my heir.
My daughter he hath wedded. I will die,
And leave him all: life, living, all is Death's.
PARIS:
Have I thought long to see this morning's face,
And doth it give me such a sight as this?
LADY CAP.:
Accurs'd, unhappy, wretched, hateful day.
Most miserable hour that e'er time saw
In lasting labour of his pilgrimage.
But one, poor one, one poor and loving child,
But one thing to rejoice and solace in,
And cruel Death hath catch'd it from my sight.
NURSE:
O woe! O woeful, woeful, woeful day.
Most lamentable day. Most woeful day
That ever, ever I did yet behold.
O day, O day, O day, O hateful day.
Never was seen so black a day as this.
O woeful day, O woeful day.
PARIS:
Beguil'd, divorced, wronged, spited, slain.
Most detestable Death, by thee beguil'd,
By cruel, cruel thee quite overthrown.
O love! O life! Not life, but love in death!

CAP.:
Despis'd, distressed, hated, martyr'd, kill'd.
Uncomfortable time, why cam'st thou now
To murder, murder our solemnity?
O child, O child! My soul and not my child,
Dead art thou. Alack, my child is dead,
And with my child my joys are buried.[55]

At this point, I am sure you will recognize several aspects of a typical lamentation ritual present within this passage. There are four lamenting individuals—an ideal number of mourners to surround a corpse. They use repetitive words and phrases; they share verse lines to build the lamenting energy; they establish the corpse's time of death; they declare how they are related to the corpse; they appear to fluctuate between emotional states of grief, anger and frustration; they each have numerous long, open, moan-like vowel sounds incorporated into their texts; and they directly address Death and Time, just as the Greeks would have cried to their gods. What might have happened if Lady and Lord Capulet, the Nurse and Paris had been directed to listen and vocally support each other in a ritualized act of lamenting? I cannot be sure, but perhaps my long-ago rehearsals of "O Woeful Day" would not have been quite as painful had we all known more about our lamentation options.

54. Dal Vera 2001, 58.
55. B. Gibbons, Ed. of Shakespeare's *Romeo and Juliet* 1980, 210-12.

Works Cited

Alexiou, Margaret. *The Ritual Lament in Greek Tradition.* Lanham, Maryland: Rowman & Littlefield Publishers, Inc., 2002.

Cahill, Betty. "Vocal Expression in Oral Traditions and Theatrical Performance with particular reference to the 'Caoineadh'." *www.ucd.ie/irthfrm/issue4.htm#bcahill*, Irish Theatre Forum, University College Dublin, 1998.

Crossley-Holland, Kevin. Programme on Keening, Radio 4, "talk on Radio 4 12/12/82 with world-wide examples: CASS-30-0616," 1982.

Dal Vera, Rocco. "The Voice in Heightened Affective States," in *The Voice in Violence presented by the Voice and Speech Review*, Rocco Dal Vera, ed. (Cincinnati, OH: VASTA), 2001.

D'Angelo, James. *Healing with the Voice: Creating harmony through the power of sound.* London: Thorsons, 2001.

Dorian, Hugh. *The Outer Edge of Ulster: A memoir of social life in nineteenth-century Donegal.* Ireland: The Lilliput Press, 2000.

Euripides. *The Women of Troy*, P. Vellacott, trans. *Euripides: The Bacchae and Other Plays*, Hammondsworth, Penguin Books Ltd., 1973.

Fewer, Michael. *A Walk in Ireland: An Anthology of Walking Literature.* Cork: Atrium, 2001.

Havelock, Eric A. "Watching the *Trojan Women*," E. Segal, ed. *Euripides: A Collection of Critical Essays.* New Jersey: Prentice-Hall Inc., 1968.

Holst-Warhaft, Gail. *Dangerous Voices: Women's Laments and Greek Literature*. London: Routledge, 1995.

Homer. *The Odyssey*. R. Fagles, trans. London: Penguin Books, 1996.

Houfek, Nancy. "Oedipus' Aiee's: Using Ancient Greek on the American Stage," *Shakespeare Around the Globe presented by the Voice and Speech Review*, Mandy Rees, ed. (Cincinnati, OH: VASTA), 2005.

Kübler-Ross, Elisabeth. *On Death and Dying*. New York: Macmillan Publishing Company, Inc., 1969.

Linklater, Kristin. *Freeing Shakespeare's Voice*. New York: Theatre Communications Group, Inc., 1992.

Macalister, R. A. S. *TARA: A Pagan Sanctuary of Ancient Ireland*. London: Charles Scribner's Sons, 1931.

O'Casey, Sean. *Two Plays: Juno and the Paycock, The Shadow of a Gunman*. New York: The MacMillan Company, 1925.

O'Connor, Frank. *An Introduction to Irish poetry: [a selection of Irish poetry from earliest times to the present with poems by Seamus Heaney, Brendan Kennelly, W.B. Yeats, Frank O'Connor, Paul Durcan, and others / selected by Sean Dunne]*. Cork: Bookmark, Ossian Publications, 1991.

Ó Súilleabháin, Sean. *Irish Wake Amusements*. Dublin: Mercier Press, 1997.

Pikes, Noah. *Dark Voices: The Genesis of Roy Hart Theatre*. Woodstock: Spring Journal Inc., 1999.

Shakespeare, William. *Romeo and Juliet*, Brian Gibbons, ed. London: Methuen & Co. Ltd (Arden Edition), 1980.

Sophocles. *The Complete Plays of Sophocles*, Sir Richard Claverhouse Jebb, trans. Moses Hadas, ed. New York: Bantam Books, 1967.

Sophokles. *Elektra*, Ezra Pound and Rudd Fleming, trans. New York: New Directions Publishing Corporation, 1987.

Synge, J. M. *The Tinker's Wedding and Other Plays*. Dublin: Maunsel and Co., Ltd., 1904.

Synge, J. M. *The Aran Islands*. Dublin: Maunsel and Co., Ltd., 1907.

Wood-Martin, W.G. *History of Sligo, County and Town, from the Close of the Revolution of 1688 to the Present Time*. Dublin: Hodges, Figgis, and Co., Ltd., 1892.

Peer Reviewed Article *by Karina Lemmer*

Accent/Dialect Coaching for a Multilingual Student Cast—
A Case Study

Introduction

Coaching a cast to perform a stage production in a specific accent poses challenges. While adhering to the director's interpretation of the accent or dialect, the dialect coach also has to consider the actors' experience, ability to imitate, and regional dialect (Raphael 1983). Such challenges increase in complexity when one prepares a multilingual student cast for their very first production in an accent. A recent student production of Arthur Miller's *The Crucible* in Pretoria, South Africa, provided such a challenge when Lesley Ferris from Ohio State University directed a student cast from Tshwane University of Technology.[1] The young cast members were diverse and reflected several indigenous South African languages. Cast members included Zulu, Xhosa, Sotho, Tswana, and Afrikaans first-language speakers—all language groups that produce unique South African English accents (only three cast members were mother-tongue English speaking). The director embraced the diversity by casting African actors in key roles, including John Proctor. The production's non-traditional nature also extended to include only certain elements of the period in which the text is set.

Karina Lemmer holds an Honours Degree in Drama and a Masters in Applied Linguistics. She is a Lecturer in Speech Sounds and Dialects at the Drama Department of Tshwane University of Technology and works as a speech and communication consultant for business executives in South Africa and various other countries on the content. Karina also conducts dialect coaching with actors and is involved in research projects that explore speech and language in the South African context.

Relatively inexperienced student actors were awarded a unique challenge. They were to perform this complex work, rich in emotional intent and ideology, using three different accents. Although each character used only one accent, the production demanded interaction between the different accents. The director indicated the majority of the characters were to use General American. RP was to be used by the actors portraying Reverend Hale, Judge Hathorne, and Deputy Governor Danforth. The actress who played Tituba used her native Tswana accent to establish a character from Barbados.

When the accent/dialect requirements for this production were discussed, it became clear the approach should be considered carefully as a uniform accent base did not exist.

Not only was the cast multi-lingual, the student actors hailed from various regions within South Africa and the dialects added to the broad variety of English accents. Raphael (1983) cites that a dialect coach may have to eliminate existing regional dialect patterns before the actor can acquire a new pattern. In this cast two sets of patterns had to be considered:

- Patterns of actors' English accents generated by first language transfer from his/her mother tongue. Example: a Zulu speaker would replace [ɜ] in /nurse/ with [ɛ] as in /dress/.
- Regional dialect patterns as the English spoken in South Africa displays distinct regional characteristics. Example: an Afrikaans speaker from certain areas in the Western Cape would replace the [æ] as in /trap/ with [ɛ] as in /dress/.

It would therefore be vital to consider each cast member's accent and dialect patterns to determine the content and format of the coaching program. In a society that embraces eleven official languages, multilingual casts have become the norm and South African audiences are accustomed to diverse accents and dialects. However, as this production would play in a non-South African accent, both accent and dialect coaching was required. The rationale for this lies in the definition of the terms. Accent could be defined as the

1. This production formed part of an exchange agreement between the Faculty of Arts at Tshwane University of Technology and the College of the Arts at the Ohio State University.

2. At the time when this production commenced, the third-year students had completed a general module on accent work and the second years had been exposed to basic phoneme adjustments following instruction in class.

3. Fourth-year students, who specialize in voice, act as voice coaches for specific productions. This is conducted under the Lecturer's supervision and guidance. It also serves as practical training exercise. Alexia Benic used the coaching of this production as the theme for her fourth-year thesis. Marth Munro is the Department's voice lecturer; she supervised the student coach.

4. The quoted comments reflect syntactical elements of the different accents present in this cast.

mispronunciation (compared to standard production) of non-native speakers. Dialect could be defined as a legitimate language variant that displays characteristic grammar, vocabulary and pronunciation used by mother tongue speakers (Meier 2005, 4). General American and RP would therefore be an accent to the second language speaking South African actors and a dialect to the mother tongue English actors. The ideal approach for this cast would be one that addressed dialect and accent acquisition or reduction. In a 1998 interview (Horwitz 1998, 1) dialect coach Deborah Hecht states that it is more difficult to lose a speech pattern than it is to gain one. She also indicates that asking an actor to reduce his/her native accent or dialect could be viewed by some as criticism on the actor's ethnicity and identity. This is taken very seriously in the South African training context. Diversity is embraced and care is taken in our training to always focus on accent acquisition rather than accent reduction. The focus is on providing the actor with skills to increase his/her range while accepting native accent rather than "changing" the actors' natural speech. In a production such as this, where the actors' native speech could affect the outcome of the accent work and ultimately the impact of the performance, first language interference could not be ignored.

Apart from its multi-lingual nature, accent/dialect coaching for this cast posed another challenge. The students selected for the project included first, second and third years. This implied various levels of exposure to voice and accent work. Students receive speech production and phonetic instruction aimed at enhancing their use of South African English and regional dialects, by means of perception and production development, as part of their training. Yet many cast members were in the early stages of their training. Their exposure to phonetic transcription and other accent acquisition techniques was therefore limited. Limited exposure to accent work would also imply that they would not have mastered South African English and would still subject English phonemes to the phonetic rules of their first language(s) (Chela de Rodriquez 1991, 356). The reality within this cast was that many students were not yet able to perceive and produce South African English and this would certainly affect their perception and production of phonemic and prosodic adjustments towards General American.

It was also noted that students had specific preconceived perceptions of what General American should sound like. Their knowledge of General American came from exposure to American television, film and music. The director was a General American speaker and her perception of her native dialect would inevitable differ significantly from the South African cast's perception. It would therefore be vital to define

the signature sounds to promote a uniform understanding of the accent/dialect.

This also raised the question: what would a South African audience's expectation of a General American accent be? Honorof (2003, 107) states that a familiar accent is judged according to the listener's historic perception of what the accent should sound like. South African audiences are exposed to American English on a daily basis, courtesy of the media. A recognizable model of the accent was therefore needed for the audience as well. Considering the diverse cast and the challenges faced it became clear that uniform accurate production of General American would be difficult to attain. Our objective was to find a model of General American that would be attainable for the cast and recognizable to the audience. This was a stage production that employed heightened text. Stage conventions accept heightened styles and demand less intense accuracy than film (Horwitz, 1998). It could be argued that since the conventions applied were heightened, the accents did not have to be naturalistic, yet there had to be an element of believability within the conventions.

This production of *The Crucible* marked most of these students' first experience of using an accent/dialect in performance.[2] It has been stated that it gets easier with each new accent (Honorof 2003, 107), implying that once an actor has analyzed and applied the process of acquiring an accent, subsequent accents are attained with greater ease. As no such experience existed, the coach had to guide the students through the accent acquisition process. This production provided a potentially rich learning experience within the tertiary education context.

It was however essential to prepare a coaching program that would aim to address this cast's unique needs while remaining sensitive to its multilingual nature and establishing a stage accent that audiences would recognize. For this reason it was decided to survey the cast's experience of the accent/dialect coaching process to assist such work in potential future productions in a multi-lingual context. A questionnaire was used to gain insight into the cast members' subjective experiences of the coaching process and performances.

This article summarizes the phonetic context and coaching process that was applied for this production. Emphasis will be placed on the coaching of General American as this applied to the bulk of the cast. RP resembles South African English and it is therefore often easier for South African actors to attain. The Barbados accent will also not be explored as it was decided to use the Tswana speaking actress' own English accent. The main tendencies noted from the results of the survey of the cast's experience will also be explored briefly.

1. Phonological Context

In order to establish a suitable coaching program for this cast, we had to understand the phonological context or the specific phonetic interferences that could be anticipated. Phonetic interference occurs in second language speakers' speech because they decode input speech signals by using their knowledge of the constraints that are imposed by the human articulatory output apparatus. This causes the second language speaker to subject the phonemes produced in the second language to the phonetic rules of the first (Heny 1994, 62; Gleaser 1995, 22).

Fledge (1978, 9) further distinguishes between "identical," "new" and "similar" phones in the articulation of second language speakers. "New" phones could be described as sounds that have no counterpart in the speaker's first language and "similar" refers to phones that differ systematically from identifiable counterparts in the first language. If phonetic interference affects the general production of a second language speaker's English, then this would certainly transfer to such a speaker's production of an English dialect. Finkle (2005, 2) states that one of the dialect coach's challenges is to modify sounds that do not exist for some cast members. This would be a very real challenge in this production and it was important to explore the potential phonetic interference patterns of the specific language groups as this could affect their production of General American.

Understanding phones that are "new" or "similar" in General American as compared to the first language(s) would assist the coaching process. Considering the broad range of languages that the cast spoke, focus was placed on the primary phonetic features of each language or dialect. For the purpose of this article the descriptions of the cast's first languages below, has been summarized and includes core characteristics only.

1.1 African Languages

The African languages represented in the cast included two Nguni languages (Zulu and Xhosa) as well as Sotho and Tswana. Although the different African languages have distinct phonological characteristics that influence first language speakers' production of English, certain general characteristics have been identified. These characteristics relate mostly to vowel phonemes (Lanham 1978, 192). For the purposes of this project these general characteristics were considered.

Such characteristics include the fact that so-called African languages have limited vowel systems, only seven primary vowels. Sound clusters are also absent. For example: the sound cluster

[ɑ] as in /far/, [ʌ] as in /fun/, [æ] as in /apple/ and [eɪ] as in /take/ is represented by the [ʌ] sound only. This could affect the English pronunciation of such speakers as they render these clusters according to their limited vowel system. Unlike the [ə] as in /agree/ and [ɜ] as in /bird/ in RP, African languages contain no true mid-vowels. Vowel substitution therefore occurs and these sounds tend to be replaced with [ɛ] or according to spelling when the [ə] is applied in weak syllables. African languages also do not have diphthongs and no distinction in vowel length occurs (Lanham 1978).

As far as consonants are concerned, the Nguni languages contain complex consonant systems that apply many consonant clusters and a variety of "click" sounds produced by the tongue and palate. Tswana on the other hand does not contain consonants in final positions (Wissing & Zonneveld 1994, 19). Consonantal phonetic transfer into English occurs as African language speakers tend to pronounce voiceless consonants as voiced in certain contexts (Wissing & Zonneveld 1994, 18). For example: the final /k/ in /think/ could be produced with a strong voiced tongue action. Jacobs' (1993) investigation of Zulu speakers' production of English consonants revealed that Zulu speakers replace voiced final fricative and plosive sounds with voiceless counterparts. These features also impact on vowel length and quality.

It is important to consider the speaker's exposure to English as this would determine the extent of their first language interference. In this cast, certain African Language speakers received their primary and secondary education in English whereas others did not. The degree to which the above phonic interferences affected their English pronunciation therefore varied.

We decided to focus on the vowel adjustments required to produce General American, since all the African languages shared a common feature, limited vowel systems. New and similar sounds were incorporated in coaching the cast members to use General American in performance. Clarity and emotive expression would be vital as first language African language speaking actors portrayed central characters in this production.

1.2 Afrikaans

In contrast to the above African languages, Afrikaans contains an extensive vowel system that includes diphthongs, and vowel length is used extensively (van Wyk 1981). The English of Afrikaans speakers is therefore more likely to be affected by "similar" phonemes rather than "new" phonemes. Meier (2004, 5–8) describes such possible phonetic interferences. These include the [ɪ] as in /bit/ that is articulated as [i] in certain consonantal contexts, shorter and more tense articulation of the [ɛ] towards [e], occasional replacement of the [æ] with [ɛ] and conscious lip-rounding of the [ɒ] resulting in [ɒ̜]. Distinctive lip rounding may also occur in the [ɑ] as in /bath/ and [ɜ] as in bird. Certain diphthongs such as [eɪ] and [ʊə] could be articulated with increased lip-rounding, open and sometimes more centrally than the RP counterparts. Consonantal characteristics of Afrikaans speakers' English include the favoring of voiceless plosive and fricative consonants in final positions and the signature trilled uvular [ʀ].

Wissing and Zonneveld (1994, 1) compare Afrikaans to Dutch and German in its characteristic devoicing of final plosive and fricative consonants. Example: /and/ will be sounded as /ant/. This phonetic habit is often transferred to Afrikaans speakers' English pronunciation. The fricative consonants [θ] as in /think/ and [ð] as in /that/ could be considered "new" sounds as they do not occur in Afrikaans. In some speakers the [θ] is replaced with [f] and the [ð] with [d]. This is however not a general characteristic of the Afrikaans accent and is more likely to occur in speakers of older generations or those who live in regions where they do not use spoken English daily.

Amongst Afrikaans speakers the extent of first language interference is mostly generational. Young Afrikaans speakers have enjoyed continued and comprehensive exposure to spoken English and this reflects in their pronunciation of English that includes fewer phonetic interferences than the English of older speakers. The Afrikaans-speaking cast members in this production ranged in age between 18 and 22 placing them in the generation able to produce English that resembles South African English. Individual actors did however display certain signature sound adjustments and such habits were taken into account during the coaching process.

1.3 General American within the Context

In developing an accent coaching program for this student cast it was important to define the signature phoneme and prosodic changes required to achieve a recognizable General American dialect. To effectively describe the phonetic features of General American to the cast, sound adjustments were noted in relation to RP. RP was used as base since South African English (as spoken by first English-speaking South Africans) resembles RP, although specific vowel and inflection adjustments occur. Many of the cast members were also familiar with RP as they studied its phonemes as part of the syllabus. It was therefore decided to describe the General American dialect by means of how it differs from RP.

Considering the cast's multilingual nature and the potential broad range of phonetic interferences, it was decided to focus on core sounds to promote results within a limited rehearsal period. The phonemes and prosodic elements selected had to meet the following criteria:

- Phonemes should reflect General American in a way that would make the dialect/accent recognizable to a South African audience
- Phonemes should resemble, or be similar to sounds that cast members could already produce, especially since African language speakers were cast in demanding roles
- Phoneme changes should not significantly affect projection and articulation during performance
- Phoneme changes should be simple to aid consistency and a degree of uniformity during performance.

After establishing the above criteria, Meier's (2005) description of General American was consulted and the following signature sounds were isolated for inclusion in the coaching program:

- The [æ] as in /pass/ which substitutes for the RP [ɑ] in certain consonantal contexts
- The [ɑ] as in /lot/ which substitutes for the RP [ɒ]
- The r-coloration as in /start/ and /first/
- The medial [d] or tapped [ɾ] as in /better/ which substitutes for the medial [t]
- The [ɚ] in word ends such as /summer/ which substitutes for the RP [ə]

The department has a strong culture of collaboration and the voice and speech lecturers often work together on projects. In this spirit, the department's voice lecturer was consulted during this process to ensure that the phoneme adjustments did not impede projection and articulation. This was an important consideration as the cast consisted of young actors whose voice training was still in a developmental phase. Once the core sounds were selected and described we developed a coaching program.

2. Coaching Program

The voice and accent coaching of this production constituted teamwork. My contribution included accent advice, developing the coaching program and conducting initial accent rehearsals. A fourth-year student was selected to assist the cast at all rehearsals, facilitate warm-up sessions and conduct individual sessions.[3] The lecturers supervised the process, held frequent feedback meetings with the student coach, attended several rehearsals and conducted individual sessions with cast members, when possible. The coaching program commenced one week prior to the production's primary rehearsal phase. Pre-rehearsal coaching could be used to familiarize a potential cast with the general characteristics and specific sounds of the dialect (Raphael 1983). The first session was devoted to describing the accent/dialect by means of discussion and clips from films and television that illustrated General American. A group session followed in which the cast members discussed, described and demonstrated their perception(s) of General American. This session served to acknowledge individual perceptions and to clarify the core characteristics of the dialect that would be portrayed in the production.

The thirty cast members were then divided into two groups to promote individual work during the coaching sessions. Mother tongue and the students' ability to produce neutral South African English were considered when the groups were established. Students then participated in daily coaching sessions for a period of one week.

Each session commenced with a physical and vocal warm-up. A specific warm-up routine was devised for this production. It included the signature sounds selected to portray the production's interpretation of General American. The reason for developing this routine was two-fold. First, it was used to reinforce the accent coaching and was subsequently used throughout the rehearsal phase and during performance. Second, it was viewed as a method to link the phoneme explorations to voice explorations the students were already familiar with.

The Lessac system is one of the primary systems used for voice development in the department and the students were familiar with the system's explorations to enhance structural energy, tonal energy and consonant energy (Lessac 1997). We also consulted the work of Kur (2005) who implements the three energies approach of this system in stage dialect studies. The structural energy that refers to the adjustable form, size and shape of the oral cavity, had specific relevance in the warm-up routine as we could focus on the signature sound changes, thus incorporating these holistically for the cast.

Consonant energy explorations by means of Lessac's instrument approach enabled us to heighten the cast's sensory awareness of the target consonants. Since this was an inexperienced cast it was essential that such connections be made for them. Additionally, the Lessac system's structural explorations are based on the General American phonemes. Incorporating this allowed us to use relevant explorations that the students were familiar with to assist in achieving the required phoneme adjustments.

In initial sessions students were provided with lexical sets that contained the selected phoneme adjustments. At this stage we incorporated phonemes that could be challenging. This was achieved by including words that contain the target General American phoneme(s) and the sound(s) that may reflect first-language interference. Example: the [ɜ] in /first/ is not used in African languages, yet the post vocalic /r/ or r-coloration as in

/first/ was identified as a phoneme adjustment required to establish General American. Such words were included as minimal pairs to promote perception development. Example: "bed – bird," "cart – cut," "bad – bat" etc. The word lists started with minimal pairs, one-syllable words then moved to two-syllable words and then featured complex words. The lists were used for perception and production practice, followed by pre-constructed carrier sentences that contained words with the target phonemes. Each phoneme was explored individually, using this format. Once produced satisfactory, carrier sentences that contain additional target sounds were introduced. This process was repeated and ultimately led to sentences that contained all the target sounds. Phonetic transcription of target sounds was applied throughout. When all the target phoneme adjustments were explored, students drafted their own sentences and ultimately applied the phoneme adjustments to spontaneous speech, in structured explorations.

At this point text was introduced. Since the casting was not yet finalized, we employed text extracts of some of the author's other works. Text extracts were transcribed focusing on the target sound adjustments. Prosodic elements of the accent was then introduced centering on volume emphasis, stress on initial parts of utterances and tonal energy as described by Meier (2005, 80).

An error analysis was conducted and each actor provided with feedback on the phonemes or prosodic elements that he/she needed to focus on. It was noted that first-language interference occurred in the case of certain second-language speakers and this was addressed, as far as possible, during individual sessions. However, the schedule did not permit individual sessions for all second and third-language speakers.

When the casting was completed and the rehearsal phase commenced, the cast was encouraged to identify signature sounds and conduct phonetic transcription as they worked with the text. Raphael (1983) comments that lines memorized in the dialect are likely to be delivered more organically and consistently than lines that are memorized without the dialect. We followed this opinion and encouraged the actors to transcribe the text as they learnt their lines. The student voice and dialect coach attended all rehearsals. She provided feedback and identified actors who found specific phonetic elements challenging and arranged individual sessions, as far as possible.

Clarity and articulation was addressed in an effort to prevent the accent work from contaminating meaning. In certain cases, an element of accent was sacrificed to maintain emotional expression and to elevate clarity. This pertained specifically to second-language speakers whose first-language patterns continued to be notable. Although it may be stated that an actor's performance in an accent could be believed as a type even if the accent is not perfect (Honorof 2003, 107) the different phonic interferences in this cast, due to a broad variety of first languages, possibly affected the "type" established.

Discussions and audience feedback made comments to this effect. It was more difficult for second-language speakers to produce the desired sound patterns and they were ultimately more susceptible to negative feedback. Since this was a training production it was important that students remain motivated and able to view criticism within the context. Therefore students were coached and counseled throughout this process. It was also decided to conduct a response survey to establish how the diverse cast experienced the process. The objective of the survey was to provide students with an anonymous forum to state their subjective experiences during the coaching process. Their experiences could then assist future work of this nature within the Department. It is our priority to provide effective education in a culturally sensitive manner within South Africa's diverse linguistic society. For this reason, the students' subjective experiences would be valued and the informal survey aimed at increasing insight into how the diverse cast experienced the process.

3. Discussion of the Informal Survey
A questionnaire containing twenty-five questions related to the cast's experience of the coaching, rehearsal and performance process was drafted. Twenty of these questions were to be answered by means of a rating scale. The scales to be selected from included "very often," "often," "sometimes," "seldom" and "very seldom." To ensure specific comments, five questions were included that provided the cast with an opportunity to express their experience in their own words. This questionnaire was made available to the voice lecturer for comment. Finally it was given to the cast for response. Precautions were taken to ensure ethical conduct. When the cast was requested to complete the questionnaire, it was emphasized that this was a voluntary and anonymous process. (Only two cast members did not complete the questionnaire). The cast completed the questionnaire directly after the production concluded. We explained the process and objective of the questionnaire to the cast and they were requested to complete consent forms on which they agreed that their comments may be quoted. The responses were then analyzed and a percentage calculated for each rated response (see Appendix A).

As stated above the purpose of the questionnaire was to gain insight into the diverse cast's subjective experiences. The results are therefore based on perception. It also became clear that the questionnaire has certain short-comings and the results can therefore not be scientifically verified. It did,

however indicate certain interesting trends that could benefit future work of this nature.

The survey revealed that the cast's overall perception of the experience seems to be positive as 95% indicated they enjoyed it "very often" and 5% enjoyed it "often." This is encouraging, as is the cast's perceived opinion that the accent assisted them in developing their characters. 60% responded "very often" and 35% percent responded "often." Another positive trend noted is that the cast seemed to feel the process increased their general awareness of accents. Although based on the students' subjective responses, this possible increase in awareness could be viewed as productive as it could promote more effective perception of phonemes and prosodic elements, thus aiding future speech work. Students also indicated an increased awareness of their articulation and voice projection habits.

The students' attitude towards the process and instruction also seems reasonably favorable. Mixed responses were noted regarding the use of phonetic transcription, the warm-up routine and linking of the accent work to familiar responses. The nature of the responses makes it difficult to interpret these results. However, within the training context this could be explored further and varied methods to aid accent/dialect acquisition could be considered in future productions.

Initially, it was anticipated that the cast would imitate their General American-speaking director. The results, however, reveal that if imitation occurred it was subconscious. Perhaps conscious imitation should be explored in future processes of this nature.

According to this informal survey the students seem to be aware of different success levels and of the audience feedback. This is indicated in their rating of the accent's perceived success during the production and their comments.

In the final questions the cast members were asked to indicate what they had learnt by using accent during this production. Many constructive comments were cited suggesting that the production served as a productive training exercise. Examples of such comments are: "That a character's accent definitely has a huge influence on who he/she is," "That it is not as difficult and I can hear the difference in accents," "Practice makes perfect," "Listening skills and increased awareness of phonetics," "How to adapt interpretation, intonation, articulation and character work to an accent," "It is not an easy task and everyone's standard, general American is different," "There's a lot more the voice can really do if you work with it," "How to do an accent," "How to articulate with General American on stage," "Helps with character building and speech patterns from other accents," "How to project, keep an accent going, working with an accent was a good challenge" and "That many people speak accents but because of our dialect will sound different."[4]

Finally when asked if they would like to participate in another production that incorporates accent work, all cast members noted "yes." It be could interpreted that they gained enough from the process to wish to attempt it again despite mixed reactions from audiences and difficulties during the rehearsal phase.

Conclusion

The use of accents in this specific production was debated by audiences and fellow students in subsequent discussions. Accordingly, the relevance of using General American and RP in the South African context was questioned. This is echoed in the audiences' responses. Although the relevance and impact of using such accents should be considered carefully in future productions, it seems that it served as a positive learning experience for the student cast. If one considers that the objective of student productions is education, it could be viewed as successful in that regard.

The multilingual nature of the cast and the fact that their experience levels differed also affected the outcome of the accent work in this production. Initially, it was feared that the experience would affect the students' confidence in and attitude towards accent work, especially in the case of second users as comparison was inevitable. Yet, the students' responses suggest that they viewed this as a valuable training experience and that their attitude towards accent work remains positive. It is however, important to state that the responses were noted in an informal survey. A formal survey that produces more interpretable results could be used in future to gauge such a cast's experiences. A questionnaire that rates the audience's perception could also be applied within the training context to evaluate the accent coaching process. Such a survey could potentially provide insight into how a multi-lingual audience experiences a play performed in a non-native accent.

Second-language speakers' ability to perceive and produce English phonemes should be considered carefully before they attempt an English dialect, in addition to their accent. This should also be a potential consideration during casting. However, an interesting (and subjective) observation was made. Considering South Africa's political and subsequent sociolinguistic heritage, resistance towards acquiring perceived Standard South African English pronunciation is often noted. That never occurred during this process. Perhaps removing the target accent from the stigma of being perceived as "correct," made the process more accessible. This may imply that the

focus on accent acquisition rather than accent reduction yielded a more positive attitudinal result. This ought to be investigated as the skills developed during this process; auditory perception, phoneme production etc. could enhance the students' vocal output.

In a linguistically complex society, accent work with diverse casts will continue to be challenging, and uniform standards difficult to achieve, especially in the training context. We should continue to explore the phonic differences to enable students to extend their range as actors. Yet, the positive experiences claimed by these students indicate that accent work has the potential to stimulate an entire cast. Perhaps we should not only focus on the differences that are highlighted by accent work but also view it as a potential unifier.

Bibliography

Chela de Rodriguez, B. "Recognizing and producing English rhythm patterns." *Teaching English pronunciation: a book of readings.* London: Routeledge. 1983.

Fledge, J. E. "The production of "new" and "similar" phones in foreign language: evidence for the effect and equivalence classification." *Journal of Phonetics*, no 15 (1986): 47-65.

Finkle, David. "Accent on Dialect Coaches." *Back Stage*, Vol. 45 (2005): 20-21.

Glaser, Robyn. "An investigation into the effects of Nguni first language interference on the identification of vowels by English and Nguni listeners." University of Cape Town: (Dissertation B.Sc), 1995.

Heny, J. "Learning and using a Second Language." *Language: introductory readings*, Clark, V. P., Escholz, P.A. & Rosa, A. F., eds. New York: ST Martin's Press, 1994.

Honorof, D. N. "Reference Vowels and Lexical Sets in Accent Acquisition." *Film, Broadcast and Electronic Media Coaching presented by the Voice and Speech Review*, Dal Vera, R. ed. (Cincinnati, OH: VASTA), 2003.

Horwitz, Simi. "Putting the Accent on Speech" *Back Stage*, Vol. 39 (1998): 37.

Jacobs, Monica. "Consonantal variation in Zulu English mesolect." *S. A. Journal of Linguistics*, no 12 (1994): 16-25.

Kur, Barry. *Stage Dialect Studies A Continuation of the Lessac Approach to Actor Voice and Speech Training.* Barry Kur, 1987.

Lanham, L.W. & Prinsloo, K. P. *Language and communication studies in South Africa: current issues and directions in research and inquiry.* Cape Town: Oxford University Press, 1978.

Lessac, Arthur. *The Use and Training of the Human Voice.* McGraw-Hill Publishers, 1997.

Meier, Paul. *Accents and Dialects for Stage and Screen.* McLouth, KS: Paul Meier Dialect Services, 2005.

Meier, Paul. *An Afrikaans Accent.* McLouth, KS: Paul Meier Dialect Services, 2005.

Raphael, Bonnie. "Preparing a Cast for a Dialect Show." *Communication Education*, No 32 (1983): 41-51.

Rosner, B. S. & Pickering. *Vowel Perception and Production.* Oxford: Oxford University Press, 1994.

Roux, J. C. "Prosodic Data and Phonological Analysis in Zulu and Xhosa." *South African Journal for African Languages*, no 15 (1994): 19–27.

Van Wyk, E. B. *Praktiese Fonetiek vir Taalstudente.* Durban: Butterworth, 1981.

Wissing, D. ; Zonneveld, W. "Final Devoicing as a Robust Phenomenon in Second Language Acquisition." *S A Journal of Linguistics*, Supplement 34 (1994): 3-21.

Appendix A: summary of rated responses

	Very Often	Often	Sometimes	Seldom	Very Seldom
Did you find the accent preparation phase prior to rehearsal phase beneficial?	50%	45%	5%		
Did your knowledge of phonetics assist you in developing the accent?	50%	17%	28%		
Did the warm-up routine assist you with developing the accent?	12%	50%	28%	5%	5%
Did you find it difficult to change the signature sounds?		5%	60%	30%	5%
Did the fact that the accent work was linked to familiar voice explorations assist you?	28%	22%	45%	5%	
Did the accent help you to develop your character?	60%	35%	5%		
Do you think the accent affected the clarity of your speech/articulation during performance?	45%	22%	5%	28%	
Do you think the accent affected voice projection during performance?	28%	28%	22%	17%	5%
Did you enjoy using the accent during this production?	95%	5%			
Did the accent work significantly increase your workload during the production?	13%	22%	29%	31%	5%
Did the accent work affect your confidence during rehearsals and performance?	17%	13%	45%	20%	5%
Did you have problems sustaining the accent?		12%	33%	22%	33%
Were you able to pick up the sound and inflection changes in the accents of other cast members?	50%	28%	22%		
Did you consciously copy the other cast members or director's accent(s)?	5%	12%	12%	33%	38%
Has the production increased your awareness of accents?	62%	28%	5%		
Did you work on your own (outside of rehearsal time) to refine the accent?	5%	57%	33%	5%	
Did you find the instruction effective?	33%	62%	5%		
Did you participate in additional/ individual sessions with the voice/ dialect coach?	12%	22%	22%	32%	12%
Was the use of accents, during this production successful?	38%	45%	12%		5%

Essay *by D'Arcy Smith*

The Issue of Vocal Practice:
Finding a Vocabulary for Our Blocks and Resistances

Introduction

As voice teachers we all understand the importance of our students creating healthy practice habits. For one, a healthy practice leads to a true ownership and to a depth of understanding of what has been taught. On a more practical level there are a limited number of hours that can be devoted to voice and speech at actor-training institutions. Patsy Rodenburg said, "If you're realistic, it's very hard to train a voice classically in under eight or nine hours a week of voice work." Few actor-training institutions have this amount of time. Rodenburg goes on to say that because of this "you're then having to ask the student to do a lot of work on their own" (Carey 2003, 230). In his article on practice David Smukler writes, "…we have to find short cuts so that the precious studio time can be harnessed around the experiential work and engage the students in actively developing their practice skills" (Smukler 1998). Yet it is the discipline of practice that eludes most students and even some teachers. I've found teaching a student to practice is as much of an art as teaching the subject of voice itself!

D'Arcy Smith is an Assistant Professor of Voice and Speech at Wright State University. He has taught voice and speech at York University and at the Toronto Film School. He also served as an associate faculty member for two years at Canada's National Voice Intensive. He holds a Graduate diploma in Voice Teaching along with an MFA and BFA in Acting from York University in Toronto. He has dialect coached numerous productions and has acted professionally in film, television, voice-over and theatre.

At the beginning and end of each quarter I have my students write a "Progress Report" outlining their specific discoveries, blocks and possible solutions. This is an opportunity for the students to take some time and do some self-assessment of their voices and their practice habits. In one section I ask the students to write about what keeps them from their vocal practice. Though the responses vary, more often than not they are vague in their description. They have trouble articulating exactly what it is that is in their way. Some write they had too little time to practice, others they had too much time on their hands, or they became bored or distracted. I began to feel that simply asking them about these blocks was not enough. Our ideas were too general. We needed to have a vocabulary in which to express these different blocks and resistances.

It was during this search for some kind of vocabulary we could share that I turned to yoga. After all, yoga relies heavily on the notion of practice. It is through practice that the student is able to find real growth. I read more about the philosophy of yoga: *the ten living principles* (The Yamas) and *the codes for living* (The Niyamas). I discovered these could be used to help us to clarify what was needed to nurture our practice. Here was a vocabulary we could use! I was struck with how these ideas, while important guides on how to live life, could be directly related to the vocal practice of the performer. My hope is by giving my students words and concepts with which to name their blocks and resistances they could become more conscious of them; with consciousness comes change.

What follows is the way in which I introduce each of the Yamas and the Niyamas in a language that applies to voice work. I make it clear that this is a structure for us to work from, not a spiritual conversation or conversion. I am interested in the categorization of our blocks and resistances to make them more understood. For that reason I have simplified the ideas to what I believe is essential to the performer, regardless of spiritual orientation. I encourage my students to create their own words for the ideas expressed here. I have found that the fact these are not English words allows them to experience these ideas in a new way.

After we have read through the Yamas and Niyamas we discuss their response to these ideas and the ways in which they might nurture their vocal practice. These words are meant to be a jumping off point to future examinations of the nature of practice.

Yamas and Niyamas: A Vocabulary for Our Blocks to Vocal Practice

As you read through the following, write a few words or phrases for your reaction to each of the Yamas and Niyamas. You may even want to create your own word for the ideas expressed if you find this helps you. The quotations are from Donna Farhi's book *Yoga Mind, Body and Spirit* (2000).

The Yamas (The Living Principles):

AHIMSA:

> First and foremost we have to learn how to be nonviolent toward ourselves. Any thought word or action that prevents us (or someone else) from growing and living freely is one that is harmful (8).

At times during, before, or after the practice we may have thoughts that silently negate the work and growth we are working on. Thoughts such as "I'm not growing fast enough," "Why bother, I'll never get it perfect," and "I don't have the vocal range that so and so has"—all of these thoughts are judgments about our self and our practice. These thoughts can build up over time and lead to a resistance to the desire to practice. An awareness of our thoughts and attitude to our own practice can strengthen the practice itself.

SATYA:

> This means that when we say something, we are sure of its truth (9).

In our voice practice it is important to remind ourselves that, as performers, we are seeking to work from a place of honesty. It can, at times, be tempting to focus only on the technical side of our practice. If we merely practice for the sake of practice we are practicing to be a robot, not a performer. We must invest our humanity, intentionality, and emotionality into our practice. By continuing our awareness of our own truth we are working towards a more expressive, open, and available voice.

ASTEYA:

> Asteya arises out of the understanding that all misappropriation is an expression of a feeling of lack. In constantly looking outside of ourselves for satisfaction, we are less able to appreciate the abundance that already exists (10).

Asteya works from the idea that we are ready now and all we need is already within our grasp. An attitude that is constantly focusing on what we don't have can prevent us from enjoying what we do have now. When we practice with Asteya we recognize we have already within us what we need to begin the practice. We may have seen a young actor gulp in a large amount of breath, or go through a lengthy process of organizing himself to begin his monologue. These "preparations" are manifestations of a feeling of inadequacy. We can begin from where we are now. Our breath, alignment, clarity of thought etc. do not need to be "perfect" to begin the practice. We can discover these elements *through* the practice. The idea of self-abundance can also help us when we are first building our practice. It may at times seem like we cannot practice without our teacher present. The performer may say, "I can't do this without my teacher here; I'll do it wrong." We can, however, *imagine* the teacher there in the practice with us. Our memory of his or her voice, image, and guidance can be with us in the practice without his or her physical presence. We already have what we need from him or her with us in order to begin. Within the Yamas this is the idea of not stealing. For us it is more important that we focus on the idea of working from a place of abundance.

BRAHMACHARYA:

> Practicing Brahmacharya means that we use our sexual energy to regenerate our connection to our spiritual self (11).

I have made the decision to interpret this area in a very broad sense. For our practice, the challenge for the performer is the ability to channel, not just sexual energy, but *all* of ourselves into our work. This includes all of our senses, intuitions, and feelings, not just the ones we feel safe and comfortable with sharing. How often do we deny our anger, jealousy, shame, and lust? As performers we must be brave enough to give voice to these feelings. This does not mean we become consumed or self-indulgent in our emotions, but that we don't deny them when they do arise.

APARIGRAHA:

> ...life does change, and it demands that we adapt and change with it. The resistance to change, and tenaciously holding on to things, causes great suffering and prevents us from growing... (12).

I remember one of my voice teachers, David Smukler, asking a group of us to examine, "What is the physical construct that you have created in which to survive today?" Are we holding on to old habits that at one time served us? By remaining open to change within our practice and ourselves, we are open to possibilities.

Change can also come from outside of ourselves. Physical, artistic, and emotional situations change, and this changes our practice habits. We must be flexible in the practice to the changes in our daily lives both internally and externally.

Niyamas (Codes for Living):
SHAUCHA:

> When we take in healthy food…the body starts to function more smoothly. When we read books that elevate our consciousness, movies that inspire…we are feeding the mind in a way that nourishes our own peacefulness (12).

Shaucha, in the broadest sense, involves our giving care for our practice and any influences on it. The idea of being healthy in our practice goes beyond the obvious association of healthy voice habits. We all know that not smoking, drinking plenty of water, avoiding loud places etc. will aid our practice and our voices. We also know that it is important to practice healthy breath and phonation habits outside of the studio. Creating a safe and healthy place to practice is important as well. Most educators know that having a set place in the home for children to study contributes greatly to their ability to do their homework. The same is true for voice practice. If you can't find a place within your home, seek other places, perhaps at school, or a music room at a nearby library.

TAPAS:

> Literally translated as "fire" or "heat," tapas is the disciplined use of our energy. Because the word discipline has the negative connotation of self-coercion, I take the liberty here of translating this central precept as "burning enthusiasm" (13).

When practicing begins to feel like a chore rather than a joy we are experiencing a lack of tapas. We have lost the burning enthusiasm.

> …it is helpful to have a kind of parental consciousness coupled with a good sense of humor (13).

Donna Farhi uses the metaphor well when she compares this to a fire:

> If we light a fire and then we let the fire go out, it will take a lot of work to get it started again. But if we care for the fire, feeding it from time to time, the flames will grow (13).

That being said, beating up on oneself for letting the fire go out is not productive. If we struggle to find tapas in our practice, we can seek out teachers who inspire us, ideas from books

on the subject, or others who have a strong practice and practice with them. We must make sure that the practice is for *us* and is rooted in the joy of discovering, realizing, and revealing our inner voice.

> Tapas keeps us on track so that we don't waste our time and energy on superfluous or trivial matters (13).

At times the manifestation of a lack of tapas comes in the form of procrastination. We argue we have no time to practice, yet we fill a half-hour with television. We argue we are too busy to practice, yet the practice can help us to function better throughout our day. Tapas means using our energy for the things that inspire us, thus the energy can fuel itself.

SANTOSHA:

> …the ability to feel satisfied with the container of one's immediate experience. Contentment should not be confused with complacency, in which we allow ourselves to stagnate in our growth (13).

The greatest challenge in our practice is to balance the ability to be satisfied with where we are in our work, yet continue to move forward and grow. This is a balancing act that continues throughout one's life. It is important to ask the questions, "Am I pushing too hard?" or "Am I being hard on myself?" Santosha means that we are patient with our growth in our practice, not driven to get results immediately.

SWADHYAYA:

> While self-study uncovers our strengths, authentic swadhyaya also ruthlessly uncovers our weakness, foibles, addictions, habit patterns and negative tendencies (14).

It is important for us in our practice to take some time to acknowledge where we are weak and need to work. This does not mean that we begin to beat ourselves up. It can be more productive to simply acknowledge this limitation and allow for the possibility of growth in this area. It is difficult at times to balance this self-scrutiny while not becoming negative about our work. We want to acknowledge our limitations so we can change and grow.

ISHWARAPRANIDHANA:

> Life is not inherently meaningful. We make meaning happen through the attention and care we express through our actions (15).

By giving attention to a vocal gesture we give it meaning. When we mindlessly move through the practice it is not meaningful. We must seek to be specific about what we are doing moment-to-moment. By being present and aware of what we are specifically doing in a given moment we can become more open to the possibility for us to become a vessel through which we can express.

Assignment:
Now that you have read through the Yamas and the Niyamas, choose one or two of them to focus on for the next five weeks. Seek to nurture these aspects in your practice. Then choose one or two new ideas to nurture for the final five weeks of the course. You will write 2 two-page reports about how these ideas have influenced your practice and the ways in which you have nurtured them.

Acknowledgements:
I wish to thank those whose advice and feedback assisted in the creation of this article: Andrea Tutt, Jennifer Hambrick, Jeffrey Simlett and Eric Armstrong.

Works Cited
Carey, David. "Interviews with Patsy Rodenburg and Cicely Berry." *Film, Broadcast & Electronic Media Coaching presented by the Voice and Speech Review*, Rocco Dal Vera, ed. (Cincinnati, OH: VASTA), 2003.
Smukler, David. *VASTA Newsletter*, Spring/Summer 1998 Vol. 12, No. 2, and Fall 1998 Vol. 12, No. 3.
Farhi, Donna. *Yoga Mind, Body & Spirit : A Return to Wholeness*. New York: Henry Holt, 2000.

Essay *by Patricia Delorey & Debra Charlton*

Negotiating the Corpus Callosum:
A Whole-Brain Approach to Teaching Shakespeare

The ideal actor moves fluidly between the rational and creative sides of the brain, connecting with equal facility to both the intellect and the body/voice. The complexities of performing Shakespeare demand this complete and flexible actor. In this essay, we share our journey toward developing a teaching methodology designed to encourage students of Shakespeare to inhabit that open and receptive place, the meeting place between intellect and intuition—the corpus callosum.

Anatomists define the corpus callosum as the arch of tissue that bridges and facilitates communication between the left and right cerebral hemispheres. In our work, we think of the corpus callosum as the actor's springboard for transport between the analytical and the creative. At the core of our teaching partnership lies the desire to cultivate a mindset in which the actor is poised upon the corpus callosum, balanced between the two cerebral realms, and ready to navigate with ease between the intellectual and the organic. Our approach to teaching Shakespeare draws on the synergy of technical, visceral, and emotional exercises designed to keep the actor in a state of alert responsiveness, ready to tap into the resources of the whole brain. The goal of this approach is to excavate and release the scholar/actor.

As a voice director and director/dramaturg, our teaching approach has evolved over several years of experimentation, in both classroom and production settings. Although we teach at institutions in different parts of the United States during the academic year, each summer we unite to co-teach a Shakespeare intensive which serves as a laboratory for our teaching process. Our approach to teaching Shakespeare is grounded in the following goals:

To engage the analytical by
• Connecting to the intellect
• Developing critical thinking
• Applying a systematic process
• Training technical skills

To uncover the organic by
• Connecting to the body
• Developing spontaneity
• Avoiding self-judgment
• Tapping into autonomic responses

Our teaching methodology first took root during rehearsals for a university production of *The Winter's Tale* for which we served as director and vocal coach. During this production, the young actor playing Florizel was struggling with phrasing problems. Our attempts to help him unlock the text—by pointing out structural cues such as parentheticals and operative words—only served to make him more self-conscious, leading to stiffness and odd physical mannerisms. As his intellectual openness declined, his physical responsiveness also suffered, creating an actor who was progressively frozen and intimidated by the text. Over the course of rehearsals, it became increasingly clear that his analytical difficulties were interfering with his engagement with the body/voice. Ultimately, we decided the best way to salvage his performance was to work to bring both sides of his brain into dialogue.

Patricia Delorey is the Resident Voice Director for the Asolo Repertory Theatre and Head of Voice at the FSU/Asolo Conservatory for Actor Training. She is a Certified Fitzmaurice Voicework Teacher with her MFA in Voice & Speech from the MXAT/American Repertory Theatre Institute for Advanced Theatre Training at Harvard University. Ms. Delorey has worked professionally in the US and internationally, including *Phaedra 4.48* directed by Robert Woodruff, *Enrico IV* directed by Karen Coonrod, *Five by Tenn* directed by Carl Forsman, and the world premieres of *Nocturne, Ohio State Murders, & Stone Cold Dead Serious* directed by Marcus Stern.

Debra Charlton is Director of Graduate Studies in Theatre at Texas State University, where she supervises the program in production dramaturgy. She holds a PhD from the University of Texas, where she specialized in Shakespeare studies and dramaturgy. Dr. Charlton has worked professionally as an actor, and has directed numerous productions, including *King Lear, The Taming of the Shrew,* and *The Winter's Tale.* Dr. Charlton is currently at work on her first book, *Holistic Shakespeare,* which explores the Renaissance concept of embodied emotion and its implications for acting process.

Since the actor was profoundly blocked both intellectually and physically (and the production's opening date was looming), we decided to radically reinvent our working process. During sessions with this actor outside of regular rehearsals, we agreed to scrap conventional director/vocal coach boundaries in favor of intensive co-coaching sessions. We left our titles at the door and simply went into each coaching session prepared to use all of our collective tools. We knew this particular actor was already in tune with his body; he moved with ease and flow. Yet, at this point in the rehearsal process (about three weeks before opening), his fear of the demands of a complex text was inhibiting his connection to his body/voice intuitions and impulses. We agreed to try to capitalize on the actor's physical grace and strong body awareness by re-teaching the fundamentals of language structure through the body.

We set to work carving out the phrasing of the text with the actor. Using intensive side-coaching, we guided him word by word, clause by clause, and thought by thought through the monologue, looking for the thought transitions or sense breaks. Once we had agreed on the sense breaks, the actor was encouraged to use shifts in pitch to offset each parenthetical phrase:

Thou dear'st Perdita,
With these forced thoughts **I prithee** darken not
The mirth o' th' feast. Or I'll be thine, **my fair,**
Or not my father's; for I cannot be
Mine own, **nor any thing to any,** if
I be not thine. To this I am most constant,
Though destiny say no. Be merry, **gentle!**
Strangle such thoughts as these with any thing
That you behold the while. Your guests are coming:
Lift up your countenance, **as it were the day**
Of celebration of that nuptial, which
We two have sworn shall come.

In order to embed these phrasing choices in the whole brain, we asked the actor to find a full body gesture to illustrate each shift in pitch. As he moved though the monologue, physicalizing and vocalizing the parentheticals, we used side-coaching to correct deviations from the phrasing score. Side-coaching was quick, intense, and immediate, allowing the actor little time to over-think, ponder, or get stuck. At each new phrase, he *had* to make a physical choice. This allowed him to respond in the moment to the power of the words, to free his impulses and emotions, and to activate his physicality. This method successfully taught the actor to understand and apply the concepts of pitch shift and pitch matching, while engraining his sense phrases in the body/voice. When the actor returned to full company rehearsals, he abandoned the full body gestures, but

retained the impulses and clarity gained by his physicalization of phrasing.

While restoring and capitalizing upon the actor's natural body confidence, this coaching method freed him of his fear of the text, and taught him a new path to bring the text to life. We, too, learned from this experience. Working with a dense and difficult text, we learned that the best route to intelligibility was through the body/voice. The discoveries we made during work on this production have served as talking points as our teaching methodology has evolved, and have motivated a long-running conversation about bridging left and right brain thinking in the actor.

The summer Shakespeare intensive serves as our testing ground for many of our experiments in whole-brain teaching. We share our experiences with this course, not as a guide to the "model" Shakespeare intensive, but as an illustration of the variety of exercises we employ to encourage intellectual, physical, and emotional interconnectedness. Each of the exercises is intended to stimulate "whole" ownership of the text, and to keep the actor firmly centered in the corpus callosum working place.

In the Shakespeare course, our students are a diverse mixture of pre-professional actors, graduate-level directors, theatre historians, and teachers in training. Despite their diverse skill sets, we assume the ideal actor. As co-teachers, we seek to open and facilitate passage between the analytical and the creative selves. We do not always agree on exactly how to do this, but we share a willingness to explore. Our teaching is unified by the core belief that emotion is housed in the body, ignited by the text, and released on the voice. This fundamental belief is central to our collaboration, and to the way in which we help the student connect with both sides of the brain.

Throughout the five-week Shakespeare intensive (two weeks at Texas State University-San Marcos and three weeks in Stratford-upon-Avon, England), students participate in a wide variety of classes and activities, ranging from research projects using primary materials, to practical workshops in fencing and period dance. Daily voice and text work unifies the course, and provides the cornerstone upon which the practical work is layered. Fitzmaurice Voicework dovetails beautifully with our goal of fluid transport between the creative and rational sides of the brain. Catherine Fitzmaurice names "breath as the vital active ingredient for physical sound-making as well as for the expression of ideas." In the Fitzmaurice Voicework, "inspiration" is that moment when the actor breathes-in and creates a thought; "expiration" is when the actor breathes-out and expresses an idea. In Catherine Fitzmaurice's work, as in our

Pedagogy and Coaching

Negotiating the Corpus Callosum: A Whole-Brain Approach to Teaching Shakespeare
by Patricia Delorey & Debra Charlton (continued)

work, both "inspiration" and "expiration" are intellectual and physical actions, and there is harmonizing of the autonomic with the conscious. During the Fitzmaurice "Destructuring," actors link themselves to impulse and to breath, and release themselves from strongholds of tension and habit within the body/voice. This work engages the organic and taps into autonomic responses which become the raw material for acting and for the process work through which we guide our student actors. During the "Restructuring," actors engage their conscious minds. "Restructuring gives the actor control over the timing and the variety of delivery choices of pitch, rate, volume, and tone, and allows approximate repeatability without loss of either spontaneity or connection to impulse" (Fitzmaurice 1997). An actor with the intellectual and creative agility that "Restructuring" fosters is ripe for the variety of work we do with language.

Daily practical work begins with simple yoga exercises, which are used to help the student connect the intellectual self with the body, stimulating and focusing the breath, energizing and releasing tension in the body, and engaging the core. The exercise "Salute to the Sun" is particularly useful, since it uses every major muscle group in the body. In this exercise, upward movement coordinates with inhalation, while downward movement corresponds to exhalation. Done in repetitions, the exercise trains the actor in flow and allowing, rather than push and forcing. The breath releases the body and the emotions, and connects the individual to both the internal self and external environments simultaneously. When performed as a group, the exercise becomes a daily ritual which builds and focuses the ensemble; students find themselves breathing together and sensing one another kinesthetically.

We begin daily language structure work following the yoga exercises, when the actor is physically warm, intellectually receptive, and emotionally open. Respect for the language structure is fundamental to playing Shakespeare; however, many students come into the class fearing this work, or believing that textual analysis is academic, difficult, and prescriptive. As teachers, one of our key challenges is to quickly overcome this misconception. In our joint text classes, we share territory, reinforcing and augmenting one another's teaching methods. Scoring work is taught through a variety of modalities, ranging from classroom discussions about the vagaries of early modern spelling and punctuation, to conversations about Renaissance printing practices, to practical and creative applications of meter. Historical and academic discussions serve to frame and provide a set of given circumstances for performance. At its core, scoring work is experiential, process-oriented, and performance-driven. As dramaturg/director and vocal coach, we work as a hands-on

unit, engaging parallel strategies for bringing both sides of the brain into dialogue.

Language structure work commences by teaching regular and irregular metrical forms. We teach scansion by relating shifts in meter to the natural rhythms of the body. We discuss the Renaissance idea that emotion resides in the body, not the mind, encouraging students to embrace the notion of interconnectedness between the visceral and the abstract. We then examine how the physical body responds to stress and emotion through variations in breath and heart rate. Finally, by contrasting metrically predictable speeches with more erratic passages, we illustrate how Shakespeare uses rhythm to create a linear chart to a character's emotional journey. Students soon grasp that meter is a *playable* tool, not simply a decorative literary device.

Since we find it most efficient to work from a common vocabulary, we require students to quickly master correct metrical terminology. Metrical forms are taught through muscle memory, since this is the surest means to permanently imprint the rhythmic patterns and their terminology in the mind and the body. We accomplish this by teaching meter through a movement and sound wheel. Working in a circle, we introduce and define the major metrical forms (iamb, trochee, spondee, anapest, dactyl, and pyrrhic). Moving quickly around the circle, we ask individual students to demonstrate the stress pattern of each metrical term through a simple physical action, such as tapping the fingers, clapping, or stamping the feet, while simultaneously pronouncing the word with its corresponding stress pattern ("i-AMB, an-a-PEST"). This rapidly progresses into more complex full body gestures that are allied with sound to illustrate each metrical form. Eventually, the students will execute a complex series of sound/gestures that correlate to the six major metrical forms. The exercise quickly becomes more individualized and free-form as students compete to find creative variations in pitch, rate, and volume that reflect the rhythms of each metrical foot. By the end of the exercise, the students "own" each metrical form, having absorbed its cadences into the body/voice.

Once the foundations of meter have been taught, we begin working with a common text to create an acting score. While some elements of scoring are fixed, objective, analytical, and systematic (such as identifying parts of speech), others are open, subjective, interpretive and organic; we strive to help students distinguish between the two. We place emphasis on the score as the medium through which the physical instrument is played, stressing its *utility*, and subjecting each scoring choice to the question: "How will it play?" Our classroom text is *The Riverside Shakespeare*, which we prefer because we find the editors' textual choices to be reliably playable. However, we encourage our students to retain a modicum of skepticism, noting occasions when editorial choices are at variance with their artistic impulses. The ultimate goal is to teach the ability to read a text both critically and interpretively; thus, creation of the score is an exercise in dual negotiation, engaging much debate and discussion as we work toward a group consensus, and requiring constant mobility between right and left brain thinking.

Working with a common monologue, we collaborate as a group to map out the meter, using shifts in rhythm as guide-posts for changes in thought, physical state, and/or emotion. Next, punctuation is used as a marker for navigating thought groupings, and for identifying parentheticals and direct address. Then, parts of speech are named and labeled (subject, verb, direct object, indirect object, modifiers), and operative words are selected, with emphasis on avoiding the trap of "too many operatives." Line endings are noted, and short, long, and shared lines are flagged. While this text work can be time-intensive and technically challenging, we find that it profoundly frees the actor by demystifying the text and providing a roadmap for the actor to follow in rehearsal.

Once the scored text is complete, the actors test their intellectual choices by carving out the language through their bodies and through variations in the voice. When physical embodiment of our scoring choices proves awkward or impossible, this is usually a clear indicator that we have missed something important in the text.

We begin with punctuation. Starting in a neutral body position, the students find a new *vocal* action (a change in pitch, rate, or volume) for every piece of major and minor punctuation. At this stage, we ask the students to make bold vocal choices, which can later be pared down into more realistic inflections. Once the punctuation has been explored vocally, we add movement, asking students to embody grammatical shifts, such as parentheticals, through changes in both physical level and pitch. This exercise is also used to get the actors to feel in their bodies the difference between sustained inflection, upward inflection, and downward inflection.

We progress to exploration of line endings, using the following exercise to illustrate the physical requirements of endstopped versus enjambed lines. While reading aloud a common monologue (*Romeo and Juliet*), students travel around the room at a sustained pace, noting variations in line endings. Lines ending with minor punctuation are illustrated through *releves* on final words, while simultaneously using inflection of the voice to lift energy of the final words and propel to the next line of text. Endstopped lines are physicalized through *plies* and

downward inflection, while sustained pace and vocal pitch are used to illustrate enjambment. By requiring a specific physical action, this exercise imprints line endings in the memory, while emphasizing the need to make a physical and vocal choice in response to each form of line ending.

Thou know'st the mask of night is on my face,↑
Else would a maiden blush bepaint my cheek,↑
For that which thou hast heard me speak to-night.↓
Fain would I dwell on form, fain, fain deny→
What I have spoke: but farewell compliment!↓
Dost thou love me? I know thou wilt say 'Ay,"↑
And I will take thy word, yet if thou swear'st,↑
Thou mayst prove false: at lovers' perjuries→
They say Jove laughs. O gentle Romeo,↑
If thou dost love, pronounce it faithfully,↑
Or if thou think'st I am too quickly won,↑
I'll frown and be perverse and say thee nay,↑
So thou wilt woo, but else, not for the world.↓
In truth, fair Montague, I am too fond,↑
And therefore thou mayst think my 'havior light,↑
But trust me, gentleman, I'll prove more true→
Than those that have more coying to be strange.↓
I should have been more strange, I must confess,↑
But that thou overheardst, ere I was ware,↑
My true love's passion; therefore pardon me→
And not impute this yielding to light love,↑
Which the dark night hath so discovered.↓

Throughout this stage of the text work, we emphasize the value of making strong physical choices. This helps the actors to grasp the size of the language, and lifts them out of subtext-centered acting conventions. At the same time, it prohibits the detached, overly cerebral style of acting that infects much classical performance. The next step is to bring the physical/vocal shifts down to a smaller "performance" level, with a focus on allowing the action/movement to originate from the spine and core.

Visual and spatial exercises are also utilized to illustrate the idea of naturalist versus heightened style, and to stimulate interplay between the eye, intellect, and imagination. Balance, composition, symmetry, opposition, and scale are concrete tools used for demonstrating structural elements such as antithesis, and for creating word pictures that reflect textual imagery. Spatial/visual exercises also serve as effective vehicles for reinforcing Renaissance notions of hierarchy, power, and alliance. The text and spatial exercises engage the whole brain, encouraging the interaction of mind, body, and voice, in which neither right nor left brain modes of access are privileged above the other.

Pedagogy and Coaching

Negotiating the Corpus Callosum: A Whole-Brain Approach to Teaching Shakespeare
by Patricia Delorey & Debra Charlton (continued)

The capstone of the course is a scene-showing in Stratford. As we move into rehearsals, our roles shift somewhat from voice director and dramaturg to voice director and stage director. Although the nature of rehearsal demands that we make this adjustment, we still do not work within a strictly traditional rehearsal dynamic. While the director spearheads the through-line, we strive to work as equal partners in the creative process. For the student, this means responding to input from two sources, which requires a change to their usual experience. As a dramaturg/director and vocal coach, we have learned to be comfortable with flexible boundaries. Likewise, in our students, we value and cultivate adaptability. The students are now on their feet acting a text, while receiving direction that requires a range of responses: intellectual, creative, physical, technical and emotional. It is the young actor's job to stay within the realm of the corpus callosum so that they can move with agility and ease between the two regions of the brain, working as both technicians and creative artists. The value of this mental litheness is the ability to make quick, targeted acting adjustments.

Admittedly, there are plenty of times when we work solely in one realm or the other; when we say, for example, "Release the body and forget the intellect." Most of the time, however, we are in navigation. We ask students to remain fluid, responsive, and open to discoveries. Just as the corpus callosum bridges separate and essential regions of the brain, the collaborative perspectives of the voice director and the dramaturg link the intellectual and the organic.

Acknowledgments
Special thanks to Nancy Houfek for introducing me to so many things, including the idea of the corpus callosum, and to Margaret Eginton for sharing with me her Yoga work with actors, and for mentoring me. P.D.

Works Cited
Fitzmaurice, Catherine. "Breathing is Meaning." *The Vocal Vision*, Marian Hampton & Barbara Acker, eds. New York: Applause Books, 1997.

Vocal Production,
Voice Related Movement Studies *Marth Munro, Associate Editor*

Vocal Production, Voice Related Movement Studies *Marth Munro, Associate Editor*

Since the last edition of the Voice and Speech Review I had the privilege to act as a peer reviewer and examiner for various articles and dissertations in the wider field of performance. In retrospect I realize how often I have indicated that an author or a student must read an article or an essay in a past *VSR*. This to me serves as a testimony of how the *VSR* is not just providing a map of the Voice and Speech territory, but how VASTA as an association impacts on the wider performance field and how we are reflecting performance issues in the true sense of the word.

In the column "Voices around the World" the reader is introduced to Lyn Darnley from the Royal Shakespeare Company. For Lyn, the essence of voice work lies in collaboration and inclusivity. Cindy Milligan provides an interesting angle on voice/physicality congruency when she shares the embodied pattern reflecting envoicing to provide believable performances in the film *Ray*. In two separate articles, John Tucker and Doug MacArthur share approaches explored with clients' male-to-female and female-to-male transgender paths. They are both reflecting on changes that did not happen in theatre but happened in life "where all the men and women are merely players." The next two articles deal with well-known body approaches that both have optimal organic functioning of the body as a main goal. Ruth Rootberg outlines the Alexander technique and it's contribution to voice work for the reader. Sheila Gordon and colleagues Goldberg, Rockwell and Netsell reflect on an experiment using the Feldenkrais technique in a Voice class in order to improve breathing. The following two essays both deal with issues around voice and violence, written respectively by Mark Ingram and by Matthew Ellis and Rena Cook. And finally, Barbara Acker's article takes a unique angle when she demonstrates the importance of researching "voice history" when she reflects on the unconventional way verse usage was explored by W.B. Yeats and Farr. Perhaps the reason for the conflicted reactions to this work is captured in the non-congruency of the voice and physicality of the Yeats/Farr approach.

As always, it was a learning curve for me to work on the material submitted to this section. I want to thank the wonderful contributors: the ones whose work was accepted and the ones who have to go back to the drawing board. I have learnt a lot from all of you. I want to thank all the peer reviewers for being willing to read, comment and read again. It is this kind of teamwork that ensures the quality of the Journal. As I pass this section on to another associate editor, I am deeply under the impression that this Journal provides quality—not just in the reading, but also in the process of putting it all together. Sharing it is true VASTA characteristic. I thank you.

Marth Munro specializes in performance voice building, body/voice integration and vocal pedagogy. She holds a PhD in which she investigated the acoustic properties of Lessac's Tonal NRG and the "Actor's formant" in the female voice. She has completed a team research project on computer-aided training of the singing voice. Munro has been recognised by the National Research Foundation (South Africa) as a rated researcher. She is a Certified Laban/Bartenieff Movement Analyst, serves on the Laban Institute of Movement Studies board, and is a Certified Lessac Voice and Movement Teacher. She teaches in the Department of Drama, Tshwane University of Technology, South Africa. She publishes in popular and scholarly journals; teaches workshops for actors, singers and musicians; and directs opera, musical theatre and theatre.

Voices From Around the World: Lyn Darnley

We were privileged to be able to ask Lyn Darnley from the Royal Shakespeare Company to be our "voice from around the world" person for this edition. Lyn is actually from two worlds—her current world of Britain, and her "birth world" of South Africa. Lyn writes so eloquently and directly that we place her replies as they came to us from her.

Where did your interest in voice and working with voice begin?
My interest in voice work developed out of an early career in radio. As a child I met a radio director at a friend's home and she contacted my parents to ask if I could participate in a radio drama. This was at a time when South Africa was a "televisionless" society, and radio was the principal entertainment. I began to work regularly in serialised dramas which were broadcast daily and in radio theatre which allowed me to perform excellent texts with very experienced actors. I continued to work very regularly in radio studios doing drama, narration, and adverts and when television in was introduced in 1976 I worked as a presenter. I believe my early exposure to radio theatre both as a listener and a performer developed my love for words and an awareness of the power of language alone, to engage with the imagination and tell stories. I think it was a very oral culture to grow up in and the multi-lingual "soundscape" was fascinating. To this day I love to listen to radio drama and readings.

What were your first formal learning experiences in voice?
I studied with Catherine King. She was an inspirational teacher who was a South African who had trained at Central School with Elsie Fogerty and Gwyneth Thurburn. She was Head of Voice at RADA and worked with Clifford Turner. When she retired she returned to Durban and her anecdotes of life in war-time London, working with actors who had gone on to become stars of stage and screen were both exciting and inspiring. These anecdotes were largely responsible for creating my interest in the history of voice teaching. I think she awakened a real desire to teach and I will always be grateful for the solid foundation she gave me in verse. What I admired about her more than anything was that whenever I returned and went to see her she was interested in discussing and debating the new developments in voice work—she never had the need to hold on to fixed ideas and welcomed the changes in thinking.

Your work in radio moved into the theatre in time. How did this happen?
I worked as an actor for NAPAC (Natal Performing Arts Council) in Durban and touring small theaters in country towns in Kwa Zulu. The work was always classic, apart from Christmas Shows—and I think (no, I know) that at the time white South African actors were in some ways in a very

privileged position—the pool was fairly small but opportunities were rich, so I did Shaw, Shakespeare and Moliere etc., all of which developed my interest in classic text. The down side was that we never really explored our own roots—I envy South African actors today who are involved in creating a theatre that comes out of their own experience. It was certainly more like the American model than the British one as multi-tasking (acting, teaching, writing, presenting) was encouraged and not viewed with "suspicion" as it tends to be in the UK. I continued to teach around my acting, presenting and radio commitments.

I also worked as part of my husband's Theatre-in-Education Company which toured schools and played in the parks. The parks were the only places during the time that were multiracial and provided the only opportunity to play to mixed audiences. Once I had children I concentrated on radio, teaching and, for three years before leaving South Africa for the UK, I worked as a television presenter, initially on a preschool programme and later on a current affairs programme.

We left South Africa in 1980 as my husband is British and he had become increasingly frustrated by the political situation and the implications of this on his ability to operate his theatre company. I was very fortunate and found work at Rose Bruford College within a week of arriving in England. At the time the College had two courses, one in traditional theatre and the other in Community theatre. Ultimately I worked as Head of Voice on both courses but initially I spent eight years teaching on the Community Arts Course and I feel that was where I really gained my education. We team-taught acting projects and I learned invaluable skills from my colleagues, the students and the work, which included reminiscence work, devising and storytelling. The forward looking approach of the course allowed tutors to be inventive and push boundaries and

Lyn Darnley teaching a public workshop on RSC Open Day. Photo by Ellie Kurttz.

there was a freedom to devise courses to suit and support the broad intake. I left Rose Bruford College in 1992 when I was invited to join the Voice Department at the Royal Shakespeare Company.

It must have been at this stage that you started developing your own approach to the work. How did this happen and where has it led you?
I was Head of Voice at Rose Bruford first on the Community Arts Course and then when the courses amalgamated, on both. It was during my 12 years at Rose Bruford that I became passionate about the need to introduce a structured programme of verse and prose to first and second year students. In their devising workshops they were learning how to structure scenes and I felt the best way to learn about the shape and rhythm of language was from the extant texts. When they studied narrative theatre, we spoke the great narrative poems, when they looked at Brecht we spoke his verse and in this way the work was "joined up." One of the most exciting projects I initiated was a political speeches festival which we presented at the end of a term in which students studied of rhetoric. This was done in the term before the Shakespeare project and I believe they still include it in the curriculum. Another memorable aspect of the work at Bruford was the link we had with Central School of Speech and Drama. For two of the three terms each year, we had students from the Voice Course placed with us and I found this was a wonderful way to keep revising and challenging my practice. I feel very strongly that we cannot be satisfied with our practice or settle into a system, we have to keep open to new ideas and new influences. That is why I have always tried to keep attending conferences and workshops. We are so fortunate to have an active and sharing voice community. When I arrived in England there seemed to be nothing for voice teachers. I was so delighted to learn about the then newly formed Voice Research Society which later became the British Voice Association. I have learned so much from colleagues and it was through the VRS that I met Stephanie Martin (we met after a Voice Research meeting because we had left our conference badges on and sat opposite each other on the train). Stephanie and I went on to work together on the *Voice Source Book* and the first and second editions of *The Teaching Voice*. The VRS became the BVA (British Voice Association). Learning about VASTA further broadened my perspective and I have been to VASTA and ATHE several times over

Lyn Darnely with colleagues Charmian Gradwell (left) and Anna Morrissey (right). Photo by Ellie Kurttz.

the years. I find contact with other practitioners nourishing and I have met many friends through conferences with whom I regularly correspond.

It was during my last two years at Rose Bruford when I began researching the history of voice work. I believe we learn so much from looking backwards and it helps us know how to move forewords. I think it is wonderful that today voice coaches have a proper place in the theatre. I think some very remarkable people (most of them women) have made this happen.

Cicely Berry is one of these women and it is a great privilege to work with her and watch how she is able to free language for actors. Actors of all ages and levels of experience respond to her particular style of work. It is totally inspiring to hear her talk about the work with such passion and common sense. I have seen her help actors, students and young directors form a relationship with classic language that transforms their approach. The work is always rooted in the theatre and the character's need to speak. It is totally connected to her politics which is what makes it so powerful.

What might be your central concern or concerns as a voice teacher or facilitator?
I believe we have to teach an actor or student, and not a system. I hope I always gear my teaching towards their needs. This does not mean I don't have a set of principles. My text teaching is based on Cicely Berry's approach—finding the muscularity of language and the physicality of sound rather than "listening to the voice" or working for beautiful speech. Clarity comes with clarity of thought and muscularity. Of course any teacher brings herself or himself to the work and I find I use exercises that worked for me as a student. I work a lot on rhythm but through speaking and assimilation rather than explanation. My voice work is physical and is very connected to movement. I love working with movement teachers. I teach the physiology if I think an actor will benefit from knowing how things work. This can be useful, depending on how an actor thinks and learns. For some actors too much information can create blocks, so you have to get to know the actor or student and trust your instincts.

I believe that voice and movement should be interrelated whenever possible. Voice and speech are based on the movement of breath and muscle and respond to changes in thought. You can't separate them. I enjoy team teaching groups and warm-up sessions with movement directors/coaches and exploring verbal and movement dynamics alongside each other. More important, actors find that the one releases the other. There seems little sense in trying to separate them. What better way is there to explore rhythm, impulse and energy?

How do you fit into the production dynamic?
When working on a production it is really important to be in the rehearsal room as much as you can be. This way you learn what the director's concept is and understand the rhythm and energy and dynamic of the production. The work the voice coach does must be part of the whole, so he or she should be part of the company. It is also important to get to understand the way in which the actors work so you can know how best to help them. It is great to work with actors on long-term contracts because you can develop a good working relationship with them and this allows you to support them.

What is your present "job description?"
My job includes the delivery of the Artist Development Programme at the Royal Shakespeare Company. Artistic Director, Michael Boyd has promoted a culture in which artists continue to develop their skills while working—a true ensemble ethic. There has always been some training offered to actors at the RSC since Peter Hall's time. Hall developed a programme in 1960 when Michele Saint Denis and Peter Brook were working with him. Saint Denis' Studio at Stratford ran for about three years. The Voice Department which Cicely Berry started in 1970 offers artists the opportunity to develop their language, verse and voice skills. Michael Boyd has extended this idea to include not only actors but all artists in the company and we provide a programme of training for all the companies within the ensemble. This can be anything from ensemble-building work which might be mask work, Meisner Training, group singing, drumming and dance work or production specific workshops or lectures on aspects of the texts being produced. At the heart of the programme is the work on language which includes the work of John Barton, Cicely Berry and distinguished visiting teachers. Some great work is done by senior members of the ensemble and it is great to be able to observe the way in which younger actors learn from those with more experience—either by observing them or more directly by discussion and suggestion. I work with Jane Hazell who co-ordinates the programme and we liaise closely with directors and also respond to suggestions by artists. The programme draws on the incredibly rich skills base within the RSC and extends the work to directors and writers. It also includes the Professional Placements in Voice and Movement which allow coaches to experience working within a large classical company. There have been moves towards closer links with the drama conservatoires, directing courses and stage management courses.

Do you work with other people besides the company?
A great thing about working at the RSC is that we work with the Learning Department on their educational projects and this allows me to maintain a link with young people—school groups, university and drama students. We work with The Shakespeare Centre doing workshops on the plays in rep for visiting university students from all over the world. I also work with school teachers on a regular basis and that too is rewarding and allows me to continue to work.

What are your current projects?
2006 has been a very exciting time to be at the RSC because of the Complete Works Festival. The visiting companies have brought with them a vibrancy and originality that has infected everyone. There always seems to be something new to see and each production reveals something new in a play you thought you knew well. The international productions have definitely fuelled the spirit of creativity in Stratford. It has been wonderful to work with many of the visitors from South Africa, Poland, India the USA and Germany. I am looking forward to the remainder of the Complete Works Festival which goes on till 2007.

Essay *by Cindy Milligan*

Performing Voice: The Voiceless Women in *Ray*

The 2004 biopic *Ray*, about aspects of the life of Ray Charles the musician, offers four strong yet very different roles for women. Director Taylor Hackford's decision to use Ray Charles' original recordings demands a certain type of vocal performance and requires the principle actors to use their voices in distinctive ways, especially for those who are not professional singers.

In this essay, I will focus attention on two female characters in the film *Ray* whose voiced performances became "voiceless"—their actual voices were "removed" during singing sequences. Highlighting their vocal abilities, the use of sound, and editing I will show how they were able to make their characters believable and therefore to get audiences to suspend their disbelief. The roles demanded the actors use their voices and bodies to communicate subtle meaning that is not always so obvious in the text.

This is a case study of the performances of Regina King, who played Margie Hendricks in the film, and Aunjanue Ellis who played Mary Ann Fisher. I provide a close textual analysis of their vocal interpretations, focusing on the concept of the embodied voice and how it is used in the film.

The challenge for the women actors in *Ray* rests with those who are not professional singers and have to lip-synch, that is to say, accurately "match" their own lip movements to the lip movements of recorded voices. For example, both Regina King and Aunjanue Ellis are not professional singers, yet their roles demanded they play the part of strong singers able to belt out a song. To do so and make their performances believable, they had to attempt to match, vocally and physically, the recorded performance of the original artists. The actors needed to mold their performances of the songs to fit those of the original artists, knowing that their own voices would be edited out and replaced by overdubbing. This voiceless performance would mean the merging of one voice with another's body. And, it had to be believable.

Through a close textual analysis of specific sections of the text, I uncover some of the issues of performing voice and show how the filmic devices of editing, overdubbing, the use of camera angles, shots, shot lengths, and use of space in the *mise en scene* can silence a very strong voice while imploring audience buy-in and encouraging a suspension of disbelief.

The notion of "performing of voice" or "voiceless performance" leads me to ask the following questions: What information can audiences glean from the sound of the actor's voices—both in the production and sound of their voices, as well as the words that they are saying? Do their body movements contribute to their voiced performance and, if so, how? What messages are conveyed in their voiceless performances? Can the sound of one actor's voice be merged effectively with another's body and create a believable and convincing performance? How does "performing" voice contribute to the overall story of *Ray*?

This study is motivated by my interest in the impact of voice in film and the rich ground the film *Ray* provides for analysis. Focusing a study on voice in performance also offers a chance to further explore how editors and sound designers effectively merged the speaking voices of one set of actors with a

Cindy Milligan is a PhD candidate at Georgia State University and teaches voice, speech, film, journalism and communications courses. Her research focuses on the use of voice in film. A former television and radio news anchor, reporter and talk show host, Cindy created a vocal warm-up CD called, *The Warm-Up Studio*. She is an actor, filmmaker, producer and Director of Media at Faith Christian Center.

completely different set of singers in a different era. Analyzing vocal performances can show the best ways the film medium can be exploited in terms of voice, particularly as it relates to audience acceptance of perceived authenticity. It also provides an excellent opportunity to study how actors can come across as believable.

There is a large gap in the literature in use of voice in both live and mediated performance. This work seeks to close that gap by highlighting the use of voice and body in film. Much of the casting in Hollywood films is based on box office draw, and an even greater portion focuses on the visual image. Voice scholar and dialogue coach Mel Churcher says filmmakers usually seek out a certain look when casting, while little attention is given to the sound of the human voice and how it can impact the meaning of the text and the film as a whole (Churcher 2003, 50). On the other hand, Sarah Kozloff in "Overhearing Film Dialogue" disagrees with Churcher, saying that casting in American films does take voice into account "not only in defining leading parts, but in creating a blend of different tones on the sound track" (Kozloff 2000, 92). But in a biographical musical film such as *Ray*, the sound of the performer's speaking voice created a different challenge because it was critical that there be some similarity of the actor's voice who would be performing the lip-synched sections of music to the original singer's voice; the original recordings demanded so. Hackford says he was not as concerned about this often neglected part of the actor's toolkit and talked about his concern for Jamie Foxx's singing and piano playing ability. However, he does not mention this consideration when referring to the casting of the female roles, particularly of Regina King and Aunjanue Ellis who had to perform as singers matching their interpretations of the songs with women who sang and toured with Ray Charles.

Two concepts are helpful in studying the performing voice: voice production and the embodied voice. The concept of voice production focuses on the sound of the voice, and the use of inflection, rhythm, tempo, pitch, volume, color, timbre, tone, resonance, and variety—all the paralinguistic features of speech that convey meaning to audiences as they hear the spoken dialogue. In many cases, studying the text involves the interpreted content of the written script as the actor looks for *meaning*, but in this work attention is focused on how an actor interprets the written words on a page of script and brings them to life—in other words, the *performance* of that meaning. The printed text is only the beginning of film dialogue. The actor vocalizes the words and the director helps the actor shape his or her performance from the plethora of aural and gestural possibilities that enhance the desired meaning

and undertones (Kozloff 2000, 96), which leads to the second vocal concept: the embodied voice.

In the film *Ray*, the embodied voice speaks to how actors lip-synch their performances and how they use their bodies to match visually what is being heard aurally so that the audience "matches" the visual cues with the aural cues to believe in the transition from spoken moment to sung moment. One must remember that the spoken voice comes from the actor, and the sung voice from recording. This process makes the actors' actual voices voiceless through editing and overdubbing of another performer's voice in the final product. In essence, this means that the actor's embodied actions need to contribute to the audience's interpretation and acceptance of the vocal performance.

There are several short portions of the film I use for analysis, all of which are mid-way through the film. I specifically chose clips that are: 1) well into the film so that they could stand alone in terms of meaning; 2) not too close to the end, giving a sense that things were wrapping up or coming to an end; and 3) rich with a variety of underlying subtext and messages.

Two clips provide substantive content highlighting the performances of King and Ellis and the notion of performing voice. In the first clip, I analyze Aunjanue Ellis's voiceless, lip-synched performance of Mary Ann Fisher singing "Drown in My Own Tears." In the second clip, attention is turned to Regina King as Margie Hendricks performing voice in "Night Time is the Right Time." Both actors' performances become voiceless when editors overdubbed them with the real Mary Ann Fisher and Margie Hendricks who were the singers on the original recordings. Both Ellis and King's performances appear to (or sound like they) address director Hackford's goals for each character.

Ellis/Mary Ann's 1st Performance—Body & Voice
Ellis/Mary Ann's first scene where she is introduced to audiences and to Ray shows Ellis' performance is multi-layered, including voiceless lip-synching, a sexually provocative, finger-snapping dance (both expertly embodied), and a vocal come-on to Ray in the dialogue. She is auditioning for Ray in a club, singing *a cappella* and alone on the stage while he and his manager Jeff drink coffee and listen in the auditorium. The scene opens in black with sound up full of Ellis/Mary Ann's fingers snapping while we hear Mary Ann singing "Drown in My Own Tears." The fact that Ellis/Mary Ann is not the first visual in this scene suggests that the visual of her singing might not synch up with the voice of the real Mary Ann singing on the soundtrack. This is a filmic device that can be used by the editor to camouflage the fact that the sound and

image are out of synch. After a few seconds, Ellis/Mary Ann emerges out of black into a beam of light and a smoky atmosphere. The director uses the haziness of the *mise en scene* to cloud the image—a device that draws attention away from Ellis' possibly mis-synched mouth and sound. The camera is slightly off center as Ellis/Mary Ann is first seen in a medium shot as she is holding a note. Since Ellis' mouth is open, it looks like she is actually singing. As soon as the words to the song change, and Ellis' mouth appears not to catch up with it, the editor cuts to a wider shot and the camera moves to the left so that her face is not clear and one cannot follow whether her voice is synched with the music. However, she continues to sway and dance on stage in front of Ray and Jeff, providing embodied clues to the "truthfulness" of the singing. She continues to sing, but the visuals cut to a waiter pouring a drink for Ray and as the waiter moves out of the picture, we see Ray talking with Jeff. Their conversation is heard over Mary Ann's song. When the editor cuts back to Ellis/Mary Ann visually on stage, Ellis' lips synch with the song for a few seconds in an over the shoulder shot with Ray in the foreground. Ray cuts her off quickly—another device used by the director to shorten the amount of time viewers would see Ellis/Mary Ann actually singing the song. In this sequence, Ellis is "performing" voice (as opposed, for example, to "giving voice"), or lip-synching. Director Taylor Hackford shows Ellis/ Mary Ann singing, but by pulling the camera away from her and taking a long shot, the asynchronization is camouflaged. The long shot becomes a filmic device used to get audiences to buy-in to Ellis' performance. A close-up of her face is not seen again while she is singing, but Ellis' body is communicating openness to her private audience of the two men, and Ellis' movement is free and unrestricted as she sways to embody the sound of Mary Ann's own voice. Starr Marcello talks about how Hollywood separates the sound and image of the actor's performance, but then tries to cover up the separation in the cinematic recording process "to preserve the illusion of reality" (Marcello 2004, 2). She explains:

> That is to say, careful attention is placed on the synchronization of the sound track and the visual track, so that correspondence of the actor's spoken words with his or her moving lips will create the semblance of a live, natural performance rather than an artificial, recorded one. This fusion of sound and image tends to generate more full-blown analyses of actors' performances—analyses that tie the sound or vocal aspect of the performance to the visual or bodily one (Marcello 2004, 2).

The use of the body cannot be ignored in this performance because the filmmaker depends on visuals and using shots of the actor's body as cutaways for creating an apparent seamless suture of the film. Ellis/Mary Ann's dance and finger-snapping slightly distracts the audience from paying close attention to

whether her mouth is synchronized to the words of the song. Ellis' body movement makes us believe that her voice is the one we hear in the film. Additionally, the waiter, Ray, and Jeff are also used as distractions from Ellis' (but not Mary Ann's) performance, but their distractions are not great enough to disturb the narrative; instead it seems like a natural part of what might happen in the club while Ellis/Mary Ann is auditioning. The three men remain an important part of the scene, but attention is slightly redirected. The reasoning behind the redirect is two-fold: to take attention off Ellis' mismatched lip-synch and to move the narrative forward in the film. The audience is able to suture the sound of Mary Ann's song with the visual of Ellis dancing, which is aided by the editor's skill at merging these two elements. All these things working together allow audiences to suspend their disbelief and accept Ellis the actor as Mary Ann the singer.

The most important part of Ellis' voiceless performance is that she had to actually sing the song as if she were auditioning for Ray on the stage. She could not "pretend" to sing. Instead, she had to give the "filmed moment" full voice no matter what she sounded like. Ellis is not a professional singer, and it did not matter that she did not sound like the real Mary Ann Fisher; her tone was close enough to be believable. Furthermore, Ellis' natural speaking voice was not so far removed from Fisher's singing voice. It was only important that Ellis looked like (embody the idea that) she was singing the song. The cinematographer had to set the camera with appropriate angles and distance as well as use the set design to enhance and/or camouflage the environment in which she was singing. Aunjanue Ellis' voice was silenced in the performance, but her body was not; it was singing loud and clear.

After Ray stops Ellis/Mary Ann in mid-song, they briefly talk. The sexual tension developing between them becomes more immediate as Ray gets rid of Jeff, suggesting he (Ray) rehearse alone with Mary Ann. Both Ray and Mary Ann's goals are clear. Her goal is to sing and perform with Ray and his band. Ray's goal is two-fold: 1) to meet another woman, maybe someone he can become intimately involved with, and 2) to add a female voice to his band. The physical space between Ray and Mary Ann has diminished. She is no longer alone on the stage, but has been joined by Ray who sits at the piano as she leans on it. Ellis' vocal tone is much lower and softer now, versus the embodied belting out of the song when she was alone on the stage. Mary Ann Doane says in "The Voice in the Cinema: The Articulation of Body and Space" that "the voice must be anchored by a given body; the body must be anchored in a given space" (Doane 1985, 164). Ellis' performance in this sequence anchors both in the space. The real Mary Ann Fisher's voice (the overdubbed one) is anchored visually in Ellis' body and embodiment. Ellis' body is anchored on the stage, leaning on the piano and then sitting next to Ray—she is settled in the *mise en scene* and clearly a part of what is supposed to be there. We can focus on her and accept her surroundings. No matter what she is doing, whether it is listening to Ray sing, or kissing him, she fully occupies the space physically, visually, and vocally. The editing process separates Ellis technically but not visually from the song, and the audience does not have reason to suspect that they are hearing another vocalist.

Margie's Performance—Body and Voice

In this scene, Margie (Regina King) is introduced to Ray and to audiences for the first time. Within a minute into the scene, King becomes voiceless—"performing and embodying voice"—singing in a recording session. It is her first voiceless performance (lip-synched). Margie, together with the band The Cookies, sings "Leave That Woman Alone." The synchronization of the voices of the Cookies with the actors playing them is very close to perfect in the beginning of this scene. Editors cut between the three female singers and Ray with tight shots of the trio singing ("performing/embodying") back-up. Since neither of the women have the lead in the song, the synchronization is not too difficult to maintain because there are fewer lyrics for the back-up singers. However, a quick cut to the studio personnel may suggest something was off, but the conversation of the producers with the engineers serves to move the narrative forward while the music continues in the background—it is another distraction from the visual and vocal attempt at lip-synching. Then the film presents a couple of quick edits back and forth between Ray and Margie as she backs him up. The shots are close-ups of both actors and it is clear that Regina King's performance of voice (lip-synching as well as embodiment) is very accurate in this sequence. The edits and performance also serve to communicate Margie's interest in Ray as she watches him during the recording session. Sound editors "silence" the actors embodying the Cookies vocally by overdubbing their voices with the original artists, but the cameras record the embodying or the "performing voice." Furthermore, the language of the actors' bodies, particularly King's/Margie's, cannot be silenced which clearly signifies that Margie is interested in more than just singing. The director shot both Ray and King/Margie head-on, showing them both in positions of power. Camera movement is minimal and the direct cuts are synchronized with the beat of the music. King's speaking voice blends well with the speaking voices of the actors playing the Cookies. Their sound makes it easy to believe that they could be the real Cookies on the recording, as they move between performing voice and embodying voice.

The sound of King's/Margie's voice is critical to the meaning communicated and received by audiences. Since there is not a lot of action and movement in this sequence, the small, subtle movements and the vocal performances of the actors present/embody a subtext which communicates intense feeling and emotion. Mel Churcher talks about the importance of the voice expressing meaning and emotion:

> We know that voice is the most sensitive indicator of feeling…If the actor doesn't use a voice that resonates with the 'ring of truth,' no amount of visual clues will compensate. Actors need to take voice as seriously as any other aspect of communication on film. Because film deals mainly in subtext, the sound of the voice doesn't seem as important as the feelings underneath. But the two can't be separated. If the thought is strong—the voice will be. If you drive what you want either through the words or under the words, a free released voice will carry your intentions or your subtext (Churcher 2003, 51).

The actor's ability to effectively use the voice is important to the messages of the narrative that the audience receives. A script develops so many further dimensions of meaning when an actor uses the paralinguistic features of speech and voice to add richness, depth and dimension to the meaning suggested by the words. Speech involves breath and muscular activity, and it utilizes a different part of the brain than physical activity, yet all are interrelated. Speaking is a physical act. King and Ellis prove in their performances that although their voices may be silenced on the editing room floor, performing voice is a physical act that strongly involves the entire body to make it believable. Turning text into meaningful and entertaining speech through embodied voice is the key, as is finding ways to turn printed music and text into believable song (Marshall 2002, 78).

Performing Voice

King's/Margie's performance of "Night Time is the Right Time" is a powerful and sexually charged sequence. Leading into this performance is an intimate love scene where Margie is explaining to Ray how she feels about him and his genius on the stage. She expresses how much she wants to be a part of his life, and the music of "Night Time is the Right Time" provides a perfect segue into the recording studio where Margie and Ray ignite the screen with a sexually charged performance. The scene is powerful and well edited to show a cohesive performance by the band. But the focus is on Margie and Ray singing to each other. The music and lyrics of the song pushes the narrative forward, telling of their relationship. There is a point when Ray belts to her, "Sing your song, Margie!" And she does just that. As the scene cuts to a close-up of her singing directly to Ray, the level of intensity heightens. Her eyes fixed on him, she responds to his call with an energy and focus that is powerful and demanding of attention.

Her expression is open and focused, seemingly leaving everyone else out of the exchange. With the accuracy of the synchronization and the interchange between Foxx and King, it is easy to believe they are both singing/performing the song. The call and response between them becomes all about Margie and Ray. The lyrics also strongly add to the sexual energy of the performance, "Nighttime is the right time to be with the one you love…" (Charles 2004). Hackford says he directed the scene to show the direct sexual connection between Ray and Margie through the music (Hackford 2004). As King performs in this scene, the intensity in her body language is strong, passionate, and powerful. Muscles in her face, neck and upper body demonstrate the soaring level of intensity with which she performs. She is belting that song out to Ray as if she means every word. There is nothing in this performance that would lead viewers to believe she is not the voice you hear in the song. Her demeanor and attitude (embodiment) is that she owns the song and the performance and all "her" energy and emotion is directed toward Ray. Hackford says that he promised King that he would never allow the vocal recording of her performance to be heard since she is not a professional singer (Sunshine, 2004, 22). However, in the sequence she clearly has the look, movement and demeanor of a pro singing from the heart.

The success of this scene can be attributed to the effective marrying of King's performance with the director's use of camera shots and angles, and to meticulous editing of the audio and visual. The cameras are strategically placed to foreground the couple singing to each other. The shots are straight on both the actors; nothing is shot off center and the cameras are positioned to fully capture their intense direct engagement.

In order for the performance to be believable, the actors had to actually give full voice to the songs. Put another way, the actors had to present a fully committed physical embodiment of the act of singing, using these songs. Full commitment was necessary in order to gain audience buy-in.

King's approach to performing voice with the song "Night Time is the Right Time" is multi-layered and multi-functional. It is more than just singing along "with" or "to" the recorded version. First of all, King had to mold her voice to fit the sound of the original singer—Margie Hendricks. In order for her to accomplish this, she had to listen to and study carefully the song, which was originally recorded in 1958—nearly 45 years prior to the production of the film. She needed to pay close attention to the lyrics as well as all the subtle nuances in the vocal stylings of Hendricks. She had to adjust her voice to meld with Hendricks and fit the image of the back-up singer who performed in New York in the 1950s. Additionally, this information had to be shaped and fit into the meaning and

context of the scene which ultimately speaks to the intent of the writer and then the director. Within the moment when the scene was being filmed, King filtered this information through what she understood the vocal signs meant in the original recording along with the objective of the film. Furthermore, she had to study very carefully the physical manifestations of singers as they were singing these types of songs, so that she could access the required embodied patterns of "singers in the process of singing." This allowed her to embody the singing voice or perform the singing voice moment. As she interpreted the song and the script, she molded all of this to the other actors in the scene—mainly Jamie Foxx, but also the other Raelettes, band members, studio engineers and producers. Her performance required a direct performed or embodied sexual connection with Foxx, but also a blending of body movement with the Raelettes.

King's physical position in the scene affected her performance since the action takes place in a set that resembles a recording studio. And finally, she had to do all this and make it believable. Her level of commitment to the singing part had to be high, and Sunshine talks about her struggle with singing the song since she was not a professional singer (Sunshine 2004, 22). King made very specific choices in the interpretation of the song as well as how she physically performed it during the filming moment with the other actors.

There are vocal markers and embodied markers that allowed her to perform the song with such commitment and make audiences believe in its authenticity. It is not possible to note the vocal markers without hearing her voice as she performed it; however, the following is a list of the embodied markers as she performed voice on the song, "Night Time is the Right Time." These are features that helped audiences to suspend their disbelief and fully accept her as the singer in the scene:
1. direct and focused eye contact with Ray;
2. upper body leaned forward slightly and gently reaching toward the microphone;
3. positioned directly between the other two, Raelettes (she faces forward as the Raelettes are turned toward her facing each other);
4. half smile;
5. neck muscles flexed;
6. face open and inviting;
7. hands to the side, lifting her dress slightly as she moves with the music.

As she gets to the solo in the song, the embodied markers intensify:
1. neck muscles are flexed harder and much more strained (as the sound of Hendricks' recorded voice suggests);
2. bigger and wider smile;
3. body leaned forward more;

4. eyebrows furrowed;

5. mouth wide open as she sings.

Additionally, as she solos, the Raelettes move slightly out of her space, but come back in during their parts as back-up. There are a variety of different types of shots—close ups, medium, wide shots, and an establishing shot of the engineers and studio space with the band. One shot gives a different perspective of her solo—which takes a camera angle slightly behind her and to the left in an over-the-shoulder shot. The sequence is intercut with two other scenes—one of Ray junior's birthday party and the other with people dancing to the music at the club.

The sounds of the actor's voices are not irrelevant to the finished product even though the editing process eliminates them, rendering them voiceless—they form part of the actors' frame of reference and point of departure. But the body movement, voice and language were critical to the success of the scene and ultimately the film. Audiences would not buy into their performances if the actors were not actually singing. The key seems to be that they were singing; engaging their bodies fully—the interpretation and the believability of the singing was fundamentally reliant on the embodying.

It is the small, seemingly insignificant and subtle movements of the singer/performer that make a performance stand out. Even the muscle movement in the face and neck as well as the intensity with which the song is performed will matter to the final edit. Michel Chion in *The Voice in Cinema* says the most striking and memorable moments are "those in which a strong link has been created between the voice and the body, the voice and face. It's in this relationship that something can emerge, and not in the voice taken in isolation" (Chion 1985, 171). King's voice gives intensity and life to the performance even though it is not heard in the final edit.

Through technology and the editing process, editors can cut together visual images to suggest that Margie, Mary Ann, and Ray are all really singing the songs heard in the film. As the story unfolds, the actors' performances prior to the lip-synching sequences contribute to the audience's suspension of disbelief. The actors are accepted in the roles and when they begin singing, the audience has already begun the buy-in. As they progress through the song, their ability to fully suspend disbelief is directly tied into the level of commitment of the actor to the character in the scene as they "perform voice." All the movements of the muscles of the neck, mouth, face, and body must communicate singing and performing; it is only in that way that the visual elements of the performance correlate and can link together with the music.

Conclusion

There is much connotative meaning communicated through the sound and use of the voice. Part of the schemata used in understanding movies comes from the signs and meaning ascribed to tones, inflection, and pitch in the voice. This is the production of voice. In the film *Ray*, some of these include conflict, jealousy, happiness, fear, and passion which can all be understood clearly. As actors utilize the paralinguistic features of speech to encode messages, audiences are able to decode that information along with the schema they have developed for watching film and understanding narrative.

However, when that opportunity to communicate through tones, pitch and inflection is removed from the actor's vocal instrument, it has to be replaced in some way by the embodiment of the intentions of that tone, pitch or inflection, as well as the very acting of voicing. Such is the case when the voice of the actor is replaced by the dubbed voice.

Blending the voice and body in performance seems like a natural act to actors, but trying to decipher exactly how actors do it is another question open for study. Nonetheless, it is clear from this analysis that the human voice and the body used effectively have the potential to carry the subtlest meaning in the most complicated of scenes and in the end, allow audiences to suspend their disbelief as well as to interpret accurately (and enjoy the performance all at the same time).

❧

Bibliography

Charles, Ray. (Night Time Is) The Right Time. On *Ray!: Original Motion Picture Soundtrack* [CD]. Rhino Records, 2004.

Chion, Michel. *Audio-Vision: Sound on Screen*, ed. and trans. Claudia Gorbman. New York: Columbia University Press, 1994.

Chion, Michel. *The Voice in Cinema*. New York: Columbia University Press, 1985.

Churcher, Mel. "Sound Speed; Voice on Film." In *Film Broadcast & e-Media Coaching and other contemporary issues in professional voice and speech training*, edited by Rocco Dal Vera, 50-53. Cincinnati: Voice and Speech Review, 2003.

Doane, Mary Ann. "The Voice in the Cinema: The Articulation of Body and Space." In *Film Sound: Theory and Practice Film*, edited by Elisabeth Weis and John Belton, 162-176. New York: Columbia University Press, 1985.

Hackford, Taylor (Director). *Ray Unchain My Heart* [Film]. Studio City, CA: Universal Pictures, 2004.

Kozloff, Sarah. *Overhearing film dialogue*. Berkeley: University of California Press, 2000.

Marcello, Starr. "Sound and Acting: Analyzing Vocal Performance in Film." Paper submitted for Film Acting Class (Professor Pamela Wojcik) at the University of Chicago, Chicago, IL, 2004.

Marshall, Lorna. *The Body Speaks: Performance and Expression*. New York: Palgrave Macmillan, 2002.

Sunshine, Linda, editor. *Ray: A Tribute to the Movie, the Music and the Man*. New York: Newmarket Press, 2004.

Breaching the Ultimate Cultural Divide—
Voice Work as the Key to Changing Gender

Since June 2004, I have been running workshops at the Central School of Speech and Drama exploring the speech and voice needs of female to male transgender people or, as they are commonly called, trans-men. Throughout this paper, I shall be referring to the participants as trans-men. A trans-man is someone who believes his gender not to be that of his biological body.[1] Many trans-men undertake a sex change operation with concomitant hormone therapy.

The voice workshops take place over the course of one year: autumn, spring and summer. Different strands of voice workshops are running concurrently, monthly and weekly strands, both for beginner and advanced participants (advanced participants are former participants returning). The monthly voice workshops consist of four workshops every term and the weekly voice work-shops consist of five workshops every term. Each voice workshop is two hours long. The two strands were set up in this manner in order to respond to the availability of the participants as well as to their divergent needs.[2]

In this world of ours, the ultimate cultural divide remaining is that between man and woman. It is still socially imperative to belong to either of the two traditional genders (Gooren 1996, Foreword). This means that a person who wishes to change gender sets him or herself the quantum task of changing from one side of the divide to the other. When undergoing gender reassignment a trans-man, the medical profession lavishes much of its attention on transforming his female exterior appearance, whilst neglecting what I believe to be the predominant medium that will carry his evolving persona, his voice.[3]

There are many misconceptions surrounding trans-man. A trans-man, or trans-woman for that matter, is someone whose gender identity is other than his or her biological one (Press for Change website). To be a trans-man is to be concerned foremost with gender identity, sexuality falling in line with that identity. For instance, the majority of trans-men are not gay. In fact, the majority of trans-men are heterosexual, having sexual relationships as men with women and living happily as fathers (Beaumont Society website). The United Kingdom's Transgender Recognition Act of 2004 protects the right of all transgender men and women to live under their chosen name pertaining to their changed gender without fear of exposure to their previous identity (Dept. for Constitutional Affairs website).

Gender Reassignment

Many trans-men seek to alter their physical appearance and certain clinics in Great Britain, such as the one at Charing Cross Hospital in London, offer gender reassignment services ranging from psychiatry to surgery (Antoni 2005, 4-5). A major part of any physical change is the administration of the male hormone testosterone. If females take testosterone, they experience many physical changes. Their bones will grow and they are likely to grow taller. They will develop muscle mass, grow beards and body hair, and can sometimes experience baldness. What impacted most upon my research is the fact that testosterone makes the larynx grow. (Whittle 1998, 1-6). The trans-man's female voice type (soprano, mezzo or alto) effectively changes into a male voice type (tenor, baritone or bass).

John Tucker, MA. John's voice work with actors and singers is at the forefront of contemporary trends in theatre, film, and television. John has taught at the Central School of Speech and Drama and Mountview Academy of Theatre Arts in London as well as the Hochschule der Künste in Berlin. At CSSD (2004-2007) John developed a voice program specifically addressing the voice needs of female-to-male transgender people. Recently, John coached 8 new plays for the "HighTide Festival" in Britain. Next, John will teach at BADA (British American Dramatic Academy) in London. John is the voice coach for "The Association of Women Solicitors" of London.

1. "Transsexuality is a complex and permanent transposition, the causes of which are not yet known" (Eicher 1992, 17-20).

2. The weekly workshops serve the needs of those trans-men living and working in London. The month-ly workshops were set up to serve the needs of those trans-men who travel to the association from as far away as Reading, Brighton, Manchester and Somerset.

3. "In addition to their outward appearance, via their main means of communication—the voice—which may be regarded as a secondary sexual characteris-tic, human beings are assigned to a particular sex by people around them. The fundamental frequency and timbre are the basic sex-specific characteristics of the voice" (Neumann & Welzel 2003, 154).

Testosterone causes the thyroid and cricoid cartilages to grow and the vocal folds to lengthen and thicken. This leads to a drop in the fundamental frequency of the voice.[4] This drop in pitch is similar to the "break" experienced by the adolescent boy during puberty. This change can last anywhere from six months to two years and is irreversible. Joseph, one of the participants in the first series, started taking testosterone two weeks before the start of the series. For the next six months, his voice seemed to be suffering from a permanent cold. He reported that his throat felt sluggish and groggy but, unlike a cold, it was not inflamed or sore (Questionnaire 01.08.05).

What now seems typical in my experience is that the doctor handling Joseph's gender reassignment offered little in the way of vocal support or therapy to follow up the effects testosterone had upon Joseph's larynx. Joseph wrote, "I haven't talked to doctors about transitioning much because they don't know much. I just knew from talking to other FTMs (female to male transgender people) that my voice would drop and that this would be irreversible." In fact, Joseph's gender reassignment doctor "talked about this as a side effect of taking t (testosterone), rather than something we would actually want to help us pass better!!" (Questionnaire 01.08.05). In conclusion, there is a misguided assumption in the medical profession today that the trans-man's male larynx will function after transition and that this new larynx will sound low like a biological man's larynx. As a result trans-men, unlike trans-women, are not offered referrals for voice therapy as part of their gender reassignment process.

From this, and other trans-men's comments, one can sense the tendency of the medical profession to assume that once a trans-man has developed his male larynx it will automatically function as such. I have found this not to be the case. Almost all the trans-men I have encountered over the past four years are vocally dysphonic, in many cases chronic. There is generally a poor use of breathing, support and vocal engagement resulting from a lack of physical alignment and physical co-ordination. Participant Jay astutely described the quality of trans-man's voices as having "a sort of helium sound" (Questionnaire 02.08.05).

Teaching trans-men to engage in lower fundamental frequencies is central to the pedagogical remit of the whole voice workshop series. Gelfer & Mikos write in a study of gender identification: "The most obvious difference between male and female voices is fundamental frequency or pitch." They conclude that "gender identifications were based on fundamental frequency"[5] (2005, 544-554).

No trans-man has come onto the programme at Central able to engage effectively or healthily the lower fundamental frequencies that his new male larynx can produce. The male larynx is a larger physical structure than the female larynx and, as such, I believe requires a subtle but profoundly different physical and acoustic engagement to the female larynx. How can the trans-man be expected to achieve this engagement effectively when he has never experienced the male larynx functioning or the acoustic properties it produces? To make matters worst, most trans-men have never, in their lives, experienced healthy voice use. Generally, all trans-men say they have "hated" their female voices since childhood and have spent their whole life abusing their

4. "The average speaking fundamental frequency for men generally falls between 100 and 146 Hz, whereas the average speaking fundamental frequency for women is usually between 188 and 221 Hz. These pitch levels help a listener correctly identify the speaker's gender" (Gelfer & Mikos 2005, 544-554).

5. "Three factors are responsible for controlling the fundamental frequency of the voice: the tension, the mass, and the lengthening of the vocal folds" (Neumann and Welzel 2004, 161).

voice trying to make it sound male: "My voice sucks," Mike Street (DVD 12.10.05); "[O]n the phone my voice lets me down," Carl Mogg (DVD 12.10.05); and "[My voice] often does not work," Lucas McKenna (DVD 12.10.05).

The older participants in the programme are confronting years of physical and emotional tensions, which inhibit and confuse their physical and vocal engagement. In contrast, younger participants have a general ease about their physical and vocal engagement. I attribute this ease to today's more relaxed and accepting attitude towards gender diversity.

Without exception, all the trans-men in the programme at Central have said that it is the voice which they fear will most expose their former female identity. Participant David wrote: "I've always felt that my voice has let me down. Before taking male hormones, I would usually pass as male in the world, in general, until I spoke—it gave me away. Therefore I've always restricted my vocality and not valued it" (Questionnaire 02.08.05). The social implications of such inadequate voice use are easy to imagine. What often follows is an increasing sense of social isolation. To many trans-men, speaking in public situations is something of a trauma. They find it difficult to speak in noisy environments, such as pubs and restaurants. Trans-men are particularly concerned about speaking on the telephone.

The Workshops

Series Overview
• The first series in the autumn term introduces physical alignment and basic techniques developing a use of breath and voice.
• The second series in the spring term starts to connect the participant to a more dynamic voice use of the breath and the voice whilst exploring support.
• The third series in the summer term explore speech structures and speech elements.

My first impression of the trans-men in the workshops was they were trying to make their voices sound "low" without any awareness of vocal function or form. The first thing I did was to develop a series of physical vocal exercises that would inject the participants' vocal efforts with an appropriate sense of "male" physicality. These physical voice exercises are similar to those devised by Cicely Berry, Patsy Rodenburg, Barbara Houseman and Kristin Linklater for training the voices of actors. Most of the exercises combine voice with physical actions such as running, walking, lying, jogging, jumping, sitting, tugging, tussling, mutual massaging and even rolling on the floor. As one participant, Joseph, put it—these physical

voice exercises take the participants "past edges that I would not (otherwise) have passed" (Questionnaire 01.08.05).

Cicely Berry has shown that when an actor is working with physical movement to connect his voice to the word, he will experience both physical and emotional responses on the level of the subconscious. When Berry gave the actors "very simple tasks to do while they were speaking…they would get in touch with their own subconscious response to the text" (Berry 2001, 38). Such subconscious responses allow the participant to discover new ways of engaging with his voice and body. If the participant keeps repeating these new physical responses, he will eventually be able to call upon them at will. This means that the new physical responses have become learnt, memorized. In effect, they turn into new "habitual" responses, in other words, the basis for a new vocal technique.

Loudness, Pace, Engagement
With the focus on engaging lower fundamental frequencies, I worked on the premise that the trans-man's habitual response to engaging and controlling his male larynx falls back onto his engagement of his former female larynx. In order to develop an approach that would engage the new male larynx and the lower fundamental frequencies it produces, I focused on what I believe to be three key aspects of male speech: *loudness*, *pace* and *engagement*. Engagement means to engage the body with a strong sense of "male" physicality, that can support pace and loudness. Pace means to give the appropriate amount of time and physical space for the lower fundamental frequencies to resonate in the larynx (the rate of speech is slower in men than in women). Loudness means to speak in a loud, but dropping off, dynamic quality, which is typical of men's voice production and which is supported by pace and engagement.

Voice Types
One of the most common misconceptions amongst trans-men is that they believe they can make their voices sound masculine simply by speaking "low" and without acquiring a more differentiated understanding of vocal function. Vincent wrote, "I didn't understand how to get my voice to sound consistent, or how to achieve a depth that I felt would be masculine" (Questionnaire 5.12.05).

I believe this can be overcome by making use of the system of voice types usually used in training the voices of classical singers: tenor, baritone and bass. It is my teaching of the spoken voice according to voice types that enables trans-men to understand that the male voice has different qualities. It also clarifies the fact that acoustically, not all male voice types function in the same manner. Once Fraser, who is a tenor, started to notice the quality of his resonance was not like David's, who is a bass-baritone, Fraser was able to accept that the quality of his voice was no less masculine than David's— just because it seemed to him to be higher. Only by intellectually and emotionally accepting this fact could he allow his voice to function healthily.

Conversely, David had previously felt uncomfortable with his low voice. He wrote: "finding out that my natural speaking voice was much deeper than I thought…was quite crucial. I held back from speaking this low before because I thought it would sound like I was 'putting it on.' It was just another restriction I was placing on myself" (Questionnaire 02.08.05). Jay's baritone voice was the most difficult to settle. When it did settle he wrote, "For me the most critical moment was when I heard my own voice take on real power and resonance in the space" (Questionnaire 02.08.05). Over time, it was agreed that all male voice types were as valid and expressive as each other.

This fine-tuning of each individual's search for his specific voice type was done entirely by using the speaking voice. At no time did any of the participants sing. The reason it worked is that I used voice type categorisation not to restrict each individual within a certain category, but to help him overcome his fixation with simply sounding like a man. This part of the training moved away from the stereotypical duality of man versus woman to simply finding the voice that is right for each individual. At no point did I see the necessity to make use of what I view to be stereotypical gender "speech elements," which is common practise when working with trans-women (Speech Language, Therapy Programme, U of Michigan website). I came to realize I was already dealing with male voices in male bodies and was simply searching for a way of connecting the two.

Being Loud
Loudness is an aspect of the male speaking pattern that I teach as part of the sessions and recommend as a teaching practice. Trans-men find it difficult to project their voices in noisy environments. This may be in part a habitual response to their old female voice type. In a study of men and women speaking against noise, it was concluded that "[s]ubjectively, women reported less success making themselves heard and higher effort. The results support the contention that female voices are more vulnerable to vocal loading in background noise" (Södersten, Ternström & Bohman 200, 29-46).

Loudness is a dynamic of speaking that is often condemned as impolite or socially unacceptable. It can also express loss of control or composure. Making loud noises is important when exploring and developing resonance and projection and releasing physical or emotional inhibitions. The workshop

participants have commented that the opportunities to speak loudly in every day life are few and far between. It is often difficult to be loud in one's own home. We worry about what the neighbours or those who share our accommodation might think. In this light, the opportunity for the participants to be loud with their voices in the workshops cannot be overestimated.

Role Play
One of my greatest concerns in devising the workshops was that the trans-men would not respond to the applied theatre techniques. After all, they were not actors but members of the public. Jay wrote: "Why is it so embarrassing to shake all your limbs violently in order to loosen up? Why is it so embarrassing to talk but not pronounce any consonants?" (Questionnaire 02.08.05). I found that it was the support they derived from working within a "group" environment that carried any such awkward moments.

I devised a physical voice exercise that involved male role-play. We staged a few of Romeo's lines from act three of Shakespeare's *Romeo and Juliet* commencing with "Eyes, look your last!" Romeo had to deliver these lines whilst engaging his whole physical being in the act of lifting the supposedly dead Juliet from the floor into his arms. As a preparatory step, we had vocally explored the masculine quality of Shakespeare's Iambic Pentameter.

The Pentameter with its strong rhythmic alternation of unstressed and stressed syllables reflects the vocal dynamic of male speech soft/loud, soft/loud. Male speech has a general tendency to exist in short term bursts of energy to support this dynamic, which gives space for the lower fundamental frequency to exist. Female speech tends towards a more even dynamic delivery supporting a higher frequency. (Denes & Pinson 2001, 175-177).

How do you support this sudden burst of energy that dies away? I did so by aligning three key elements of the male speaking pattern: loudness, pace and engagement. Loudness and its distribution we have just dealt with. Its facilitator is pace. A man speaks slower than a woman because his frequent bursts of energy, delivered in short term soft/loud, soft/loud patterns, need to allow for sufficient time for the lower frequencies to resonate. This is where the participant has to enter into the right physical engagement, which is to engage his body with an appropriate sense of male physicality, put in vocal terminology—an appropriate sense of support.

The response of the participants to our staging of a scene from *Romeo and Juliet* along with the preparatory exercises brought some interesting insights: Joseph said, "I feel more 'Joe' when I am being physical" (Questionnaire 01.08.05). David wrote, "It somehow brought me more together. I understood on a physical level (rather than just a mental one) how parts of the body and the functions it performs are related to each other" (Questionnaire 02.08.05). Jay's response was, "It...makes you wish for a freedom, an unrestrainedness. When you start moving towards this unrestrainedness is the moment when you can start changing your voice" (Questionnaire 02.08.05).

FTM Voice Research

It has been a surprise to me is that there has been little research conducted on the voice issues of female-to-male (trans-men) transsexuals. The voice issues of male-to-female (trans-women) transsexuals are extremely well served. In one such study of trans-women, Neumann and Welzel claim that voice reassignment strengthens the "sexual identity, the way they relate to their bodies, their self-esteem, and consequently, improves their general well-being" (2004, 154). Neumann and Welzel argue that "for male-to-female transsexuals, the function of the voice remains the main obstacle to their finding a new sexual identity as, in contrast to female to male transsexuals, hormone therapy does not make a significant difference to, or have a lasting effect on, the pitch of the voice."

This statement implies that for trans-men hormone therapy removes voice function as an obstacle to finding a new sexual identity. My findings do not bear this out. They show that gender-specific voice training should be as much part of voice reassignment for trans-men as it is for trans-women. Hormone treatment is the first step and must be part of an integrated long-term retraining program if it is to strengthen, in trans-men, the "sexual identity, the way they relate to their bodies, their self-esteem, and consequently, improve[s] their general well-being."

My findings also run counter to the theory that hormone therapy provides the trans-man with a functioning male larynx. Unless the trans-man receives vocal support as part of his voice reassignment, he cannot make sense of the new physical structure in his throat. For instance, in moments of stress, habitual female sounds and muscle reactions reoccur in a trans-man's voice use. Lucas spoke in class of losing the lower tones in his bass baritone voice when he is "talking to my mum" (DVD 11.01.06). Andrew said in class that his voice still rises and constricts when he is talking on the telephone (DVD 11.01.06). The anticipation of being mistaken for a female is so great that his voice responds habitually and his vocal tract constricts.

In discussing her work with transsexuals at Charing Cross Hospital, London, speech therapist Christella Antoni writes:

> In female to male transsexuals, testosterone hormones...[lead] to a thickening of their vocal folds and a corresponding shift in fundamental frequency resulting in a lower pitched voice. In male to female transsexuals however, the oestrogen treatment they are given...has no effect on the structure of the vocal cords and therefore no vocal changes occur in the client. The bulk of our work with this client group therefore is with Male to Female transsexuals who wish to feminise their voice and communication (2005, 4).

Again we find the view that trans-women need speech therapy more than trans-men. To state that since oestrogen treatment does not change the vocal cords in the way that testostorone treatment does is in my experience misleading. Such a statement will restrict what voice care trans-men can expect or receive. Trans-men are left unaided and unsupported in their physical vocal adjustment after testosterone treatment. Doctors are unaware of the fact that the trans-man's larynx does not simply slot into its proper use after the changes brought about by testosterone treatment but requires voice care after vocal reassignment just as a trans-woman does. Let me reiterate, the most common statement I have heard from trans-men during the programme at Central is Andrew's "the one thing that lets me down is my voice" (DVD 12.10.05).[6]

6. "Unless suitable measures are taken, the transsexual…will encounter numerous problems in an attempt to become fully integrated into society. This will lead, in turn, to serious internal mental conflict, which often results in long periods of psychotherapy" (Neumann and Welzel 2004, 154).

I have never told the trans-men how to behave like men—unlike speech therapists working with trans-women, who traditionally engage with "secondary [speech] factors" such as hand gestures or the use of grammar. The transwoman has to mimic female vocal qualities whereas the trans-man has the potential to produce organic male vocal sounds. Trans-men do not have to "mimic" or learn gender specific behavioural rules of communication to sound or appear male. If a trans-man's voice lets him down, it is a technical not a behavioural shortcoming. All this boils down to the fact that trans-men are men with male larynxes, each learning to exploit the full sound potential of his new, individual and unique voice.

Conclusion

Voice work is never just about the voice alone, in dealing with the voice one is dealing with the person as a whole (Rodenburg 200, 36-86). Our workshops did just that by offering a space where those taking part felt they were being socially accepted. For Joseph, this was crucial. For the first time he was "being accepted as Joe and having people call me that all the time, especially before I had legally changed my name. Getting the feeling that people liked me OK as a man" (Questionnaire 01.08.05).

There are, however, other issues to be faced and questions to be answered. Jay wrote that the workshop space "was a sort of sanctuary, a special place outside of the world that I occupy. The most difficult thing about all of this is that sort of jolting back to reality" (Questionnaire 02.08.05). One of the tasks I face over the next year is to find ways of bridging the cultural divide between the workshop sanctuary and the world without. To that effect, I have arranged for past participants to be able to "pop in" at any of the new workshop series.

Today, making use of conventional voice types as a teaching tool in the training of speech and voice is out of fashion. To me, the fact that within one year every single course participant could recognise not only his own spoken voice type, but also the spoken voice types of his colleagues, indicates that the convention of voice categorization can still serve a very significant purpose. It helps release, not restrict, individual vocal identity and realise individual vocal potential. I am convinced that my work with trans-men could be applied on a much wider scale in Drama Colleges. It could help young actors and actresses, whether or not they wish to change their gender, find the whole depth of a truthful, flexible vocal identity. I leave you with one further comment from

Jay. It encapsulates for me the raison d'être of the whole project: "I pass all the time on the telephone now when I didn't before, so much as a year ago" (Questionnaire 02.08.05).

Bibliography

Berry, C., *Text in Action*, London: Virgin Books, 2001.

Denes, P., B., and Pinson, E., N., *The Speech Chain*, New York: W.H. Freeman, 1993.

DVD: Every voice workshop was recorded on DVD

Professor Gooren, L. J., "Foreword." in Rees, M., *Dear Sir or Madam :The Autobiography of a Female-to-Male Transsexual* (Sexual Politics), London: Cassell, 1996.

Houseman, B., *Finding your Voice*. London: Nick Hern Books, 2002.

Linklater, K., *Freeing the Natural Voice*. New York: Drama Book Publishers, 1976.

Questionnaires: There were questionnaires handed out at the end of every term

Rodenburg, P., *The Need for Words*, Methuen Drama, London, 2001.

Whittle, S., *The White Book*, Press for Change for the FTM Network, 1998.

Web Bibliography

The Beaumont Society, *www.beaumontsociety.org.uk/page4.html*

Press for Change, *www.pfc.org.uk/campaign/pfcissue.htm#wherediscrim*

The Speech, Language and Therapy Programme, University of Michigan, *www.med.umich.edu/transgender/speech.htm*

Department for Constitutional Affairs, *www.dca.gov.uk/constitution/ transsex/legs.htm/*, October 2005.

Journals, Publications And Newsletters

Antoni, C., "Working with Transsexuals." *The Newsletter*, The British Voice Association, Vol. 5, Issue 3, April, 2005.

Eicher, W., ed. *Transsexualismus: moeglichenkeiten und grenzen der geschlechtsamwandlung*. Stuttgart: Fischer 1992.

Gelfer, M. P., Mikos, V.A., "The Relative Contributions of Speaking Fundamental Frequency and Formant Frequencies to Gender Identification Based on Isolated Vowels." *Journal of Voice*, Vol. 19, No. 4, 2005.

Neumann, K., and Welzel, C., "The Importance of Voice in Male-to-Female Transsexualism." *Journal of Voice*, Vol. 18, No.1, 2004.

Södersten, M., & Ternström, S., & Mikael Bohman, "Loud Speech in Realistic Environmental Noise: Phonetogram Data, Perceptual Voice Quality, Subjective Ratings, and Gender Differences in Healthy Speakers." *Journal of Voice*, Vol. 19, No. 1, 2005.

Essay *by Douglas MacArthur*

Transgender Voice: An Unexpected Journey

Doug MacArthur is a voice, speech and acting teacher in the Department of Theatre and Dramatic Arts at the University of Lethbridge in Lethbridge, Alberta, Canada. He graduated from York University (Toronto) with an MFA in Acting along with a Voice Teaching Diploma. During the spring of 2000 and 2001 he worked as an associate faculty member at Canada's National Voice Intensive. Doug has participated in numerous stage productions as a voice coach and as an actor. Recently, he has been applying his specialty in voice and acting to transgender voice training. Doug has also dedicated a significant amount of time to collecting dialect resource material for student and professional actors.

As voice teachers, we help students, actors and clients in all facets of life to fulfill their potential and desire as speakers and communicators in a variety of venues and for a wide variety of impelling reasons. We are sometimes confronted with clients that push the boundaries of our experience and invite us to work outside the traditional routine of theatre-style voice training. As a result, we are often given the extraordinary opportunity to witness the power of the human spirit as these clients struggle to reveal and release a voice within them that is unrestrained by circumstance, ideology, psychology or physical limitation. A voice they can call their own.

The following paper is a description of my experience training someone who faced and faces layers of difficulties not usually encountered in routine theatre-style voice work: a Male-to-Female (MtF) transsexual. Attention will be directed to issues surrounding voice feminization for the MtF transsexual by documenting my experiences training one MtF transsexual's voice. Throughout the paper references will be made to literature, as well as voice and performance techniques that influenced the direction of the voice training. Challenges arising from this experience are presented and discussed. Finally, the importance of the theatre voice trainer in clinical models of transgender voice therapy is suggested. Also, a call is made for theatre voice trainers to share their experience, expertise and research in transgender voice training with other voice trainers and clinicians.

An Unexpected Client

The journey I am about to relay to you took me by surprise. I did not leave graduate school intending to declare transgender voice training as an area of research for myself, nor did I expect to be presented with such a research opportunity in the heart of rural Canada. However, as it has already been pointed out, voice trainers have the fortunate opportunity to work with a wide variety of people, in and outside the performing arts.

In the fall of 2001 I was contacted by one of my voice students in an anonymous email message. In this email the student indicated they had a special voice issue they needed help with, but didn't know how to proceed or where to go for help. It was obvious from the anonymity of the message the stakes were high for this student. After a reassuring reply on my part the student revealed in a second email that he was an MtF transsexual in the very earliest stages of transition and that he needed help feminizing his voice.

After a significant number of email exchanges and my assurance that anonymity would be respected, the student revealed to me his identity. For the purposes of this paper we will refer to the student as John. We scheduled a preliminary meeting where we would discuss his situation in more depth as well as my role as a voice trainer. John presented himself in this meeting, as he had done in his email, as a man. The psychological dynamics a transsexual must work through are complex and demanding. However, John made no verbal or non-verbal presentations that caused me to question the authenticity of his gender identity dysphoria or led me to believe that he was not sufficiently prepared to participate in voice training. This was further supported with the revelation that he was receiving medical support from a psychiatrist and a family physician in Calgary, and that his family, although troubled by his gender issues, were generally supportive of his move towards transition. As part of my own disclosure, I drew attention to the fact that I was a voice trainer and not a Speech and Language Pathologist (SLP). Also, that this was new territory for me as a voice trainer and there would come a point in the training process where I would become as much an investigator as a trainer. This was satisfactory to John and the training plans proceeded.

Initial Response and Important Preliminary Information

My initial response of course was to acquire preliminary information on transgendered persons, and in particular on an MtF transsexual. I quickly found that I had many questions regarding voice training for clients seeking to permanently feminize their voices. Where does the voice teacher begin? Can the process begin with the natural voice? What then is the natural voice? What role can the theatre voice trainer play in the complicated puzzle of creating the female identity?

While accumulating information I gathered a heightened appreciation of the importance of voice to the transgendered person. The transgendered person, and more specifically the MtF transsexual, must negotiate her way through complicated stages of transition in order to become the gender, and finally the person, she knows herself to be. One of those transition processes, or stages, is the development of a feminine voice. The voice is like a fingerprint in many ways. It is almost an "infallible form of identification" (Rodenburg 1992). There are endless numbers of testimonies from MtF transsexuals who feel their voice betrays them. Lynn Gold highlights one such testimony in a VASTA newsletter. "I feel I am a woman, but if I can only speak with a man's voice my whole identity is shattered" (Gold 1999, 10). In the stark reality of this statement we see how key the voice is in the MtF transsexual's gender identity journey. A transsexual is then highly motivated. Voice is often the final piece of the equation.

It is important to note that both John and I were living in a community quite some distance from a large urban centre, where support groups and helpful resources might normally be readily available to either a member of the transgender community or a professional voice specialist. In many ways we were both isolated.

On an initial assessment of John's voice and body, I found him to be soft-spoken and somewhat withdrawn. He had a minimal investment in sound production, frequently devoicing. He was quite tall, but did not extend his spine to its full length and he collapsed in the sternum. As a result, he thrust his jaw forward and diminished the length of the back of his neck. His breath support was weakened and his vocal instrument had very little openness or freedom to it. Naturally, his inner

dilemma was evident in his body and voice. Up until recently, John always presented himself as male in all voice training sessions. In fact, he presented as a man in all public situations that I was aware of. He very rarely presented as a woman, other than in the privacy of his own residence. He made no request that I call him by his female name and for that reason I will continue to use his masculine identifier and the masculine pronoun as I describe these first stages of our professional relationship.

My email discussions and initial meeting with John revealed to me how very little I knew about the transsexual and transgender situation. One of my first tasks was to become much more familiar with the proper terminology, beginning with the terms transsexual and transgender.

It would be useful to define these terms at this juncture. A transsexual (TS) can be described as a person who has a deep long standing and irresistible longing to become a member of the opposite sex (Bailey 2003). The MtF transsexual is an individual who is biologically male but identifies himself as a female, and may or may not seek sexual reassignment surgery (SRS). The MtF transsexual often has a profound sense of dysphoria. The term transgender (TG) is an umbrella term used to refer to those with various forms and degrees of cross gender practices including the transsexual (Meyerowitz 2002). John very rarely referred to himself using either term. He hoped that one day he would be a full and complete woman and that the prefix "trans" wasn't really necessary.

As I continued to seek a basic understanding of the TG/TS situation and sub-culture, I became cognizant of the fact that the TG/TS individual walks a complicated path on their quest for wholeness, a path that is confounded with a complex array of physical, psychological and psychosocial influences and obstacles. Discrimination, employment trouble, family issues, religious issues, medical complications, legal and civil issues are just a few of these (Adler, Hirsch and Mordaunt 2006). Aware that core voice work has its own psychodynamic to it, I knew that it was important I proceed with sensitivity and caution. With an undergraduate degree in psychology and 11 years experience working in that field, I felt I had sufficient understanding to recognize the need to refer to other professionals should the work surpass my area of expertise. I am glad to report that this was never required.

Beginning with the Natural Voice

Patsy Rodenburg (1992) begins her book *The Right to Speak* with the short but powerful statement, "Voice work is for everybody." Rodenburg, like many other voice teachers is concerned with training the speaking voice, with a specific interest in training actors. But as she clearly states in the opening sentence of her book, voice training is for everybody, not just actors. Rodenburg does not invite her readers to sound like Maggie Smith or James Earl Jones. In fact, she cautions her readers not to attempt to recreate the beautiful voice of someone else, but instead, to realize that, "every human voice has thrilling potential waiting to be discovered and unleashed. And [she does] mean *every* human voice" (Rodenburg 1992, 14).The process that voice teachers like Rodenburg invite students to embark on is one designed to uncover the natural sound of the individual human speaker. The natural sound, or what is often referred to as the natural voice, is the unrestricted and supported sound that is unique to every individual. It represents the vocal equipment each of us is born with and the potential we have to respond fully in a vocal manner to any given need for self-expression.

This concept of uncovering the natural voice of the speaker is a shared ideal for many preeminent voice teachers. Kristin Linklater, whose work I am most familiar with and practice myself, is one such teacher. Her landmark voice training text is simply titled *Freeing the Natural Voice*. Linklater makes a basic assumption that everyone possesses a voice capable of expressing a multitude of complex emotions and thoughts through a vocal range of two to four octaves but a combination of physical and psychological "tensions" impede the natural voice from its most expressive and unadulterated form (Linklater 1976). At first impression, a two to four octave range would be quite sufficient to handle higher feminine sounds.

Like Rodenburg, Linklater starts with the human vocal instrument and through her pedagogy helps the client reach a level of voice capacity, the natural voice, that already exists and then helps the client adapt to their vocal needs, actor or not. Voice training begins with the discovery and the development of the natural voice—"your own God-given voice" as Rodenburg (1992, 16) so aptly puts it.

My experiences and training as a voice trainer led me to believe that it was vital we begin John's training with the development and release of his natural voice. This of course raised the question what was John's natural voice? If the natural voice is what Rodenburg calls "our God given voice" how would that definition be described by, or to, a transsexual or transgendered person? Linklater (1976) suggests that freeing the voice results in freeing the person, and that each person is indivisibly mind and body. Would the investigation of the natural voice lead to or away from my client's desired sound? The decision to begin with traditional voice work would not have caused me concern if it were one of my male voice students seeking to prepare to play a female character in a play, but in the case of my client, I knew this suggested course of action

157

could be unsettling. Exploring the natural voice for this client meant he would have to reveal his maleness because the natural voice for him will fall somewhere in the male spectrum. This was incongruent with his gender destination as a female.

Despite the troublesome questions related to the natural voice and gender identity, it was vital that John develop awareness and proficiency of his vocal instrument, as well as develop healthy voice practices, especially if he was going to attain his desired voice target and maintain that voice on an ongoing basis. I presented this concept to John and he objectively responded with, "I hate the sound of my voice, but I know that I am going to have to put up with this voice for a while until I find my female voice, so it's okay." This was a most difficult response for John but an encouraging response for our training program.

Over the course of the next six months I led John through a voice training sequence based predominantly on the work of Kristin Linklater and David Smukler. Key elements of this sequence included physical awareness, breath awareness, breath support, connecting breath and impulse with sound, freeing the channel for sound, developing mid, facial and head resonance and an exploration with vocal range. Throughout all our investigations unnecessary physical tensions impeding the voice were identified and, where possible, released through a variety of physical /sound related exercises. The material we covered in our coaching sessions was much like the curriculum of an introductory voice course in an undergraduate acting program. We met for an hour and a half once every two weeks, on the average.

The Training Proceeds
During these first six months of work the client revealed some very deep, rich sounds that in any other situations would have been immediately celebrated. Since the client was biologically male, but his identity was female, there would be no celebration. It was just hard work for him to get where he needed to be. Gender became more than a word. I witnessed the angst.

The revelation of this new sound experience was a key indicator that John was investing himself in the full potential and use of his natural voice. From a trainer's point of view this observation meant that a proper vocal foundation was being laid. Future voice work could continue towards the feminine sound explorations. Up to this time I have been unable to find any study where the male vocal instrument was well developed as a planned precursor to the voice training for female gender identity to follow. Most studies I found focused on pitch and its importance in being perceived as female (Spencer 1988; Wolfe et al. 1990; Pausewang-Gelfer and Schofield 2000).

It would be helpful to know the success rate approaching gender voice training by first developing the full range of the client's vocal instrument (i.e. natural voice) in MtF clients as opposed to moving directly to frequency alteration.

After laying down the fundamental building blocks of vocal technique the next step in our investigation was to look towards creating a feminine sound. What then are the characteristics of the feminine sound? The first and most apparent characteristic is pitch or frequency. Much of the research I found on voice feminization focused on frequency and its relationship to being perceived as feminine. Intuitively I knew there was much more to creating a feminine sound than just pitch and subsequent readings supported this (Gold 1999; Dacakis 2000; de Bruin, Coerts and Greven, 2000; Van Borsel, De Cuypere and Van den Berghe 2001) but increasing John's pitch seemed to fit well with the natural progression of our work to date.

The fundamental pitch of a woman is most often perceived as higher than a man's. These pitch values are usually represented in measures of frequency. This fundamental pitch is referred to as the speaking fundamental frequency (sf_0), which generally means the habitual speaking frequency of an individual (Adler, Hirsch and Mordaunt 2006). Frequency ranges in males and females are about two octaves (65 Hz to 262 Hz for males and 128 Hz to 523 Hz for females) (Gold 1999). This indicates an overlap of about one octave. Spencer (1988) and Wolfe et al (1990) indicate that a speaking fundamental frequency of 156-160Hz is the dividing line between male and female voices. An MtF transgendered person must reach this dividing line or beyond to be perceived as a female (Spencer 1988). Michelle Mordaunt refers to this interval as an area of gender-ambiguous pitch, but after a literature review she expands this interval to include fundamental frequencies as high as 185Hz. She cautions clinicians to set realistic goals in regards to pitch modification stating that a "natural sounding voice" will be more suitable than a high voice (Adler, Hirsch and Mordaunt 2006).

With an overlap of frequency values of about an octave between male and female voices, and a reasonably low dividing line, raising John's fundamental frequency seemed attainable. In voice training terms this meant expanding the accessible range of the client's voice, establishing a target speaking fundamental frequency, sustaining that target frequency in a healthy manner and finally introducing the articulation of vowel sounds, words and phrases within and around the target frequency. It was this course of action I took with John.

A Challenge for Both of Us

During our early explorations of head resonance, placement and pitch I thought John might be ready to explore words and/or phrases on some higher frequencies. We had just been creating some falsetto sounds on the vowel /i/ with good success so I introduced the idea of speaking in a falsetto by doing so myself with a short nonsense phrase. I knew this was not a voice we were striving to find. This was just an exploration with sound. As I began to create the falsetto sound myself he suddenly got self-conscious and mumbled out "I don't think we need to go there right now. I am not sure if I want to do that at this stage." He exhibited no particular angst about his decision to "not go there" right away. I determined to go ahead slowly and carefully without pressure. I expected and hoped the client would move to where he really desired to be as soon as he was ready.

By now I had some deepening insight into the difficult journey to "truth" in voice that the trangendered client must travel. There were many psychosocial considerations. For the most part he was alone in this journey to becoming a whole woman. Furthermore he was about to give voice to his deepest joy and perhaps his greatest fear.

This whole situation caused me to pause in the process. I began to have doubts about my place in all of this. Did we move too fast too soon? Was I prepared for these next steps in our journey? I wondered what I had to offer as a man to the process or at what point my effectiveness as a voice teacher might be limited by my male experience. On the other hand, if an individual came to me and asked for my help acquiring an Irish dialect I wouldn't hesitate on the basis that I wasn't Irish. Voice coaches are often asked to assist actors in the creation of character voices that are unfamiliar and push the boundaries of the human voice. However, John was not an actor in a play. I think that is what was most troubling for me. I realized this was real life for John and the stakes were high. Even still, I recognized that I had skills that were useful to his journey. John had invited me on this journey and I accepted the offer. I had a deep desire to assist him. It was important that I continue with him and support him as long as I could. Admittedly, a whole new experience of voice training had opened up to me, an experience that was causing me to reevaluate my perception of the natural voice and its relationship to gender. At this point I didn't feel like I had stepped outside the boundaries of my training or profession. My conclusion was that it was vital I carry on.

I later consulted with Sandy Hirsch, a Speech/Language Pathologist, voice clinician and co-author of the recently published text *Voice and Communication Therapy for the Transgender/Trannssexual Client: A Comprehensive Clinical Guide* (Plural Publishing 2006) about this event. She reminded me that John, although perceiving himself identifying as a woman, has been experiencing life heretofore as a man. Even though there may be nothing more pressing for him than moving along in the transition, leaving his male experience behind can still be difficult and produce, among other manifestations, hesitancy.

We took a break from the regular training during the summer and met again several times over the course of the next school year. John had a heavy workload at school and was trying to work on the side to pay his rent. We met only once a month on average, sometimes more frequently and sometimes less. As a result, we spent a lot of time revisiting the basic vocal work we had begun in the first six months of coaching. John began to make minor cosmetic changes to his appearance such as removing facial hair permanently from his face and chest through the process of electrolysis, nothing that affected his voice or the production of sound. It was during this time we began to work again on raising his fundamental pitch. There was no reservation on either of our parts as we revisited this work. Perhaps we were both more prepared for embarking on the next stage of our journey.

Internet Resources
About the time John and I resumed work on raising his fundamental frequency he indicated that he had discovered what seemed to be a reputable voice training program for MtF transsexuals. This was an Internet resource available in a video or DVD format. I had already begun collecting numerous resources as part of my investigations, so it seemed prudent of me to familiarize myself with as many voice training methods for transsexuals as possible, clinical or otherwise. However, I remained cautious given the source of the material, the Internet. John, whose lifeline in many ways was the Internet, was more optimistic about the program and anxious to see what it offered. Arrangements were made to purchase a copy of the DVD and additional materials.

John was first to receive the material, an instructional booklet, DVD and audio CD titled *Finding Your Female Voice*, produced by Deep Stealth Productions, Inc. He gave me the instructional booklet and audio CD to review while he kept the DVD. By this point John had already read through the booklet and watched the DVD several times. After reading through the booklet and listening to the audio CD I remained cautious but curious about some of the concepts and approaches presented in the material. I knew John was already exploring these concepts and approaches in his own practice so I decided we should investigate them together in our voice sessions.

Some of the introductory material was informative giving the user practical information about vocal anatomy and hygiene as

well as a very cursory description of a vocal warm up. Time and commitment to vocal exercises were also discussed and highlighted.

Attempting to walk through the material as if we were beginners, investing ourselves as objectively as possible in each new exercise, was challenging to say the least. I guess what concerned me the most was the emphasis in the exercises on moving from a pinched sound to a breathy sound as a way of discovering proper placement and resonance for a feminine voice. An endless number of exercises involving constricting pharyngeal and laryngeal muscles to create a "pinched voice" and then moderately releasing that tension into a breathy sound were outlined. The instructor on the DVD, Andrea James, pointed out that the optimal feminine sound lay between the pinched sound and the breathy sound. After spending two or three sessions exploring these exercises I suggested we discontinue the use of the material. I was very concerned that prolonged participation in these exercises would lead to the use of unnecessary laryngeal tension during speech. John's voice would soon be pushing the boundaries of his range. In order to maintain his vocal health over a long period of time (a lifetime) his larynx needed to be free of as much tension as possible during feminine speech. I could understand where the instructor was headed in regards to resonance and tone, but I was aware of other vocal exercises that could be used to reach the same results with less risk to the voice. My concerns were confirmed as I shared them with a Speech and Language Pathologist.

There are several voice training systems available online designed to assist the transgender community with vocal transition. These systems are disseminated by well meaning people seeking to serve a community that receives only minimal support at the best of times. For many transgender persons these voice training systems represent their only resource to make the necessary changes to their voices. However, it is important to recognize that individuals that have been successful with their own vocal transition, but don't necessarily have the credentials or training required to be trainers or clinicians, design many of these programs. Anyone using these programs should be encouraged to follow up with a professional voice clinician or voice trainer.

Back on Track
After a short side-track with the Internet we returned to the work we had resumed earlier. Exploring pitch could not take place effectively without exploring resonance and placement. Prior to this type of investigation with John, I had spent three days with Richard Armstrong at the International Voice Intensive at the Banff Centre, Canada. Two key focal points of

our three-day intensive were range and resonance. Armstrong led us through an array of vocal explorations that seemed to extend the possibilities for range in the human voice. His work is often referred to as "extended voice," but in Armstrong's opinion, "a multi-octave expression is in fact the normal healthy range of the human being" (Armstrong 2004, under "the voice is the muscle of the soul"). Armstrong demonstrated this with all the participants of the workshop. In each exploration we discovered the potential to experience and create pitch in a variety of resonating regions in the body: head, neck and upper chest, rib case and lower torso. Using a variety of character images that Armstrong insisted we embody as we created sound, a clear sensation of each resonating area was established—always on the same pitch. After a clear sense of placement and sensation was established Armstrong began to explore range within each region through a variety of individual and group exercises. Singing-type explorations were frequently employed. The end results were outstanding to observe. All participants experienced an unexpected growth in the range of their voices. From my own perspective, I was able to release sound in a free and open manner unlike any notes, higher or lower, that I had sounded in the past. There was no doubt this experience would have profound influence on my work with John in the area of resonance and range.

After incorporating this introductory work of Richard Armstrong's into my own practice and teaching, I felt ready to introduce John to some of the explorations (I had been introduced to Armstrong's work in several workshops and voice intensives prior to working with him directly). Of course, at this stage in the journey there was no need to explore lower regions of resonance or lower pitches. Generally speaking, higher vocal sounds are experienced in the face and head and lower vocal sounds are experienced in the chest. Literature indicates increasing and maintaining head resonance and reducing chest resonance is important to feminization of the voice (Gold 1999; de Bruin, Coerts and Greven 2000; Adler, Hirsch and Mordaunt 2006). Richard Armstrong's work became invaluable in helping John identify and maintain a generally head/face centred voice.

Other exercises and explorations employed to establish face and head resonance, increase the range of his voice and establish an increased sf_0 included simple singing exercises, chanting phrases and slowly raising the pitch on each repetition of a phrase and focus exercises emphasizing the continuant /m/. I followed my original plan of working with sound, then using words and short phrases and eventually lengthening phrases into larger thought groups in conversation.

The measuring equipment we had to use did not include the high-tech frequency measuring tools used to determine sf_0

values and other measurements in referenced scientific studies. I simply employed a piano and a sense of pitch. Using this scientifically crude method of evaluation I determined John's sf_0 to be approximately 110 Hz. After a period of approximately ten voice coaching sessions, John's sf_0 was increased to 185 - 196 Hz. A proper assessment has yet to be conducted to determine our accuracy. However, the client's ability to converse for increasing lengths of time during the hour-long sessions continued to improve.

A considerable amount of time was spent developing the client's ability to place and sustain a targeted sf_0 and head resonance during speech. Frequently the client's sound had a nasal quality to it, which diminished the authenticity of the sound. Placing the sound in the head without a dominant nasal sound was a difficult challenge to overcome. Many sessions were spent on reducing the nasal quality, with reasonable success. Strangely enough, an in-depth exploration of nasality with the /m/ sound was very useful in reducing the nasality. By having a clearer sense of hyper-nasality in the continuant consonant /m/, John was able to better identify sounds that were not hyper-nasal. Constant encouragement to allow the sound to move through his full mask (head and mouth) proved especially useful. Whispering phrases before voicing them was also productive. But the problem was not completely resolved. This was one of several stumbling blocks we encountered at this stage of our journey. Not only was it difficult to avoid a predominantly nasal sound to the voice, it also became difficult for the client to maintain the new sf_0. His voice in my opinion sounded affected and not at all natural.

Beyond Pitch and Resonance

Up until this point most of our work had been dedicated to pitch and resonance, but I knew all along that an increase in the speaking fundamental frequency of a voice alone would not ensure a feminine sounding voice. A study by Spencer (1988) with eight MtF transsexual subjects, all with an sf_0 above 160 Hz, had only four subjects recognized as female and three of these were judged low on a femininity scale. Obviously there are other characteristics that need to be considered. My continued investigations had determined that fundamental frequency and resonance focus are only two of many gender related markers that could affect the male-to-female transsexual passing as a woman. Lynn Gold indicates ten markers that should be considered. These include: raising fundamental frequency; higher functional intonation range and pitch variability; more expression with a variety of pitch, stress and duration patterns; occasional breathy phrases and breathier voice; tag questions for consensus; use of modals such as can, will, trust, may; light but precise articulation; wider range of qualifiers e.g. such a little, quite cute; compound polite requests e.g. "Would you—please?" (Gold 1999, 13-14)

Gold also identifies several nonverbal markers that need to be considered such as maintaining eye contact, increased use of hand, arm and body gestures and spatial proximity to other speakers. Gold, of course, warns that stereotypical use of non-verbal gestures will result in a reduced perception by others as an authentic woman. Several recent publications support most of, if not all of Gold's observations in regards to verbal and nonverbal markers. These include *Changing Speech* by Shelagh Davies and Joshua Mira Goldberg, a resource paper prepared for the Trans Care Project in British Columbia, Canada and *Voice and Communication Therapy for the Transgender/Transsexual Client: A Comprehensive Clinical Guide* by Richard Adler, Sandy Hirsch and Michelle Mordaunt. Unfortunately, these publications weren't available at this juncture of my work with John, but each publication supports the understanding that creating a feminine voice has a broad group of influences outside of pitch and resonance.

The Actor Client Connection

As a voice teacher dealing primarily with actors, and being an actor myself, it was impossible for me not to think of the actor's work in relationship to gender transition and specifically the vocal transition. Gold (1999) suggests that fem-inization of a voice can be enhanced significantly by three major factors, one of which is talent or experience in the per-forming arts. I believe this to be true partly because the per-forming artist, and stage actor specifically, recognizes the inter-play between the body and voice and invests a good amount of time and effort exploring this interplay. As voice teachers in the theatre we are constantly emphasizing the relationship between the body and the voice. Many voice training systems combine physical movement with sound production in order to free a restricted voice, develop awareness of vocal processes within the body or for the creation of character voices. Theatre voice trainers witness, almost on a daily basis, the significant change that occurs in the voice of an actor when he or she commits to the physical body of a character. The detail work an actor must participate in when building character is very similar to the work a transgender person must participate in. I am highly sensitive to the fact that the transgender per-son is not creating a temporary role and that the art of creat-ing persona for the TG/TS person has high stakes attached to the process and is often complicated by a number of significant physical, psychological and psychosocial influences most actors will never have to consider when creating a role. However, my experience and sensibility as an actor and theatre trainer caused me to nudge John into the next and most vital stage of our journey.

During one of our more challenging, but productive sessions, I shared my observation that our voice work, although

successful so far, was now being limited by his masculine personae during our voice sessions. I suggested, that when he was ready, he should consider embodying his feminine personae during our voice sessions. He agreed with my obser-vation and said he would consider my suggestion.

John was still presenting as a male in public situations. I real-ized this next step for him was huge and needed to take place only when he felt ready. My experience with John thus far was that he did things at his own pace, with thought and always with full commitment. I left him to consider my suggestion and didn't bring it up again. We continued with our work, meeting when we could, sometimes with less regularity than we had in the past.

Within about three months John informed me that he had started taking hormones and had set a date to live fulltime as a woman. Of course, he had consulted with his psychiatrist and family physician about this change. (In Canada, a transsexual person wanting to be considered for Sexual Reassignment Surgery must first live fulltime as their desired gender for one year.) He had already met with his manager at work and explained his situation and plans for transition. His manager was supportive and plans were put in place for John to begin this transition at work. Naturally both John and I felt an urgency to continue with our work and meet on a more regular basis.

My opinion was that vocally John was ready for this next step. He had made incredible gains with the development of a feminine voice. It wasn't perfect by any means and still needed work, but I felt that it was ready for this next step in transition. There were still many feminine markers we hadn't yet covered or even considered. I sensed that a few of these markers would take care of themselves as the transition unfolded. The other markers we would have to address after he went fulltime.

As part of our final preparation for John's transition we began to look at inflection and the feminine voice. Mordaunt (2006) points out that studies suggest woman tend to have more inflection and pitch variation than men during speech. I thought it might be useful to listen to and imitate a woman's voice as a way of incorporating more natural feminine inflection into John's voice. It is not uncommon for actors preparing a dialect role to listen to samples of native speakers of a dialect and then imitate the subjects as a way of learning the proper inflection and cadence associated with the dialect. Dialectician Gillian Lane-Plescia frequently encourages her subscribers to imitate the tune of select phrases she offers in her dialect samples, insisting that by doing this the tune or cadence of the dialect will naturally become part of the dialect during speech (Lane-Plescia 2002). I thought this concept might transfer well to our work with the feminine voice.

It was important that we choose a subject that modeled a voice that suited John's sensibility and vocal range. John suggested we consider using his roommate Mary (her name for this purpose) as a vocal model. They shared a lot of similarities and interests, and more important her sf_0 seemed close enough to John's feminine voice that he could imitate her vocal range in speech without too much challenge. John spoke with Mary and she agreed to help. Plans were made to record her during a natural conversation.

After recording about 40 minutes of conversation with Mary we then extracted short phrases for practice. John spent a considerable amount of time on his own repeating and imitating these phrases. I supplied John with a copy of the conversation in CD format so that he could also practice any sections of the recording that interested him. Two voice sessions were dedicated to listening and imitating specific phrases from the recording.

Only minor changes in John's speech were observed such as a slight raising at the ends of declarative phrases. It is important to note that John had only been practicing with the recording for a few weeks at this point. More significant, John was still presenting as a man in our sessions and when our work was completed at the end of a session he would resume use of his masculine voice. I was curious to discover what affect studying with a voice model might reveal after he had gone fulltime as a woman. Could there be more assimilation taking place than was being expressed at this time?

I met with John for the last time a few days before his transition date. Everything was set. He had a written an informational letter for his colleagues at work, which was to be distributed and read out at a Friday afternoon staff meeting. John would not be present at this meeting. His manager would answer any questions colleagues might have and facilitate discussions as needed. The following Monday, Sandy (John's female personae) would arrive at work. John was also planning to meet with his family over the weekend and introduce them to Sandy. His family had been well informed about his transition date and anticipated his arrival that weekend.

Transition
Despite all the work we had done and the accomplishments John had made with feminizing his voice, I was still very nervous about this next step. I was as much nervous for John as I was thrilled for him. We had been working together for

several years by this point and all my attention had been on preparing John's voice for transition almost forgetting that a transition day would and should actually arrive. My goal had always been to assist John with vocal transition, but the true goal was really larger than that. It involved an entire person— voice, body, mind and spirit. Like the actor, John was indivisibly all these things. The goal had always been bigger than just feminizing a voice. It was to help someone find wholeness.

On November 25, 2005 John was transformed into Sandy. Unfortunately, I was unable to meet with Sandy for quite some time after her transition date. I was directing a play for a local theatre company and we were in our last week of rehearsals before technical rehearsals began (an all consuming time in a theatrical production). In actual fact I didn't speak or see Sandy for several weeks after her transition date.

My first contact with Sandy was a call on my cell phone. I wasn't expecting to hear from Sandy by phone as most all our communications were through email. Any phone conversations I'd had with Sandy in the past were always brief. She didn't ever seem to have much to say while on the phone. I was completely taken by surprise when she called. In fact, I didn't even recognize her at first. It took me several moments to connect the name with the voice. She sounded very convincing and naturally feminine on the phone. And she was very talkative, which I found surprising and fascinating.

A week or so after this phone call I met with Sandy for the first time in a voice session. By this point she had been living as a woman for over a month. The voice elements we worked so hard on such as speaking fundamental frequency and resonance were being well maintained. I did observe further inclusion of feminine inflection in her speech and a lighter and more precise articulation pattern as well. Of course, there was more work to do in these areas, but a solid foundation had clearly been laid, and as I suspected, fully embodying the feminine personae made a significant difference in her voice.

Sandy and I continued to meet on a semi-regular basis for general vocal maintenance and to address vocal issues that arose from living fulltime as a woman. Issues surrounding volume, laughing, coughing and crying were predominant. There is still other work that needs to done in regards to the development of her voice. Feminine verbal markers outside of speaking fundamental frequency, resonance and intonation need to be addressed. (Although intonation does need further investigation.) Non-verbal markers that affect feminine perception also need attention. A vocal maintenance program should be established so Sandy can maintain the vocal characteristics she has already mastered.

Having said that, Sandy is indeed passing as a woman. She told me of an incident where she was filing some forms at a government office. She indicated that she normally leaves the boxes blank where you are asked to indicate your sex. The clerk she had been talking to when checking the forms, noticed the open boxes related to gender identification and checked the one indicating female without any query. The client was very encouraged and excited at this modest success. In the same time frame the client reported that she is most often perceived as a woman when on the phone. Progress had been made!

Final Reflections

The journey will continue from here with emphasis on incorporating other specific feminine verbal markers. Although I had some reservations in the beginning with "natural voice" training as a launching ground for our journey, it had proved most valuable in the process. Indeed, the expanse of the natural voice has room in it for an authentic feminine sound. Several voice clinicians recognize the importance of theatre oriented voice training to the TS/TG client, but few have the theatre background or training to incorporate these techniques into their therapy programs. The need for concrete discussions between voice trainers and voice clinicians (SLPs) is far overdue. The inclusion of voice trainers in the team of "transition professionals" for transgendered persons is warranted. Finally, a call for other voice trainers to document and share their study of the transgender voice training is most needed.

References

Adler, Richard A., Hirsch, Sandy and Mordaunt, Michelle. 2006. *Voice and Communication Therapy for the Transgender/Transsexual Client: A Comprehensive Clinical Guide.* San Diego: Plural Publishing.

Armstrong, Richard. 2005. The voice is the muscle of the soul. http//www.richardarmstrong.info/stmt.html (accessed July 2005).

Bailey, J.M. 2003. *The Man Who Would Be Queen: The Science of Gender-Bending and Transsexualism.* Washington: Joseph Henry Press.

de Bruin, M. D., Coerts, M. J., and Greven, A. J. 2000. Speech Therapy in the Management of Male-to-Female Transsexuals. *Folia Phoniatrica et Logopaedica* 52(5): 220-227.

Dacakis, G. 2000. "Long-Term Maintenance of Fundamental Frequency Increases in Male-to-Female Transsexuals." *Journal of Voice*, 14(4): 549-556.

Davies, Selagh and Goldberg, Joshua Mira. 2006. *Changing Speech.* The Trans Care Project. Vancouver Coastal Health, Transcend Transgender Support & Education Society and Canadian Rainbow Society. http//ww.vch.ca/transhealth/resources/library/tcpdocs/consumer/speech.pdf

Gold, Lynn. 1999. Voice Training for the Transsexual. *VASTA Newsletter*, 13 (Spring/Summer):10

James, A. and Adams C. 2003. *Finding Your Female Voice.* Deep Stealth Productions, Inc/tsroadmap.com. Accompanied with a CD-ROM and DVD.

Lane-Plescia, Gillian. 2002. *Cockney and Other Accents of London and the Home Counties.* England: The Dialect Resource. Accompanied with CD-ROM.

Linklater, Kristin. 1976. *Freeing the Natural Voice.* New York: Drama, Quite Specific Media Group Ltd.

Pausewang-Gelfer, M., & Schofield, K.J. 2000. Comparison of acoustic and perceptual measures of voice in male-to-female transsexuals perceived as female versus those perceived as male. *Journal of Voice*, 14(1): 22-33.

Meyerowitz, Joanne. 2002. *How Sex changed: A History of Transsexuality in the United States.* Cambridge, Mass.: Harvard University Press.

Rodenburg, Patsy 1992. *The Right to Speak: Working with the Voice.* London: Methuen Drama.

Spencer, L. E., 1988. Speech characteristics of male-to-female transsexuals: A perceptual and acoustic study. *Folia Phoniatrica* 40: 31-42.

Van Borsel, J., De Cuypere and G., Van den Berghe, H. 2001. Physical Appearance and Voice in Male-to-Female Transsexuals. *Journal of Voice*, 15(4):570-575.

Wolfe, V. L., Ratusnik, D. L., Smith, F. H., & Norththrop, G. E. 1990. Intonation and fundamental frequency in male-to-female transsexuals. *Journal of Speech and Hearing Disorder*s. 55: 43-50.

Peer Reviewed Article *by Ruth Rootberg*

The Relation of Head Balance to Vocal Use:
An Alexander Technique Point of View

Introduction

Allow the head to go forward and up. This is a phrase common to all students of the Alexander Technique. The words invoke the intention to balance the head on top of the spine so there is the least amount of vertebral compression[1] and the least amount of effort required to keep the head away from the ground.[2] A balanced posture also enables optimum freedom in the voice.[3] Actors and singers have studied the Alexander Technique for over 100 years and claim improved vocal use, reduced performance anxiety, lightness and ease among the many benefits. After providing a brief introduction of the Alexander Technique to set context, this article will focus on the value of head balance to vocal users and explain from the Alexander point of view the semantic difference between "forward head" and "forward neck" when describing one kind of misalignment.

Brief history and tenets of the Alexander Technique

Frederick Matthias Alexander (1869-1955), himself an aspiring actor, suffered chronic hoarseness and respiratory ailments until he succeeded in re-educating his sensory awareness, thereby improving the use of his whole self.[4]

When Alexander began to observe himself in the mirror, hoping to help himself where doctors had failed, he noticed that his larynx depressed and he gasped for breath.[5] His hoarseness was undoubtedly related to these behaviours. He also noticed his head tilted *back and down*.[6] At first he didn't know whether it too was related to the hoarseness. When he learned to prevent his head from going back and down, it moved *forward and up*; his larynx didn't depress; he didn't gasp for breath.[7] Eventually he taught himself to think in such a way that he could prevent the neck tension associated with the back and down movement of the head from moment to moment.[8] He developed a series of principles as he worked on himself over a period of nine years.[9]

The essence of the principles and educational value of the Alexander Technique can be summarized in the following points:

- The Alexander Technique uses three tools: Awareness, Inhibition and Direction[10] so that the individual gains Conscious Control.[11]
- There is a fundamental assumption that if the head balances *forward and up*[12] of the atlanto-occipital joint and if the head and neck come into dynamic relation with the rest of the back, the individual's *use* will improve. This relation of the head, neck and back is referred to as the *Primary Control*.[13]
- If use improves, any function that deteriorated because of *misuse*[14] has an opportunity to improve.[15]
- We are a whole psycho-physical organism, and therefore, we will more likely change if we look at the whole self rather than at one particular part.[16]
- It is not easy to change one's habitual movement, posture, or reaction, because our sensory system by which we determine those things becomes unreliable by the very nature of the habit.[17] We can, however, re-educate ourselves to improve the accuracy of our sensory awareness.[18]
- It is possible for any one to learn these skills without the aid of a teacher, if one does what Alexander did. However, in today's world, it is assumed that the Alexander teacher, who uses gentle hands and words as the primary pedagogical tools, will vastly speed the learning process.[19]

Ruth Rootberg, is an AmSAT certified Alexander teacher, a designated Linklater voice teacher and Certified Laban/Bartenieff Movement Analyst (CMA). She has performed as actress, singer, clown and puppeteer. She taught/coached voice at the Yale School of Drama/Yale Repertory Theatre, Northern University of Illinois, DePaul's Theatre School, Center Theater, and Shakespeare & Company. Currently she presents integrated voice/movement workshops around the world and has written for *The Voice and Speech Review* and *The Complete Voice & Speech Workout*. Ruth conceived and edited *Teaching Breathing: Results of a Survey* (www.mov-ingvoices.us). Ms. Rootberg has a teaching studio in Amherst, Massachusetts.

1. Palastanga, *Anatomy & Human Movement: Structure & Function*, 582.

2. Roberts, *Understanding Balance*, 96.

3. Sataloff, Chapter 7, "Care of the Professional Voice," 141-142.

4. Alexander, *The Use of the Self*, 47-48.
5. Ibid., 27.
6. Ibid., 27.
7. Ibid., 27.
8. Ibid., 45-46.

9. A review of introductory articles on the Alexander Technique shows a variation in the length of time—either three or nine years—as the time it took Alexander to develop his technique. According to his biographer, Michael Bloch, the hoarseness—catalyst to his experiments—that Alexander refers to in *The Use of the Self*, occurred in the second half of 1892, and by 1894, a mere 18 months later, Alexander began teaching some of his early discoveries. Bloch goes on to suggest that although Alexander began publishing in 1900, "almost a decade after he embarked on that process," his ideas were still not fully developed (34-36), and that using the term *Primary Control*, the underlying principle of the work, was not named in print until 1924.

10. Vineyard, Missy, "An open letter to the National Institutes of Health," written on behalf of AmSAT, June 21, 2000.

11. Alexander, *Constructive Conscious Control of the Individual*, 27.

12. − − − , *The Use of the Self*, 30.
13. Ibid., 30.
14. Ibid., 71; "the misdirection of use."

15. − − − , *Constructive Conscious Control of the Individual*, 78-80.

16. − − − , *The Use of the Self*, 35.
17. Ibid., 34-38.
18. Ibid., 36.
19. Ibid., 20.

20. − − − , *Constructive Conscious Control of the Individual*, 43.

21. Bloch, Michael. *F.M.: The Life of Frederick Matthias Alexander, Founder of the Alexander Technique*, 40.

22. Ibid., 42, 48. Alexander offered voice lessons, and then advertised acting lessons.
23. Ibid., 43, 49-51.
24. Ibid., 59

25. Author unknown; probably Walter Carrington, *F. Matthias Alexander, 1869-1955: A Biographical Outline*, 5, 7.

26. The Affiliated Societies' Web Site claims 3,000 teaching members. <http://www.alexandertechnique-worldwide.com/whoweare.html>

27. The writer knows the teachers who work at each of these institutions. AmSAT has formed the Higher Education and Professional Training Outreach Committee (HEPTOC) to research what the national status is of all performing institutions in the United States.

28. Alexander, *The Use of the Self*, 28, 45-48.

29. Zemlin, *Speech and Hearing Science*, 4-5.

30. Palastanga, op. cit., 2.

31. The range cited as average weight of the head varies from source to source: Kapit & Elson, *The Anatomy Coloring Book* (21) reports 6-8 lbs; Gorman, *The Body Moveable* (170): 10-15 lbs; Dr. Dennis O'Hara, "Chiropractic and Posture," <www.posturepage.com/chiropractic>: 12 lbs; The Back Shop <www.back-shop.com/faq/neck.htm>: 14 lbs.

32. Palastanga, op. cit., 580.

• The Alexander Technique is an education.[20] The student is an active participant on the road to change. Many people first learn the Alexander Technique when they are in pain, have lost range of motion, or cannot accomplish daily life tasks such as sitting or climbing stairs with the ease of days gone by. Other students take lessons to increase their coordination so they can continue to build skills with a minimum of tension or anxiety.

When Alexander was able to coordinate himself using his guiding principles, his hoarseness never returned, he never suffered from respiratory ailments again, and he went on to achieve great acclaim on stage.[21] He began to teach others. Actors, curious as to how he had solved his problem, were among his first pupils.[22] Physicians, also curious, sent him people with a variety of ailments.[23] As he taught his technique, people improved skills requiring coordination and also resolved functional problems that the physicians were not able to help. Eventually Alexander turned to teaching his technique full time.[24]

Alexander emigrated from Australia to England in 1904, and in the 1930s began training teachers.[25] Today there are thousands of certified Alexander Technique Teachers, affiliated under the umbrella of a 15-nation organization, the International Affiliated Societies of the Alexander Technique.[26] In the United States several drama departments have AmSAT (American Society for the Alexander Technique) certified teachers on faculty (e.g., on the East Coast: North Carolina School for the Arts, Yale School of Drama, Juilliard, Trinity Rep).[27]

Because Alexander first noticed an improvement in his voice when his head balance changed to what he called a *forward and up direction*[28], this instruction is central to the teaching of the Technique. In order to discuss where the head balances in relation to the spine, it is important to have a consensus defining spatial terminology. The next section will provide that contextual framework.

Spatial directions defined

Spatial and directional terms describe a relation to the self, rather than to the room or gravity. This is the same reference point anatomists use.[29] Up is head-ward, forward is in front of you, and wide is side-ward, to the left and right. This referencing is used no matter what position you are in[30], (when lying down, up is not towards the ceiling, but towards the head; while doing a back flip off the diving board, up is the headward orientation as the head revolves in space). These directions describe a relation of one part to another (the head is above or up in relation to the neck; a balanced head is forward and up of the joint) and also convey the aim or continuous thought ("I look forward in space"). A combination of directions such as forward and up creates a diagonal stream or vector.

The importance of head balance to overall posture

The head weighs 6-15 pounds.[31] It meets the top of the spinal column at the atlanto-occipital joint. When standing, the weight of the head travels through the spinal column, then is distributed through the pelvis and continues through the two legs to the floor.[32]

The center of gravity of the head, where 3-7.5 lbs. would balance on either side, does not lie in the same vertical plane as the neck; it is not directly up from the neck. It is forward and up from the joint, approximately behind the eyes.[33] That means there is more weight in front of the joint than behind. Without help from muscles, the imbalance of weight at the joint would pull the head toward gravity. The head would flop forward and down onto the chest.[34]

In order for the head to balance, the muscles in the back of the neck (extensors) work to keep the head erect (away from the chest). If the muscles work too hard, they pull the center of gravity over the joint. This back and down pull puts too much weight on the spinal column. That means there will be more compression through the vertebral column. The intervertebral discs will bulge more, and the front muscles (flexors) will have to work harder to return the head to the vertical, or at least prevent the head from falling back. The pelvis may thrust forward or tilt back to rebalance the weight of the whole column. The legs may also adjust by bracing the knees or ankles, gripping the toes, or the weight may simply shift too far to the heels or toes.

If the extensor muscles are not working enough, the pull of the head towards gravity tends to shorten muscles in the front, taking the neck forward with it. Muscles in the back, and ligaments, can overstretch, and the pressure on discs will again be uneven, ultimately leading to bulging or herniation.[35] The spinal column will lack the support to maintain its curves. If the postural muscles of the back are stretched rather than working, the weight of the head will tend to pull the head, neck and torso down towards gravity. Other muscles (phasic) in the back will then engage to keep the body from falling.

When there is a balance of the head, the extensors and flexors work in coordination to establish a tonus in the muscles that provides ease of movement.[36] Because the center of gravity is forward and up of the joint (Figure 1), there will be a slight upward lengthening of the extensor and flexor musculature. There will be less disc and joint compression; less bracing—less energy expended to prevent falling. The Alexander Technique teacher uses hands to encourage an improving head/neck relationship, thereby gaining the desired lengthening. The muscles tone[37] and students report suppleness that energizes, makes movement easier, and prevents many harmful situations.[38]

Head balance is thus essential to maintain the curves in the spine, to avoid herniation, and to use muscles optimally with the least effort. This balance also affects the voice, by impacting the laryngeal area and respiration.

The anatomy of vocal and respiratory production as it relates to head balance

Although one can see examples of perfectly poised heads in many young children, by the time these toddlers have reached the age of theatre voice training, they will have developed their unique patterns of misuse.[39] This will affect their learning in voice class. The anatomy of the extrinsic muscles clearly demonstrates how optimal alignment helps vocal use, and how misuse can lead to faulty alignment, beckoning the converse. One can see the necessary relationships in terms of muscles that attach directly and indirectly to the hyoid bone, which in turn suspends the laryngeal cartilages.

33. Kapandji, *The Physiology of the Joints*, 216-217.

34. Ibid., 216.

35. Ibid., 122-124.

Figure 1: Head forward and up. (Credit: Clive J. Mealey)

36. Jones, *Freedom to Change*, 5.

37. Kapandji, op. cit., 216.

38. Anecdotal evidence comes from numerous books and articles about the technique.

39. Alexander, *Constructive Conscious Control of the Individual*, 78-79. Alexander considered work with adults as "re-education" and work with children "preventive."

The hyoid bone is not jointed to another bone, but rather finds its placement through a series of muscular connections to several other bones above, below, and behind it. The laryngeal cartilages are suspended from the hyoid bone via the thyrohyoid.[40] Muscles attached to the hyoid also attach to the head at the styloid (stylohyoid) and mastoid (digastric) processes. The hyoid also connects to the sternum and clavicle (via the sternohyoid) as well as to the scapula (omohyoid). Indirectly the hyoid connects again to the sternum (thyrohyoid and sternothyroid). The hyoid is also the attachment site for muscles in the floor of the mouth that will affect tongue and jaw movement (mylohyoid, geniohyoid). It is the seat of tongue muscles (hyoglossus, genioglossus).[41]

When the head is in balance, these muscles can work in coordination to provide a relatively stable arena within which the intrinsic muscles of the larynx will do what they do, which is to relax, tense, lengthen, shorten or vibrate.[42] As the vocal user learns to coordinate varying pitch, dynamics and resonance, it simplifies the learning and provides an anatomically correct environment for the physiological necessities of respiration, phonation, resonance and speech to function with more ease and less effort.

In the absence of well-coordinated head balance, the body struggles to maintain itself away from gravity. The neck would be the first place to brace against the imbalance. When the head is not in balance, the muscular shifts will change the positioning of the hyoid which in turn may change the position of the larynx, or bring undue tension into the area. As the extrinsic laryngeal muscles are called on to maintain balance, positioning of laryngeal cartilages must change or be held under greater tension.[43] This can make a difference in the amount of effort needed to create pitch, resonance, power and speech. Sometimes the effort may just mean the vocalist tires easily. Sometimes it means there is a loss of range, a dulling of sound, a strident or metallic edge, a sluggishness in articulation—the variety and extent of possible problems is vast.

The relation of the hyoid to structures below the larynx demonstrates the importance of head balance to respiration and posture, which in turn will affect voice. The sternohyoid attaches to the sternum, clavicle and hyoid bone. The sternum is also the site of attachment for the sternocleidomastoid (attaching back and up to the head) and the sternothyroid, which indirectly connects back to the hyoid via the thyrohyoid. The hyoid also relates to the scapula via the omohyoid.[44] (See Figures 2 and 4[45]).

As the sternum, clavicle and scapula all relate to the hyoid and head through muscles, as the clavicle attaches to the sternum, and as ribs connect between the sternum and vertebrae, the head balance will affect not only the laryngeal structure, but respiration as well. This is a potential two-fold problem, because an improper head balance will affect the curves of the spine[46], as well as change the tensions in the shoulder girdle. If any trunk muscles brace, if there is a pulling down, the ribs and diaphragm will be less free to move.

40. Zemlin, op. cit., 102-103.

41. Ibid., 103, 121-126.

42. Ibid., 127-128.

43. Heirich, *Voice and the Alexander Technique*, 62.

Muscles attaching between hyoid and head	
At Styloid Process:	At Mastoid Process
Stylohyoid	Digastric
At Mandible	
Mylohyoid	
Geniohyoid	
Muscles attaching between hyoid and tongue	
Hyoglossus	
Genioglossus	
Muscles attaching between hyoid and structures in turn attaching to spine or head	
At Sternum	
Sternohyoid	
Sternothyroid (+thyrohyoid = indirect)	
At Clavicle	At Scapula
Sternohyoid	Omohyoid

Figure 2: Muscles with hyoid attachments.

44. Zemlin, op. cit.,121-126.

45. Figure 4 Illustration from Heirich, 108. Artist credit: Jaye Schlesinger.

46. Gorman, *The Body Moveable*, 167.

The resulting postural defects mean reduced capacity and/or lung compliance.[47] It is not difficult to then infer that subglottal pressure, even if consistent, will be diminished in duration, therefore altering the maximum artistic potential for choosing phrasing and dynamics.

The exact combination of imbalance and bracing is quite individual, and the examples given do not represent the complete array of misuse that is caused by improper head balance. The descriptions have focused on the head balance as the primary place where tension and resulting bracing begin to occur. One can also notice tensions that initiate elsewhere in the body (e.g., gripping the feet, locking the knees, tightening the fist) that travel up towards the neck, causing it to tense and pull the head back.[48]

Thus head balance becomes exceedingly important to the vocalist. In the Alexander Technique, the teacher guides the head in a forward and up direction, and asks the student to think "*head forward and up.*" Position is not as important as direction, because thinking of a static position can lead to holding patterns that would initiate further misuse. By learning the technique one can improve both head balance and freedom of rib movement. It follows then that laryngeal and respiratory functions can improve as well.

Anecdotal evidence[49] of the impact the Alexander Technique has on vocal improvement when there is a change in head balance outweighs clinical studies, but nevertheless there is scientific evidence to support this theory.

Scientific basis for accepting head balance

The importance of head balance is not an opinion of the Alexander Technique. It was experienced empirically by Alexander, and soon after, unbeknownst to him, Rudolf Magnus described it: "the head leads, the body follows."[50]

Frank Pierce Jones published research demonstrating an improvement in resonance of a singer when head balance was restored.[51] In other research, he demonstrated that improved head balance reduces the activity in the sternocleidomastoids during movement.[52]

The principles of head balance are accepted among Alexander teachers and other professions such as physical therapy and chiropractic. However, when describing a misalignment, there is a semantic discrepancy that needs to be addressed.

Semantic differences using directional terms

As was stated in the introduction, Alexander teachers use the phrase *head forward and up* quite frequently. If the head (center of gravity) is *forward* of the neck, one can also say the neck is *back* of the head. If the neck sheers forward at any place along the seven vertebrae, losing the natural curve, we can then say the neck is forward, or *forward neck.*[53]

A chiropractor or physical therapist, seeing the neck pulled forward (usually accompanied by a caving in of the chest, a hump in the back), will call this relation of the neck to the spine *forward head.*[54] This can lead to confusion, and one might think the various practitioners had different ideals in mind. It

47. Zemlin, op. cit., 81.

48. Alexander, *The Use of the Self*, 32-33.

49. See Heirich for several success stories.

50. Magnus, "Some results of studies in the physiology of posture," 531-536.

51. Jones, "Voice Production as a function of Head Balance in Singers," 209-215.

52. Jones, "Head Balance and Sitting Posture II: The Role of the Sternomastoid Muscle," 363-367.

53. Class notes, Alexander Technique School New England, 2000-2003, Missy Vineyard, Director.

54. Kendall, *Muscles testing and Function with Posture and Pain*, 66. In some instances, Alexander Teachers will also describe the *head* as forward rather than the *neck*. See Heirich, Figure 4.1C: caption, 62.

55. Alexander, F.M. *The Use of the Self*, 29.
56. Ibid., 29-30.

57. Class notes referring to unpublished letters between Alexander and Frank Pierce Jones, Alexander Technique School New England, 2000-2003.

58. Kapandji, op. cit., 16, 20.

59. The author fell err to this problem before beginning Alexander teacher training.

is a semantic problem. *Forward head* is descriptive of the head resting farther forward *in space* than it should, but this is because of the misplacement of the neck. The seven vertebrae of the neck can and do move out of their natural curve, taking the head with them forward in space. Thus anatomically, the misalignment is a problem of a forward neck, not a forward head.

In fact, when the anterior muscles of the neck and thorax pull down sufficiently to shift the neck forward, one's gaze tends to sink below the horizon towards the ground. This, in Alexander terms, is called head *forward and down*.[55] Should one want to see ahead to walk down the street, or look at the person one is addressing on stage, one will pull the head *back* and *down in relation* to the top of the neck. The neck is *forward* and the head is back and down. (Figure 3). Note that Alexander eventually expanded his principle of head balance to include the whole spine, calling it Primary Control.[56] It is a certain relation of the head to the neck and a relation of the head and neck to the rest of the spine.[57] Thus, if the neck is out of alignment, losing or increasing its natural curve, head orientation and balance is affected.

Some students will over-straighten the neck, thinking (incorrectly)[58] a straight neck is the norm; others may be attempting to overcorrect the forward neck without the aid of an Alexander teacher. When the neck is pressed back, the head tends to fall forward and down, which can also depress the larynx and tighten the jaw.[59] One voice teacher commented:

> I seem to see students whose heads are too far forward and, in an effort to reach 'up' they are putting pressure on the front of the throat. Do you see ones who need their heads to go up and forward?"[60]

If the teacher had written there was too much pressure at the back of the neck, it would be probable that the head was pulled back and down. It seems more likely the neck was over-straightened, and then the head pulled forward and down.

It is interesting to note that beginning students of the Alexander Technique will often observe the head going back and down, but describe it as going up, possibly because the face tilts up towards the ceiling (when sitting or standing).

Conclusion
The Alexander Technique has been used by actors and other performing artists. This paper discusses a fundamental concept of the Technique, which is that because the center of gravity of the head is forward and up of the atlanto-occipital joint, one's intention is to direct the head forward and up. This alignment is useful for the vocal student, and misalignment can create various problems in vocal production. The principle of the head going forward and up is scientifically sound, but semantically there is a problem because some professions (e.g., physical therapists and chiropractors) use *forward head* to name a misalignment.

When voice students learn to apply principles of the Alexander Technique, there are numerous benefits that have been reported anecdotally. More

Figure 3: Neck forward, head back and down. (Credit: Clive J. Mealey)

60. VastaVox e-mail correspondence, October 1, 2003, Lissa Tyler Renaud to Ruth Rootberg.

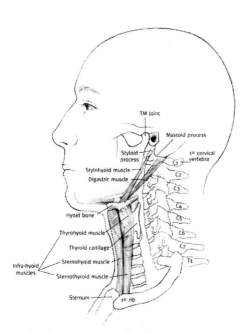

Figure 4: Illustration by Jaye Schlesinger. Used with permission. See Heirich, 108.

research would be useful and welcomed to determine more specifically what the Technique provides, and to what degree it affects beginning and advanced vocal users.

Books by F. M. Alexander
Articles and Lectures. London: Mouritz, 2000.
Man's Supreme Inheritance (1910). London: Mouritz, 1996.
Constructive Conscious Control of the Individual (1923). London: Mouritz, 1997.
The Use of the Self (1932). London: Gollancz, 1932.
The Universal Constant in Living (1941). London: Mouritz, 2000.

Other Books about the Alexander Technique
Author unknown; probably Walter Carrington. *F. Matthias Alexander, 1869-1955: A Biographical Outline*. London: The Sheildrake Press, 1979.
Bloch, Michael. *F.M.: The Life of Frederick Matthias Alexander, Founder of the Alexander Technique*. London: Little Brown, 2000.
De Alcantara, Pedro. *Indirect Procedures: a Musician's Guide to the Alexander Technique*. Oxford: Clarendon Press, 1997.
Gelb, Michael. *Body Learning: An Introduction to the Alexander Technique*. New York: Henry Holt, 1994.
Heirich, Jane Ruby. *Voice and the Alexander Technique*. Berkeley: Mornum Time Press, 2004.
Jones, Frank Pierce. *Freedom to Change: The Development and Science of the Alexander Technique* (originally *Body Awareness in Action*, 1976). London: Mouritz, 1997.
MacCallion, Michael. *The Voice Book*, Revised Edition. New York: Routledge, 1998.
McEvenue, Kelly. *The Actor and the Alexander Technique*. New York: Palgrave Macmillan, 2001.
Vineyard, Missy. *How You Stand, How You Move, How You Live: Learning the Alexander Technique to Explore Your Mind-Body Connection and Achieve Self-Mastery*. New York: Marlowe and Company, 2007.

Other References
The Back Shop. <www.back-shop.com/faq/neck.htm>
Gorman, David. *The Body Moveable*. Canada: privately printed, 1981.
Jones, Frank Pierce, "Head Balance and Sitting Posture II: The Role of the Sternomastoid Muscle." *Journal of Psychology*, Vol. 52 (1961): 363-367.
Jones, Frank Pierce. "Voice Production as a function of Head Balance in Singers," *Journal of Psychology*, Vol. 82 (1972): 209-215.
Kapandji, I.A. *The Physiology of the Joints, Volume Three: The Trunk and the Vertebral Column*. New York: Churchill Livingstone, 1975.
Kapit, Wynn & Lawrence M. Elson. *The Anatomy Coloring Book*, Second Edition. New York: Addison-Wesley, 1993.
Kendall, Florence Peterson, Elizabeth Kendall McCreary & Patricia Geise Provance. *Muscles: Testing and Function with Posture and Pain*, Fourth Edition. Baltimore: Williams & Wilkins, 1993.
Magnus, Rudolf, "Some results of studies in the physiology of posture." *The Lancet* CCXI Vol.II.5376, (September 11, 1926): 531-536.
O'Hara, Dennis. "Chiropractic and Posture." <www.posturepage.com/chiropractic>
Palastanga, Nigel, Derek Field, Roger Soames. *Anatomy & Human Movement: Structure & Function*, Third Edition. Boston: Butterworth-Heinemann, 1998.
Roberts, Tristan D.M. *Understanding Balance: The mechanics of posture and locomotion*. London: Chapman & Hall, 1995.
Sataloff, Robert Thayer. *Performing Arts Medicine*, 2nd Edition. San Diego: Singular Publishing Group, 1998.
Zemlin, Willard R. *Speech and Hearing Science*. Boston: Allyn and Bacon, 1998.

Peer Reviewed Article

by Sheila Gordon, Lynette R. Goldberg, Jessica A. Rockwell & Ronald Netsell

Feldenkrais-based Sensory Movement Technique and Breathing for Voice Production for the Stage

The purpose of this study was to investigate the effects of a Feldenkrais-based sensory movement approach (FM) on breathing for voice production in students who are planning a career in stage performance. All participants were young adults who had no documented difficulties with breathing, voice, or speech production. However, when asked about issues they might like to change, these participants had expressed some concerns related to their breathing and voice production in their work on the stage. These concerns are detailed in Table 1. As positive results of Feldenkrais intervention have been documented in a variety of disorders (e.g., Gilman 1998; Kolt & McConville 2000; Lundblad, Elert, & Gerdle 1999), it appeared possible that students who are planning a career in stage performance could benefit from this approach.

Sheila Gordon is an Assistant Professor of Acting and Voice in the Department of Theatre Arts at Saint Edward's University. She is a member of SAG, AEA, VASTA and ATME. She is a certified practitioner of the Anat Baniel Method (based on Feldenkrais), and a certified Pilates trainer. Her primary research focus is in integrating somatic movement techniques with voice and acting.

Lynette Goldberg is an Associate Professor in Communication Sciences and Disorders (CSD) at Missouri State University. One of her specific research interests centers in interdisciplinary collaboration and the effects of this approach on student learning.

- "On stage I feel that I just want to talk and talk and often forget to breathe until it is almost too late and I have to gasp in a breath."
- "I feel like I have to breathe a lot and sometimes I don't take enough breath to get through a complete thought."
- "I run out of breath sometimes when speaking. I just don't judge the right amount of breath."
- "I feel like I have good control but sometimes when I'm nervous I have trouble exhaling."
- "I think sometimes when I get nervous I start breathing faster and perhaps more shallow—but I know I can project and breathe normally."
- "At times I'm lazy and my speech is not supported."
- "I feel that my breathing is sometimes shallow and inefficient."
- "If I feel comfortable, my breathing is deep and the pitch is usually lower. When I'm excited my voice and breath become high pitched and faster and I find myself short of breath."
- "I feel I don't sound the same as I do when I hear it on a tape recorder, video camera, etc. I feel sometimes I mispronounce words or talk too fast."
- "I am pleased with my speech breathing, although I would like to extend my length of exhale."
- "I feel as though most of the time I speak on my exhales. However, some situations cause this to change, such as excitement or anger."
- "I feel that I have good breath control and volume, but I want to control my pitch more."

Table 1: Concerns expressed by students related to their breathing and voice production in their work on the stage.

A Review of Research Regarding Outcomes of the FM Approach

If we do not know what we are actually enacting then we cannot possibly know what we want (Feldenkrais 1981, xi).

The Feldenkrais Method is a system designed to use movement and perception to foster individualized improvement in function. The underlying premise of FM is to promote a more conscious direction of the self and, in doing so, find the most efficient ways for movement (Apel 1992; Buchanan & Ulrich 2001). The method strives to improve individuals' awareness of how they make certain movements, and with this awareness, allow an opportunity to change these movements and produce them more efficiently. To do this, individuals are required to make differentiations between unnecessary and necessary muscular effort during a given movement. Efficient movements are believed to be better organized and decrease the risk for stresses on other systems on the body (Spire 1989). Feldenkrais advocated that distributing effort equally and evenly throughout the body could create the sensation of effortless execution of movement, often resulting in greater outcome. He believed that this process would positively affect both thinking and feeling

(Gutman, Herbert, & Brown 1977). Subsequent research with children with neurological impairment (Reilly, Skuse, Wolke, & Stevenson 1999) and in the area of experiential learning (Eyler 2005; Kolb 1984) has shown the importance of the link between emotional awareness (through thinking and feeling) and learning in retaining new information.

Lundblad et al. (1999) sought to investigate if Feldenkrais intervention could provide relief from neck and shoulder pain in 97 female industrial workers (mean age 33 years). These workers were randomly assigned to three treatment groups: physiotherapy intervention, Feldenkrais intervention, and a control (no treatment) group. The 32 participants in the physiotherapy group received intervention for 50 minutes twice a week during a 16-week period. In addition, each subject also was asked to practice exercises at home. The 33 participants in the Feldenkrais group received individual intervention four times and group intervention 12 times during the 16 weeks. The 32 participants in the control group did not receive either type of intervention. Participants who received the Feldenkrais treatment reported significant decreases in pain, while participants in the control group reported that their neck and shoulder complaints were unchanged. Participants in the physiotherapy group had greater complaints of neck and shoulder pain.

Kolt and McConville (2000) investigated the effects of the Feldenkrais program on anxiety. Anxiety was assessed using the *Composed-Anxious* scale of the Bipolar Form of the *Profile of Mood States* (POMS-BI). This scale described how participants were feeling at a particular moment in time. Participants were 54 undergraduate physiotherapy students (35 female and 19 male) ranging in age from 17 to 38 years. They were randomly assigned to an FM group, a relaxation group, or a control group for a two-week period of intervention. Results indicated that the Feldenkrais program was effective in reducing anxiety, as measured by scores on the POMS-BI. After the fourth session of Feldenkrais intervention, participants in this method demonstrated lower anxiety scores, showing an immediacy of the effect of the intervention. The anxiety reduction also was maintained one day later. However, similar results may not have been achieved if the sample had been more equal with regard to gender and if the participants had a diagnosed clinical problem with anxiety. It also is interesting to question if the noted reduction in anxiety was maintained over time. This is important for actors, as anxiety is a hefty component of stage fright, which can have an adverse effect on voice production. The Feldenkrais program incorporates the elements of centering, focus and increased awareness—all principal components of actor training methods utilized in order to address stage fright and/or anxiety.

Gilman (1998) investigated the effects of FM in two adult females with a history of chronic stuttering. These two women participated in an 8-week series of Feldenkrais treatment. During this time, no other stuttering treatment was administered. Results of the study showed a minimal reduction in verbal disfluencies. However, both women reported the sensory movement technique positively influenced and reduced their anxiety levels and tensions during speaking situations. The sensory movement education in FM was thought to promote relaxation through increased coordination and facilitate new behavior patterns. Gilman & Yaruss (2000) are continuing to investigate the use of this approach for people who stutter.

Jessica Rockwell is a recent graduate of the CSD program at Missouri State University and is working as a speech-language pathologist for Summit Care Rehab in Kansas City, MO. She also has a background in dance. This paper is based on a series of studies she completed for her Master's degree.

Ronald Netsell is a professor in the CSD department at Missouri State University. His research and teaching areas relate to brain and vocal tract function of typical and atypical speakers. His clinical interests are in developing better methods for evaluation and treatment of children and adults with neurological speech disorders.

Professional Voice Users and the Vocal Risks of their Professions

Benninger (1995) defined professional voice users as individuals who rely on their voices to perform job-related tasks successfully. These professional voice users include actors, singers, broadcasters, teachers (especially sports teachers), military servicemen, clergy, telemarketers, businessmen, customer service advisors, industrial workers, and speech-language pathologists. These people are at a high risk for voice problems due to overuse, other types of vocal abuse, poor education on optimal vocal hygiene, and/or limited understanding (Roy et al. 2004; Titze, Lemke, & Montequin 1997). As an example, some people in the broadcasting profession may attempt to use a habitually lower pitch than is normal to obtain a more dramatic "vocal signature" (Benninger 1995, 9).

Actors and singers rely on the effective use of their voice for a living. Many of these individuals either a) may not have had proper training in how to do so effectively and safely or b) when given vocal education, do not use optimal vocal behaviors even when they know these are necessary (Timmermans et al. 2002; Timmermans, DeBodt, Wuyts, & Van de Heyning 2004). When actors or singers have difficulty during a performance, they may react naturally by increasing their speaking or voice output effort. This, in turn, contributes to more vocal function problems (Vilkman 2004). These problems may be cumulative over a period of years. A positive effect of Feldenkrais technique for actors and singers could be in integrating unrestricted breathing and muscular effort during higher volume demands to ensure that any needed increased vocal effort is distributed evenly and equally throughout the respiratory and speaking mechanisms.

In addition to prolonged voice use, factors such as background noise, acoustics, and air quality, including humidity, dust, mold, or vapors can have an adverse effect on the voice. Further, gender, endurance of the body and vocal folds, health condition, life habits, vocal skill and experience, the amount of vocal work done, and personality can contribute to the load on the respiratory and vocal systems (Vilkman 2004). Vocal loading affects the fundamental frequency, type and loudness of phonation, the vibratory characteristics of the vocal folds, and the external frame of the larynx. Vilkman speculated that difficulties with vocal loading arise when the loading factors are out of balance with the speaker's vocal mechanism capacity. Improper breathing techniques also can play a role in vocal loading and subsequent voice problems. If vocal loading factors are affecting voice production and individuals are not breathing efficiently for performance, these factors could lead to inefficient voice production and subsequent compensatory efforts to improve vocal quality. These compensatory efforts

could, in turn, lead to voice problems. Actors and singers are at risk for problems related to vocal loading and respiratory imbalance. Strain on the vocal and respiratory systems to produce sound and sustained vocal fatigue may lead to an inability to produce voice at all (Vilkman 2004).

Treatment Techniques

Vilkman (2004) advocated that balanced vocal loading should be considered the primary outcome measure in studies on voice treatment outcomes. He suggested that a short period of vocal rest can be used to achieve significant positive changes in various vocal parameters, including fundamental frequency. However, results of studies by Andrews (1999), Roy et al. (2002), and van der Merwe (2004) provide evidence that absolute voice rest should not be practiced for more than three days because of the chance for decreased muscle tone and negative psychological reactions of the client.

Treatment techniques of voice amplification, respiratory muscle training, and resonance therapy have been investigated by Roy et al. (2003). Sixty-four teachers with vocal difficulties were randomly assigned to one of three different treatment groups. Teachers in these three treatment groups received (a) electronic amplification, (b) respiratory muscle training, or (c) resonance therapy. Electronic voice amplification was proposed to reduce the vocal loading effects on the voice and larynx by reducing loudness levels and the demands posed on the voice from extended use. Respiratory muscle training was designed to strengthen the muscles of exhalation to help voice users increase their ability to generate exhalation pressures. This technique was proposed to lessen the burden on the larynx and help prevent further trauma to laryngeal tissues. Previous investigators (Baker et al. 2003; Hoffman-Ruddy, Sapienza, Lehman, Davenport, & Martin 2001; Olson, Davenport, Sapienza, Martin, & Knafelc 2001; Sapienza, Brown, Martin, & Davenport 1999; Sapienza, Davenport, & Martin 2002) had suggested that respiratory muscles would respond to strengthening and conditioning programs to help improve vocal quality and voice production. Lastly, resonance therapy was employed to teach individuals to produce voice in an easier, more resonant manner and to achieve the strongest possible voice with the least amount of effort, thus reducing the likelihood of injury to the vocal folds. Results showed that voice amplification and resonance therapy were the more favorable approaches to treating these teachers. Participants in the voice amplification group reported overall voice improvement, greater vocal clarity, and greater ease of speaking and singing voice post-treatment. The resonance therapy group also reported significant lowering of the degree of voice handicap and voice disorder severity after the treatment phase. Participants in the respiratory muscle training group did not report any significant improvements in their self-perceived level of voice handicap or voice severity ratings.

While the results of this study demonstrate the clinical significance of voice amplification and resonance therapy with teachers with voice disorders, the question remains as to whether preventive respiratory/voice education could have a positive effect and whether Feldenkrais techniques could be an integral aspect of such preventive education. Respiratory/voice education is one of several fundamental components used to improve sustainability of voice production and long-term vocal stamina for actors and singers. The purpose of adapting Feldenkrais to voice and speech work is to introduce the actor and singer to unrestricted breathing during all patterns of functional human movement. This could be useful in situations during which actors must move their bodies in multi-directional patterns on stage while speaking at high volume. The results above verified those found in a previous study conducted by Roy et al. (2002) where the effectiveness of voice amplification was compared to vocal hygiene instruction for individuals with voice disorders. Results of this 2002 study revealed that individuals who used voice amplification experienced significant lowering of their degree of voice handicap and voice disorder severity post-treatment. Vocal hygiene instruction was deemed effective, but only produced modest results. The researchers concluded that vocal hygiene instruction might have been more effective if it were coupled with another treatment approach.

Timmermans et al. (2004) explored a similar treatment technique involving professional voice users. During this study, the actors and radio directors in the "trained" group received vocal hygiene education and voice training for 18 months, while the "untrained" group did not receive either. In the trained group, the individuals learned basic skills such as relaxation, natural posture and healthy breathing, all of which are considered to contribute to efficient vocal production. The researchers judged the speakers in the trained group as having significantly better vocal quality than those who did not receive vocal training. These judgments were based on subjective vocal judgments by the clinicians. One problem encountered by Timmermans et al. (and by Roy et al. 2003), is that of the *adaptation* of the new behaviors learned during the training. Both groups of investigators found that participants understood what they were supposed to do, but were unable to maintain the newly learned behaviors.

Proponents of sensory movement techniques developed for children and adults with movement difficulties argue these techniques of integration facilitate greater awareness and understanding of efficient movement. This awareness and understanding enables the learning and effective use of new movement patterns (Apel 1992; Feldenkrais 1972). This approach to learning appears ideal to counteract the adaptation difficulties documented by Timmermans et al. (2004) and Roy et al. (2003). To date, there is no report in the literature that documents the use of the Feldenkrais approach to motor learning and education regarding breathing for voice production for professional voice users, particularly students who are planning a career in stage performance.

The Feldenkrais Method: A Sensory Movement Approach
The Feldenkrais Method advocates two basic forms of teaching: (1) *Awareness Through Movement* (ATM) and (2) *Functional Integration* (FI). ATM is a technique that is taught verbally. Individuals learn by following directions from an instructor. As they are following directions, they are executing specific movement tasks, getting a feeling for the movements through kinesthetic awareness, exploring associated sensory information, and modifying their movements accordingly (Apel 1992; Buchanan & Ulrich 2001). These movement tasks usually are first practiced while lying down, but also are experienced sitting and standing. The entire repertoire of ATM includes a wide range of functional human activities, including: rolling, twisting, spiraling, bending, kneeling, reaching, kicking, arching, looking, grabbing, falling, breathing and all the movements of the jaw, tongue and lips. A Feldenkrais instructor may select ATM lessons with a broad goal in mind or to change behavior more specifically for a sensory movement function (Buchanan & Ulrich 2001; Feldenkrais 1972). ATM lessons proceed slowly to allow every individual enough time to assimilate the idea of the movement (Feldenkrais 1981). While ATM does not include voicing in its repertoire, many of the lessons focus on the motor functions of muscles involved with voicing, speaking or singing. All ATM lessons encourage the coordination of unrestricted breathing to facilitate the movement tasks. The lessons also incorporate verbally guided rests to facilitate deeper awareness and perceptual gain of breathing changes occurring in the body.

Functional Integration (FI) lessons rely on touch to enhance awareness (Gilman & Yaruss 2000; Ginsburg 1999). The instructor facilitates gentle movements causing impulses through the skeleton, muscles and Central Nervous System with the aim of producing a better organization of the body. In both ATM and FI techniques, Feldenkrais instructors avoid showing participants how to move in order to encourage them to experiment and explore their own sensory movement options (Fortin, Long, & Lord 2002). Individuals are encouraged to notice differences in internal and external pressures while moving, the position of their bodies in space and time, and changes in their breathing patterns (Buchanan &

Ulrich 2001). Using a Feldenkrais approach, instructors believe new movement patterns are learned and used more effectively. Schmidt (1998) defined motor learning as "the processes of acquiring the capability for producing skilled actions" (345). Effective motor learning is believed to result from task-specific activities. In simple terms, this refers to the fact that when learning a certain movement, it is necessary to practice the specific tasks that are going to help one achieve the particular targeted movement. Sensory movement feedback is an important component of motor learning. At first glance, FM may appear not task-specific. It focuses on the body as a whole and relies on sensory and kinesthetic awareness through feedback from one's explorations and adaptations as to how the body moves in space. However, Feldenkrais and practitioners of the method argue that it does include task-specific sensory movement techniques (Buchanan & Ulrich 2001; Feldenkrais 1972, 1981; Lundblad et al. 1999). If so, the inclusion of both general awareness and task-specific techniques may make the FM a powerful intervention tool.

Methodology

Participants

There were two groups of participants in this study. Seventeen students registered for THE 326, *Advanced Voice for the Stage I* comprised the experimental group. Eight students were men and nine were women. Their ages ranged from 19 to 23 years (mean = 20.31 years). These students were matched with 11 students who were not registered for THE 326. There were seven women and four men in this control group (mean = 18.72 years). Students in the control group had not previously taken THE 326 or THE 226, *Voice and Movement for the Stage II*. All 28 participants in the experimental and control groups were full-time undergraduate students seeking a degree in Acting or Musical Theatre.

All participants were free of any abnormalities or deviations in the structure of their oral, laryngeal, respiratory, and hearing mechanisms, as documented by their responses on a *Participant Questionnaire*. On this questionnaire, all participants also indicated they gained experience in reflective journaling in other classes and all reported their writing skills were average or above average. All participants spoke intelligibly as judged by the investigators. All participants signed an

Informed Consent Form prior to their involvement in this study. The study was approved by the Institutional Review Board of the university at which it was conducted.

Data Collection Focus and Measures

The aims of the collection of both quantitative and qualitative data are summarized in the following table.

Aim	Type of Data	Activity	Class Period[2]
1. To evaluate the voice quality of a group of students who are planning a career in stage performance and compare measurements to those of a control group of students who did not receive FM training	Objective evaluation of jitter, shimmer, and voicing duration (*t*-test analysis)	Repeated production of sustained /a/[1]	Pre: 2 - 3 Post: 22-23
	Objective acoustic evaluation of minimum and maximum fundamental frequency (F_0), F_0 range, speaking F_0, and dynamic range (dB) (*t*-test analysis)	Reading the *Grandfather Passage*[1]	Pre: 2-3 Post: 22-23
	Perceptual self-rating of voice quality (*t*-test analysis)	Ranking of seven parameters on a vocal quality rating scale	Pre: 2-3 Post: 22-23
2. To investigate students' perception of FM as a supportive technique for voice production on the stage	Subjective evaluation (thematic analysis - ongoing)	Reflective comments in journals maintained during the study	6-29
	Subjective evaluation (thematic analysis - ongoing)	Participatory lessons with movement and voice tasks, lectures, and in-class discussions of FM	6-21
	Subjective evaluation (thematic analysis - ongoing)	Reflective comments on a post-FM questionnaire	30

Table 2: Aim and type of data collection before and after FM training.

Note. 1. To control for the effect of practice, participants were instructed not to perform any vocal warm-up exercises; tasks were counterbalanced across participants to control for order or fatigue effects.
2. The course was scheduled twice per week throughout the 16-week semester (N=32 classes). Each class period was 110 minutes in length. Focused FM techniques were introduced sequentially and taught periodically over seven weeks. These techniques then were integrated into group voice and movement warm-ups for the remainder of the study.

Movement Tasks Chosen

All of the movement tasks chosen for this study were based on FM-ATM lessons learned through the Anat Baniel Method Training Program (a school of FM practice, Spire 1989) and the work of Baniel (1994) and Wildman (2004). These lessons incorporated combinations of flexion, rotation, lateral flexion and extension of the torso. The movement patterns were chosen in order to bring awareness to the area of the body housing the greatest portion of respiratory functioning.

First Aim: Tactile referencing during respiratory functioning

Most lessons were executed while lying on the back or side, with supplemental assignments given for seated experimentation. The purpose of choosing the lying down lessons was to facilitate a tactile reference for the student. The area of body-contact that the student has with the mat throughout a given lesson can be enhanced by gravitational force. This way the student can become kinesthetically aware of many areas of the torso that move during respiration.

Second Aim: Diminishing unnecessary muscular effort during voicing

The secondary goal of the lessons was to reduce unnecessary muscular effort surrounding the jaw, throat and tongue during voice and speech production. Students were asked to become aware of the respiratory valving that occurs during various vocal tasks. These exercises included /a/, counting, conversational speech and speaking Shakespearean text during various lessons.

All of the students in THE 326 already had experienced an introduction to different FM-ATM lessons prior to taking the class, but many had not revisited the practice since their last semester of voice class (which varied from three months to two years). The following lessons were taught over a period of seven weeks (between classes six and 21). One class period per week during this time was devoted to experiencing an FM-ATM lesson, while the next class period focused more on performance of text and incorporating principles from the FM-ATM lessons.

Lesson One: Pelvic movements and breathing

Purpose: 1) to coordinate equal distribution of effort between breathing and movement, and 2) to increase awareness of the abdominal and thoracic areas during respiration and voice production.

FM-ATM Task: While lying on the back with knees bent, the student was asked to move the pelvis slowly in a clockwise pattern, to notice the points of contact with the mat and to become aware of muscular effort during the movements. The student then was asked to repeat the action in a counter-clockwise pattern. The student was asked to execute these movements without tightening the abdominal muscles or holding the breath. Rest was encouraged if any strain was detected.

Vocal Task: The student was asked to hum, produce /a/ and speak two lines of Shakespearean text at various intervals throughout the movement lesson.

Lesson Two: Thoracic movements and visualization

Purpose: To facilitate a tactile and visual association between vocal production and respiratory muscles of the ribcage. To experience (through kinesthetic means) how the size and shape of the posterior ribcage changes during respiration and voicing.

Preparation: Before the movement task was given the student was asked to create a visual image (called the *Inkblot*) of his/her body-contact with the mat. Throughout the movement lesson, the student was repeatedly asked to rest and notice whether the size and shape of the *Inkblot* had changed throughout the lesson. The *Inkblot* was referred to throughout the subsequent lessons.

FM-ATM Task: While lying supine with knees bent, the student was asked to make small and gentle circular movements with the ribcage, defining the perimeter of an imaginary clock he/she was lying on. The student was asked to notice the points of contact with the mat and the quality of muscular effort used as he/she passed through each hour of the clock. After resting, the student was asked to move the ribcage in a way that would define a diagonal line from 10 o'clock to 4 o'clock. The same task was requested for the diagonal line between 8 o'clock and 2 o'clock. After resting and visualizing the *Inkblot*, the student again was asked to make the circular movements to explore the perimeter of the clock. The student was asked to execute this action a few times in a counter-clockwise direction and then in a clockwise direction. Again the student was asked to perform these movements without tightening unnecessary muscle groups and without holding the breath. Students were encouraged to rest if they felt any strain or discomfort.

Vocal Task: During rests each student was asked to change the shape and size of the *Inkblot* only by breathing. Then the student was asked to change the size and shape of the *Inkblot* by producing a series of vocal sounds (open /a/ and humming). The student also was asked to produce these sounds during the movement lesson without compromising the equal distribution of effort.

Lesson Three: Lateral flexion of the torso

Purpose: To help students have greater experience of the depth of the ribcage as well as the effect on breathing while shortening one side.

FM-ATM Task: The student was asked to lie on one side with support underneath the head and to slowly lift the head by shortening the distance between the hip and shoulder that were not resting on the mat. As the student executed the movement, she/he was asked to become aware of breath leaving and entering the lungs. Each student was encouraged to minimize the effort made in the neck muscles in order to distribute the effort more equally throughout the torso. Rest was taken periodically to notice changes which may occur in the *Inkblot* of the lateral portion of the ribcage. After a series of rests on the side and the back, the student was asked to repeat the movement and to turn the head downward after lifting. The same task was explored while lying on the opposite side.

Vocal Task: Humming and /a/ were used during movement and during rest. Gradually, memorized text was incorporated into the movements.

Lesson Four: Movements of the diaphragm and intercostals

The following lesson was executed while lying on the back, on the side, and while sitting and twisting.

Purpose: To develop greater awareness of 1) the depth of the thoracic cavity between sternum and spine, 2) excursion of the diaphragm and 3) the three dimensional expansion and contraction in the abdominal and thoracic regions while breathing and voicing.

FM-ATM Task: While lying supine the student was asked to notice his/her breathing, without altering duration or effort. The student then was asked to inhale normally and hold the breath while performing the following actions: create greater volume in the abdominal/pelvic region, and transfer this volume to the thoracic region while diminishing volume in the abdominal region. The student was asked to repeat this action several times. Emphasis was given to work within a comfortable range of effort and duration, so releasing the breath could occur at the student's will. After breathing normally for several cycles, the task was repeated. This breathing/movement task of volume transference also was executed after exhaling comfortably and holding the breath. This sequence was repeated while varying the position of the body (in the above mentioned configurations).

Vocal Task: Before initiating the FM-ATM movement tasks but after the initial breathing awareness, the student was asked to speak some memorized text (*King Henry V*, Shakespeare) in an easy manner, while noticing any volume changes which may occur in the torso. After finishing the speech, the student was guided through the FM-ATM movement task. The text was spoken during the resting intervals, with variations in loudness, pitch and duration. Each student was asked to maintain an even distribution of effort during voice and speech exploration.

Lesson Five: Movements of the jaw and tongue

Purpose: To facilitate awareness of how to release unnecessary tension of the jaw, tongue and surrounding areas of the larynx during voice and speech production.

FM-ATM Task: While supine, the student was asked to open and close the jaw gently and slowly, while allowing the breathing to remain normal and unrestricted. Instruction was given to become aware of whether the head was moving relative to the mat during these jaw movements. The student then was asked to purposely roll the head up and down (like nodding yes) on the mat while opening and closing the jaw. After resting with guided awareness, the student repeated the simple jaw movements without nodding the head. Additional lateral and anterior jaw movements were added. Functional movement of the tongue was introduced after primary investigation of the jaw movements. The tongue movements investigate the inside structure of the mouth. While making various small movements of the jaw and tongue, the student was asked to become aware of all sensations of the respiratory, neck and facial muscles.

Vocal Task: Conversational speech was improvised before and after the lesson. A supplemental assignment was given to practice the lesson while sitting and to speak memorized text before and after the lesson. Many students reported a more pleasant experience undergoing the movements while sitting compared to being supine.

Lesson Six: The lumbar region and breathing

Purpose: To let go of muscular contractions that may shorten the lower spine during respiration and voice production. Because the diaphragm is rooted posteriorly (through the crura) to the lumbar spine, performers who are able to release tension in the lower back area may benefit from greater excursion of the diaphragm and thus improved respiratory function (Stough 2001).

FM-ATM Task: In a supine position with both legs bent, the student was asked to slowly and gently rotate one hip externally and then straighten the leg on the same side. This action was coordinated with one exhale. As the student was straightening the leg, he/she was asked to keep the foot within the width of the hips. The student was then asked to reverse the movement of the leg (to the starting position) during another exhale. These movements were to be executed with uninterrupted breath flow and with minimal amount of muscular effort in the chest, jaw, neck and shoulders. The student was asked to repeat the same movement task with the other leg. Rest intervals were used (with both legs extended) to become aware of changes that may have occurred in the *Inkblot*, particularly in the area of the lumbar region.

Vocal Task: Once the student sensed that the movement task was harmonized with his/her breathing, voice and speech were introduced. In this class, individual monologues from *Romeo and Juliet* were used.

Note: A supplementary lesson was assigned (without supervision) for the student to explore similar movements of the arms in a seated position.

Lesson Seven: Scapular movement in relation to the ribcage

Purpose: To combine complex movements of the spine with simultaneous actions of arms, liberate the movements of the scapula, and alleviate tension in the shoulders and chest during respiration and vocal production. Because the muscles and ligaments of the arms are interwoven with the ribcage and clavicles (both involved with respiratory function), it would seem valuable for actors to utilize the arms during speech without adversely affecting respiratory flow.

FM-ATM Task: In a supine position, the student was asked to bend one leg and leave the other leg straight. The student was asked to place one arm (same side as straight leg) above the head (on the mat) and keep the other arm down along the side of the body. The student then was asked to gradually roll the pelvis in the direction of the lengthened side, and to simultaneously reach the arms in opposition to one another. The student was asked to slowly shorten one side of the torso in order to facilitate the rolling and lengthening of the opposite side. The approximations were developed in the following order: a) reaching the arms in opposition, b) rolling the pelvis, c) combining a and b, d) turning the head and looking up, and e) combining a through e.

Vocal Task: Students were asked to introduce a range of voicing according to their individual breathing comfort. Those who experienced even distribution of effort were asked to speak memorized text. Those who exerted more forceful and abrupt movements were asked to diminish range of motion in the movement task and use /a/. During this lesson, students had particular difficulty with diminishing range of motion in order to harmonize with comfortable breathing. Reported outcomes of this lesson included a more open sensation in the chest and a more naturally upright posture once standing.

Results

Voice Quality of Students Planning a Career in Stage Performance Compared to Controls: Objective Measures

The means and standard deviations for each objective acoustic parameter used to measure voice quality during the production of sustained /a/ and reading of the *Grandfather Passage* are presented in Table 3. Two-tailed *t*-tests for independent samples documented statistically significant differences between the experimental and control groups for jitter, duration of /a/, and for dynamic range. For the parameter of jitter in the production of sustained /a/, the experimental group showed significantly less variability in F_0 (pitch) than the control group (t [df=31, p<0.05] = -2.30). Statistically significant differences between the two groups also were evident for the duration of /a/. The experimental group sustained this vowel longer than the control group (t [df=31, p<0.05] = 1.85). With one exception, no significant differences were evident between the two groups on F_0 values when reading the *Grandfather Passage*. The dynamic range of amplitude (loudness) was significantly less for the experimental group (t [df=31, p<0.05] = -2.18). These results are shown in Table 3.

Task	Mean		Standard Deviation		Group Comparison	t value
	EG	CG	EG	CG		
Sustained /a/						
Jitter	0.63	0.93	0.45	0.54	EG<CG	-2.30*
Shimmer	3.19	3.21	1.34	1.54		-0.04
Duration of /a/	16.38	14.58	4.63	2.85	EG>CG	1.85*
Grandfather Passage						
Min F_0	90.67	91.72	20.88	25.20		-0.17
Max F_0	273.53	282.12	69.03	68.84		-0.61
F_0 Range	183.95	190.10	61.44	62.49		-0.45
SF_0	165.94	176.84	40.56	41.88		-1.24
Dynamic Range (dB)	66.55	68.78	3.76	4.60	EG<CG	-2.18*

Table 3: Group means, standard deviations and *t*-test analyses for objective measures of voice quality for students in the experimental and control groups.
Note. EG=Experimental group, N=16; CG=Control group, N=11.
* Critical value of *t* (*df* = 26, *p* <0.05) = 1.71.

Voice Quality of Students Planning a Career in Stage Performance Compared to Controls: Descriptive Measures

Data from the experimental and the control groups' self-ratings of seven parameters of vocal quality, as documented from their responses on a 9-point *Vocal Quality Rating Scale*, are presented in Table 4. Two-tailed *t*-tests for independent measures documented statistically significant differences between the two groups for *loudness* and *inflection*. Mean loudness ratings for the experimental group were closer to optimal than the loudness ratings of the control group (t [df=26, p<0.01] = -4.20). Similarly, mean inflection ratings for the experimental group were closer to optimal than those of the control group (t [df=26, p<0.05] = -2.30). These results are presented in Table 5.

Vocal Parameter	Mean	Standard Deviation	Range
Breathiness			
Control	4.91	1.24	2.25-6.25
Experimental	5.36	0.99	3.50-7.50
Loudness			
Control	6.43	1.05	4.25-8.00
Experimental	4.73	1.02	3.25-7.75
Pitch			
Control	4.47	1.33	2.50-7.00
Experimental	4.73	0.97	2.50-6.50
Inflection			
Control	5.50	0.54	4.75-6.50
Experimental	4.81	0.88	3.25-6.75
Nasal Resonance			
Control	5.20	1.02	3.75-6.75
Experimental	5.02	1.03	3.50-6.75
Rate			
Control	6.36	1.13	4.25-8.50
Experimental	5.75	1.04	4.00-7.75
Speaking Effort			
Control	4.84	1.27	3.25-6.50
Experimental	4.84	1.42	3.50-9.00

Table 4: Experimental and control group mean ratings on the seven vocal parameters of the *Vocal Quality Rating Scale* , adapted from Myers et al., 2002.
Note. Experimental group N=16, Control Group N=11.
*4.50 is considered optimal on this scale.

Vocal Parameter	Group Comparison	df	t value	Sig.
Breathiness		26	1.05	0.31
Loudness	EG<CG	26	-4.20	0.01**
Pitch		26	0.58	0.57
Inflection	EG<CG	26	-2.30	0.03*
Nasal Resonance		26	-0.47	0.64
Rate		26	-1.45	0.16
Speaking Effort		25	1.41	0.17

Table 5: t-test analyses of self-ratings of vocal quality for experimental and control groups.
Note. Experimental Group N=16, Control Group N=11
*Critical value of t (df=26, p <0.05) = 2.06
**Critical value of t (df=26, p<0.01) = 2.78

Discussion

Experimental vs. Control Group

At the conclusion of the Feldenkrais-based course, interesting differences were evident between the two groups with regard to *acoustic measures*. Participants in the experimental group demonstrated more vocal stability and longer vowel duration than participants in the control group. Feldenkrais (1981) argued that the sensory movement techniques integral to his method improve individuals' awareness of how they execute movements. Efficient movements are better organized and decrease the risk for stresses on other systems in the body (Spire, 1989). With this awareness, individuals gain insight into their movements and how to change and produce them more efficiently. In their investigations of sensory movement techniques on the speech of people who stutter, Gilman (1998) and Gilman and Yaruss (2000) speculated that the awareness from Feldenkrais intervention increased confidence during speech. In turn, this confidence positively affected respiration and its relationship to fluent speech. In the current study, the increased vocal stability and vowel duration evident in the experimental group may reflect the influence of Feldenkrais techniques on participants' integration of sensation and move-ment. This synthesis may facilitate their ability to use these sensation and movement patterns for increased breath coordi-nation and support for voicing. This insight was evident in participants' comments in their ongoing reflective journals and on the *Post-Feldenkrais Questionnaire*. Examples include:

- "I understand how the techniques aim to move your muscles with your breath. I understand better how it works."
- "I have learned better ways to support my breath."
- "I'm certainly more aware of my breathing and how connecting with that breath helps create the vocal quality I want."
- "Everything involved with Feldenkrais is body awareness."
- "More fluidity of breathing muscles. They move easier and I feel it is more open and comes out with ease and I don't have to strain."
- "I feel a lot more powerful and loud with my voice. I also feel that my breath is deeper. I also feel a greater understanding of my pitches."
- "I think it has made me breathe a lot deeper so every breath I take can last longer."

When comparing *perceptual measures*, additional differences were evident between the two groups on their self-ratings of the parameters of *loudness* and *inflection*. Participants in the experimental group perceived their loudness and use of inflection as closer to optimal (4.50 on a 9-point scale) com-pared to participants in the control group. These perceptual

Vocal Production, Voice Related Movement Studies

Feldenkrais-based Sensory Movement Technique and Breathing for Voice Production for the Stage
by Sheila Gordon, Lynette R. Goldberg, Jessica A. Rockwell & Ronald Netsell (continued)

differences appear to support the differences found between the groups on acoustic dimensions. Participants' experience in THE 326 appeared to provide them with the knowledge and awareness to integrate sensory and movement issues for optimal loudness and inflection, as they perceived these parameters. Whether this positive change was reflective of Feldenkrais intervention and/or other influences is difficult to determine. In their investigation of three approaches to voice treatment (voice amplification, respiratory muscle training, and resonance therapy), Roy et al. (2003) found that respiratory muscle training was the least favored approach by teachers. Results of the current study suggest that it would be interesting to explore the effects of a Feldenkrais paradigm to strengthen and condition respiratory muscles. In the study by Roy et al. (2003), teachers preferred electronic voice amplification to reduce vocal strain. While the use of electronic voice amplification was positive, one could argue that an amplification device does not increase teachers' (or actors and singers') awareness of the most optimal way to use the voice. If replication of the current study verifies the positive effect of Feldenkrais-based intervention on loudness and inflection, this technique to integrate sensory information with efficient laryngeal movement could be a valuable complement to vocal intervention strategies.

Should the acoustic data showing increased vocal stability and breath support be related to optimal perceptual ratings of loudness and inflection, these findings strengthen the argument for the positive effect of Feldenkrais-based sensory movement techniques—for both the *prevention* of vocal difficulties, and *intervention* once vocal difficulties have been identified. Support for this speculation also is evident in participants' comments. Examples include:

- "I never realized before how much having proper breath support can increase not only inflection, but proper pitch."
- "Once I have rid my body of tension, my voice is free to travel."
- "I am so much freer with my voice. It's easier to access where to get air."
- "I think the techniques have given my voice more clarity and power because I am now able to connect my voice to my breath."

An in-depth categorical analysis of the descriptive data from students' reflective journals is underway to provide valuable insight into the students' perspective on the FM technique and assist in further interpretation of the acoustic and perceptual data.

Conclusions and Recommendations
The inclusion of Feldenkrais-based technique in methods to prepare students for a career in stage performance appears

warranted and worthy of continued investigation. The present study has provided interesting preliminary evidence to support the use of Feldenkrais-based technique to facilitate breathing for voice production in students who are planning a career in stage performance. Acoustic and perceptual quantitative measures and reflective commentary documented positive changes in participants' breathing and voice production and may suggest that with a focus on the integration of sensory and motor performance, Feldenkrais intervention provided these participants with knowledge and awareness to better control and use their voice in stage performance.

These changes also may reflect the effects of Feldenkrais-based technique on participants' increased awareness of the effects of tension in stage performance and ways in which this can be relieved. When asked if Feldenkrais-based technique had affected their bodies and movements, all participants responded positively. One participant stated, "I am aware of where I hold my tension in my body." Another stated, "I am much more aware of my body being tense and also how to release that tension. I am also more in tune to how my body is responding to certain movements and whether it feels desirable or not."

Several issues may have influenced the findings of this study and it would be important to address these issues in future work. Specifically:

Participant Groups. At the beginning of the study, the experimental group consisted of 17 students, eight men and nine women. During the post-test measurements, the experimental group consisted of 16 students, seven men and nine women. The control group consisted of 11 students, four men and seven women. Data were analyzed per group. The greater number of women in the two groups may have biased the acoustic measurements as women have a higher F_0 than men and generally a smaller lung capacity. In addition, the groups were unequal regarding number of participants. Replication of the study would be valuable with equal numbers of participants in the experimental and control groups and equal distribution of gender within these groups.

Dynamics of the THE 326 Course. The course was taught by an instructor undergoing Feldenkrais certification. While Feldenkrais-based intervention was the foundation for each class, additional techniques were included as the students moved into actual stage work. Future research may want to focus on the outcomes of a course for theatre students wholly-based on Feldenkrais intervention technique.

Ratings of Vocal Quality. Accurate ratings of self-perception of vocal quality were integral parts of this study. There was a wide range of ratings on the 9-point Likert-type scale.

Although the value of training is debated, continued research using this scale may consider the inclusion of training sessions for the participants to promote optimal use of the scale.

Activities Outside of Class. Two of the participants in the experimental group were majoring in musical theatre. In courses for this major, these participants may have been exposed to additional breathing techniques for singing. If these additional breathing techniques increased these participants' knowledge of vocal performance, their performance may have influenced the overall group results. The remaining 14 participants were not involved in musical theatre, but were not asked about associated activities in vocal performance. Continued investigations of the effects of Feldenkrais-based technique on vocal performance would be strengthened by documenting all participants' outside activities relating to vocal production and stage performance.

Notwithstanding these limitations, results of the current study provide valuable insight into the potential effects of Feldenkrais-based technique in the preparation of students who are planning a career in stage performance and the use of both quantitative and qualitative data. Previous studies of vocal intervention techniques have been limited by a reliance on either quantitative or qualitative measures. Results of the current study suggest the importance of using both measures and illustrate how each type of data can complement the other and provide a comprehensive view of the effects of Feldenkrais-based sensory movement technique on breathing for vocal performance.

Acknowledgments: We would like to extend sincere thanks to two anonymous reviewers for their valuable suggestions to strengthen the presentation of this work.

References

Andrews, M.L. *Manual of voice treatment: Pediatrics through geriatrics (2nd ed).* San Diego, CA: Singular Publishing Group, Inc., 1999.

Apel, U. The Feldenkrais Method: Awareness through movement. *World Health Organization Regional Publications, 44* (1992): 324-327.

Baker, S., Sapienza, C., Davenport, P., Martin, D., Hoffman-Ruddy, B., & Woodson, G. "Inspiratory pressure threshold training for upper airway limitation: A case of bilateral abductor vocal fold paralysis." *Journal of Voice, 17*(3), (2000): 384-394.

Baniel, A. *Dr. Moshe Feldenkrais at Alexander Yanai, 1*(1), (1994): 111-115. Translated from Hebrew.

Benninger, M.S. "Voice dysfunction in the broadcasting professional." *American Journal of Speech-Language Pathology, 4*(1), (1995): 8-10.

Buchanan, P.A., & Ulrich, B.D. "The Feldenkrais Method: A dynamic approach to change motor behavior." *Research Quarterly for Exercise and Sport, 72*(4), (2001): 315-323.

Colton, R.H. & Casper, J.K. *Understanding voice problems: A physiological perspective for diagnosis and treatment.* Baltimore, MD: Williams & Wilkins, 1996.

Darley, F.L., Aronson, A.E., & Brown, J.R. *Motor speech disorders.* Philadelphia, PA: W.B. Saunders, 1975.

Eyler, J. "Reflecting on service learning." Presentation at Southwest Missouri State University. Springfield, MO, February 2005.

Feldenkrais, M. *Awareness through movement: Health exercises for personal growth.* New York, NY: Harper & Row, 1972.

Feldenkrais, M. *The elusive obvious.* Cupertino, CA: Meta Publications, 1981.

Fortin, S., Long, W., & Lord, M. Three voices: Researching how somatic education informs contemporary dance technique classes. *Research in Dance Education, 3*(2), (2002): 155-179.

Gilman, M. "The reduction of tension in stuttering through somatic re-education: A multiple baseline single subject design study." Presentation at the 38th annual convention of the Illinois Speech-Language-Hearing Association, Arlington Heights, IL, Feb. 1998.

Gilman, M., & Yaruss, J.S. Stuttering and relaxation: Applications for somatic education in stuttering treatment. *Journal of Fluency Disorders, 25,* (2000): 59-76.

Ginsburg, C. "Body-image, movement and consciousness: Examples from a somatic practice in the Feldenkrais Method." *Journal of Consciousness Studies, 6*(2-3), (1999): 79-91.

Gutman, G.M., Herbert, C.P., & Brown, S.R. "Feldenkrais versus conventional exercises for the elderly." *Journal of Gerontology, 32*(5), (1977): 562-572.

Hoffman-Ruddy, B., Sapienza, C., Lehman, J., Davenport, P., & Martin, D. "Expiratory pressure threshold training in high risk singers." Presentation at the Voice Foundation 30th Annual Voice Symposium: Care of the Professional Voice, Philadelphia, PA, June 2001.

Kolb, D.A. *Experiential learning.* Englewood Cliffs, NJ. Prentice-Hall, 1984.

Kolt, G.S., & McConville, J.C. "The effects of a Feldenkrais awareness through movement program on state anxiety." *Journal of Bodywork and Movement Therapies, 4,* (2000): 216-220.

Lundblad, I., Elert, J., & Gerdle, B. "Randomized controlled trial of physiotherapy and Feldenkrais interventions in female workers with neck-shoulder complaints." *Journal of Occupational Rehabilitation, 9*(3), (1999): 179-194.

Myers, F.M., St. Louis, K.O., Bakker, K., Raphael, L.J., Wiig, E.K., Katz, J., Daly, D.A., & Kent, R.D. "Putting cluttering on the map: Looking back." American Speech-Language-Hearing Association Annual Convention, Atlanta, GA, 2002.

Netsell, R. "Speech physiology." In F.D. Minifie, T.J. Hixon, & F. Williams, eds. *Normal aspects of speech, hearing, and language.* Englewood Cliffs, NJ: Prentice-Hall, 1973, 211-234.

Olson, D., Davenport, P., Sapienza, C., Martin, D., & Knafelc, M. "Specific expiratory muscle strength training in adult male deep water US Navy divers." Presentation at the Experimental Biology Spring Conference, Orlando, FL, April 2001.

Reilly, S., Skuse, D., Wolke, D., & Stevenson, J. "Oral motor dysfunction in children who fail to thrive: Organic or non-organic." *Developmental Medicine and Child Neurology, 1* (1999): 115-122.

Roy, N., Merrill, R.M., Thibeault, S., Parsa, R.A., Gray, S.D., & Smith, E.M. "Prevalence of voice disorders in teachers and the general population." *Journal of Speech, Language, and Hearing Research, 47,* (2004): 281-293.

Roy, N., Weinrich, B., Gray, S.D., Tanner, K., Stemple, J.C., & Sapienza, C.M. "Three treatments for teachers with voice disorders: A randomized clinical trial." *Journal of Speech, Language, and Hearing Research, 46,* (2003): 670-688.

Roy, N., Weinrich, B., Gray, S.D., Tanner, K., Walker Toledo, S., Dove, H., Corbin-Lewis, K., & Stemple, J.C. "Voice amplification versus vocal hygiene instruction for teachers with voice disorders: A treatment outcomes study." *Journal of Speech, Language, and Hearing Research, 45* (2002): 625-638.

Sapienza, C.M., Brown, J., Martin, D., & Davenport, P. "Inspiratory pressure threshold training for glottal airway limitation in laryngeal papilloma." *Journal of Voice, 13* (1999): 382-388.

Feldenkrais-based Sensory Movement Technique and Breathing for Voice Production for the Stage

by Sheila Gordon, Lynette R. Goldberg, Jessica A. Rockwell & Ronald Netsell (continued)

Sapienza, C., Davenport, P., & Martin, D. "Expiratory muscle training increases pressure support in high school band students." *Journal of Voice, 16* (2002): 495-501.

Schmidt, R.A. *Motor control and learning: A behavioral emphasis* (2nd ed.). Champaign, IL: Human Kinetics, 1998.

Spire, M. "The Feldenkrais Method: An interview with Anat Baniel." Reprinted from *Medical problems of performing artists.* Philadelphia, PA: Hanley & Belfus, Inc., 1989.

Stough, C. *Breathing: The source of life.* The Stough Institute, 2001. (contact: <Info@Breathingcoordination.com>

Timmermans, B., DeBodt, M.S., Wuyts, F.L., Boudewijns, A., Clement, G., Peeters, A., & Van de Heyning, P.H. "Poor voice quality in future elite vocal performers and professional voice users." *Journal of Voice, 16*(3), (2002): 372-382.

Timmermans, B., DeBodt, M.S., Wuyts, F.L., & Van de Heyning, P.H. "Training outcome in future professional voice users after 18 months of voice training." *Folia Phoniatrica et Logopaedica, 56,* (2004): 120-129.

Titze, I.R., Lemke, J., & Montequin, D. "Populations in the US workforce who rely on voice as primary tool of trade: A preliminary report." *Journal of Voice, 11*(3), (1997): 254-259.

van der Merwe, A. "The voice use reduction program." *American Journal of Speech-Language Pathology, 13,* (2004): 208-218.

Vilkman, E. "Occupational safety and health aspects of voice and speech professions." *Folia Phoniatrica et Logopaedica, 56,* (2004): 220-253.

Wildman, F. 2004. *The intelligent body: TMJ for head, neck and jaw pain.* Berkeley, CA: Feldenkrais Movement Institute, 2004.

Essay *by Mark Ingram*

Speaking Physical Sentences

Mark Ingram has been an actor, director and fight choreographer working in Canada and the USA for the past twenty-five years. He is the Artistic Director of the Rogue and Peasant Theatre Company (Toronto, Ontario), and a member of the Society of Canadian Fight Directors. He received his MFA (plus voice teaching diploma) from York University and currently teaches voice and acting at the Toronto Film School and York University. He gratefully acknowledges the influences of his voice mentor, David Smukler (York University, one of the first teachers trained by Kristin Linklater) and fight mentor, Tony Simotes (University of Wisconsin/Madison, the first teacher trained by B.H.Barry).

Overview

One of the key goals with every fight sequence is to engage the audience—to allow the audience a visceral (i.e. emotional, physical, physiological and/or breath) response to a fight. The importance of breath and voice in fight sequences and their impact on the audience cannot be overstated. The voice has the ability to inform the character and define the story; it can connect both the actors and the audience into the truth of the moment. Take, for example, a common stage slap. One can more than double the impact of the move on the audience by adding in the character's vocal response. The sharp inhalation of shock or the cry of surprise can be both unexpected and highly dramatic. Similarly, in any kind of fight to the death, the specific sounds of exhaustion, pain and rage can heighten the audience's experience beyond what is possible by watching the physicality from a slightly removed and unengaged position (Lowry 2001, 107), in other words, the vibrations of sound are physical, tangible links between the actors and the audience.

From interviews with eighteen SAFD (Society of American Fight Directors) fight directors, it was noted that, in general, fight directors know that "a silent fight is often indicative of poor breathing" (Harding 2001, 91). There are many manifestations of poor breathing—be it held breath, high/shallow breathing, a restricted pharyngeal cavity, or any other variation where the air channel is constricted and one's ability to communicate is reduced—and the fight director must find and address the cause/root of the problem for the fight to be most effective.

This essay will investigate stage-fighting techniques from the perspective of voice work. As a fight choreographer and a voice coach, I am continually made aware of the interrelation of these two disciplines. When working on a scene I tend to see moments of checked movement or sudden vocal grip/grab; either of these suggest the action is hitting some kind of a block. This essay will describe my technique as a fight instructor as it has evolved over the past sixteen years, my observations of how it incorporates voice work, and how it enhances the actor/audience relationship.

A Brief Job Description

I've learned from my own experience and from conversations with other fight directors that a basic definition of a fight director's job is to tell a story. To do so, fight directors need to assess the actor/fighter's skills and learning style, and then teach all the skills required for the fight sequence. They must choreograph the sequence(s)—using ideas from their imagination and the script, as well as input from the actors and director. Furthermore they must ensure the safety (physical, vocal, emotional) of all involved—it is important to foresee any possible mishaps and establish proper guidelines and contingencies.

One of the voice coach's roles is to help the actors to allow their thoughts, ideas, impulses and emotions to reach the audience. The root of most voice techniques, and certainly the Linklater technique in which I trained, is breath work. The breath allows the actor to tap into his/her own emotional depth and range, and ensures the communication of these thoughts and feelings. The freer the breath is and the more unrestricted the channel that it travels, the greater the connection with the audience.

Vocal Considerations In Stage Fighting

Usually, a character will move into physical communication (i.e. fight work) when verbal communication isn't effective in achieving one's objective. This move is not merely a switch from one to the other: it is an addition of the physical to the verbal/vocal. A physical gesture not only illustrates what is being said, but it adds depth and meaning that the words themselves simply cannot provide (Sewall 1998, 76). This point is crucial. Viewing the physical work as an addition helps keep the breath and voice alive. The fight is not separate, but an outgrowth and enlargement of the verbal aspect of the scene; the two work hand in hand, and the voice can heighten the impact of the physical blow.

Beginner fighters tend to use the same sound for everything. If the same sound is made when grasping, attacking and parrying, the audience can be forced into their heads in order to intellectually interpret confusing sounds. This confusion arises from an innate understanding that we, as human beings, make different sounds for different activities. As Lise Olsen states: "At the most basic, we grasp a particular weapon at a specific effort level, attack at one effort level and parry at another" (Olsen 2001, 30). Part of a fight director's job is to help the actor shape these sounds and find the specificity that will help tell the story clearly. One solution is to view each move as a separate *physical sentence* which requires a separate intention and voicing; this approach will be expanded below.

More and more, the importance of a crossover between fight director and voice coach becomes apparent. For example, a two-hand broadsword has weight and is used with a certain style that forces the fighter's chest to become more closed, thus forcing actors to breathe more into their back ribs. Costumes can also restrict breathing, requiring adjustments that will allow proper vocal support (Wiley et al. 2001, 36). These are instances where it is advantageous to have knowledge of voice work in order to help the actor to solve potential problems. However, weapons and costumes are not the only causes of poor vocalizing during a fight. A lot of performers, especially when first learning new moves, pull down on their voice in order to show the effort; they place the full burden of the illusion on their voice rather than allowing the complete picture on stage to tell the story. For example, they will virtually close down their throat and pharynx to demonstrate a strangle. Whereas, the image of someone's hands around your throat during a struggle, and the addition of quick intakes of breath (similar to soft palate stretches) can create the illusion without damaging the actor's voice, plus give the audience a very visceral breath experience.

Poor breathing may also be apparent when it is obvious in a scene where the fight director's work starts and stops—through a noticeable change in the way the actors move, speak or relate to one another. The voice/body connection shifts and is evidenced, most obviously, by a change in breath and vocal patterns. A technique that is useful for connecting voice and body in fight moves is similar to training methods used for martial arts, such as Kendo. "In delivering a blow or thrust, the kendoist calls out the point he is contacting, showing that he has struck the opponent mentally as well as physically. The kendoist places great emphasis on *eye contact* and the ki-ai [shout or cry]" (Draeger 1969, 102). By having the actor name the target this ensures s/he must send vocal intention and breath at the opponent. This helps focus the transfer of breath/vocal energy from the aggressor to the victim. It also helps in directing the audience's focus.

A silent fight may also result if an actor is concentrating on learning a new skill. A fight director is usually required to work very quickly. For some actors, this necessity for speed adds pressure that can, unfortunately, equate to added physical tension. As Patsy Rodenburg notes, "Any useless tension, anywhere in the body, can restrict the freedom of the voice" (Rodenburg 1992, 20). Aside from the obvious implications for the voice work, this statement also points to the necessity of teaching fight movements with a *building block* approach. The building block approach allows the actor to add each new skill to one previously learned—much as a baby learns to walk in increasingly complex stages. This reduces the apprehension that can stifle/inhibit an actor's physical/vocal work as they learn to find the lightness and ease in the body that allows for a free clear voice while still presenting an image that appears to be full of tension: that of a fighting body.

Another manifestation of poor breathing is either going off-voice or just lacking support for the large vocal energy that is required to be sent to the other actor(s). When working to get an actor grounded and centered, the image of the fighter as the bleeder valve on top of a pressure cooker can be very useful. Their power source is the earth; the need to lash out, to hit, comes up from the ground, through their entire body and out through breath, voice and physical action. Not only does this work to get the body in a centered position, it also encourages deep, supported breathing for each move. This thinking has been around for centuries; martial arts master Chuang Tzu wrote that the "pure man of old...could scale heights without fear, enter water without getting wet, and go through fire without feeling hot... He breathed deep breaths. The pure man draws health from the great depths of his heels, the multitude only from their throats" (Draeger 1969, 32).

Fear or discomfort of the fight world's vocabulary may also be a factor contributing to a silent fight. By having the actors verbalize their targets, physical and vocal integration is achieved while using terminology they know. This is a particularly useful technique for swordplay. Instead of using the number system to identify hits and parries (which is useful for recording sequences), using basic body parts utilizes words that the actors won't have to translate. For example, actors can *parry high 5*, or they can *protect their head*, or they can have a breath/emotional response to the attack—which manifests itself in a physical defense. In essence, the goal is to keep the actors connecting the physical movements to the acting versus allowing them to think "here comes the fight sequence."

Speaking Physically

From my experience, a fight director is usually brought into the rehearsal process relatively late. The actors are off-book and have been working the scene up to the point where they say, "And the fight goes here," and then they continue the scene. So they have inadvertently rehearsed a break in their breathing and vocal patterns. Now the fight director has to find a way to shift this *break* into a *build*. An approach I have found to be useful is not so much a shift in technique but rather in perspective and terminology.

When I met Tony Simotes at Shakespeare & Company in 1989, he was teaching stage fighting as *physical lines of dialogue*. While still using some of the technical fight terms he encouraged the actors to think in terms of motivation, objective, intention and similar acting terms and to speak the text with their bodies. This approach put what could be challenging, frightening and foreign work into a language that actors already understood. From this my work has now evolved into working in *physical sentences*. Each move is a *sentence*. Each sequence is a *paragraph*, *dialogue* or *argument*. I have found that using this terminology eases tension in the actor who is not completely physically comfortable on stage. It removes some of the concentration from the unfamiliar skill and places it on the communication.

Each sentence has an inspiration (both idea and breath), an intention, a motivation, and an execution (both a physical and vocal expression). There is also a *punctuation*, (the actor must deal with the consequences of speaking or receiving this sentence). These are terms that actors use daily—it's our own language and therefore doesn't require translation. Approaching the work in this way allows actors to continue their text analysis and implementation without a break in the through-line. Now the only difference (if one chooses to view it that way) is that a physical gesture has been added to the execution of the objective.

Breaking moves down into physical sentences forces specificity of each move, and this can help to prevent a fight from

moving at *street speed* rather than *stage speed*. By making each engagement, hit, movement and reaction into separate sentences, a fight will progress at a pace that allows the audience to breathe along with the actors—similar to the effects of traditional punctuation.

An issue that seems to be popping up more and more these days—one that can be dangerous, if not deadly—is realism. Eugenio Barba states, it "is a fundamental principle of the theatre: on stage, the action must be real, but it is not important that it be realistic" (Barba 1995, 32). The effect of this real action is that the audience remains engaged with the actors and is given a visceral experience, which includes emotion, communication and breath. It is usually fairly easy to convince actors of this when dealing with most fight moves—except for the slap. For some reason a lot of actors feel they must *feel* a slap to portray it properly. This brings up a lot of issues: Why does it have to be real when the audience is sitting in chairs watching, programs on their laps, and lighting instruments hanging from the grid (which are visible to the naked eye)? How can it be real when the slap will leave a mark on the face well into the next scene (which happens two weeks later)? And what about the actor playing the aggressor—maybe s/he doesn't actually want to take the victim's career into their hands (as one's face is their calling card in this business)? For the slap the breath, intention and movement of the arm are real, but the spacing is not realistic. Yet the move can still work very effectively as long as these first three elements are present. This is true for all fight moves—the breath and intention are real, yet the action that would, in reality, cause harm is simulated to approximate a realistic image. When the actors complete— punctuate—each physical sentence before moving onto the next one, their breathing, intentions and physicality will be accurate to a real fight and yet they will not have the realistic pain in the next scene (which could be a flashback scene before the fight even occurred).

If a sequence has a series of repetitions of the same move, it can easily be related to the actor's text work. When speaking Shakespeare, for example, we frequently have to repeat a word two or three times, and each repetition of the word is different because the intention and motivation are different. The same is true in a fight: in each physical sentence the intention/motivation has to be different, if for no other reason than the first hit didn't achieve what it was supposed to and a second attempt will be made, or it did and there is a desire to inflict more.

By using sentence imagery the breath and voice work is also facilitated. When the actor finishes the thought with a *punctuation mark*, s/he has to realize and react to the consequences of that action. A question must then be answered: is this sentence finished with a period, a question mark, an exclamation mark, an ellipsis or some other punctuation? This forces the actors to fully inhabit and fill each physical exchange as an acting moment and not just a fight—it becomes an extension of their acting work. The punctuation mark can also act as a reminder to breathe, and this will help maintain a breath connection with the audience and other actors who hear and feel us breathe, and breathe themselves in response.

Frequently, in rehearsal, one hears, "you're playing the end of the scene at the top," or "you're giving away the punch line before you actually get there." Structure of writing dictates how a scene will build, and the actor must be sensitive to this. The same is true of a sequence of physical sentences. The acting of each sentence has to occur in the moment; the punctuation of the first sentence must be realized before the idea of the second sentence occurs. Thought builds on thought, (each though grows out of the one that came before). This allows the fight sequence to become a tight, reasoned argument of *physical rhetoric* rather than one long run-on sentence.

Conclusion

Experienced fight choreographers continue to return to the breath and voice as a necessary complement to the physical skill that helps maintain the actor/audience relationship on a visceral level. A fight sequence's believability involves the use of auditory elements. "The very sound of weapons clashing, knaps, footfalls, the breath and the voices of the people involved in the action guide the audience to follow and enhance the visual story, to understand the 'impact of the blow', to accept the fight as real and believable" (Wiley et al. 2001, 34). Whenever one of these elements is missing, the audience is forced out of the visceral and into the intellectual element of the experience; they must mentally complete the image for a full understanding. At that moment, the audience has temporarily been lost and the actors have to work that much harder to re-establish the connection.

Working fights as *physical sentences* is a shift in approach that can make the fight world less threatening to the actor. It uses terminology that is consistent with familiar acting techniques helping to integrate the choreographed sequence with the rest of the story. It brings it back to acting, which in turn helps in opening up the breathing and the voice. Using physical sentences also helps the actors to experience an intuitive fight because voice, breath and physicality are specific and integrated. As a result, the audience is also included in the theatrical event, by way of the breath, and has their own emotional, physical, physiological and breath response.

Works Cited

Barba, Eugenio. *The Paper Canoe*. New York: Routledge, 1995.

Dal Vera, Rocco, ed. *The Voice in Violence presented by the Voice and Speech Review*. (Cincinnati, OH: VASTA), 2001.

Draeger, Donn F., and Robert W. Smith. *Comprehensive Asian Fighting Arts*. New York: Kodansha International, 1969.

Harding, Matt. "Voice and the Choreography of Staged Violence: a Survey." *The Voice in Violence presented by the Voice and Speech Review*, Rocco Dal Vera, ed. (Cincinnati, OH: VASTA), 2001.

Lowry, Marya, and Robert Walsh. "Voice/Combat Conversation." *The Voice in Violence presented by the Voice and Speech Review*, Rocco Dal Vera, ed. (Cincinnati, OH: VASTA), 2001.

Olson, Lise. "Some Personal Discoveries Regarding Vocal Use in Stage Combat." *The Voice in Violence presented by the Voice and Speech Review*, Rocco Dal Vera, ed. (Cincinnati, OH: VASTA), 2001.

Rodenburg, Patsy. *The Right To Speak*. Great Britain: Methuen Drama, 1992.

Sewall, Ian William. *The Folkloral Voice*. Edmonton: Qual Institute Press, 1998.

Wiley, Elizabeth, Marth Munro and Allan Munro. "Orchestrating the Music of the Fight." *The Voice in Violence presented by the Voice and Speech Review*, Rocco Dal Vera, ed. (Cincinnati, OH: VASTA), 2001.

Voice Coach & Fight Coach:
A Collaboration in Physical Effort, Free Breath and the Open Voice
A Dialogue by Matthew E. Ellis and Rena Cook

Rena Cook (RC): Violence has always made me uncomfortable.

Matthew Ellis (ME): On the other hand I have always found it exciting and even compelling.

RC: Consequently, given my own lack of exposure to staged violence, when it was time to create a unit on "Voice and Violence" for an advanced voice class, I turned to my colleague, Matthew Ellis, to help me create a unit of study that integrated voice and choreographed fights.

ME: I readily accepted this challenge as I thought my own work could be enhanced by having vocality incorporated into the initial creative process: "along with" rather than an "add on later." I was inspired by a quote by Fight Master J. Allen Suddeth in which he states:

> An actor shouldn't try to layer these vocalizations on too late in the rehearsal process. An actor should experiment from the first day to create a vocal score for the character. Heavy breathing, shouting, screaming, and physical effort, as well as pain, fear, and triumph are all human traits that help the audience become involved in the struggle (Suddeth 1996, 163).

My mentor, David Leong, spoke fondly of his collaborations with the esteemed voice trainer, Bonnie Raphael, as he said that the voice added energy; activating the voice encourages the body to open more freely to physical impulse.

RC: My current pedagogical obsession is breath, specifically how breath inspires not only the voice but the authentically acted moment as well. K. Jenny Jones shares her belief in the importance of breath when she says, "Most of what I am currently exploring is less voice work and more breathing…the performing of stage fights directly contributes to its own unbelievability; tension, stress, even anxiety. All these elements interfere with the free flow of the breath, hence the voice" (Coetzee 2001, 96). Her references to unbelievability, tension and stress reflect my apprehensions each time I face this particular issue of integrating voice and violence.

ME: It has been my contention that breath must co-exist side by side with effort, effort here meaning the force of energy used to accomplish a specific task. Adding breath to the motion increases the effect of ease and flow. In my personal practice I have intuitively known the importance of deep central breathing. An article by Matt Harding supports this notion, "…a silent fight," he states, "is often indicative of poor breathing. The breath is either inappropriate, unsupported or non-existent" (Harding 2001, 91). I have observed similar situations with actors I have worked with, realizing that tension is the enemy, but without a type of controlled tension we can't have conflict. Nicholas Sandys is quoted in Harding's article, "If the actor does not breathe, then tension builds, the body losses flexibility, the techniques become stiffer and contact too hard—and there is, of course, no noise!" (92).

RC: I knew of Bonnie and David's 1997 VASTA workshop and have long been an admirer of the amount of knowledge they both have contributed to this

Matthew E. Ellis is an Assistant Professor of Movement and Acting at the University of Oklahoma. He holds an MFA in Theatre Pedagogy with an emphasis in Movement and Fight Directing from Virginia Commonwealth University. Matthew has worked as both a professional actor for the past ten years and a professional fight director for the past six years. His fight direction credits include *Hamlet*, *Noises Off!*, *Man of La Mancha*, *Breath, Boom!*, *As You Like It*, *Macbeth*, *Come Back Little Sheba*, *Quay West*, *Beauty and the Beast* and *Taming of the Shrew* among others.

Rena Cook is an Associate Professor of Theatre at University of Oklahoma where she teaches Voice, Speech and Dialects. She has served as vocal coach for the Illinois Shakespeare Festival on *The Merry Wives of Windsor*, *Richard III*, and *Wild Oats*. She has directed *Dancing at Lughnasa*, *The Prime of Miss Jean Brodie* and *Medea*. Rena holds an MA in Voice Studies from the Central School of Speech and Drama. Her theatrical reviews have appeared in *The Journal of Dramatic Theory and Criticism* and *Theatre Journal*. She is on the Board of Directors for VASTA and assumes the role of Editor-in-Chief for the next issue of *VSR*.

body of work. It was her words that finally inspired Matthew and me to begin to develop our own way of integrating the voice with physical violence:

> I think actors need to develop skills related to physical violence before they go into rehearsal for a production in which those skills will be needed. In the same way that some actors take singing lessons or dancing lessons or learn to juggle or whistle or to use different stage dialects, it's a great idea for them to learn the basics of both unarmed combat and doing the wrong (vocal) things the right way. The best time to refine and habituate skills relating to grunting, groaning, coughing, choking, sobbing, screaming, etc. is not while you are in rehearsal for a show. It's far more productive to bring these special skills into the rehearsal process with you (Meyer 2001, 20).

I wanted to explore staged violence and its relationship to breath and voice in the studio in a relaxed, organic way. When I have worked with fight directors in the past, my contribution was often limited to grunts and groans produced as safely as possible. I was eager to explore a vocal coach/fight coach partnership.

In determining what to include and how best to structure the sessions, I looked to Marth Munro's editorial in the *Voice and Speech Review*:

> In real life conflict situations, highly emotional moments (and definitely situations where violence is taking place) the voice is involuntarily 'in service of' the unmediated emotion. Consequently, intense emotions like aggression or sadness usually lead to constriction in the laryngeal area, as the emotion 'overcomes' the whole body (Munro 2001, 14).

Having observed a regular pattern of vocal constriction during intense emotion and physicality in my experience as well, I determined that some lamentation work (inspired by Marya Lowry's 2003 presentation at Voice and Speech Trainers Conference) might lay the foundation of breath and the free, open voice during heightened circumstances.

ME: Rena invited me to participate in her lamentation exploration. I observed how comfortable the ensemble was with physicality and how committed they were to vocality while being drawn into the emotionally intense circumstances. I saw bodies *sharing* vocality, actors sharing a vocal language. It was two people sharing a vocal effort or impulse, as if a single set of sounds was shared by two bodies. I remember one moment when the students, in pairs, were moving back to back, feeling and sensing the sound vibrations together. You can't wail without breathing. As I saw them commit to the lamentation, I saw the bodies activate automatically to meet the vocal stakes.

It made me aware that in the same way the voice can match physical stakes, the body can match vocal stakes. The way I have worked in the past was to establish the physical stakes, then bring the vocal stakes up to match it.

As a result of this exploration with Rena and her students, I now believe it is better to build the physical and vocal in tandem. Raphael speaks clearly to this point, "If…both sound and movement emanate from the same aggressive or defensive impulse and if the impulse originates from the actor's center, then the voice will respond spontaneously and will not have to be added on later because the fight seems oddly quiet" (Raphael 1989, 13).

RC: This speaks to the primary question of how, in the studio, can we help actors explore a process of integrated voice and movement, deeply supported by breath, in heightened or extended circumstances? K. Jenny reiterates the same question when she says, "…we can talk and discuss about breathing from a grounded center, meanwhile, our students and actors are turning blue from the cardiovascular, aerobic and emotional demands of the choreography…One of my fears is how easily we get caught up in our ideologies of what 'ought to be,' while allowing ourselves less time for being practical" (Coetzee 2001, 97). Matthew and I resolved that through this collaboration we would move beyond discussion into a practical exploration that might yield tangible performance application.

What follows is a discussion and description of three sessions, each two hours in length, in which the voice coach and fight coach worked side-by side with eighteen voice students with the goal of creating simple repeatable violence accompanied by healthy open sounds fully supported by breath.

ME: To provide an outline of the path we followed, I used a series of organic exercises, first introduced to me by David Leong, a Fight Master within the Society of American Fight Directors. "Water Meets Water" is the central concept to which all variations within this workshop return. As a basic exercise in physical objective and partner-induced obstacle, it contains the essence of any physical conflict. Next in this sequence is an exercise called "Push/Pull" which, like "Water Meets Water," contains a single objective and a single simple obstacle with the addition of specific scripted elements, lending itself to ease of repeatable action, which is vital to performing violence within the confines of a scripted dramatic work.

We then put the application we learned in "Push/Pull" back into "Water Meets Water" so that motion or actions in the first exercise can be recreated thus leading to repeatable action and set choreography. The contrast between this exercise and conventional unarmed fight choreography, where the fight director prescribes action, is clear. "Water Meets Water" allows the movement to be created from the actor's own understanding of character need, objective and impulse. It is important to note here that beyond the confines of this classroom situation, the "Water Meets Water" sequence can also include conventional staged combat such as non-contact masking and knaps; however traditional elements provide highlighted moments and not the sole basis for choreography.

Throughout the work, safety, both physical and vocal, was a prime concern. The students were reminded to keep the pace slow at Tai Chi speed. A warning was repeated often to be aware of any potentially dangerous moves such as an elbow in face that can easily be modified to insure safety. Likewise, a sharp ear was kept for sounds that were open and supported by breath. Side coaching was continuous in an effort to keep the environment safe.

"Water Meets Water," A Description

Two actors, hereafter called A and B, face one another and gently make hand contact, not necessarily "holding hands" but gently touching one another. A begins by choosing an objective that resides on the opposite side of B. For early demonstrations, the students are encouraged to maintain an energy level of one to two (on a scale of 1-10, 1 being the least amount). Conflicting objectives are as simple as "A: To get the cookie on the other side of B. B: To keep A from achieving success." It is important that each actor listen to the physical impulse of his or her partner. Therefore, when A goes for the cookie, B cannot just stop him/her cold. This is the equivalent of saying "No" in an improvisational exercise. B has to recognize that A's objective has value, but then must "suggest" an alternative. This becomes a sort of Tai-Chi-like dance in which:

1. A goes for his objective.
2. B lets A pass, while maintaining a physical connection.
3. B gives A a physical "suggestion" that redirects A back to where he started.
4. A and B stay in physical contact, and A picks a new physical tactic, such as going around the other side of B or under B's legs. The process begins again.

All the while, the two actors are maintaining a slow, easy flowing rhythm, like water meeting water. While A works to achieve getting his cookie, there are some simple rules:

1. The exercise is about a single objective with one tactic applied at a time. Therefore, when A goes to get the cookie, he does not try to "fake-out" his partner.

2. Once A receives the effort from B that suggests going back, he must do so. The amount of effort that A needs to "convince" him is dependent on the effort level at which the pair is working. For instance, at effort level 2, it should not be difficult for B to turn A around, but at effort level 7, B will have to work a great deal to turn A around.

It is important that both A and B proceed slowly! An increased effort level can be independent of speed. The students should stay at a slow "Tai-Chi Speed," but retain the energy and effort level no matter where they are on the spectrum.

RC: During the actual sessions, I noticed that the actors had a tendency to hold their breath. I suggested that they exhale on an easy "ah" as they physicalized their tactic, asking them to give the sound the same attention as if both body and voice were working together in the common pursuit of need.

ME: It's important to note that the actors should use their voices to match their physical effort level. For instance, when pushing with an effort level of 10 and vocalizing with an effort level of 3, the vocalization is actually restricting the amount of helpful breath. On the other end of the spectrum, when pushing with an effort level of 5 and vocalizing with an effort level of 10 a restriction can occur in the vocal tract that is potentially damaging to the voice. When these two elements are out of sync, the disconnection produces a forced and synthetic performance.

"Push/Pull"

After the completion of the basic "Water Meets Water," another exercise is introduced to produce an honest physical effort to achieve an objective.

The students clasp hands while standing. Both students push into one another and find an equilibrium of force, with a warning to avoid so much force that it overpowers the partner and pushes them down or back, or conversely makes it too easy. The key is to find the most force without the whole structure collapsing, to establish a sense of stasis. Next, actor A chooses an intention. This can be abstract, such as "pushing my way through a relationship" or "convincing my father that acting is a valid profession," anything that carries a moderate amount of emotional weight. Once that choice is made, A pushes B across the space. This time B must let himself be pushed slowly across the space, without making it too easy for A.

RC: We explored this exercise with and without focused breath. We found that breath assists effort and sound becomes more natural. With the addition of a low "oh" or an "ah," the

Vocal Production, Voice Related Movement Studies
Voice Coach & Fight Coach: A Collaboration in Physical Effort, Free Breath and the Open Voice
by Matthew E. Ellis & Rena Cook (continued)

voice stays open and connected. Physical effort and the sound work together, and the sense of effort is actually reduced. After a trip across the space, the actors switch roles, exploring various effort levels.

ME: The same exercise is repeated with pulling instead of pushing. Each pair is given a towel and instructed to pull their partner across the space. Even though the concept of actual effort and breath is the same, it allows the students to explore a different type of effort and therefore a different experience with the use of their body.

RC: The "Push/Pull" sequence was altered by adding a voiced fricative, "v" or "z," and comparisons between vowels and fricatives were discussed. Students noticed that the resistance offered by the fricative helped to manage the breath. One student observed that she could monitor her partner's effort level more easily.

A commonly-memorized sonnet, "Batter My Heart" by John Donne, was introduced with an admonition to monitor effort levels. With the addition of text, students noticed they had a smoother journey across the floor. They could more easily monitor their own effort levels as well as their partner's.

ME: The final variation prior to returning to the main construct of "Water Meets Water" is an opportunity to use real opposing effort in a simple repeatable scenario. In this variation of "Push/Pull," B sits on the ground while A attempts to push B from their spot. The partners are given a prescribed scenario:
1. A tries to move B from the spot and fails.
2. A tries to move B from the spot a second time in a different way and fails.
3. A tries to move B from the spot a third time in a different way and succeeds, after great effort.

After the actors are comfortable with this they are asked to repeat each of the actions as accurately as possible, such as same hand placement, same stakes, same motion, each time using as much effort as can be given yet fulfilling the requirements of the script. As in "Water Meets Water," the actors are encouraged to give authentic effort to match the effort of their partner. In the repetition of this action, the actors have choreographed a scene of physical struggle.

RC: This scenario was repeated with a focus on breath, exhaling first on simple vowel sounds, then voiced fricatives. Previous discoveries were reinforced as it became clear that the presence of intentional breath assists and clarifies the effort, making the action more easily repeatable, providing another muscle memory hook.

ME: The final step is to take this concept of creating repeatable action back to "Water Meets Water," using the scenario above: try, fail; try again with a different tactic, fail; try a third time with a new tactic and succeed. To raise the stakes, actor A is given a prop such as a belt or a shirt with the instructions to "tie up your partner." B is instructed to resist until the third tactic when A succeeds. The exercise is escalated one more time with the addition of vocalization in the form of "yes," "no" or "you son of a bitch."

The use of "yes" and "no" clarifies and heightens intention for both audience and performers. These words take the exploration away from merely movement or voice, adding an element of narrative which leads to an escalation of stakes.

RC: It was clear, however, that restricting the text to these simple words was essential in order to keep the actors connected to the moment without intellectualizing improvised text.

What emerged from this series of exercises was a group of individual scenes of physical and vocal violence, each reaching a level of theatrical specificity, in which elevated stakes in both body and voice were equally and safely engaged.

RC: Normally, when I teach the voice and violence unit without the presence of a fight coach, the bodies of the actors are only partially engaged. The meager attempts at creating violent acts fall short of the reality that the voices seem to be conveying. Bonnie Raphael makes a similar observation when she states, "Whenever the movement is limited to arms and legs and centered breathing is not behind it, any urge to make sound will not be organic and whatever sounds are produced may appear phony and unconvincing" (Raphael 1989, 13). What I perceived that Matthew's work brought to this project was a confidence in the physicality with extended body lines and pictures that evoked far more, bringing body and voice into an integration of theatrical authenticity.

ME: When I have done this work in the past, I have observed the degree of conflict that the actors achieve is stronger than much staged combat; however, I have always felt it lacked an extra something that pushes the violence to a visceral place. By integrating the body and Rena's voice work together, the product achieves a heightened degree of need, making it more dramatically captivating.

Conclusion

RC: At the conclusion of the three-session workshop, we reflected on our initial questions and the subsequent outcomes. We looked first at the collaborative process that we undertook, voice and fight coach working side by side. In this particular instance, Matthew took the lead and I supported his directives with side coaching that brought the students back continuously to breath and voice. As the collaboration progressed, Matthew's focus broadened to encompass not only the physicality but the breath as well. An ease, an ebb and flow, of coaching voices became almost seamless from the students' perspective.

Within the exploration of the relationship of effort to breath, the exercises provided not only a vocabulary, but a practical application reinforcing that the two are inextricably tied. Over the three days the students learned, both intellectually and kinesthetically, that one cannot exist efficiently and safely without the other.

ME: I was particularly interested in the outcome of building vocal and physical stakes in tandem. This collaboration reinforced my desire to explore the simultaneous creation of the physical and vocal score. Building the two scores together raises the physical stakes during the initial choreography, one beat at a time. This avoids the need to back pedal when adding on the vocality. Rena and I confirmed what Dale Girard spoke of saying:

> The voice, like all action within a fight, must be built from the ground up. It cannot be superficially laid onto an action or it will sound artificial and unconvincing. The actor must be grounded and centered in order to command force or energy. If you are relaxed and properly centered in the execution of your actions, allowing your energy to come from the ground up and support from the diaphragm, you should find the voice naturally freed with the action. If the action and the sound originate from your center, then the response will be spontaneous and organic (Girard 1997, 445).

Last, we returned to the question that originally inspired our dialogue, "how, in the studio, can we help actors explore a process of integrated voice and movement, deeply supported by breath, in heightened or extended circumstances?" From a vocal standpoint, the actors created a more varied tapestry of textured sounds all of which were open and healthy. From a physical standpoint, the violence was unpredictable from an audience's view but safe and repeatable for the actors. At the final performance it became clear that the "Water Meets Water" sequence, jointly taught, provides a solid model that moves the actors nearer to the goal of physical effort, integrated with the free breath and open voice.

Bibliography

Coetzee, Marie-Heleen. "Voicing the Visceral: an Interview with Erik Fredericksen and k. Jenny Jones." *The Voice in Violence presented by the Voice and Speech Review*, Rocco Dal Vera, ed. (Cincinnati, OH: VASTA), 2001, 95-104.

Girard, Dale Anthony. *Actors on Guard*. New York: Routledge, 1997.

Harding, Matt. "Voice and Choreography of Staged Violence: a survey." *The Voice in Violence presented by the Voice and Speech Review*, Rocco Dal Vera, ed. (Cincinnati, OH: VASTA), 2001, 87-94.

Meyer, Ursula. "Bonnie Raphael." *The Voice in Violence presented by the Voice and Speech Review*, Rocco Dal Vera, ed. (Cincinnati, OH: VASTA), 2001, 16-21.

Munro, Marth. "Vocal Production, Voice-related Movement Studies." *The Voice in Violence presented by the Voice and Speech Review*, Rocco Dal Vera, ed. (Cincinnati, OH: VASTA), 2001, 14-15.

Raphael, Bonnie. "The Sounds of Violence, Part 1: The Real Thing." *The Fight Master*, XII, no.1 (Winter 1989): 13.

Suddeth, J. Allen. *Fight Directing for the Theatre*. Portsmouth: Heinemann, 1996.

Peer Reviewed Article *by Barbara Acker*

The Verse Delivery Experiments of William Butler Yeats
and Florence Farr

William Butler Yeats was, of course, a Nobel Prize winning lyric poet. He was also a poet who nurtured a life-long enthusiasm for the theatre. Yeats was the chief architect and spokesman of the Irish literary theatre movement and was one of the founders of the Abbey Theatre. As a playwright, he had a poet's concern for how his words were spoken. In his quest for the perfect actor and style of delivery for literary drama, Yeats had help from his friend, actor Florence Farr. They wanted to create an evocative style of vocal delivery that would illuminate poetic language.[1] In the 1899 production of *The Countess Cathleen* and in the early years of the Irish National Theatre Society, Yeats and Farr experimented with *speaking* lines of verse to a simple melody. This speech, they claimed, was not chanting or singing, but real speaking. Some critics and audience members liked the delivery of verse, while others rejected it. In Yeats' early plays, the partners came up against two obstacles. The first was a pragmatic one: having the authority and sufficient rehearsal time to train the actors. The second obstacle was more elusive and, perhaps, more important: convincing the company of amateurs that the half-chanted, half-spoken style they advocated was an effective way to speak verse. As much as Yeats said he wanted tragic power and passionate actors in his plays, many actors and audiences found this style of slow, sonorous delivery more like poetic recitation than taut dialogue suitable for drama.[2]

In a series of lectures, Yeats and Farr tried to generate enthusiasm for their approach to verse delivery. Farr demonstrated speaking poems to melodies she played on a psaltery. The audiences they reached, artists and professionals of the educated middle class—people who cared about theatre, Yeats' verse, or Irish culture—they were not the ones who had to be convinced. Yeats needed to reach the Irish actors who performed his plays, and he needed Farr to do the practical work of instructing and coaching. Though Farr could have trained the actors, she was never hired for the task. Ultimately Yeats depended on an intermediary, Frank Fay, to teach the actors his method of speaking. Frank Fay was a member of the Abbey acting company and the elocution teacher who trained the actors. Yeats felt the company could not measure up to Frank Fay's delivery. Later he went so far as to say Fay's delivery was not good enough. Disillusioned, Yeats gave up the hope of hearing his dramas spoken the way he wanted and turned to plays for dancers. Given the continued interest in Yeats' plays and his ideas of theatrical production, his experiment with vocal delivery is important: it can shed some light on his particular approach to theatre, and what he believed would make his early plays work.

W.B. Yeats wrote extensively about his theories of poetic drama and how such drama should be staged. Interest in Yeats' plays and theories about theatre have generated an impressive body of scholarship. Much less has been written about Yeats' actual practice: what he said to actors at rehearsals to influence blocking and line delivery. The rehearsal record is further obscured because Yeats tended to look at his own past in a way that displaced certain contributions of his collaborators. For example, he did not fully acknowledge Lady Gregory's collaboration in writing some of his early scripts until the 1924 publication of *Plays in Prose and Verse: Written for an Irish Theatre and Generally with the Help of a Friend*.[3] In his reminiscences, *Four Years: 1887-1891*, Yeats described Farr as an amateur, dismissing her years of professional experience in the theatre and her help with speaking to the psaltery.[4] Looking

Barbara Acker is an Associate Professor at Arizona State University, where she teaches voice and acting. She holds a PhD from Wayne State University in Theatre with a minor in Speech Science. Acker studied with Arthur Lessac and Sue Ann Parks. She directed *Wheel of Fire: The Bacchae* as part of a Roy Hart intensive taught by Ivan Midderigh. Acker has presented at the Care of the Professional Voice conference and ATHE, and published in *The Journal of Voice* and the *Journal of American Drama and Theatre*. She co-edited of *The Vocal Vision*. She has served as President and Member of the Board of VASTA.

back on the early days of the Abbey, Yeats did not acknowledge Frank Fay's contribution to the voice work or the good opinion he once held of Fay's own verse speaking. It reveals another facet of Yeats' theories to examine them in the light of the realities of his productions: to see how Yeats' managed the means at his disposal to gain acceptance for his experiment. Theatre depends on time; space; personnel; the way playwrights, directors and actors work together; and how the audience receives the work. The exigencies of production can defeat or support a new approach to acting. This paper will look at the first production of *The Countess Cathleen* to put Yeats' theories in the context of an actual production. Since the record of rehearsals is scanty, further evidence has to be gleaned from several other productions; the correspondence between the Abbey voice coach, Frank Fay, and Yeats; and the observations of audiences from several different plays and lectures. As always, a production begins with the aspirations and dreams of the playwright and his voice coach, about the ideal acting style and vocal delivery.

Yeats and Farr looked to the past to recover the method of speaking verse to music that the bards and minstrels of ancient Greece and Ireland used to evoke a religious awe in their listeners. "We have forgotten," Yeats wrote, "that the Drama began in the chanted ode, and that whenever it has been great it has been written…to delight our ears more than our eyes."[5] Yeats wanted to subordinate everything else on stage to the speaking of his verse: "the actor should be a reverent reciter of majestic words."[6] Yeats described his ideal actor as one able to keep the "keenness and salt" natural to words, and not, like a singer, turn them into "honey and oil." Ordinary singing, Yeats believed, subordinated poetic rhythm and the meaning of words to the melody. "A lyric which is spoken or chanted to music should…reveal its meaning, and its rhythm to become indissoluble in the memory." To restore poetic drama to its full beauty, he advocated speaking verse with a musical emphasis. He disliked actors who spoke verse with conversational prose rhythms that turned poetry into mere "talk." He also cautioned actors not to sing poetry because singing sacrificed the words to the rhythmical beat. "No vowel must be preserved unnaturally, no word of mine must ever change into a mere musical note. What was the good of writing a love-song if the singer pronounced love 'lo-o-o-o-ve,' or even if he said love, but did not give it its exact place and weight in the rhythm?" "When speech becomes song, it must do so imperceptibly as if mere speech had taken fire."[7]

Florence Farr, as a professional actor, took issue with the poor verse delivery she heard in contemporary theatre. For an interview in the *Daily Express* (Dublin), Farr complained how difficult is was to find actors who could speak verse other than

as "bad and florid prose."[8] At a deeper, mystical level, she believed that style was the only thing that endures and "style is the appreciation of words as *sounds*, not merely as symbols for conveying ideas; style is the appreciation of phrases as *melodies*, not merely as the expression of thought."[9] Spoken slowly and simply, Farr believed that words could magically bridge the inner essence or soul and outer reality of physical form. The most powerful words, she believed, were intoned chants that take the listener to a deep meditative state in which it is possible to unite with the infinite.[10] Yeats' and Farr's ideas were slightly different: Yeats wanted actors to imitate his emphasis, intonation and rate of speaking, while Farr wanted the actor to create a simple tune that released the power of the words. But both agreed that words have power to transform the listener if spoken simply. Farr was happy to devise tunes that pleased Yeats.

Styles of acting do not appear out of the blue: playwrights and actors such as Yeats and Farr react to the traditions of their contemporary theatrical aesthetic, so it is worthwhile to consider how their backgrounds shaped their taste in theatre. Yeats' earliest ideas about the theatre came from reading plays and listening to the drawing room discussions of his father, the artist, John Butler Yeats and his friends. WBY was deeply influenced by the Pre-Raphaelite, romantic, school of poetry and art of his father's circle.[11] Although John Butler Yeats was himself a graduate of Trinity College Dublin, he disliked the educational practices of the time and went so far as insisting that anything written for the average boy or man would stunt one's growth.[12] Not surprisingly, W. B.Yeats, who attended school for only about six and a half years, had little hope and less money for a place at Trinity College.[13] WBY joined his sisters, Lilly and Lolly, at the inexpensive Metropolitan School of Art in Dublin. With such an erratic and limited formal education, William Butler Yeats felt his father's influence more keenly than most middle-class young men of the time did.

Yeats' father was a painter who worked at home and had the time to indulge his interest in educating his children, especially young Willie. John Butler Yeats read his young son novels such as *Ivanhoe* and the poem *The Lay of the Last Minstrel*. Later John Butler Yeats read only poems and plays, choosing passages of "the most passionate moment," and never reading anything that smacked of generalized emotions or abstract thought.[14] And father and son endlessly discussed style. Yeats absorbed his father's credo: "All must be an idealization of speech, and at some moment of passionate action or somnambulistic reverie."[15] Yeats' habit of speaking aloud as he composed poetry points to his sensitivity to the sound of words; his habit may also owe a debt to his father's relish for the spoken word. Theatre going was a luxury the Yeats family could ill afford, but Yeats remembered his father taking him to Irving's 1879 production of *Hamlet*.[16] There is no record of WBY's play going between 1879 and 1888, but the professional theatre did not matter that much to the young poet. By the late 1880s, he had already written two journeyman plays: *The Island of Statues*, "An Arcadian Play in imitation of Edmund Spencer" (1885), and *Mosada* (1886). His father's rendition of *Prometheus Unbound* and *Coriolanus* arguably carried more weight in defining WBY's tastes in vocal delivery than professional actors of the commercial theatre. Yeats claimed he always heard his father's voice in one vivid scene of *Coriolanus*, not Irving's or Benson's.[17]

In May of 1890 Yeats saw his future friend and collaborator, Florence Farr, perform in *A Sicilian Idyll* at the Bedford Park Clubhouse. Farr had a lovely voice. According to Yeats, "She had three great gifts, a tranquil beauty like that of Demeter's image near the British Museum Reading-Room door, and an incomparable sense of rhythm and a beautiful voice, the seeming natural expression of the image."[18] He recognized Farr as his ideal actor. He wrote of her and her fellow amateur actor Heron Allen in *A Sicilian Idyll*, praising their musical speech, the distinction and majesty of their poetical lines. He angrily condemned other actors in the play who mangled their verse, delivering it like banal conversational speech.[19]

Florence Farr was a professional actor with some 300 performances to her credit when she began the collaboration with Yeats. Her father was a recognized statistician and an ally of Florence Nightingale on public health issues. He supported the formal education of women and saw to it Farr attended Cheltenham, and the first institute of higher learning for women, Queen's College in London. Florence Farr had a college education, though she did not take the exams to get her external degree from the University of London. Farr disdained her advanced education: her studies did not shape her theatrical consciousness. But one course she took in college, singing, helped her as an actor and reciter. Admittedly singing was not her strength: during performances she sometimes missed her note.[20]

Farr began her career in the theatre in the usual manner for a late nineteenth-century aspirant. She apprenticed for eight months in 1882 with the actor-manager J. L. Toole at his little playhouse in King Williams' Street. The training, such as it was, consisted of step dancing and Shakespeare. Presumably apprentices recited the Bard's speeches to learn good vocal quality, projection and clear diction, perhaps even how to handle blank verse.[21] When the stage manager deemed the apprentices ready for small parts, he gave them their blocking on a Friday, and they opened the next day, Saturday, in one of Toole's stock comedies. In this rough and ready method,

novices were thrown into the deep end of the pool to sink or swim: a process Farr liked because it guaranteed a "fresh spontaneous performance."[22] She believed Toole's comedies were antediluvian relics, the oldest kind of theatrical entertainment for the masses. She continued making a living in comedies, playing small roles in W.F. Hawtrey's productions from 1884 to the mid-1890s. By the age of 30 she was no longer an ingenue; she no longer wanted to play the coquettes of her youth. She was ready to take on serious drama that offered women substantial roles with complex characterizations.

Farr joined the coterie of the New Drama enthusiasts in England when she organized the production of the Ibsen drama *Rosmersholm* in 1891, and played the leading female role, Rebecca. The following year her friend George Bernard Shaw persuaded her to take the role of an "unwomanly woman," Blanche Sartorius, in the Independent Theatre production of his play *Widowers' Houses*. Her major contribution to the new drama, however, was the groundbreaking season at the Avenue Theatre in 1894. She commissioned WBY's *The Land of Heart's Desire* (16 performances) and Shaw's *Arms and the Man* (75 performances), and so introduced both playwrights to the British public. Her foray into poetic drama began with *A Sicilian Idyll* by John Todhunter (1839-1916) and an excerpt of Shelley's *The Cenci*. Her poetic delivery was unquestionably good. In the early nineties she consciously developed her vocal quality for a fuller sound. In her novel *The Dancing Faun* she described the way she herself worked:

> Something about her voice struck her. She listened, it sounded different, a new beauty had come into it. She read on and on, wondering at the pathos of the tones she uttered…it seemed to her some inspired spirit had entered her body and was making use of her voice to reveal to her what life, and love and divine sorrow meant.

> From that day she settled down to hard work. She heard that some of her words sounded little and thin, and she resolved to work away until she got all alike resonantly beautiful.[23]

It was in verse drama that Farr and Yeats began to wrestle with vocal delivery. Yeats believed that a poet unconsciously wrote verse to a melody. According to Yeats, poetry should not be chanted, sung, or spoken like everyday conversation. He described his ideal delivery as speaking to notes with a "delicate sense of rhythm with a perfect respect for its [poetry's] meaning."[24] Sufficient practice, he argued, should allow a speaker to hold a fixed note and give the words expressive variety. Everyday speech, Yeats argued, is "formless," so conversational delivery of his verse would destroy the poetry.[25] Beautiful verse for Yeats depended on rhythm: it was rhythm that separated good writing from bad. He heard rhythm in prose, too, and he praised Milton's writings and great orators who knew how to use "a subtle monotony of voice that runs through the nerves like fire." He did not see a contradiction between his insistence on monotony *and* variety. "All art is, indeed," Yeats continued, "a monotony in external things for the sake of an interior variety, a sacrifice of gross effects to subtle effects, an asceticism of the imagination."[26] Yeats mixed prose, iambic pentameter, lyric verse, chants, and songs in his plays: each form of writing demanded a different style of delivery. Prose, lyric verse and iambic pentameter he wanted *spoken* to notes. He wanted an actor to "understand how to discriminate cadence from cadence, and so to cherish the musical lineaments of verse or prose that he delights the ear with a continually varied music."[27] To prove he was not asking actors to speak prose or verse like a monotonous chant, Yeats pointed to Frank Fay as an example of an actor who could infuse the rhythm and melody of his lines with subtly nuanced meaning. Yeats wanted chanting for some lyrics, such as the Angel's lines in *The Hour-Glass* and the Chorus of Singing Women in *On Baile's Strand*. Finally, Yeats wanted clear diction in his songs, so everyone in the audience could understand the words.[28] He publicly avowed knowing anything about music, "I do not even know one note from another. I am afraid I even dislike music…"[29] Since Yeats was tone deaf and Farr was not musically adept, the partners needed the help of a musician to create melodies for speaking, chanting, and singing. They were fortunate to find an enthusiastic collaborator in Arnold Dolmetsch.

Dolmetsch was an early music expert who built replicas of early musical instruments. When Yeats and Farr approached him in 1901 with a request for a harp-like instrument to accompany verse, Dolmetsch created a psaltery with 13 metal strings and a range of semi-tones from G below middle C to G above middle C to suit Farr's low-pitched speaking voice.[30] The psaltery had a pentatonic scale of 5 tones, a scale arranged like a major scale with the fourth and seventh tone omitted. Dolmetsch showed them how to play the psaltery and how to use a few simple musical notations to write notes on a musical staff to indicate pitch and to mark short and long syllables. Farr's pentatonic melodies had a very narrow pitch range. They sounded dissonant and grounded in a minor key, especially when compared to the popular music of her time, which was based on the octave scale. Farr would begin with "the most impressive way that occurred to me," to say the first line of a poem and wrote down the notes she used as a starting point. "I do not chant…or use the singing voice except in refrains…I simply speak as I would without music and having discovered the drift of my voice in the phrase, indicate that on the psaltery."[31] At times she played chords under words, although in other instances she played the specific note of a

word as she spoke it. She insisted that she spoke words, and did not chant them, since she believed that chanting is "a monotonous singing sound on notes" that ruined the inflection that carries meaning. For her, the difference between speaking and singing was that the spoken word had an inherent melody based on meaning. Singing sacrificed words to the melody of the music.[32]

James Flannery analyzed the melody Farr composed and performed for Aleel's song in *The Countess Cathleen*. He described the music as a "*chant-like* delivery of verse: a speech melody wavering through half and quarter tones, varying no more than one pitch per line; a subtle modulation of dynamics within phrases; a lingering over vowels to give slight emphasis to important words; and a careful rhythmic stressing of strong and weak beats to give the whole lyric a sense of inner body and life."[33] Flannery's analysis describes Farr and Yeats aesthetic for a *chanted* song. Yeats believed an actor could also *speak* to specific notes and that this was an old art he was reviving. The melody for spoken verse, he said, must be kept simple enough to accommodate different emotions, but above all, he believed it was possible to speak to notes without drifting into chant.[34] The melodies Farr composed for the poems used in their lecture-demonstrations are the clearest evidence of how Yeats wanted his verse spoken. The spoken melodies have the same kind of dissonant harmonies and narrow pitch range that Farr used in Aleel's song.

Yeats recited his own verse to friends and to actors to demonstrate the way he wanted his lines spoken. The poet John Masefield described Yeats' unique way of reciting poetry as follows: "He stressed the rhythm until it almost became a chant. He went with speed, marking every beat and dwelling on the vowels. That ecstatic wavering song…was to remain with me for years."[35] Yeats' sister Lolly gave an account of his recitation style when she described his attempt to speak French:

> Willie's dramatic intense way to saying his French with his voice raised to telling distinctness and every pronunciation wrong as usual, seemed to amuse Mr. Sparling more than ever. He simply doubled up when Willie commenced. Willie of course divided it up into any amount of full stops where they weren't any, so Madam [the French teacher] 'Mr. Yaytes, you don't read poetry like that, do you?' 'Yes, yes,' he does, volunteered Mr. Sparling, and in truth [it] was rather like his natural way of reading.[36]

The journalist H.W. Nevinson described Yeats as talking constantly, "[M]oving his hands a good deal, & sometimes falling into a chant: says 'D'y see?' every sentence." One scholar heard three contemporaries of Yeats imitate his rolling cadences and long vowels and wondered if Yeats had imitated

Irving's curiously rhythmical manner of speech he used in the role of Hamlet.[37] Another hint of Yeats' voice comes from the indefatigable Dublin theatre-goer Joseph Holloway:

> Certainly Mr. Yeats in speaking acts up to his opinions, as he chants most of his remarks in a monotonous recitative most slumberful in result; only he is so erratic or over-laden with ideas, that he continually breaks off at a tangent from a rhymed idea to a commonplace quite foreign to the previous sentence…I assure you that three gentleman of the line of chairs with me were almost lulled to rest and peacefully closed their eyes as Mr. Yeats' chanting fell on their ears.[38]

A verse drama demands adequate rehearsal time, especially if the actors are untrained. Adequate is an elastic term for a director that can mean several years, months or weeks, but the usual state of affairs for the Irish theatre in these early days meant rehearsals lasted for a little more than a month or two. Yeats and Farr were in a position to dictate the acting and vocal style of *The Countess Cathleen* because they controlled the casting and rehearsing—at first. Yeats asked Florence Farr to direct the play, which was to rehearse in London and transfer to Dublin to open on 8 May 1899. In late March she gathered a group of amateurs that included her niece Dorothy Paget who was to play the role of the Countess. With Yeats' approval, Farr took the role of Aleel, the bard, a companion of the Countess. By mid-April Edward Martyn and George Moore, fellow playwrights of the Irish Literary Theatre, convinced Yeats that Farr was a terrible director and the amateurs were not good enough. Yeats took their advice and hired English professionals, the F.R. Benson Company, to replace most of the amateurs. Farr kept her role of the bard, but May Whitty took up the leading part of the Countess and Farr's niece was given the prologue to recite. Farr and Yeats arrived in Dublin on 4 May to rehearse the minor characters. In the first issue of the program *Beltaine*, Yeats prepared prospective audiences for something new: "the speaking of poetic words…to music, [is] so perfectly among the lost arts that it will take a long time before our actors, no matter how willing, will be able to forget the ordinary methods of the stage or to perfect a new method."[39] This warning was hardly necessary, since only Farr and Dorothy Paget were using the new method. May Whitty as the Countess and the rest of her company were opposed to Farr's psaltery and invocations of the poetic muse.[40] Lady Gregory, who did not care for Farr, rejected WBY's suggestion that Farr teach the actors elocution. Farr did not have anything to do with the Irish theatre productions after *The Countess Cathleen*. Afterwards her presence was only felt in the music she composed for songs in *The Land of Heart's Desire, On Baile's Strand, The King's Threshold,* and *Deirdre*. The one chance Yeats and Farr had to create a company of actors speaking to melodies disappeared in the exigencies of the production when the English professionals replaced the amateurs. But Yeats did not give up his dream; he talked to the Abbey vocal coach about his method of delivering verse.

There is little evidence that Yeats had much opportunity to teach the Irish actors how to speak to a melody, except through an intermediary, Frank Fay. Vocal training for the Irish actors was in the hands of Frank Fay from 1899 until he left the Abbey Theatre Company in 1908.[41] Yeats instructed the actors during rehearsals, but he typically did not spend much time at rehearsals. He tended to arrive toward the end of a rehearsal period to give actors notes a week or two before productions opened.[42] It is difficult to piece together what actually happened at rehearsals. As prolific as Yeats was, turning out manifestos and explanations of his ideal theatre, there are few accounts of his exchanges with actors. WBY tried to demonstrate what he wanted, but his illustrations, more often than not, were frustratingly subtle for the actors. Unlike Yeats, William Fay and his brother Frank Fay were always at rehearsals, coaching and directing the actors.

In December 1902, William Fay's Ormond Dramatic Society and some amateurs from Maud Gonne's society, Daughters of Ireland, joined forces with Yeats, George Russell, Lady Gregory and some others of the Irish Literary Theatre to form the Irish National Theatre Society. This company became the famed Abbey Theatre. Frank Fay and William Fay were actors in the Abbey Company. William directed the plays, designed and painted scenery, and handled the lighting. Frank Fay was the vocal coach. Frank also wrote dramatic criticism for the Dublin newspaper *The United Irishman* for three years. Both men had studied acting and elocution with the English actor Miss Randford. William Fay was theatre-mad, an avid play reader and theatre-goer, who acted for years with travelling companies. Frank Fay had developed a beautiful speaking voice, and exhaustively studied acting and voice.[43] Frank trained the actors in projection, quality and diction; much of their practice material was Shakespearean verse.[44] Seamus O'Sullivan in an interview spoke of, "the grueling course of voice-production at the hands of Frank Fay, before he [O'Sullivan] made his bow as an in actor in AE's *Deirdre*.[45] Udolphus Wright, who was with the Abbey Theatre from 1902, recalled, "Frank would make us sound a's and o's for hours, raising and lowering the key. He insisted on distinct final d's and t's. The ends of our sentences had to be well out. Sharp! He saw to it that we took breathing exercises."[46] Padraic Colum described "Sunday walks in the hills or along the streets after a rehearsal, repeating verse in the way that Frank Fay taught us to repeat it, giving full value to all the vowels. Frank Fay was in his element declaiming and instructing in declamation. He reveled in the poetry of WBY.

Rehearsing with him was a memorable training in vocalization and verse-delivery."[47] Sara Allgood, one of the finest actors of the Abbey Theatre, credited her vocal success to Frank's training. In an interview with Gerard Fay, Allgood explained, "Frank Fay emphasized clearness of speech, strength without loudness, and particularly the greatest possible tone variety."[48]

Frank Fay concerned himself with more than the mechanics of clear diction, good vocal quality, and projection: he wanted actors to understand what they were saying and to deliver the verse with emotional and dramatic power. He admired the French tradition of stage speech that honored rhythm and rhyme in verse. In July 1901, he began an extensive correspondence with Yeats on methods of speaking dramatic verse, laying the groundwork for their collaboration.[49] When WBY asked Fay about the French methods of declamation and intonation on the stage, Fay recommended, "Raymond Solly's *Acting and the Art of Speech at the Paris Conservatoire*, Talma's *The Actor's Art*," and he sent WBY his own copy of Coquelin's *L'Art de dire le monologue*, marking the pages that dealt with the delivery of verse. Fay described a practical exercise to show students how to say poetic lines intelligibly. Conservatoire students, he told WBY, like their English counterparts, are asked to paraphrase a line of verse in colloquial speech, than use the colloquial intonation in the poetic line. Fay went on: "I imagine the French practice to go deeper and to say "Consider how the *type* of man or woman you are representing would say so and so. That is certainly the basis on which Coquelin works and to my way to thinking is the only sound one in acting, as by it as little as possible of the actor's personality gets into the part."[50] Considering that Fay enjoyed Yeats' poetry and Shakespeare, he could easily have been the ideal voice coach for Yeats plays. Did any of Yeats' ideals about speaking reach the stage through Fay's teachings?

Joseph Holloway attended the first performance of the Irish Literary Theatre on 8 May 1899. About *The Countess Cathleen* he wrote in his diary:

> It was weirdly, fantastically, pathetically, or picturesquely effective by turns; and, as I followed its progress, Poe's words, 'all that we see or seem is but a dream within a dream,' floated in on my mind, and a spiritual, half-mystic, visionary sensation crept over my senses as I watched enraptured, as if I were in fairy land. Miss Florence Farr as 'Aleel,' a bard, declaimed all her lines in majestic, beautiful, rhythmic manner good to listen to—most impressive, if occasionally indistinct.[51]

The critic of *Irish Daily Independent* also had kind words for the production; claiming the acting did justice to the verse performance and he singled out Dorothy Paget's delivery of

the prologue and Farr: "The rhythms, beat and cadence of the verse stole on the ears like music sweetly played…Miss Florence Farr was a charming Aleel. Hers is the best delivery of verse that we have heard upon the modern stage."[52] The English professionals were fine, the chorus passed muster and Yeats' chanting and speaking garnered praise. But after Farr's direct influence passed from the scene, Yeats objected to the company's style of speaking, except for Frank Fay's and Sara Allgood's delivery.

Even later Yeats contended that the Fays were good in peasant comedy but not up to the demands of his verse drama. The Dublin playgoer Holloway did not report any such disparity in quality between the company's speech in poetic and prose plays. The reactions of critics and audiences were decidedly mixed. Charles Ricketts admitted to Yeats that although the [Yeats'] play held his attention, he was, "[O]nce or twice annoyed by the intoning of pieces which were quite delightful enough in themselves, without the vocal form of limelight."[53] Another correspondent commended the excellent acting in Lady Gregory's plays performed in London (1903), but did not like the intoning.[54] Max Beerbohm was one of the London critics who praised the Irish company on their 1903 visit to London. He wrote of the pleasure of hearing the "artless" speech of the Irish, which inscribed the Irish company as a colonial "other," not professional actors, but merely exciting interest as exotics.[55] While public praise for the productions was music to Yeats' ears, critics did not single out his particular style of vocal delivery as noteworthy. William Archer, who heard a demonstration/lecture in London, described Farr's fragments of melodies as more singing than speaking. The Greek scholar Gilbert Murray thought the experiment was pretty but had little scientific or historical interest.[56]

Yeats' friend Annie Horniman, who later gained fame as the manager of the Manchester Repertory Theatre, supported the Abbey financially from late 1903 until 1910. She complained of the acting under William Fay's direction. She acknowledged, "[T]he right of authors stage-managing [directing] their works; this is quite right when practicable, but something must be done to make it certain that their orders will be carried out *in their absence*. Until this is done all your toil is just making ropes of sand! Fay will never do this…" The company, she insisted, could not be made first rate "until everyone *acts* instead of simply using themselves. This was perfectly shown in the case of Barlow. He was so good as the red-haired Jack Smith at first when he was fresh & natural but when he got used to the part he became dull wooden useless amateur for he had no *Art* to fall back on."[57] This is a perennial problem of companies that cast both professionals and volunteers—quality is uneven within productions and between productions. Horniman quarreled over conditions that were out of her control and the company's. She dreamed of a professional company like those she saw in Germany and in London, but there were no Dublin theatres doing contemporary Irish plays teaching Irish apprentices, nor was there a training school attached to the early Abbey.

Whatever the actors' limitations in capturing the elusive sound of Yeats' verse, Yeats knew what he wanted, and he struggled to demonstrate it clearly. Joseph Holloway's report of a rehearsal hints at the problem that daunted Yeats:

> *On Baile's Strand* was gone through with the ever-restless W. B. Yeats at the helm, and I say without fear of contradiction that a more irritating play producer never directed a rehearsal. He's ever flitting about and interrupting the players in the middle of their speeches, showing them by illustration how he wishes it done, droningly reading the passage, and in that monotonous preachy sing-song, or climbing up a ladder onto the stage and pacing the boards as he would have the players do…Anon he would rush on and erase or add a line or two to the text, but ever and always he was on the fidgets, and made each and all of the players inwardly pray backwards. Frank Fay, I thought, would explode with suppressed rage at his frequent interruptions during the final speeches he had to utter.[58]

Seaghan Barlow confirmed this tension at rehearsal. WBY interrupted Frank Fay so many times in one speech that Fay lost his temper and asked Yeats how "he [Fay] was expected to deliver his lines properly, when he did not know what he was talking about."[59] Actors struggled to master whatever Yeats heard in his head, but the line readings eluded his powers of demonstrating. The BBC producer George Barnes worked with WBY in action in a 1937 series of broadcasts on modern poetry. "The pleasure of rehearsals was to hear him trying to convey the sounds which were running in his head, and when he succeeded they remained unforgettably in the ear."[60]

Gradually Yeats grew disenchanted with the Fays' work in his plays: actors coached and trained by the Fays lacked an inner fire and passion and could not hold the audiences with their words. Perhaps even more important, nothing in the scanty record of rehearsals Yeats had with the Irish actors suggests that Yeats convinced the actors (many of them amateurs) that his method would make the verse sound better and thus, make them better actors. In spite of all the advice Frank Fay gave WBY about acting in their lengthy correspondence, Yeats did not *apparently* talk about dramatic action to the cast. Cicely Berry, a renowned voice teacher and coach, is reported to have said actors want to be better actors, not better speakers. Actors generally respond well to advice couched in terms

of what the character and dramatic action demand, rather than to requests to imitate a line reading. The first kind of advice appeals to actors' imaginations and is holistic: it can influence actors' readings throughout the scene or play. The second approach, asking an actor to imitate a line reading, can be useful when the playwright helps the actor understand the operative words that move the action forward. Sometimes, though, asking an actor to change one line reading disrupts a pattern of exchanges between characters that builds to the climax of a scene, so the changed line upsets an entire scene. The actor also might take offense at the suggestion that the playwright wants a tape recorder rather than an artistic partnership.

As for audiences, they were not always taken with the Yeats/Farr style of delivery. The dreamy wavering semi-tones Farr spoke, chanted, or sang to the psaltery grated on the ears of audiences who were used to romantic music of the time. And the pentatonic tunes were not musically or dramatically gripping. Yeats wanted intensity, but the tunes were too somnolent and too much like religious chant to stir intensity, as the writer discovered in a public demonstration of the chants. WBY compounded the problem by insisting on few gestures. At one point he felt the body should "disappear" to heighten attention on speech. He wrote that he wanted to "rehearse them [actors] in barrels that they might forget gesture and have their minds free to think of speech for a while. The barrels, I thought, might be on castors, so I could shove them about with a pole when the action required it."[61] But far from inhibiting passionate dialogue, physical tension in the body creates and supports dramatic tension; take, for example, Constantine Stanislavsky's later theories of the body and Tadashi Suzuki's work. The Abbey actors could have learned to maintain physical and emotional intensity, even in exchanges that had no overt conflict. But, to train the actors, Yeats would have had to win the battle with Lady Gregory, who opposed the idea of Florence Farr working with *her* poet. Lady Gregory supported Yeats financially and artistically in so many ways that Yeats could not argue with her. Farr was never invited to Dublin to teach the new art to the company. And there was no money or will in the early days to establish an acting training program. Flannery points out that the literary people running the theatre, including Yeats, never gave directors or teachers the authority to shape the company or take plays in more theatrical directions.[62] This lack of trust, never allowing good directors to create strong staging, undercut Yeats' goal. His verse needed theatrical, not just literary, imagination to give it life on stage.

Yeats said later in life that only three actors could speak his verse the way he wanted it to be spoken: Florence Farr, Sara Allgood, and a pupil of Farr's, Miss Taylor. In 1911 he wondered if his rejection of "vitality," and insistence on a few gestures and little blocking had "imposed too statuesque a pose" together with "too monotonous a delivery."[63] Perhaps he realized—to some extent—that the physical tension of the body, voice, and emotions support each other, that theatrical life is more than speaking.

Frank Fay did not believe Yeats had created new art: speaking to the psaltery was basically singing or chanting, not speaking.[64] G. B. Shaw dismissed the speaking to the psaltery as mere cantilation or intoning. "Yeats thinks it is something new only because he does not go to church. Half the curates in the kingdom cantilate like mad all the time…Toastmasters …public speakers…and Sarah Bernhardt's abominable 'golden voice,' which has always made me sick, is cantilation, or, to use the customary word, intoning. It is no use for Yeats to try to make a distinction, no novelty, no nothing but nonsense."[65] Yeats had come to agree with his audiences: the sound Yeats heard when he composed was lost in translation. He found a cold reception for the melodies of his dream world.

W. B. Yeats and Florence Farr seem to have tried something along the minimalist lines in speaking the verse in Yeats' early plays at the Abbey. The passionate acting and speech WBY longed to see in his plays were inhibited by his insistence on gentle, dissonant melodies. If only three women, in Yeats' estimation, could adequately speak his verse, Yeats and Farr had created a new art of speaking to notes that was liable to slip into the old arts of chanting or singing. Audiences did not appreciate their innovation except in the acting of Frank Fay, Florence Farr, and Sara Allgood. As much as Yeats and Farr would have liked to popularize their method, they did not initiate enough actors into their work or stage it vigorously and imaginatively enough to make a success of their experiment. Frank Fay's more traditional way of speaking verse triumphed. Producers of Yeats' drama may want to investigate the Farr melodies for hints of Yeats' method, but twenty-first century theatre has moved beyond the gentle measures of this lost art, except for productions of Yeats' early plays.

Endnotes

1. Yeats, *Samhain: 1906—Literature and the Living Voice* In *W.B.Yeats:The Irish Dramatic Movement*, 212.
2. Flannery, *W.B.Yeats and the Idea of a Theatre*,193-195.
3. Yeats, *Plays in Prose and Verse*.
4. Yeats, *The Trembling of the Veil. Book I*, 118.
5. Yeats, *The Collected Letters of W.B.Yeats*, 349.
6. Yeats, "A Symbolical Drama in Paris," 237.
7. Yeats, *Plays in Prose and Verse*, 435.
8. Yeats, *The Collected Letters of W.B.Yeats*, 389, foot note #1.
9. Farr, *The Music of Speech*, 23.
10. Ibid., 18,19.
11. Foster, *W.B.Yeats: A Life I*, 85.
12. Yeats, *Reveries Over Childhood and Youth*, 69.
13. Foster, *W.B.Yeats: A Life I*, 16, 25, 32; Kelly, *A W.B. Yeats' Chronology* 5, 6.
14. Yeats, *Reveries Over Childhood and Youth*, 80.
15. Ibid., 81.
16. Ibid., 69.
17. Ibid., 80.
18. Yeats, *The Trembling of the Veil. Book I*, 118.
19. Ibid., 118.
20. Johnson, *Florence Farr*, 10, 13, 18; Greer, *Women of the Golden Dawn*, 23, 24.
21. Ibid., 19.
22. Ibid., 20.
23. Farr, *The Dancing Faun*, 53.
24. Yeats, "Speaking to the Psaltery," 15.
25. Ibid., 21.
26. Ibid.
27. Yeats *Samhain: 1903* In *W.B.Yeats:The Irish Dramatic Movement*, 27.
28. Yeats, *Samhain: 1904* In *W.B.Yeats:The Irish Dramatic Movement*, 74-75.
29. Yeats, *The Collected Letters of W.B.Yeats*, 158.
30. Johnson, *Florence Farr*, 16.
31. Farr, *The Music of Speech*, 16.
32. Ibid., 17.
33. Flannery, *W.B.Yeats and the Idea of a Theatre*, 197.
34. Yeats, *The Collected Letters of W.B.Yeats*, 197.
35. Flannery, *W.B.Yeats and the Idea of a Theatre*, 197.
36. Murphy, *Family Secrets*, 67.
37. *Yeats Annual, 7*, ed. Warwick Gould (London, 1990), 91, cited in Foster, *W.B. Yeats: A Life I*, 207; Ellmann, *Yeats:The Man and the Mask*, 8.
38. Holloway, *Joseph Holloway's Abbey Theatre*, 5.
39. Yeats, *Beltaine: May 1899* In *W.B.Yeats:The Irish Dramatic Movement*, 145. Yeats published the *Beltaine*, a journal-like collection of articles to promote the spring productions of the Irish Literary Theatre. Later for the autumn seasons of the Irish National Theatre Yeats published *Samhain*.
40. Webster, *The Same Only Different*, 205.
41. Fay and Carswell, *The Fays of the Abbey Theatre*, 231; Mikhail, ed., *The Abbey Theatre*, 65, 88.
42. Kelly, *A W.B.Yeats' Chronology*, 56-58 62-64, 76-77,79.
43. Hogan and Kilroy, *The Abbey Theatre*, 9.
44. Mikhail, ed., *The Abbey Theatre*, 88.
45. Ibid., 12.
46. Ibid., 19.
47. Ibid., 63.
48. Ibid., 65.
49. Yeats, *The Collected Letters of W.B.Yeats*, 93.
50. Ibid., 287, foot note #1.
51. Holloway, *Joseph Holloway's Abbey Theatre*, 6, 7.
52. Johnson, *Florence Farr*, 104.
53. Finneran et al., eds., *Letters to W.B.Yeats*, 141.
54. Ibid., 123.
55. Beerbohm, *Around Theatres*, 316.
56. Farr, *The Music of Speech*, 3, 9.
57. Finneran et al., eds., *Letters to W.B.Yeats,*, 165.

58. Holloway, *Joseph Holloway's Abbey Theatre*, 45.
59. Mikhail, ed., *The Abbey Theatre*, 95.
60. Flannery, *W.B. Yeats and the Idea of a Theatre*, 203.
61. Yeats, *Samhain: 1902* In *W.B. Yeats: The Irish Dramatic Movement*, 12.
62. Flannery, *W.B. Yeats and the Idea of a Theatre*, 351.
63. Yeats, *Plays for an Irish Theatre*, x.
64. Frank Fay, *Towards a National Theatre: Dramatic Criticism*. Ed. Robert Hogan *The Irish Theatre Series 1*, ser. eds. Robert Hogan, James Kilroy and Liam Miller. (Dublin: Dolmen Press, 1970), 95, 96.
65. Bax, ed. *Florence Farr, Bernard Shaw, W.B. Yeats*, 15.

Works Cited

Bax, Clifford, ed. *Florence Farr, Bernard Shaw, W. B. Yeats: Letters.* London: Home & Van Thal, 1946.

Beerbohm, Max. *Around Theatres.* London: Rupert Hart-Davis, 1953.

Farr, Florence. *The Dancing Faun.* London: Elkin Mathews and John Lane. Boston: Roberts Brothers, 1894.

— — —. *The Music of Speech, Containing the Words of Some Poets, Thinkers and Music-Makers Regarding the Practice of Bardic Art Together with Fragments of Verse Set to its Own Melody by Florence Farr.* London: Elkin Mathews, 1909.

Ellmann, Richard. *Yeats: The Man and the Mask.* London: Faber & Faber, 1961.

Fay. W. G., and Catherine Carswell. *The Fays of the Abbey Theatre: An Autobiographical Record.* London: Rich & Cowan, 1935.

Flannery, James W. *W.B. Yeats and the Idea of a Theatre: The Early Abbey Theatre in Theory and Practice.* New Haven, CT; London: Yale University Press, 1976.

Finneran, Richard J., George Mills Harper, and William Murphy. *Letters to W.B. Yeats.* vol.1. New York: Columbia University Press, 1977.

Foster, R.F. *W.B. Yeats: A Life I : The Apprentice Mage*, 1865-1914. Vol.1. Oxford; New York: Oxford University Press, 1997.

Greer, Mary K. *Women of the Golden Dawn: Rebels and Priestesses.* Rochester, VT: Park Street Press, 1995.

Hogan, Robert, and James Kilroy. *The Abbey Theatre: The Years of Synge, 1905-1909.* vol. 3. *The Modern Irish Drama: A Documentary History.* Dublin: Dolmen Press, 1978.

Holloway, Joseph. *Joseph Holloway's Abbey Theatre: A Selection from His Unpublished Journal: Impressions of a Dublin Playgoer.* Robert Hogan and Michael J. O'Neill, eds. London, Amsterdam: Feffer & Simons; Carbondale, Edwardsville: Southern Illinois University Press, 1967.

Johnson, Josephine. *Florence Farr: Bernard Shaw's 'New Woman.'* London: Colin Smythe, 1975.

Kelly, John. S. *A W.B. Yeats Chronology.* Houndmills, Basingstoke, Hampshire, UK; New York: Palgrave Macmillan, 2003.

Mikhail, E. H., ed. *The Abbey Theatre: Interviews and Recollections.* Totowa, NJ: Barnes & Noble Books, 1988.

Murphy, William M. *Family Secrets: William Butler Yeats and His Relatives.* Syracuse, New York: Syracuse University Press, 1995.

Russell, George [AE]. *Some Passages from the Letters of AE to W.B. Yeats.* Dublin: Cuala Press, 1936.

Webster, Margaret. *The Same Only Different: Five Generations of a Great Theatrical Family.* London: Victor Gollancz, 1969.

Yeats, W.B. "A Symbolical Drama in Paris." In *W.B. Yeats: Early Articles and Reviews: Uncollected Articles and Reviews Written Between 1886 and 1900.* John P. Frayne and Madeleine Marchaterre, eds. Vol. IX of *The Collected Works of W. B. Yeats.* Richard J. Finneran and George Mills, eds. Harper. New York; London: Scribner: 2004.

— — —. *Dramatis Personae: 1869-1902. W.B. Yeats: Autobiographies.* William H. O'Donnell and Douglas N. Archibald, eds. Vol III of *The Collected Works of W.B. Yeats.* Richard J. Finneran and George Mills Harper, eds. New York: Scribner, 1965.

— — —. *Essays and Introductions.* New York: Macmillan, 1961.

— — —. *Plays in Prose and Verse: Written for an Irish Theatre, and Generally with the Help of a Friend.* New York: Macmillan, 1924.

— — —. *Reveries Over Childhood and Youth.* In *W.B. Yeats Autobiographies.* Vol. III of *The Collected Works of W.B. Yeats.* William H. O'Donnell and Douglas N. Archibald, eds. New York: Scribner, 1999.

— — —. "Speaking to the Psaltery." In *Essays.* London: Macmillan, 1924.

— — —. *W.B. Yeats: The Irish Dramatic Movement.* Mary FitzGerald and Richard J. Finneran, eds.. Vol VIII. of *The Collected Works of W.B. Yeats.* Richard J. Finneran and George Mills Harper, eds. New York; London: 2003.

— — —. *The Trembling of the Veil. Book I. Four Years: 1887-1891.* In *W.B. Yeats: Autobiographies.* William H. O'Donnell and Douglas N. Archibald, eds. Vol III of *The Collected Works of W.B. Yeats.* Richard J. Finneran and George Mills Harper, eds. New York: Scribner, 1965.

— — —. *The Trembling of the Veil. Book IV. The Tragic Generation.* In *W.B. Yeats: Autobiographies.* William H. O'Donnell and Douglas N. Archibald, eds. Vol III of *The Collected Works of W.B. Yeats.* Richard J. Finneran and George Mills Harper, eds. New York: Scribner, 1965.

— — —. *The Collected Letters of W.B. Yeats. 1901-1904*, Vol 3. John Kelly and Ronald Schuchard, eds. Oxford: Clarendon Press, 1994.

Ethics, Standards and Practices *Barry Kur, Associate Editor*

Introduction to Ethics, Standards and Practices *by Barry Kur, Associate Editor*

The Diversity of Diversity

An administrative colleague of mine recently arranged a diversity retreat for the faculty of his theatre department. His reason for doing this was that too many of his faculty, who decades ago lived through the events of the civil rights movement, believed that their diversity awareness was complete and that many had put the issue of diversity away on their shelf of accomplishment. They neglected to sense the evolving scope of diversity awareness that must become a common element of our work places. Gender identity, religious faith, physical challenges are just a few of the increasing number of diversity issues gaining our attention.

In this issue of the *VSR* we are addressing the issues of gender—a complex diversity issue and certainly a current hot button topic of moral, professional, social and political discussions.

Professor Steve Satta's article addresses issues related to LGBT students in theatre training. Dr. Robert Sattaloff and his associates' article informs us of the surgical options for those dealing with transgender identity. Professor Tara McAllister-Viel relates her experiences of teaching in Korea and the dilemma of working with students who possessed cultural gender performance expectations that did not align with the expectations of the methods of training most familiar to her.

These three articles offer anecdotal experiences, research data and scientific practice that may all contribute to a holistic awareness necessary for our voice/speech work and its relationship to the complex topic of gender identity.

Barry Kur is the Associate Director of the Penn State School of Theatre and serves as the Voice/Speech Specialist of their Professional Actor Training Program. He is the founding Artistic Director of the University Park Ensemble, a Penn State based outreach theatre company that addresses academic, social and health issues for which he is the recipient of awards for excellence in teaching and service. He has coached over 100 theatre productions for both professional and academic theatres. Kur is the Director of Certification of the Lessac Training and Research Institute, the author of *Stage Dialect Studies: A Continuation of the Lessac Approach to Actor Voice/Speech Training*, and Past-President of the Voice and Speech Trainers Association.

Peer Reviewed Article *by Steve Satta*

Steven J. Satta is Associate Professor of Voice/Acting at Towson University where he is currently directing a production of *Angels in America: Perestroika*. He is the Co-Chair of the Towson Committee on LGBT Issues which works to promote a safe and supportive environment for LGBT students. He has presented his workshop on gender—"Marlboro Men and Cover Girls"—at various conferences. He is an active member of ATHE's LGBT Focus Group where he presented the dramaturgy behind his cross-gendered production of *Twelfth Night*. His production of the original work *Tara's Crossing* for Houses on the Moon Theatre Company dealt with transgender issues and immigration and was nominated for a New York Innovative Theatre Award.

OUT AND LOUD:
The Queer Student in Undergraduate Actor Training Programs

INTRODUCTION

Within a few months of my arrival as an Assistant Professor on my new campus, after I had become acclimated more or less to the building and the schedule and my colleagues, I noticed something I hadn't expected: a real absence of a vocal or visible gay presence in the department. Having attended NYU in the early 80s, I expected a sizeable theater department to have a radical element that included some real sex and gender transgressors, but this did not seem the case. Cautiously I asked, "Where are the queer kids?" Faculty members identified two students in a department of 180 majors—this was way below Kinsey's 10%! I was stunned.

Eventually, I decided that I was just going to have to make some noise all by myself, so I did. Soon they came out (pun intended) to see what was going on and now four years later they make lots of noise all on their own, not only in the theater department, but many of them have become leaders in the Queer Student Union.

I tell this story to make a point: I assumed that because this was a theater department in an east coast university near a large urban center and because the faculty was open-minded and forward-thinking, gay students would feel comfortable and nurtured and accepted. They would grow and develop into *gay adults* with a mature, healthy understanding of their sexuality and the role it plays in their overall identity and even, perhaps, in their lives as artists. This was not the case. It took some real effort and attention to address the needs and concerns of these students. Despite my identification as a gay man and a gay artist, I had a real learning curve around being a teacher of gay students.

In the next few pages, I would like to touch on what it means to be a sexual or gender minority in American culture, then address teaching undergraduates in general, then more specifically undergraduate actors and then finally, address some topics in voice training.

As teachers of university undergrads, we must realize these young people are at a crucial point in their lives—many are testing their wings in solo flight for the first time. They are just beginning to figure out who they are as adults. While curricula is priority-one much of the time, we cannot avoid the impact of students' identity development processes on our classrooms. Like it or not, these processes are taking up a lot of our students' time, energy and attention and come into the classroom with them.

As teachers of theater (in general) we most likely encounter more students struggling with their sexuality than many of our colleagues in other departments. More specifically, as performance teachers we must acknowledge that the very nature of actor-training means we are more deeply engaged with students' personal identities and development than in many other academic disciplines. So, there are even more possibilities for identity-development issues to surface in the classroom and impact work.

Finally and most specifically, as teachers of voice, I believe we tread what is for many student-actors some of the most sensitive ground around issues of identity. Our voice literally announces our presence to the world. The word "persona" is sometimes traced back to the Latin "personare" which means "to sound through." This originally referred to an actor's mask in ancient times which had a megaphone built into it (http//encyclopedia.jrank.org/). I believe that this etymology is not universally accepted but it makes sense to me. Our voice, our sound is the manifestation of our selves that travels furthest away from our bodies without technological assistance. To work with a student's voice is to work with his/her very sense of identity. Referring to the happy gurgles of a baby, Kristen Linklater tells us "The voice IS emotion" (Linklater 1992, 5). I would say when working with the voice, one must consider that to a great extent the voice IS the baby (or the student) as well.

A Note on Terminology

At times I may use the term "queer" rather than "LGBT" which stands for "lesbian/gay/bisexual/transgender." "Queer" was used as a slur for many years but began to be reclaimed by the more radical element of the LGBT community during the AIDS activism of the 80s and 90s, most prominently by the group Queer Nation. Those who accept the term usually see it as inclusive of all those who live outside the social norms of gender and sexuality, even if only in specific situations. Many also find it preferable to the ever-growing "alphabet soup" of LGBT to which more letters must be added to include "questioning," "curious," etc.

There are others who see "queer" as inclusive of all those outside the mainstream, including those living with uncommon psychological or physical issues or even those with radical political agendas. In this article when I use the word "queer" I will be confining my meaning to those who live outside the social norms of gender and sexual identity and expression.

"Queer" is not universally accepted; many within the LGBT community find the term offensive still. Unless people specifically refer to themselves as "queer" it is probably safer to stick to "LGBT." If you're really unsure of how to proceed in a conversation you can always ask "how do you identify?" The concept of "identifying" is empowering and communicates the sense that the individual actively chooses the words that describe him or her rather than being labeled by society. "How do you identify?" is the sensitive way to ask for information rather than "are you a…[insert presumptive label here] ?, or something awkward like "so…what are you?"

BEING QUEER IN AMERICA

Before we proceed into classroom issues, let's lay a little groundwork about what it means to be an LGBT individual in the USA.

Living in a Straight World

First we must acknowledge that we live in a heterosexist culture—that "the sexual identity of heterosexual students is shaped by an environment that is characterized by a fear of homosexuality, the denigration of gay persons and cultures, and either the invisibility or outright oppression of gay relationships" (Sullivan 1998, 3).

This heterosexist ideology has some core beliefs which have been found through research to be consistent:
- Heterosexual relationships are right, normal and loving.
- Homosexual relationships are inferior, abnormal and exclusively sexual.
- Gay men are weak.
- Lesbians want to be men.
- Gay people need counseling.
- Society must be protected from gay people.
- Gay people should keep their orientation to themselves.

These beliefs may be passively held or actively pursued (Sullivan 1998, 5).

It is important to remember this is the prevailing culture, meaning that queer people are taught these beliefs as well. They may internalize these teachings into their own personal belief structure until—and often after—they realize and acknowledge their own identities. This is known as "internalized homophobia" and it can make the realization and acceptance of one's difference very difficult and complex.

Coming Out

"Coming Out" in LGBT individuals is commonly known as the realization and acceptance of one's difference. Coming out is not a single event but an ongoing process that may be life-long. In 1979, Vivienne Cass outlined a six-step developmental model which has served as the foundation for additional research. The model I would like to look at—developed in 1992—uses Cass' model as a springboard, so it will be helpful to look at this model briefly.

Coming out – the Cass Model (1979) six stages:
1. Identity Awareness
2. Identity Comparison
3. Identity Tolerance
4. Identity Acceptance
5. Identity Pride
6. Synthesis (www.glbtq.org)

The original "Identity Pride" finds queer individuals defining themselves through a determined rejection of the dominant culture. This stage is marked with anger and a re-evaluation of values and norms in which there is a complete and concerted rejection of the dominant heterosexist culture. In this stage everything "gay" may be highly valued and everything "straight" may be completely devalued. The student covered in rainbow regalia and confrontational or provocative slogans might be in this stage, prompting the common complaint "must they shove it down my throat?"

"Synthesis" is the stage when the individual integrates sexual orientation or gender identity into the rest of his or her psyche and identity, striking a positive balance with the dominant culture.

Patricia Sullivan integrates this model with a Racial Identity Development Model (Hardiman and Jackson, 1992) and talks of the difficulty of moving from Identity Pride into Synthesis. She reconfigures Cass' "Synthesis" into "Redefinition" and "Internalization."

Sullivan Racial Identity Development Model
1. Naiveté
2. Acceptance
3. Resistance
4. Redefinition
5. Internalization

The "redefinition stage" indicates a focus on the new community rather than attacking the old. Students may self-segregate, re-evaluate friendships or extra-curricular activities in favor of staying within their newfound community. While Sullivan dispenses with Cass's idea of this stage being marked by anger and rejection, the "self-segregation" she describes may still seem provocative to some.

"Internalization" is the integration of a positive LGBT identity into the whole, recognition of orientation as one facet in a spectrum of identity. How large a facet orientation is in one's whole identity varies from person to person (Sullivan 1998, 9-11).

Sullivan points out that: "Unfortunately the achievement of the internalization stage by LGBT students is made extremely difficult by the pervasive heterosexism of the campus environment" (Sullivan 1998, 11). Likewise it may be difficult for students to move out of the angry, "us" vs. "them" aspect of Identity Pride because "negative responses from heterosexual persons and/or society only confirm their dichotomous perception"(Sullivan 1998, 9). This can sometimes be a stage where students get stuck. The kid covered in rainbows finding every opportunity to identify publicly as queer may be in this stage. Support and affirmation is the way to help them move through this. Telling them to "tone it down" may only keep them stuck longer. I'm not saying to endure disruptive behavior in class but consider the dynamic you are entering into when you have that one-on-one talk.

BEING QUEER IN COLLEGE
Obstacles to Coming Out

The obstacles to the "internalization" stage Sullivan articulates become even more daunting when we consider the following statistics:

97% of all students report hearing homophobic comments.

80% of gay and lesbian youth feel severe social isolation.

80% of prospective teachers report negative attitudes toward gays and lesbians.

66% of guidance counselors report negative feelings toward gays and lesbians.

42% of homeless youth self-identify as gay or lesbian.

30% of completed teen suicides are done by gay or lesbian youth.

11.5% of gay youth report being physically attacked by family members (www.glsen.org).

The stress caused by harassment and fear of harassment puts LGBT youth at a significantly higher risk for alcohol and drug abuse, suicide, missing school and risky sexual behavior (Cianotto 2003, 47-9). Combine this with the general stress that university students experience—first time away from home, first time living full time in a community of peers, separation from friends and support network of home, etc.— and you've got a group of students greatly at risk for academic failure on top of everything else.

Depending on where your institution is located, you may have students arriving never having experienced any of this. Many recent authors and articles have commented that many LGBT youth experience the coming out process as immensely positive and empowering nowadays and that not everyone has the struggles that Cass outlined in her 1979 coming out model. But you will also have a great many students coming from more conservative and/or provincial backgrounds whose coming out experience will not differ much from mine back in the late 1970s when Cass was formulating her model.

Coming Out as a Beginning, Not an End

But somehow many, many LGBT students manage to take those steps out of the closet. As educators, we can't assume just because a student identifies themselves as gay or lesbian that they are now at the Integration stage. It is a long journey and once out, the student is then confronted with a whole other set of issues.

1. How out is out?—Are they out just in the department, the college, in the residence? To friends at home? To select family members? To the entire family? To the world at large? Once out to him or herself the student must decide to whom and when to disclose their identity.

2. Finding and adapting to community—how easy is it to find others who also identify? On campus? In the surrounding area? Do they find commonality with those they meet?

3. When to speak up?—Often the out student must keep coming out. Teachers or fellow students may ignore or disrespect their experience as an LGBT individual. The out student may hear homophobic comments in the cafeteria or in their residence. The out student may have to decide on a daily basis whether or not to speak up or remain silent with all the fear, stress, anger or guilt that comes with that choice.

Numbers 2 and 3 are certainly issues for many other minority students as well. One significant difference for LGBT students is that unlike students of color (for example) LGBT students cannot identify each other by sight all the time. In addition, even if a student senses or knows another student is LGBT, both students must claim that identity publicly to some extent (even if only with each other) to facilitate contact and to make a sense of support and community possible. Buddhists or feminists might have the same issue, but one could argue that LGBT culture has a lot less support in this country than either of those identities. Also one might discreetly ask another student if s/he follows Buddhist teachings without the same sort of social repercussions or stigma of inquiring about sexual orientation or gender identity.

THE CHALLENGE FOR THE EDUCATIONAL INSTITUTION
Adjusting our thinking/Maintaining our perspective
I address this not because I think all educators are guilty of insensitivity. I address this not to accuse anyone but to articulate the enormous burdens these students may face. It is easy for us in our little oases of free-thinking, new-age, artistic-types to allow ourselves to think that it has gotten easy for these students to make their way in the world or even on campus in safety and with dignity. It has not.

Even if your classroom is safe and supportive, not every classroom may be so. Even if the entire academic environment is safe and supportive, the dorms may not be. Even if your entire campus is safe and supportive, the families which these students come from and which they still look to for validation may not be safe or supportive. It may have gotten somewhat easier in the last decade but it is certainly not easy.

Is your silence interpreted as complicity?
Our challenge is to remind ourselves of that struggle, lest our sense of well-being allows us to become complacent in confronting homophobia and makes us not implicit but complicit

with the negative forces working against these students.

While overt victimization of LGBT students is clearly a problem on campuses and in classrooms, students encounter other negative experiences resulting not from conscious acts of aggression but rather from a passive stance on the part of faculty. LGBT students' needs are unknown, unmet, or ignored by well-meaning but uninformed individuals. Paradoxically, in a study at Oberlin College, Norris (1992) found that students, faculty, and staff of all sexualities expressed strong positive attitudes toward their LGBT peers and colleagues, but these same LGBT people were subject to widespread harassment and violence. In explanation, Norris presents evidence that while these supportive students and employees are not the same people who are engaging in specific anti-gay actions, they are not actively preventing or discouraging these activities. By not acting to interrupt the pattern of LGBT victimization these students and employees are contributing to it (Renn 1998, 234).

How does this impact learning?
Clearly students that have all this going on in their lives may find it especially challenging to focus on their studies.

Learning Theory: The Four Pillars
- Involvement—in academic and extracurricular life.
- Motivation—linked to student needs (self-actualization, achievement, competence, self-worth and goals) and expectations (self-efficacy, previous experiences, success of others and feedback).
- Emotion—students' emotional lives can enhance or impede their progress. Feelings of pride may increase motivation and involvement while, anger or fear may decrease it.
- Constructing meaning—the process by which students unlearn false paradigms and learn new ones; this allows students to make meaningful connections between their own lives and experience and curricular content. This is at the heart of the learning process.

Impact of LGBT Identity Development on the Four Pillars
Involvement may be curtailed because
- student feels too threatened or isolated.
- student spends more energy dealing with harassment than their straight peers.
- *alternately*, the student who is further along in their coming out process may find additional opportunities for involvement through LGBT student groups or organization.

Motivation
   The learning environment must help motivate students by

supporting their sense of self-worth and their ability to succeed. Negative images of LGBT individuals (or the absence of any images) lower LGBT students' expectations of their own success and worth, diminishing motivation and negatively impacting learning.

Conversely, positive images and inclusion of LGBT individuals maintain or increase motivation and support learning. Additionally, those students who have begun "coming out" may view that process as an accomplishment which enhances their sense of their ability to achieve.

Emotion
- It is imperative to have a classroom that is deemed safe and secure for all involved. Studies show that students who do not feel secure or who feel actively threatened on an ongoing basis learn less. For LGBT students there is also often anger and frustration at curriculum which does not reflect their lives and experiences, making them feel invisible or marginalized (Renn 1998, 234-5).
- *Alternately*, the student who feels encouraged to express themselves and receives positive feedback will feel pride and be more deeply invested.

Constructing Meaning
Kristin Renn in her article "Lesbian, Gay, Bisexual and Transgender Students in the College Classroom" writes: "For many students, college represents the first opportunity to explore their sexual orientation and the implications of identifying as LGBT (D'Augelli, 1989d, 1992; Sloane, 1993). Students who seek to make meaning of new academic material by connecting it to this salient aspect of their identity may be discouraged from doing so by faculty who are not aware of the importance of LGBT issues to the student or of the possibilities for building connections and meaning based on LGBT development, culture, or experience. In some cases discouragement may be passive or unintended on the part of the teacher, but in another case, it may be the result of the teacher's open disrespect for LGBT people and/or lesbian and gay studies. In either case, the teacher is missing or denying an opportunity for the student to make new connections and to learn.

The development of an LGBT identity gives students opportunities to learn new paradigms and models for understanding the world. They interpret their academic surroundings differently from their heterosexual peers (Ghaill, 1991). Whether or not they identify publicly, LGBT students who identify personally have a heightened consciousness of self versus others (D'Augelli, 1992) that

may influence the way they create cognitive structures or the elements to which they attach meaning. As they come to see themselves as healthy, normal and productive, they challenge and unlearn negative messages they have internalized about LGBT people (D'Augelli, 1992; Massachusetts Governor's Commission 1993; Uribe & Harbeck, 1992). These students are not strangers to the process of reformulating information into new structures" (Renn 1998, 235-6).

Students who connect curricular material to their own lives in a meaningful way learn more, so it can be extremely powerful for the LGBT student to connect to material as an LGBT individual. When a queer student connects curricular content to their world it is a queer world they are connecting to. They must be allowed to speak their "queerness" in class and write their "queerness" in assignments and even perform their "queerness" on stage because that is part of their learning process.

How many of us, even those of us who identify as lesbian, gay, bisexual, transgender or queer, can truly say we are prepared to support these particular students in their work? In their campus life?

Do you know if:
- your institution has a non-discrimination policy which includes sexual orientation and gender identity?
- there is an LGBT student group or LGBT studies classes?
- there is an LGBT center with knowledgeable staff and resources? (not a counseling center but an LGBT cultural or student center!)
- there is faculty development and student programming that deals with diversity and helps create a positive atmosphere on campus for LGBT students?
- the residence life office and the RAs are capable of maintaining physically and emotionally safe dorms?

As LGBT youth become self-aware earlier and earlier—in high school or even before—these policies and resources will become greater and greater factors in recruitment and retention of undergraduate students. Those of you involved in recruitment activities may want to have this information ready. In addition to addressing this in classroom work and curriculum, you may want to become involved at an institutional level. Please realize that straight allies are important in creating change around this issue.

Recommendations to Strengthen the Learning Experience
- Create a classroom climate that supports dialogue, debate and disagreement within a context of personal respect;

call prompt attention to both malicious and unintended homophobic remarks by students.

• Incorporate LGBT material in your curriculum and support the development of queer studies curricula; conduct research on LGBT topics; voice your support for visible LGBT faculty and staff and work through institutional committees and forums to support LGBT issues.

• Support students in their academic exploration of LGBT issues. Faculty should encourage all students to research and write about LGBT issues; become a knowledgeable resource for students doing LGBT academic work; and learn more about LGBT issues by attending campus and community events as well as LGBT sessions at academic conferences (Renn 1998, 234).

Not all of these suggestions may seem immediately applicable to your situation on your campus. If you are an adjunct or an itinerant workshop leader, the scope of your influence may be too limited for many of these suggestions. But whatever way you can embrace the spirit of these suggestions in your own work would mean the world to an LGBT student or client. If you are a tenured or tenure-track faculty member, these suggestions may require more involvement in the life of your campus. However attending one event, making one comment in a meeting, or reading and sharing one article accomplishes more in your institution and educates you more than you might imagine.

BEING QUEER IN A COLLEGE THEATRE DEPARTMENT

How Issues Of Gender And Sexuality Impact Actor Training

We must acknowledge that theatre does not just hold the mirror up to nature, it holds the mirror up to society as well. In the case of the United States and most other places, society is overwhelmingly hetero-normative (assumes heterosexuality and is largely designed to support heterosexual individuals) and frequently homophobic, as we stated earlier. The process of learning to perform in the theater, then, is largely one of learning to reflect accurately heterosexual values, beliefs and behaviors. For queer students this is fraught with problems. Jill Dolan, a noted theorist and out lesbian, relates her experience:

> When I turned twenty-one, coming out into my own sexuality meant beginning many years of relative exile from theater production, even though acting and directing first breathed life into my sense of the possibilities of this both public and private forum. I grew from a teenager who, at a local theater school, had enthusiastically played roles across gender and across generation (Mrs. Malaprop in Sheridan's *The Rivals*, for instance was one of my famous

performances) to a frightened college freshman in a professional theater training program, who was being indoctrinated, through the theater practice that had once liberated her, into gender and sexuality roles she was ill equipped to play. Ingénues, and what I read as their utter submission, their vacuousness, their weakness, were anathema to me for reasons I could barely articulate in 1976. I only knew that my inability to do well in movement classes was somehow related to my alienation from my own body, which was somehow related to my thorough incompetence at the heterosexual role-play the professors in Boston University's theater program were casting me to do.

> After one particularly painful experience playing the ditzy female in a scene from *Lovers and Other Strangers*—cast across from a young man I'm now sure was gay, although I didn't have those words at that time—I dropped out of the theater program and declared English my new major. My self-imposed exile from theater practice created a critic, and later a feminist and a theorist, whose perspective was fueled by her desire to recapture or at least to describe what had so seduced her about the theater, and what had then so wretchedly been snatched away (Dolan 1993, 185).

Jill Dolan's story indicates that issues of sexuality can be tied to issues of culturally appropriate gender expression, i.e. the performance of "masculinity" or "femininity." But, these performances may be problematic for many students, not just LGBT students. Some straight students may be too identified with their gender expression. In my voice classes, I see many examples: the young man with a tight jaw and monotonous vocal cadence of the stereotypic male facade; the young woman with the "little girl" voice who believes she cannot make low or dark sounds. Such students are as inhibited by these cultural ideas as some queer students.

Sensitivity to Issues of Sexual Orientation and Gender Identity is Good for Everyone

Almost all students come into actor training programs with personal habits that limit their range and expression as performing artists. Many of these limitations may be the result of or the response to the gender indoctrination that occurs in our society. Smashing the strictures of the "acceptable and appropriate range of gender expression" is important and difficult for ALL students. But there are additional difficulties which LGBT students face. Perhaps as a teacher you've had the experience of looking for the euphemism to address the "feminine boy" or the "tomboy girl." Perhaps you've seen the pained response in students when a teacher directly applied those descriptors in class. The other difficulty is perhaps more subtle to notice: when limiting behaviors are finally addressed, usually LGBT students are being brought into line with hetero-normative expectations without being given permission to explore their *difference* from that culture, without exploring what it means to be an LGBT individual.

One of the most devastating effects of the injunction to remain silent and invisible is that LGBT young people are denied the freedom to talk openly about their feelings and experiment openly with new ways of being. It is in part by experiencing their own and others' reactions to new roles, ideas and behaviors that young people develop a sense of who they are and what they want. By providing for the open exchange of ideas and opinions about sex and sexuality and creating a space within which LGBT youth can express themselves, verbally and behaviorally, *as LGBT youth*, LGBT/queer studies can enrich the developmental experience of all students, especially of LGBT and questioning ones (Chestnut 1998, 227).

THINGS YOU CAN *DO* WITH STUDENTS:
The general academic approach to this issue is to use curricular materials that present a wide range of cultures and attitudes about gender and sexuality. How does this play out in the acting studio? I suggest finding exercises that "unpack" the loaded ideas of "appropriate masculine behavior" and "appropriate feminine behavior" for everyone. Some of the approaches and exercises I use are below. They happen in my voice studio but the concepts (and some of the exercises themselves) transfer easily into an acting studio.

1. **Primal Work:**
    a. *Take language away for a few weeks*: Work only with abstract and unsocialized sound. This usually gets students into the "reptile" part of their brain. They begin to experience sound and behavior as expressive apart from any cultural benchmark. (Within a few days of this work I ask them if they miss being able to use language; most of the time they laugh because they don't miss it and hadn't noticed its absence.)

    b. *Break the class into smaller groups* so that while one group explores, another can watch objectively. Comment on what's happening and help the watchers understand what they are seeing.

    c. *Things to watch for and open for discussion:*
    i. *The Crucible*: In my experience "female energy" tends to play out in a way reminiscent of Arthur Miller's classic play in which a group of young women claim to be attacked by the witches in Salem, and respond to these invisible attacks spontaneously and simultaneously as a group. This plays out in the exercise as groups (usually initially of women) moving in unison, often in a circle facing in, with little body-to-body contact beyond hand-holding. There is incredible connection here with members of the group very acutely attuned to each other and moving in sympathy and empathy.

    ii. *The Lord of the Flies*: "Male energy" tends to look more like *The Lord of the Flies*—chaos and physical competition between groups or individuals (usually men initially) whether serious or playful; lots of wrestling.

    iii. **Dropping in age**: Often students will regress in age and the first attempts at a primal group activity will look like grade-school recess. This is a common way students avoid committing to the exercise fully. Encourage them to remain the age they are, which usually brings in an awareness of sexual energy and the idea that their actions have serious consequences within the exercise. Coaching from the sidelines is helpful. I'll sometimes coach the most aggressive player to try to "attack" the least aggressive player. This usually has interesting and dramatic results and of course requires trust and maturity among the players.

    iv. **The Trickster or The Space Between**: At least one of your students will shift their energy or occupy the space between "male" and "female." The man who tries to stop the fighting or effect a reconciliation; the woman who steps forward when her group is "threatened" by an outsider; the man who assimilates himself into the women's circle easily, etc. Sometimes this person delights in simply disrupting the energy of the group by shifting his or her own energy to move counter to the group. This phenomenon is usually acknowledged by the class as being fascinating to watch.

    d. *Present "male" and female" as energies that everyone is able to access*: Once students move into a more primal, unsocialized expression they begin to relate to each other in terms of human energy and human impulse rather than culturally dictated behavior. At this point, they usually aren't threatened by a loosening of the cultural concepts of "male" and "female" because they've already experienced these energies out on the studio floor. Colleagues have told me that they avoid the charged terms of "male" and "female" by referring to "warrior energy" and "nurturer energy" but my aim is to unpack these specific words for students and redefine them.

e. *Notes on Primal Work*:

• The space "between male and female" is the queer space, and in this context "queer" signifies "outside social boundaries or norms." "Queer" energy is the energy that belongs to the "trickster" figure in tribal cultures that delights in disrupting whatever the majority is doing. The trickster breaks the rules and (according to many stories) brings gifts such as fire to humanity or even starts the human race itself in the process. Identifying that there is a place for this energy, that there are more choices than just "male" and "female" (one can be neither or both at once) is important for all students and can be particularly powerful for LGBT students. The concept of "trickster" is helpful as a label for this energy because the group may not be ready for the word "queer" and because it encompasses disruptions of many different social norms, not just gender and sexuality. I'm also careful when I discuss this not to point out a specific individual who made this energy manifest, but the students usually can identify it when they see it. Sometimes a student will proudly claim that energy…and it's not always the student you think it will be!

• It becomes clear through this work that male and female energy can have little or nothing to do necessarily with the individual's sex or sexuality. Everyone has access to the full spectrum. This also leads you to other really interesting observations about group dynamics and "otherness" in general.

• There are lots of approaches to this work. Two which I draw inspiration from and which I recommend highly are Richard Armstrong's approach to teaching the Roy Hart voice work and the lamentation work which Marya Lowry teaches. The Roy Hart Theater teaches what is sometimes called "the extended voice" and approaches voice work as a function of the imaginative life of the actor rather than through a technical manipulation of the physical vocal apparatus. This work explores an entire range of vocal expression outside the western ideal of bel canto and good speech for classic texts, including animal and multiphonic sounds. Because it taps into the imaginative life directly, it moves students outside their cultural context and into an unsocialized expression fairly quickly. At the VASTA conference in New York some years ago, Marya presented her lamentation work as, in part an exploration of "the mother tongue"—the intuitive, free-flowing voice of grief versus the "father tongue" of the structured and limited eulogy. This work also moves students outside the cultural strictures they know.

2. **Cross-Gendered Work**

a. *Fairy Tales*: A great, simple exercise is to have students act out a fairy tale (or section of a fairy tale) in which they must play multiple characters—men, women, dragons, etc. This is great for lots of aspects of vocal expression, presence and energy, etc. but it also opens up the gender divide. I insist my students have at least one non-human character but you could also insist they cross genders.

b. *Real-life observations of members of another sex*: Have students bring in a character study of a gender they don't identify with. This requires really sharp skills of observation and imitation. The point is not a full-blown "gender illusion" (rarely possible without makeup and full costume) but to expand physical and vocal range. The conversation within the class surrounding the exploration of gender and gender expression and gender roles is immensely valuable. The acting task of finding characteristics (or sounds) within themselves that are usually associated with the other sex will be profound for many of them.

3. **Acting Across The Gender Line**

Find a piece of common text that expresses eternal love for the scene partner in non-gender specific terms. I use Jerry's text from the final scene of *Betrayal* by Harold Pinter. (This exercise was introduced to me by David Rotenberg of the MFA program at York University in Toronto. He used it for slightly different reasons than those outlined here.) I have all the students memorize it and then put them in improvisational situations on the spot in class and after a while I purposely include outlandish and outrageous situations. They must speak the text to one another. The focus is on finding the emotional state of "I love you" easily and authentically with any scene partner at any time. I never address the pairings as either gay or straight but simply require the actor to play authentically off the other actor.

Ultimately these are valuable ideas for any actor to work with and they will stretch all of your students by challenging both their technical facility and their understanding of themselves and the world around them. This can address any student who is trapped in a very narrow idea of his/her identity concerning gender orientation and especially can provide a sense of belonging and validity to the out LGBT student looking for opportunities to bring more authenticity to his/her work.

The closeted or questioning student is also given the freedom to try new modes of expression or identity safely, within the context of the class work without having to make any public declarations. It will also make the room safe by making it clear that you will be accepting and encouraging of work that breaks or blurs norms of gender and sexual expression. I must stress that you can never assume that your LGBT students know this about you. Consistent negative reinforcement outside your classroom may make them wary. Despite clear demonstrations of your open-mindedness on other issues, until you address the issue of sexuality somewhat directly, they may not assume they are safe.

BEYOND SAFETY

When a young woman enters an acting class she is encouraged to play a wide range of roles that explore the wide range of her identity as a woman and how our society has viewed women. We see this as important to her development into a mature actress. We are thrilled when students of different ethnicities or races bring the dramatic literature of their culture into class. Not only is it good for those students to deepen their understanding of themselves through work on this material, it broadens the horizons of every student to see such work being performed.

But time and time again, I am contacted by LGBT students I have known through my work with various high schools and told that their university teachers have specifically forbidden them to work on queer material. These students are always confused, often shamed and sometimes devastated. I understand these teachers' impulses to help students become viable commodities in the commercial marketplace—an actor who reads clearly as "gay" will have trouble finding work. But is pushing these students away from queer material really the way to help them grow into mature actors and actresses?

It is important to remember that gay children are rarely born into gay households. There is no one at home to tell them their history or model a place in the world for them. When they finally come out, they don't get a packet in the mail that tells them what it means and who they are as an LGBT person. They must find that out themselves and the knowledge is hard won. With the advent of university resources mentioned earlier and more media presence (generally a positive thing but often a double-edged sword) it may be easier but the issue isn't fully resolved.

So even if students are "out" that does not mean they have arrived at a deep, positive or stable understanding of this aspect of themselves and/or integrated it into their psyche. I remember a colleague of mine discussing a gay student who was having a tough time in class; when I asked if his sexuality was an issue, she confidently responded that it couldn't possi-

bly be an issue because he had already come out! As we have seen, that "synthesis" stage can be hard to reach. Making sure queer students can continue their exploration and identity development in their acting training (not only apart from it) will allow them to grow further as actors.

I believe that the most important thing is to be supportive and encouraging when we see students exploring what it means to be queer through their work in class.

Acting is about entering into fictional worlds, finding truth there and expressing that truth to an audience. In order to find truth in a fictional setting, an actor must be able to make meaningful connections between that fictional world and his or her own experience of the world. (This is one of the pillars of learning theory mentioned earlier.) The queer student's experience of the world is *a queer experience* and thus he/she must be connected and knowledgeable about that experience in order to make connections to material and find the truth of the material.

Hopefully it is the rare teacher these days who forbids queer material in the classroom. But even the most sensitive and aware teacher will sometimes articulate or display the values of the heteronormative culture at large. One young gay male high school student very recently told me that a teacher who had otherwise been very supportive became concerned when it was time to prepare material for college auditions. The student had chosen two very different contemporary monologues (I coached him and the pieces contrasted beautifully) but both characters were gay men. Despite the fact that one character's sexuality was not in any way made clear, the teacher advised changing one of the pieces. The student's confidence was shaken and he came to me for coaching. I wondered if that teacher had similar conversations with straight students who had chosen to perform two heterosexual characters. Are we always careful that we assign queer material to heterosexual students as often as we assign "straight" material to queer students? Are we sure we don't unwittingly indicate that we place a higher value on "straight" material and "acting straight," even if that isn't our conscious intention or personal opinion?

TECHNICAL ISSUES OF VOICE AND BODY:

But, we do at some point need to address the concerns of the commercial marketplace (provided that is where the student wishes to go, but that is another topic) and make our students viable and "castable." The big issue here for us as voice teachers is that old bugaboo, "appropriate pitch and tone"—boy's voices can't be too high and girl's voices can't be too deep. How do we deal with this?

Address the Source

Many times the limiting vocal and physical characteristics that worry us are the result of the student's limited understanding of him or herself as a queer person. "Soft" movements, sibilant sounds or a light voice may be the only way a young gay man knows to express an important aspect of his identity. Flamboyant clowning may have been his only way to find some acceptance. A young woman's obvious athleticism and ability to "hang with the boys" may have served the same purpose. These are valuable, perhaps life-saving behaviors which will not be dispensed with casually. As Patsy Rodenburg says: "It is so easy for groups who do not fit clear gender definitions and who have been mocked and repressed, to then hide behind a vocal caricature of themselves" (Rodenburg 1992, 75).

Research shows that self-perception plays an important role in changing vocal expression (Andrews and Schmidt 1997, 312). We cannot change the outward manifestation of identity until the identity is secure. We cannot remove the familiar voice until the student has something to take its place. The more the queer student explores the range and diversity within his or her community, the startling and proud heritage he or she is part of, the more he or she will be able to own a three-dimensional identity and sense of self. At this point, the outward expression may alter on its own. The student, who understands him or herself as more than a stereotype, will be less inclined to behave in stereotypical ways.

Timing is important

In the case where it really is necessary to adjust someone's sound technically, voice teachers will have a much easier time if they wait until their students have a secure sense of self. If a student's sense of identity is fragile he/she will resist or feel threatened by an attempt to change his or her sound drastically. Once students know who they are, hopefully they'll perceive the technical adjustment, as just that—a technical adjustment rather than an attack on their identity. Of course just because they may be ready, doesn't mean that old defenses won't come into play—it can be a bit of a dance. Establish trust and keep the lines of communication open.

Watch out for the shame button

If the student's need for vocal adjustment is too severe to wait and/or the student has not given you the appropriate cues to speak freely about their orientation, then make sure you separate the work from his/her personal identity. If you approach this from "you sound too light for a boy" you will push the shame button and both you and your student will have a bad time. This is that "negative reinforcement" that can prevent "synthesis" which we discussed earlier. Work on this in the context of a specific role rather than in general. You can then discuss a more "effective sound" for the character rather than

making comments about the student's personal vocal expression. When dealing with sensitive issues of any kind, I find myself frequently repeating this phrase in class: "I'm not telling you how to live your life outside this studio but regarding this monologue/scene/song etc…"

Are you sure you're hearing what you think you're hearing?

We all have, to some extent, internalized the negative messages about homosexuality that pervade the dominant culture. We may have to confront bits and pieces of cultural homophobia time and time again no matter how open-hearted and well intentioned and well educated we are. We may have to check in with ourselves to make sure that your dissatisfaction with a student's sound is not a socially conditioned response to a "gay" sound.

Technical Issues

Really examine if the problem is what you think it is. Is the voice really too high-pitched or too low? Research shows that the difference in pitch between voices that are perceived as male and voices that are perceived as female is almost non-existent. That is, there is huge overlap in the range of pitch between male-sounding voices and female-sounding voices—notice I did not say "male voices" and "female voices." The difference is usually one of resonance, timbre and melody and not pitch. "…[A]lthough men and women tend to use the extremes of pitch differently, they both share an extensive middle range. It seems that it may be the movement of the voice with respect to frequency shifts and contours rather than the location of the habitual pitch level that influences the perception of gender" (Andrews and Schmidt 1992, 308).

But there is even some research showing that "some adjective descriptors that are usually thought to be gender specific (e.g. soothing, smooth) were not found to be gender specific" (Andrews and Schmidt 310). Marlon Brando's performance in the film of *Streetcar Named Desire* is widely thought of as the quintessential performance of heterosexual masculinity. But technically his voice is somewhat light and his movements are oddly graceful and feline rather than brutish as Blanche describes him. So where does the perception of a voice as "inappropriate" come from?

Connection

As voice teachers we strive to balance out *all* our students' voices to give them the greatest flexibility and range—so finding the upper resonators for the "husky-voiced" woman and the lower resonators for the "light-voiced" man should be part and parcel of our work regardless of concerns of gender and sexuality. All voice teachers have techniques to adjust resonance, placement, sibilance, etc. There is no technical secret to working with the LGBT voice. Yet, we still end up stumped in these cases, if the number of times someone posts a question about this to the VASTAVOX (the Listserv for VASTA) is any indication. Why?

Rather than the technical attributes of the voice, are we responding to the information or lack of information the voice is carrying? As Rodenburg says there is a vocal mask or "caricature" that many queer students carry. It's a vicious cycle. Queer students may deny who they are (at least on stage if not in life) and attempt to technically approximate a more "masculine" or "feminine" sound. But it may be the denial of their true voice that creates the vocal issue. Are we hearing the disconnection in the voice rather than the voice itself? Are we put off by the fact that the queer student seems to be hiding something or "lying?" If we attempt to correct this exclusively through technique we will fail. We can lower pitch, shift resonance, adjust melody but a disconnected voice is disconnected on every pitch and in every resonator. Instead, get the student to connect to the truth.

A PROVOCATIVE THEORY

The actor who has no understanding of love because she is not connected to where she finds love in her own life, has no hope of playing Juliet.

The actor who has no understanding of sexual pleasure because he is not connected to where he finds his own sexual pleasure, has no hope of playing Stanley Kowalski.

But the queer actor who understands her/his own unique experience of love and sexual pleasure (which in this case is queer love and queer sexual pleasure) has what he or she needs to begin work on either role. Remember that the Four Pillars of Learning tell us that learning takes place when students connect curricular material to *their own lives*. This is what also makes the "Magic If" work. Only if an actor understands his or her own experience first can he or she begin to work towards understanding Juliet's or Stanley's experiences.

So, rather than having gay and lesbian students work on appearing straight, encourage them to first work on exploring the depth and range and reality of being gay, of being fully themselves and, ultimately they may understand what it means to be fully human. This furnishes them with the understanding they need to approach any role.

SOME REAL LIFE CASES

Michael:

Michael was a student director when I arrived on campus and I had heard of him but never worked with him (he was much,

much more firmly established in the department than I was at this point). At that time, he was directing and co-writing an original solo show with another male student.

One day the faculty advisor of this solo project asked me to look at a piece of writing and to speak to Michael as she was stumped about what to say. The piece was intended as a "comic" indictment of the behavior of gay men. It traded on and perpetuated negative stereotypes and relied on verbal gay bashing for its laughs. I found it extremely troubling and sat down with Michael to discuss it.

I realized quickly that Michael, despite being out, was conflicted about his identity. He accepted his own orientation but didn't seem to like it at all. He disliked most members of the gay community that he had met and kept saying he never wanted to be like them. I asked how he thought this piece would impact students in the audience who were struggling with their own sexuality—whether this would make it easier or harder for them. I knew Michael had befriended a freshman who was in the midst of such a struggle. I asked him to see his actions as connected to his friend and to a larger community he could be part of if he chose. He cut the piece (the solution he chose, not one I suggested) and we established a bond.

The next year I was directing *Twelfth Night* and he asked if he could assist me. At our meeting I explained that I intended to do a trans-gendered re-visioning of the piece and would take him on if he still wanted to do it. "Oh, I thought you were REALLY doing *Twelfth Night*." I replied that my choices were based firmly in research, supported by the text and, in my opinion, true to the spirit of the piece. Confounded, he said he would have to think about it for a while.

Eventually he signed on and I gave him and the entire cast books by Kate Bornstein—a noted transgender author, artist and activist. The books upset and angered him deeply. They challenged his view of the world. By now we knew each other well enough to have frank and open discussions. I continued to point out the rigidity of his thinking and the homophobic attitudes he had internalized. He stuck with the project. When we were lucky enough to raise the funds to bring Kate in to work with the cast, she and Michael became fast friends.

The next semester it came time for Michael to write his senior thesis. He decided to write the paper on Tim Miller, a queer solo artist whose work straddles art and activism. We had long, intense discussions about Tim's work and other queer artists. It was clear to me that Michael's concept of himself as a gay man was becoming fuller and more integrated as he explored his identity through his work.

The next year he decided to direct a student production of *Shakespeare's R&J*. This is an adaptation of the Shakespeare classic in which four young men in a boarding school secretly act out *Romeo and Juliet* in their rooms after classes are over. It was a major sea-change for Michael to take on a show with such clearly homoerotic content. We worked together on that piece (he asked me to be his advisor on it) and the show was beautiful, finely drawn, unabashed and unapologetic—a far cry from the monologue two years earlier. The show was so good in fact that it was invited to the KCACTF Region II Festival[1] and then was invited to the National Festival at the Kennedy Center.

Michael and I have talked about this progression extensively and he has said there was no way he could have directed that show without the previous experiences which challenged him to expand his concept of himself and his work to include a mature understanding of being gay.

The growth of two young gay actors
Two of the actors on that production of *Shakespeare's R&J* also identified themselves as gay—one had been out a while and the other had just come out. Both were promising actors but with some real challenges. Both were tentative and intellectual in their choices and always seemed to be holding something in reserve. One played Romeo and the other played Juliet.

Drawing on the cross-gender work we had done with Kate Bornstein on *Twelfth Night*, Michael and the cast arrived at an understanding of how to play the emotional truth of a scene without descending into stereotype since three of the four cast members played women at some point in the show.

Over the weeks I watched as the work of these two actors grew and opened as I had never seen it before. They became passionate, expressive and dangerous on stage—things that had always been lacking in their work. Other faculty members were astounded. Both actors were nominated for Irene Ryan Acting Competition (sponsored by KCACTF) and one made it all the way to the final round of the competition. I am completely convinced that it was the experience of performing in a show in which they could bring their own unique, queer experience of the world directly to bear that allowed them to open up and take much greater risks than they had before. Once they had that experience—and been given tremendous positive feedback—it was easier to find their way back to that place of freedom and passion in their next roles.

The most important thing is that since then they have played a variety of roles in the department—gay and straight—and

their work has stayed open and passionate since that time. One has also become an extremely prominent activist on campus as president of the Queer Student Union and has gone from being a borderline student to an academic success.

Two Freshman—one in and one out
My final anecdote is my observation of two young actors, one who publicly identified as gay and the other who (in my opinion) was struggling privately. Both chose to work on monologues that dealt with the end of a romantic relationship with a woman.

As the out actor worked in class I saw that he understood the material but was having no success in finding a place of passion or deep connection. His scene partner was a woman—a close friend who had not at that point manifested any sexual energy in her work. I asked his permission to change his scene partner and he agreed. I chose a very tall, handsome and charismatic young man. The energy of the young actor shifted dramatically as he confronted this version of the lover he was leaving—he found the struggle to leave, and the pain that goes along with that decision. The work gained more emotional depth and became much more personal and dangerous. When he returned to a female scene partner, he was able to retain a good amount of what he had found. This actor is small and small-boned, with a boyish voice and yet we never for a moment questioned his sexuality—we believed him because he was connected to some internal truth.

The other young actor was (in my estimation at the time) the more talented of the two. He had a lot of the same acting issues as the first actor but I could not address him in the same way. This actor struggled to push his voice deeper, overemphasized the profanity in the speech and really did everything he thought believable as an aggressive heterosexual male. It did not work. I coached him away from pressuring his voice and strove to help him find a more personal connection. While it was a very simple scene that was clearly within this actor's realm of intellectual understanding the trouble was that he was lying and disconnected from his own impulses the entire time. He attempted to build a convincing mask rather than reveal the truth of what he knew about love and loss. He was hiding the entire time and his audience of classmates we knew it, too.

Some Outside Support
Jill Dolan found cross-gender work to be valuable in expanding the range of an actress in her production of *Etta Jenks*. In the production the actress played both male and female roles. I include this brief anecdote because I find the difference in the audience's perception and the actor's experience to be enlightening.

For Susan McCully, playing James in pointed-toed boots and a tasteless red jacket, and playing Shelly in spiked heels, a skin-tight short skirt, and the leather outfit and garters of a dominatrix, the experience marked her relationship to gender differently. Performing Shelly's frank and open femininity was much harder for McCully to achieve as an actor. Although many spectators assumed that James was the stretch for her, since the role crossed gender, Shelly's masquerade was more profound. McCully jokes that she was typecast as James, but that from playing Shelly, she learned to appreciate the power of femininity. I was gratified that such experiences were possible within our cast. As given my own history as an acting student, the process for these actors was as important to me as the product for the audience (Dolan 1993, 194).

TOWARDS A QUEER THEATER

Beyond the concept that a gay actor with a fully realized and healthy connection to the entirety of his/her identity is much more capable of playing a wide range of roles than someone who denies who he/she is before performing on the stage, there is another perhaps even more provocative idea:

Queer theater is valid theater.

Some of your queer students may not opt for the existing commercial marketplace. They may decide to make and participate in theater that reflects their queer experience of the world and is meant for their queer community. They may choose to celebrate and revel in all that is deemed "inappropriate" about themselves. If this makes you uneasy, sit with that uneasiness for a moment before you form a response or an opinion. Isn't good theater often theater that makes you uneasy? Don't we often profess to our students that universality lies in the specifics? Is this any less true when the specifics they find are queer specifics? "Think of those who ride over the gender lines—Dietrich, Prince, Madonna, even the contemporary "metro-sexual" male—David Beckham, Brad Pitt—we are fascinated by them. And can we offer our students support in finding the most compelling versions of themselves, whatever that may be. The authentic, rather than the expected will be the most striking, compelling choice the artist has to offer" (Simlett 13).

While we must prepare our students for "the business of 'Show Business'" we cannot forget that art is a medium of personal expression. We cannot focus on what students have to "sell" to the exclusion of what it is they want to *say* to the world.

Charles Ludlam started out as an acting student at a university, running afoul of his acting teachers. His acting was too eccentric and outrageous for his teachers but for him it was the true expression of his authentic impulse. Rather than obey his teachers he delved into his difference and found there a vision of theater that extended beyond his approach to acting. Rather than wait for someone to create a play in which his unique acting could be supported, he created the Ridiculous Theatrical Company. He created a new theatre specifically because his interests and his acting were too outside the mainstream. How much richer the art of theatre became because Charles Ludlam embraced and created from his queerness.

❦

Endnotes

1. The Kennedy Center American College Theater Festival is broken into regions across the US. Each region sponsors a festival every year which includes works selected from colleges and universities in that region as well as workshops and scholarship competitions.

Bibliography

Andrews, Moya L., and Charles P. Schmidt. "Gender Presentation: Perceptual and Acoustical Analyses of Voice." *Journal of Voice* 11.3 (1997): 307+.

An Encyclopedia of Gay Lesbian Bisexual Transgender and Queer Culture. <http://www.glbtq.org>.

Cianotto, J. *Education Policy: Issues Affecting Lesbian, Gay, Bisexual and Transgender Youth*. New York: n.p., 2003.

Chestnut, Saralynn. "Sexual Identity Development: The Importance of a Target or Dominant Group Membership." *Queering the Curriculum or What's Walt Whitman Got to Do with It?* Ed. Sanlo, R. Westport, Connecticut: Greenwood Press, 1998.

Dolan, Jill "Gender, Sexuality and 'my life' in the (university) Theater." *Kenyon Review*, 15.2 (1993): 185+

Gay, Lesbian, Straight Educator's Network Online Resource Library. <http://www.glsen.org>.

Linklater, Kristin. "Introduction." *Freeing Shakespeare's Voice*. First ed. New York, New York: Theatre Communications Group, 1992. 5.

Ludlam, Charles, *Ridiculous Theatre: Scourge of Human Folly: the Essays and Opinions of Charles Ludlam*. Steven Samuels, editor, 1st edition New York, Theatre Communications Group, 1992.

Online Encyclopedia. Net Industries. <http://encyclopedia.jrank.org/>.

Renn, Kristen. "Lesbian, Gay, Bisexual, and Transgender Students in the College Classroom." *Working with Lesbian, Gay, Bisexual and Transgender College Students: A Handbook for Faculty and Administrators*. Ed. Sanlo, R. Westport, Connecticut: Greenwood Press, 1998.

Rodenburg, Patsy. *The Right to Speak*. New York, New York: Routledge, 1992.

Simlett, Jeffrey. final research project for diploma in Voice Teaching at York University. n.p.: n.p., 2005.

Sullivan, Patricia. "Sexual Identity Development: The Importance of a Target or Dominant Group Membership." *Working with Lesbian, Gay, Bisexual and Transgender College Students: A Handbook for Faculty and Administrators*. Ed. Sanlo, R. Westport, Connecticut: Greenwood Press, 1998. 3.

Peer Reviewed Article *by Tara McAllister-Viel*

Casting Perceptions: The Performance of Gender as a Career Strategy

Six years ago in Seoul, Korea, actor Hong Suk Chun became the first public figure to announce he was gay. He promptly lost his job as a children's television presenter.[1] I happened to be in Seoul during that time, training actors' voices at The Korean National University of Arts [KNUA], School of Drama. Hong's announcement and his subsequent mistreatment by his television employers dominated the Korean news and eventually entered my Voice classrooms. We discussed Hong's particular situation but also talked about the larger issues his announcement raised: the way homophobia functions in Korean society, pressure placed on Korean men to fulfill cultural expectations of "masculinity" and the particular pressures Korean actors face to portray themselves as "macho." We also discussed the cultural/gender issues Korean women faced, such as the casting emphasis on youth and beauty, as well as the difficulty of fulfilling expected social roles like motherhood while trying to develop a career as an actress.

These in-class discussions prompted me to investigate the cultural and gender relationship my students had with images of Korean masculinity and femininity and how those relationships were realized in vocal gender performance. This article details only a small part of my investigation—which lasted over the course of four years—by focusing on one particular issue, the training and performance of the "macho" voice. By choosing such a narrow focus I am not implying that other gender voice issues are less important, or the vocal issues of Korean men somehow deserve more attention than the vocal issues of Korean women. I wish to concentrate on this issue alone because it lays the foundation for discussing the larger ethical questions I faced teaching overseas: when introducing my Western Voice praxis into a Korean acting training program based in a very different socio-cultural system with its own values and practices, how do I balance what I feel is necessary in training the actors' voice with Korean gender and cultural expectations? What is my place as a white American female voice teacher training Korean male voices for the commercial Korean marketplace? By presenting my own classroom as case study, this article adds yet another perspective to on-going conversations about the ethical implications of teaching overseas in culture/language systems outside of one's own experience.

The methodological approach I used in my Korean Voice classrooms to investigate gender and the voice was adapted from the work I had done in the US on the performance of gender and acting training. As part of my Masters of Fine Arts-Acting thesis I explored adapting feminist theories as strategies for the embodiment of female roles by female actors, particularly using the scholarly work of Judith Butler to critically analyze what she calls the "performance of gender."[2] This theoretical approach underpinned my practice and was integrated into a voice assignment called Vocal Self-Assessment. This assignment was given to both BFA and MFA level KNUA Voice classes over the course of four years.[3] The responses I received demonstrated that KNUA acting students clearly understood the vocal gender expectations of the profession for which they were training. As an outgrowth of the assignment, my students wanted to use their awareness of Korean gender expectations in combination with my voice training techniques to influence casting and commercial acceptability.

The Self-Assessment assignment raised several ethical questions for me and for the students about the professional consequences of upholding or thwarting

Tara McAllister-Viel received her PhD in Performance Practice-Voice from the University of Exeter and her Masters of Fine Arts-Acting from the University of Wisconsin-Madison, Asian/Experimental Theatre Program. While a Visiting Professor of Voice at The Korean National University of Arts, School of Drama, Tara also studied a traditional Korean vocal art form. Tara's research and teaching focus is adapting p'ansori training techniques, Hatha yoga and tai chi chuan (Wu form) into an intercultural/interdisciplinary approach to training actors' voices. Currently, Tara is Voice lecturer at The Central School of Speech and Drama, London.

1. Macintyre, Donald. "Hung Suk Chun: Breaching a Social Barrier," *Time Asia*, October 2, 2004. *www.time.com/time/asia/2004/heroes/hhong_suk_ch un_.html*.

2. Butler, Judith. *Gender Trouble: Feminism and the Subversion of Identity*. New York and London: Routledge, 1990, 1999: 12.

3. I taught voice full-time as Visiting Professor, voice to MFA and BFA acting students (2000-2002), then returned to teach for the summer of 2003, and then again for the fall semester, 2004.

vocal gender expectations and the place of "technique" in training for a certain kind of actor's voice within a larger socio-economic context. The quotes from students' Self-Assessment assignment offers some insight into the way these students, at a particular point in their learning development, understood how gender vocal performances "work" in a job market with explicit gendered voice expectations.[4] My critical analysis between students' self-observations throughout this article is my attempt to understand a larger pattern of cultural and gender influenced vocal function within the male students in my class. The conclusions I drew at the time have influenced the way I approach training actors' voices and my perspective of the voice teacher's role in the construction of vocal gender representation for commercial markets.

"Gender *is* performance"[5]

Judith Butler argues, "The acts by which gender is constituted bear similarities to performative acts within theatrical contexts."[6] When applied to training actor's voices, performative gender acts as "cultural construct[s] made up of learned values and beliefs" that can be perceived through "vocal pitch and intonation."[7] If the listener does not *perceive* the speaker's performance as fulfilling culturally-specific gender expectations, the speaker risks "punishment" for failing "to do their gender right."[8] In this way, the performance of gender becomes a cultural survival "strategy"[9] that knowingly plays with "learned values and beliefs," performed and perceived between speaker and listener.

When vocal survival strategies leave the daily sphere and enter the voice classroom, the process of performing gender in the voice is "doubly fraught with implication" because the voice classroom is a place "where presentation invariably entails representation."[10] The moment the student actor enters voice training, gender vocal strategies are no longer negotiated only between speaker and listener but now intimately involve the voice trainer. What we teach and how we teach is as integral to crafting the voice for the performance of gender on-stage as helping students become aware of the ways in which socio-cultural expectations "craft" the construction of the gendered voice in daily life.

Most mainstream contemporary voice training approaches address these survival strategies as vocal habits in order to explain the many ways vocal function is blocked through the use of excessive or unnecessary muscular contraction, or tension.[11] Since the 1970s contemporary voice training has focused on exercises to release these blocks and help the student actor develop a "free" voice.[12] But how much freedom does a "free" voice have in any given socio-cultural context that regularly "punishes" acts that do not fulfill certain expectations? If vocal gender performance in daily presentation must "pass," in other words must successfully be perceived to fulfill socio-cultural gender behaviors in order to avoid "punishment," are the vocal gender representations of actors punished when their performances can not pass the audition, fulfilling the expectations of casting directors and other employers? Are voice trainers also punished if they do not produce actors that meet casting expectations for the performance of gender in the voice?

For voice trainers, success is often measured by the number of students they train who become working actors in the industry. Many canonical voice texts

4. KNUA students granted permission to use their comments and first names only. I have chosen to further safeguard their identity by abbreviating their first names into initials. Also, some excerpts from the Vocal Self-Assessments were written in English as a Foreign Language [EFL] while others were translated for me by in-class translators, or translated by me. I take responsibility, however, for all translations that appear in this article.

5. Senelick, Laurence (ed.). *Gender in Performance: Presentation of Difference in Performing*. New England: Tufts University Press, 1993: introduction.

6. Butler, Judith. "Performative Acts and Gender constitution: An Essay in Phenomenology and feminist Theory," in Sue-Ellen Case, ed. *Performing Feminisms: Feminist Critical Theory and Theatre*. Baltimore: Johns Hopkins, 1990: 272.

7. Senelick, *Gender in Performance: Presentation of Difference in Performing*, ix.

8. Butler, *Gender Trouble: Feminism and the Subversion of Identity*, 273.

9. Ibid.

10. Senelick, *Gender in Performance: Presentation of Difference in Performing*, ix.

11. Linklater, Kristin. *Freeing the Natural Voice*. New York: Drama Book Publishers, 1976: 1.
Berry, Cicely. *Voice and the Actor*. New York: Collier Books, 1973: 7-8.
Lessac, Arthur. "From Beyond Wildness to Body Wisdom, Vocal Life, and Healthful Functioning: A Joyous Struggle for Our Discipline's Future," *The Vocal Vision: Views on Voice*. (eds.) Marion Hampton and Barbara Acker. New York: Applause, 1997: 17.
Rodenburg, Patsy. *The Right to Speak*. New York: Routledge, 1992: 8.
McCallion, Michael. *The Voice Book: for actors, public speakers, and everyone who wants to make the most of their voice*. London: Farber and Farber, 1988: 4.

12. Berry, *Voice and the Actor*, 23-28. Rodenburg, *The Right to Speak*, 19-20. Linklater, *Freeing the Natural Voice*, 24.

are introduced by famous actors or directors who have studied or worked with the author/voice trainer, suggesting directly or indirectly that the trainer's approach "works," or is commercially successful.[13] Voice trainers have a vested interest in training actor's voices to fulfill commercial expectations, not only for our own careers but also for our students' careers. But when we train actor's voices to fulfill gender voice expectations in an attempt to make available job opportunities in mainstream markets, do we also re-inscribe gender stereotypes and typecasting, further *limiting* job opportunities?

"Big boys don't cry"
In chapter two of *Freeing the Natural Voice*, Kristin Linklater suggests that developing an awareness of how social messages become embodied is a necessary part of training the actor's voice. She points to certain social messages in the US that create ways of shaping or inhibiting vocal production: "'Big boys don't cry.' 'Nice little girls don't shout'."[14] However, the embodiment of gender messages by the actor is only part of the performance of gender. Laurence Senelick argues that gender "exists only in so far as it is perceived." How acts are performed, perceived and placed along a "scale of masculinity and femininity" determine gender attribution.[15] Perception can apply to both the listener as well as the student actor embodying and performing learned gender messaging. Korean acting students, like their US counterparts, receive very clear gender messages both on and off-stage. I understood that in training the KNUA student actor's voice I would have to investigate the act of perception as well as the act of vocally embodying performative acts.

Some of the messages within the Korean market, perpetuated by other Korean male actors and directors, encouraged male KNUA Voice students to perceive and perform "masculinity" in very specific ways: One male student commented in his Self-Assessment assignment, "In small theatres my voice is ok, but in big theatres my voice is not strong enough for a male Korean actor. Some Korean male actors have some expectations for male actors that they must have a certain amount of volume" (J. H. 2000).

One of my male students studying towards an MFA explained how he was bullied by a Korean male director who ridiculed him regularly throughout rehearsals. "When I was in a production the director named me 'mosquito' because he thought I had such a small voice. I didn't perform for a long time after that" (D. S. 2000). Eventually, this student changed career plans and became a mime artist to avoid vocal issues altogether. Only after receiving awards for his work in mime, did this performer feel confident enough to return to acting and enrolled in KNUA's MFA acting program. He trained with me for two years and currently works as a professional physical theatre artist integrating both voice and mime techniques into his performances.[16]

For this student, the clear messages he received from other industry professionals affected not only his off-stage perceptions of male gender vocal performance, but greatly affected his vocal gender performance for the stage, and limited his access to jobs. Only when his perception of his voice changed over the course of his career was he able to re-conceptualize the function of a voice in performance and the place of voicing in his artistic work.

"If I sound 'macho' then they will think I am 'macho'"[17]
In regards to hiring within the profession, many male KNUA students looked

13. Berry, Cicely. *Voice and the Actor.* New York: Collier Books, 1973. Forward by Peter Brook.
— — —. *The Actor and the Text.* New York: Applause Books, 1987, 1992. Forward by Trevor Nunn.
— — —. *Text in Action.* London: Virgin, 2001. Forward by Adrian Noble.
Rodenburg, Patsy. T*he Right to Speak.* New York: Routledge, 1992. Forward by Ian McKellen.
— — —. *The Need for Words.* London: Methuen, 1993. Forward by Antony Sher
— — —. *The Actor Speaks.* New York: St. Martin's Press, 2000. Forward by Judi Dench.
— — —. *Speaking Shakespeare.* London: Methuen, 2002. Back cover quotes by Anthony Sher, Trevor Nunn, Ralph Fiennes, Simon McBurney and Judi Dench.

14. Linklater, *Freeing the Natural Voice*, 11. For more "masculine" gender messages and a discussion on how these messages change historically and are affected by race, culture and class, refer to Mangan, Michael. *Staging Masculinities: History, Gender, Performance.* New York: Palgrave Macmillan, 2003: 207-212.

15. Senelick, *Gender in Performance: Presentation of Difference in Performing*, introduction.

16. D.S's story raises interesting questions about the way volume and breath support indicate performances of "masculinity" and the way silence and silencing are used as tools of power. Due to this article's length requirement I cannot investigate here issues surrounding certain homophobic anxieties or issues of Asian masculinity within a modern Korean performance industry. Refer to Deborah Cameron (ed.), "Speech and Silence," and "Talking gender: dominance, difference, performance," in The *Feminist Critique of Language.* London: Routledge, 1998, 1999, and Robin Tolmach Lakoff's essay "Cries and Whispers: The Shattering of the Silence," in *Gender Articulated*, Kira Hall and Mary Bucholtz (ed.). New York and London: Routledge, 1995.

17. Vocal Self-Assessment assignment by male KNUA student C., 2000. In order to stay focused on training actors' voices and the performance of gender, I do not cross-culturally compare "macho" and "machismo" here. Refer to Haywood, Chris and Mac an Ghaill, Mairtin. *Men and Masculinities.* Buckingham and Philadelphia: Open University Press, 2003: pp. 83-100.

to film, TV and music industries as examples of vocal gender performances that "worked" for Korean male actors. One student wrote in his Self-Assessment, "I have a husky and low voice and this quality is really great! People tell me I have a similar voice to an action actor in the [Korean] movies, Kim Po Sung. So if I encourage my voice for the stage I could have this very good voice like his" (G. W. 2001). Another student wrote in his Self-Assessment, "I am very influenced by other actors. Others say my voice is pleasant because it is a low voice. Others may feel that this sound is a 'macho' sound so maybe that is how I want them to see me. If I sound 'macho' then they will think I am 'macho'" (C. 2000).

Many of the male KNUA students were attracted to the "tough guy" image and "macho" vocal performance. A good example of this macho voice was represented in a popular gangster film called, "*Chingu*"[18] [trans. "Friend(s)"], which had been released during the time we were exploring gender and voice in my voice classes. The actors in *Chingu* represented a particular kind of "macho," influenced by the subculture of the Korean mafia. To correctly perform this vocal representation, the actor adds jaw tension as though the character would say something but was restraining his desire to speak. The actor also pitches his voice in his lower range, allowing the sounds to resonate in the chest. The actor uses more support than is necessary, contracting the intercostals limiting rib swing and breath capacity, and constricts the muscles in the vocal tract to "catch" the sound in the throat. The resulting sound has a husky quality that my male KNUA students found engaging.

Pitching the "macho" voice

In their Vocal Self-Assessment assignments, students generally pointed at first to simplistic understandings of gender through pitch: men had low pitched voices and women had higher pitched voices. Pitch was treated as a "fixed" stable element in performing gender, not as a culturally perceived vocal element that read as "macho." In mainstream voice training, pitch is rarely discussed as a culturally perceived phenomenon. Contemporary voice training prioritizes scientific evidence to guide the training of actors' voices. Jacqueline Martin writes:

> Scientists have determined that an individual's natural pitch level, which is often referred to as 'optimum,' lies somewhere near the third or fourth tone above the lowest which can be produced clearly. Many teachers now realize that locating this 'natural' pitch level constitutes a basic step towards improving voice and a number of methods are easily available for its determination.[19]

"Optimum pitch" does not conceptualize a framework for the ways in which pitch is culturally interpreted and manipulated. Eduardo Archetti writes, "It is important to capture the diversity of these signs and forms of behavior by understanding that masculinity cannot be treated as something fixed and universal."[20] If pitch cannot be fixed to indicate masculinity in a Korean male's daily life, pitch becomes even more unstable in the representation of masculinity in the performance of gender. Chris Haywood writes, "A recent conceptual framework has emerged that focuses on uncoupling masculinity from male bodies, that is, uncoupling *what men do* from *what men are* (emphasis his).[21] In this way, even female actors can perform the aural indicators of the macho voice in the performance of gender.[22] In regards to culturally-

18. In July 2000, the Korean government through the Ministry of Culture and Tourism [MOCT] introduced the MOCT Hangeul Romanization System to replace the formerly used McCune-Reischauer system. In this article I have used the new MOCT system.

19. Martin, Jacqueline. *Voice in the Modern Theatre.* London: Routledge, 1991: 39.

20. Archetti, E.P. *Masculinities: Football, Polo and the Tango in Argentina.* Oxford: Berg, 1999: 113.

21. Haywood and Mac an Ghaill, *Men and Masculinities*, 15.

influenced gender performances, should voice trainers reconsider this notion of training actors towards natural or optimum pitch?

Tonal quality of the "macho" voice

According to scholar/practitioner Pamela Hendrick, "How we use our voices to convey gender would chiefly address the phonology (the pitch and intonation patterns) of masculine and feminine language" but "simple alternations in intonation and pitch lead only to partial and inadequate 'gendering.'"[23] Besides the pitching of the macho voice, KNUA male students were also attracted to the tonal quality, the huskiness of the voice. Students sought out this vocal quality not only in Korean film representations but also the overseas films that ran in their local cinemas. "I am engaged by Antonio Bandera's voice—his husky quality" (H.Y. 2000).

Because Seoul is a cosmopolitan city, KNUA students were exposed to a variety of overseas gendered voice representations from many different cultures. But, for some male students, the vocal standard had been set— the husky quality worked, it fulfilled vocal performance expectations of Korean macho masculinity and obtained work for male actors in Seoul. Korean (pop) culture not only influenced which voice qualities were valued by the KNUA students but also influenced the ways KNUA students interpreted and valued the vocal qualities of performers from other cultures.

Certainly, a husky or raspy vocal quality has been similarly valued by American performers in the US. However, current mainstream voice training is dominated by warnings against vocal strain from such master teachers as Kristin Linklater, Cicely Berry, Patsy Rodenburg, Michael McCallion and Arthur Lessac. According to Jacqueline Martin, "A condition of 'spontaneous relaxation' of the…larynx, mouth and tongue is now considered to be of prime importance in the production of a good vocal quality."[24] Notice how a certain kind of anatomical function is considered "good." Voice praxis develops exercises to fulfill shared cultural or aesthetic values of what is considered "good," suggesting what the voice *should* do, not only what vocal anatomy is capable of doing. As a result, the voice training traditions I brought with me from the US had an arsenal of techniques I could employ for releasing excessive muscular contraction, or tension, but did not have a similar number of techniques for teaching how to place tension in the throat in order to create huskiness.

Most voice practice in the US does not train students for a husky vocal quality or the use of tension [excessive muscular contraction] in the vocal tract in part because tension and huskiness are thought to signal vocal misuse or a possible vocal health problem. Tension, as excessive muscular contraction, is not "good." Vocal health became an important underlying principle of voice praxis as early as 1885 when Manual Garcia discovered a way of examining the vocal folds during function through a series of mirrors.[25] Voicing moved away from the art of rhetoric into the science of phonation, (re)conceptualizing the voice and its potential through a scientific, anatomical perspective. Vocal health as a basic principle of current voice praxis has helped encourage the development of exercises designed to release excessive muscular contraction so as not to damage vocal fold function. Release of excessive muscular contraction is "good."

22. Queer theory has explored this area, as well as theorist from transgender study and feminist theatre critics in regards to drag/cross-dressed performance. Refer to Shapiro, Judith. "Transsexualism: Reflections on the Persistence of Gender and the Mutability of Sex," pp. 142-166 and Straub, Kristina. "The Guilty Pleasures of Female Theatrical Cross-Dressing and the Autobiography of Charlotte Clarke," pp. 248-279 in Epstein, Julia and Straub, Kristina. *Body Guards: The Cultural Politics of Gender Ambiguity.* New York and London: Routledge, 1991; Dolan, Jill. "'Lesbian' Subjectivity and Realism: Dragging at the Margins of Structure and Ideology," in Case, Sue-Ellen (ed.). *Performing Feminisms: Feminist Critical Theory and Theatre.* Baltimore and London: Johns Hopkins University Press, 1990: pp.40-53; Senelick, Laurence. "Lady and the Tramp: Drag Differentials in the Progressive Era," in Senelick, Laurence. *Gender in Performance: The Presentation of Difference in the Performing Arts.* Hanover and London: Tufts University, University Press of New England, 1992: pp. 26-45.

23. Hendrick, Pamela R. "Two Opposite Animals? Voice, Text, and Gender on Stage." *Theatre Topics.* September 1998, vol. 8 no. 2: 114.

24. Martin, *Voice in modern theatre,* 38.

25. Ibid., 37.

Balancing vocal health and socio-cultural factors

Voice exercises built for the anatomical health of the vocal folds produce particular kinds of sounds and generally do not value sounds that are restricted in the throat. However, such sounds may be important aural indicators for the performance of masculinity within a given socio-cultural or marketplace context. If the performance of masculinity via excessive muscular contraction is part of a tradition of performing gender that comes with severe consequences and rewards, then socio-cultural factors become as important as vocal health for an actor's career survival.

Within seminal texts, voice praxis suggests not only what the voice can do (e.g. anatomical potential), but also suggests what the voice should do. Linklater writes, "Sometimes throat tension, coupled with an unconscious need to sound manly or in control, can push the larynx down so that the sound only resonates in the lower cavities, and a monotonously rich, deep voice is developed that cannot find light and shade from the upper part of the range."[26] However, finding "light and shade from the upper part of the range" was simply not a priority for many of the male KNUA students that I taught. They had a different perception of what their voices should do to "correctly" perform Korean masculinities.

26. Linklater, *Freeing the Natural Voice*, 13.

This experience created an ethical dilemma for me. As a voice teacher I had always trained towards keeping my students' voices healthy and while teaching in the US I was surrounded by a teaching culture that gave vocal health the highest priority. By accepting a position to teach voice at KNUA I relocated myself in another cultural and learning community that asked me to reprioritize and balance Korean socio-cultural expectations with my own teaching expectations. What was my place in asserting what the voice *should* do?

As an American woman I reconsidered my role in training actor's voices through the experience of training male KNUA students' voices to represent Korean masculinities. The personal experiences my students wrote about in their Vocal Self-Assessments, reinforced by larger events such as the news stories surrounding Hong's dismissal, demonstrated the tangible economic and social consequences my students would face if they failed to meet expectations for Korean men in performing assumed heterosexual masculinities. Certainly my male KNUA students were as capable of training their vocal anatomy towards "light and shade from the upper part of the range" as were my US students, but given the socio-economic climate why would they want to? I wondered if some of my US techniques would have a life outside of my KNUA classroom. These larger socio-cultural and economic influences challenged me to reconsider not only the training techniques I taught (e.g. techniques that required excessive muscular contraction to achieve huskiness) but the underlying principles of my voice teaching praxis.

Mimetic training and "self-expression"

In the Vocal Self-Assessment assignment, many of my KNUA male students desired to imitate male voices they admired. Their focus was not on finding their "own" voice or perceived "natural" voice, but to train towards virtuosic imitation of a voice they perceived would land them a certain kind of role. They looked to technique as integral to this virtuosic imitation. But the techniques I brought with me from the US did not develop from a desire to mimic. In fact, most of the training techniques I used in my classes developed out of the radical politics of the 1960s and 1970s in the US and UK which rejected previous mimetic training exercises from the 1950s "Voice Beautiful" era in order to cultivate the "individual"[27] voice of the student, or find one's own "natural"[28] voice for "self-expression."[29]

Deborah Tannen, noting how actors often "find art in an impulse to imitate" asks, "Why do humans experience a drive to imitate…what purpose could be served by the drive to imitate and repeat?"[30] She suggests that in regards to language, and I would add the voicing of that language, "we are dealing with a delicate balance between the individual and the social, the fixed and the free…The elements [of language and voice] can be manipulated, interpreted, rearranged, and synthesized precisely because they are familiar and fixed."[31] As a result, she concludes, "speakers repeat parts of prior talk not as mindless mimics but to create new meanings. Paradoxically, it is the individual imagination that makes possible the shared understanding of language [voicing].[32]

If I apply Tannen's argument to my experience teaching male students at KNUA, then perhaps the impulse to imitate macho vocal gestures were instances of a gender/cultural negotiation between fixed socio-cultural expectations (within a given historical moment) and the individual. Freeing one's individual voice during training must be in relation to understanding these fixed social expectations. Students should not only examine the negative ways gender inhibits vocal function (i.e. how gender can "taint the sound we make"[33]) but also the positive ways gender helps to construct character voices that communicate common cultural meaning between performer and audience. Gender is not simply a limiting force but instead a material condition of training and performance that negotiates larger fixed economic and social structures.

At KNUA, I made certain pedagogical modifications in my teaching in an attempt to realize Tannen's assertion that "utterances do not occur in isolation" but are created and recreated within socio-cultural contexts between speaker and listener, actor and audience. Mimicking male gender voice performances was one way KNUA male students created new meanings from pre-patterned vocal forms, and perhaps found their own "individual" voice in relation to their society.

For instance, one student wrote in his Self-Assessment, "I performed in a play called 'Play' and my character's name was 'The Man.' The character voice I used for this play was nothing special—I used my own voice. I was told I don't drop my jaw so the sound doesn't come out. Now, whenever I'm on the stage my voice is monotonous and stuck in lower pitches so I feel like my character is stuck—I want to be free" (S.U. 2001). This student mimicked the jaw/throat tension of "M/man" modeled on the Korean masculinities around him and in the end decided that he wanted to be "free," perhaps implying more than vocal freedom, or a release of excessive muscular contraction? To me, this response is an indication that this student is finding his own voice in relation to his society, finding "self-expression" in pre-patterned forms.

How much freedom does a "free" voice have in any given socio-cultural/economic context? Judith Butler refers to "the bind of self-expression" that is the

27. Ibid., 185.

28. Ibid., 2.

29. Rodenburg, *The Right to Speak*, 19.

30. Tannen, Deborah. *Talking Voices: Repetition, Dialogue, and Imagery in Conversational Discourse.* Cambridge: Cambridge University Press, 1989: 94.

31. Ibid., 95.

32. Ibid., 96.

33. Rodenburg, *The Right to Speak*, 8.

34. Butler, *Gender Trouble: Feminism and the Subversion of Identity*, xxiv and 12.

"polarity between free will and determinism."[34] Students and voice trainers alike are caught in this bind between our free will, developing the "free" voice, and determinism, the larger structures that influence vocal production and reception that must be taken into account. Within the larger economic structures in which I taught in Seoul and now teach in London, I know that the effectiveness of my teaching has been and continues to be measured by how well my students meet gender voice expectations to land the job. However, I do not measure myself exclusively against the marketplace. Success is also measured in very personal ways, through self-discovery. For me, the Self-Assessment assignment challenged me and my students to reconsider certain principles in current voice training praxis, such as vocal health and freeing the voice in relation to socio-cultural expectations. I also reconsidered the way I trained actor's voices in relation to pitch in presentation and representation, along with the larger notion that relying on scientific, anatomic understandings of vocal function, e.g. what the voice *can* do, does not necessarily help to conceptualize what the voice *should* do for the performance of gender as a cultural construct playing with "learned values or beliefs" between speaker and listener.

Essay *by Reinhardt J. Heuer, Margaret Baroody & Robert Thayer Sataloff*

Management of Gender Reassignment (Sex Change) Patients

Modified from: Sataloff RT. *Professional Voice: The Science and Art of Clinical Care*, 3rd *Edition*. San Diego, CA: Plural Publishing, Inc., 2005: 1359-1363; with permission.

Introduction

Transsexualism is a gender dysmorphic disorder characterized by persistent feelings of inappropriateness of biologic sex and preoccupation with eliminating primary and secondary sexual characteristics. Male-to-female transsexualism is encountered more commonly than female-to-male transsexualism and demonstrates more difficult communication problems. In most cases, these patients benefit from communication therapy. Female-to-male transsexuals, due to the influence of hormonal treatment on the larynx and related structures, are less likely to have vocal problems. Male-to-female transsexualism occurs in approximately 1 out of 37,000 births.[1,2]

Dr. Reinhardt Heuer is a full professor in the Department of Communication Sciences, School of Health Professions, Temple University. He is also affiliated with the American Institute for Voice and Ear Research. Dr. Heuer's particular areas of interest are voice disorders, communication problems associated with transgenderism and neurological disorders of speech and language. He received his PhD from the University of Oregon, his MA from Brooklyn College, NYC and his undergraduate degree from the University of Wisconsin.

Other related groups of individuals require similar communication assistance. Transgenderists are men who wish to live full time as women but are not so concerned with body issues. Interestingly, in the American culture, it is easier for women to live full time in a masculine role. Cross-dressers are men who enjoy part-time dressing and behaving as women. However, individuals frequently will vacillate from one classification to another over a lifetime. Persons who are primarily cross-dressers will move toward transsexualism or will abandon (purge) their feminine accoutrements. Most males falling into these categories report periods of rejection of the entire issue and work toward becoming hypermasculine, usually early in their lives. Most are married, and many have children. The authors believe that therapy for voice and communication issues is most appropriate when the patient has been diagnosed with gender dysphoria and is living 90 to 100% of the time as a woman. When working with cross-dressers, treatment should be behaviorally based and focus on developing "stage" accent and scripts for use during social events. Other subgroups, such as transvestites and female impersonators, are less likely to look to voice and communication specialists for assistance, but they can be helped similarly when they do.

When developing a program of therapy for the male-to-female transsexual (M/FT), it is important to keep in mind which aspects of communication are based in biology/genetic structure (male/female) and which aspects that are based in learned/social behavior (masculine/feminine). Biologic and genetic aspects include, of course, primary and secondary sexual characteristics. Specifically related to communication are lung size and capacity, laryngeal size and configuration, vocal fold mass, resonating cavity sizes, muscle mass of the tongue, and oral orifice size and thickness. These differences affect the pitch, loudness, quality and resonance of the voice and some aspects of articulation. Learned or social aspects of communication include melody/intonation in voicing, patterns of syllabic emphasis/stress, word choice, sentence structure, semantic structure, gestural communication and dress.

Margaret Baroody is a singing voice specialist in the voice medicine practice of Dr. Robert T. Sataloff and Associates, and Instructor in the Department of Otolaryngology—Head and Neck Surgery at Drexel University College of Medicine. Widely recognized for her work with injured voices, Ms. Baroody is also a highly respected singing teacher who maintains a busy private studio. Ms. Baroody has written frequently on the subject of singing, with particular regard to the injured voice and vocal health. She is the author of over 25 published articles on voice as well as main author and contributing author of numerous book chapters. Ms. Baroody is a professional mezzo-soprano with extensive performance experience.

The major goal for most M/FTs is sexual reassignment surgery with modification of the primary sexual characteristics. This surgery is expensive (over $20,000) and is considered elective by many insurance companies. Most responsible sexual reassignment surgeons require psychiatric proof of gender dysphoria and practical evidence of the patient's ability to live successfully in a feminine role prior to consenting to do the surgery.

Robert T. Sataloff, MD, DMA, FACS is Professor and Chairman, Dept. of Otolaryngology-Head and Neck Surgery and Associate Dean for Clinical Academic Specialties, Drexel University College of Medicine. Dr. Sataloff is Chairman of the Boards of Directors of the Voice Foundation and of the American Institute for Voice and Ear Research. He has served as President of the International Association of Phonosurgery, the American Laryngological Association and the Pennsylvania Academy of Otolaryngology-Head and Neck Surgery. Dr. Sataloff is Editor-in-Chief of the *Journal of Voice* and the *Ear, Nose and Throat Journal*, Associate Editor of the *Journal of Singing*, and on the editorial boards of numerous otolaryngology journals. He has written over 600 publications, including 36 books. His medical practice is limited to care of the professional voice and to otology/neurotology/skull base surgery.

There are no really good surgical procedures to lower the voice in female-to-male transsexuals. The mass of the vocal folds can be increased by injection of substances, and the vocal folds can be shortened by type III thyroplasty; but neither technique results consistently in both substantial decrease in habitual pitch and retention of good vocal quality. Procedures to feminize the biologically male voice are more successful.

Non-surgical Therapy for Pitch Modification

Ninety five percent of the more than 400 M/FTs the author (RJH) has seen had a primary complaint of excessively low pitch. Although this is a male/female trait, the patient frequently elects to work on pitch behaviorally. Surgical considerations for pitch change are discussed later in this chapter.

Gelfer and Schofield[3] report that speech fundamental frequencies above 155 Hz (D3) are more likely to be perceived as feminine. Oates and Decakis[4] are more generous in reporting a gender ambiguous range between 128 and 260 Hz. The goal of pitch modification in M/FTs is to develop a speaking fundamental frequency high enough to allow down-glides that remain above the masculine/feminine cutoff. Initial evaluation of the M/FT involves determining current speech fundamental frequency and the patient's frequency comfortable range. It would be difficult to modify the pitch range upward for an individual who has little flexibility in the upper voice ranges. Behavioral modification of habitual pitch is not easy. It involves development of vocal flexibility, breath support, relaxation, and practice.[5,6] Several approaches have been successful in raising speech fundamental frequency, hopefully allowing the patient to continue using modal voice. Again, this is possible only if the patient has an adequate range. A series of up, down, and up-and-down glide exercises is helpful in extending the patient's range and flexibility. Exercises may include glides on the vowels /ɑ/, /i/, and /u/. One would like to establish a pitch range of at least four semitones above 155 Hz. Drills on words and phrases following upglides are very helpful. Visual feedback using the Kay Visipitch or Kay Real-Time Pitch programs is also very helpful. The majority of patients who seek help do so because they are unable to modify or monitor their own voices acoustically. A program of practice with and upglide + phrase with visual cues, upglide + phrase without visual cues, followed by fading of the upglide and visual cues have been effective in our clinic.

Patients with limited upper ranges are not good candidates for behavioral modification of modal voice or for surgical modification of voice. A voice modification program called "Melanie Speaks" advocated the use of low falsetto voice.[7] The author describes exercises gliding down from natural falsetto to lower falsetto pitches and modifying pharyngeal tension. This is similar to a classical Bel Canto exercise used for centuries by singers to integrate registers into a "mixed" voice.

Surgery for Pitch Modification

Once the diagnosis has been established, the patient is living as a female, psychiatry clearance has been obtained, and voice therapy has been completed, pitch modification surgery may be reasonable. Transsexuals often request this surgery even if they have been extremely successful at modifying voice gender recognition through voice therapy. If such patients are awakened suddenly,

Ethics, Standards and Practices

Management of Gender Reassignment (Sex Change) Patients
by Reinhardt J. Heuer, Margaret Baroody & Robert Thayer Sataloff (continued)

talk in their sleep, or are startled, they are often "revealed" through unthinking, sudden bursts of masculine phonation. This can be extremely embarrassing; and surgical correction in such patients is appropriate.

Many techniques have been proposed, and none is ideal for all cases. Isshiki's type IV thyroplasty has been used for this indication.[8] Unfortunately, even with overcorrection, vocal pitch tends to drop over time. The author's (RTS) cricothyroid fusion[9] produces better long-term results. However, it is only suitable for use in young transsexuals. The cricoid cartilage must be sufficiently flexible to permit its placement just inside the lower border of the thyroid cartilage. When pulling the cricoid toward the thyroid cartilage, it is extremely important to exert all forces under the cricoid arch laterally. The cricoid arch is thin in the midline. If attempts are made to pull the cricoid superiorly with hooks placed in or near the midline, midline fracture is likely to occur. In patients under 40, this operation tends to work well. In patients over 60, ossification is usually too advanced to permit subluxation of the cricoid arch behind the thyroid cartilage. In those between 40 and 60 years old, success depends on the degree of ossification. In such patients, Issiki's technique can be used as described originally or with suture placement as modified by Lee et al.[10] Anterior commissure advancement was described by LeJeune and coworkers in 1983.[11] LeJeune created a cartilage window that was pulled forward, along with the vocal folds. The space between the advanced cartilage and the rest of the thyroid cartilage was maintained with a titanium splint. Tucker modified the procedure by placing the cartilage window in a more cranial position.[12] However, both of these procedures result in increased prominence of the thyroid cartilage. Because many transsexual patients have already undergone laryngeal shave to reduce the thyroid prominence, this cosmetic disadvantage may be unacceptable to the patient.

A few authors have used scarring obtained by parallel cuts near the vibratory margin[13] or vocal fold stripping[14] to elevate pitch. Although increased stiffness does elevate pitch, it is also associated with decreased volume and substantial hoarseness. This author (RTS) does not advocate these procedures. Abitbol has utilized endoscopic thyroarytenoid myomectomy successfully (Jean Abitbol, MD, Paris, France, personal communication, 2001). In this operation, a large ellipse of thyroarytenoid muscle is removed using a CO_2 laser, through an incision placed laterally on the superior surface of the vocal fold. The vibratory margin is not disturbed. This procedure results in decreased mass and, consequently, elevated pitch. The voices are slightly breathy but clear. This procedure can be done unilaterally or bilaterally and has a place in the management of these patients.

Another approach to pitch elevation involves shortening of the vocal folds. Initially, Donald proposed performing such surgery through an external approach.[15] The anterior commissure was divided, the anterior portion of the vocal folds was de-epithelialized, and the vocal folds were sutured together. This procedure was modified by Wendler[16] and Gross[17,18] and more recently by the author (RTS, unpublished data). The procedure described by Wendler and by Gross essentially creates a web, as did Donald; but it is created endoscopically. The anterior portion of the vocal fold is de-epithelialized, and the vocal fold are sutured together firmly through the laryngoscope, creating a V-shaped anterior commissure but a shorter vibrating vocal fold. As in patients who have vocal fold webs for other reasons, this usually results a clear voice of higher pitch; because the remaining vibrating segment is short, but the vibratory margin has not been disturbed. This author (RTS) has modified the procedure slightly, preserving approximately 2 mm of mucosa adjacent to the anterior commissure. This small area does not interfere with the result. However, although it is unlikely that anyone would elect to have this procedure reversed, should it ever be necessary to try to correct the surgically created web, retaining the anterior commissure will probably prove helpful. To elevate pitch substantially, it has been necessary to de-epithelialize at least one-third to one-half of the musculomembranous vocal fold. This author prefers to accomplish this procedure by marking the anterior and posterior limits of the intended resection with a CO_2 laser. Submucosal infusion is then performed. Flaps of mucosa can be elevated bilaterally using cold instruments or the CO_2 laser. However, because the intention is to scar the vocal fold together, there is no disadvantage to using the laser during this procedure. The vocal folds are approximated using one or two Vicryl sutures. The procedure can be performed under local or general anesthesia. This operation has proven useful as a primary procedure and as a secondary procedure when cricothyroid approximation has proven insufficient for the patient's needs. Following successful pitch modification surgery, it is reasonable to expect an increase in pitch of about 5 to 9 semitones (about one-fourth to one-sixth of an octave). Pitch elevations as low as 3 or 4 semitones and as high as about 12 semitones occur occasionally. With the increase in pitch, there usually is some decrease in pitch range, particularly loss of a one-fourth or one-fifth of an octave on the lower end of the pitch range. The highest notes that can be produced do not tend to change much as a result of the surgery.

Therapy for Other Aspects of Voice Gender Identification
Speech fundamental frequency is not the sole answer to a more feminine voice, even following surgical modification. As noted above, Oates and Dacakis[4] reported the gender ambiguous frequency range as quite large. Probably of more importance to gender identification is the inclusion of

increased melody within the spoken syllable. This voice attribute appears to be learned and is an aspect of the masculine/feminine continuum not the male/female continuum. The more feminine individual tends to utilize increased intrasyllabic melody on vowels within the syllable. The more masculine individual tends to utilize a flatter, less melodic pattern. Listen to the way masculine individuals say "Hello" or "Good morning," and this difference is obvious immediately. Pitch modification does not change this voicing attribute and may only create the impression of a masculine individual with a high-pitched voice.

Practice in melodic intonation should include visual feedback using a device such as the Kay Visi-Pitch overwrite feature for short phrases and sentences. Initially, vowels may need to be elongated, and consonants may have to be shortened and made more precise to allow time to shift pitch on each vowel. Extensive drill is necessary. Practice on varying intonation patterns (particularly upglides) within phrases is also helpful. Over time, visual feedback should be faded, speaking rate increased, and carryover procedures should be initiated. Matching melody to emotional content should be encouraged once the patient is able to free herself from the more monotone masculine pattern. Phrases and sentences taken from the patient's own corpus of frequently-said sentences should be used for practice purposes. Melanie Phillips[7] suggests pharyngeal constrictions similar to that obtained when mimicking "the wicked witch of the west" voice and then relaxing the throat to the point of resonance desired. Moya Andrews[19] discusses elevation of the larynx and pharyngeal constriction as another possibility. Currently, there is no evidence of safety from vocal discomfort or disorders in developing these vocal misuse patterns.

Using a relaxed jaw and gentle smile is very effective in reducing the strength of the lower partials in the voice. More feminine individuals are found to smile more frequently during speech in any case. Better oral resonance and a relaxed open jaw can be facilitated by an exercise that involves clenching the jaw while monitoring the masseter muscles with the fingertips and then relaxing the jaw until the muscle bulk has diminished but the muscle is not stretched. Mirrors and videotapes are helpful feedback devices for practicing smiling speech. Over-rounding of the lips or a chimneylike anterior resonance chamber should be avoided.

The female oral cavity is somewhat smaller in most cases than the male oral cavity. Tongue bulk is also less. More feminine articulation is characterized by lighter contacts and shorter articulatory gesture distances that result in less impact on contact. The patient should practice reducing the vowel triangle both posteriorly/anteriorly and inferiorly/superiorly; moving the posteriorly articulated consonants /k/ and /g/ and /ŋ/ forward may create a more feminine articulatory production. Utilizing a modified paired-stimuli approach is helpful. The target consonant-vowel (cv) syllable /ki/ can be contrasted with /ku/ and other back vowels, striving to keep the place of articulation of /k/ and the vowel in the forward position. These modifications in articulation tend to change the positioning of formant II, which is correlated with more feminine speech. Extensive practice at home is necessary to modify these basic speech patterns. Drilling on words from the Thorndike/Lorge Lists of the 1000 Most Frequently Used Words[20] may be helpful.

In addition to working on anteriorizing vowels and consonants, narrowing the productions of sibilants may also improve femininity of speech. More masculine sibilants tend to be more dull and strong. All of these aspects of voicing, resonance, and articulation benefit from singing as well as speech practice.

Carol Gilligan, in her book *In a Different Voice* discusses the differences in developmental patterns of boys and girls and how these affect a person's worldview, what he or she talks about, and how he or she phrases speech.[21] Women develop other-orientation, oligarchical superiority, and relationship maintenance preferences. Apparently differences between boys' and girls' attitudes begin very early in life and are probably related, at least in part, to differential parental patterns. Gilligan demonstrates these differences even in the play patterns of young children. More feminine individuals tend to soften the harshness of their speaking patterns by including more tag question sentences such as, "It's time to go, isn't it?" They tend to use more psychological verbs, such as "I feel, I think," and so on. These kinds of changes are difficult to train later in life when we work with gender dysphoria, because they are related directly to the person's mindset. However, the patient should be aware of these kinds of differences, as well.

Gesture and body language also may need to be modified. More masculine individuals tend to take up all the available space with their bodies; whereas more feminine individuals tend to compact themselves with more upright posture, crossed legs or ankles, and arms held close to the body. More masculine individuals tend to walk with a broad-based gait and the palms of the hands facing backwards; more feminine individuals walk with the feet placed in front of each other and the palms of the hands facing toward the thighs. Feminine arm gestures tend to be more lateral and less often

Ethics, Standards and Practices

Management of Gender Reassignment (Sex Change) Patients
by Reinhardt J. Heuer, Margaret Baroody & Robert Thayer Sataloff (continued)

in front of the gesturer. Arm gestures focus on the wrists and fingers of more feminine gesturers.

The major goal in behavioral therapy with male-to-female transsexuals is the development of comfort and a feeling of confidence in the patient's femininity. If a true relationship exists between communicating partners, after about five minutes of conversation, the voice and speech patterns of the individual become irrelevant and/or are simply part of that person's persona. A conundrum always exists within the male-to-female transsexual because of the feeling of being "female" trapped in a "male" body. "If I already feel as though I am a woman, why do I have to change my behavior?" Yet, there is an anxiety about "passing" and "being ready" as the opposite sex. The development of confidence and the ability to recognize what constitutes more feminine behavior assist patients in developing comfort and ease with whatever level of feminine voice and speech they are capable of reaching.

References

1. Brown GR. "A review of clinical approaches to gender dysphoria." *J Clin Psychiatry* 51, no. 2 (1990): 57-69.
2. Landen M, Walinder J, Lundstrom B. "Prevalence, incidence and sex ratio of transsexualism." *Acta Psychiatr Scand* 93 (1996): 221-223.
3. Gelfer MP, Schofield KJ. "Comparison of acoustic and perceptual measures of voice in male-to-female transsexuals perceived as female versus those perceived as male." *J Voice* 14, no. 1 (2000): 22-33.
4. Oates JM, Dacakis G. "Speech pathology considerations in the management of transsexualism-a review." Br J of Disord Commun 18, no. 3 (1983): 139-151.
5. Heuer RJ, Rulnick RK, Horman M, et al. "Voice Therapy." In: Sataloff RT. *Professional Voice: The Science and Art of Clinical Care, 3rd Edition.* San Diego, CA: Plural Publishing, Inc., 2005: 961-987.
6. Raphael BN, Sataloff RT. "Increasing Vocal Effectiveness." In: Sataloff RT. *Professional Voice: The Science and Art of Clinical Care, 3rd Edition.* San Diego, CA: Plural Publishing, Inc., 2005: 993-1005.
7. Phillips M. "Melanie Speaks!" Burbank, CA: Heart Corp (P.O. Box 295, Burbank, CA 91503). [Video]
8. von Leden H. "The Evolution of Phonosurgery." In: Sataloff RT. *Professional Voice: The Science and Art of Clinical Care, 3rd Edition.* San Diego, CA: Plural Publishing, Inc., 2005: 1095-1115.
9. Sataloff RT. "Voice Surgery." In: Sataloff RT. *Professional Voice: The Science and Art of Clinical Care, 3rd Edition.* San Diego, CA: Plural Publishing, Inc., 2005: 1137-1215.
10. Lee SY, Liao TT, Hsieh T. "Extralaryngeal approach in functional phonosurgery." In: *Proceedings of the 20th Congress of the IALP.* Tokyo, Japan: The Organizing Committee of the XXth Congress of the International Association of Logopedics and Phoniatrics (1986): 482 483.
11. LeJeune FE, Guice CE, Samuels PM. "Early experiences with vocal ligament tightening." *Ann Otol Rhinol Laryngol* 92 (1983): 475-477.
12. Tucker HM. "Anterior laryngoplasty for adjustment of vocal fold tension." *Ann Otol Rhinol Laryngol* 94 (1985): 547-549.
13. Tanabe M, Haji T, Isshiki N. "Surgical treatment for androphonia. An experimental study." *Folia Phoniatr (Basel)* 37(1985): 15-21.
14. Hirano M, Ohala J, Vennard W. "The function of laryngeal muscles in regulating fundamental frequency and intensity of phonation." *J Speech Hear Res* 12 (1969): 616-628.
15. Donald PJ. "Voice change in the transsexual." *Head Neck Surg* 4 (1982): 433-437.
16. Wendler J. "Pitch elevation after transsexualism male to female." Presented at the XVI UEP Congress in Salsomaggiore, Italy (October 10-14, 1990).
17. Gross M, Fehland P. "Ergebnisse nach operativer Anhebung der mittleren Sprechstimmlage bie Transsexuellen durch Verkurzung des schwingenden Stimmkippenanteils." In: Gross M (ed). *Aktuelle phoniatrisch-padaudiologische Aspekte 1995.* Berlin, Germany: RGV, 1996: 88-89.
18. Gross M. "Pitch-raising surgery in male-to-female transsexuals." *J Voice* 13, no. 2 (1999): 246-250.
19. Andrews, ML. *Manual of Voice Treatment: Pediatrics through Geriatrics.* San Diego, CA: Singular Publishing Group, Inc., 1995: 391-404.
20. Thorndike EL, Lorge I. *The Teacher's Wordbook of 30,000 Words.* New York, NY: Teacher's College, Columbia University; 1944.
21. Gilligan C. *In A Different Voice: Psychological Theory and Women's Development.* Cambridge, MA: Harvard University Press, 1982.

Heightened Text, Verse and Scansion *David Carey and Rena Cook, Associate Editors*

Heightened Text, Verse and Scansion *David Carey and Rena Cook*
Associate Editors

The issues surrounding voice and gender are not new to the area of Heightened Speech, Verse and Scansion. Shakespeare laid a firm foundation for the joy and pathos that can arise from gender confusion when he wrote roles for male actors who play women who then pretend to be men in such plays as *Twelfth Night* and *As You Like It*.

In this issue of *The Voice and Speech Review* three authors have addressed the challenges of achieving believable and healthy vocal cross-gender transformations. "Sonic Trans-Dressing: Somewhere in Between," a peer-reviewed article by Terri Powers, examines a psycho-physical approach to aid women playing men's roles in performance, using Native American Vocables as a component. Author Jane Vicary, in her peer-reviewed article "Cross-Gender Vocal Transformation," outlines the practical research she undertook to isolate vocal variables—pitch, resonance, physicality, and volume—that performers can safely adjust to affect the audience's perception of gender. Mel Churcher also explores voice and gender in the article "What is a Sexy Voice?" in which she examines what western culture considers the "sexy" vocal attributes of men and women.

In this issue we are fortunate to have the fourth in a series of columns by Jacqueline Martin called "Rhetoric Revisited." In this installment, entitled "Stanislavki's Rehearsal Process Re-Visited," Ms. Martin reviews several of the major tenets of the Stanislavki system as seen through the eyes of a group of international theatre artists who, in 1986, assembled in Sweden to discuss how The Master's work translates into a modern theatre, how strictly his principles are adhered to, and where misinterpretations and incorrect use of terminology may have taken place.

A frequent contributor to *VSR*, Ros Steen provides an inspiring overview of the pedagogical underpinnings of voice training and its role in actor training in Scotland, specifically at the Royal Scottish Academy of Music and Drama and in the formation of the National Theatre of Scotland in "Seein Oursels As Ithers See Us."

Charmian Hoare chronicles her journey as dialect coach for a landmark production at Shakespeare's Globe Theatre in London. In "Pronouncing Shakespeare: The Globe's Production of *Romeo & Juliet*" she paints a challenging and exciting picture of using Original Pronunciation, working with director Tim Carroll and renowned linguist David Crystal.

A third peer-reviewed article, "Examining the Use of Lessac in Shakespearean Text" by Lessac Master teacher Kathryn Maes, explores Shakespearean text using Lessac's three Derived Energy States.

Finally, Scott Kaiser leaves us with a chuckle and a shudder as he explores the distinction between "Malaforms and Malaprops in Shakespeare," quoting not only The Bard but a contemporary political figure as well.

Finally, I want to say a heart felt thank you to my Co-Associate Editor David Carey whose prompt and thoughtful response to our authors for the last five years has been an inspiration to me. I am thrilled that, as I move into my new position as Editor of *VSR*, he has agreed to do one more issue as Associate Editor in the area of Heightened Speech, Verse and Scansion.

David Carey is Voice Tutor at the Royal Academy of Dramatic Art, London. He trained at the Royal Scottish Academy of Music and Drama, and has degrees from both Edinburgh and Reading Universities. David has worked nationally and internationally within higher education and the professional theatre, including 4 years as assistant to Cicely Berry at the Royal Shakespeare Company. As Course Leader of the Voice Studies course at the Central School of Speech and Drama he trained over 200 voice teachers from around the world. He recently coached at the RSC, the Oregon Shakespeare, and summer 2007 at the Stratford Ontario Festival.

Rena Cook is an Associate Professor of Theatre at University of Oklahoma where she teaches Voice, Speech and Dialects. She has served as vocal coach for the Illinois Shakespeare Festival on *The Merry Wives of Windsor*, *Richard III*, and *Wild Oats*. She has directed *Dancing at Lughnasa*, *The Prime of Miss Jean Brodie* and *Medea*. Rena holds an MA in Voice Studies from the Central School of Speech and Drama. Her theatrical reviews have appeared in *The Journal of Dramatic Theory and Criticism* and *Theatre Journal*. She is on the Board of Directors for VASTA and assumes the role of Editor-in-Chief for the next issue of *VSR*.

Column *by Jacqueline Martin*

Rhetoric Revisited:
Stanislavski's Rehearsal Processes Re-Viewed

Dr. Jacqueline Martin is currently a Senior Research Fellow in the Creative Industries Faculty at the Queensland University of Technology, Australia, and former Head of Theatre Studies. She has been an Associate Professor of Theatre Studies at the University of Stockholm since 1991. She has conducted master classes for the European League of Institutes of the Arts, Amsterdam, and for the Centre for Performance Research, Cardiff. Monographs include *Voice in Modern Theatre* (1991) and *Understanding Theatre: Performance Analysis in Theory and Practice* (1995). She is a member of the Executive Committee of the Federation for International Theatre Research where she co-convenes a working group on Performance as Research.

1. The Audience Development Project is an Australian Research Council funded project for which I am the Chief Investigator. It is nearing conclusion after 3 years looking into audiences in outback Queensland and the Northern Territory.

Background

One of the cornerstones of good acting, and one of the most difficult, is that of mastering a text-based approach to acting. It is not new; the rules for *actio*—or "speaking to the ear" and "speaking to the eye"—had been established by the rhetoricians during the Greek and Roman periods of antiquity and reached their peak in the Shakespearean era, laying down some rules for vocal delivery, which this column has reported on in previous editions, and which I have written on widely in *Voice in Modern Theatre* (Routledge, London and New York, 1991). Nowadays, as rhetoric has fallen from favor and visual and physical performances have assumed prominence in theatrical style, a text-based approach to acting has been called into question. Nevertheless, audiences consistently report that they cannot hear nor understand what actors are saying on stage (Report on Audience Development project—Talking Theatre[1]). This has instigated a research project into investigating rehearsal processes. Seeing as Stanislavski's System has been such a dominating force and formed the basis for actor training in many drama academies in the world, an international group of respected directors, all schooled in the Stanislavski approach, agreed to participate in a symposium in Stockholm in 1986 in order to investigate Stanislavski's legacy. This essay is a report on that symposium.

The Rise of the Stanislavski System

It took many years for Stanislavski to develop workable rehearsal processes. The main reasons for this were that Russian theatre of the 19th century was actor-driven; the idea of a director shaping a production was unheard of. In a repertoire where actors were cast to type and a "star system" flourished, quantity ruled over quality; sets were used over and over again, there being no attempt at historical accuracy, and costumes depended on the actor's purse. Worst of all acting was reduced to imitation, with the actors having to follow the prompt—situated down stage centre—as rehearsal time was practically non-existent.

By 1899 when the infant Moscow Art Theatre staged *The Seagull* Stanislavski had had seven years to establish his particular directing style, which toppled dangerously towards dictatorship. Although he did not understand Chekhov's play well he created an unforgettable nuance-filled mise-en-scene, replete with the barking of dogs and croaking of frogs, the likes of which had never been seen on the Russian stage before. Unfortunately the many details he had worked out on paper for his actors did not translate to the rehearsal room—so he was left with a revolutionized outer form for staging without any truthful portrayal of life on stage by the actors.

The Drama of Life (1907) was the first production in which Stanislavski consciously examined "the inner character" of the play and its roles. However he was still at the "demon director" stage of development—forcing a blend of analysis and spirituality on his actors—asking them to follow hieroglyphics denoting their various emotions and inner states! He maintained that these littered the text to signpost the character's emotional journeys, which the actors were then expected to experience.

By 1910 Stanislavski's rehearsal methods had been simplified: the actors were now asked to identify the rather more attainable "bits" of a text (often translated as "units") and "tasks" of a character (often translated as "objectives"). This combined what Stanislavski called the three **inner motive forces** of thought, will and action. This meant that through intellectual analyses (via the thought centre) the actors determined what they were doing (in the action—or will centre) and why they wanted to do it (through the emotion—or feeling centre). At this time the major components of **bits, tasks, affective memory, inner motive forces and communion** had been identified—in other words **Stanislavski's System** was in place. He never stopped searching and towards the end of his life when he discovered how important the **Method of Physical Actions** was, he insisted on **Active Analysis** as the only way to rehearse.

From being one of the most feared directors at the MAT Stanislavski became an inspirational director, whose processes became *de rigeur* and were slavishly followed, even though Stanislavski himself was always looking for improvements and change. As Soviet Realism under Stalin became the favourite genre, Stanislavski's methodology and approach was upheld as supporting Revolutionary ideology. Perhaps it is for this reason that the Stanislavski System rather than Meyerhold's Biomechanics came to be regarded as the cornerstone of Russian Theatrical excellence.

The Stockholm Stanislavski Symposium

Half a century later the Swedish National Touring Theatre Company, together with Teater Scharazad, Stockholm City Theatre, the Theatre High School in Stockholm, the Dramatic Institute and the Institute for Theatre and Film from Stockholm University decided to hold a symposium in Stockholm in 1986, whose theme was Stanislavski's view of theatre. Teater Scharazad had earlier arranged a similar symposium around Meyerhold and were now keen to learn what they could from the opposite court—the Stanislavskian tradition—to see how it could offer a methodical way of working for Swedish theatre practitioners and even to see what it could offer contemporary theatre.

The symposium was divided into two sections—a section which was open to the general public, containing lectures, demonstrations of Russian training films with Tovstonogov and Moniukov as well as guided tours from the Stanislavski Museum in Moscow; the other was a closed section, where invited lecturers, or master directors, worked with groups of actors on the floor. Lectures were given by Stanislavski experts—including the actress Angelina Stepanova, who had performed under Stanislavski's supervision for a long time, the theorists Jean Benedetti from the UK, Freddy Rokem from Israel, Martin Kurten from Finland, as a translator and author of *Att Vara Akta pa Scen* (Being Truthful on the Stage)—which addressed many misconceptions and incorrect uses of

terminology for the first time in the Swedish language—and Robert Cohen, from the USA, a self-confessed post-Stanislavski theorist and author of *Acting Power: An Introduction to Acting* (1978). As a doctoral candidate at the Institute for Theatre and Film Science in Stockholm I had the privilege of being asked to co-edit a report on this Stanislavski Symposium.

Mindful of the fact that since 1986 further re-evaluations of Stanislavski's teaching and rehearsal processes have appeared (Benedetti, 1990,91,94,99; Gorkachov, 1994 and Merlin 2003) and inconsistencies in translation been addressed (Carnicke, 1998)—the questions I am seeking to answer with my current research are:

- What can be learned from this 1986 symposium about the working methods for rehearsing as demonstrated by directors trained at the MAT in the Stanislavski tradition?
- How were these methods received by contemporary Swedish actors not trained in the System?
- How strictly did their approaches follow Stanislavski's model and where did the differences lie?

The four master pedagogues who worked with a group of actors and directors in the closed rehearsals on the floor for five days working on special scenes from different texts were Oleg Efremov and Anatolij Efros both from Russia; Alexander Bardini from Poland and Robert Cohen from the US. The observers in each group consisted of actors, directors, drama pedagogues, acting students and University students of Theatre. I was assigned to Cohen's group, where I worked as translator between Cohen and the acting cohort. I have direct observations from these days, whilst the other groups reported back to a group leader. These rehearsals have been video recorded. Access to these video recordings will be made available to me from the Archive for Sound and Moving Images and the Dramatic Institute in Stockholm pending funding support from an Australian Research Council grant application to further this research. What follows is a summary of the main points from the Symposium report where the groups are presented one at a time:

Oleg Efremov

Efremov received his actor training at the Moscow Arts Theatre School, where he also taught from 1949. He became artistic director of the MAT, where today he is still engaged as director and actor. He has also made a number of films. The chosen text used was Chekhov's *Ivanov*—Scene One.

As a practical theatre person Efremov had a vast experience about how to apply Stanislavski's theories. Even though he spoke directly to the group through a translator, he had such intensive and living body language—speaking only one sentence at a time, he was able to keep close contact with his group.

Efremov's working process was just like a rehearsal. He began by giving the actors very simple circumstances, e.g. Ivanov is sitting out in the garden reading. He wants to leave; Borkin comes and tries to attract his attention. By defining their objectives and lines of action, Efremov built up their mutual relationship, emphasizing that when conflicts occur something happens.

Efremov constantly asked questions of the actors—e.g. "What is Ivanov thinking about this evening? Sunset—what does that mean?" He asked for volunteers to come out on the floor and try things out. Efremov broke the act up into a number of "bits" sometimes very small ones and encouraged etyds (or improvisation) as a working method. (In Stanislavski's terminology this is **Active Analysis**—through the simple sequence of reading the text, discussing and improvising, the actors find that their words and actions move closer to the playwright's script, with the formal reading of the text reduced to a minimum).

Efremov held Stanislavski in great respect but indicated that some of his principles were today rather outmoded—like relaxation exercises, because today's actors are too relaxed; they need to gather themselves more. He never dictated what the playwright meant, but during these days laid the ground for a methodical way of working by constantly posing questions which stimulated the actors' creativity. In this way he was successful in arriving at truthful and logical action as well as believable characterizations, even in such a short time. It was also most obvious that this way of working for the Swedish actors was entirely new. Efremov demanded more of them than the external cliché-ridden first attempt at rehearsing a scene which they had obviously been used to. His methodology followed Stanislavski's recommendations closely—where the director was to be regarded as being able to help actors if they did not understand the super-objectives of their roles. It was clear that this master teacher had a deep understanding of human behavior and used psychology freely.

Anatolij Efros

The text chosen for this practical work was Moliere's *Don Juan.*

On the floor were just a table and two chairs for Efros and the translator. Those actors who participated were those who answered Efros' leading questions and whose answers he

considered worth taking up and performing. Efros decided to run the workshop in "slow motion" so that the different steps in the analysis process would be clearly understood by the participants.

Analysis of the text through "action" was the process by which Efros rehearsed with the actors, as he believed that this increases the actors' understanding of the play. During the analysis process the actors should open themselves intellectually and emotionally. Thought and action are the two sides of the same coin for Efros. The analysis is carried out in small steps; the elementary actions are placed beside each other—like pearls on a string. Efros believes the director should be very careful about when he reveals his interpretation of the text and the characters for the actors, comparing it to opening a parachute—"if you do it too early then everyone gets stuck in the wings; if you do it too late everyone is likely to crash. The director must know the overall objectives—the actors do the rest!"

His way of working is the way he rehearses a play for production: he begins with the text—goes quickly over to action—works through each scene—only to come back to the text at the end of one month, when the **line-of-action** is clear. Then he has, what he calls a **partitur**. The next month is spent rehearsing this partitur. He does not like the actors to use the words of the text in the early stages of rehearsal believing that when theatre is good the audience should be able to follow the action with their eyes—even if they don't understand the text.

Efros' way of working created enormous uncertainty among the actors. Some of them were surprised at the freedom they had during the analysis process: they would rather have analysed each scene and immediately performed the results of their analysis. The fact that he demanded artistic discipline was also unpopular.

Aleksander Bardini

During his long artistic career he has worked as theatre and opera director, actor, musician, theatre director and theatre pedagogue as well as film director in particular (*White, Blue and Red*). Since 1950 he has been a professor at the State Theatre High School in Warsaw.

The chosen texts were from Chekhov's *Uncle Vanja* and *Three Sisters.* Surprisingly he began the first session with an explanation about the hidden side of Chekhov—sexuality. Bardini explained that in Chekhov's plays one constantly meets people unhappy in love, but no one ever speaks about sex.

Bardini begins his analysis with a short general description of the circumstances and the characters. It can often be a short psychological sketch of the performers, a description of their situation and a hint about the special conflict situation in which they will be acting.

The actor is placed in a definite situation (in Bardini's case this is directed as a mise-en-scene). He gives suggestions for the action; then as the actors play the scene he stops the action often to ask them for explanations for their actions. Bardini explains that exactly as with Stanislavski the actor is expected to have a logical, controlled and proper action.

During his rehearsals Bardini tried to explain his way of working. He spoke about "an analysis through action" which was to be done on the floor as opposed to "around the table." He spoke about thematic exercises, which would develop the through line of action. For Bardini **tempo-rhythm** was a very important aspect of the play, the different characters and their interaction. This relates to Stanislavski's **Method of Physical Actions**. As with Stanislavski he too "coached" while the actors performed.

Bardini maintained that the actor should first act in his own name in order to then go over to the character's way of thinking—the **magic if**. Impulses to the actions are focused on at this stage of the analysis. The work on the role becomes a sort of seeking after motivation.

Bardini follows Stanislavski in the main, particularly in his deep psychological investigations, but he differs from Stanislavski in the following ways:
  • He leads the analysis work
  • He gives the stage directions

Robert Cohen
Robert Cohen is Professor and Head of the Drama Department at University of California, Irvine. He has written a number of books on acting and translated a number of plays. He refers to himself as a post-Stanislavskian theorist, because he believes that the driving force for an actor in a situation is not what "caused" the situation to exist, but what the "purpose" is for the character's actions: ask "what for"—not "why"; the character is "pulled by the future," not "pushed by the past." In other words, in all action on stage Cohen believes one should progress from the deterministic to the cybernetic way of thinking. The actor should look forward—rather than backward.

The texts chosen were some scenes from Shakespeare's *Hamlet* and *King Lear* as well as a scene from Sam Shepherd's *Fool for Love*.

Four terms form the basis for his working method. *Victory*—what the actor is striving to attain, which will determine his actions and his characterization. He explained this was what Stanislavski referred to as "tasks." *Realcom*—a portmanteau word meaning "a relation" and "a communication"—where the actor and his fellow actors stand in a constant "sender" "receiver" situation. The flood of information created is transformed into a "feedback-loop." (Cohen maintains this is what for Stanislavski was "the undertext.") Realcom victories are those victories we consciously or subconsciously strive for in our relationships with other people. *Obstacles* are things that stand in the way of the actor attaining his goal—these can come from the text, other actors or the director. For Cohen this is the director's main task—to establish where these are. *Tactics*—are what each actor chooses in order to attain his goal. He must also work with effort and have expectations.

Robert Cohen uses three levels in his rehearsal process, the situation, the style and the performance. I will develop these briefly as follows:
  • The **situation**: (here Cohen uses a downhill skier as a metaphor) who must reach his goal and win. There are obstacles in his path, but the actor must ask himself what he can do in order to overcome these and win.
  • The second level in the process is **style**: the dramatic level (here he likens these to the flags on the ski-run, within which the actor must work). Also in this aspect belong the literary, social and political aspects of the role.
  • The third level the actor must pass through is the **performance**: theatrical level (here he refers to the importance of developing a relationship with an audience).

Perhaps the most outstanding aspect of Cohen's working process was his constant "coaching" of the actor whilst he was working on the floor (as with Bardini). This was a great irritation to some of the actors, but Cohen explained that eventually they were all working to become their own coaches.

Conclusion
The Stockholm Stanislavski Symposium certainly introduced this way of working to the Swedish Theatre community—most of who had been trained according to the Brechtian aesthetic. As the political climate changed, artists realized that there was a lack of real emotional and truthful acting on the Swedish stage, which prompted this Symposium, where through the master classes Swedish actors and directors were introduced to the fruits of Stanislavski's life-long labours to promote truthful acting and the "spirit of humanity" in all productions. More details about the reception of this praxis will be possible with a closer interrogation of the rehearsal tapes housed in Stockholm.

What this research has revealed to date is the delayed
approach to using the text in rehearsals. Earlier interpretations
of Stanislavski's System demanded of the actors that they try
to do everything at once in rehearsal—work on the action,
work on the subtext and work on the text and this was in a
very long rehearsal period, compared with today's short ones.
Later interpretations, and those workshops witnessed in this
Stockholm Symposium advocated delaying the work on the
text and concentrating on getting the action of the scene
secure first—often by improvisation—then when the whole
play was built up "like pearls on a necklace" the actor would
be invited to use the playwright's words from the text. In this
way the text is based on something very secure and is not
"empty" or lacking action. I would recommend this practice
for contemporary actors who seem to be grabbing at one acting method after the other, seeking instant results in ridiculously short rehearsal times, whilst the delivery of their spoken
texts remains limp and unconvincing.

Peer Reviewed Article *by Jane Vicary*

Cross-Gender Vocal Transformation

*"Girls will be boys and boys will be girls,
It's a mixed-up, muddled-up, shook-up world."*
Lola: The Kinks

In 2002 I sold a Ben Nicholson picture to fund my place on the MA Voice Studies (MAVS) course at Central School of Speech and Drama (CSSD). This was to be an eventful year of commuting between family in the English Lake District and the close-knit group of MAVS students, who were my weekday companions in London. I had been a drama teacher in Adult Education as well as a performer for over 20 years. A rediscovery of my singing voice had led to more professional work which increasingly seemed to focus on vocal technique. An awareness of my ignorance on matters vocal, combined with a desire to know more, led to the sale of the Ben Nicholson and my big voice adventure in London.

Unlike most of my fellow MAVS students, who seemed to know exactly which area of voice they intended to research for their dissertation, I had no such area of inquiry planned. My exploration into the cross-gendered voice was as much by chance as design.

My journey began with a gossipy chat with an actress friend who had been less than overwhelmed by a performance of Viola in *Twelfth Night* that had received rave reviews and nominations. The production was magnificent, but my friend commented that Emily Watson's voice—for she was the actress—"had never changed, not even in 'characterful' slips where Viola forgot to maintain her male persona."

This started me thinking about voice and character in "trouser roles," but after wrestling with the permutations of boys playing women who then disguise themselves as young men who then reveal themselves as women (aaagh!), I found myself being drawn towards the "straight" gender swap—of men playing women and women playing men in single sex productions. Fortuitously for my research project, there seemed to be a positive rash of cross-gendered productions receiving high profile publicity in the UK during 2003.[1]

I began to wonder how the actor might approach such a role vocally and preliminary enquiries led me to unpublished material written by Edda Sharpe, an actress and dialect coach who was also a graduate of the CSSD Voice Studies course. She had played Macbeth in an all-female production of that play and wrote:

> …although I worked with some degree of success, achieving the production aim and not hurting my voice, I struggled with the balancing act of developing masculinity of voice while maintaining vocal freedom and sensitivity.[2]

Edda seemed to have identified a vocal issue that was not simply solved by the usual actor's work on characterization but which required some fundamental awareness of what it is to be male or female and how that is expressed vocally. I decided to build on her insight and explore how a vocal coach might assist in the process of cross-gender vocal performance.

Jane Vicary (MAVS) has a degree in Theatre Studies and English from Lancaster University and an MA in Voice Studies from the Central School of Speech and Drama. Based in the Lake District, Jane works as a freelance vocal coach and theatre director in the North West of England. She worked for many years as a drama tutor in adult education and on projects with special needs students. She is currently directing a graduate student production at Cumbria Institute of the Arts.

1. London Globe 2003 season; all-female *Richard III* and *Taming of the Shrew*, director Barry Kyle; all-male *Richard II* director Tim Carroll; Marlowe's *Edward II*, all-male production, director Timothy Walker; Propeller Theatre Company, all-male *Midsummer Night's Dream*, director Edward Hall. At Brighton and at the Edinburgh Festival 2003 *The Lady Boys of Bangkok*.

2. Sharpe, E. unpublished preliminary notes, date unknown, for putative dissertation at CSSD given by the author to me. Our dissertation subjects overlapped and Edda shared some of her research notes with me.

This article is a record of my journey of discovery and a distillation of the work that became my dissertation. I met some extraordinary and generous people whom I interviewed and made some fascinating discoveries in practical workshops; I hope this will add something to the body of knowledge on voice and gender.

As a first step on my journey I decided to narrow my exploration. I identified three types of cross-gender performance styles:

Base gender never forgotten and exploited usually for comedy, e.g. in traditional British pantomime or performers such as Edna Everage and Danny La Rue.

Deceptive—gender intended to deceive, e.g. in the film *The Year of Living Dangerously* where Linda Hunt played a man, Billy Kwan, and fooled the film industry, winning an Oscar for best supporting actress.

Suspended disbelief—the audience know the base gender but accept the theatrical "lie" or convention, e.g. all female or all male productions of Shakespeare and other classic plays.

It was this third and final theatrical convention that interested me most and made my enquiry more specific.

My aim was to explore the vocal issues involved in cross-gender performance and to try and answer the following questions:

- Could a vocal coach be useful on a cross-gendered production and if so in what way?
- Is it possible to access femininity or masculinity vocally?
- If it is, can one do it in a healthy way?
- Can one maintain truthfulness and avoid caricature or mimicry?
- Can the vocal coach work in harmony with an actor, respecting their process whilst offering vocal choices?
- Does playing cross-gender remove an actor one step further from the role and could the vocal coach help to close that gap?

With these questions in mind I set out to conduct a series of workshops that explored voice and gender. I anticipated and identified four possible vocal issues—or problems—that might be encountered in this work:

A. Constriction for higher pitches.
B. Pushing down for deeper sound.
C. Hitting the general; playing the caricature rather than the truthfulness or specificity.
D. Forcing for volume and authority.

And I realized these related to the four main vocal elements of difference between the sexes:

1. Pitch and range (including tune and inflection)
2. Resonance
3. Physicality and movement
4. Volume and directness/commitment

In the practical workshops, these four elements provided the structure for my exploration. I had chosen them because to me they covered the most obvious vocal differences between the sexes and seemed as good a place as any to begin.

I wanted to see if one could isolate and identify masculine and feminine voice qualities in order to ascertain whether they could be heightened, played down or transferred. I also felt it would be valuable to identify one's own habits as man or as woman, in order to avoid bringing them to one's character. Over the period of my research and reflection, these four elements were refined and their order of import (in my thinking) changed as well.

THE WORKSHOPS

The workshop participants were all acting students from either Central School of Speech and Drama (CSSD) or Manchester Metropolitan University's acting school (MMU):

Workshop 1: 3 hours, 2 men and 2 women (CSSD)
Workshop 2: 3 hours, 2 women (CSSD)
Workshop 3: 3 hours, 2 men (CSSD)
Workshop 4: 2 hours, 5 women and 7 men (MMU)

Every session began with a full physical and vocal warm-up and, after familiarization with the particular text I had chosen for them to work on, I asked the actors to perform a scene and I recorded the extract. This was to be the control version against which I compared a second version. This second version of the scene was carried out after a series of specific, "gender-bending" exercises that targeted the four areas I wished to investigate:

1. Pitch and range (including tune and inflection)
2. Resonance
3. Physicality and movement
4. Volume and directness/commitment[3]

WORKSHOP 1

(2 Men & 2 Women; Text: *Bouncers* and *Shakers* by John Godber)
After a general vocal warm-up to free the breath and to wake up abdominal support, resonance, range and articulation, we came to the text. The scripts were performed and recorded.

While they had a coffee break, I asked the actors to observe men and women in the café to find the "most masculine man" and the "most feminine woman" and to note gestures and body language. This was to address physicality and movement (element no. 3). After the coffee break, these observed gestures and movements were copied, played with, exaggerated and then refined. This work was incorporated in their characterization and performance of the extracts. I showed the group photographs of gangs of young people similar to the characters in the play, and the actors took elements of stance and physical expression into their characterization. From the images they chose a character, a gesture, decided where their character breathed from, voiced the sound of that breath, turned it into a laugh, then a word, then a line. On an impulse I asked the women to stuff socks down their trousers to give them a physical sense of their power and energy coming from the groin.

We explored five different ways of finding centre note or optimum pitch (element no. 1) so that the actors found a method which worked for them including: creak into voice, finding one's lowest singing note and going up

3. Perhaps I should clarify a little about what I mean by directness/commitment; I feel it is connected to a quality of being definite, of what one says being taken note of. In a patriarchal society, men have a natural authority, a tone that brooks no question, a tune that has no questioning or rising intonation. Women may have a softer, less definite or sure tonal quality. For further discussion see Deborah Tannen, *Talking From 9 to 5: Women and Men at Work: Language, Sex and Power.* (UK: Virago, 1996)

five notes, humming and finding the place of most vibrations, sirening (police car siren sound on a "ng") with fingers in ears and finding place of most volume. We worked on resonance (element no. 2) using exercises to open chest, oral, head and face resonance. We played with sounds and then lines of text, rolling and throwing them (metaphorically) across the space to a specific point (for female to male cross-gendering) then to a more general area (for male to female cross-gendering), to explore volume and directness (element no. 4). Finally we repeated the same extracts as before and recorded them again.

When observing the work, I felt that the physicality and movement exercises had been the most effective in effecting cross-gender changes (and the participants' responses confirmed this), but when I listened to the recording of the session I could detect no actual vocal changes. The acting had become clearer, the females became more masculine in presence and energy—likewise the men had become more feminine physically. A colleague of mine, a speech and language therapist, who listened to the recordings made both before and after targeted exercises, confirmed that overall, all four voices were freer and more released after the gender-specific exercises but that they still sounded like their own sex.

I felt the text was probably responsible for the success of the physicality and movement exercises. The plays (*Bouncers* and *Shakers*) do ask for a "broad brush-stroke" style of acting, where the actors quickly snap from one character to another, so it was hardly surprising that physical characterization was the most productive starting point.

Alarm bells rang for me when one of the men said that he felt more like a transvestite than a real woman. This made me feel that I was working at the level of superimposition; so, in order to plumb greater depths of characterization and gender, I decided to change the kind of text I was using in the second workshop as well as some of the exercises. I also felt it would be simpler to hear what was happening vocally if I used a monologue and a richer text. Dialogue is tricky, and vocal energy drops if cues are not picked up, which can affect overall vocal quality and connection to text.

I also wondered about the response of one of the females who said that after doing the gender-targeted exercises she felt that "when I came to speak it was a different voice which I almost couldn't identify as my own." My response to this was, "Where was this voice on my recording? Was it actually an inner perception of the voice sounding or feeling different from within? Or a bit of teacher pleasing?" Workshop 2 aimed to find this "different voice" or to at least see if we could access and record some vocal transformation.

WORKSHOP 2
(2 Women—Lottie and Clare; Female to male transformation; Text: *Henry V*)

I repeated the first workshop's format of a general warm-up, reading and becoming familiar with the text and then performing and recording it. Once more this was followed by gender-targeted exercises on pitch & centre note, resonance, physicality & movement and volume & directness/commitment.

In the physicality section we played with archetypes: king, hero, warrior. We improvised being men in the pub, at a football match and other "male" environments, finding a sound and a gesture, being aware of where the breath was as we improvised. We used props to act as swords, braced ourselves and became heroic statues which then came to life. Then we let the breath come on to sound—any sound—and allowed that sound to give an impulse for movement, letting the sound take us through the space. We spontaneously used words that for each individual felt connected with masculinity and allowed them to take us through the space. We read the speech "as if" the sword was speaking, "as if" we were a general speaking to an army in a contemporary conflict.

Again we found centre note/optimum pitch using the method that worked most easily for the individual and then worked on chest resonance, tapping the chest to release tension and encourage vibrations. I introduced an exercise using the sensation of a laugh to retract the false vocal folds to create more space in the pharynx and thereby enhance the lower harmonics. We used the yawn and a sigh of pleasure, again to release and open the vocal tract.

Working on volume and directness we played with sounds, making them ebb and flow like the sea, then like a radio with the signal fading and returning. We stretched out our hands and sent sounds, words and phrases to those points. The goal of the work was to try and remove focus from the larynx and to increase power and precision and a masculine, forward, thrusting energy. I also used some of Nadine George's[4] work using the "Deep male quality" for volume and directness. I had just participated in one of Nadine's workshops and had found the belly-connected, "deep male" vocal quality accessed a very different sound and sensation in my own voice. Nadine George is a direct link through Roy Hart to Alfred Wolfsohn who had done pioneering work on voice during the first half of the twentieth century. He believed both sexes were capable of accessing an eight octave voice—which would be seriously useful for cross-gender performance and an approach that I would certainly like to explore in future research.

Outcomes

This was a much more satisfactory workshop as I could concentrate on just the one gender transformation of female to male. I felt the actors also took more risks vocally in the all-female environment and were generally less inhibited. When I listened to the recordings, voice quality changes were apparent. This was a very exciting workshop with results that made me more confident in feeling that the specific exercises were transforming voices in the direction of the desired gender.

I asked my speech and language therapist colleague to listen to the recording of Lottie's voice before any exercises were done. She identified creak, occasional glottal onset and pharyngeal constriction. Work on pitch and centre note transformed her voice quality, reducing glottal attack and "headiness" (an over-reliance on head resonance), and her pitch also lowered. Her delivery became slower with more appropriate emphasis. She responded less well to the volume and directness exercises. She seemed to be trying too hard. She speeded up and returned to the heady, higher resonant sound, although the glottal attack remained reduced. The physicality & movement exercises

4. Nadine George workshop at CSSD 2003 in which the author participated. See also Nadine's article, "My Life with Voice" in the: *Shakespeare Around the Globe* presented by the *Voice and Speech Review*, Mandy Rees, ed. (Cincinnati, OH: VASTA), 2005.

5. Gillyanne Kayes, *Singing and the Actor* (London: A&C Black, 2000), 69.

6. In a worst-case scenario, pressed voice can lead to muscle tension dysphonia and/or contact ulcers. In addition, Lesley Mathieson in *The Voice and its Disorders* (London: Whurr, 2001) says, "In cases where the larynx is forcefully depressed in the vocal tract, speaking on residual air is also a common feature accompanying the 'pressed' voice production" (159).

seemed to make Lottie rather forced vocally. Again she seemed to be trying too hard, but gradually she began to take more space and breath, her pauses became more appropriate, articulation became more muscular and the lower resonances could be heard. Lottie found the physical exercises for characterization and the use of props very helpful saying that she "*made sense of the speech and kept a pulled up neck.*" (It was interesting that she was here describing "anchoring," a technique used by Jo Estill for the "belt" quality in singing.) I decided to incorporate that into the work on female to male transformation in future workshops as it is a technique that helps to access power and volume. Gillyanne Kayes[5] describes it as "postural anchoring" that involves grounding and rooting the body thereby making a "firm scaffold for the vibrating mechanism of the voice."

I felt that Lottie was helped most in her vocal characterization by the work on centre note/optimum pitch. She tends to press her larynx down, a not uncommon tendency for women who want to have more vocal gravitas and authority and who are sub-consciously mimicking deeper male voices.[6] Finding a neutral position for her larynx accessed a more easy vocal quality.

Clare's voice was very smooth and mellifluous. Her pitch sits naturally around her centre note and vocally she has an "easy on the ear quality," but her articulation is not sharp. The speech and language therapist described it as, "Plum-velvet, a cuddly voice with no sharp edges." Her articulation improved dramatically after work on centre note/optimum pitch, and had more "edge," although it became monotonous as she tried consciously to stay on centre note. She sounded a lot more open, and her articulation improved again after the volume and directness work.

Clare seemed to respond most positively to the physicality and movement work and to acting exercises that brought her on to the word. She accessed some "edge" in her tone that gave her delivery bite and attack. Her voice on the tape, and as heard in the workshop, became huge. In the questionnaire she described the change in her voice as, "Much bigger, lower (in pitch), dropped in support, louder." I would agree with her description but would say that the lower pitch was actually due to increased resonance because the lower tones were being enhanced in the vocal tract. More space, more vibrations. In fact, after the resonance work, both voices seemed to have more colour and expressivity, which would make sense as the exercises had opened the pharynx and made more resonant space.

From their feedback, the general feeling was that the physical exercises had helped with a sense of characterization. Both women said that the sense of being bigger and taking up more space had also helped characterization and playing male.

WORKSHOP 3
(2 Men—John and Ennio; Male to female transformation;
Text: *A Midsummer Night's Dream*—Titania's "These are the forgeries of jealousy" speech)

I kept very much to the format of the previous two workshops but I replaced the vocal section on volume and directness (which I associated with masculine voice quality) with exercises using different onsets to access different vocal qualities. In my research I had noticed that "breathy" voice quality has been identified as being used by more women than men.[7] Using an aspirate onset, i.e. allowing breath to precede the sound, was an effective way to access this soft, breathy voice quality. I also used the simultaneous onset[8] which results in thinner folds and therefore a higher pitch. It is accessed by using a silent laugh or "sob" to cause the false vocal folds to retract, making little crying, mewing or whimpering sounds and then holding that laryngeal posture to come on to the sound "eee" then on to word. I also used some pieces of costume to help with the physicality and movement and, during an early exercise, had them dress each other in a practice skirt and a bum roll to give a sense of having hips. These they wore for the duration of the session. I felt that wearing appropriate "practice" clothing would assist gender transformation.

I wanted the men to immediately begin work on waking up the imaginative, instinctive, "right brain" thinking that is traditionally associated with the female. I went straight into a general warm-up followed by an imaginative exercise, where each actor embodied the spirit of a tree using images from nature. From this we came to the text, reading it through together, sorting out any word or phrase that we didn't understand. Next the actors "walked" the text, changing direction on each punctuation mark. Then one of the actors became a "handmaiden" to the other actor playing Titania, and read all lines of the speech with the Titania-actor repeating any phrases or words that he felt were especially feminine. During this exercise, the handmaiden dressed Titania. The actors changed roles and repeated the exercise.

For the next part of the workshop we looked at the gender-specific exercises on voice qualities with exercises on vocal set-up and onset. I used Gillyanne Kayes' methods which are based on the techniques of Jo Estill.[9] I used the sob or cry onset (as described above). This tilts the larynx and has the effect of lengthening and thinning the folds thereby accessing a higher pitch. To access a breathy vocal quality I used the aspirate onset, accessed by first releasing a little breath on an "h" sound and then coming on to word. I recorded the speech after each exercise. The two men shared Titania's speech by speaking alternate lines. I did this so they had a chance to reconnect to the feeling of breathiness and recollect the onset device while the other was speaking a line. Perhaps it is worth pointing out that this technique might not be useful for performing in a large space, but as part of a workshop I felt it was useful for the men to play with this breathy, sexy voice quality.

For the next exercise I asked the men to use a rising inflection at the end of lines including those with full stops. I wanted to see if it could be used as the opposite of the "masculine" directness and although this is more to do with the tune of speech, I felt it was appropriate to try this alongside the work using the aspirate onset and the tilted vocal set-up. The rising intonation conferred a slight hesitancy to the delivery. One man found it useful, one did not.

For resonance I concentrated on exercises targeting head and face resonance, lots of humming and sounding into the mask of the face and imagining the sound pouring out of the top of the head and through the bridge of the

7. Monique Biemans, *Gender Variations in Voice Quality* (Netherlands: LOT, 2000), 25.

8. Kayes, *Singing and the Actor*, 17-19.

9. Jo Estill—Estill Voice Training Systems developed in the 1970s. www.evts.com

nose—all to try and move the men away from the more masculine chest resonance.

In the physicality and movement section I used Stanislavski's "Magic If" exercise to bring back a connection to text after all the technical work they had been doing. I also wanted to see if any of the vocal qualities they had accessed reappeared when they weren't thinking about it. The actors said the speech as if they were a wronged wife, as if a queen, and as if… their own choice. I also showed the actors still images of women and they experimented with copying a stance or a gesture, and then moving in the space in an indirect way as opposed to directly, which I had identified as the more masculine approach.

Outcomes

After the general physical and vocal warm-up (i.e. before the targeted exercises), my colleague, the speech and language therapist, identified John to be slightly pressing his larynx down and Ennio as using lots of head resonance with some pharyngeal constriction. There was a cumulative effect of the exercises on vocal quality in that both men became more adventurous vocally and entered more and more willingly into exploring notions of femininity.

The work on onset was very interesting in that it does transform voice quality so radically and so quickly. For John, the simultaneous onset (using the tilting of the thyroid and thereby thinner folds) didn't work for him at all; there was something false in his sound. On the other hand, using the aspirate onset really helped him to find a feminine quality that could be developed for performance. He retained some chest resonance but it was reduced, and he seemed to be on support whilst producing a softer, breathy sound. This may be a sound more appropriate for use with an intimate rather than large acting space. Breathy onset is simply allowing some breath to be released prior to onset of tone which alters the vocal quality or tone of the speaker. Breath is used less efficiently but it can still be managed (supported) muscularly at sub-glottic level. John found the sensation and the sound exciting. It was a new vocal quality he could use playing cross-gender, whilst staying connected to breath and support. Interestingly, he found the language-based exercise of a rising intonation most useful, but I had combined this exercise with the aspirate onset, and I felt it was this that had effected the change.

Ennio found most connection to femininity through the imaginative acting game "As If," particularly "The woman preparing the dinner and living the text as a woman." Vocally I heard a real connection to the word and a wide variety of tone and delivery. He identified it as the exercise that had helped him most in vocal characterization.

WORKSHOP 4
(5 men & 2 women; Text: *Henry V* & *A Midsummer Night's Dream*)

Using acting students from Manchester Metropolitan University, this was a concentrated class that covered a lot in the time available to me. I wanted to use the exercises which had seemed to effect most change in vocal quality in the previous workshops, that is, mainly the vocal set-up and onset work. I added in glottal onset for the women, in order to counteract the more feminine aspirate onset and access a more direct, masculine quality. Glottal onset sets up the folds in a thicker configuration, mimicking the naturally thicker folds of the male. With hindsight, I would also try the simultaneous or "glide" onset for the women as it counteracts a tendency for breathiness as the breath and the tone start together and it avoids slapping the folds together with a glottal attack—hence "simultaneous." I think the simultaneous onset is about finding a balance between a glottal and an aspirate onset.

I included physicality and movement exercises where the actors observed the walk and gestures of the opposite sex. Work on centre note helped each actor to find a neutral laryngeal position and place of optimum resonance and we also used exercises to access head resonance for the males and chest resonance for the females. But it was the work on onsets and laryngeal settings which created the most interesting vocal results.

The men found the aspirate and the simultaneous onsets useful in accessing different voice quality; two in particular seemed to find a comfortable new sound. Of the simultaneous onset, one commented: "It felt very good…didn't feel strained, but felt it was a different part of the voice." A female participant said she heard more desperation in the words and delivery of one of the men. The breathy quality seemed to open upper resonance. Some lost connection to the text, probably because they were concentrating on holding on to the sensation of the onset, and some found it easier than others. Comments included: "I can accommodate female pitches without sounding fake or put on. I can sustain this, which I haven't done before."

The women both felt they tended to sit on their voices and push down for a lower sound. When I used the glottal onset with centre note, they both sounded easier, less "shouty," as one had described her previous rendition of the speech.

Female 1, after the acting exercises, lost connection and sounded higher in pitch, due to change in resonances. It sounded as if she was trying too hard, and as if she was experiencing a little performance anxiety. After exercises on resonance, my fellow professional listener felt she sounded "a bit fake." With the glottal onset, we both remarked on a more relaxed and pleasant quality that was less pushed. Both women accessed a more masculine sound, with improved muscularity and improved speech rate that was more appropriate. Generally, the acting got better with a deeper connection to text and a more engaging and affecting delivery.

SUMMARY OF PRACTICAL WORKSHOPS
All the participants found the work on centre-note useful, in that each individual could both feel and hear the ease and freedom which that place gave them as a starting point.

In the two mixed-sex workshops, it was noticeable that each sex learnt from each other through observation, collaboration and encouragement. The voice work was also cumulative in its effect, as the channel (both vocal and emotional) was opened and released through all the practical work. In the later workshops I had introduced exercises for onsets and vocal fold set-up. This was revelatory, in that it gave quick results and a new voice quality which, although sometimes extreme and inappropriate for performance use, did open up vocal possibilities that continued to affect and influence the individual's sound afterwards. Different methods worked for different individuals. No one exercise accessed the masculine or the feminine, but different combinations of the physical, the imaginative, the vocal set-up and the language-based exercises, offered a choice for the individual to experiment with.

Furthermore, as a result of the practical work and my on-going reading and research, my focus on the original 4 Elements shifted:

	From...		To...
1	Pitch & Centre Note	1	Centre Note & Pitch
2	Resonance	2	Placement & Registration
3	Physicality & Movement	3	Physicality & Space
4	Volume & Directness	4	Acting & Truth to Characterisation

Centre note became more important in that it connected the actor to their optimum pitch. Consequently resonance became more about release and relaxation and I replaced vague terms of head and chest voice with placement or registration of the voice working at vocal fold level. This gave the performer vocal options with gender significance—e.g. breathy, glottal,

etc. Physicality and movement was still very much connected with how a character, whatever gender, moves but with greater awareness of the physical and verbal space the sexes claim. Volume became of very little import and directness became a clearer manifestation of focus on characterization and truthfulness and how that affected vocal production.

This refinement of the original four Elements was further supported by the discoveries I made interviewing practitioners with practical experience of cross-gender performance.

FINAL THOUGHTS
When I began my research to explore how a vocal coach might assist in the process of cross-gender vocal performance my main concern was that all that might be required was a free and open vocal technique. Throughout my study I became more and more aware of a double tension that constantly pulled at the work: a tension between the "hardware" (the physical—the blood, guts, muscles, larynx, lungs, the bones) and the "software" (the artistic, the aesthetic, consciousness, the unconscious, the processes of mind). In an ideal performance these two areas are integrated so that mind, body and spirit create a complete whole, a piece of art ("What a piece of art is a man!" says Hamlet.) And in writing that last sentence I am aware that I have mentioned a third element, "spirit." Where does that reside? In the mind or in the body? Philosophers and scientists have argued over soul or spirit since time began and I am certainly not going to resolve it here…but I would like to draw attention to the word "spirit" which comes from the Latin *spirare* meaning "to breathe." Therefore if "spirit" and "breath" become synonymous, breath becomes the element that links the mind and body.

Voice is a physical entity, as well as an external manifestation of how we feel and how we present ourselves to the world. With specific anatomical knowledge that is backed up by gender studies research and the work of practitioners with relevant experience, I believe the voice coach can offer an informed and detailed approach to playing cross-gender, which avoids the straitjacket of stereotypical acting.

So, if talking about yin and yang, the animus and the anima, the myth of Hermaphrodite, (and here, rather outrageously, I throw in a whole lot of new thoughts/names/concepts that I have not had time or space to discuss here but which do, annoyingly, keep bubbling up in my brain) or working on physicality or vocal quality through laryngeal onsets—whatever helps to release an actor's imagination to access masculinity or femininity, use it. The discussion of vocal cross-gender transformation is in its infancy and this enquiry has only just scratched the surface of what is a huge and complex subject.

I hope to offer some suggestions in reaching vocally across the gender divide and to this end offer a list of ingredients which you may fashion into a recipe of your own.

A RECIPE

Using my research outcome (the "refined" 4 Elements), what follows is a summary of what I found to be relevant and most useful to work on when trying to access masculinity and femininity. I do not advocate using all the methods at once, but rather suggest trying some of them, to see what helps the individual embody a more truthful characterization of a cross-gendered role. What may be interesting and effective in a workshop may not always translate to a stage performance but most journeys open up new vistas and possibilities.

RECIPE FOR CROSS-GENDER TRANSFORMATION
Pick and mix ingredients as required.

1. Centre Note & Pitch
- Find centre note, place of optimum pitch
- Be aware that pitch is determined by size of folds
- Work to increase range and vocal flexibility, as in singing
- Be aware that constriction and tension cut out lower harmonics, creating impression of higher pitch
- Using muscular effort to raise the larynx (for higher pitches), or depress the larynx (for lower pitch) is artistically limiting and potentially harmful

For female actresses playing male:
- Glottal onset—accesses thicker folds
- Creak, harshness, nasality, tense voice, loudness, less precise articulation

For male actors playing female:
- Aspirate onset—accesses breathy voice
- Simultaneous onset—accesses thinner folds & falsetto quality

2. Placement & Registration
- Connect with resonance
- Release & open primary resonators—oral, pharyngeal, and nasal
- False vocal fold retraction
- Locate sympathetic resonators for kinaesthetic feedback—head and chest vibration

For female actresses playing male:
- Create pharyngeal space, retract false vocal folds, release upper body tension, tongue, lips, face—freeing the channel
- Engage abdominal support muscles—sense of breath dropping lower—grounding work

- Work from centre note, place of ease, loose thicker folds, place and imagine resonance lower
- Exercises to increase chest resonance

For male actors playing female:
- Explore secondary resonators, developing strong sense of head resonance linked to onset work on thin folds
- Cry and aspirate onset, awareness of using tilt, exercising crico-thyroid mechanism

3. Physicality & Space
For female actresses playing male:
- Take up more space—forward energy—puff out chest
- Lower centre of energy—stuff pants!
- Observe masculine gesture and body use
- Speak without rushing—take verbal space without giving room for debate
- Get louder to hold attention
- Look without apology—assume power
- Disguise shape—bind breasts

For male actors playing female:
- Reduce space you take up—denial, reduction, giving way
- Observe female gesture & body use
- Speak co-operatively, giving room for debate
- Look, without assuming you have power
- Use costume early in rehearsal, if applicable

4. Acting & Truth to Characterization
- Use the word and the text to connect to characterization
- Be aware of socio-linguistic language features—useful for improvisation games
- Use imaginative acting games

For female actresses playing male:
- Interrupt interaction partner
- Use a falling intonation at end of phrases

For male actors playing female:
- Use tag questions at end of statements
- Use a rising intonation

Suggested further reading:
Drass, Kriss A. "The effect of gender identity on conversation." *Social Psychology Quarterly* Vol. 49, no. 4 (1986): 294-301.
Key, Mary Ritchie. *Male/Female Language.* Metuchen N.J.: Scarecrow Press Inc., 1975.
Laver, John. *The Phonetic Description of Voice Quality.* Cambridge: Cambridge University Press, 1980.
Mulac, Anthony. (1986) "Linguistic contributors to the gender-linked language effect." *Journal of Language and Social Psychology* Vol. 5, no. 2 (1986): 81-101.
Rodenburg, Patsy "Powerspeak," in Armstrong, Frankie and Pearson, Jenny (Eds.) *Well Tuned Women.* UK: Women's Press, 2000.
Tripp, Anna (Ed.) *Gender: Readers in Cultural Criticism.* New York: Palgrave, 2000.

Peer Reviewed Article *by Terri Power*

Sonic Trans-dressing: Somewhere in Between

Somewhere in between the waxing and the waning wave,
Somewhere in between what the song and the silence says,
Somewhere in between the ticking and tocking clock,
Somewhere in a dream between sleep and waking up,
Somewhere in between breathing out and breathing in.[1] -Kate Bush

Recently I participated in a butoh workshop in London with renowned practitioner Endo Tadashi.[2] The workshop took place in a Buddhist Art Centre which was significant because Endo practices his unique style of butoh dance, called butoh-MA. MA is a word derived from Japanese Zen Buddhist philosophy and means "emptiness" or "the space between." It describes a state of being that, as Endo explains in dance terms, is "…the moment just at the end of a movement and before the beginning of the next."[3] I was drawn to Endo's workshop because he is known as the master of being "in between" and his physical expressions of the tension between yin and yang, masculine and feminine, male and female held personal interest for me. Like Endo Tadashi, I too am exploring the in between space in performance. My interest and exploration of the intersection between gender categories is considered a *butohist*[4] quality as butoh dance "befuddles the rational mind…it survives on images that continually change, riding the moment of meaning in transition."[5] I believe that the future of gender performance, like butoh, will be the art of metamorphosis, of crossing back and forth, in and out, up and over, between and beyond the gender binary and its prescriptive categories. As we continue to explore gender in performance, interrogate its conventions, introduce new media, and participate in cross-cultural artistic exchanges that influence our cross-dressing future, a big question emerges. As our (trans)gendered performance future can clearly be viewed, we must now ask: how will it be voiced?[6]

It is the in between space of sonic gender performance (masculinity and femininity), of its physical production (breathing in and out), of its external and internal influences (personal and cultural) and of its experiential effect (psychological and physical) that this paper aims to address. Over the last four years I have been developing a psycho-physical vocal approach to aid women playing male roles in performance. The in between space, or what I refer to as *Sonic Trans-dressing*, is the emphasis of my work as I demonstrate and highlight *other* possibilities in our sonic gender production. This technique has developed as part of my research towards a PhD in Performance Practice at the University of Exeter and incorporates cross-cultural influences such as Japanese performance training methods, Asian Yoga technique, and Native American drumming and voice work.[7] In this paper I aim to set the backdrop to this growing performance trend, describe my personal experiences in developing my approach, introduce topical theoretical and academic arguments, and describe my practice through examples with students and professional artists.

Crossing the Gender Divide

"This was a Shylock who sometimes left the Rialto but never the Contralto."

This quote taken from a 1920s newspaper review of Lucille Laverne's performance as Shylock in a production of *The Merchant of Venice* easily echoes the current critical view of cross-cast performances. In the last decade there

Terri is finishing a PhD in Performance Practice at the University of Exeter where she was awarded an MFA in Staging Shakespeare in 2004. She also holds a BA in Theatre from UCLA and is the founder of the Shake-scene Players. Her plays *Drag King Richard III* and *Possession: Macbeth* have garnered many awards and accolades. Terri is a member of AEA, AGVA, BASSC, IATSE and has worked with such reputable companies as Shakespeare's Globe Theatre, RSC, SITI Company, the Wooster Group, The Queen's Company, Knightsbridge Theatre, Cleveland Public Theatre, Disney, Universal Studios, and in film and television.

1. From Kate Bush's Album *Aerial*, EMI Records Ltd., 2005—*A Sky of Honey*, song title "Somewhere In Between".

2. Butoh is a form of dance that originated in post-war Japan as a response to the highly technical and rigid expressions and influences of western ballet and modern dance as well as traditional Noh and Kabuki performance. Sometimes referred to as "post atomic spectacle" and "dance of darkness," butoh seeks to reject social mores and express the inexpressible and imperfect through a gestural body, shaped and shifting through the politics of identity. Endo Tadashi is a well-known butoh solo dancer and teacher. He specializes in a form of butoh dance that he calls butoh-MA. The workshop I attended took place in London at the Buddhist Arts Centre, September 16-24, 2006.

3. Taken from Endo Tadashi's workshop materials.

4. One who lives and dances butoh. I use this term in reference to Sondra Fraleigh and Tamah Nakamura's description of the ethos/ethics that define butohist philosophy. This is an ethos of becoming, a rejection of modern categories and appreciation of the "nature of life and the life/death/life cycle…because it comes from emptiness, itself not really empty, but in the process of emptying and filling, like the process of breathing." Fraleigh, Sondra and Tamah Nakamura. *Hijikata Tatsumi and Ohno Kazuo*, 72.

5. Fraleigh, Sondra and Tamah Nakamura. *Hijikata Tatsumi and Ohno Kazuo*, 3-4.

6. Throughout this paper I will use the prefix "trans" to evoke the sense of crossing over, between and mostly beyond states and categories. My use of "trans" is influenced by transgender attentive politics derived from the queer community.

7. PhD in Performance Practice at the University of Exeter, due to be submitted in the autumn of 2007. The topic of my PhD is staging masculinities with female performers.

8. Throughout this paper I refer to cross-dressing, not in terms of the social-psychological terminology found in queer, gender and psychological discourse, but in terms of a distinct performance convention at play with an audience.

9. Kathryn Hunter as King Lear at The Young Vic, 1997. Fiona Shaw as Richard II at The National Theatre, 1995 and the Queen's Company production of *Taming of the Shrew*, at the Walker Space NYC, 2005.

10. Propeller is an all-male Shakespearean company. Rylance's productions: *Antony and Cleopatra*, Shakespeare's Globe Theatre, 1999; *Twelfth Night*, Shakespeare's Globe Theatre, 2002; *Measure for Measure*, Theatre for a New Audience, 2005.

11. *Theatre Record* Volume XX: 2000, 20 May- 2 June 2000 pgs 690-694.

12. *Theatre Record*, Vol;XXIII: Issue 11-12 productions from 21 May-17 June 2003) pgs 739-742.

13. John Peters, *Sunday Times*, 31-08-03.

14. From a description of the technique Valerie Lilias Arkell-Smith, most notably known as Colonel Barker, used to gain her "manly" sound on stage when she lived and worked professionally as a "male actor" (Ivor Gauntlett) in *Colonel Barker's Monstrous Regiment* by Rose Collis. Collis goes on to write about the Bamboula tour Barker appeared in; "Halfway through the tour, the strain of singing in a low register took its toll: Ivor Gauntlett's voice broke down and he had to leave the play", 106.

247

has been a rise in the numbers of all-female Shakespeare productions, companies and female performers cross-dressing the boards to portray classically male roles.[8] Some of these companies and performers have been extremely successful at swapping genders and staging masculinity such as Kathryn Hunter's portrayal of King Lear, Fiona Shaw as Richard II, and the recent Queen's Company production of *Taming of the Shrew*, whilst others have been ridiculed by audiences and the press.[9] In fact, several gender-bending performances have been artistically criticized as "resembling a girls' school play" and few all-female companies have gained the artistic credibility and financial sponsorship as their male original practices counterparts such as Edward Hall's *Propeller*, and Mark Rylance's productions of *Antony and Cleopatra*, *Twelfth Night* and recent *Measure for Measure* on tour.[10] Of particular note is the part voice has played in the success or failure of these performances and how the well-crafted appropriation of the masculine voice is neglected yet imperative for the future of these transformative acts to be sounded and inspired.

Looking at the critical response a few of these cross-dressed performances have garnered reveals a symbiotic relationship between successful voice production and perceived artistic achievement. Vanessa Redgrave is an actor well known for her "imposing voice," "beautiful diction" and her ability "to speak verse." However when she played the role of Prospero in *The Tempest*, her voice was ridiculed as the critics wrote that "Her speaking is lifeless, colourless, and monotonous" and it was argued that "Perhaps gender-bending damages at least one vital organ—the voice."[11] In contrast, the critical focus on Kathryn Hunter's voice as Richard III in Shakespeare's Globe Theatre 2003 production, resulted in favourable mentions and, as inferred in the reviews, led to the production's success. Her sonic quality was described as "low voiced," "husky," "smoky" and "If you close your eyes, you might believe the deep rasping voice was a man's."[12] Yet the all-female *Taming of the Shrew*, also starring Hunter (as Kate) and staged at Shakespeare's Globe Theatre in 2003 was not so highly received. Of particular note is the critical emphasis on the physicality of the performances. John Peter of the *Sunday Times* writes about the over emphasis on the physical performance of masculinity "Apart from Amanda Harris (Tranio), none of the cast knows how to play men…Janet McTeer's hulking, laddish Petrucchio does a lot of rubbing of the genital area; also harrumphing and hoarse grunts, usually at the expense of the words."[13]

As these critical examples indicate, the expense of the words in cross-dressed performances of women playing men occurs primarily because to physically signify masculinity is much easier than to vocalize it. In these performances, the over-articulating of the physical semiotics of gender acts to re-direct the audience's attention away from the lack of vocal craftsmanship. In the cases wherein artists attempted to produce a "masculine" sound, it was predominately accomplished not only at the expense of the words but at the risk of damaging their voices altogether; as they routinely "chain smoked cigarettes,"[14] growled and shouted through lines, and discarded vocal warm-ups in order to maintain their morning "huskiness" as method to their spoken manliness.

Problems Voicing Gender

In 2004, as part of my practice towards an MFA in Staging Shakespeare from the University of Exeter, I worked in a residency at Shakespeare's Globe Theatre in London through the Globe Education department. The core of the residency focused on exploring acting challenges induced by performing on the Globe's stage. Inspired by the fore-mentioned performances, I decided to play the part of Romeo in a cross-cast exploration of the balcony scene from *Romeo and Juliet*.[15] As my male partner (playing Juliet) and I began staging and rehearsing our scene, vocal questions and complications arose. How important is gendering the voice in cross-cast performance? Should we affect our voices to match our gendered presentations? Does gendering the voice inspire "camp" readings of our scene? How could we portray truthful cross-dressed performances through gendered vocal appropriation? We decided to try to affect our registers without "indicating" that effect. We theorized that this act would help in our transformations without sliding into parody and therefore making our scene humorous, which was not our intent. This idea was good in theory but when practiced within the size and multi-dimensional space of the Globe, nearly impossible to execute without technique and training.

Let me explain that I take great pride in my voice and practice good vocal hygiene daily. I never work on a cold throat and as a professional actor having made my living with my voice, I have adopted a very good warm-up regime. Specifically I practice variations on exercises taught to me by a number of vocal coaches and incorporate them into Chuck Jones' Vocal Workout.[16] My previous vocal practice was not enough however to cope with the demands sonic trans-dressing introduces. Without any insight into appropriating the "masculine" in voice safely, I proceeded to do what most women do in this instance: to push, to clench, to manipulate into deeper tones, and ultimately damage the voice. Within days, I had lost my most valuable tool as a Shakespearean actor.

Not long after my cross-dressed performance at the Globe I was again to play a male role in an original appropriation entitled *Drag King Richard III* for the Shake-scene Players.[17] Half Shakespearean text, half auto-biographical drama about a FTM (female to male) trans-sexual, I played the lead role as Laurence (Richard).[18] Unlike the Globe experiment, I had to portray a "believable" man in an intimate professional production and anything short of a transformative attempt would negate the serious nature and intention of the piece.[19] To add depth to my performance, I spent months researching and training myself to walk, move and perform as a man. I even went so far as to shave my head and began to wear suits and ties in my daily life.[20] "Because we can walk and talk, we assume we can act. But an actor actually has to reinvent walking and talking to be able to perform those actions effectively on the stage."[21] My walking and physical performance as a man was easier to reinvent, as I was able to research and study the semiotics of gender and practice drag and cross-dressed techniques.[22] At times I even passed for a man on the street…until I opened my mouth. I soon discovered that reinventing my voice for the performance would become my biggest and most valuable challenge.

Sonic Trans-dressing
Elizabeth Wood in her seminal work *Sapphonics* describes the female voice as applied to singers that cross the sonic gender divide as Sonic Cross-dressing

15. As part of my MFA in Staging Shakespeare at the University of Exeter we worked in a two week residency as part of a module at Shakespeare's Globe Theatre in London. Working with practitioners such as Stewart Pearce and Patrick Spottiswood of Globe Education division we staged practical explorations on the SGT stage. The residency ran from March 1-19, 2004.

16. From the Chuck Jones book *Make Your Voice Heard* and as described in the chapter entitled "The Daily Voice Workout."

17. *Drag King Richard III* written and directed by Terri Power was produced by the Shake-scene Players and had its world premiere at the Edinburgh Fringe Festival 2004. The production was critically acclaimed and was commended by Amnesty International for highlighting the plight of the transsexual community. The production went on to tour the UK including a return to Edinburgh with new casting specifically trained for the performance in 2005.

18. The role of Laurence requires an actor capable of portraying a (FTM) female to male post-operative transsexual with great conviction and sensitivity. At times Laurence appropriates Richard III's Shakespearean dialogue in order to express how "Laurence" felt in the wrong body when he was "Laurie" and reflects upon his pre-operative life. The title of the play uses "drag" with several interpretive meanings: drag referring to "drag king" performance in which women play men in performance, to pull with force or violence (part of the play looks at sexual reassignment surgery as a violent act), and the colloquial slang for "annoyance" (as "Laurie" views her female parts as obstacles pre-surgery).

19. The aim of the directorial approach was for the queer and straight audience to identify and/or sympathize with Laurence's sexual conundrum. By portraying a "believable" male character, it was thought that the actor could be perceived as male rather than as a female actor playing a male role. This performance would then highlight the serious sexual dysphoria that is at the heart of the play's narrative.

20. In order to prepare for the role I researched materials on the transitioning periods of FTM (female to male) transsexuals. The transition period is usually the time that the individual begins to live and dress in the opposite sex before sexual reassignment surgery. Many pre-operative transsexuals attend coaching sessions, workshops, begin hormone treatments and psychological therapy. I interviewed FTM's pre- and post-operation, attended meetings, and participated in many actions as though I was transitioning. I also studied with drag king performers and eventually incorporated their techniques in my work.

21. Bogart, *A Director Prepares*, 96.

22. I define these two performance conventions in my paper "Trans-dressing the Stage: From Drag King to Female Player," first presented at the Gender conference at Leeds University in June 2006. Through my practice I have found that drag is "the hyper performance of the socially prescribed performance of gender...(and) is predicated upon an assumption of a 'fixed' sexed body and its prescriptive social attributions wherein sex, sexuality and gender performance are 'normative' and congruent...Drag interrogates this assumption by revealing the performance as a performance through an absurd theatrical enactment that re-renders gender, sex, and sexuality beyond prescriptive terms." In contrast I define the convention of cross-dressing in the same paper as "simply crossing the material stylization of the 'fixed' body in order to re-gender a performer for performance." The audience, through suspension of disbelief, understands the sex/gender performance belongs to the character, as the actor's fixed sex/gender is not part of the actor/audience dialectic.

23. Wood, Sapphonics, from *Queering the Pitch*, 28.

24. Jones, *Make Your Voice Heard*, 74.

25. Although the voice is physically produced by the body, there are many voice specialists that believe it is affected by internal and external influences. The voice has been argued to have transformative and healing powers and has been used in a variety of therapies. I define the voice as metaphysical because in my work it is expressed through the intersection of the physical body and the liminal spirit. It is not material in matter, yet carries weight and substance.

and Saphonnic sound:

> I call this voice Sapphonic for its resonance in sonic space as lesbian difference and desire. Its sound is characteristically powerful and problematic, defiant and defective. Its flexible negotiation and integration of an exceptional range of registers crosses boundaries among different voice types and their representations to challenge polarities of both gender and sexuality as these are socially—and vocally—constructed.[23]

Her concepts around the argument of Sapphonic sound and Sonic Cross-dressing define a lesbian and erotic discourse between performer and listener. Obviously Wood's theories can be applied to work in which women are appropriating masculinity and "other" gender variant sounds in spoken performance, but I argue that what is important is not the erotic effect of this vocal performance but the transformation that is staged in the ear of the listener.

My current practical research is focussed upon the voice's "flexible negotiation and integration" of gendered ranges (voice types) as applied to spoken cross-cast performances of women playing men. It is not the voicing of lesbian difference and desire that is the focus of my research but the transformative performance possibilities the Sapphonic voice produces. I call this production of the voice in spoken performance sonic trans-dressing. Through my experience in practice, I have found that voicing "masculinity" is not a crossing over into the sonic territory of men or a masking/costuming of the normatively gendered voice (as is implied in the term cross-dressing), but rather an expanding of the actor's tool to transcend territories and properties by transforming into a multi-tonal and flexible voice trained for variant gender readings.

Also imperative to Sonic Trans-dressing is an understanding of how socially prescribed gender performance (as learnt behaviour) limits vocal possibilities. As Chuck Jones writes "It helps to understand the gender-based restrictions society has placed on you all your life and observe how these restrictions are manifested in your voice and body."[24] These gender observations can be made in many sonic spaces; between the actor and her vocal identity, the actor and her instrument, the actor and her character, and the actor and her audience. Indeed as the gendered voice is interrogated, a truth emerges. The voice, as a metaphysical occurrence, is not fixed nor bound by any gender demarcations other than those imposed by our personal suppositions.[25] Sonic Trans-dressing is a metamorphosis that occurs through the symbiotic relationship between practice/training of the instrument in non-normative gendered sonic territory and the mercurial inspiration of psycho-physical vocal awareness.

Gender and Text

Having completed an MFA in Staging Shakespeare before my work in *Drag King Richard III*, I was adept at applying in-depth text work to Shakespearean performances. I had a strong foundation in the techniques of voice luminaries such as Cicely Berry, Patsy Rodenburg, Kristin Linklater and Chuck Jones. One major observation I had as I tried to appropriate a masculine sound for my performance, was that as I applied the skills of text work to the Shakespearean soliloquies, prose and poetry (making up ½ the script), I effectively sounded and conveyed the vocal masculinity I was seeking. However, this was not happening within the auto-biographical sections of the play. I soon made the connection that the language used in Shakespeare's text was constructed of powerful words and "masculine" authority that originated in a deeper place within my body and in turn affected my voice.

A further example of this phenomenon of textual masculinity was made as I observed the table work of the all-female Queen's Company when rehearsing *Taming of the Shrew* in Autumn of 2005.[26] When we sat down for the initial reading of the script "re-imagined" by director Rebecca Patterson, I had reservations as to whether some of the more feminine women could ever sonically affect masculinity. I noted that their voices were pitched high, expressive, and at times sounded soft and melodic. I feared that they could not convey the deeper qualities, tones and power demanded by the text and portrayal of leading male characters. Yet as the performers began dissecting the text methodically through their table work, within the first week, sonic transformations took place as the women collectively began to embody masculinity through voice.

26. I served as the assistant director and actor in the original NYC Queen's Company Production.

Textual cues, such as those crafted in Shakespeare's playwriting, can be a major factor in how people perform and communicate gender through voice. As I researched transitioning periods of FTM (female to male) transsexuals for my performance as Laurence (Richard), I soon learned of the numbers of vocal coaches employed to work with the trans community in order to help them achieve an appropriate sonic performance.[27] These coaching sessions and workshops serve not only to train participants to re-gender their voice by expanding their tones and placements, but to highlight that gender differences are conveyed not simply in the tone and pitch of men's and women's voices but in their use and voicing of language. Gender cues are conveyed in voice production through the words we choose, the energy we place behind them and the multiple ways through which we communicate.

27. My reference to the trans community means pre- and post-operative transsexuals, transgendered men, women, and everyone in between.

Kate Bornstein in *Gender Outlaw* refers to these cues as Power Dynamics and explains that they are conveyed through our modes of communication; communication techniques; and degrees of aggressiveness, assertiveness, persistence, and ambition.[28] Power dynamics are constantly conveyed through our use of everyday speech in our selection and articulation of words, intentions behind them, their delivery and production, and the conscious and unconscious reification of gender cues. Deborah Tannen in her book *You Just Don't Understand* reasons that these textual gender cues occur because "women speak and hear a language of connection and intimacy, while men speak and hear a language of status and independence."[29] Tannen explains that men and women have speech differences she terms *genderlects*. Women "rapport talk," using conversation to connect with others and negotiate relationships; men "report talk," using speech to hold center stage, maintain status, and get and keep attention.

28. Bornstein, *Gender Outlaw*, 26.

29. Tannen, *You Just Don't Understand*, 42.

In Norah Vincent's book *Self- Made Man*, she describes living undercover as a man for 18 months and in the first chapter recounts her process for *becoming* a man. Of particular interest is her description of a session with a vocal coach from Julliard. The professional voice coach was hired to help Vincent vocally *pass* as a man.[30] Curiously Vincent does not mention learning exercises that

30. "Pass" is often used in the gay and trans community to mean someone (usually homosexual or transgendered) that can dress and act as the opposite sex publicly and undetected.

re-gender pitch and tone of voice, or re-placement of resonators or applying any vocal training techniques; she writes about the coach's instructions about gender textual cues in social interactions. Instead of concentrating on Vincent's sonic range, the coach's intent is on instructing Vincent to speak and interact as a man, which through the coach's example, is learnt by not speaking as a woman. Vincent explains:

> My Tutor said 'women tend to bankrupt their own breath.' She described and demonstrated the process by thrusting her chest and head forward when she spoke, and cutting off the rhythm of her breathing as she forced a stream of words from her mouth. 'Admittedly this is a stereotype' she said 'but generally women tend to speak more quickly and to use more words, and they interrupt their breathing in order to get it all out'…Women often lean into conversation and speak in wordy bursts, asking to be heard. Men often lean back and pronounce with terse authority.[31]

31. Vincent, *Self-Made Man*, 14-15.

These examples highlight how social gender programming is found in our interpersonal communication and textual cues resulting in genderlects. Applying Shakespearean vocal text work can help to eliminate "feminine" communication and vocal cues as it serves to employ male behavioural and speech cues. A well-trained actor, as in the Queen's Company example, can embody sonic masculinity simply by scoring the script, maintaining breath control, and speaking with authority.[32] This is perhaps why Shakespearean text has historically lent itself to cross-dressed performance. But what happens when an actor is performing with other texts? And, as in the case of Vanessa Redgrave playing Prospero, what if textual technical proficiency is not enough? These are a few of the questions that I have begun to answer through my psycho-physical vocal approach.

32. Scoring the script is the technique of methodically analysing the structure of the text for vocal performance with concentrations on such areas as meter, masculine and feminine endings (pentameter), rhythm, breathing, alliteration, pauses, irregularities of rhythm, assonance, onomatopoeia, rhyme, antithesis and so on.

Of Breath, Spirit and Psycho-physical Vocal Awareness
In my practice and training of students and artists, we begin the work by focusing on breath. We use breath to relax our bodies from the pressures of the outside world, to rouse our state of readiness, to develop an active awareness of the "geography of the body" and inspire our internal and sonic transformations.[33] As we develop our connection to breath, we strengthen our psycho-physical awareness of how breath affects us, and its location and production in our bodies. This psycho-physical awareness will eventually aid in inspiring deeper relaxed tones and pitches in our vocal register to be resonant and articulated.

33. Oida and Marshall, *The Invisible Actor*, 14. The Geography of the body is described as active awareness of the physical body as it is theorized that "every tiny detail of the body corresponds to a different inner reality."

Breath also serves a metaphysical and *spiritual* place in our practice. Spirit: from the Latin *spiritus* meaning "breathing," also defined as "breath of life."[34] Breath brings life to our characters in the microcosmic action of breathing in (in)spire and out (ex)spire. There is a duality between life (inhale) and death (exhale): between breathing in and out. Most important to our work is to highlight the in between space; the space of rest and balance that lies between life and death. This is the transitory transversing agency we aim to develop and acknowledging this space through our breathing exercises allows the performers to see that within all of us exist spaces between oppositions, between masculine and feminine, life and death. This space constitutes diverse possibilities within each of us and foregrounds balance and truth. As Anne Bogart writes "Truth, which is an experience and not something easily defined,

34. Taken from the *Shorter Oxford English Dictionary*, Volume II.

mostly exists in the space between opposites." She then goes on to write that "opposition, or dialectic, sets up alternative systems of perceiving."[35]

It is in perceiving this alternative space in breath work that the foundation of my work with women appropriating "masculine" sonic territory is predicated. We build our bodies, breath, and voice in this in between space, discovering that voice does not have to be tonally fixed and can be fluid in locality. The body becomes the instrument of breath, a vocal resonator, rendered gender fluid through the space of the body; transforming its interior, exterior, and liminal sonic articulation.

Of course, I realise that I am referring to a metaphysical transformation using breath as a catalyst that for many may be too alternative/new age for their purposes. However, in the new millennium and as new challenges present themselves for performers such as cross-dressed and what I term *Trans-dressed* performances[36], these issues must somehow be addressed and experimental methods practiced. At the heart of this work is simply a deeper connection to breath as an agent for transformation and the insistence of my practical focus on breath ultimately creates a relaxed body. A body that becomes more resonant, flexible, and (in)spired which reflects in holistic voice production and empowers not only the voice in quality but the actor in form. "If we breathe consciously, focusing our thoughts through the rhythm of our breath, the breath becomes a powerful energy for creation, inspiration, and change."[37]

The next step in our process is to focus on the *hara*; energizing this area with breath for movement and voice. Used in many forms of Asian martial arts, spiritual and theatrical practice, the hara holistically connects the body, mind and spirit as one unit. Many western practices refer to this area as the core, center or belly. It is located a few inches below the navel, and when working with new students I will request that they wear a loose hanging belt with a big buckle to help indicate the hara throughout our work. Lorna Marshall helps to describe it further: "the Japanese concept of the hara is seen as something more than a physical location; it is the core of the entire self. It is the centre of a person's strength, health, energy, integrity, and sense of connection to the outside world and the universe."[38]

Another source of connection to the world and universe that I use in our psycho-physical vocal practice is an emphasis on the feet. As we work and begin with breath and hara awareness, we remain barefoot; establishing our connection to the earth through the soles of our feet. I sometimes ask the students to "breathe through their feet" and this aids in getting them to breathe more deeply. At this stage in the approach, we use several simple Suzuki exercises, such as walking and stamping of the feet to build the connection between our breath and our feet. As Tadashi Suzuki suggests "There are many cases in which the position of the feet determines even the strength and nuance of the actor's voice."[39] Also, in the case of stamping the feet, we begin to feel our own power through the relationship between breath and body. Another key benefit of stamping the feet is that "It is a gesture that can lead to the creation of a fictional space, perhaps even a ritual space, in which the actor's body can achieve a transformation from the personal to the universal."[40]

35. Bogart, *A Director Prepares*, 56.

36. In my paper "Trans-dressing the Stage: From Drag King to Female Player," first presented at the Gender conference at Leeds University in June 2006, I describe and define performative difference between Drag, Cross-dressed, and what I term Trans-dressed performance. Trans-dressed performance has its roots in drag and cross-dressed performance but sets itself apart from these conventions by "(trans)cending the fixed body to highlight a fluid site that cannot only cross back and forth between masculinity and femininity but transcend gender altogether, revealing multiple gender readings in a single performance or production."

37. Pearce, *The Alchemy of Voice*, 36.

38. Oida and Marshall, *The Invisible Actor*, 10.

39. Suzuki, *The Way of Acting*, 6.

40. Oida and Marshall, *The Invisible Actor*, 12.

Key to the work is finding these transformative spaces, not only from the personal to the universal but to the uni-gendered. In the next step, we begin to neutralize the performer's gender cues by working the body and breath together through Astanga Vinyasa Yoga practice.[41] This highly technical and aerobic Yoga form ungenders the body and forces the body-mind connection. Through *Vinyasa* (the process of linking breath with movement) sequences and *Asanas* (physical positions) the breath is active and audible as *Ujjayi* "victorious" breathing is practiced. The lungs work more efficiently, the heart pumps oxygen to all the cells, and the performer becomes hyper-aware of their life force. They embody a state of readiness, genderlessness, extreme focus and transformation.

41. Many of the sequences and positions I have incorporated into my voice work have derived from private training sessions and the book *Ashtanga Yoga for Women* by Sally Griffyn and Michaela Clarke.

Native American Vocables

In autumn of 2004, I began creating an original play around a part Native American youth named Tom A. Hawk. As I developed Tom's persona for a solo performance, I created his narrative through experimental projects that incorporated ceremonial dance, drumming, song and storytelling alongside Native American history and current social struggles. The resulting performance *Tom A. Hawk: War Within* was well received and introduced new performative changes into my growing training method.

One of the major changes in my work that I experienced in the academic year 2004-2005 was in the quality and sound of my voice. As I documented my work on digital video and sound recordings, I immediately recognized that my voice had grown more powerful, flexible, resonant and masculine in its sonic range. As I had been working exclusively with Native American male songs, dances and the vocables contained within, it was clear that (like the Shakespearean text work) applying vocables in voice work created a dynamic sound that made sonic trans-dressing a vocal possibility.

It is difficult to give an exact definition of vocables as many Native American tribes are committed to their oral traditions and are adamant about not publishing any piece of their culture in written forms. Many of the descriptions I have uncovered about vocables have been interpretive and usually defined by someone outside the culture. However, one of the most thorough descriptions comes from Charlotte Heth, a Cherokee, who writes:

> Although most songs are performed, for the most part, in native languages, some include vocables (non-translatable syllables) used to carry the melody in the same way that "fa-la-la" and other vocables do in European folk songs. These vocables are fixed and are indeed the words to the songs. Many of the melodies start high and descend throughout the renditions; others undulate from beginning to end. Variations in vocal style identify tribal and regional differences and genres of songs. A few songs sound like recitations on one or two pitches. Besides the sounds of the drum, bells, and an occasional whistle, the 'pulsation,' or intentional quavering of the voices, enhances the texture...[42]

42. From the chapter/article by Charlotte Heth "American Indian Dance: A Celebration of Survival and Adaptation" contained in *Native American Dance Ceremonies and Social Traditions*.

As Heth describes, the "pulsation" or intentional quavering of the voice is created by an intensive practice of using the core of the body (the hara) to produce sound and a heightened state of awareness of the active nature and transformative power of breath.

The vocables themselves also serve as a site for metaphysical transformation, which is quite possibly why they are vital to sacred ceremonies. In practice, one finds that as they are devoid of any literal and specific meaning, vocables in song and spoken voice communicate spiritual and universal meanings. They communicate the essence of the performer (the spirit) and an audience is not required to have knowledge of vocables in order to understand the experiential effects of joy, loss, anger, etc. that they embody. Vocables also serve to release the critical mind of the performer in the same esoteric connection that mantras have on eastern practices. The voice becomes the manifested sacred site, between the physical body and the liminal spirit, an embodied articulation of the in between space of transformative and sonic possibilities.

Using Vocables
Native Americans use the vowel sounds A ("Ah") and ("Ay"), E ("Ee"), I ("I"), O ("Oh"), U ("oo") in combination with rich consonant sounds to create vocables. Vocables range in variety and combinations but the ones that I work with most unite consonants such as H, N, Y, L, D and W with the vowel sounds. Together they create vocables such as Ha, Ne, Yo, Lu, Di and many of these strong combinations can be found in Native American songs, dramas, and storytelling. Using vocables in spoken form as in singing activates the hara, as the sounds created originate and resonate from a deeper place within the body and spirit. As they are voiced, vocables are unifying not only through their uni-vocal and multi-lingual function, but in their ability to fuse the body and spirit in a gender-neutral and metaphysical state. Stewart Pearce writes about how Native Americans use the vowels sounds "as sound energies for transformative purposes, because they accomplish a great connection with the spirit world and therefore a healing of the mind and body."[43]

43. Pearce, *The Alchemy of Voice*, 105.

In my practice with students and professional artists, we incorporate vocables into our hara breath work by beginning with an exercise that I call *Fire Breath*. This exercise has been adapted from the Breath of Fire Yoga technique and integrates the Native American vocable "Ha" (H-ah).

The exercise begins as follows:
Like Yoga's Breath of Fire, we breathe in through the nose rapidly, pause a moment, and out through the nose rapidly. We pause when we have fully exhaled, breathe in through the nose again rapidly, pause, and this time release the breath while making a "Ha" sound.

You will note that "Ha" or rather "H-ah" is the first in the line of Native American vowel sound energies. By adding the H to the vowel sound "ah," we create a vocable that sounds like the beginning of the word "hot." This is what I tell my students to imagine as they execute the Fire Breath exercise, "Think Hot, but say 'Ha.'"

I ask the students to repeat the Fire Breath exercise a few times and to note changes as we add pyscho-physical positions to the work. For example, after a few Fire Breaths, the students are asked to repeat the exercise but this time placing their hands upon their haras. They are instructed to focus moving their breath to and from this physical point and note changes, if possible, in their sound. Next, they are asked to assume the asana yoga position, the plank, and resume Fire Breathing with the vocalized "Ha," again noting any sonic changes.

Our next step in the process is to use the vocables made by combining the consonant sounds (H, N, Y, L, D, W) with the vowel sounds (a, ay, e, i, o, u) whilst we move through a Vinyasa sequence that incorporates asanas. In this exercise we move using active breath from downward facing dog to plank, from plank to right arm triangle, from right arm triangle to left arm triangle, from left arm triangle to plank, and from plank back to downward facing dog. As we execute this vinyasa sequence we inhale breath into the hara whilst physically moving into the next asana, then each set of vocables are voiced as we exhale.

The sequence can be described like this:
(Begin from seated position and remember to execute all breathing and vocalizations engaging the hara and releasing on one continuous breath.)
—Inhale through the nose and move to downward facing dog.
—Exhale through the mouth and gently vocalize (Ha, Hay, He, Hi, Ho, Hu).
—Inhale through the nose and move into plank position.
—Exhale through the mouth and gently vocalize (Na, Nay, Ne, Ni, No, Nu).
—Inhale through the nose and move to right arm triangle.
—Exhale through the mouth and gently vocalize (Ya, Yay, Ye, Yi, Yo, Yu).
—Inhale through the nose and move to left arm triangle.
—Exhale through the mouth and vocalize (La, Lay, Le, Li, Lo, Lu).
—Inhale through the nose and move to plank position.
—Exhale through the mouth and vocalize (Da, Day, De, Di, Do, Du).
—Inhale through the nose and move to downward facing dog.
—Exhale through the mouth and vocalize (Wa, Way, We, Wi, Wo, Wu).
—Inhale through the nose and return to seated position.

Working with a Drum

The drum is a very important element in my work with women appropriating masculine tones for performance. As an ancient and ceremonial instrument it contains universal meanings and has always inspired creativity and acts of transformation. In the modern era the drum has been linked to men, male rituals, and masculine endeavours such as war and hunting festivities. However, archaeological and anthropological studies have uncovered that before the fall of Rome, women had a strong connection to the drum and drumming was an integral part of their spiritual practice. Through its symbolic representation and metaphysical properties, the act of striking a drum and setting rhythmic scores in sonic trans-dressing practice can deeply affect the performer, and uniquely inspire her to respond by matching the drum in tone, power, pitch, rhythm, and resonance. This act of one rhythm drawing another into harmonic resonance in music is termed *entrainment*. In our work, the drum leads and we follow.

Mental and physical concentration on rhythm connects (us) at times with a universal energy, both internally and externally. This energy conveys a feeling of timelessness. Drumming engages the conscious mind, and like meditation, cuts back on its continual chatter. As a result, as happens after practicing meditation, the habitual patterns of thinking that drive behaviour become less powerful.[44]

This work can be done by using a variety of drums but in my practice I have found that using a hand held Native American hoop drum (tom-tom) or frame drum with one or two mallets works best. As a hoop drum can easily be held with one hand and struck with the opposite, it allows a freedom of movement for the instructor to move about the room and assist students. The drum I routinely use is handmade from stretched cow hide and wood, about 14 inches in diameter and executes a deep rich tonal quality. Different skins will create different tones and generally the larger the drum the deeper the emanating sound will be. It would be ideal to have a separate drummer during practice but it is not necessary.

Usually when working with female performers I will wait a few weeks into our training process before introducing the drum. My aim is to allow them time to develop their psycho-physical awareness, supporting breath, execution of vinyasa sequences, and inner ear listening skills. I want to be sure that they have developed listening skills that are attune to the inner rhythms of their own breath and starting voices before they are externally influenced by the drum. When I feel they are fairly prepared, I introduce the drum as a new company member; an important member that they must listen and respond to as they would anyone else. Our first day is spent as a day of silence wherein no one speaks as they practice and all exercises are indicated and initiated through the striking of the drum. The students are also encouraged to listen intently to the external sonic voice of the drum and its rhythms and note how the drum affects their breathing and internal processes during their practice.

Initially we begin with expressive movement and voice as the drum leads and we follow. We work toward freedom of movement and voice in relation to the rhythms and power of our new company member.[45] The drum pauses and so do we. The drum beats faster and slower and we respond. There are no rules; no right or wrong in this exercise, just an emphasis on listening and responding using kinaesthetic awareness. The goal is to once again create a safe environment for unique transformative practice, as many women will initially feel uncomfortable as they step closer to voicing masculine tones. This work with the drum inevitably silences the critical mind and works to develop an ability to explore new physical and sonic territory through organic impulsive expression.

In most of our drumming sessions we work on resonating the body. I will invite the students, after a vigorous session using movement and free voice with the drum, to lie down with their backs to the floor. I instruct them to close their eyes and to reinvest in their breath and hara awareness. Then I will ask them to relax different parts of their bodies through tension and release exercises. When I feel that they are adequately relaxed I strike the drum and ask them to focus on how the drum vibrates sound through the room. What does vibration sound like? How does it feel in our relaxed bodies? How does the tone and mood of the drum sound and feel? I strike the drum several times and then instruct the students to imagine that their body is the drum and as I strike it (the drum) to gently vibrate (the body). I repeat this exercise several times and then ask the students to hum with a closed mouth in the

44. Redmond, *When the Drummers Were Women*, 13.

45. Most of the rhythms I use revolve around simple variations on the heartbeat. Usually I employ four strikes of the drum in ¾ time with a stronger strike on the fourth or (two bars) eighth beat. I try to stay away from complex rhythms as I am trying to create a meditative environment in this practice. I want my participants to feel the rhythms rather than think about them.

same tone and with the same vibration as the drum. They are working toward becoming the drum; to use their bodies to vibrate sound. The effect is amazing as the women gently lower their pitch and through the vibration of a relaxed body they sound more powerful and sonically masculine.

The exercises continue in this manner as we move the closed mouth hum, into an open mouthed vocable "Ha" (H-ah). We will work through several vocables in this way and I will place the drum on their bellies just over their haras and strike it as they work, so they can more easily feel the drum's vibration. I also ask them to continue to work and combine vocable sounds such as "Ha Ya" (H-ah, Y-ah), "Ni Yo," "Le Wa," etc. Then I ask them to slowly move into seated position and make a circle. In our circle we begin our next exercise which is to create nonsense words out of our vocables. The first student makes up a two vocable combination such as "ha hey" and delivers it to the student to her right. The student to the right repeats it in agreement and creates a new vocable combination for the student on her right and the process continues all around the circle.

When this exercise is completed we continue to work in the circle on an exercise that I call *Chief Circle*. I explain to the students that they are to imagine that they are all great and powerful chiefs and they are representing their tribe at a very important meeting. Each student is asked to speak in only vocables but convey the important message that they must give to the Chief Circle. Inevitably the students will become self-conscious at first and find difficulty remembering the vocables, but the aim of the exercise is to speak with meaning and power through the sounds they have practiced. These sounds, through routine conditioning, will eventually convey masculinity as they are placed with resonance and freedom in the deep location of the hara.

Applying Technique to Text

As the students work and their psycho-physical awareness of producing vocables develops, they will be able to make the leap and use their work in dramatic texts. When my students and artists start to work with Shakespearean monologues for example, they will go through shortened versions of the drum and voice work and then be asked to work on their text. As they perform they will discover places in the text where they can feel their voices *lifting* out of its newly trans-dressed placement. I call this return to "feminine" and/or "normatively gendered" voice production "lifting" because as Chuck Jones describes, women predominately use "facial-mask resonators, (nasal passages, sinuses, and cheeks)"[46] to create sound. This sonic production occurs largely upwards in physical locality, as opposed to my encouragement of using the lower hara and entire body to produce sound. I will ask her to mark where the lifting occurred so that together we may work toward understanding the reason behind the lift and relocate its origination.

The majority of the time the problem is the deep vowel sounds inherent in the vocables are lost, or the performer is not able to embrace the masculinity of a word and play it to its full advantage. I encountered a moment like this with an actor in my *Women Playing Men* workshop working on the St. Crispian's Day speech from Shakespeare's *Henry V*. She kept lifting into feminine tones and facial-mask resonators on specific words like *honour, manhood* and phrases like *band of brothers*. When we encounter problems like these

46. Jones, *Make Your Voice Heard*, 71.

257

examples, I encourage the artist to return to the exercise of the chief circle and to say the same words amidst the vocables. How would the chief use the word honour? How would he create that sound in his body? How would he use it for meaning, power, and emphasis? These questions and this exercise help a great deal. If not, then there's always the drum!

Working with monologues is the first step. From there we usually move onto dialogue and more complex texts. When I directed an all-female *Romeo and Juliet* project, I trained the actors playing the male roles in my vocal approach. Their monologues sounded commanding, deep, and resonant but I noted that as soon as they began to interact with the female characters, such as Romeo interacts with Juliet in the balcony scene, their voices lifted into higher pitches and the deeper resonance was lost. I realized that this was again a result of socialized communication patterns between women.

Women as caregivers and nurturing supporters tend to match one another in pitch, tone, resonance, and quality in order to assimilate and affect our understanding. This is a type of social entrainment. We adopt similar speech patterns in order to make the speaker and/or listener feel safe and comfortable to communicate. The actors in the production had become friends during the course of their training and rehearsal periods and as they performed together, these off-stage socialized patterns emerged through their on-stage sonic expression and rendered their sound "effeminate." As I cited this in their work, we all became aware of those patterns and continually worked toward eradicating them from the performance altogether. In making the actors aware of these potential problems and asking them to reinvest in their psycho-physical vocal awareness, a positive process is developed that is essential to this type of performance and its demands.

In my experience, women are drawn to this work because it helps them to develop the challenging performances that they crave and tests their abilities as artists. However, one major problem frequently arises in every performer at some point in the process: her relationship to the social stigma still attached to cross-gender performance. Therefore, in order to assist women on their sonic trans-dressing journey I find that it is integral to create a safe and supportive exploratory environment, to recount the history of the performance convention, to discuss gender and its physical and vocal prescriptions, and share performance tools that assist in transcending gender limitations. These steps lead the actors as they discover the breadth, challenge and importance of this work and prepare them on how it may impact socially, psychologically, and artistically.

As my approach is still growing as an on-going learning practice, I know there will be a great deal of obstacles and pitfalls that will present themselves that I have not yet encountered. However it must be noted as I have personally practiced and taught this approach to students and artists over the last four years, nearly all the challenges we have faced have been either individual to the performer (usually derived from self-consciousness, close-mindedness, stubbornness, or fear) or are social patterns or prescriptions that can obstruct the work making us redefine our aims and re-examine our process. I do not see these pitfalls as hindrances but rather as opportunities to learn more about our connection to voice production, gendered voice stereotypes, personal growth and artistic development.

A Final Note

As I continue my work I find that sonic trans-dressing enables the actor to safely develop a process towards a re-gendered, un-gendered, or uni-gendered voice. If an actor has a daily (personal), and an extra-daily (performative) relationship with her voice, then it can be argued that this approach creates another sonic connection for the performer. Many of the women that I have trained call it their "masculine" voice, and although I sometimes use the term masculine to define the new sonic space trans-dressing the voice produces, I recognize that categorising and labelling it as such is limiting. Despite what label we give this new voice, call it masculine or transgendered, as a result of the sonic psycho-physical training the performers experience the "in between" and it is this practice that gives voice to "other" gendered performances.

"As butohists they move past modern categories altogether...one enters into morphing states of awareness through performance."[47]

47. Fraleigh, Sondra and Tamah Nakamura. *Hijikata Tatsumi and Ohno Kazuo*, 72.

As we highlight the in between space in our breathing, in our voices, in our perceptions of gender and in our way of performing and being, we become like the butohists; rejecting social mores and vocally dancing toward more truthful and universal performances. These performances potentially have transformative power beyond that of masculine and feminine sonic readings. Staged in the ear of the listener is "something else," something not yet defined and therefore all the more truthful; re-shaping and transforming our sense of what is possible.

Bibliography

Bassett, Kate. "Independent on Sunday." *Theatre Record*, Volume XXIII, Issue 11-12 (May 21- June 17, 2003): 740.

Bogart, Anne. *A Director Prepares*. London: Routledge, 2001.

Bornstein, Kate. *Gender Outlaw: On Men, Women, and the Rest of Us*. New York: Routledge, 1994.

Collis, Rose. *Colonel Barker's Monstrous Regiment: A Tale of Female Husbandry*. London: Virago Press, 2001.

De Jong, Nicholas. "Evening Standard." *Theatre Record* Volume XX, Issue 11 (May 20- June 2, 2000): 690.

Fraleigh, Sondra and Tamah Nakamura. *Hijikata Tatsumi and Ohno Kazuo*. New York: Routledge, 2006.

Griffyn, Sally and Michaela Clark. *Ashtanga Yoga for Women*. Great Britain: Godsfield Press Ltd, 2003.

Heth. Charlotte and National Museum of the American Indian. *Native American Dance Ceremonies and Social Traditions*. New York: Fulcrum Publishing, 1994.

Jones, Chuck. *Make Your Voice Heard: An Actor's Guide to Increased Dramatic Range Through Vocal Training*. New York: Backstage Books, 1996.

Oida, Yoshi and Lorna Marshall. *The Invisible Actor*. London: Methuen, 1997.

Onions, C.T. ed. *The Shorter Oxford English Dictionary*, Volume II. London: Book Club Associates, 1983.

Pearce, Stewart. *The Alchemy of the Voice*. London: Hodder and Stoughton, 2005.

Peter, John. "Sunday Times." *Theatre Record* Volume XXIII, Issues 16-17 (July 30-Aug 26, 2003): 1039.

Redmond, Layne. *When the Drummers Were Women*. New York: Three Rivers Press, 1997.

Suzuki, Tadashi. *The Way of Acting*. New York: Theatre Communications Group, Inc., 1986.

Tannen, Deborah. *You Just Don't Understand: Women and Men in Conversation*. London: Virago Press, 1991.

Vincent, Norah. *Self-Made Man*. London: Atlantic Books, 2006.

Wood, Elizabeth, Philip Bret, and Gary C. Thomas eds. "Sapphonics." *Queering the Pitch: The New Gay and Lesbian Musicology*. New York: Routledge, 1994.

Essay *by Mel Churcher*

What is a Sexy Voice?

What do we hear as a sexy voice? Recently I was asked to supply some comments for a Channel Four television programme listing the 100 sexiest film voices. I was asked to offer some thoughts on a list of famously "sexy" voices, including Marilyn Monroe, Marlon Brando, Joanna Lumley, Sophia Loren, Alan Rickman, Gerard Depardieu, Kim Basinger, Antonio Banderas, Angelina Jolie and the changing voices of James Bond.

I was tickled to be asked as, some years ago, I did a research MA through Central School of Speech and Drama focusing on what seemed to be the most desired voice qualities for female performers. Funnily enough, some of the actors above had been the subjects of my research too—and Joanna Lumley had come top of my small research poll, just as she has in so many others. So I was not surprised by the programme's choices, as there seems to be some consensus of opinion when it comes to the sensual quality of voices. But what gives them this erotic appeal?

If I were asked to give a recipe, in generalised terms, for what might be perceived as the archetypal sexy voice for women, it might be: low, resonant, possibly husky or breathy, "centred" and not "disconnected" from the physical person (I'll try to explain what I mean by that in the next paragraph!), engaged and part of the performer's "presence." The recipe would be very similar for men, except, perhaps, without the breathy quality.

As there are a large amount of sympathetic and parasympathetic nerve endings congregated around the solar plexus, perhaps by "centred" we imply that the voice seems to have a direct connection to this area where we "feel" emotion and that it is not blocked off from this emotional channel. So when voices are being driven by a diaphragmatic-abdominal breath and are not disconnected from this area by constrictions, we feel that speakers are alive to their emotions and feelings. Thus they are more likely to arouse ours. If the voice is powered by this "centred" or "grounded" breath, the speaker will be engaging the whole body and not be merely a "talking head." Without this grounding, however, the speaker will be more likely to throw the chin forward, collapse at the chest, round the shoulders or otherwise disconnect from his/her physical self. This disconnection will make the voice sound higher and thinner and make the person look "needy." We are drawn towards people who seem comfortable in their own skins and any tension or neediness that is seen in the performer is unlikely to come across as sexually appealing.

I am not suggesting that sexuality in its most obvious form is necessarily a desirable or important quality in a performer. And yet I am sure we would recognise some of this centred and connected quality in our greatest actors so that, at some deep level, we are very aware of their physical and emotional presence and are attracted to it. I am also aware of how imprecise our definitions are when trying to define this presence and its causes. And yet, to discuss these issues, we have to launch into some kind of language. I am hoping that by using a range of definitions, I will get somewhere towards describing what I mean!

There is an old adage that when a cat crosses a stage, the audience will look at the cat and not at the actors. This is because the cat is content in its own being and is not trying to please us. Therefore an actor who is rooted and at

Mel has worked for many years at the Actors Centre, in drama schools and theatres including the Royal Shakespeare Company, Manchester Royal Exchange and London's West End. She has been resident Voice Coach at the Open Air Theatre, Regent's Park for the last twelve years. Coaching on movies includes *The Secret Garden, The Fifth Element, Joan of Arc, The Count of Monte Cristo, Lara Croft: Tomb Raider, 102 Dalmations, Unleashed, King Arthur* and *Eragon.* She is part of the British Voice Association Education Working Party and her book *Acting for Film: Truth 24 Times a Second* was published by Virgin Books in 2003.

ease with his/her self will attract our interest more than one who strives to please. The voice will reflect this ease when it is coming from a centred abdominal-diaphragmatic breath without strain or constriction. We will also feel the actor is connected to thought and feeling. (This does not preclude the use of sub-text. If you are hiding feelings, there are still feelings there to hide.)

As well as those around the abdominal area, there are also parasympathetic fibres within the larynx itself responding to subtle chemical changes, so, at that level too, our voices are subtle indicators of our emotion and feelings. Therefore, theoretically, merely thinking about sex should produce biological changes in the larynx that make the voice acquire the same characteristics that actual physical sexual activity provokes.

During sexual excitement, the vocal folds become swollen due to increased blood supply or hormonal changes. Or perhaps it is because the excited, clavicular breath rasping across the larynx prevents approximation of the vocal folds. Whatever the physiological reasons for the aroused husky voice, this quality, heard in other contexts, seems to evoke pleasurable memories of the voice of passion to the listener.

If you doubt that merely thinking about something could cause the body to produce hormonal and chemical changes—try this test. Imagine a bright yellow, juicy lemon sitting on your kitchen worktop. Cut into your imaginary lemon with an imaginary knife and pick up one half of it, seeing the glistening surface of the lemon. Hold it up to your nose and smell the fresh, zingy, lemony smell. Now suck hard on that lemon. Did that imaginary lemon bring real saliva into your mouth? Scientists have found that athletes running an imaginary race produce the same chemical changes in their bodies as they produce when they are running in a real race.

Of course, a husky voice may have nothing to do with sex. Many different physiological reasons may impart the same quality. Some minor voice damage, such as a nodule, might impart a husky quality to the voice, or leaving a slight posterior chink in the vocal folds may give the voice a breathy quality. Many young women, particularly in Britain, develop this "breathy" tone in their teens and twenties. There is weak medial compression of the vocal folds with a posterior chink allowing too much breath to pass through the vocal folds during voiced sound. This is sometimes attributed to a lack of confidence but it may also be a way of appearing more feminine or less aggressive. For an actor working in a large space, this voice quality can cause voice damage and it can also carry a degree of huskiness, which can also be a sign of vocal damage. Therefore, many voice practitioners will, quite rightly,

discourage a breathy or husky tone in their clients and seek to rectify this quality.

And yet we cannot deny the appeal of this husky or breathy quality. Marilyn Monroe is the classic example of this kind of voice. She has one of the most imitated of "sexy" voices. Think of her singing "Happy Birthday, Mr. President" and you capture this breathless, vulnerable, childlike voice. The singer appears aroused and capable of arousal. Blossom Dearie, the jazz singer, is another example of this breathy quality, and many jazz singers, like Cleo Laine, Eartha Kitt and Joss Stone, sing with a husky quality to their voices. The British presenter, Mariella Frostrup, has a husky voice and is in great demand for her voice quality. Judi Dench, whilst her voice is flexible and clear, has a heart-stopping crack in her voice from time to time and many, many successful female movie actors over the years have had elements of this quality.

The male version of this quality would be the famous rasp of Rod Stewart and Louis Armstrong or the raw, edgy sound of many pop singers (and adopted by some female singers—Janis Joplin being a famous example!). Here, the lack of constraint to the sound adds a danger, which excites the listener even as it disturbs the conscientious voice coach.

Pitch is another voice quality associated with sexuality. Again, during passion, the voice tends to be deeper because of the vocal fold changes mentioned above. As a coach working in both film and theatre, I am often asked by directors to "make the voice lower," particularly in the case of women. The idea that a woman's voice should be low has been with us for as long as writers have documented attitudes to voices. Shakespeare famously described Cordelia's voice as "ever soft, gentle and low," echoed by a tract in 1881 called "Girls and Their Ways" that urged women to "cultivate a low voice, that 'excellent thing in a woman.'" Female movie stars with low voices or a combination of low voice together with the husky quality have long been considered sexy: Joan Greenwood, Glynis Johns, Lauren Bacall, Ann Bancroft and Jodie Foster, to name but a few.

A lower voice suggests an adult (and grown up women are sexual beings), whereas a high voice imparts a childish quality (which is pre-sexual). Strength, power and "attitude" are traditionally male sexual qualities and as women move into powerful male dominated professions, they often strive for the lower quality to the voice that is associated with these traits.

The voice tends also to lower in pitch during relaxation as the larynx comes to rest in its natural position in the pharynx. Perhaps this is another reason why it is easier to listen to a lower voice. Hearing a relaxed performer speak imparts a sensation of ease in the listener. And incidentally, sexuality combines high energy with a curious sense of relaxation and release from tension.

(We also seem to associate resonant lower pitched tones with truthfulness and depth of emotion. Cicero reports that in Ancient Rome, an eminent pleader, Gracchus, had a servant placed behind him with a pitch pipe. If his voice rose too high, the servant sounded a lower note at which the speaker's voice would descend to his melodious and "truthful" tone!)

Just as for female movie stars, a low resonant voice has been a desirable quality for leading men. Actors like Robert Mitchum, Marlon Brando, Humphrey Bogart, Sean Connery, John Hurt, Russell Crowe and the new James Bond— Daniel Craig have all had bass, resonant and, sometimes, husky voices.

For the voice practitioner, it is important that these seemingly desirous qualities are achieved in a healthful manner. Men often push lower than their natural resonant position to sound more "manly." I find when working in The Open Air Theatre, Regent's Park, male actors are often the ones who lose their voices because they push too hard and speak below their most resonant position. In spite of having the strongest voices, they are the most apt to push and use laryngeal constriction because, with so little auditory feedback in the open air, they still want the reassurance of their big, deep voices.

Of course there are other things that affect our voice perception. Accents, especially French and Spanish, seem to rate highly with British men and women as sexy. We like to hear Antonio Banderas, Yves Montand or Gérard Depardieu. In the list I was asked to choose from for the television programme, I was not surprised to find Gina Lollobrigida and Brigitte Bardot. Apart from the obvious sexuality of their appearances, they also had the exotic appeal of a foreign accent. Greta Garbo, Marlene Dietrich, Penélope Cruz and many other female performers for whom English is, or was, a second language have exploited this appeal. Perhaps it is because, when heard in a new accent, words strike us as newly-minted. We hear language freshly and with a new energy. According to my research, some listeners find a carefully articulated British accent sexy—for example the young Julie Andrews, or Angelina Jolie's accent as Lara Croft, or the precise articulation of Alan Rickman. The highly rated Joanna Lumley uses a warm, rich, slightly breathy voice, which also has extreme clarity of diction. We also seem drawn to voices that carry the melody and strength of a Celtic accent like Scottish, Irish or Welsh. This has been an undoubted part of the success of, say, Sean Connery, Richard Burton, Anthony Hopkins or Colin Farrell.

It is always difficult to separate the voice from the personality and the physicality of the speaker. In all these actors, male and female, the sound of the voice evokes the strong physical presence that gives rise to it. This physical presence does not have to be beautiful in the accepted sense. Bette Davis, Judi Dench, Walter Matthau or Gerard Depardieu are not traditionally good-looking but their sensuality is undeniable. The way they inhabit their own bodies has an awareness, an energy and a sensitivity.

I have been talking, in the main, about the overtly sexy voice but true vocal attractiveness comes from a well-produced, flexible voice with an attractive warmth and richness. A voice does not need to be husky or breathy to be sexy and, indeed, in many situations that quality would be a dangerous choice for vocal health. Voices should find a natural pitch from the lack of constriction in the larynx and from good resonance.

In the end, a voice does not have to adhere to any fixed recipe to be perceived as sexy. But it is likely to be an easy, comfortable well-produced sound that suits the speaker's physicality. It is unlikely to be tense or constricted to be rated as attractive.

And incidentally, no-one in the TV programme's list of sexy voices that I was asked to choose from had a nasal, or an abnormally high pitched voice and both of these qualities were rated as the most unattractive when I did my own research.

So where does that leave us as voice trainers? I think we have to recognise the appeal of individual voices with all their so-called faults and not try to obtain a uniformly "safe" and, therefore, bland voice. We have to encourage speakers to show their personalities, thoughts and feelings through their voices but at the same time to help them to do this without voice damage. We have to assist in the communication of text and to help the actor to be free to be vocally able to achieve whatever their vision dictates without vocal hindrance or pain. This means understanding the circumstances in which they are going to use their voices. A tone suitable for use with a close microphone may not be suitable in a large performing space. Even within the same medium, the voice used for pillow talk may cause vocal damage if used to call the army to battle.

One of my first jobs as an actor, newly out of drama school, was in a film called *Cromwell*. The star of this, Richard Harris, deliberately made himself hoarse by yelling in an old quarry to give himself a rasping voice. It is our job to help actors find whatever quality will best serve their roles without them having to go to these damaging lengths. The strong gravelly tones of the action hero or the husky sexuality of the leading lady will continue to be sexy and to thrill their audiences. We can't change their appeal and we wouldn't want to—but we can be there to give the best vocal advice possible.

Peer Reviewed Article *by Kathryn G. Maes*

Examining the Use of Lessac Exploration in Shakespearean Text

Kathy Maes is the Interim Dean, College of Arts and Media, University of Colorado-Denver. Kathy served as dialect coach for four productions for the Royal Shakespeare Company and co-dialect coach with Joan Washington on the Royal National Theatre's Olivier Award-winning production of Arthur Miller's *American Clock*. Kathy has coached such notable actors as Ralph Fiennes, Brenda Blethyn, Sir John Wood, and Pierce Brosnan. In summer 2003, Kathy served as vocal/dialect coach for Sir Peter Hall Company's in London and Bath, England. She served as Head of Voice at the Denver Center Theatre Company prior to coming to UCD in 1992.

I began studying the Lessac System in 1974 when I attended my first summer intensive workshop in Binghamton, New York. Since that time, I attended a second voice and body intensive workshop in 2002 in Mercersburg, Pennsylvania. This bio-dynamic approach to the human voice and body opened up alternatives to the exploration of text in ways I previously couldn't have imagined possible.

Working with Lessac's three *Derived Energy States* (hereafter referred to as NRG), structural NRG, tonal NRG and consonant NRG, I quickly discovered a new way of exploring Shakespeare's texts. Combining these three vocal NRGs with their allied body NRGs (buoyancy, potency, and radiancy) (Lessac *Body Wisdom* 1990, 34), I began linking the vocal and body explorations and came to realize that my previous interpretation of Shakespeare's text came from the neck up, rather than being integrated throughout my entire body, voice, mind and soul. This system is a true gestalt in every sense of the word. As Arthur Lessac states:

> Vocal life cannot stand alone; it is integrally ensembled with physical life, emotional life, and spiritual life. These entities organically synergize each other so that the combined whole is always fresh, unique, intriguingly creative, and infinitely diverse in its body, voice, and speech communication, transmission, and intelligence gathering....
>
> Body support for creative vocal life implies a perception and awareness of what it is that 'turns you on' and 'tunes you in' when you feel the reality of weightlessness, floating, or smooth-flowing currents inside your body; or when your body experiences 'inner sparks,' humor-sensing, electricity, or childlike eagerness; or when your muscle-yawning strength and power, your ecstasy, or your inner vivid intensity pervades and courses through your body.
>
> (In exploration of text) you will be working with your vocal NRGs more definitively, with more imagery. You'll be more inter-involved with the different qualities of each NRG state, which should lead to deeper sensing, perceiving, and responding. You will learn to 'taste' the 'sound-feel' of the words with more relish and to 'touch' the music of the consonants more evocatively.... (Lessac *Human Voice* 1997, 203, 208-209)

In the Exploration Discoveries presented after each NRG exploration, I will rely heavily on my experiences while personally exploring each piece for the vocal and physical NRGs in the selection. I am not inferring that mine is the definitive and only possible interpretation of this text or character. I am certain that others who have previously undertaken a similar exploration of this text have had far different experiences and interpretations than what I present here, but this is the value of exploration. It will always elucidate a variety of different possibilities, and it is then for the actor and director to choose the most meaningful elements found in the exploration based on the action and objective of the character. Regardless, exploration always has led me to surprising and unexpected meanings that I may well have previously missed through the use of scansion and intellect alone. Lessac exploration incorporates the use of the muscles of the body and face, the vibrations and resonances of the sound, the rhythms created by allowing the various NRGs (both physical and vocal) to activate and inhabit the actor's center. The *memory* of the experience of exploration, therefore, becomes centered in the actor's very being as a *familiar event*, and the recurrence of the activity of exploration will allow the actor to recreate the emotions in the moment-to-moment life of the character.

Before I begin the Lessac exploration, I have undertaken both my character preparation and have fully scanned the text for an understanding of what is being said, the ideas being presented and the issues of debate. When beginning the Lessac exploration, the text is first "scored" by searching out the various NRGs inherent in the text. The structural NRG vowels are identified, thus locating the opportunities for the use of structural NRG found in the text; the opportunities for Tonal NRG are sighted—i.e., finding the vowels in the text that allow the production of the most concentrated sound with the least amount of effort; and the "playable" consonants are discerned which permit the detection of the consonant NRG contained in the text.

I have been asked why the Lessac System doesn't use the IPA in the identification of the sounds of the language rather than the system Lessac has created. Because of the nature of the Lessac training, a notation system was needed that not only identified the sounds, but one that would also support the fundamental constructs of the training. Lessac refers to his training as kinesensic training—i.e., "an intrinsic sensing process where energy qualities are physically felt and perceived, then tuned and used for creative expression." (Lessac *Human Voice* 1997, 3) He created this term "kinesensic" in order "to better describe the neurophysical sensing process: *kine*, for movement and motion; *esens*, for spirit, inner energy involvement; *sic*, for familiar occurrences." (Lessac *Human Voice* 1997, 4) Most vocal training I had previously encountered relied most heavily on an individual's hearing as the means of determining the accuracy and aesthetics of the voice and sound production. Since the Lessac System is based on this *kinesensic* training, auditory monitoring is no longer the primary assessor of the accuracy of sound production. Rather, this system requires that a student learn to rely "on a new sensitivity to—and a new concentration on—other perceptions: the vibratory, kinesthetic, and tactile sensations." (Lessac *Human Voice* 1967, 15-16) The IPA, on the other hand, presents a collection of symbols that represents particular sounds, so it does not address the kinesensic needs of the Lessac System. The Lessac System of notation, then, is a *tono-sensory* indicator that acts as a guide as to how to actually produce the sound, rather than a *phono-sensory* one such as the IPA that just *represents* the sound. In other words, the notation system that was developed by Arthur Lessac is built on a kinesensic rather than a symbolic base alone. For example, the #1 Structural NRG vowel represents a specific size of lip opening which creates a particular shape within the oral cavity. Once phonation is

added to this lip opening and corresponding oral cavity shape, only one vowel sound can be produced. The production of this #1 structural vowel (or u:) is thus produced through a kinesthetic trigger (#1) rather than a memory of how the vowel sounds which is controlled by the ear. This *kinesensic* concept is true of all Lessac notation. This kinesensic-based tono-sensory notation helps in achieving Lessac's objective of "overriding the outer ear." (Lessac *Human Voice* 1997, 18)

In an attempt to make identification clearer for all readers (not just those trained in the Lessac System) and to assist in identifying the repetition of vowel sounds in the selection (i.e., Shakespeare's use of assonance), at first I will use the Lessac numeric notation with an IPA key rather than the notation Lessac usually uses in exploration: 1) structural NRG exploration—a horizontal arc over the structural vowel, and 2) tonal NRG exploration—a heavy dot over the tonal vowel (in the final tonal NRG exploration, however, I have used a simpler means of identifying the tonal NRG vowel similar to Lessac's, i.e., a bold asterisk [*] over the vowel). Additionally, because I am limited to the use of letters and symbols on a standard computer keyboard, I am not able to reproduce the symbols Lessac uses for the consonant NRG exploration, and out of necessity I had to create a parallel system of marking the playable consonants. The goal is to help the reader visually locate the playable consonant possibilities found in the text. I have included the symbols I use with a key that will precede the selection to be explored in the consonant NRG section.

I fully realize what I am attempting to do in the next portion of this article is to explain a process that is so much larger than the simple sum of its parts. It is not my intention to teach the reader how to *do* Lessac exploration, but to underscore how this process can help an actor understand the *meaning* of the text in a more profound and holistic way. It is my intention, therefore, to focus on the *value* of the process rather than on the *mastery* of the process. One must first take the time to learn the Lessac approach before one can begin to incorporate the exploration of text. To any who are unfamiliar with the Lessac work, at first glance this exploration process may appear to be too complicated or too academic for actors. It is quite the contrary, in fact. The Lessac work relies on and expands the actor's kinesthetic sensitivity, and awakens an awareness, perception and comprehension of sound, vibration, and muscle memory that is rooted within the actor's very being. It is a system not limited to—or by—the actor's intellect.

Structural NRG

Structural NRG refers to the mold, shape, and size of the human voice and speech instrument and its sound-box structure. The first step...is to mold and shape the instrument; to establish the form and function of the oral cavity and to develop the optimal facial posture.... (Structural NRG) means three things: (1) the muscle activities in the oral cavity, cheeks, jaw, and lips that control the sound box; (2) the kinesthetic action of perceiving these muscle activities and controlling them through sensory recall; and (3) the kinesensic application of these concepts to our communicating behavior and personality both onstage and offstage....

We all know that the larger the sound box, the fuller, richer, and warmer are the tone and quality emanating from the instrument....a simple experiment will demonstrate that you can and should maintain the cavity size unchanged while sounding all of the ensuing structural vowels—and that you can consistently maintain a sensible and optimal space capacity in the oral-vocal sound box... (Lessac *Human Voice* 1997, 160-61).

If a yawn sensation is induced in the cheek and lip muscles, a comfortable two-finger space between the upper and lower side teeth will result, and:

...you will observe that the muscles within the triangular area of the cheeks—along with the yawn component—control the experiment. There are four muscles on either side of the face: one beginning at the nasal bone just under the eye, one starting from directly under the eye, and two originating at the cheekbone....All of these muscles converge just above the gum ridge and insert bilaterally into the upper portion of the rounded lip muscle. When you extend or elongate these bilateral muscles and add a yawn-felt facial posture, you can easily maintain the maximum space within the oral cavity while reducing the rounded lips to their smallest opening. Be aware that the yawn feel is part of the natural familiar event to teach yourself the structural NRG facial posture....you have created an image of the inverted megaphone shape... (Lessac *Human Voice* 1997, 163)

When the inverted megaphone shape is fully achieved, a space approximately the size of the middle and ring finger will have been created between the upper and lower teeth (referred to as two-finger space). The structural NRG vowels, then, are the result of a specific lip opening, the full inverted megaphone shape (with the full two finger space created between the teeth), and phonation. Phonetically, the structural vowels are designated in numbers, based on the size of the lip opening, going from the smallest lip opening to the largest. They include:

Lessac		IPA
#1	(s*oo*n)	u:
#21	(b*o*ne)	oʊ
#3	(f*a*ll)	ɔ:
#4	(d*o*ll)	ɒ
#5	(f*ar*m)	ɑ:
#51	(h*ow*l)	aʊ
#6	(f*a*st)	a
#3y	(f*oi*l)	ɔɪ
#6y	(f*i*ne)	aɪ
#R/-derivative	(b*ir*d or wid*er*)	ɜ/ɚ

Before beginning this first exploration, a word needs to be said about the use of weak versus strong forms of words. Words like "was" and "and" can—and should—be explored using both the weak and strong pronunciations of the words (i.e., [wɒz – wəz] [ænd – nd]), which I did in my own explorations. I generally found that I gravitated toward the use of the weak form as is evidenced by the markings found in my final trinity exploration.

Constance from *King John*, Act III, Scene 3:

6y 6 4 6   6y   6y
I am not mad. This hair I tear is mine,
6y   4   6y   6y
My name is Constance, I was Geffrey's wife,
      5   6y   6   4
Young Arthur is my son, and he is lost.
6y 6 4 6 6y   1   6y R/
I am not mad, I would to heaven I were!
    3   6y 6y   6y
For then 'tis like I should forget myself.
21 6y   6y
O, if I could, what grief should I forget!....
                  1   6y 6   6y
Grief fills the room up of my absent child,
6y   3   6   51
Lies in his bed, walks up and down with me,
      4   R/
Puts on his pretty looks, repeats his words,

         3   5
Remembers me of all his gracious parts,
    51   5   3
Stuffs out his vacant garments with his form;
     6 6y   1   4
Then, have I reason to be fond of grief?....
21 3   6y 3y 6y 5   6y
O Lord, my boy, my Arthur, my fair son!
  6y 6y   6y 3y 6y 1   6y 3   R/
My life, my joy, my food, my all the world!
  6y   21   6   6y 4 21
My widow-comfort, and my sorrows' cure!

Exploration Discoveries

What is quite striking in the first six lines is the heavy usage of the larger opening structural NRG vowels, especially the #6 and 6y:

6y 6   4   6   6y   6y
I am not mad. This hair I tear is mine,
6y   4   6y   6y
My name is Constance, I was Geffrey's wife,
     5   6y   6   4
Young Arthur is my son, and he is lost.
6y 6   4   6 6y   1   6y R/
I am not mad, I would to heaven I were!
    3   6y 6y   6y
For then 'tis like I should forget myself.
21 6y   6y
O, if I could, what grief should I forget!....

The repeated use of these two structural NRG vowels has always had a strong effect on me in my explorations, both vocally and physically. I first encountered this emotional effect while I was exploring Hermione's speech in *The Winter's Tale*, Act III: Scene 2, which begins:

Sir, spare your threats.

This speech, like the one from *King John*, contains a quantity of structural NRG vowels. It never failed that every time I reached the line in this speech:

        51 6y
        N*ow*, m*y* liege,
           6y 6   6y
Tell me wh*at* blessings *I* have here al*i*ve,
  6 6y   1 6y
Th*at I* should fear t*o* d*i*e....

I would begin to cry. The use of the yawn-stretch in the formation of the structural NRG somehow equated at my center

with Hermione's struggle and grief over the loss of her children. It didn't surprise me, then, when the very same thing happened to me when I began exploring Constance's speech from *King John* with structural NRG. The use of the structural NRG became the familiar event that triggered the response to Constance's pain and grief in the form of tears.

In the second six lines of Constance's speech, there is a lesser number of structural vowels, but there is a heavier use of both consonant NRG and tonal NRG, especially in the Y-buzz, +Y-buzz as will be seen below in the sections relating to tonal NRG:

             1   6y 6   6y
Grief fills the room up of my absent child,
   6y   3   6   51
Lies in his bed, walks up and down with me,
   4   R/
Puts on his pretty looks, repeats his words,
          3   5
Remembers me of all his gracious parts,
     51   5   3
Stuffs out his vacant garments with his form;
     6 6y   1   4
Then, have I reason to be fond of grief?....

It is not uncommon in Shakespeare that when the use of one NRG is lessened then the use of another NRG will increase.

The final three lines of this speech return once again to the focus on the use of structural NRG:

21 3   6y 3y 6y 5   6y
O Lord, my boy, my Arthur, my fair son!
  6y 6y   6y 3y 6y 1   6y 3   R/
My life, my joy, my food, my all the world!
  6y   21   6   6y 4 21
My widow-comfort, and my sorrows' cure!

Note especially:

  6y 6y   6y 3y 6y 1   6y 3   R/
My life, my joy, my food, my all the world!

Every word in the line but one contains some form of a structural vowel. Once again, her pain and grief reaches a new depth and moves into insanity, ultimately resulting in her death.

Tonal NRG

Simply put, tonal NRG allows the creation of the most concentrated and vibratory tone that can be produced with the least amount of effort. Tonal NRG can be achieved on all vowel sounds, extended over the vocal range of the voice. There are two component parts of tonal NRG: 1) The Y-buzz (i:) and it's related variation diphthong the +Y-buzz (eɪ), and 2) the Call (which can be achieved on all other vowels). While the Y-buzz and +Y-buzz support and are developed in the lower third of the vocal range:

> The Call goes beyond the Y-buzz and +Y-buzz in tonal NRG and is designed to expand and develop range, pitch, volume, production, and quality of practically the entire speaking voice, most of the female singing voice, and approximately two-thirds of the male singing voice.

> While the Y-buzz is explored with a reduced facial form and shape and with minimal space between the teeth, the Call technique requires a fuller forward facial posture, a more definite yawn feel, and, therefore, a wider space between the teeth. The Call is precisely that—a calling out—but it is a rounded, robust Call, a ringing Call, a rich Call, a singing Call...

> In practicing the Call sensations, the vowel sounds must be treated with considerable latitude—an approximation is all that is necessary...(as) it (the vowel) will certainly differ phonetically or phonemically from its sound in normal speech.

> The Call is always governed by a characteristic vibratory, ringing sensation—a fully concentrated tonal feeling—that expands the technical and emotional ranges of the voice (Lessac *Human Voice* 1997, 137).

Additionally, there is one rule of thumb that needs to be incorporated in finding pure tonal NRG that applies to both the Call and the Y-buzz: the larger the lip opening, the higher the pitch; the smaller the lip opening, the lower the pitch. Since the Y-buzz and +Y-buzz are found in the lower third of the vocal range, not surprisingly, the Y-buzz vowels (including the +Y-buzz) use a smaller lip opening that is somewhat lateral (not rounded) in shape, with minimal space (approximately one-finger space) between the upper and lower teeth. Calls on structural vowels #1 through #3 and the R-derivative (R/) are also found in a lower range of the voice, though they are pro-duced slightly above the Y-buzz pitch range continuing to mid pitch range of the voice. Since it is most common to use mid to lower range in normal everyday conversation, it is reason-able to assume that these lower number vowels are the most readily and naturally accessible to tonal NRG without significant distortion of the vowel (i.e., a balance is easily found between clarity of the vowel sound and the carrying power of the voice in this pitch range)—though tonal NRG can

be achieved on any vowel. So long as the emotion of the exploration is appropriate and allows the actor to naturally access the vocal range necessary to achieve the Call, the actor should feel free to explore the tonal NRG possibilities on the larger lip opening vowels as well as the more readily accessible smaller lip opening vowels.

Oftentimes, however, rather than choosing to raise the pitch to the required level for the larger lip opening vowel, the actor finds an "emotional" compromise between the necessary pitch and the required lip opening and achieves a "Call-like" tone as a means of keeping the distortion of the vowel to a minimum while producing a more vibrant and ringing tone on the vowel. As the lip opening becomes larger, the pitch will have to rise to accommodate the specific lip opening and space in the oral cavity necessary to achieve pure tonal NRG in order to keep distortion of the vowels to a minimum. To produce the pure Call, in addition to the appropriate lip opening and pitch, the full inverted megaphone (complete with the two-finger space) must be achieved. Additionally, the structural diphthong vowels #51 (aʊ) and 6y (aɪ) will give a "bonus tone" as one moves from the larger lip opening structural vowel to the smaller lip opening structural vowel or to the Y-buzz. As the larger lip opening reduces to the smaller lip opening (e.g. #51 moves from the #5 lip opening to the #1 lip opening), there is a moment when the pitch of the voice finds the appropriate lip opening and a Call is produced, and creates what Lessac refers to as a "bonus tone" on the vowel.

For purposes of clarity, I will focus on the opportunities for *easily* accessible tonal NRG (either achieving the Call or Y-buzz) with minimal distortion found in the mid to lower range in the voice by using the following smaller lip opening vowels:

Lessac		*IPA*
Structural Vowels:		
#1	(s*oo*n)	u:
#3	(f*a*ll)	ɔ:
R/-derivative	(b*ir*d or wid*er*)	ɝ·/ɚ·
Structural Diphthongs:		
#21	(b*o*ne)	oʊ
#51	(n*ow*)	aʊ
#3y	(f*oi*l)	ɔɪ
#6y (bonus tone)	(*ai*sle)	aɪ
yɪ	(c*u*be or men*u*)	ɪu

Y-buzz Vowels:

Y-buzz	(h*ee*d)	i:
+Y-buzz	(m*a*de)	eɪ

Neutral Vowels (or Short Vowels):

N1	(b*oo*k)	ʊ
N2	(h*i*ts)	ɪ
N3	(g*e*ts)	ɛ
N4	(c*u*ps)	ʌ
N4	(*a*bout)	ə

Neutral Diphthongs:

N1n	(p*oor*)	ʊər
N2n	(p*ier*)	ɪər
N3n	(p*ear*)	ɛər
3n	(p*ore*)	ɔər

Constance from *King John* (Act III, Scene 3)

6y N2 N3n N3n N2 6y
I am not mad. This hair I tear is mine

6y +Y N2 N4 6y N4 N3 Y 6y
My name is Constance, I was Geffrey's wife,

N4 N2 6y N4 Y N2
Young Arthur is my son, and he is lost.

6y 6y N1 ɪ N3 R/
I am not mad, I would to heaven I were!

3 N3 N2 6y 6y N1 3 N3 6y N3
For then 'tis like I should forget myself.

21 N2 6y N1 N4 Y N1 6y 3 N3
O, if I could, what grief should I forget!...

Y N2 N4 ɪ N4 N4 6y N3 6y
Grief fills the room up of my absent child,

6y N2 N2 N3 3 N4 51 N2 Y
Lies in his bed, walks up and down with me,

N1 N2 N2 N1 Y Y N2 R/
Puts on his pretty looks, repeats his words,

N2 N3 Y N4 3 N1 +Y N4
Remembers me of all his gracious parts,

N4 51 N2 +Y N4 N3 N2 N2 3
Stuffs out his vacant garments with his form;

N3 6y Y N4 ɪ Y Y
Then, have I reason to be fond of grief?....

21 3 6y 3y 6y 6y N3n N4
O Lord, my boy, my Arthur, my fair son!

6y 6y 6y 3y 6y ɪ 6y 3 N4 R/
My life, my joy, my food, my all the world!

6y N2 21 N4 R/ 6y 21 yɪ
My widow-comfort, and my sorrows' cure!

The marking of the vowels above is the initial way the actor begins a tonal exploration as this helps the actor identify the specific lip opening of the vowel. Once this is done, however, it is easier for the Lessac actor to go through the text once again, marking the easily accessed tonal NRG opportunities with an asterisk (*—or a black dot as Lessac does) over the vowel rather than the specific number of the vowel. Through practice, the visual cue of the location of the opportunity is all the trained Lessac actor will need. Bonus tone will be marked with ^ over the 6y and the #51:

Constance from *King John* (Act III, Scene 3)

^   * * ^ * * ^
I am not mad. This hair I tear is mine

^ * * * ^ * * * ^
My name is Constance, I was Geffrey's wife,

*   * ^ *   * *
Young Arthur is my son, and he is lost.

^   ^ * * * ^ *
I am not mad, I would to heaven I were!

* * * ^ ^ * * * ^ *
For then 'tis like I should forget myself.

* *^ * * * * ^ *
O, if I could, what grief should I forget!....

* * * * * ^ * ^
Grief fills the room up of my absent child,

^ * * * *   ^ * *
Lies in his bed, walks up and down with me,

* * * * * * * *
Puts on his pretty looks, repeats his words,

* * * * * * *
Remembers me of all his gracious parts,

* ^ * * * * * * *
Stuffs out his vacant garments with his form;

*   ^ * * * * * *
Then, have I reason to be fond of grief?...

* * ^ * ^ * ^ * *
O Lord, my boy, my Arthur, my fair son!

^ ^ ^ * ^ * * * *
My life, my joy, my food, my all the world!

^ * * * * ^ * *
My widow-comfort, and my sorrows' cure!

Exploration Discoveries

The first thing to observe is that there is a large number of vowels with lower number lip openings—structural vowels, Y-buzz related vowels, neutral vowels, and neutral diphthong vowels. There are also numerous opportunities for bonus tone, especially through the repetitive use of the 6y—28 times in total—14 times in the word "my, myself, and mine"; ten times in the word "I." Tonal NRG is rooted in power of the voice, concentration of the tone, and the strong vibrations of the sound being produced.

Through my tonal NRG explorations of this piece, I have found that it allows me to easily connect with Constance's enormous strength which has been put to the test beyond human endurance. The opening line contains none of these easily accessible tonal vowels (with the exception of some bonus tone), but it is loaded with structural vowels which help me connect with and reveal her pain and grief. With the beginning of the second half of line 1—

N2 N3n 6y N3n N2 6y
This hair I tear   is mine,
6y +Y N2   N4 6y   N3 Y 6y
My name is Constance, I was Geffrey's wife,
N4   N2 6y N4   Y N2
Young Arthur is my son, and he is lost.

through my tonal exploration, I discovered that Constance has moved beyond her pain (structural NRG) to clarity of thought with a full grasp of the reality of her situation. As the selection goes on—

6y   6y N1   1 N3 6y R/
I am not mad, I would to heaven I were!

I discovered a change in the structural NRG from pain and grief to adamant statement of fact ("I am not mad,") which builds through the tonal NRG to an anger filled with irony. The following two lines are full of short vowel sounds and four structural vowels (all easily accessible for tonal NRG as well as structural NRG), and the exploration tended to allow me to incorporate both NRGs giving her the freedom to experience the pain and grief as well as the reality of her loss and her current situation:

3 N3 N2 6y 6y N1   3 N3 6y N3
For then 'tis like I should forget myself.
21 N2 6y N1 N4 Y N1 6y 3 N3
O, if I could, what grief should I forget!

The following six lines seemed to me to take Constance in a new direction being comforted by her clear memory of her lost child:

Y N2 N4   1 N4 N4 6y N3 6y
Grief fills the room up of my absent child,
6y N2 N2 N3   3 N4   51 N2 Y
Lies in his bed, walks up and down with me,
N1   N2 N2 N1 Y Y N2 R/
Puts on his pretty looks, repeats his words,
N2 N3   Y   3 N1 +Y N4
Remembers me of all his gracious parts,
N4   51 N2 +Y N4   N3 N2 N2 3
Stuffs out his vacant garments with his form;
N3   6y Y N4 1 Y   N4   Y
Then, have I reason to be fond of grief?

The tonal vibrations I experience are particularly strong and are notably reinforced through the repetition of the Y-buzz vowels. Additionally, the "bonus tone" words (i.e., "my," "child," "Lies," and "I"—all 6y) all have a short Y-buzz as a component of the diphthong which can be accessed as tonal NRG by allowing the pitch of the voice to enter the lower third of the range as the word is uttered. These vibrations from the Y-buzz vowels and the Calls on the smaller lip opening vowels and neutral diphthongs (especially the #1, #3, N1, and N2) stirred a sense of comfort and consolation in my exploration in this section of the piece.

Finally, in the last three lines—

21 3   6y 3y 6y 5   R/ 6y N3n N4
O Lord, my boy, my Arthur, my fair son!
6y 6y 6y 3y 6y 1   6y 3 N4 R/
My life, my joy, my food, my all the world!
6y N2 21 N4 R/   6y   21 y1
My widow-comfort, and my sorrows' cure!

there is a return of the heavy use of structural/tonal NRG vowels, again reviving for me her conflict between the near insanity of her pain and grief versus the clear realization of her loss. At that moment, it became clear to me that her sanity, irretrievably, was lost.

Consonant NRG

To Arthur Lessac:

Consonants are the anatomical 'spine' of words in vocal life. They are the interpreters that convey the meaning of speech—they make the spoken word intelligible. But they are also the instruments that provide musical accompaniment to speech; they produce rhythmic patterns, melodies, and sustained tonal colors. They provide contrasts and variations. To the single sustained note of the vowels they add percussion and sound effects. They can also bring healthful, enlivening energy to our speech when they are felt, tasted, and enjoyed as sensory, or kinesensic, experience.

Consonants form the skeletal structure of words and are responsible for intelligibility....Although there is room for error in the formation of vowel sounds, there is none in the formation of consonant sounds (Lessac *Human Voice* 1997, 67).

Lessac's view as to the musicality of the consonants extends to his creation of a consonant orchestra:

Once you learn how to produce the feel of the orchestral consonants, you can focus your attention on playing them lightly, smoothly—musically.

The instrumental approach is most important where a consonant precedes another consonant or is the final sound before a pause or semipause....The consonant before a sounded vowel, however, requires less attention because the vowel that follows maintains the vocal line and keeps the sound of the whole syllable moving forward....

(The consonant orchestra contains)...a full complement of strings, drums, woodwinds, and cymbals and a fair representation of sound effects and brass (Lessac *Human Voice* 1997, 68-69).

Consonant NRG, then, is found by identifying the "playable" consonants when: 1) they are the final sound on the word followed by a pause, or 2) they precede another consonant.

I have also found that one of the most significant advantages to this musical approach to consonant NRG is it will invariably help student actors break locked-in, habitual rhythm patterns. Further, since there is such variety in the rhythm patterns in the production of consonants (i.e., some are sustainable and some are percussive), this allows a student actor to explore these differences as they are found in the words, and provides an opportunity to connect with the emotion experienced in the production of the sound itself and as it releases its NRG within the word. I often remind my students that: "Once you have uttered a word it becomes history—and you can no longer kinesensically experience the meaning and emotion of the word you just uttered. This can only happen at the moment you articulate the word." This is what I understand that Cicely Berry means when she talks about the "energy of the word" (Berry *Voice* 1973, 43).

The following is a key to the symbols used in the consonant NRG exploration. Hopefully it will help the reader create a visual image of the rhythmic possibilities found within the text of Constance's speech:

Consonant NRG Key:

1. Sustainable consonant—   so**N**
   (consonant played capitalized and underlined, both in bold)
2. Percussive consonant—   ma<u>d</u>
   (consonant played underlined)
3. Direct link—   Arthur~is
   (~ in bold connects a final consonant that is linked to an initial vowel)
4. Play and Link—   no**t~m**ad
   (consonant played underlined with ~ connecting to the following consonant, all in bold)
5. Prepare and Link—   woul**d~t**o
   (~ connects consonant prepared with the underlined consonant that is fully released, all in bold)
6. Two Consonants that are playable are separated by /

Constance from *King John* (Act III, Scene 3):

I a**M** no**t~m**a<u>d</u>. Thi**S** hair~I tear~i**S** mi<u>**N**</u>e,

My name~i**S** Co<u>**N**</u>/**S**ta<u>**N**</u>/**C**e, I wa**S** Ge**FF**rey'**S** wi**F**e,

Young~Arthur~i**S** my so<u>**N**</u>, a<u>**N**</u>/**d~h**e i**S** lo**S**/<u>t</u>.

I a**M** no**t~m**a<u>d</u>, I woul**d~t**o heaven~I were!

For~the<u>**N**</u> 'ti**S** like~I shoul**d~f**orge**t~m**yse**L**/**F**.

O, if~I coul<u>d</u>, wha**t~g**rie**F** should~I forge<u>t</u>!....

Grief~**fi**<u>**LL**</u>/**S** the room~up~o**F** my abse**Nt~chi**<u>**L**</u>/<u>d</u>,

Lies~i<u>**N**</u> hi**S** be<u>d</u>, wal<u>k</u>s~up~a**Nd~d**ow<u>**N**</u> wi**TH** me,

Puts~o<u>**N**</u> hi**S** pretty loo<u>k</u>/**S**, repea<u>t</u>s~hi**S** wor<u>d</u>s,

Reme**M**ber**S** me of~a<u>**LL**</u> hi**S** graciou**S** par<u>t</u>s,

Stu**FF**s~ou<u>t</u>~hi**S** vaca<u>**N**</u>/<u>t</u>~garme<u>**N**</u>/ts wi**TH** hi**S** for**M**;

The<u>**N**</u>, have~I reaso<u>**N**</u> to be fo**Nd~o**F grie**F**?...

O Lor<u>d</u>, my boy, my Arthur, my fair so<u>**N**</u>!

My li**F**e, my joy, my foo**d**, my a**LL** the wor**L**/**d**!

My widow-co**M**for**t**, a**N**/**d** my sorrow**S**' cure!

Exploration Discoveries

I found that the consonant NRG exploration in the first three lines revealed yet another side of Constance's emotions. Through the predominance of fricative (e.g., Z bass fiddle, S sound effect, and F sound effect) and nasal (M viola and N violin) sounds, I discovered a strong sense of her agitation and anger in this opening section:

I a**M** not~**m**a**d**. Thi**S** hair~I tear~i**S** mi**N**e,

My name~i**S** Co**N**/**S**ta**N**/**C**e, I wa**S** Ge**FF**rey'**S** wi**F**e,

Young~Arthur~i**S** my so**N**, a**N**/**d**~he i**S** lo**S**/**t**.

While some consonant NRG exists in the next three lines, it became clear to me through my exploration that the structural NRG takes the lead, followed by the tonal NRG. The consonant NRG seemed to lose an emotional focus or center, as the playable consonants did not have a notable or remarkable pattern.

The next six lines, however, exploded once again for me with the vibration of the fricatives and nasals, with heavy emphasis on the Z bass fiddle and the S sound effect, supported further by the F sound effect and TH clarinet:

Grie**f**~**fiLL**/**S** the room~up~o**F** my a**b**se**Nt**~**chi**L/**d**,

Lies~i**N** hi**S** be**d**, wal**ks**~up~a**Nd**~**d**ow**N** wi**TH** me,

Puts~o**N** hi**S** pretty loo**k**/**S**, repea**ts**~hi**S** wor**ds**,

Reme**M**ber**S** me of~a**LL** hi**S** graciou**S** par**ts**,

Stu**FF**s~ou**t**~hi**S** vaca**N**/**t**~garme**N**/**ts** wi**TH** hi**S** for**M**;

The**N**, have~I reaso**N** to be fo**N**d~o**F** grie**F**?...

What I discovered that was different in this section compared to the first three lines was the consonant NRG shifted the emotion from one of anger to one of soothing, consolation and comfort of Constance's loss. These emotions were further reinforced by the vibratory sensations of the N violins and M violas.

Finally, the last three lines once again had very few significant playable consonants, with two extraordinary exceptions: the

sustainable F sound effect in the word "life" and the M viola in the word "comfort." Both words took on a vital new emotional meaning for me, both of which are at the core of her loss.

Trinity Exploration

The final step—the trinity explorations using all three vocal NRGs—in the exploration process is best expressed in Arthur Lessac's own words:

> Communicate and perform with your own unencumbered, undirected, indulgently personal trinity exploration—with full options!...
>
> As you become totally involved with the moment-to-moment reality, let the NRG you intuitively feel do the leading; let the interpretation and the use of the NRGs remain free and unstructured...let your vocal life both inspire and express your emotional life....
>
> Take a risk! If you never take a risk, if you never violate the rules of taste, order, or form, you will never truly investigate the range of possibilities within a role or, more importantly, within yourself. The new, the exciting, and the true often lie outside the accepted boundaries....
>
> When vocal life takes its proper place in this trinity, it both expresses and helps to create emotional life; it becomes a discriminating force that explores the possibilities and determines the degree and quality of an actor's emotional life onstage (Lessac *Human Voice* 1997, 223-24).

The following represents a trinity exploration based on the discoveries I had made through my previous structural, tonal, and consonant NRG explorations. The use of structural NRG will be marked with the appropriate structural vowel; the use of tonal NRG will be marked by an * above the opportunity for a Call, and a Y-buzz and +Y-buzz will be indicated by a Y or +Y; and the use of consonant NRG will be marked as indicated by the Key presented in the consonant NRG section:

Constance from *King John* (Act III, Scene 3)

```
6y 6   4     6                        6y
I aM not~mad. ThiS hair~I tear~iS miNe,
   6y  +Y                          *      6y
My name~iS CoN/StaN/Ce, I waS GeFFrey'S wiFe,
        5                            4
Young~Arthur~iS my soN, aN/d~he iS loS/t.
        ^   *        *             *
I aM not~mad, I would~to heaven~I were!
```

```
    3              6y        *  *       *
For~the**N** 'ti**S** like~I shoul**d**~for_forget_~myse**L**/**F**.
 21            *                    6y      *
O, if~I coul**d**, wha**t**~grie**F** should~I forge**t**!....
     Y      *      1        6y         6y
Grief~**fiLL**/**S** the room~up~o**F** my abse**Nt**~**chiL**/**d**,
 6y          4          51           Y
Lies~i**N** hi**S** be**d**, wal**ks**~up~a**Nd**~**d**ow**N** wi**TH** me,
                   Y   Y    *     *
Puts~o**N** hi**S** pretty loo**k**/**S**, repea**ts**~hi**S** wor**ds**,
   Y    R/  Y           +Y      5
Reme**M**ber**S** me of~a**LL** hi**S** graciou**S** par**ts**,
            +Y       5                3
Stu**FF**s~ou**t**~hi**S** vaca**N**/**t**~garme**N**/**ts** wi**TH** hi**S** for**M**;
         6    Y      Y   4
The**N**, have~I reaso**N** to be fo**Nd**~o**F** grie**F**?...
    *    *   6y  3y   6y  5   *  6y  *
O Lor**d**, my boy, my Arthur, my fair so**N**!
 6y 6y 6y  3y 6y  *   6y  *        *
My li**F**e, my joy, my foo**d**, my a**LL** the worL/**d**!
 6y      *         6      4   21    *
My widow-co**M**for**t**, a**N**/**d** my sorrow**S**' cure!
```

Enjoy these explorations! Don't shy away from the outrageous or lose your curiosity regarding them. At the same time, never distort or regiment them into preconceived or habit-patterned, imitative, mechanistic exercises; these are actor's explorations in search of unrevealed subtext, yet 'unborn' inner images, and brand new discoveries. The search requires a constant connection with your innocent and your healthy, vulnerable imagination and innovative originality. Surprise, excitement, and unanticipated energy surges with them (Lessac *Human Voice* 1997, 210).

In my experience, I find that once these exploratory discoveries have been made, the energy of the discovery is retained, and it fully innervates the iambic pentameter—and certainly does not distort or eliminate it! The Lessac exploration infuses Shakespeare's language and emotion with life and vitality *within* the framework of the given rhythm of Shakespeare's poetry which often changed in order to reveal the emotional life of the character. The Lessac exploration only helps support the information Shakespeare's rhythm is revealing.

Bringing Scansion and Lessac Exploration Together

As can be seen through the individual explorations of structural, tonal and consonant NRG, structural and tonal NRG will reveal Shakespeare's use of assonance, while consonant NRG reveals the poetic use of consonance within his work. Scansion on its own will help the actor determine what possibilities Shakespeare had in mind as far as what might be stressed within a line leading to clarity of meaning, which will assist the actor in making specific choices of action. Since scansion has latitude as to how a given line may be scanned following my keys dictated by the standard rules of scansion, there is rarely only one choice that can be made. Did Shakespeare realize that great acting is based on an actor's ability to make great choices? Did he consciously write his poetry in such a way as to make certain that these varieties of choices were there to be made? The more I work with Shakespeare's text, the more inclined I am to answer "yes" to both questions.

Some may be concerned that the Lessac exploration appears to artificially work against the natural rhythm of the iambic pentameter in Shakespeare's poetry. Admittedly, in the early exploration phase it might well have this effect on the natural rhythm inherent in the poetry of Shakespeare. The goal of the Lessac exploration at this stage, however, is to fully open up the possibilities of the sounds, language, imagery and vocal NRGs, and discover how these elements holistically and organically are integrated into the meaning, emotion and the character. As Lessac instructs:

Bibliography

Berry, Cicely. *Voice and the Actor*. London, England: George G. Harrap & Company, 1973.

Lessac, Arthur. *Body Wisdom: The Use and Training of the Human Body*. Second Edition. San Bernardino, CA: Lessac Institute Publishing Company, 1990.

Lessac, Arthur. *The Use and Training of the Human Voice*. New York, NY: DBS Publications, Inc./Drama Book Specialists, 1967.

Lessac, Arthur. *The Use and Training of the Human Voice*. Mountain View, CA: Mayfield Publishing Company, 1997.

Essay *by Charmian Hoare*

Pronouncing Shakespeare: The Globe's Production of Romeo & Juliet

Charmian trained at the Central School of Speech and Drama gaining a Bachelors of Education from London University and the Advanced Certificate in Voice Studies. She has taught at the Guildhall School of Music and Drama, RADA, and Penn State University. Since 1990, she has taught and coached both voice and dialects at the Royal Shakespeare Company. She has also worked profusely in British theatre. Most recently she worked on the RSC production of *Coriolanus* which also played at the Kennedy Center in Washington and the London production of the *Lord of the Rings*. Her film work includes *An Ideal Husband, Scandal, Othello* and *The Butcher Boy*. She also spent a season working at the Festival Theatre in Stratford, Ontario.

This article is an account of my experience of working on the original pronunciation (OP) of Shakespeare with David Crystal in the summer of 2004 at Shakespeare's Globe in London. I will not be describing the particular features of OP or the background to the research material used. I leave all that up to David in his excellent book *Pronouncing Shakespeare* (Cambridge, 2005), which includes a full phonetic transcription of OP and description of the Globe Experience. What follows is the dialect coach's story and the process that I went through to interpret, communicate and teach David's wonderful work to the actors.

Early in the summer of 2004 Mark Rylance, then artistic director of Shakespeare's Globe, rang to check my availability. He was looking for a dialect coach who could become part of a team of specialists who were going to teach and help to produce a production of *Romeo and Juliet* spoken entirely in the original pronunciation of Shakespeare. The production (in modern pronunciation) was already in rehearsal at that point and would play as part of the regular repertory, but at some point during the run there would be four special performances of the play spoken in the original pronunciation.

This was a very unusual request and, although I had been teaching dialects and accents for over twenty years, I had never been asked to do this before. It was also a form of speech that I was unfamiliar with. I had heard John Barton's original pronunciation while working at the RSC but had never had the opportunity to study it or teach it to others. Not only was it a sound completely unfamiliar to me but it was also a sound for which there was no reference. As far as I was concerned it was a "text book" sound created by academics and linguists and I wasn't too sure if it had any relevance to the speaking of modern Shakespeare.

However not being someone who turns a good job down, not least the opportunity to work at the Globe, I accepted and found myself called in to a meeting shortly after with the director Tim Carroll and David Crystal, the linguist and creator of the original pronunciation that we were going to use. I was immediately put at ease. David was a delightful man with a passion for language and a deep love and knowledge of Shakespeare. He was also an expert in the original pronunciation of Shakespeare and would be our teacher and guide on this project.

He had transcribed the whole of the play into phonetics, and my job would be to act as a translator or interpreter for the actors. I would take the transcription and teach it to the actors in a very similar way that I would any other accent. Sessions would be fitted around their busy performance schedule and then Tim would direct a couple of runs to put the whole piece together with David and me in attendance. So far so good.

However, there were several points that caused me concern.

The transcription would inform us of the specific vowel shifts and consonant placements, and we had the iambic to lay down the rhythm, but because this was not a living accent there was no record of the tune or intonation;

nothing for the actors to identify the accent with and no tapes of native speakers for them to listen to. A hard task for both myself and the actors. They would have to rely on David and me. Would that be enough?

I was also very concerned that the original pronunciation was going to be introduced to the actors well after the rehearsal period was over and the production was up and running. I've always thought the learning of an accent should be embedded into the rehearsal process so character and voice can grow together organically. I couldn't envisage how this would work, and realized that it would need an enormous amount of good-will and co-operation from company members but that, nevertheless, it would be a very hard task and could cause serious problems.

Another concern was a simple one shared by both David and Tim. Would it work and was it possible to speak Shakespeare in the original pronunciation and make it still relevant and accessible to a modern audience? Would they understand it?

I also had one final concern and that was for myself. Would I be able to learn the OP in time to teach it with confidence and familiarity? As it happened, I reverted to an old teaching technique—a recognizable one to many—which was to be one step ahead of the actors in every session and to make each session a learning experience for all of us, including myself, and somehow it seemed to work!

So having committed myself to the project, work commenced. Some of my concerns were addressed and answered by David but others would have to wait until I started working with the actors. David immediately cleared up the problem of the intonation. He had a very free and open attitude to the speaking of the original pronunciation. He always said that Elizabethans weren't as "bound" by rules of speech as we are and he encouraged all the actors to bring their own regional tones and tunes to the OP. He said that at the court of Queen Elizabeth there would have been many regional speakers and that there was no set "standard speech" at that time—no "Queen's English" or "Received Pronunciation." This he claimed would give us the permission to add our own regional overtones to the accent while still following the guidelines of the vowel and consonant placements that he described. He also suggested that the speech was generally less articulate—certain medial consonants being dropped, the /h/ consonant dropped and final "ing" becoming "in"; fortunately he agreed with me that certain consonants particularly the /h/ should be maintained for clarity, but it was interesting to know that a more casual, less "reverential" approach was taken to the speaking of the text originally and reminded me of Cicely

Juliet Rylance (Cressida) and David Sturzaker (Troilus) in *Troilus and Cressida* at Shakespeare's Globe, 2005. Photo by Stephen Vaughan.

Berry's work, always encouraging the actor to make the language their own and to speak it through their own natural voice and regional sound.

So work commenced with the actors. David produced the full phonetic version of the text on the first day of rehearsal and the actors freaked! Once we'd calmed them down and reassured them that they didn't have to become phonetic experts and that I would be acting as their interpreter things settled. David taught them some basic phonetics to explain the various vowel shifts and consonant changes and by the end of the first session they were reciting the prologue to *Romeo and Juliet* in perfect OP.

For the next six weeks I continued the work in groups and individual sessions, assisted by David's fantastic recording of the whole play in OP which remedied my concern about not having any native speakers for the actors to listen to. His recording was incredibly helpful and gave the actors the reference point that they needed.

During our time together the actors responded in all sorts of different ways. On the whole with good will and enthusiasm; but, as I had expected, for many it was a hard task, and even a very frustrating one for some whose performance depended on the voice quality and accent that they had chosen for the production in modern pronunciation. To suddenly change that choice of voice would inevitably change the whole nature of the performance and character and did cause concern and some confusion.

This happened particularly with the character roles. For instance, the actor who played the nurse in a broad London accent found that his performance changed completely when speaking in the OP. The London nurse was a harder more urban, "street-wise" character whereas the OP nurse had a more earthy, rounded, softer feel to her, so inevitably this was going to affect the performance. This was a dilemma we had to face and deal with on this particular project but which I thought would not be a problem the following year, when we did a production of *Troilus and Cressida* in the OP from start to finish. But yet again there were problems where actors really didn't see their characters speaking in this particular way and wondered how they were going to realize a truthful performance speaking in a tongue that had no reality or reference point for them. Some actors really struggled to accomplish this and maybe never felt entirely comfortable with their performance and use of OP.

Other actors, like our Scottish Juliet and our Northern Irish Peter, really loved the sound of the OP and in some way it allowed them to really explore and enjoy their own accents through this other sound. They brought their own Celtic tunes and placement to the accent with great success.

Interestingly enough I think the actors who enjoyed the accent most were those for whom RP was their native accent. For them this completely foreign dialect gave them a vocal freedom that they had never experienced before. I heard new resonances and more released sound from many of the actors. The language had a freshness and vitality to it that I hadn't heard before. Using the post vocalic /r/ really helped to define the language and give it new weight and texture. And I think, like children who on discovering the sound of a new word love to play with it, the actors found a playfulness with these new sounds. And unlike learning a specific dialect where one feels an obligation to "get it right" there really was no such pressure with the OP. As David kept on telling us, "Who in the audience would be able to judge?" And that was certainly true.

After two great runs in the rehearsal room it seemed like everything was ready. My next concern was for the audience.

How would they receive it and more important would they understand all of it? Chief of these problems was the very foreign sounding pronunciation of certain words like /flo:r/ for "flower" and /di:l/ for "devil." Would they understand such words? Then there was the ambiguity created by the /i:/ vowel moving to /e:/ in all positions—so /ni:d/ ("need") becomes /ne:d/ and /si:d/ ("seed") becomes /se:d/, /fi:ld/ ("field") becomes /fe:ld/—this could completely change the sense of the line. Actors were sensitive to the problem and on the whole changed the word back to the modern one if it was essential for meaning to be maintained. However, when we did hear this new language it was rather like hearing Chaucer read in the original; there is a sound and music to it that brings a freshness and originality to the text, draws one in and makes one listen and work a bit harder, and I think our audience enjoyed doing just that!

And so the four performances were completed. We had two wonderful discussion events between actors, Tim, David, myself and the audience, at which Cicely Berry was present. Feedback on the whole was generous. Out of the many points raised at the discussions one comment stands out and that is that many people enjoyed an "RP free" production. Rather like going to a concert and hearing a fresh piece of music, they had enjoyed hearing this new sound and I think it had made them listen to the text in a different way.

For me this doesn't necessarily mean that we have to do every production of Shakespeare in OP to find a freshness in the text. Far from it. The lesson for me is that, as always, the language is the key into the play and if we ignore it or allow the language to become stale and inactive then we lose that vital physical connection with our audience that vocally draws them into the world of the play. And it really doesn't matter what language or accent is brought to the text, it's our connection to the word which is all important.

❧

Rebusing the Fartuous Word: Malaforms and Malaprops in Shakespeare

You won't find the word "malaforms" in the dictionary, but it most certainly ought to be there.

What do I mean by a malaform?

A malaform is the unintended creation of a new word by a speaker who has mangled the pronunciation of a perfectly good existing word.

A good example of a malaform in Shakespeare is this line spoken by Dogberry, in *Much Ado About Nothing*:

> *Dogberry*: Adieu. Be vigitant, I beseech you.　　　*ADO* 3.3.94

Dogberry's mangling of the perfectly good word "vigilant" into a word that does not appear in any dictionary is what I would call a malaform.

But isn't that a malaprop, you ask? Well, yes and no.

Let me explain the distinction I'm advocating between a *malaform* and a *malaprop* by first reviewing the history and use of the malaprop.

The word *malaprop*, you will remember, originally comes from the French *mal à propos*, meaning inappropriate. The use of the term malaprop to describe perfectly good words used imperfectly can be traced back to the appearance of Mrs. Malaprop in 1775 in the play *The Rivals*, by Richard Brinsley Sheridan.

Most of Mrs. Malaprop's verbal gaffes still resonate in the theatre as if they were written for a hot new TV sitcom, like this one:

> *Mrs. Malaprop*: He is the very **pine-apple** of politeness!

She means "pinnacle," of course, not pineapple. Here's another doozy:

> *Mrs. Malaprop*: She's as headstrong as an **allegory** on the banks of the Nile.
>   (*She means alligator*)

Since *The Rivals*, most people know a malaprop when they hear one, and many can be heard in modern life. The living baseball legend Yogi Berra is famous for making ludicrous statements such as this:

> It ain't the heat; it's the **humility**.
>   (*He means humidity*)

And modern politicians are often found guilty of mouthing this type of misstatement:

> *Dan Quayle*: Republicans understand the importance of **bondage** between
>   a mother and child.　　　　　(*He means bond*)

Scott Kaiser is Head of Voice and Text at the Oregon Shakespeare Festival in Ashland, where he has served as Voice and Text Director on over 80 productions. He is the author of two books, *Shakespeare's Wordcraft*, published by Limelight Editions, and *Mastering Shakespeare: An Acting Class in Seven Scenes*, published by Allworth Press. Both texts are being used in actor training programs throughout the United States. Scott has also created several critically acclaimed adaptations for the theatre, including *Splittin' the Raft*, a retelling of the Huck Finn story through the eyes of African-American abolitionist Frederick Douglass.

Our forty-third president has created a cottage industry with his prolific use of malaprops, which have been faithfully recorded in Jacob Weisberg's book *Bushisms*:

> *George W. Bush*: Reading is the **basics** for all learning.
>   (*He means basis*)

> *George W. Bush*: We cannot let terrorists and rogue nations hold this nation hostile or hold our allies **hostile**.
>   (*He means hostage*)

> *George W. Bush*: I am mindful not only of preserving executive powers for myself, but for **predecessors** as well.   (*He means successors*)

Of course, Shakespeare, never having seen *The Rivals*, and never having heard George W. Bush, would not have called these slips of the tongue *malaprops*.

According to Sister Miriam Joseph, in her sublime study *Shakespeare's Use of the Arts of Language*, he might have known them as a form of the rhetorical device *cacozelia*. Sister Miriam defines *cacozelia* as "the ignorant misapplication of words," such as in this line, where Dogberry unwittingly misapplies not just one word, but two:

> *Dogberry*: Marry, sir, I would have some **confidence** with you that **discerns** you nearly.   *ADO* 3.5.2
>   (*He means conference and concerns*)

Another definition of cacozelia is provided by Richard A. Lanham in his book *A Handlist of Rhetorical Terms*: "a vulgar error through an attempt to seem learned," which Dogberry demonstrates in this example:

> *Dogberry*: Comparisons are **odorous**.   *ADO* 3.5.16
>   (*He means odious*)

Or, Shakespeare might have studied the rhetorical figure *acyron* in school, which Sister Miriam defines as "the use of a word repugnant or contrary to what is meant," as in this Dogberry example:

> *Dogberry*: Dost thou not **suspect** my place? Dost thou not **suspect** my years?   *ADO* 4.2.74
>   (*He means respect*)

No matter what he called them, Shakespeare loved to use them. Most often we hear them in the comedies, with characters like Dogberry, who proves, without question, that

he is the very pine-apple of Shakespeare's malaprop-makers in examples like these:

> *Dogberry*: You are thought here to be the most **senseless** and fit man for the constable of the watch; therefore bear you the lantern.   *ADO* 3.3.23
>   (*He means sensible*)

> *Dogberry*: Only get the learned writer to set down our **excommunication**, and meet me at the jail.   *ADO* 3.5.63
>   (*He means examination, or communication?*)

> *Dogberry*: O villain! Thou wilt be condemned into everlasting **redemption** for this.   *ADO* 4.2.57
>   (*He means damnation*)

> *Dogberry*: By this time our sexton hath **reformed** Signor Leonato of the matter.   *ADO* 5.1.254
>   (*He means informed*)

Bottom, of course, is the other champion mal-appropriator, as illuminated in these examples from *A Midsummer Night's Dream*:

> *Bottom*: But I will **aggravate** my voice so that I will roar you as gently as any sucking dove. I will roar you an 'twere any nightingale.   *MND* 1.2.81
>   (*He means moderate, or mitigate*)

> *Bottom*: We will meet, and there we may rehearse most **obscenely** and courageously.   *MND* 1.2.108
>   (*Perhaps Bottom means unseen, without being seen?*)

> *Bottom*: O, wherefore, Nature, didst thou lions frame, Since lion vile hath here **deflower'd** my dear
>   (*He means devoured*)   *MND* 5.1.292

> *Bottom*: But I pray you, let none of your people stir me. I have an **exposition** of sleep come upon me.
>   (*He means disposition*)   *MND* 4.1.39

Launcelot Gobbo and his father clearly share a genetic propensity for malaprop-making, as seen in these examples from *The Merchant of Venice*:

> *Gobbo*: He hath a great **infection**, sir, as one would say, to serve.   *MV* 2.2.125
>   (*He means affection*)

Launcelot: In very brief, the suit is **impertinent** to myself, as your worship shall know by this honest old man
(*He means pertinent*)   *MV* 2.2.137

Gobbo: That is the very **defect** of the matter, sir.
(*He means effect*)   *MV* 2.2.143

Launcelot: I do beseech you, sir, go. My young master doth expect your **reproach**.   *MV* 2.5.20
(*He means approach*)

And Elbow, like Dogberry, enforces the law with these pronouncements in *Measure for Measure*:

Elbow: My wife, sir, whom I **detest** before heaven and your honor—   *MM* 2.1.69
(*He means protest*)

Elbow: I do lean upon justice, sir, and do bring in here before your good honor two notorious **benefactors**.
(*He means malefactors*)   *MM* 2.1.50

Elbow: First, and it like you, the house is a **respected** house; next, this is a **respected** fellow; and his mistress is a **respected** woman.   *MM* 2.1.162
(*He means suspected*)

Costard reaches above his station with these winners in *Love's Labor's Lost*:

Costard: Sir, the **contempts** thereof are as touching me.
(*He means contents*)   *LLL* 1.1.190

Costard: And therefore welcome the sour cup of **prosperity**.
(*He means adversity*)   *LLL* 1.1.313

And Launce delivers these ill tidings in *Two Gentlemen of Verona*:

Launce: Sir, there is a proclamation that you are **vanished**.
(*He means banished*)   *TGV* 3.1.218

The Merry Wives of Windsor boasts several superb malapropmakers, such as Bardolph, who stumbles over his tale with this retort:

Bardolph: Why, sir, for my part, I say the gentleman had drunk himself out of his **five sentences**.
(*He means five senses*)   *WIV* 1.1.175

Or, the Host of The Garter Inn, who serves up this palatable sample:

Host: For the which, I will be thy **adversary** toward Anne Page.   *WIV* 2.3.94
(*He means emissary, or advocate?*)

Or Slender, a suitor to Anne Page, who makes this engaging statement:

Slender: But if you say, "Marry her," I will marry her; that I am freely **dissolved**, and **dissolutely**. *WIV* 1.1.251
(*He means resolved and resolutely*)

Or Mistress Quickly, who puts out these juicy morsels:

Quickly: She does so take on with her men; they mistook their **erection**.   *WIV* 3.5.40
(*She means direction*)

Quickly: Good faith, it is such another Nan; but, I **detest**, an honest maid as ever broke bread. *WIV* 1.4.150
(*She means protest*)

Shakespeare did not restrict his use of malaprops to the comedies alone. They appear in the histories as well, such as when the self-same Quickly commits these verbal misdemeanors in *Henry the Fourth, Part Two*:

Hostess Quickly: And he is **indited** to dinner to the Lubber's Head in Lumbert Street, to master Smooth's, the silkman.   *2H4* 2.1.28
(*She means invited*)

Hostess Quickly: Murder! Murder! Ah, thou **honeysuckle** villain, wilt thou kill God's officers and the King's?
(*Perhaps she means homicidal?*)   *2H4* 2.1.50

This vice of Quickly's continues after marriage, in *Henry the Fifth*:

Hostess: O well-a-day, Lady, if he be not hewn now, we shall see willful **adultery** and murder committed.
(*Perhaps she means assault, or battery?*)   *H5* 2.1.37

Shakespeare also used malaprops in his romances. The Clown in *The Winter's Tale* offers up this jewel:

Clown: Ay; or else 'twere hard luck, being in so **preposterous estate** as we are.   *WT* 5.2.148
(*He means prosperous a state*)

And sometimes malaprops worm their way into Shakespeare's tragedies, such as when the Clown slays 'em with this one in *Antony and Cleopatra*:

Clown: Truly I have him, but I would not be the party that should desire you to touch him, for his biting is **immortal**. Those that do die of it do seldom or never recover. *ANT* 5.2.247
(*He means mortal, or deadly*)

Each of these examples contains a malaprop, because, as the *OED* says, it demonstrates a "ludicrous misuse of words, especially in mistaking a word for another resembling it."

A *malaform*, on the other hand, is the unintentional *distortion* of a word or phrase, often with humorous consequences.

In other words, where a *malaprop* is the imperfect use of perfectly good words, a *malaform* is the mangling of perfectly good words into imperfect ones.

Once again, for modern examples, it is easiest to cite statements made by George W. Bush, whose rare talent for malaforms is well documented. In each of these examples, GWB has coined a word that *sounds like* the word he intended to say, but would be impossible to find in any dictionary:

George W. Bush: They **misunderestimated** the compassion of our country. I think they **misunderestimated** the will and determination of the commander-in-chief, too.
(*He means underestimated*)

George W. Bush: The United States and Russia are in the midst of a **transformationed** relationship that will yield peace and progress.
(*He means transformational, or transforming?*)

George W. Bush: Governor Bush will not stand for the **subsidation** of failure.
(*He means subsidization*)

George W. Bush: Whether it **resignates** or not doesn't matter to me, because I stand for doing what's the right thing, and what the right thing is hearing the voices of people who work.
(*He means resonates*)

In Shakespeare, it is Dogberry, already the canon's maestro-of-malaprops, who holds the high office of malaform-maker-in-chief. As evidence, witness each of these examples, in which the officer mangles a perfectly good word into a trans-formationed mess:

Dogberry: Yea, marry, that's the **eftest** way. Let the watch come forth. *ADO* 4.2.36
(*He means deftest*)

Dogberry: Our watch, sir, have indeed comprehended two **aspicious** persons *ADO* 3.5.46
(*He means suspicious*)

Dogberry: This is your charge: you shall comprehend all **vagrom** men *ADO* 3.3.25
(*He means vagrant*)

Dogberry: It shall be **suffigance**. *ADO* 3.5.52
(*He means sufficient*)

Dogberry: Is our whole **dissembly** appeared? *ADO* 4.2.1
(*He means assembly*)

Dogberry isn't the only word-warper in Shakespeare. Mistress Quickly, who misuses many a proper word in *Merry Wives*, is also quick to corrupt virtuous words into malaforms, such as these:

Quickly: But indeed she is given too much to **allicholy** and musing. *WIV* 1.4.154
(*She means melancholy*)

Quickly: She's as **fartuous** a civil modest wife, and one, I tell you, that will not miss you morning nor evening prayer, as any is in Windsor *WIV* 2.2.97
(*She means virtuous*)

Quickly also shamelessly perverts this modest word in *Henry the Fourth, Part Two*:

Hostess Quickly: Your **pulsidge** beats as extraordinarily as heart would desire *2H4* 2.4.23
(*She means pulse*)

In addition, we have characters like Sir Hugh Evans, the Welsh parson in *Merry Wives*, who makes an ungodly muddle of this English word:

Evans: You must speak **possitable**, if you can carry her your desires towards her. *WIV* 1.1.236
(*He means positively*)

And Petruchio's servant Grumio, who makes hash of a word in *The Taming of the Shrew*:

> *Grumio*: Is there any man has **rebused** your worship?
> (*He means abused*)   *SHR* 1.2.7

And Sir Andrew, who foolishly flubs a word in *Twelfth Night*:

> *Sir Andrew*: We took him for a coward, but he's the very
>   devil **incardinate**.   *TN* 5.1.182
> (*He means incarnate*)

And Lepidus, who loses control of a word in *Antony and Cleopatra*:

> *Lepidus*: Nay, certainly I have heard the Ptolemies'
>   **pyramises** are very goodly things; without
>   contradiction I have heard that.   *ANT* 2.7.35
> (*He means pyramids*)

Now that you know the difference between a *malaform* and a *malaprop*, I urge you to be vigitant, to make certain that you use the two distinct terms in the eftest possible manner, and to be aspicious when hearing someone rebuse the proper terminology.

Then, perhaps, we shall see the word *malaform* appear in a suspected dictionary on a bookshelf near you.

❦

Bibliography

Bevington, David, ed. *The Complete Works of William Shakespeare*. New York: Addison Wesley Longman, 1997.

Brown, Leslie, ed. *The New Shorter Oxford English Dictionary*. Oxford: Oxford University Press, 1993.

Evans, G. Blakemore, ed. *The Riverside Shakespeare*. Boston: Houghton Mifflin, 1974.

Harbage, Alfred, ed. *William Shakespeare: The Complete Works*. New York: Viking Press, 1969.

Joseph, Sister Miriam. *Shakespeare's Use of the Arts of Language*. New York: Columbia University Press, 1947.

Kaiser, Scott. *Shakespeare's Wordcraft*. New York: Limelight Editions, 2007.

Lanham, Richard A. *A Handlist of Rhetorical Terms*. Berkeley and Los Angeles: University of California Press, 1991.

Proudfoot, Richard, A. Thompson, and D.S. Kastan, eds. *The Arden Shakespeare Complete Works*. London: Arden Shakespeare, 2002.

Schmidt, Alexander. *Shakespeare Lexicon and Quotation Dictionary*. New York: Dover Publications, 1971.

Sheridan, Richard Brinsley. *The Rivals*. London: Oxford University Press, 1968.

Spevack, Marvin. *The Harvard Concordance to Shakespeare*. Hildesheim, Germany: Georg Olms Verlag, 1973.

Weisberg, Jacob. *Bushisms: The First Term in His Own Special Words*. New York: Simon and Schuster, 2004.

Essay *by Ros Steen*

Seein Oursels As Ithers See Us

Ros Steen trained at the Royal Scottish Academy of Music and Drama, Scotland's national conservatoire, and holds an MA(Hons) from the University of Glasgow. She is Centre Leader of the Centre for Voice in Performance at the RSAMD and Guest Lecturer at Athanor Akademie, Germany. She has spent many years working with the techniques of Nadine George of the Voice Studio and pioneered the use of that voice work as a medium of rehearsal in professional theatre. She is Scotland's foremost voice coach having worked extensively in Theatre, Film and TV, most recently for the National Theatre of Scotland.

1. Scots for "forward into the game." *Voices of Scotland.* Unpublished paper by Ros Steen for the VASTA conference August 2005.

2. Ros Steen, "Introduction to the Day," *The Contemporary Voice*, Bruce Wooding, ed., (ICV, 2006). Chapter 3, 20-21.

3. E-mail from Joe Windley, Course Leader for MA in Voice Studies, Central School of Speech and Drama, Nov 28th 2005.

4. Sarah Lyall, "Angry Plays Become Hit Shows in Edinburgh," *The New York Times*, August 26, 2006.

5. Lyn Gardiner, "Black Watch," *The Guardian*, August 8th 2006.

6. Joyce McMillan, "Black Watch," *The Scotsman*, August 7th 2006.

7. Thom Dibdin, "Black Watch," *Edinburgh Evening News*, August 7th 2006.

Observers can see a chess game more clearly than the players. (Chinese proverb)

Introduction

Since the summer of 2005, three events have allowed me to see what is happening with theatre voice in my country through different eyes. The first was an opportunity I had to present a short paper at the VASTA annual conference in Glasgow in August of that year. This was the stimulus for a reflective consideration of the present state of voice work in Scotland and how it had been achieved, both in teaching and in the theatre profession. The very positive interest and reaction of colleagues and peers to both the paper and the confidence expressed in the way Scotland was moving 'forrit into the gemme'[1] gave food for thought. One of those colleagues was Joe Windley, Course Leader for the MA (Voice Studies) at Central School of Speech and Drama, and as a direct result of that day's presentation I was asked to give the keynote address[2] at the International Centre for Voice the following January because:

> I was profoundly impressed by your account of the new energy coming out of RSAMD through your work and that of your students and colleagues. The new liberties, opportunities and identities present within Scottish voice work and training when relayed by you gave tacit permission for all to begin to identify their own process.[3]

The honour that afforded me was simultaneously a wake-up call. What was going on in Scotland was being seen as sufficiently and significantly different from what was going on in voice teaching elsewhere and was deemed to offer a useful model for a wider consideration about the nature of voice teaching now.

The third and last event was *Black Watch*, the fledgling National Theatre for Scotland's first production to step into the international spotlight of the Edinburgh Festival. Its runaway success took everyone by surprise, performing from the minute it opened to *rapturous reviews with sellout crowds and standing ovations every night.*[4] Based on the real-life experiences of the Scottish Black Watch regiment's young soldiers in Iraq, it:

> places the audience in the very heart of the war zone. John Tiffany's storming, heart-stopping production is all disorientating blood, guts and murder, threaded through with history and songs of the regiment and intercut with lyrical moments of physical movement, like some great dirty ballet of pulsating machismo and terrible tenderness.[5]

while for the Scots it soared:

> up to and beyond the gold standard we can expect from our National Theatre. Far more important, though, is the ground-shaking energy with which it announces the arrival of the National Theatre as a force.[6]

Having worked on voice and text for the production, *Black Watch* realised in performance much of what voice work in Scotland had been moving towards for a long time, embedding it at the centre of the country's culture. *Black Watch* struck a deep chord with its audience, reflecting back to it that pride in itself it longed for:

> This is exactly the sort of theatre that the National Theatre should be putting on. It is theatre for the people whose history it is, portrayed with panache, humour and utter, bloody, realism.[7]

A far cry, then, from the cultural cringe of 18th century Scotland when even James Boswell, well-known biographer of the famous Dr. Johnson had to admit:

> I do indeed come from Scotland, but I cannot help it.[8]

Nicholas Hytner, the artistic director of the National Theatre in London who invited *Black Watch* to play there, admitted the show had made him "respectful, admiring and envious,"[9] giving rise to some discussion as to whether NTS:

> could prove a more exciting and urgent proposition than even its hyper-successful counterpart in London.[10]

To understand how voice work came to be part of that exciting proposition, we need to trace the journey of its place in actor training and in professional rehearsal practice within the current Scottish theatrical context.

The nature of the voice work and its role in actor training

In a recent article for the VASTA journal[11], I discussed the voice work I taught in some detail. The article described my own training in the mainstream British tradition best exemplified by Cicely Berry, and the subsequent influence on my work, sixteen years ago, of the technique of Nadine George of the Voice Studio. George had been one of the founder members of the Roy Hart Theatre but had taught independently since 1990, developing her own vocal technique about which she subsequently wrote.[12] The essence of George's work, as both articles explained, was the development of the four different qualities of voice, two male and two female, which existed within every human voice. These were first explored as sung notes, using the fixed intervals of the piano for guidance, and then connected straight into text with Shakespearian lines being used as a bridge between the two. Once these connections had been made, a more extended exploration of the voice took place in direct conjunction with the text being spoken:

> My work, at the Academy and in theatre, focuses on enabling actors to enter the text and embody it, literally; that is, the whole text is vibrated through the body and voice of the actor in order for it to be transmitted to the body of the listener, in the moment of speaking. This vibration of the text in the body means that the text, rather than simply being understood intellectually or felt emotionally and then "acted," is connected deeply to where the voice actually comes from: to the physical source of the creative energies and impulses of the actor.

> The work that I do in rehearsal connecting the actor to the source of the voice and the impulse to express, allows the thoughts and feelings of the text to be contacted physically, worked with consciously, and then embodied or channelled by the voice and body. Matters such as the intellectual discussion of the text, what characters are feeling or experiencing and so on, happen internally through the body connection, rather than externally as ideas which are then acted out. It puts the body and voice, rather than the head, at the centre of the acting process and rehearsal period, redresses any imbalance between them and re-connects both in the act of speaking itself.[13]

The work was described by one director as "ultrasound for the point of impulse."[14]

8. James Boswell, *Life of Johnson* Vol. I. 1763.

9. Charlotte Higgins, "Hytner fails to tempt Black Watch to National Theatre," *The Guardian*, September 13th 2006.

10. Ibid.

11. Ros Steen, "Helena, Hitler and the Heartland," *Shakespeare Around the Globe* presented by the *Voice and Speech Review*, Mandy Rees, ed., (Cincinnati, OH: VASTA), 2005, 43-58.

12. Nadine George, "My Life With Voice," *Shakespeare Around the Globe* presented by the *Voice and Speech Review*, Mandy Rees, ed., (Cincinnati, OH: VASTA), 2005, 33-42.

13. Steen, "Helena, Hitler and the Heartland," 43.

14. Nicola McCartney, writer and director, verbatim, summer 2005.

This vocal technique became an established part of the training of actors in the mid-nineties at the Royal Scottish Academy of Music and Drama, Scotland's national conservatoire where I worked, although the use of the voice work as a medium of rehearsal was one that I pioneered in professional theatre in Scotland before introducing it to the Academy. There it had led to an enhanced role for the voice practitioner working alongside directors in productions, and in this way innovative practice in the profession led directly to innovative practice in actor training. The voice department of Scotland's national conservatoire, the Royal Scottish Academy of Music and Drama, under the guidance of its then Head, Jean Moore, had already secured a strong reputation for its voice work nationally and internationally. With settled, permanent full-time staff, the department was able to evolve a shared philosophy and practice for over twenty-three years. At the heart of this philosophy was the recognition of the uniqueness of each individual voice and the inseparable connection between the voice and the individual. While recognising that today's creative artists needed to have a flexibility of vocal expression in order to accomplish the many demands of an extremely demanding market, the department trained actors who were recognisably their own person in their voice, that is, who had ownership of a voice that was distinctively and exclusively theirs.

The relationship between the acting department and the voice department within the Royal Scottish Academy of Music and Drama had also grown to be very strong, with the voice work instrumental to this process of integration, especially when acting tutors and directors began to engage with it on a personal level. Through its work in rehearsals, the voice department moved from being seen as a "skills" department (voice as compartmentalised classroom subject) that "serviced" the acting courses (voice as handmaiden to the production) to one where voice practitioners became an equal partner in the creative process, even to the point of co-direction of productions.

Until recently, the voice work that George and I taught sat alongside more traditional approaches within the department and was only introduced towards the end of the first year[15] once a foundation in mainstream technique had been established. George's vocal technique was introduced by George herself and in second year taken on and taught by me, mediated by my own experience and practice, where it formed the basis of the voice work for the next two years within both class and rehearsal situations. How it worked was as follows: Within the context of classes, everyone took part in group breath and energy work, and warmed up in the four qualities and placing lines.[16] Then each individual researched one quality per class, on a cyclical basis, in ever increasing depth. Within the context of production rehearsals, the day would begin with the foundation group work on breath, energy, quality of sound and placing lines which was followed by one of two approaches, depending on what was being rehearsed that day. If it was a scene, the text would have vocal energy "broken through" it; that is, the text would be spoken on full voice with highly physically vibrated energy. Again, this is described elsewhere.[17] As the text was repeated, these vibrations tapped into underlying, even subconscious creative impulses connected to the thoughts and feelings of the text which were first physically experienced and then consciously repeated. After a while, the actors explored when and where to move in the performance space as suggested by the internal physical and

15. The BA (Acting) is a three year programme in Scotland.

16. Steen, "Helena, Hitler and the Heartland," 45-46.

17. Ibid., 49.

psychological impulses for the words. The embodied pool of choices was then available to the director who had been observing the whole process and who could then work with them further in the knowledge that the work had cut to the chase, short-circuiting hours of discussion or "playing around." If the rehearsal explored detailed character work with individuals, I would work with the actor in a more extended way at the piano to open up the voice through one quality. He or she would immediately use the vibrated, embodied voice s/he had been contacting to open up and release the acting possibilities for them in their text. Sometimes two actors would work in this way, tuning in to each other's vibrations and connections to text before playing their scene together. In these ways the voice work was fully integrated into the rehearsal process of the Shakespearian productions which were the core of study of the second year's summer term and the central events of Scotland's *Shakespeare in the City* Festival. In the third and final year, actors had individual half hour lessons where their vocal development continued, tailored to their particular artistic and personal needs. Texts used in the lessons came directly from their final year productions and professional auditions selections.

The value and importance of this work for young actors—actually for all actors—was that it quickly and simply helped them to confront and accept their own particular body and voice in order to develop its use. At the same time it directly addressed how they worked, that is, what it was that facilitated or limited what they permitted themselves to accomplish. As we know, the desire to be creative and exciting is often tempered by the fear of exposure that these things imply, and the balance of risk to comfort is one that has to be negotiated all the time. This technique holds young actors—at an often insecure stage in their lives as artists and people—within a clear, safe structure that allows them to go into themselves and their voices slowly, bit by bit, in order to explore and embody that exploration securely. The result is they know what they are doing, where they are going and how they can get there, not just with a teacher but, crucially, by themselves, through having a technique able to support them both as actors in training and throughout their working lives. Our graduates, possessing this technique, could find when they joined an acting company in Scotland that they were working side by side with experienced actors who had continued training in the work as part of their continuing professional development. When that happened, an ensemble was not only swiftly built up, but was able to function at a different and deeper level because it shared a common language and way of working, rather than the normal company set-up of actors with differing approaches and levels of training.

One of my visions for Scotland had always been the establishment of a generation of trained actors and directors who not only shared a common understanding and language of theatre but a shared practice. One part of the vision had begun to take shape but the other half required directors willing to share this practice and the insights it afforded about their actors, if theatre was to move forward into the future:

> We know that relationships between voice people and directors, while being very fruitful in many cases, are not always unproblematic. Difficulties are likely to arise because we share the common territory of the interpretation of the text more closely than any other members of the production team. Certainly the territory of the voice specialist is, as Cicely

Berry has articulated, '*an ability to listen and hear words with a heightened awareness of their underlying sound, rhythm, cadence and form, along with an ability to open this out physically and imaginatively and in this way allow it to inform meaning.*'[18]

18. From a reference given by Cicely Berry for Ros Steen's application for an AHRB grant for research into the arts.

But, if we come clean, this is not all we do and voice work cannot be entirely divorced from interpretation. For that reason there is the potential for a clash of readings of the text and therefore a clash of roles which could prove disastrous. That we as a profession have assiduously avoided such a collision course is a commonplace but I don't think it has been achieved without some risk to our own voice as creative practitioners...we have got to get our work out of rooms into where it matters most—the badlands of the rehearsal room. We need to put our work and ourselves on the line if we are to work with directors in new ways. Directors, for their part, must move as well, even if it means calling into question the traditional hierarchies of relationships in theatre. If we want to realign the working relationships in the rehearsal room we are questioning how theatre is made today. And not everybody wants to have that conversation with us. But if it is allowed that there are two stories told when the audience watches a play—the story of the text and the story of the production process—then the change of relationships within the rehearsal room influences the finished product itself. New theatre for a new millennium.[19]

19. Ros Steen, "Introduction to the Day," *The Contemporary Voice*, Bruce Wooding, ed., (ICV, 2006). Chapter 3, 20-21.

The other half of my vision would demand directors prepared to be open enough and vulnerable enough to move the profession forward.

The role of the voice work in professional rehearsal practice
Over many years, I had worked at building relationships bit by bit with such directors and forging partnerships to the point whereby they were willing to give over their rehearsal room to me because of what the work offered them creatively. One such partnership was at the internationally renowned Traverse Theatre in Edinburgh where the work became an integral part of the rehearsal process for many productions over many years. Some of these productions, in addition, gave me the opportunity to explore the different energies and musicalities of Scots as opposed to English, whether it was the language of different historical times (wonderfully re-imagined in David Harrower's modern classic *Knives in Hens*) or a range of subtly different social registers such as the Scots translation of Michel Tremblay's *Solemn Mass for A Full Moon in Summer* (co-directed by myself and Philip Howard, Artistic Director of the Traverse) or a broad spectrum of dialects such as Shetland in Sue Glover's *Shetland Saga*.

How the process worked in professional rehearsal practice was as follows. The director and I had an initial conversation about which areas s/he was seeking help with, based on the nature of the text, the challenges of the writing and the actors that had been cast. Each day before I began any voice work, I led a conversation with the actors—with the director listening—about their agenda items and concerns. In this way I not only took the temperature of the rehearsal room but could reconcile what the actors were after, what the director was after and my own agenda items—what I thought was going on in the text musically, say—so we arrived at the most useful things to work on by consensus. Next we did the voice work—breathing, four qualities and individual work for each actor on voice leading into text—which would be directed by me, sometimes physically in the space, while the director observed and listened. We paid particular attention to the actors' reflections on what the work had accomplished. The director might then have talked about the work's connection to what s/he was interested in developing, or s/he might take what had happened and immediately stage it, or s/he might add a further practical suggestion to be tried then and there. Sometimes the actors' discoveries were all that needed to happen and s/he simply moved on. All the time we were checking in with one another and reading each other to ensure that together what we were doing remained useful to the actors. In finding new ways of sharing the territory of the text with directors I was not frightened that my work bordered on direction. Bordered on it, but wasn't. By physically opening up the possibilities inherent in the text in rehearsal, I shared the territory of the text with the director but my excavation of the text in the voice became a creative contribution to the director's excavation of the text and not a challenge to it. The writer Jules Horne, who watched the voice sessions during rehearsals of her play *Glorious Avatar*, wrote the following observations of the proceedings:

> Phil Hoffman [playing Dan] climbs the scale, and Ros draws his notes in the air, pulling them longer and stronger. At one point, there's a clear shift in power. It's as though Phil's airwaves have suddenly punched clear. His note rings out with a different intensity. Hard to describe, but it's almost spiritual—as though he's an instrument being played by natural forces… The voice session goes way beyond physical technique, though. Ros also opens up the characters with questions about their world…. And—particularly fascinating for a playwright—she brings fierce insights to the dialogue and what's going on emotionally…What makes the characters tick and how is that expressed in how they speak? There's a strong affinity between music and dialogue—rhythm, tone, texture—and Ros's work goes straight to the core of that.[20]

20. *Glorious Avatar* weblog posted by Jules Horne 4/10/2006. http://www.gorgeous-avatar.co.uk/archive/2006_04_01archive.html.

While this collaborative practice was first evolved at the Traverse, it was not limited to it. Another important collaborative partner was lookOUT theatre company where, under the artistic directorship of Nicola McCartney, I worked on seven new plays. Each helped to evolve my role as theatre voice practitioner but perhaps the fullest expression of the voice work as rehearsal practice was *Home*, a play about Jo, who suffers from a communication disorder based on Asperger's syndrome, and her all-female family of mother, sister and aunt. The inner life of the characters, but especially that of Jo, is refracted through a poetic form that brilliantly captures each person's emotional rhythm and disjunctions as she interacts with the others or retreats into her personal space. Company work not only forged a working ensemble but helped the actors to form the family relationships at the heart of the play by the way they tuned into each other and absorbed the vibrations and connections from each other's sung and spoken work. Much individual work was done on different qualities suggested by the varying emotional territories of the text. As an example, Jo has a long monologue that charts a relationship she has managed to make when she was younger and her subsequent feelings when she is later abandoned for "normal" friends. Here is the second part of the speech:

Sometimes
But most times
We'd just watch.

I went to her house
She came to my house
And I'd talk
And talk
She laughed at me
Her laugh was okay
Safe.

Sometimes
When I wasn't
When she was with
The
Other ones
I used to follow her
To just
Watch
Touch
The soft
Soft
Blue
Or the long long blonde
She said that was a bit
Weird.

Suddenly she
She stopped
Especially when she was with
The boy in the sand dunes
He didn't
Didn't
And I think that's why
She stopped
Pretending
Because of
The boy in the sand dunes.[21]

21. Nicola McCartney, *Home*, Traverse Publishing, 2000, Scene 7, 35.

22. McCartney, *Home*, Scene 11, 62.

23. "Peever" is the Scottish name for the children's game of hopscotch.

By the time we approached this monologue, the sixth full voice session in rehearsals, the actor playing Jo, Kate Dickie, had had enough experience in the work to intuit for herself the right quality starting point for her individual vocal exploration for the text. My journal entry for the session reads:
Kate wants to avoid the higher female head quality of /ha/, the obvious 'child' spot, and opts instead for the deeper of the two female qualities, the /hoo/ in the chest. It's an area she has also used for the journey of her drowning attempt in session four.[22] As we stay in the deep female quality she has to really work to hold into the chest spot as she takes it higher and higher up the piano towards the head and you can hear the voice opening. Then she took the text and peevered it[23], i.e. physically played the game once or twice while speaking with huge energy, then she sat to do the speech on the set. It was still slightly outward until I asked

her to keep hugging the words to herself and then she got to a wonderful chested spot of feeling and real searching for the words, surprising herself by her discovery about the boy in the sand dunes changing everything.[24]

24. Ros Steen, *Home: personal voice journal*, 2000.

Lastly, the expressive sung and spoken vowels of the text were used as the basis for the music of the production. Each actor took a text that was key for their character and the quality they felt where it was initially located, and we worked with piano, voice and speaking of the text as usual.

Jo: female chest, her end speech sc. 14.[25] It is full of space and depth and she says she feels very rooted and open.

25. McCartney, *Home*, Scene 14, 85-86.

Jen :   (Gillian Kerr) deep male, her trapped in a glass coffin speech, sc 9[26] has real abandonment.

26. Ibid., Scene 9, 44-45.

Kath : (Hope Ross) chooses the high female head spot for her speech about childlessness[27] childish and very emotionally moving area as a woman.

27. Ibid., Scene 12, 70-71.

Annie : (Mary McCusker) also chooses the high female spot for her panic attack speech[28] where the same area opens to a high head scream.[29]

28. Ibid., Scene 12, 71-72.

29. Steen, *Home: personal voice journal*, 2000.

After that, they voiced only the sung sounds of the feeling places of these texts which were recorded and subsequently treated for the final score thereby adding another layer to the overall soundscape of the production.

The Scottish context for the voice work

I micht hae screived yon airticle in Scots, yin o Scotland's three heidmaist leids (the ither twa bein English and Gaelic) gin I thocht ye wid hae unnerstood it but, tae be mair comprehensible, I decidit tae owerset it intil English.[30] Scotland is another country with its own language, Scots, and though still part of the United Kingdom, has a strong sense of itself as the proud and independent nation in Europe it once was. In 1998, constitutional reform in Britain led to the Scotland Act which made provision for a Scottish parliament with devolved power for domestic policy and laws for Scotland in "response to hundreds of years of Scottish nationalist sentiment."[31]
On July 1st 1999, the Parliament was duly opened by the Queen and in September 2003 it announced the creation of the National Theatre of Scotland:

30. Scots for: "I might have written this article in Scots, one of Scotland's three main languages (the other two being English and Gaelic) if I thought you would have understood it but, to be more comprehensible, I decided to translate it into English."

31. Luis Rivera, "Scottish Devolution : A Historical and Political Analysis," *Loyola University New Orleans Student Historical Journal*, Vol 30, 1998-1999.

For over 100 years, the theatre community in Scotland has been campaigning for a National Theatre. Now it is finally happening.[32]
Vicky Featherstone, the first artistic director of the National Theatre of Scotland [NTS] wrote in its opening programme of events:

32. The Manifesto of the National Theatre of Scotland. Website: <nationaltheatrescotland.com>.

We have spent many hours debating the notion of a 'national theatre' and the responsibility that entails. It is not, and should not be, a jingoistic, patriotic stab at defining a nation's identity through theatre. In fact, it should not be an opportunity to try to define anything. Instead, it is the chance to throw open the doors of possibility, to encourage boldness.[33]
She also declared:

33. Ibid.

Scottish theatre has always been for the people, led by great performances, great stories or great playwrights. We now have the chance to build a new generation of theatre-goers as well as reinvigorating the existing ones; to create theatre on a national and international scale that is contemporary,

34. Ibid.

35. Ibid.

36. The Tattoo is an annual spectacle held on the esplanade at Edinburgh Castle during the International Festival, featuring the military bands and display teams of Scottish regiments as well as international regiments. Over 200,000 visitors see it live and an estimated further 100 million watch it tel-evised. The highlight of the show is the massed pipes and drums and each evening ends with a floodlit lone piper playing from the Castle walls <www.edin-burgh-tattoo.co.uk>.

37. Associate Director (New Work) of the National Theatre of Scotland.

38. The squaddies spoke in Fife and Dundonian dialects and the vocal characteristics of real life politi-cians Alex Salmond and Jeff Hoon, who were repre-sented by two of the actors in the play, were also explored.

confident and forward-looking; to bring together brilliant artists, composers, choreographers and playwrights, and to exceed our expectation of what and where theatre can be.[34]

This last was particularly important. NTS was not to be building-based but would put its money purely into the creation of work which would tour throughout Scotland and abroad. From its inception it set out to produce work not only in established theatre buildings but in *site-specific locations, community halls and sports halls, car parks and forests*[35] and its inaugural pro-ductions (curiously entitled *Home* as well) were ten shows happening simulta-neously all over the country including a show on a ferry in Shetland, a per-formance that took place in an 18-story tower apartment block in Glasgow and an old peoples' home in Caithness. *Black Watch* itself was mounted in an empty former drill hall in Edinburgh turned into a traverse configuration with two rising seating banks reminiscent of the Edinburgh Tattoo.[36]

Black Watch

When John Tiffany[37], with whom I had worked for over ten years, asked me to work on voice and text for *Black Watch*, he had a number of different vocal issues to discuss. These ranged from the importance of the ensemble nature of the company which had to portray a very close-knit group of squaddies, the physical use of the voices in the large site-specific location, the speaking of verbatim text in the post-Iraq scenes and some particular vocal usages.[38] The voice work thus had several roles to play but its main function became to contribute to the ensemble nature of the company at the same time as building an extended use of the voice that would carry the naturalistic speech out into the space and allow the speaking to balance with the sound track, the video screens and the movement. However, it also allowed for some inter-esting and unexpected developments. The breath work, for example, did not simply support the actors' voices but provided a counterpoint to the intensive physical and military training the actors underwent. It allowed them essential time, after the effortful breathing experienced during exercise, to release breath and energy and be put in touch again with their own deeper breathing centres. In turn, the energy work not only allowed access to the flow of life energy in the performer but also focused it in a very precise way that balanced the precision of movement they were to use in the space. When opening up the voice at the piano, time was spent on ensuring the actors could access feminine energy, not only for the purpose of opening up the male energy needed for the macho characters and setting of the play, but in providing an important balance for the actors themselves in their voices. *Black Watch* provided a good example of how Scotland had been resourcing itself in voice in theatre by drawing together a body of practitioners—actors trained as students in the vocal work, actors new to it, myself as vocal practi-tioner and a director interested in and committed to the voice work as rehearsal practice—with a shared technique and experience. All this was brought to bear upon a piece of new Scottish writing to create a fresh and exciting possibility for theatre.

My next project involves working on a trilogy of new plays linked by a com-mon theme and cast with the Traverse's associate director Lorne Campbell. Campbell first encountered the work as a directing student on RSAMD's Masters in Directing programme and subsequently asked me to work on his professional productions. He has also experienced the voice work first hand in the workshops I run for directors.[39] With this project the voice work will not only open up the possibilities of the text, but will again be used specifically to create an ensemble through a shared energy and approach that will link the performance of the three texts and contribute to a coherence of acting style within a unified world. This is particularly necessary as the three plays are individual pieces by three different writers, grouped as a trilogy because of a similarity of theme. Any two plays may be given in any evening and occasionally all three will be performed together.

Future Directions

The voice work is in growing demand. For some time now I have run independent workshops for actors dedicated to pursuing advanced development of their voices as a group. The company nature of the exploration has been crucial to the workshops' success. Writers are becoming interested in what the voice work can offer them in terms of developing the voices of their characters. Directors who have had some experience of the work in their rehearsal rooms want to study it themselves in order to pursue a deeper understanding of the actor's process and to share a vocabulary and language of body and voice with them. There are plans to collaborate with NTS Workshop, the developmental arm of NTS, as I continue to research the work. Can it be integrated more fully into the rehearsal process? Could a production be completely rehearsed through the voice work only? The proposed establishment of a Centre for Voice in Performance at the RSAMD is further evidence of a serious commitment to this voice work which is rooted in Scottish practice but looking out beyond to —as yet—unkent airts.[40]

Robert Burns famously wrote:

O wad some Power the giftie gie us/To see oursels as ithers see us![41]

I am grateful for what the chess players have seen and reflected back to me in this last year. It is because of these observations that I am redd up by hoo ma natioun, smaa, galus, gleg oan its feet and licht eneuch tae manouvre is already rinnin wi the baa forrit intae the gemme.[42]

39. The workshops for directors are for those who wish to understand the work further by the most direct means possible—experiencing it physically for themselves. They not only understand how it engages the imaginative and emotional sources for the actor in the moment of performance, they explore their own unique voice in the process.

40. Scots for "unknown horizons."

41. Robert Burns, "To a Louse," *Poems and Songs of Robert Burns*, James Barke, ed., Collins, 1955, 138.

42. Scots for "I am fired up by how my nation, small, impish, sharp on its feet and light enough to manoeuvre is already running with the ball forward into the game." Ros Steen, *Voices of Scotland*, unpublished paper for the VASTA conference August 2005.

Private Studio Practice *Jack Horton, Associate Editor*

Beyond the Ivy Walls

Diversity Begins With You...in Your Private Studio Practice

While attending a VASTA meeting in Chicago last Summer, a friend and I took a side trip to Evanston to hear a talk about diversity. Instead of speaking mainly about organizational policy with regard to diversity, this young speaker chose to get really personal. He wanted each member of his audience to imagine the scene at one's own memorial service. Where would it be and who would be there? Would it be a college educated all-one-race group? Would everyone be in the same basic income bracket? You can see where he was going with this.

Building on that theme, I began to think in terms of my own personal life and my own private student roster. I wondered who I might refuse to teach and then what reason I might give for not accepting an application for professional-cultural voice/presentation development lessons. It was very sobering to think about it in terms of really practicing diversity as an artist and private teacher. My mind flashed back to what I had learned during concert tours in the South back in the 1960s. Those deeply personal and ugly experiences informed my actions as I began to do more private teaching. I knew just talk without action would not make diversity a reality in a teaching studio.

In this market place beyond the ivy walls of formal education there are those among us who have cross-gender vocal issues that need to be properly addressed by a caring and experienced voice coach/teacher. Then, there are business people who have hitherto been divorced from what the arts could give them that would greatly enhance their ability to communicate. There are actors who want to be able to sing and singers who seek actor voice training. There are media people who write well, but need more training to improve their visual and vocal impact on audiences. Also, there are talented potential students for whom English is a second language. There is much to consider as we address the real vocal needs of those who seek us out for help. Are we ready and properly prepared for the task?

Questions for the modern teacher: Have you ever taught a blind person? How do you view emotional illness? Do you reach out to folks who have disabilities? Is your studio user friendly? How many countries are represented as you survey your teaching roster. Does sexual orientation disqualify anyone from taking voice training from you? How would your ability, experience and qualifications be in the best interest of any potential student?

Finally, in this spirit of diversity, I hope you will explore all the articles in this private studio practice section. There is much to ponder here as you modernize your business. And let a key aspect of that modernization be to literally embody diversity in your thinking, attitude and actions. It will enrich all of us and those we seek to help.

❦

After 23 years performing and touring out of New York City, Jack Horton relocated to Louisville, KY in 1988 to establish Presenter's Studio. He teaches professional-cultural voice/presentation development for singers, actors, business, clergy, education and media professionals...all who desire to sing and/or speak well in public. His years on stage and in business inspire his private teaching. A member of New York Singing Teachers Association (NYSTA), Natl. Association of Teachers of Singing (NATS) and VASTA, Horton enjoys the honor of an appointment by the state governor to serve as a Kentucky Colonel.

Gender Voice Issues:
Voice and Communication Therapy for Transsexual/Transgender Clients

Richard K. Adler, Ph.D, CCC, SLP, Fellow, ASHA is a speech-language pathologist and professor of Speech Language Hearing Sciences at Minnesota State University Moorhead. Dr. Adler has been a therapist, professor, researcher, supervisor, and administrator in the field of Speech-Language Pathology for over 38 years. He has worked with both MtF and FtM Transsexuals for voice and communication therapy and research for the past 24 years. He, along with two other colleagues published the very first book of its kind entitled *Voice and Communication Therapy for the Transgender/Transsexual Client: A Comprehensive Clinical Guide*, March, 2006, from Plural Publishing Company, San Diego.

Introduction

Speech-language pathologists (SLPs) are trained in all aspects of assessment and treatment for a variety of communication disorders including but not limited to the areas of articulation, phonology, language, fluency, and voice. An area of clinical need and interest that has developed in the past 10-15 years, primarily in the United States, is working with Transsexual/Transgender (TS/TG) clients. Many SLPs have been approached by potential transsexual clients who are in search of efficacious and outcome-based voice therapy. While some literature has been published in the past 20 years on this topic (Adler, Hirsch, & Mordaunt 2006; Battin 1983; Challoner 2000; deBruin, Coerts, & Greven 2000; Freidenberg 2002; Gelfer & Schofield 2000; Hooper 1985; Oates and Dacakis 1983, 1986, 1997; Pausewang-Gelfer 1999), this area within the scope of practice for speech-language pathologists remains a mystery to many and a major challenge to some.

Consumers who seek either voice masculinization (FtM or Female to Male) or voice feminization (MtF or Male to Female) go through a multi-faceted transition process. Many of these potential clients seek changes in their fundamental frequency ranges as the "catch-all" to their goal of sounding like their new gender role (Adler, Hirsch, Mordaunt 2006). However, voice modification is far more complicated than just working on pitch. Many SLPs feel comfortable providing therapy for clients who present with vocal nodules or polyps, unilateral paralysis of the vocal cords, vocal cord bowing, spastic dysphonia, and a variety of other voice disorders typically seen in university or hospital/medical center clinics. Although no empirical evidence is found in the literature, most SLPs usually do not feel comfortable working with MtF or FtM clients for voice modification. Whereas, other disciplines such as Psychology, Social Work, Counseling, and Psychiatry have worked with the MtF and FtM populations for many years. Currently, the World Professional Association for Transgender Health (WPATH), formerly the Harry Benjamin International Gender Dysphoria Association (HBIGDA), sets standards for practitioners of Transsexual Medicine including psychology, endocrinology, and surgery. There are, however, at this time, no standards set for working on voice or communication therapy. Some SLPs are hesitant to work with this population due to moral, religious or personal reasons while many SLPs, who have been interviewed in the past, have indicated that they do not know what to do for this particular therapy genre.

What is Transsexual/Transgender voice?

There is some disagreement as to whether voice therapy with an MtF or FtM transsexual client should be considered voice modification, a voice disorder, or a cosmetic change. Sometimes it is merely a case of semantic differences. Stemple, Glaze, and Klaben stated that a voice disorder exists "when a person's quality, pitch, and loudness differ from those of similar age, gender, cultural background, and geographic location" (2000, 2). By this definition, MtF or FtM clients who seek voice feminization or masculinization would present with a voice disorder since their natural, biological gender voice is different than the voice they wish to convey that would match their new gender. For an MtF client, the more masculine biological voice that is present differs from those who are already in the feminine role he wishes to portray and this would affect the pitch, quality, and loudness levels culturally and by age and gender. Hence, by definition, this person would have a voice disorder.

However, another way of looking at TS/TG voice modification is not as a voice disorder per se, but rather as a therapy process that ultimately affects the psychological, emotional, spiritual, sociolinguistic and psycholinguistic aspects of an individual who is going through transition. The process would involve all aspects of transition to the new gender role—including voice. Many patients who are in transition, express dissatisfaction with their current voice and state that it has an adverse affect on their psychological, spiritual, emotional, and linguistic well being. Many psychologists who treat transsexuals for the year they are living full time in their new gender prior to gender reassignment surgery, help them prepare for the surgery. Often, voice is brought up as the final stumbling block to this transition process. The patient seeks a modification of the current voice so that he/she can fit into the gender that the individual wishes to become. One of the biggest challenges for the SLP is to help the client match a new voice to the new outward gender appearance.

A major dilemma that exists for both the SLP and the client is that most insurance companies view TS/TG voice therapy as a cosmetic alteration which is not normally covered under an insurance policy. Cosmetic alteration, like cosmetic surgery, is often looked upon by the insurance industry as elective and those types of treatments are not covered by insurance. Perhaps as more evidenced-based practice emerges within this aspect of the voice therapy milieu, there can be some agreement of how to classify TS/TG voice therapy so that it will be acceptable to all parties—including reimbursement sources.

Transsexual clients generally do not receive a specific voice disorder diagnosis. Instead, they may come to the voice clinic with a referral/diagnosis of transsexualism or Gender Dysphoria Disorder. Transsexualism is a medical term that defines people who present in their opposite gender, who dress as such and who desire to undergo some physical transformation (hormonal treatment, surgery, cosmetic treatment, etc.) to change their body (Meyer, et al). It is wise for the SLP to consult with the referral source. This will foster an understanding of how transition affects the client's life. Before beginning a voice therapy program, the SLP should understand the client's current level of transition. A person with a diagnosis of Gender Dysphoria, as defined by the American Psychiatric Association's DSM-IV manual of mental disorders, is someone who experiences extreme discomfort with his or her own socially, biologically, or culturally assigned gender role (Adler et al 2006, 3). It is interesting to note as Christianson pointed out, that the category of transsexualism was dropped in the DSM-IV and Gender Identify Disorder in Children and Adults was listed for the first time. She further explained that Gender Identity Disorder in adults includes a strong desire for cross-gender identification by the person expressing a desire to be the other gender.

Voice Therapy for the Transgender Client: Is that all there is?

Often the SLP receives a referral for voice and communication therapy for a transsexual individual when there is no indication that the voice has already been abused or misused to the point that intervention is needed. We, as SLPs, are often the first professional individual to help the MtF or FtM client with stabilizing his/her voice in order to precede with a smooth transition to his/her true identity.

Most MtF or FtM clients, who approach an SLP or arrive at a clinic ready for therapy, assume that pitch is the ultimate parameter that requires change and that it will be the "cure-all" for their voice during the transition process. Clients are quickly advised by the SLP that therapy is more than pitch work. A total training program for the MtF or FtM client usually includes work in many, although not necessarily all, of the areas listed below:

   a. Pitch
   b. Resonance
   c. Intonation
   d. Rate/Volume
   e. Language: Syntax, Vocabulary, Pragmatics
   f. Articulation
   g. Vocal Hygiene Programming
   h. Non-verbal Communication
   i. Carry-over
   j. Voice and Speech Counseling

As an SLP we can make sure the voice and communication therapy, that is so often needed to complete transition, proceeds smoothly and efficiently with an understanding of how to avoid two major potential voice crises during that time period—vocal abuse and vocal misuse. With a clear understanding of what abuse and misuse entail, MtF and FtM clients can proceed with their therapies. They now have a better understanding of how the voice works, how voice and communication entail more than just pitch, and how verbal and non-verbal communication are complimentary. It is our job to bring those premises to the forefront and ethically help the transsexual individual.

Adler, Hirsch, and Mordaunt stated that none of the above is mutually exclusive for the client who receives voice and communication therapy as part of his/her transition. In addition to educating clients that pitch is not the complete answer to changing one's voice, SLPs and the rest of the medical team must also counsel the client that psychosocial issues play a tremendous role not only in the transition but also in the total success of the client's process.

Many SLPs may not be certain as to what kind of therapy to plan with MtF or FtM clients, despite having significant experience in working with voice disorders. Professionals have an ethical obligation to research the literature on transsexual voice therapy, aging, gender, and psychosocial issues in order to devise an appropriate individualized treatment plan. In addition to information derived from the literature, SLPs will also need to plan treatment based on each individual's situation, including the client's age, lifestyle, work/school environment, and family involvement. All of these aspects will have an impact on the success of the treatment plan. Social workers, psychologists, physicians, and counselors are good resources with whom the SLP should consult when a transsexual is referred to their service. Some insights into how psychologists, psychiatrists, or counselors work together with the SLP to ensure that psychosocial and psychotherapy issues are addressed are found in literature by Bockting and Coleman; Hubble, Duncan, and Miller; Meyer, et al; and Rachlin.

There are three case studies at the end of this article that describe some aspects of SLP assessment, treatment, and interaction with the psychologist. This approach serves as part of the broad transition process for many TS/TG clients. Readers are urged to use these cases as references and resources in order to become more comfortable treating the TS/TG client.

Furthermore, Christianson stated that treatment plans are usually shaped by three aspects of the care for the TS/TG client. They include adhering strictly to the Harry Benjamin *Standards of Care...* and *The Standards of Care for Gender Identity Disorders* (Meyer, et al)—shaping the treatment plan according to the uniqueness of the person presenting with Gender Dysphoria, and third, taking into consideration the other people in the client's life that would help influence treatment and progress.

Ethical and Scope of Practice Issues

King, Lindstedt, Jensen, and Law, as cited in Dacakis, stated that "it is vital that the clinician is aware of the possibilities for tacit discrimination, and ensures that the transsexual client is given 'full regard' and is treated with the courtesy and respect provided to every client who attends a speech-language clinic" (1999, 103).

ASHA addresses the religious, moral, and personal conflicts that many SLPs have with regard to working with the TS/TG client. The *Code of Ethics* states that "...any violation of the spirit and purpose of this Code shall be considered unethical" (1). Furthermore, ASHA Principles of Ethics I, Rule C, states that "Individuals shall not discriminate in the delivery of professional services or the conduct of research and scholarly activities on the basis of race or ethnicity, gender, age,

religion, national origin, sexual orientation, or disability" (*Code of Ethics* 2003, 1). Finally, Principle of Ethics II states that "Individuals shall honor their responsibility to achieve and maintain the highest level of professional competence" (*Code of Ethics* 2003, 2). These statements bring to light the implication that the SLP should be properly trained to work with particular clients, including the MtF or FtM client who seeks voice modification. In summary, ASHA indicates that the SLP has an ethical obligation to provide services to a person who seeks speech, language, voice, or fluency therapy despite the SLP's personal beliefs.

Knowledge and Skills

The question that is often asked is "what knowledge and skills are necessary for the SLP to work with the transsexual population?" One needs to look at the ASHA document, *Knowledge and Skills for Working with Culturally and Linguistically Diverse Populations*. According to this document, the SLP is required to become culturally competent and culturally sensitive to work with CLD (Culturally and Linguistically Diverse) clients. This is substantiated in the ASHA document entitled *Cultural Competence*. This would include not only the five traditional racial/ethnic groups as defined by both the federal government and ASHA but also a sixth category on the CLD spectrum: transsexual individuals who are seeking voice modification and who are included in the GLBT (Gay, Lesbian, Bisexual, and Transgender) cultural group. SLPs must be reminded that ASHA's *Knowledge and Skills* Document (2) states that "thus, this ethical principal [Ethics II Rule B] mandates that SLPs continue in lifelong learning to develop those knowledge and skills required to provide culturally...appropriate services rather than interpret Rule B as a reason not to provide services" (Adler, et al 2006).

Goals and Objectives of Therapy Planning

SLPs write treatment plans and goals and objectives for all clients regardless of the reason for the therapy. As professionals, SLPs use the referral source as well as their knowledge and skills to write the most appropriate treatment plan for their client.

Many MtF or FtM clients are referred to a speech/voice clinic by their endocrinologist, psychiatrist, or peer. The SLP should be aware of the fact that many clients self-refer and come to the clinic without a diagnosis of transsexualism or Gender Dysphoria. There is a misconception that only MtF clients need referral to an SLP to work on voice modification. It is true that—physiologically—the female larynx will undergo latent adolescent changes once testosterone is introduced as part of the new hormone regimen. However, this does not occur for the MtF client who introduces estrogen therapy as part of the transition process. Many SLPs and others believe that the FtM client experiences voice changes due to the increase in testosterone through hormone replacement therapy, but several authors (Dacakis; Scheidt, Kob, Willmes & Neuschaefer-Rube; and Van Borsel, De Cuypere, Rubens, & Destaerke 2006) have claimed that voice change in FtM transsexuals is not without problems and voice assessment of these clients is recommended.

Medical management of the transition process may or may not involve a formally organized team of professionals. In some large medical centers with speech and hearing clinics, there often is a Gender Dysphoria Program or at least a gender team who often administers a battery of assessments as part of the initial stages of the transition process. Team members often include the psychiatrist, psychologist, surgeon, social worker, internal medicine physician, speech and voice clinician, and endocrinologist. In an average or small community in which a gender team may not exist, there might only be a private SLP practitioner or a university speech and hearing clinic without a medical center. The SLP in consultation with the local psychologist, psychiatrist or other physician, is often the person who, by default, becomes the case manager of the patient's transition care. This alone makes it essential for the SLP to educate him/herself to the larger picture of what transition involves and how voice training becomes an essential part of that process (Adler, et. al. 2006, chapters 1 and 2).

It is important for the transsexual client to undergo an ENT evaluation including a laryngeal examination (e.g. laryngoscopy) in order to rule out pathology or a potential voice disorder. A detailed case history must be taken by the SLP due to the fact that traditional histories might not include information that is very relevant when working with an MtF or FtM client. For example, most case histories do not reveal the fact that the client is still working in the "male mode" during the day and only presents as female in the evenings or weekends. This would have a direct bearing on a carry-over schedule and, in general, just how much the client will be able to practice. Updating case history information periodically while therapy is ongoing will help the SLP with an awareness and understanding of changes in financial, social, psychological, and spiritual status of the client. These changes would have a direct bearing on progress within the treatment plan.

The SLP, according to Dacakis (2006), is able to give the client information about gender differences in communication. Each client will bring with him/her a particular set of circumstances that the SLP may use to help set goals and objectives. It is essential for the SLP to empower the client to "take charge" of this part of his/her transition, to allow for ownership of the goals and objectives that will, in turn, make the process more meaningful.

Typical goals that are usually addressed (but are not inclusive here) include establishing a safe optimal fundamental frequency of pitch, teaching new intonation patterns, understanding vocabulary and sentence structures, learning new non-verbal cues and practices, and establishing a vocal hygiene program during the transition process (Adler, et al 2006).

Case Studies

Since evidenced-based practice is the basis for which SLPs are now doing therapy (as was noted by the theme of the 2005 ASHA convention, San Diego, CA) the reader is referred to Oates, 2006 (Adler et al 2006, chapter 3) for a thorough discussion of evidence-based practice considerations. Furthermore, Dacakis (2006, chapter 7), provides a wonderful discussion on writing goals and objectives for the TS/TG client's treatment plan. The reader is referred to the numerous chapters in Adler, Hirsch, and Mordaunt (2006) that discuss the areas of pitch and intonation (Mordaunt, chapter 10); establishing effective resonance (Hirsch, chapter 11); articulation and rate/volume parameters (Boonin, chapters 12-13); and language including syntax, semantics, pragmatics, and discourse (Hooper, chapter 14, and Hooper and Hershberger, chapter 15). Furthermore, there is information on non-verbal considerations (Hirsch and Van Borsel, chapter 16, and Hirsch, chapter 17) and group therapy considerations (Mordaunt, chapter 18) all which explain the various voice and other parameters that must be taken into consideration when treating the TS/TG client.

B.R. (36 years old, Male to Female (MtF)

B.R. came to the university speech and hearing clinic after attending a local Transgender/Transsexual support group. B.R., age 36, was living full time as a woman except on the weekends when she saw her three children at which time she was forced by court order to appear in her male mode. Instrumentation (VisiPitch IV) was used to establish pitch range and habitual pitch, S/Z ratio, Maximum Phonation time, and jitter and shimmer levels. B.R. presented with a hoarse, raspy voice with an average speaking fundamental frequency (sf_0) of 113Hz with a range of 98Hz to 129Hz.

Mordaunt (Adler, et al 2006, chapter 10) explained that a conversational average fundamental frequency for females would be 220 Hz with a range of 165Hz to 311 Hz. The male average is 120Hz with a range of 93Hz to 175Hz. According to Mordaunt, striving for a gender ambiguous conversational pitch range is a safe way of introducing voice/pitch change in an MtF client. The gender ambiguous (a pitch that makes the gender of the individual indefinable) conversational pitch range has an average of 180Hz with a range of 131Hz to 247Hz. Andrews stated that it might be unrealistic to expect TS/TG clients to achieve a female sf_0 which is documented as

220Hz +/- 20Hz or a male sf_0 of 120Hz +/- 20 Hz. Others have indicated that research lists sf_0 for the gender ambiguous range to be 155-160Hz (Spencer 1988; Wolfe, et al 1998). Therefore, starting with the gender ambiguous average might be more realistic. Of course this will depend on the client's voice when he/she first presents in the clinic.

As an army veteran, B.R. was planning on having her Gender Reassignment Surgery (GRS) through the VA hospital but was currently completing her undergraduate degree and therefore she chose to wait until she finished her education, obtained a good job, and saved more money. Non-verbal communication parameters—including clothing choice, make-up and sitting and standing posture—were deemed appropriate for her appearance at that time. Therapy was scheduled twice a week for 50 minutes each session. One goal included stabilizing a fundamental frequency range of 140Hz to 175Hz. Using some of the literature that considers sf_0 in the gender ambiguous range, it was felt that B.R. would be able to achieve an optimum, safe pitch in that range. Additional goals included teaching B.R. a more feminine vocabulary and a softer articulation pattern, both of which B.R. expressed interest in learning. Working on these goals helped B.R. so that she would not be "read" each time she either spoke on the phone or would present herself in class or in her part time job.[1] The reader is referred to Hooper (chapters 14 and 15) for a thorough discussion on vocabulary, language usage and discourse. Additional goals included the areas of non-verbal communication that compromised sitting and standing posture, gestures, upper and lower extremity positioning, etc. During therapy sessions, it appeared obvious to the therapist that B.R. was struggling with some other issues that seemed to interfere with her ability to practice her goals on a daily basis (Adler, et al 2006, chapter 17). It was determined after some probing, that B.R. was struggling with her spouse's resistance to this transition and her spouse's attempts at blocking B.R. from seeing her children.

B.R. attended therapy for three semesters while attending school. After graduation, B.R. moved to the Minneapolis-St. Paul area where she hoped to find full time employment so that she would no longer need public assistance and would be able to save money for the surgeries needed to complete her transition. Therapy goals were successful as B.R. stabilized her average sf_0 at the 145Hz level and she developed a softer articulation pattern (Boonin 2006, "Rate and Volume"). B.R. reported that she was starting to be called "ma'am" each time she would use the phone or would present in public. She was however, unsuccessful in winning the fight to see her children and to find full time employment. A phone call came into our clinic last spring that told us B.R. was found dead of suicide

in her apartment. Although she achieved her voice and communication goals successfully, she was unable to deal with the loss of her rights to see her children as well as the inability to find suitable employment that would allow her to pay for her GRS and to live her life as a woman.

G.N. (58 years old, MtF)

G.N. presented with a fundamental frequency range of 99Hz to 146Hz with an average fundamental frequency of 123Hz (see the case history on B.R. above). G.N. also had a noticeable repaired cleft lip and palate. She reported having multiple surgeries through her 13th birthday. Current nasometer readings indicated a nasalance level of 97. Dalston, Warren, and Dalston (1991) studied 117 patients to determine what would constitute more than just mild hypernasality. The study found that a high nasalance score was operationally defined as 32 or greater. Therefore, G.N. was referred to a local ENT physician for evaluation and possible treatment of her severe hypernasality. Further evaluation by the ENT indicated a mild to moderate mixed hearing loss bilaterally. The ENT evaluation also reported that G.N. did not achieve velopharyngeal closure and that most of her breath stream escaped nasally during all speech situations. A diagnosis of Velopharyngeal Insufficiency (VPI) was noted and pharyngeal flap surgery was recommended. G.N. put speech/voice therapy on hold in order to schedule the surgery and to allow adequate recovery time. After six months, G.N. received medical clearance to resume voice therapy. Nasalance was still at the 96% level and therapy began to work on reducing her hypernasality.

Transsexual voice and communication therapy was put on hold at that time in order to address the nasality issue and to increase intelligibility of her speech. The TS/TG goals to stabilize an average speaking fundamental frequency, establish head resonance, establish appropriate feminine intonation patterns, and establish a more feminine articulation pattern and vocabulary usage were included in the treatment plan but were put aside to work on reducing hypernasality.

After four months of therapy, G.N.'s nasalance level was reduced to 47%. This made a significant difference in the way G.N.'s voice was perceived by herself as well as peers, co-workers, and others. Fundamental frequency stabilized at 180Hz and G.N. was pleased. She decided to go full time as a woman and proceeded to make plans to tell her co-workers and supervisor. Within one week of notifying her supervisor in a private meeting that she would begin to appear at work as her female self, G.N. was given a "pink slip" at her job and her employment was terminated. In her state, there is no statute protecting GLBT individuals so she was unable to sue her company for discrimination based on gender identity, sexual orientation, or general human rights violations. Fortunately after only five months of unemployment, G.N. found a new job that she interviewed for as a woman and voice therapy resumed. Upon her resumption of employment and voice and communication therapy, G.N. scheduled her GRS overseas. She is now discharged from speech services and has stabilized at an average sf$_0$ of 179Hz without vocal strain and has worked successfully at using appropriate feminine vocabulary, intonation patterns, as well as articulation and resonance.

K.G. (80 years old, MtF)

K. G. came to our clinic at the age of 75 to discuss the possibility of voice modification therapy. Her sexual reassignment surgery was scheduled for just after her 76th birthday. As an army veteran, K.G. had served in the Second World War and was married until her 70th birthday after which she became a widower. She decided to finally become the woman she thought she should have been all along. She began transition at age 70. At 76, just after her GRS, she came to our clinic for voice modification therapy. She had been previously diagnosed with a sensori-neural hearing loss as well as decreased cognitive functioning due to the aging process. She began voice and communication therapy at age 76.

Upon evaluation, K.G. presented with a hoarse, raspy, and thin voice quality with a noticeable vocal tremor. Volume was noticeably soft and her rate of speech was markedly slow. She attended sessions through her 79th birthday having had completed her goals each term. Her new voice was thin, slightly hoarse, yet she was able to maintain an average sf$_0$ of 170Hz with a range of 160-279Hz. She had successfully learned new feminine vocabulary, a more feminine intonation and articulation pattern as well as non-verbal aspects of communication including sitting and standing postures that matched her new gender role. She stated that her only regret was that she did not begin her transition at a much earlier age. Of course she now recognizes that she has difficulty participating in conversations in a noisy environment due to her hearing loss but is willing to do what she can to interact socially. She comes to our clinic about every six months for a re-check and is most concerned that she is sometimes "read" on the phone. During phone conversations, K.G. appeared to have lowered her fundamental frequency pitch level. Upon testing for that in our clinic using the Kay Elemetrics VisiPitch IV, it was determined that if not aware of how her pitch changed, K.G. usually conversed at a speaking fundamental frequency of 141 Hz. This would most likely explain why she was "read" while speaking on the phone.

Conclusions

The voice is an entity that many people take for granted until they have to change their voice to match who they really are.

The pursuit of changing one's voice can be even more challenging for transsexual clients. During a client's quest for his/her true identity, many MtF and FtM clients rely on the speech-language pathologist's therapeutic guidance and counseling that includes the voice, one of several identification markers that reveal someone's personality. SLPs are the professionals who not only take into consideration psychosocial issues that affect an individual's well being, but also take the client's voice and help transform it into a safe, efficient, and appropriate communication parameter.

Therapy for the MtF and FtM client takes a great deal of hard work, courage, and drive to be completed successfully. As Julius Fast once hypothesized, our verbal and nonverbal communication makes us a whole person. That is the goal of the Transsexual client; for the client to view him/herself in the new gender role that they have always wanted to be with appropriate verbal and non-verbal skills. We as SLPs play a major role in the transition and execution of that goal. Fast stated there have been clinical studies that indicated the extent to which body language would actually contradict our verbal communication. MtF or FtM clients want to be accepted in their new gender role and voice coupled with communication skills (verbal and non-verbal) help make that transition positive and natural.

❦

Endnotes

1. Being "read" refers to a male-to-female or female-to-male individual who is spoken to or perceived as their biological gender even though they appear in their chosen gender; he or she may be read due to clothes, voice or mannerisms including gestures and overall appearance.

Works Cited

Adler, R. K., Hirsch, S., and Mordaunt, M. (Eds.). *Voice and Communication Therapy for The Transgender/Transsexual Client: A Comprehensive Clinical Guide*. San Diego: Plural Publishing Co., 2006.

American Speech-Language Hearing Association. *Code of Ethics*. American Speech-Language Hearing Association, Rockville, MD: 2003. <http://www.asha.org/about/ethics/>.

American Speech-Language Hearing Association. *Cultural Competence*. American Speech-Language Hearing Association, Rockville, MD. <http://www.asha.org>.

American Speech-Language Hearing Association. *Scope of Practice in Speech-Language Pathology*. American Speech-Language Hearing Association, Rockville, MD: 2005.

American Psychiatric Association. *Diagnostic and Statistical Manual of Mental Disorders IV*. Washington, D.C.: American Psychiatric Association, 1999.

Andrews, M. L. *Manual of Voice Treatment. Pediatrics to Geriatrics*. 2nd ed. San Diego: Singular. 1999.

Battin, R. R. "Treatment of the Transsexual Voice." *Voice Disorders*. Ed. W.H. Perkins. New York: Thieme-Stratton, Inc., 1983. 63-66.

Bockting, W. and E. Coleman. "A Comprehensive Approach to the Treatment of Gender Dysphoria." *Gender Dysphoria: Interdisciplinary Approaches In Clinical Management*. Ed. W. Bockting and E. Coleman. New York: Haworth Press, 1992.

Boonin, J. "Articulation." *Voice and Communication Therapy for the Transsexual/Transgender Client: A Comprehensive Clinical Guide.* Ed. R. K. Adler. San Diego: Plural Publishing, 2006.

— — — . "Rate and Volume." *Voice and Communication Therapy for the Transsexual/Transgender Client: A Comprehensive Clinical Guide.* Ed. R. K. Adler. San Diego: Plural Publishing, 2006

Challoner, J. "The Voice of The Transsexual." *Voice Disorders and Their Management.* 3rd ed. Ed. M. Freeman and M. Fawcus. London: Whurr Publishers, 2000. 245-267.

Christianson, A. *"Psychotherapy." Voice and Communication Therapy for the Transsexual/Transgender Client: A Comprehensive Clinical Guide.* Ed. R. K. Adler. San Diego: Plural Publishing, 2006. 69-90.

Dacakis, G. "Assessment And Goals." *Voice and Communication Therapy for the Transsexual/Transgender Client: A Comprehensive Clinical Guide.* Ed. R. K. Adler. San Diego: Plural Publishing, 2006. 101-126.

Dalston, R.M., D. Warren and E. Dalston. "The Use of Nasometry as a Diagnostic Tool for Identifying Patients with Velopharyngeal Impairments." *Cleft Palate Journal* 28 (1991). 184-188.

deBruin, M.D., M.J. Coerts and A.J. Greven. "Speech Therapy in the Management of Male-to-Female Transsexuals." *Folia Phoniatrica et Logopaedica* 52 (2000). 220-227.

Fast, Julius. *Body Language.* New York: M. Evans and Company, Inc. 1970.

Freidenberg, C.B. "Working with Male-to-Female Transgendered Clients: Clinical Considerations." *Contemporary Issues in Communication Sciences and Disorders* 29 (2002). 43-58.

Gelfer, M. P. and J. J. Schofield. "Comparison of Acoustic and Perceptual Measures of Voice in Male-to-Female Transsexuals Perceived as Female Versus Those Perceived as Male." *Journal of Voice* 14 (2000). 22-33.

Hooper, C. R. and I. Hershberger. "Language: Pragmatics and Discourse." *Voice And Communication Therapy For The Transsexual/Transgender Client: A Comprehensive Clinical Guide.* Ed. R. K. Adler. San Diego: Plural Publishing, 2006. 269-282.

Hooper, C.R. "Changing the Speech and Language of the Male to Female Transsexual Client: A Case Study." *Journal of the Kansas Speech-Language-Hearing Association* 25 (1985). 1-6.

— — —. "Language: Syntax and Semantics." *Voice And Communication Therapy For The Transsexual/Transgender Client: A Comprehensive Clinical Guide.* Ed. R. K. Adler. San Diego: Plural Publishing, 2006. 253-268.

Hubble, M., B. Duncan, and B. Miller. *The Heart and Soul of Change: What Works In Therapy.* Washington, DC: American Psychological Association, 1999.

King, J.B., D.E Lindstedt, M. Jensen, and M. Law. "Transgendered Voice: Considerations in Case History Management." *Logopedics Phoniatrics Vocology* 24 (1999). 14-18.

Knowledge and Skills Document for Working with Culturally and Linguistically Diverse Populations. American Speech-Language Hearing Association, 2004. <http://www.asha.org>.

Meyer, W., W., Bockting, P. Cohen-Kettenis, E. Coleman, D. Di Ceglie, H. Devor, L. Goren, J. Hage, S. Kirk, B. Kuiper, D. Laub, A. Lawrence, Y. Menard, J. Patton, L. Schaefer, A.Webb, and C. Wheeler. *The Standards of Care for Gender Identity Disorders,* 6th vers. Düsseldorf: Symposium Publishing.

Oates, J.M., and G. Dacakis. (1986). "Voice, Speech and Language Considerations in the Management of Male-To-Female Transsexualism." in Walters, W. A. W. and J. Oates and G. Dacakis. "Voice Change in Transsexuals." *Venerology. The Interdisciplinary, International Journal of Sexual Health* 10 (1997). 178-187.

— — —. "Speech pathology considerations in the management of trans sexualism- A review." *British Journal of Disorders of Communication* 18 (1983).139-151.

Pausewang-Gelfer, M. "Voice Treatment for the Male-To-Female Transgendered Client." *American Journal of Speech-Language Pathology* 8 (1999). 201-208.

Rachlin, K. "Transgender Individuals' Experience of Psychotherapy." *The International Journal of Transgenderism* 6.1 January-March. (2002).

Scheidt, D., M. Kob, C. Willmes, and Neuschaefer-Rube. (2004). "Do We Need Voice Therapy for Female-To-Male Transgenders?" *26th World Congress of the International Association of Logopedics and Phoniatrics.* Brisbane, Australia 2005.

Standards of Care for Gender Identity Disorders. 6th vers. Harry Benjamin International Gender Dysphoria Association. <www.hbigda.org>.

Stemple, J.C., L. E. Glaze, and B.G. Klaben. *Clinical Voice Pathology: Theory and Management.* 3rd ed. San Diego: Singular Thomson Learning, 2000.

Van Borsel, J., G. De Cuypere, R. Rubens, and Destaerke. "Voice Problems In Female-To-Male Transsexuals." *International Journal of Language and Communication Disorders,* 35.3 (2001). 427-442.

When Bodies Bring Forth More Than Speech:
Voice Teachers and Pregnancy

> Pregnancy
> 1. The condition of being pregnant.
> 2. The quality or condition of being rich in significance, import, or implication.
> 3. Creativity; inventiveness.
>
> *—American Heritage Dictionary*

Prologue

I have never been pregnant. This fact unavoidably shapes my identity as a woman and as an artist.

I may imagine that I know what it means for spirit to seek expression through the body: I have occasionally glimpsed, in creative work, a kind of merging of flesh and life-spark. I have felt inspiration take hold of my being to make something out of nothing.

As Madeleine L'Engle writes, "The artist is a servant who is willing to be a birth-giver. …Each work of art, whether it is a work of great genius or something very small, comes to the artist and says, 'Here I am. Enflesh me. Give birth to me.'" Nevertheless, actual pregnancy and birth—the most quintessentially female acts of creation—remain unknown to me.

On whim, I search a Shakespeare archive, recalling a theater professor's reverent declaration that the Bard gave words to every imaginable human experience. He was wrong! In the Complete Works, "pregnant" appears only as a metaphor; "birth" refers to social class; and women "with child" are described rarely, from a distance, and by men. Nowhere does Shakespeare offer words, vulgar or noble, to women's own experiences of carrying and delivering children.

I turn from the bookshelf, back to the personal question. How would I feel if my body and soul spent most of a year building and then releasing another complete human being? What would happen to my voice, my breathing, and the intuitive body that informs teaching, if my actual body were so profoundly occupied?

My speculations are as empty as my library; I cannot change my fundamental ignorance. So I invite stories from women who know: mothers, teachers, women committed to vocal creativity who have also experienced this other, astonishing, physical-and-spiritual enterprise.

Through their tales, I peek through the doorway of this realm, glimpse its mystery and mundaneness. I am entrusted with intimacies, and "labor" in turn to edit them with care. Like an awkward but hopeful child, I fashion a collage.

ACT I: Heightened Awareness of the Interior

Deborah Sale Butler (DSB): The very first thing I felt was that the abdominal wall relaxes and the organs sort of slosh forward. It's not the baby showing yet; at that point the baby is only about as big as a lima bean! But the whole body is already reacting, preparing for the expansion that will come. If anything, there was a short while when I felt like I had more [breathing] room than usual.

Joanna Cazden, MFA, MS-CCC is a speech pathologist, voice therapist, singer, and intuitive healer in Southern California. She holds theater degrees from CalArts and the University of Washington, and she currently serves on VASTA's Board of Directors. She had an active career as a singer/songwriter in the women's music movement of the 1970s, releasing six solo albums and performing at major folk music, women's music and women's theatre festivals. She has written on vocal health issues for *Electronic Musician, Onstage, Folkworks, Whole Life Times,* and the 2003 issue of VASTA's *Voice and Speech Review.*

CONTRIBUTORS:

Lissa Tyler Renaud, PhD is a Master Teacher: Actors' Training Project, and Professor of Directing, Acting & Voice, Taipei National University of the Arts. She was the English Editor for the IATC Congress, Seoul 2006.

Crystal Robbins is a Lessac specialist who teaches Voice Production for the Stage at Santa Monica College, in California. Her comments are adapted from "The Ecstatic Birth: Lessac Training and Childbirth Preparation," which appeared in the VASTA newsletter in 2002.

Deborah Sale-Butler has coached voice, speech and dialects for over 19 years. She currently teaches at Stella Adler Academy in Hollywood and privately throughout Los Angeles. She is also a working voice actress, appearing in dozens of games and animated series. For more information, visit www.deborahsale-butler.com.

Meredith Scott is a Voice/Dialect coach and Theatre educator. She is currently the Director of the Foote Theatre School at the Citadel Theatre, where she frequently coaches, and is a graduate of the Central School of Speech and Drama. She lives in Edmonton, Alberta with her husband David and their son, Max.

Rene Urbanovich is a singing instructor, a creativity teacher and a mother of four. She holds a BA in Creativity and lives in Santa Clarita, CA. Comments excerpted with permission from "Motherhood and Creativity," unpublished essay © 2005.

Lissa Tyler Renaud (LTR): The first big challenges to my voice and breath came from nausea. It was as if there was a dead rat decomposing in my solar plexus. This is from the baby displacing digestive areas with juices we don't usually taste. I had far more saliva than usual, and was puzzled that I had never heard any mention of such an increase in the literature.

DSB: I didn't have any morning sickness, so I actually gained weight from the outset. I didn't feel bad; I was just hungry. I had some new levels of congestion, like allergies possibly kicked up by hormones, and of course I wasn't taking any medication. I did get some heartburn, not just from spicy foods, but from anything other than really small meals.

LTR: From my movement and alignment training, I had an exaggeratedly heightened awareness of the interior of my body, and could feel the baby fluttering much earlier than the nurses said I would.

Overall, the center of my mental focus was lower—shifted from the areas around the frontal sinus cavity and the sternal joint—to where I imagined The Baby to be, and this didn't so much change the quality of my voice as give me a different vocal sensation to enjoy.

ACT II: A Giant Instrument Surrounding Her

Crystal Robbins (CR): During my pregnancy, Arthur [Lessac] took me step by step through his voice text, *The Use & Training of the Human Voice*. I played the consonant orchestra, much to the growing child's delight. She responded to the percussive taps, the lilting strings and most enjoyed the vibrating and resonating Ybuzz and +Ybuzz.

DSB: When I had my amniocentesis, which is around week 15, I still had pretty good breath control. I was trying to stay relaxed, and they told me I was breathing too deeply! The position of my uterus kept changing so they couldn't stay at the right place. I didn't want that huge needle to hit something it shouldn't, but it took a lot of concentration to breathe shallowly…knowing how to adjust my breath did help.

LTR: The single biggest release in my voice came from releasing my lower abdomen in the second trimester. After a lifetime of trying to flatten the abdomen, pregnant women are doing the opposite for the first time—trying to get their tummies out in front of everyone to show off. Breathing and resonance improve.

DSB: Around my fifth month I think, breathing changed a lot. I couldn't get a deep breath; it just stopped at some point because it was tight. The uterus and the fluids and everything felt like having a basketball shoved up in there, and the digestive organs were pushed up under my lungs. It felt so weird. Just a lot of pressure. The only thing I could do was to think about expanding my back ribs, the back part of my lungs. Even that felt a little tight, and I had to really concentrate or I would get winded really quickly.

Meredith Scott (MS): I didn't notice any significant change in my breathing capacity until close to seven months. However, I carried my son fairly low. I certainly noticed a big change around seven months, give or take. The sensation was like trying to take a real breath but having a lock around my diaphragm and lower front ribs.

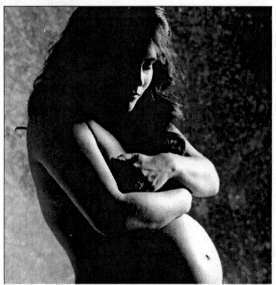

Rene Urbanovich, photograph by Kate Burroughs.

LTR: I only had problems with shortness of breath when the baby got huge and pushed against my diaphragm or got his feet caught in my ribs.

MS: I have to admit there were times when I felt genuine panic over my inability to breathe fully. I found that accessing my back ribs was helpful and eased this panic and tension. If I had not had voice training, I don't know if I could have coped in quite the same way using my back ribs. However, if I had not been acquainted with the sensation of deep, full breathing, I also might not have panicked when I felt unable to breathe deeply.

CR: I Ybuzzed my days away, calming her when she kicked furiously, and I delighted in feeling my entire body as a giant instrument surrounding her in sound. She had her own personal stereo; one that not only gave joy with sound, but one that actually massaged with vibration and tone.

ACT III: Little People Factories

DSB: I learned to monitor my energy level day to day. The speech and dialect work, the accent reduction, were no problem, but the voice work became a lot harder. As my belly got bigger I couldn't bend over. If I demonstrated something on the floor, it was awkward to get up. So if someone was working on the floor, I had to squat. Mostly I just sat and put my feet up.

LTR: I was just shy of 40 when I prepared to give birth to my only child. I had already been teaching for 20 years. I found my bel canto breathing way more useful than the Lamaze breathing, which was, of course, developed by a man who was clearly clueless.

CR: So many of the prescribed exercises in Lamaze seemed to be anesthetic, rather than esthetic and seemed to create tension in order to achieve relaxation. One Lamaze technique called Progressive Relaxation does just that. The mother is asked to tense each part of the body, one section at a time, then release that tension, exhaling on the release. In Lessac Training, we ask, "how can we achieve this effect without bringing tension into the body?"

DSB: I had a planned C-section, so I didn't need the Lamaze stuff on getting through labor. But in the class about breastfeeding, I did have an "aha" moment, realizing what the alveolar ridge is for: It's what the baby uses to hold on to the breast, because of course he doesn't have any teeth.

MS: I looked at the birthing techniques being taught in prenatal classes, and realized that I wouldn't learn anything I didn't already know about breathing.

DSB: My memory and concentration changed. I don't know if that was hormones, or fatigue, or both. I did shorter sessions. There just comes a time when you need to take a nap instead of taking a new client!

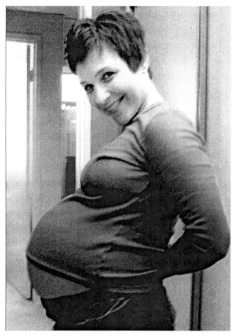

Deborah Sale-Butler, photograph by John Butler.

Rene Urbanovich (RU): In Steinbeck's book, *To a God Unknown*, the pregnant Elizabeth sits in her rocking chair day after day, and someone has the nerve to call her idle. Steinbeck retorts that her inactivity is not useless but creation in the making: *bone casting bone, flesh forming flesh.* I too sat in my rocker alongside my sister-in-law, on my patio. Both of us were expecting. Little people factories, we were.

MS: During my last trimester, although my physical agility was a challenge, the regular attention to breath while I was teaching was a good reminder, and so useful in handling the general strain and exhaustion while pregnant. I think, perhaps, I was less likely to get very breathless while teaching or, say, climbing stairs, because I was able to control my in-breath and out-breath nicely.

CR: [Arthur Lessac and I had] worked on squats and the process gave my legs such a workout that even at nine months I could squat in any position at a deliciously slow pace…these explorations would be beneficial to the physical work required in labor…I was flooded with energy and fueled with strength.

DSB: There came a point when I just off-loaded half of my private students. I didn't have the stamina. But finding back-up teachers, for classes and private work, meant making choices in a hormonally-heightened emotional state.

I wanted to nurture my students, and I also felt scared that they'd be snatched away. I didn't want someone who would elbow into my business while I was on leave and make it harder to build back up when I was ready. On the other hand, this was an opportunity to give back to colleagues who'd sent me referrals in the past.

ACT IV: Creativity at its Most Powerful

LTR: I went into early labor when it was too late to cancel a six-hour acting workshop. I made it through three and a half hours of teaching before I had to quit.

MS: I went into the whole [labour] process fully prepared to make lots of noise, and to scream, wail, chant, etc. my way through it if necessary. Interestingly, vocalizing was less helpful to me than slow, controlled breathing. I tried moaning/intoning but that made me feel less in control. Breath was my anchor.

Staying connected to the breath, and to the movement of my ribs, staying focused on my centre, helped me focus on the baby and not the pain. Keeping my breathing under control made me feel calmer, more in control of what was happening.

LTR: Natural childbirth is supposed to be with the woman moving around and vertical. For some reason, I was strapped to a bed, not only horizontal but with my head lower than my hips…So I was giving birth to a 10-pound baby uphill—unimaginable…There was chaos and it wasn't how they'd promised it would be and there wasn't any help. I almost died. There was exactly one thing that kept me sane and alive: my voice.

I found that if I intoned on a very low pitch, on very long exhales, I could keep going. Everyone looked at me like I was crazy, but I know it worked against what happens to many women—they panic and start hyperventilating and making a high-pitched squealing sound. The nurses were amazed that my shoulders were completely relaxed when I was making this low, long sound.

CR: I found Lessac Training doesn't discount or cover up pain, but fully embraces it and assists the body with all its natural and organic ways of dealing with pain…Why moan as Lamaze teaches? Why not create pleasurable full tone? Many moms are vocal anyway in birth, but the tones are out of restriction, tightness and pain. I tried to translate the tones into useful sound.

LTR: I really think [the vocal intoning] helped the baby, too—kept him calm but also stimulated by the vibration of the bones. It made a transition for him between hearing my voice from inside me to outside. It reassured him that we were in it together.

MS: As the pain got worse, and contractions got longer and closer together, both the breathing and moving into positions that I knew were good for deeper breathing were the most useful and comforting techniques. I don't know if I would have done this naturally without my voice training. The benefits were that I never hyperventilated or felt panicked and breathless.

Pushing was the only phase where the nurse instructed me to breathe a certain way—to hold my breath for ten seconds while I pushed, then take another deep breath and push for

ten seconds more, etc. It didn't make sense to me to hold my breath while I tried to push. I believe the rationale is that they think you can't maintain pressure on your pelvic floor and breathe in at the same time. This is where my voice training came in, as I was able to isolate the action pelvic floor muscles while taking a quick top-up breath.

CR: The CD played our favorite music constantly and as the labor became more intense and my concentration more total, my husband hummed, my labor assistant chimed in and the nurses noticed that between pushes the only thing that completely relaxed my body was to "go to low tones."

Before I knew it, the doctor was Ybuzzing along with the rest of them and I was surrounded by a cacophony of sound…Everybody was vibrating gently, the air was filled with that accompanying energy and the baby seemed to recognize that the comfortable buzzing she was so accustomed to was also going on in that strange outside place. [When] Miss Fiona Maeve was born, she didn't cry. She blinked her eyes and stared right at me.

RU: At the instant [my son's] frame was pulled from mine, maternal love filled my saggy womb. His own heartbeat set the cadence for mine. His hungry body fed on mine. It was the whirl of creativity at its most powerful, allowing me a glimpse of the transcendence that can stretch from one body to another, one soul to another—both inseparable from the glorious Idea who conceived the incredible process.

CR: Twelve hours after giving birth, I found I couldn't breathe easily. My nurse told me I was just nervous about being a mom…Soon, I noticed I couldn't breathe at all lying down. I grew more and more unsure of what was happening. I drew in long slow breaths, worked on expanding gently into the back. When my body suddenly cut short the time I could inhale and would not allow any reserve, I calmly called the nurse for the fifth time and told her to get me oxygen. I smelled the familiar-event flower and my short gentle sips of air sustained me while she walked in, still not believing me, and measured the amount of oxygen in my blood.

Her face went white. The oxygen level in my blood was very, very low. Within in a few hours I was transferred to ICU…The stress of labor had affected my heart [and] my lungs had begun to fill with fluid. Had I accepted the nurse's explanations and drugs, it is very likely that I would've suffocated.

Breathing continued to be difficult and painful for four days and I called upon all my Lessac knowledge to keep calm, to fuel the body with energy and to manage pain. Both my OB and the heart doctors commented on my physical strength and commended my body and breath awareness.

ACT V: Astonished Gratitude

MS: Since giving birth I have noticed an effortlessness in breathing, even more so than before. This is due, I'm sure, to relaxed abdominal muscles…the freedom of breath is remarkable. I feel that I have even greater access to deep abdominal and pelvic breathing. When speaking or singing, I feel that I can root the sound deep in my centre with far less thought or effort to do so than before.

LTR: There was a clear continuity for the baby and me between our way of being together when he was inside me and then when he was out. I had taught many hours per day when my son was lying inside me, and that litany of sounds had been reverberating all around him. As an early infant, he lay on his back and murmured brief strings of sounds, ending each one with a resounding "T" sound—unquestionably imitating the final consonant diction drills!

MS: Because everything I do is based in the creative spirit, I simply presumed creativity would be at the heart of pregnancy, childbirth and motherhood for me. I don't think giving birth has changed that for me—although getting an angry toddler through a grocery store does require endless creativity and patience.

RU: Before my first pregnancy, I had no inkling that the act of childbirth could bring me that close to Perfection, to the Divine; that the daily discoveries experienced by my newborns, my fairies, my toddlers, my children, would expand me again and again—like the belly that billowed before me—that they would become my gurus into the world of the imagination and unseen truth; that they would be the gauge for my spiritual health, the yardstick to track my inner transformation against their own growing, thriving bodies.

MS: The single greatest joy of parenthood recently is listening to my son's voice and vocabulary emerge. He experiments with sound in a way I wish I could get my adult students to. He delights in finally discovering the meaning of a word and, although he cannot say the words, he sings the melody of the alphabet song.

RU: Once I experienced the overwhelming phenomenon called motherhood, I was content to connect with a higher creativity, a kind of significance that reaches beyond time, generations, cultures, symbols. To properly interpret a great work of art or literature, one must take into account the historical references and cultural metaphors. But everyone recognizes the divinity of a baby.

LTR: The first time I sang for my infant son, his face took on a look of astonished gratitude. I could see from him that the voice is a kind of magic and that its purpose is to touch another person where mere fingers cannot touch.

Epilogue

Contemplating these stories, from within a body never so transformed, some descriptions are as I expected. Some are beyond imagining.

As time passes, I visit with babies and their parents, and hear more tales: sleep deprivation and Omnish-ent* babbling; breastfeeding timed between studio classes. If every mother is a working mother, every child is an improvisation.

My own path remains distinct, but somehow more at peace.

*Editor's Note: Developed by Dudley Knight, "Omnish" refers to a form of Gibberish comprised of all the language sounds in the IPA, including non-pulmonic ones.

Essay *by Antonio Ocampo-Guzman*

The Journey of a Bilingual Voice Teacher: Linklater Voice Training in Spanish

Antonio Ocampo-Guzman earned an MFA in Directing and a Diploma in Voice at York University having first trained with the Teatro Libre in Colombia. He spent three years with Shakespeare & Company, and after training with Kristin Linklater, he spent six years teaching at Emerson College. Antonio has been on faculty at Arizona State University, Florida State University, Boston College, The New Theatre Conservatory, Exiles Theater (Ireland), the Canadian National Voice Intensive. Antonio is adapting Linklater's work into Spanish and has offered training workshops at the Estudio Corazza (Madrid), the Teatro Libre (Bogotá) and CEUVOZ (Mexico City). He joins the faculty at Northeastern University in Boston this Fall, where he hopes to practice what he teaches.

In January 2006 I was invited to teach a series of Linklater Voice classes at the *Estudio Corazza para el Actor*, a private training studio in Madrid, Spain. For three amazing weeks I taught the full progression of exercises known as "Freeing the Natural Voice" exclusively in my first language, Spanish. Ever since training with Kristin Linklater in the mid-nineties, I have found teaching this work in English, my second language, to be a very empowering experience. But being able to offer it in Spanish was magnificent: my voice was free in my own language—I was free in my own language. As I came full circle as an artist and as a teacher, my understanding of voice expanded in many ways and my creativity has been ignited. This article is an attempt to fully understand and articulate how Linklater's progression has helped me identify myself as a truly bilingual person: an artist and a teacher who is able to express, train others and create compelling theatre in two languages.

Spanish is my original language, having been born and raised in Bogotá, Colombia. I learned English at an early age at the Anglo-Colombian School in Bogotá, a private school sponsored by The British Council. As a Designated Linklater Voice Teacher, my experiences at undergraduate and graduate academic programs and professional training workshops both in the US and abroad have thus far included:
- Teaching in my second language to native English speakers;
- Teaching in my second language to students for whom English is their second-language;
- Teaching bilingually to students with diverse bilingual abilities; and
- Teaching in my first language to native Spanish speakers.

My own training as a voice teacher started at the Teatro Libre School in Bogotá, where I trained as an actor, under the guidance of Livia Esther Jiménez. Her unique pedagogy was a result of her own self-taught experience, her explorations with the professional theatre company and the numerous workshops she had been able to participate in, including sessions with Cicely Berry in England, and Kristin Linklater in the United States. In 1990, during my third year at the school, Livia Esther invited me to become her apprentice. I eagerly accepted: her voice classes had been essential in my understanding of myself as an artist. It was mostly in Livia Esther's classes that I became aware of how my socio-economic and cultural background had shaped my body, my voice, my intellect and my acting sensibilities; and I began to ask questions about the sort of artist I wanted to one day become. I translated the introduction to *Freeing the Natural Voice* to share with my fellow students, and was so enthralled by the directness and clarity of the Linklater practice that it became evident that I was to become a voice teacher myself. My first steps in that direction were taken in Spanish, leading tutorials and introductory sessions.

In 1993 I arrived at Shakespeare & Company in Lenox, Massachusetts to further my training as an actor at the famous Month-long Intensive Workshop. Although Kristin Linklater was no longer the company's Director of Training, after the initial Master Class with Andrea Haring, I confirmed my desire to train to teach this voice work: the physical sensations of my free voice in my body were exhilarating, pleasurable and liberating. I started the training immediately after the Intensive, spending three years in Lenox. In 1998 I obtained my Linklater Designation—the first Latino and the first native

Spanish-speaker to be designated. The training and my first teaching experiences here in the US were, of course, in my second language.

It is clear to me now, in hindsight, that during those years I appropriated English to assert my own identity as an artist and teacher. To me, English had always been a symbol of cultural superiority ever since the Anglo-Colombian School. And being a Colombian actor who was able to perform even Shakespeare in English and a Colombian teacher who was able to teach voice in English was a source of great pride and accomplishment. It didn't matter that I was leaving a significant part of my psyche and my sensibility dormant. Even if I didn't fully reject my Latin American identity, I merely used it as a touch of exoticism. Indeed, during those first years in the Berkshires, I seldom spoke Spanish and strove hard to build an artistic and personal life centered on an English-only identity. I was so blind and so deaf that I didn't even acknowledge that my English was certainly accented.

Things changed when I left the Shakespeare woods. Kristin Linklater invited me to join the faculty at Emerson College in Boston in 1996. I was starting to realize and accept that here in the US I had the potential of building not only a career but also a life. I wasn't going back to Colombia. In Boston I met other Latin American immigrants who had strong senses of themselves as people and as artists and they taught me about what it means to be an immigrant in this country. Among the many opportunities available in the US there is the unique possibility of being respected as a bilingual, bicultural artist, and such a notion was very enticing to me. It has taken me a few years and the unique experience of my free voice in Spanish to finally embrace that opportunity.

At Emerson, I encountered students whose first language wasn't English either: students from Japan, Cyprus, Panama, even two fellow Colombians. Training them to free their voices in our shared second-language broadened my thinking and my understanding of my own bilingual experience. Freeing one's voice allows one to indeed feel a sense of belonging, a sense of accomplishment that transcends language. It makes one aware of how one operates in this world, and in so doing, helps one accept oneself with respect and curiosity and at the same time, challenging one to find more efficient ways of communicating and operating. Though I was guiding the exercises in English, my students and I were internalizing the freeing experience into our own languages. The Linklater voice training was allowing us not only to master our second language but even more important, it was solidifying our sense of identity as theatre artists.

At some point during those Boston years, I was faced with the notion that the English I claimed as my own was too accented

and might be questionable for a voice teacher, especially at an academic institution. No question—I handle English extremely well grammatically and expressively, but I do have an accent when I speak it. The Linklater training guides one to have a physical sensation of the voice, not to hear the sound of it, since we are not accurate judges of how we sound. I knew my voice felt free in English, but I was unaware of the actual accented sound I had when speaking it. Being faced with the possibility of taking an accent-reduction class in order to appease my critics, I made the political choice not to eliminate my accent, a fierce choice that has served me well all these years. If my voice is to be truly free, it must reveal my own experience of speaking English as a second-language without pretense. This choice is anchored in what I believe are the most important goals of a free voice: to be heard, to be understood and to be able to meet any vocal challenge with utmost efficiency. The notion of my accent is irrelevant as long as I am intelligible and revelatory. Furthermore, teaching voice in my second language gives me an added edge: I am able to guide students of whatever linguistic background to discover their own voices, freedom and potential for expression without the possibility or the temptation of modeling for them how to sound, but rather by truly focusing on the physical sensations of the voice. Once again I confirmed that English was the main vehicle to assert my teaching persona, even if it was accented.

In 2001 I left Boston to attend graduate school at York University in Toronto to pursue an MFA in Directing. I also pursued a Graduate Diploma in Voice Teaching under the guidance of the wonderful David Smukler, himself one of the very first teachers ever to be trained by Kristin Linklater. I had two significant experiences at York: teaching voice to a larger percentage of students who were immigrants and coming to terms with the notion of teaching speech in my second-language. As a Teaching Assistant at York, I had students from Greece, Indonesia, China, Russia, Ukraine, Bangladesh, Pakistan, Venezuela and several other countries, with a very wide spectrum of ability in spoken English. I needed to help these students achieve those basic goals of the voice—help them be intelligible as well as guiding them through the freeing process. Since we were doing this in our shared second-language, I had to be extremely clear. Thanks to David's indefatigable support and guidance, I now accept the importance of teaching speech as a way to help actors be intelligible, not as a way to arbitrarily standardize their speech sounds. Linklater's notion of the free voice being the alchemy between thoughts, feelings, breath and language is the connector between the freeing process and the practice of intelligible speech, one that I acquired in my second-language. This of course applies to all students, regardless of their language of origin and their language of operation: intelligibility is non-negotiable. The best way I have found to teach speech is through the use of Phonetic Pillows, the practice devised by Louis Colaianni. What I love best about this playful system is that I'm able to see language, not just to hear it. In this way, I'm able to guide my students to discover their own speech sounds, clarify them if needed, and become much more eloquent in their speaking without resorting to any sort of corrective or prescriptive methods.

Moving south, my next adventure brought me closer to my own Spanish. After graduate school I accepted a position at Florida State University in Tallahassee, where I met a large number of Latino student actors. By this time I was ready to explore being a bilingual theatre artist in a nation whose ethnic configuration is rapidly changing. I began to wonder what would happen if I were able to adapt the progression of exercises into Spanish and offer these students training in our own language. I facilitated the creation of a bilingual theatre troupe, offered them workshops simultaneously using Spanish and English which culminated in the creation of an evening of bilingual theatre. I also was invited to visit FSU's campus in the Republic of Panamá, and offer some of these bilingual training workshops there. These first experiences in bilingual theatre training were very rewarding and revelatory. Both in Tallahassee and in Panamá, I observed how empowering it was both for the students and for me to be able to use our two languages creatively—to be creative in two languages at the same time. There is a wide spectrum in the bilingual experience: from those of us who are able to go from one language to the other easily, being able to formulate and articulate thoughts, feelings, impulses and images in both languages, to those who think in one language and translate to the other. Among younger people such as many of my FSU students, the most common experience is that Spanish is the language of their family sphere, but their social lives are conducted primarily in English. Thus, these bilingual theatre adventures were helping those young artists not only to free their own voices, but also reclaim their language of origin in a creative way. Although most of us end up speaking a seamless combination of both languages, what is commonly known as "Spanglish," I chose to conduct most of the sessions in Spanish only—to have it be the backbone language. It was a challenge for some of us, but the universal language of theatre helped us create alchemy and allowed us to communicate and to create within that wide spectrum of bilingualism. The culmination of these adventures was a bilingual production of Shakespeare's *Romeo & Juliet,* which I adapted and directed at FSU in April 2005.

Most of these Latino students had been raised here in the US and I found it intriguing that I witnessed similar vocal challenges in them to those I found in non-Latino students. Overall, most of the people I have come in contact with in

training programs here in the US have little connection to the core of their bodies, living as far away from their pelvises as possible, with very tight jaws compensating for the lack of breath available from the core, and very tight and nasal voices as a result. However, Latino students who had been raised in Latin America, or whose family life was more Spanish-dominant, seemed to have more energy in the core but their tongues were tighter. Could it be that living in Spanish allows one to have more core energy, but dealing with two linguistic influences confuses and therefore tightens our tongues?

I was fortunate to meet a wonderful colleague, Micha Espinosa, in 2004 through the Voice & Speech Trainers Association, the only other visible Latina in the organization. Micha, an Associate Teacher of Fitzmaurice Voice work, had been conducting very specific research about how Latino students were being trained in US academic training programs. Our sensibilities, curiosities and passions merge together seamlessly and we have since collaborated on several projects centered on the professional training of Latino actors. Micha and I led a roundtable discussion on the subject at the 2006 ATHE Conference in Chicago and are in the process of writing further about that same issue. The predicament is that although Latinos continue to grow in numbers, and there is a plethora of Latino theatre companies, writers and scholars of incredible promise all around, the training of actors continues to be conducted under Euro-centric sensibilities. My collaboration with Micha has expanded my understanding not only of my own linguistic voice journey, but more significantly, of the great impact my own experience and my teaching may have on a generation of Latino theatre artists in this country. As it were, I have also started to free my bilingual political voice.

I moved to Phoenix in the summer of 2005 to coordinate the MFA in Performance program at Arizona State University's School of Theatre & Film. I was drawn to the southwest for the potential it offered to my adventures in bilingual theatre. Although I do not have as many bilingual theatre students at the university, there is a wide base of community actors centered at Teatro Bravo, a thriving Latino theatre company, which has invited me to explore with them. Micha Espinosa and I offered a weekend workshop for them in February 2006 including acting, voice and self-scripted storytelling and it was great to witness the power of training in two languages. Most impressive for me was witnessing Micha reclaiming her own Spanish, which had been stripped off her in elementary school. Voice work was not only empowering us—it was returning our identity.

And then, I was invited to teach in Madrid. For the first time I was able to teach the full progression of "Freeing the Natural Voice" exercises in my own language. The *Estudio Corazza para el Actor* is a very well known private training studio run by distinguished Argentinean teacher Juan Carlos Corazza, who has coached several of Spain's most famous actors including Javier Bardem and Marisa Paredes. I taught the third-year actors who had previously had some Linklater Voice Training from my colleague Leticia Santafé, and the fourth-year actors who hadn't. The very first session was an adventure in linguistic differentiation. It went smoother than I thought, although I did find myself blanking on certain words or expressions. But by the end of the second session, I was fully fluent, precise and energized in my own language. I noticed that in general, these Spanish students had a great amount of energy in the core of their bodies but had very tight tongues. I think it is a cultural phenomenon, especially in Madrid where the common accent pushes the voice into the throat. A most incredible breakthrough for a male student in releasing his tongue shed some light. After being able to release the back of his tongue and fully breathe, he connected with the memory of his First Communion, and how terrified he felt at the huge responsibility of receiving the body of his Lord into his mouth. He remembered the exact moment in which his tongue froze. Another student experienced a similar breakthrough as he released the back of his tongue and was able to limber up his soft-palate muscles. After wailing for a bit he told us of the horrific experience of having his tonsils removed at age seven, without anesthesia and after hearing the painful screams of other patients as he waited with his mother in the doctor's waiting room.

I came full circle. I would describe the physical sensation I felt as I led the exercises in Spanish as elation—I sensed my body following my own instructions and lengthening, opening and releasing at a very deep level. I was breathing with more fullness, releasing sound with much more ease, thinking with more precision, and more important, I was reaching the students more accurately, more incisively. It was as if teaching in my language had unleashed an undiscovered ability to be succinct and efficient. Or maybe, having practiced being efficient and precise in my second language for such a long time allowed this to happen. At any rate, I cannot recall a time in which my teaching was so successful or a time in which I felt so truly myself.

In Spanish, Kristin Linklater's carefully systematized work remains basically the same although there must be some changes. The most specific one is the use of the sound of sigh of relief (huh). Spanish vowels tend to be much more open when one thinks about them. From an early age we are taught that there are only five pure vowel sounds in Spanish /a/, /e/, /i/, /o/, /u/. Of course there are a myriad of variations, but usually a schwa sound is associated with exhaustion and non-committed sound, which is not at all what the initial Touch of Sound ought to be. When first introducing that notion I have

had to be even more adamant about the differentiation of relaxation as collapse versus relaxation as release of energy. Having to find language to guide Spanish-speaking students to release that initial touch of sound with energy has informed me how to make the same instruction even clearer in English. Now I refer to tension as the concentration of energy and to relaxation as the release of energy, and that has proven to be quite accurate in both languages. The other main difference is in what the vertebral column is called. I like the English word "spine." It gives a sense of support, of structural support but also a sense of movement, or sinewy movement. In Spanish the possibilities are *columna vertebral* or *espina dorsal*, which both evoke notions of stiffness. When I introduce Physical Awareness in Spanish I have to be very clear about how moveable, flexible and strong the spine truly is. I have had to increase the number of exercises that support this notion and am now following Linklater's suggestion of naming it the "thinking spine" in both languages—*la columna pensante*.

After returning from Spain I decided to fully embrace my identity in two languages and to center my career on the experience of being a fully bilingual teacher and artist, and to offer training across the whole spectrum of my bilingual experience. With her benediction, I have begun adapting Kristin Linklater's book into Spanish, which I will do in close cooperation with Leticia Santafé in Madrid and hope to have published and available by 2008. I am continuing to collaborate with Micha Espinosa on refining bilingual training curriculum, to offer workshops across the US sponsored by Latino theatre companies, and to disseminate our experiences to the larger US theatre community. I will also begin to offer Linklater Voice Training workshops exclusively in Spanish here in the US, and am setting up workshop series elsewhere in Latin America. This past August I was invited to lead Master Classes at the newly inaugurated *Centro de Estudios Para el Uso de la Voz* (CEUVOZ) in Mexico City and am hoping to develop a voice-teacher training program exclusively in Spanish in collaboration with CEUVOZ and Arizona State University.

I am ready to fully inhabit this experience of being a bilingual voice teacher, a bilingual theatre artist and a bilingual member of the theatre community. I would not have been able to get here without the intense linguistic journey I have taken with the Linklater practice as my pilot. More than anything else, what I appreciate about the journey is the clarity I have gained concerning what is truly important about training an actor's voice. The most essential discovery: voice is about communication...reaching the other person with my thoughts, feelings, impulses and my desire to be understood, listened to and acknowledged. I firmly believe this is universal, and transcends languages. I will venture to assert that the more languages we speak and create in, the more sensibility we will have to human communication.

Essay *by Bettye Zoller Seitz*

The Freelance Dance: A Private Studio Teacher Talks

Bettye Zoller Seitz is an award-winning broadcaster and voiceover/studio singer, live performer in cabarets and theatres, vocalist on recordings for Disney, Sony, and MGM, and an RCA Recording artist/EMI Screen Gems published songwriter. She holds post-graduate degrees in both music and communications from the Univ. of Missouri at Kansas City, the Univ. of North Texas, and the Univ. of Texas at Dallas. She has served on speech communications and music faculties at SMU, the Univ. of Texas at Arlington, Dallas County and Collin County Community Colleges. She owns a digital audio recording studio in Dallas and produces audio books, voiceovers, and demo CDs. She has written 11 non-fiction audio books in the speech communication and show business fields including *Speaking Effective English.*

Despite periodic forays into living the academic or corporate life, I've always found great personal and monetary rewards being a freelancer. The last time I accepted a corporate position (Creative Director with a large music production house), my accountant reminded me of a client who had agreed to sell his products exclusively to Sears. When Sears stopped ordering abruptly, the man was bankrupted! It is a cautionary tale and true. I was dismissed on one week's notice in a stock takeover. It took almost a year to rebuild my company. I'll never relinquish freelancer status again!

Many say, "ah, but I want the security of a steady paycheck." It has been my experience that there is seldom security in being someone's employee. While, as a longtime member of the Screen Actors Guild and the American Federation of Radio TV Artists, I have always had health coverage for my family, a great plus today. The self-employed can obtain insurance and have many advantages that were not available when I first began my freelance career. Childcare was in its infancy then. I had to find caregivers to come into my home. Daycare centers did not even exist on a national basis.

As a voice, speech, actor's and singer's coach, I encourage self-employment. I feel it is the only path to success if you are a performance-oriented individual. Be not afraid! As film producer/director Francis Ford Coppola is quoted as saying, "I have to succeed! What am I going to do? Fire myself?" I like controlling my life, my money, my projects. I enjoy each day and feel as if I've never "had a job" (when I've been freelance, that is...).

While teaching in major university systems (six) over the years, I discovered that salaries simply were not commensurate with the number of hours required. I admit that I greatly enjoy classroom teaching and still accept occasional adjunct assignments. It fills my need for variety as a teacher and yields new clients as well. It is a great way to be seen and to advertise one's business. My studio is valuable to the singers and actors I teach. Also, non-students in the community who want to produce audio books, singer's and voiceover talent's demo CDs, commercials, and other audio projects can rent the studio.

Although I still sing professionally (as the spirit moves me), my days as an entrepreneur usually begin early and end late. I am often working past midnight (and loving every minute). I enjoy the chase. I relish the hunt. I'm eager to try new things, teach in new ways, learn new information and acquire new skills. The "go back to school" itch infects me about every three or four years. As a freelancer, I believe that lifelong learning is a "must." We're often isolated when we're freelance except at conferences or meetings. We desperately need comradeship, our colleagues' input.

Trying to decide what would benefit you most, I have compiled the following list of discussion points. Remember: it is not within the scope of this article to provide in-depth information. Browse the "miles of aisles" at your local bookseller and see and buy many of the wonderful books that are available on every facet of freelance and business life.

As you will see, the first requirement of a successful freelancer is self-motivation and self-discipline. Organization is important to your freelance success too. If you can't organize an office properly, hire someone to help you do it.

Your files and books must be in order. If you can't rise early each morning and enthusiastically enter your office to return calls and make new acquaintances, you will need to learn more about how to become a fully functional freelance entrepreneur. No one will "fire you" for your shortcomings. Only your checkbook will show a deficit. Soon, your life will reflect that deficit too!

Here is my list:

Important Issues for Freelancers

1. *General pricing strategies*. Do I price my services differently to corporations than to individual clients? Do I charge higher fees to attorneys or physicians or executives than to college students? Yes. Just as retail merchants charge more for goods and services in affluent than in economically depressed areas. I charge more per day to large corporate clients than to small hometown store owners.

2. *Pricing long-term or "package" jobs*. What do I want as my per-hour wage? I add 20% more to assure that I receive adequate payment should unforeseen problems occur.

3. *No-shows and tardy clients*. I've adopted a "three strikes and you're out" rule. I inform problematic clients if they are no-shows for appointments or arrive late more than twice, I will refuse to teach or consult with them in the future. I have this rule in writing on my "Studio Policies" sheet. **Be sure you formulate a policies sheet and give it to all your clients! Post it on your studio wall too.**

4. *Bounced checks and other money problems*. In writing, clearly state those insufficient funds checks will be reported and the maker charged $25.00. I accept MC and VISA too (with a 5% added service fee). I process cards online while the client is present. Credit charges can be used as installment payments too. By agreement, charge the client's card on pre-arranged dates.

5. *Advertising—what works and what doesn't?* Find what methods of advertising work best. Then, pursue those methods exclusively. My best advertising is for me to appear on radio-TV talk shows. I also mail and post eye-catching fliers, e-mail newsletters and notes, attend industry networking functions, conventions, symposiums and hand out business cards everywhere.

6. *Become an organizational animal!* Join every organization in your field and become an active member. Wait at least one year to judge the effectiveness of your membership. Offer your services as a free speaker or entertainer. Present mini-workshops if the potential for advertising seems great. Sell your books, audio products, and manuals at events.

7. *Hire others with expertise*. A friend told me that I should stop performing brain surgery. He was criticizing my attempts at bookkeeping. He urged me to use my time more wisely to make money. I've hired bookkeepers and accountants ever since! Hire others to stuff envelopes, post fliers, answer telephones, run errands and be your assistant. It pays off!

8. *Get insured*. You will need liability insurance if your homeowner's policy or renter's policy does not cover client mishaps. You may want liability insurance in case someone claims you injured his/her voice or body in some way. When you train large corporations, you'll be required to have insurance they mandate. They'll be specific and you'll have to obtain the insurance required before they'll permit you to enter their premises or teach any of their employees at your studio.

9. *Protect your company name*. First, at your local courthouse, search records to determine if someone else already has the business name you've chosen. Next, if you're not incorporating, file "doing business as" papers—"dba." Whether you copyright your business name is up to you. This usually requires an attorney's assistance although online legal websites are becoming more and more helpful to do-it-yourselfers.

10. *Office at home or rent studio space?* You decide—is your home or apartment suitable for teaching or consulting? You will need adequate space, a bathroom for client's use, a quiet environment, an entrance that clients can use without invading others' privacy in your home. If your living quarters are not suitable, rent studio space nearby. Sometimes, sharing rented space is possible if you can also share a teaching schedule with another person. If you do rent space, be sure the landlord knows what you do, that he/she has no objections concerning your business activities and sees no conflict with neighboring businesses.

11. *Get savvy about today's electronic revolution!* I cannot possibly begin to fully address this subject here. Suffice it to say that you need to read and study and attend seminars to stay up-to-date in your field about recording devices, computers, and all of the other electronic advances that have taken us into the electronic age. Seek advice from experts and get wired for success! My digital recording studio at home, plus other up-to-date devices provide needed tools for a modern business. I feel it is a "must" in today's world!

12. *Maintain a website presence!* If you're not "internet educated," hire someone to build your website, simple or complex, because everyone in every field of endeavor today

needs a presence on the internet. You may want an online store too from which you can sell your goods and services.

13. *Think about how you can expand your repertoire of services.* How can you diversify so that when you don't have adequate income from teaching singers you can teach actors? If you don't have sufficient book or audio book sales, then present workshops to bring in extra cash. What areas of expertise are you not now using in your business? Diversify! This can be your all-purpose answer to cash-flow problems. All businesses have peak periods and slow times. What are yours? You should know!

14. *Make your public image professional.* Your branding, your public image, should be professional…it is your face to the world. Your letterhead, business cards, postcards, notepads, and informal notes all should be uniform and polished. Provide a logo for use on everything you do.

15. *Sponsor or contribute support to worthy causes.* It's your best advertising to support telethons, charity fundraisers, serve on phone banks, be a fundraiser, and help with organizational projects. It gives you the right kind of visibility and I believe it's building karma—give and ye shall receive!

16. *Freelancers can have paid vacations but only if they figure out ways to do it!* My family and I have enjoyed many wonderful vacations over the years. Each was not only a welcomed getaway, but I was able to continue with some important work as well. That way, my trip could be tax deductible—legal deductions are a great benefit to being self-employed.

17. *If what you're doing isn't making enough money, do something else.* It need not mean you have to stop freelancing. Diversify. Find new ways of selling your expertise. Get creative with your entrepreneurship. Find out where the need is, serve that need and you can succeed.

18. *Your telephone system must be professional.* Record a professional message on your answering machine. Obtain a voice mailbox from your local telephone company if you don't want to release your personal numbers to the public. Think carefully before giving out your cell phone number. I only give mine to good customers and students.

19. *Whatever it takes, stay positive!* Stay away from negative people and negative self-talk. Find and participate in activities that encourage you. Be proud of your business. Your business is YOU!

20. *Maintain a paper trail of every penny spent that is deductible!* For tax purposes, if ever audited, you'll need to prove you spent the money you claimed you spent for business reasons. The IRS will examine in minute detail every receipt, every statement and monthly bill. Know this material when you go to an audit session. More important, don't go to an audit alone. Hire your attorney or CPA or advisor to go with you to speak for you and to be your defender. It will be worth the money you spend! If possible, keep your accounts on a computer program such as "Quick Books" or if you don't want to keep your own books, hire a bookkeeper who understands the freelance life and your business area too. It's not your job to educate a bookkeeper. It is too time consuming. Find someone who already operates in your area by asking friends about who they use. Many creative "types" do not think much about the nuts and bolts of business, but when push comes to shove, it is the lack of business expertise that usually kills a creative venture. Get smart and get your business information from a pro!

Essay *by Sally Morgan*

Marketing for Artists

Wow, I can't believe I was asked to write this column! I've always considered myself rather lousy at marketing, but other artists do ask me for advice, which only goes to prove there is a need for more marketing information. I will be glad to share my knowledge about how I market myself as an artist with services and products.

Begin rejecting the starving artist concept. You are what you think. Replace this negative concept with a plan to become a financially secure artist. See yourself as someone who has something to offer that others need and are willing to pay good money for.

Presentation is the key. Assume no one else knows about your product or services. In order for you to become financially secure, let the world know about your work through business cards, a website, fliers, organizations of your peers, and organizations that need your skills to succeed.

These promotional materials come with a cost. Be prepared to spend money. There are hungry graphic arts students out there who can help, but if you want a professional look, hire a real professional. Be careful to make a business choice and not an emotional choice, as the emotional choice will cost you money in the long run—believe me…I know.

Present your product in an attractive manner. Make it easily accessible and understandable to your potential buyer. Devise a matching color scheme for all of your promotional and product materials. You will then look much more professional.

Take your time! Marketing yourself is a process that requires much fore-thought and planning. Begin with a brain dump. Write down everything that comes to mind about yourself and your product—no matter how strange or crazy it sounds. Get a friend to help you and bounce ideas off one another. Or you can hire a professional to help ignite your ideas and guide you through implementation.

The most important aspect of presentation is your point-of-view. Potential clients will respond to your attitude toward your services and products. How much do you value your expertise? Who needs your expertise? Look at your product as fulfilling a specific need or as solving a particular problem.

Never sell, always solve a problem for your client. Look at your products as tools to help your clients build essential skills that solve their problems. For instance, I have a CD for my business clients. Yes, I want to sell the CD so I can make money, but what I really want is to give my clients an accessible, convenient way to build their speaking skills.

The bottom line is to make sure the product you are marketing reflects *you*. All the slick promo materials and fabulous products will not yield a great career if you present yourself as a starving artist! People want to work with someone who is successful.

Sally Morgan is a New York City based author of *Morganix Method,* ™ *Your Key to Vocal Excellence* and *125 Secrets to Help You Speak Like a Pro.* She is also an award-winning composer singer and master vocal trainer. She coaches business professionals to "Speak Up and Win!" through workshops and private training. Her website is *www.MorganixMethod.com*

An artist has passion and enthusiasm—otherwise you would not be an artist. Let it shine. "Other" folks are fascinated by someone in the arts and find passion very attractive. It makes you memorable. This is where I think artists have a distinct advantage. Play a very wealthy, successful character if you need to when presenting yourself to potential clients.

When people ask you what you do, don't be shy—tell them in a way that relates to their business. For instance, if you are talking to a plumber then tell the plumber how you can help him build his business or enhance his life. Let him know what you have to offer to help build the business or to help him become more visible in his particular field…or help to build his self-confidence. Then the focus will be on your potential client and not on you—makes it easier.

Join at least one good networking group—one full of successful business people and dynamic speakers who can teach you how to run a business. Their business brains work differently from artists, I swear! My favorite networking group is the National Speakers Association. My brain hurts after four hours of meeting and lecture, yet I have learned so much.

You might want to check out a wonderful book and training program led by a former actor, Michael Port, called *Book Yourself Solid*. Michael's system of marketing is the only one I've experienced that does not give me a headache.

Work on just one tiny piece of the marketing puzzle at a time as you begin to put things together, otherwise you run the risk of becoming overwhelmed and stuck. You can even set a timer for ten minutes. Work for ten minutes, and then take ten minutes off. Work your way up to fifteen minutes with just a five-minute break and so on. An enormous task is doable in small chunks.

Good luck!

Voice and Speech Science, Vocal Health *Ronald C. Scherer, Associate Editor*

Editorial Column *by Ronald C. Scherer, Associate Editor*

Welcome to the "Voice and Speech Science, Vocal Health" section of this issue of the *Voice and Speech Review*. This issue offers a variety of topics important to our everyday pedagogy and art.

Dr. Joseph Stemple and Ms. Lisa Thomas ("Vocal Health and Hydration: Fact or Fiction?") provide a thorough review of the research literature on hydration for healthy voice and speech that leads to an informed common sense about hydration for health. They make it clear there is still much yet to be known. It is also a reminder that advice on health matters within our purview needs to be based on what is scientifically known if at all possible, not on tradition, habitual thinking, or personal bias.

The other three papers of this section are scientifically-oriented and deal with the effects of applied Lessac pedagogy, subglottal pressure in the speech of the actor on stage, and an interdisciplinary orientation to psychogenic voice and gender.

Dr. Marth Munro and Professor Daan Wissing ("Testing the Use of Lessac's Tonal NRG as a Voice Building Tool for Female Students at a South African University—A Perceptual Study") examined whether or not applying a Lessac approach to voice building over 14 weeks actually produced better voices. The results strongly suggest that the sound quality of the stage voice, perceived by theatre experts, is significantly improved via this teaching method. The study helps to establish research protocols and support the important "outcomes research" imperative needed for essentially all techniques we wish to apply to improve voice and speech. The follow-up study on the acoustic recordings related to the perceptions of voice in this work will further identify the pedagogical targets from this approach.

Ms. Malin Abrahamsson and Dr. Johan Sundberg ("Subglottal Pressure Variation in Actors' Stage Speech") offer a study on subglottal pressure dynamics in actors' stage speech. They come to some very interesting conclusions. We know that in English syllable stress is often related to intensity, frequency, and duration increases. These authors found that stress was related primarily to duration, and that unstressed syllables as well as consonants often appear to have received increases in subglottal pressure, apparently as an attempt by the actor to increase intelligibility on stage. Thus, respiratory control for stage speech is perhaps a different phenomenon than for spontaneous speech.

The final paper of this section is by Ms. Amanda Loy-Jung ("Psychogenic Voice Disorders and Gender: An Interdisciplinary Look at the Prevention, Identification, and Treatment of the Voice in Disequilibrium"). It is an in-depth view of psychogenic voice disorders related to gender. She reviews the basic concepts related to psychogenic voice problems, the various etiologies associated with these problems, and the relationships to feminine and masculine stereotyping. This is a most informative article that effectively ties the disciplines of theatre actor training, speech-language pathology, psychology, sociology, and gender and interpersonal communication to the "voice in disequilibrium." This erudite article has significant worth for diagnosis, therapy, and pedagogy of voice and speech, as well as character analysis for actors.

Dr. Ron Scherer, Professor in the Department of Communication Disorders, Bowling Green State University, teaches voice disorders and speech science courses. His research interests include the physiology and mechanics of basic, abnormal, and performance voice production and intervention, and the methodologies involved in such research. He was Senior Scientist at the Denver Center for the Performing Arts and taught in the DCPA's voice and speech trainers program. He received his PhD from the University of Iowa, a master's degree from Indiana University in speech-language pathology, and also spent two years as a music major at Indiana University.

Column *by Joseph C. Stemple & Lisa B. Thomas*

Vocal Health and Hydration: Fact or Fiction?

Dr. Stemple received his PhD in Communication Disorders from the University of Cincinnati in 1977. Prior to becoming Professor of Communication Disorders at the University of Kentucky in 2005, he served as founder and Director of the Blaine Block Institute for Voice Analysis and Rehabilitation. Dr. Stemple is the author of the texts *Voice Therapy: Clinical Studies* (2nd ed) and *Clinical Voice Pathology: Theory and Management* (3rd ed) as well as research articles and text chapters related to clinical voice disorders. An active speaker and lecturer, Dr. Stemple also holds adjunct faculty status with the Departments of Speech Pathology and Communication Sciences and Disorders of Miami University of Ohio, and the University of Cincinnati, respectively. He is a Fellow of the American Speech-Language-Hearing Association.

Lisa Thomas completed her MA Degree in Communication Disorders at Marshall University in 1992. After graduation, she began work at Cabell Huntington Hospital in Huntington, West Virginia, where she established the region's first voice center. In 2002, Ms. Thomas joined the faculty of Marshall University as an Assistant Professor in the Department of Communication Disorders, teaching primarily in the areas of voice and neurogenic disorders. She is currently pursing her PhD at the University of Kentucky and conducting translational research related to the aging voice.

Background

A discussion of vocal health is not complete without a thorough review of the issues related to laryngeal hydration. These issues may be found in numerous articles, texts, and websites related to professional voice care (Rubin, Sataloff, & Korovin 2006; Stemple, Glaze, & Klaben 2000). Hydration of the vocal folds may be described in terms of systemic or atmospheric. Systemic hydration refers to the internal hydration of the entire body that keeps the skin, eyes, and all other mucosal tissues healthy. Appropriate levels of systemic hydration are said to be dependent upon the amount and types of liquids consumed related to the amount or level of physical activity. Atmospheric or external hydration refers to the environmental influences on the respiratory system that may contribute to the surface lubrication of the respiratory tract, including the vocal folds. The rapid vibration of the vocal folds creates friction which in turn results in the production of heat. As oil reduces friction in a motor, well-lubricated vocal folds provide for the optimal tissue environment for maintaining the most efficient vibratory characteristics of the vocal folds. This lubrication is said to be dependent upon adequate internal and external hydration.

Professional voice users are often challenged by busy schedules, diets, travel conditions, working environments, personal stress, and other lifestyle habits that challenge the ability to maintain adequate hydration. However, based on observation of the large numbers of professional voice users who walk into our clinical voice centers with water bottles in hand, the message of the importance of laryngeal hydration appears to be resonating with this special population. But, does scientific evidence actually support the clinical suggestions made regarding hydration and voice care? In other words, does the evidence for dictating liquid intake actually support the practice?

Hydration Research

Lubrication of the larynx and vocal folds has long been considered in the literature. In 1974, Punt noted "considering certain singers' throats over a period of years, I have often noted that those which are well lubricated survive longer" (287). In the article, Punt went on to review systemic, local, and atmospheric methods of enhancing vocal fold lubrication. His suggestions of liquid intake and the use of humidifiers to enhance vocal health continue to be espoused in the vocal care literature. Since that time, several studies have scientifically examined the influence of hydration on voice production (Chan & Tayama 2002; Fisher, Ligon, Sobecks, & Roxe 2002; Sivasankar & Fisher 2002; Solomon & DiMattia 2000; Verdolini, Titze, & Fennell. 1994; Verdolini-Marston, Sandage, & Titze 1994; Verdolini-Marston, Titze, & Drucker 1990; Yiu & Chan 2003). Let us examine these studies which focused primarily on the systemic and environmental manipulations of hydration.

Verdolini-Marston, Titze, and Drucker (1990) used a 3 x 3 factorial design to examine the influence of both systemic and atmospheric hydration on the phonation pressure thresholds (PPTs)[1] of six healthy adults. PPT refers to the minimal air pressure necessary to initiate steady vocal fold vibration. Subjects were exposed to three conditions—dry, wet, and control. Under dry conditions, subjects were placed in an area of 30 to 35% humidity for four hours and given three teaspoons of a decongestant (drying) medication. Subjects in wet conditions were placed in an area with 85 to 100% humidity, given two teaspoons of a mucolytic agent along with water upon request. For the control condition, no manipulations of humidity were made by investigators, no medications were taken, and water intake was not controlled. Phonation pressure thresholds were taken at low, medium, and high pitches at the close of each condition. Results suggested that PPTs were lowest (desired direction) for the "wet," or hydrated condition. The authors concluded that hydration had a positive influence on the phonation pressure threshold of subjects by altering the viscoelastic properties of the vocal folds. Following this logic, it could also be concluded that vocal folds subjected to drying conditions may not vibrate as efficiently as those that are well hydrated.

In a 1994 follow-up study, Verdolini, Titze, and Fennell replicated the previous study using a double-blind, placebo-controlled, counterbalanced design. Twelve nonsmoking adults were each exposed to three conditions—wet, dry, and control. Measurements of phonation threshold pressure and perceived phonatory effort were taken prior to and following each of the above conditions. Results suggested that phonation pressure thresholds decreased with an increase in hydration and vice versa. Thus, an inverse relationship between hydration and phonation pressure threshold was identified. Furthermore, subject ratings of perceived phonatory effort increased following the dehydration ("dry") condition. Ratings of effort did not change with the hydration ("wet") or control conditions. The authors concluded that level of hydration does play a role in voice production by altering the pressure required to initiate phonation.

Results of the previous studies indicated that, in individuals with normal voice production, adequate hydration had a positive impact on one measure of vocal function (PPT) and that a condition of dehydration increased perceived effort. The next study was conducted using individuals with voice disorders. Verdolini-Marston, Sandage, and Titze (1994) used a double-blind, placebo-controlled, subject crossover design to determine if there was a benefit of internal and external hydration over a placebo treatment in the management of vocal nodules. Subjects were six adults with the diagnosis of vocal nodules or vocal polyps. The hydration condition included a two-hour exposure to a high humidity environment, the intake of eight glasses of water, and the intake of one teaspoon of a mucolytic agent three times over the course of the day. Placebo conditions included two hours in a room with filtered air and lighted, scented candles, eight sets of finger exercises, and one teaspoon of an "herbal medicine" (actually cherry syrup) three times per day. The authors identified statistically significant pre- to post-treatment differences for the hydration group in the areas of perceived phonatory effort, appearance of the

vocal folds, and the acoustic measure of shimmer. No such pre- to postcondition differences were identified in the placebo group. Furthermore, no statistically significant pre- to post-condition differences (improvements) were observed in either group for phonation threshold pressure, auditory perceptual ratings of voice, and the acoustic measures of jitter and signal-to-noise ratio. The authors concluded that the study provided early evidence in support of the use of hydration as a form of treating vocal nodules and polyps.

Solomon and DiMattia (2000) studied the impact of hydration on the phonation threshold pressures of four women during periods of prolonged reading. Subjects served as their own controls in a single subject ABAC design. Two treatments were applied. One treatment condition was considered "high hydration" and one condition was considered "low hydration." The high hydration condition delayed the onset of elevated phonation threshold pressures in three of four subjects. Interesting to note, the opposing dehydration condition did not produce increases in phonation threshold pressures. The authors concluded that hydration may be able to reduce vocal fatigue secondary to prolonged talking.

In 2001, Fisher, Ligon, Sobeecks, and Roxe hypothesized that body fluid reduction, without dehydration, would increase phonatory threshold pressure (P(th)) and be associated with patient-perceived increases in phonatory effort and worsening voice quality. The authors used a single-subject, full reversal design. A controlled volume of body fluid was repeatedly removed via ultrafiltration from six adults with end stage renal disease. The results demonstrated that the P(th) increased significantly with fluid volume reduction and reversed to baseline with fluid replacement in four of the six subjects. Fluid loss also accounted for 40% variance in perceived vocal effort. These results indicated that substantial systemic body fluid reduction without body dehydration causes voice symptoms.

In a follow-up study, Sivasankar and Fisher (2002) examined the effects of superficial dehydration on voice production by comparing the effects of short-term oral and nasal breathing on the P(th) and perceived vocal effort. Twenty female subjects were randomly assigned to oral and nasal breathing groups. Following 15 minutes of oral breathing, P(th) increased at comfortable and low pitches ($p < 0.01$) with six of ten subjects reporting increased vocal effort. Nasal breathing reduced P(th) at all three pitches ($p < 0.01$), and seven of ten subjects reported decreased vocal effort. These results demonstrate the role of superficial or external hydration on the efficiency of vocal fold vibration.

Using a basic science animal model, Chan and Tayama (2002) examined the effects of hydration on the viscoelastic shear properties of vocal fold tissue in vitro. Osmotic changes (both hydration and dehydration) of five excised canine larynges were induced by sequential incubation of the tissues in isotonic, hypertonic, and hypotonic solutions. Vibratory characteristics were examined as a function of frequency. The results demonstrated that vocal fold tissue stiffness and viscosity increased significantly (by four to seven times) with osmotically-induced dehydration with the same measures decreasing by 22% to 38% on the induced rehydration. These findings supported the hypothesis that hydration affects vocal fold vibratory characteristics and that appropriate levels of hydration may improve the biomechanics of phonation.

Finally, Yiu and Chan (2003) studied the impact of combined hydration and periodic voice rest on 20 nonprofessional Karoke singers. Subjects were randomly assigned to a hydration + voice rest experimental group or a nonhydration + non-voice rest control. Subjects in the experimental group received 100 ml of water and one minute of voice rest following each song. The control subjects did not receive water or voice rests. Results demonstrated that subjects in the experimental group were able to sing significantly longer than subjects in the control group (*p* <0.001). Furthermore, subjects who received the hydration treatment saw no changes in acoustic or perceptual measures from the pre- to postsinging conditions. Subjects in the experimental group experienced mild acoustic changes following singing. In noting one limitation of the study, the authors reported that neither hydration nor vocal rest could be causally linked to the improvements in the experimental group due to the combination of the two measures in the study. However, the authors concluded that hydration, when provided along with periodic vocal rest, was beneficial in reducing the vocal fatigue of singers.

Conclusions

Careful reading of the results and conclusions of these studies leads one to conclude that this body of evidence supports the need for adequate internal and external hydration for efficient voice production. As voice clinicians, the research is reassuring as we suggest hydration programs to our professional voice users. Certain questions, however, do remain. For example, what is adequate liquid intake to maintain normal voice production? Is it sixty-four ounces, two liters, or half of an individual's body weight in ounces of water? As researchers in vocal health, should we be more concerned in studying effects of dehydration both functionally and biologically? Because many of our professional voice users are so invested in following our every recommendation to maintain vocal health, is it possible for individuals to over-hydrate to the detriment of normal vocal function? In other words, when is enough, enough? Are we asking individuals to consume large amounts

of liquid based on solid data? Until we know the answers to these questions, we would suggest that professional voice users consume just enough non-caffeinated/non-alcoholic liquids so as to follow the sage advice of Van Lawrence (1991) when he stated "pee pale" for your vocal health.

❦

Endnotes

1. The most common term is phonation threshold pressure (PTP), though this varies across studies and is variably represented by (PPT) and P(th).

References

Chan, R.W., & Tayama, N. "Biomechanical effects of hydration on vocal fold tissues." *Otolaryngology and Head and Neck Surgery*, 126(5), (2002), 528-537.

Fisher, K.V., Ligon, J., Sobecks, J.L., & Roxe, D.M. "Phonatory effects of body fluid removal." *Journal of Speech and Hearing Research*, 44(2), (2001), 354 - 367.

Punt, N. A. "Lubrication of the vocal mechanism." *Folia Phoniatrica*, 36, (1974), 287-288.

Rubin, J.S., Sataloff, R.T., & Korovin, G.S. *Diagnosis and Treatment of Voice Disorders*, (3rd. ed.). Plural Publishing, Inc, San Diego, CA., 2006.

Sataloff, R.T. & Titze, I.R. *Vocal Health and Science: a Compilation of Articles for the NATS Bulletin and the NATS Journal*. The National Association of Teachers of Singing: Jacksonville, FL., 1991.

Sivasankar, M., & Fisher, K.V. "Oral breathing increases Pth and vocal effort by superficial drying of vocal fold mucosa." *Journal of Voice*, 16(2), (2002), 172-181.

Solomon, N. P., & DiMattia, M. S. "Effects of a vocally fatiguing task and systemic hydration on phonation threshold pressure." *Journal of Voice*, 14, (2000), 341-362.

Stemple J, Glaze L, Klaben B. *Clinical Voice Pathology: Theory and Management*, (3rd ed.). Delmar Learning, Clifton Park, NJ, 2000.

Verdolini-Marston, K., & Titze, I. R., & Drucker, D. G. "Changes in phonation threshold pressure with induced conditions of hydration." *Journal of Voice*, 4, (1990), 142-151.

Verdolini, K., Titze, I. R., & Fennell, A. "Dependence of phonatory effort on hydration level." *Journal of Speech and Hearing Research*, 37, (1994), 1001-1007.

Verdolini-Marston, K., Sandage, M., & Titze, I. R. "Effect of hydration treatments on laryngeal nodules and polyps and related voice measures." *Journal of Voice*, 8, (1994), 30-47.

Yiu , E. M. L., & Chan, R. M. M. "Effect of hydration and vocal rest on vocal fatigue in amateur karaoke singers." *Journal of Voice*, 17, (2003), 216-227.

Peer Reviewed Article *by Amanda Loy-Jung*

Psychogenic Voice Disorders and Gender: An Interdisciplinary Look at the Prevention, Identification, and Treatment of the Voice in Disequilibrium

All tension comes from anxiety to please, and eventually you have to come round to the view that what you have to offer is good enough.—Cicely Berry[1]

Let us start with an extreme example. A mousy wife is talking with her verbally abusive husband. Her vocal quality is breathy and weak; his is loud and pressed. She has asked for an evening off from her childcare responsibilities, which has made him extremely angry. He yells at her for being so selfish. During the conversation, he lets her know not only is it unacceptable for her to "abandon" the children, but also his ill mother will be moving in with them the following week, and she will be responsible for taking care of her. The wife feels this is unfair, but she says nothing for fear it will make him angrier. The next morning she awakens with aphonia.[2] She consults a speech-language pathologist, who suspects a diagnosis of psychogenic voice disorder.

PSYCHOGENIC VOICE DISORDERS
Definition
Within the field of speech-language pathology, disorders are broadly divided into organic and functional. Organic voice disorders are those in which a structural[3] or neurological cause is identifiable. In contrast, functional voice disorders are those for which no physical cause for the disorder can be found, or in which any physical symptoms are judged to be less severe than the perceived dysphonia.[4] Psychogenic voice disorders (PVDs) are a subset of functional voice disorders. Aronson (1990) offered the classic definition of psychogenic voice disorder:

> A psychogenic voice disorder is broadly synonymous with a functional one but has the advantage of stating positively, based on the exploration of its causes, that the voice disorder is a manifestation of one or more types of psychologic disequilibrium, such as anxiety, conversion reaction, or personality disorder, that interfere with normal volitional control over phonation (121).

This definition has largely determined which clients meet the criteria for a diagnosis of PVD. The predominance of subsequent research on PVDs has been based primarily on this definition as well (Andersson & Schalen 1998; Baker 1998; Rubin & Greenberg 2002; Duffy 2005). It has also been noted that patients with PVDs tend to exhibit hyperfunction[5] in the extrinsic laryngeal musculature, resulting in a high held larynx (Rubin & Greenberg 2002), as well as "a disturbed capacity for emotional verbal expression" (Andersson & Schalen 1998, 104).

Several conditions have been categorized as PVDs. These have been based largely on the pioneering work of Aronson (1990) and include:
- Musculoskeletal Tension Disorders
- Mutational Falsetto
- Childlike Speech in Adults
- Conversion Aphonia and Dysphonia

Musculoskeletal tension disorders (MTDs) are defined primarily by the habitual hyperfunction, as a result of psychological stressors, which is present in most all PVDs (Duffy 2005). Mutational falsetto pertains to prolonged use of high fundamental frequency[6] after one has gone through puberty. Whereas mutational falsetto is a diagnosis reserved primarily for men who maintain

Amanda Loy-Jung , MA, CF-SLP is a voice/speech pathology fellow at Brigham and Women's Hospital in Boston. She earned her MA in speech and hearing sciences from Indiana University. She completed the Summer Vocology Institute at the Denver Center for the Performing Arts, where she received a certificate in Vocology from the University of Iowa, in 2005. She also holds a BA in Gender and Interpersonal Communication from Kenyon College. Ms. Loy-Jung has studied theater voice work with Janet Rodgers, Matt Harding, and Nancy Lipschultz. She is a member of VASTA and the American Speech-Language-Hearing Association.

1. As quoted in Maley (2000), page x.

2. Aphonia is loss of voice, characterized by whispery vocal quality caused by lack of vocal fold closure and vibration of the vocal folds.

3. Structural refers to any abnormality in anatomical structures. This includes additive lesions on the vocal folds.

4. Dysphonia is any vocal quality judged to be abnormal (e.g., hoarseness, breathiness, harshness, pitch abnormality, monopitch, monoloudness, etc.) compared to gender and age norms.

5. Hyperfunction is the hypercontraction of muscles, so that more energy is being used than necessary to perform a motor task (e.g., voicing).

6. Fundamental frequency is the rate at which the vocal folds vibrate per second. This is perceived as pitch.

high-pitched voices into adulthood, childlike speech in adults is the diagnosis assigned to women who maintain into adulthood a youthful communication pattern relative to stress, intonation, and resonance. Notably, the way diagnoses are defined determines what clients, with what voice and speech characteristics, will fall into which diagnostic categories.

7. Conversion reactions, broadly defined, are disorders where psychological difficulties manifest as physical symptoms. Conversion aphonia and dysphonia are the two types of conversion reactions pertinent to voice.

8. Somatic is another word for body-based, or physical.

By the same token, the original definition of conversion reactions[7] has determined the course of research and clinical practice regarding this diagnosis. Aronson (1990) defined conversion voice disorders as the translation of interpersonal conflict into somatic[8] symptoms. Voice loss then serves as a metaphor for the inability to communicate one's personal beliefs, needs, wants, or emotions. Although the patient experiences loss of voluntary control of voicing, she benefits from the voice problem, in that it exempts her from confronting the problem directly through verbal communication (Duffy 2005). Since the process of converting psychological conflict into abnormal vocal symptoms is an unconscious one, many of these patients believe the problem is organic in nature (Aronson 1990).

The phenomenon of *la belle indifference*, or not caring that one has a voice problem, has traditionally been associated with conversion reaction (Butcher, Elias, & Raven 1993). This notion is based on Freud's "unacceptable impulse theory," in which he attributed conversion reactions to women's suppression of their sexual desires (1920). Using this theory as a basis for the diagnosis of conversion reaction, estimates of percentage of PVDs that are conversion disorders fall in the 4-5% range (Butcher, Elias, Raven, Yeatman, & Littlejohns 1987; House & Andrews 1987). Similarly, Roy (2004) attributes most PVDs to social inhibition, rather than to conversion reaction, because of lack of la belle indifference. However, there are examples in the literature of patients who are very concerned about their voice loss; yet, clinicians still diagnose them with conversion reactions (Baker 2003; Duffy 2005). As a result, the distinction between conversion reactions and PVDs becomes difficult to make.

Prevalence

Several studies have cited the fact that PVDs are diagnosed much more often in women than in men (Butcher et al. 1987; House & Andrews 1987; Baker 2003; Andrews 2006). More specifically, estimates of the ratio of females to males diagnosed with PVDs have ranged from 4:1 (Aronson 1990) to 5:1 (Andersson & Schalen 1998) to 8:1 (Baker 2002). When men have been diagnosed with the disorder, they have typically found themselves in situations where they felt powerless and helpless, such as in futile combat situations (Baker 2002). Importantly, although most people diagnosed with PVDs are women, being a woman does not predispose a person to developing a PVD per se. Therefore, the question underlying the present paper is: *Why might women be diagnosed more often with PVDs, and what factors predispose some women in particular to develop PVDs? How can understanding these factors aid in the prevention, identification, and treatment of these disorders?*

Etiologies

Currently, the predominant theory regarding the etiology[9] of PVDs is "conflict over speaking out" (CSO), a phrase coined by House and Andrews (1987) to describe the inner turmoil which arises from wanting to express something verbally but not believing that it is advantageous to do so. In their follow-up

9. Etiology is another word for cause.

study, House and Andrews (1988) found that 54% of subjects with PVDs had recently experienced CSO, whereas only 16% of the controls had.[10] Oftentimes, individuals find themselves in a state of chronic stress or anxiety, at which time an "antecedent event[11]," such as an upper respiratory tract infection, triggers an episode of aphonia or dysphonia (Rubin & Greenberg 2002; Duffy 2005). Other co-occurring reasons for voice loss include taking on too much responsibility to care for others, interpersonal conflict, recent stressful life events, poor coping skills, poor social network, inhibition around self-assertion, feelings of powerlessness, and a sense of futility in trying to change the situation (House & Andrews 1988; Butcher et al. 1993; Andersson & Schalen 1998). Additionally, Aronson (1990) suggested that some people may be *laryngoresponders*, or those who react to emotional stressors by over-contracting their laryngeal muscles.[12] If this pattern of hyperfunction becomes habitual, then vocal symptoms may remain after the interpersonal difficulties have been resolved (Duffy 2005).

While CSO offers an explanation for the majority of PVD cases, it does not account for all of them. For example, Baker (2003), a clinician with dual certification as a psychologist and a speech-language pathologist, presented two case studies of women with psychogenic aphonia who were not experiencing any significant life stress at the time. Through careful psychosocial interviewing and the creation of an atmosphere of trust, it was revealed that each of these women had been sexually abused four months or 38 years previously. Recent precipitating events had triggered episodes of aphonia as an expression of Post-Traumatic Stress Disorder (PTSD). Although neither of these women exhibited indifference, Baker (2003) diagnosed them with conversion reaction. She favored an alternative explanation for the diagnosis: the "affect-trauma model" put forth by Janet (1920), over Freud's "unacceptable impulse theory." In the affect-trauma model, patients seek to dissociate themselves from real-life traumatic experiences, rather than suppress imaginary sexual fantasies. For these women, recent reminders of sexual abuse triggered an abrupt change in their emotional state, represented by voice change.

PSYCHOLOGY, VOICE, AND GENDER
Feminine and Masculine Stereotypes for Voice
The current distinction between sex and gender is an important one, especially since they are so often confused. Sex refers to one's biological category: usually male or female. Gender, on the other hand, refers to a set of culturally defined behaviors that are associated with manly or womanly characteristics: typically masculine or feminine. Since gender stereotypes apply to fluid traits, roles, appearances, and voice use patterns, it is possible for any man or woman to choose to act in stereotypically feminine, stereotypically masculine, or androgynous[13] ways (Six & Eckes 1991).

Research on gender and voice has revealed some interesting patterns. For example, in public contexts, frequent voice use is considered masculine, while infrequent voice use is considered feminine (Tannen 1990). Moreover, feminine voicing patterns have been associated with childlike voice, given the higher pitch; lower vocal pitch has been associated with masculinity, greater levels of seriousness, and maturity (Pemberton, McCormack, & Russell 1998). Indeed, womanhood and adulthood are often viewed as mutually exclusive concepts (Gilligan 1985). As a result, some women may use a lower

10. This difference was found to be statistically significant.

11. Typically, an antecedent event is defined as the starting point of a disorder, before which point a state of health is assumed. The antecedent event is therefore viewed as the cause of the disorder. With regard to voice disorders, upper respiratory tract infections and periods of intense voice use are cited as common antecedent events.

12. Others might tense a different part of their bodies (e.g., lower back, stomach muscles, etc.).

13. Androgyny may be defined as a state that is neither strictly masculine nor strictly feminine, but a combination of the two.

fundamental frequency in order to be taken seriously. Oftentimes, women who sound vocally confident have simply taken on a masculine pattern of voicing, which lacks vocal variety and upper range (Aston 1999). In fact, many assertiveness training programs are geared toward teaching women to adopt a masculine style of speaking. However, for women to express themselves fully, they need to find their own unique ways of using their voices, not simply take on stereotypically masculine patterns (Rodenburg 1992).

Psychogenic Voice Disorder as a Feminine Diagnosis

Clearly, in order to examine PVDs closely, we need to place them in their broader socio-cultural perspective. Women choose their vocal style based on both their individual preferences and societal expectations for acceptable behavior patterns for women. Psychogenic voice disorders, as they have been defined in the literature, coincide with stereotypically feminine vocal behaviors (i.e., listening, passive, quiet, without a voice). In his definition of PVDs, Aronson (1990) stipulated that loss of "volitional control over phonation" (121) is a diagnostic feature. House and Andrews' (1987) concept of "conflict over speaking out" highlights an inherent choice between vocal self-expression and maintenance of relationships in the stereotype of femininity. Since femininity is a set of behavior expectations for women, it is not surprising that the majority of people who choose a feminine vocal style are women. Although both men and women have devalued loss of voice, many women choose to devoice in order to maintain their relationships with other people. In these cases, *women fear that to truly speak their minds would result in abandonment.* In long-term relationships, this anxiety becomes protracted so the lack of expression, coupled with the effects of accumulated fear on the body, sets the stage for the development of a PVD, which can be triggered by a common head cold. This is then the physical manifestation of their current psychological state of not having a "voice" (i.e., not expressing themselves fully). Therefore, given what we have learned about stereotypically feminine voice patterns, it stands to reason that PVD (as defined by Aronson) is a feminine diagnosis, which is likely to produce more female sufferers than male.

Other psychological diagnoses have also been found to have a feminine gender bias. Jimenez (1997) claimed that some psychiatric disorders—including hysteria, dependent personality disorder, and borderline personality disorder—have served to reinforce societal norms regarding appropriate behavior for women.

In the case of hysteria, Jimenez illuminated the diagnosis as a "caricature of exaggerated femininity," including childishness,

emotional instability, dramatic displays of emotion, attention seeking behaviors, self-centeredness, seductiveness, and an abnormally high level of dependence on others (3). One theory behind these behaviors is that women can exert power over men only through an irrational display of histrionics, rather than by direct force or aggression (Jimenez 1997). Similarly, a woman diagnosed with a conversion reaction can indirectly exert control over an interpersonal conflict by taking on the sick role, rather than confronting the problem directly through verbal communication (Butcher et al. 1993). Frequently, conversion reaction and hysteria have been referred to as similar diagnoses (Duffy 2005). Aronson (1990) distinguishes between hysteria as a set of behavior patterns and conversion reactions as somatization of emotional conflicts. However, the ways in which people deal with emotional conflict are reflected in both their behaviors and their overall health and well-being, so it makes sense that the two are closely connected. In effect, these diagnostic labels both delineate appropriate feminine behaviors and penalize women who take them to an extreme.

As stated above, the primary difference between PVDs and conversion reactions, as defined in the literature, is la belle indifference. It may be that the majority of women with PVDs are not diagnosed with conversion reaction because they are concerned about their voice problem. This could be a reflection of the way both men and women devalue feminine communication style. During the women's movement in the 1960s, traditional femininity became undesirable for many women (Jimenez 1997). Correspondingly, these women may find the extreme dependence on others and lack of assertiveness inherent in a PVD undesirable.

Jimenez (1997) found that people who are diagnosed with borderline personality disorder, also diagnosed primarily in women, exhibit exaggerated feminine characteristics as well as overt expression of anger. Expression of anger is considered masculine (Tannen 1990). Therefore, these women are penalized both for exaggerating feminine behaviors and for daring to take on a masculine communication style. Aronson (1990) claimed that women with conversion voice disorders display "difficulty dealing maturely and openly with feelings of anger" (132). However, if women are expected not to express anger, they may suppress it or over-express it, which leads to perceptions of immaturity and theatricality (Jimenez 1997). Since expression of anger is considered masculine, it is acceptable for men to express anger in a greater number of social contexts (Jimenez 1997). Similarly, when men speak using hyperadduction, it is not considered pathological (i.e., abnormal) until it becomes a vocal fold lesion.

Psychogenic Voice Disorders and Gender: An Interdisciplinary Look at Prevention, Identification,
and Treatment of the Voice in Disequilibrium by Amanda Loy-Jung (continued)

Vocal Fold Lesions as a Masculine Diagnosis

If PVD is a feminine diagnosis, then benign vocal fold lesions[14] are its masculine equivalent. While PVDs are associated with lack of control and underuse of the voice, vocal fold lesions are typically associated with hyper-control and overuse of the voice. In other words, vocal fold lesions typically result from a combination of phonotrauma[15] and excessive voice use over time. Immoderate use of the voice means the vocal folds are coming together more often, and phonotrauma means they are coming together with greater impact. If produced habitually, this phonatory style can result in the development of swelling at the mid-membranous portion of the folds, or the point of maximum impact (Andrews 2006). As an exception, professional voice users often present with vocal fold lesions that reflect only overuse of the voice, without any misuse. It is emphasized that the following discussion pertains to vocal misuse patterns only and does not reflect other factors that may influence the development of vocal fold lesions, such as smoking, allergies, post-nasal drip, intubation, laryngopharyngeal reflux[16], and so on.

In some cases, vocal fold lesions have been referred to as a psychosomatic disorder, in which stress turns into organic disease by way of pressed vocal fold closure at the glottal[17] level (i.e., hyperadduction[18]) (Duffy 2005). In contrast, PVDs are associated with incomplete vocal fold closure at the glottal level (i.e., hypoadduction[19]), and hyperfunction develops at the supraglottal[20] level in order to compensate (Baker 2003). Both of these physiological states involve hyperfunction; the difference is in *the muscles involved and the amount and type of voice used.* As we have seen, societies determine acceptable norms for feminine and masculine voice use. Individuals then, consciously and unconsciously, choose whether they want to sound more feminine or more masculine (Andrews 2006). Gender is one powerful way in which voice is linked to personal identity.

In a seminal work on personality and voice, Roy, Bless, and Heisey (2000) associated specific personality characteristics with particular voice disorders. They found that 71% of the subjects with functional voice disorders were introverted, with 49% being neurotic ("neurotic introverts") and 22% not being neurotic ("stable introverts"). Conversely, they found that 75% of subjects with vocal nodules were extraverted, with 32% being neurotic ("neurotic extraverts") and 43% not being neurotic ("stable extraverts") (757). In the case of neurotic introverts and neurotic extraverts with voice disorders, it seems that high levels of anxiety accompany the act of communication (refer to Berry's description of the "anxiety to please"). As we have seen, anxiety is pertinent to voice use if it results in hyperfunction at the glottal level or at the supraglottal level. It can be surmised that neurotic introverts with functional voice disorders have reacted to their anxiety by devoicing, whereas neurotic extraverts with vocal nodules have expressed their anxiety in voice overuse. In either case, musculoskeletal tension disorder (MTD), of which hyperfunction is the defining diagnostic feature, co-occurs with the development of a PVD or of vocal fold lesions.

It is possible for a man to develop a PVD and for a woman to develop vocal fold lesions. These clinical cases provide support for the notion that these diagnoses are linked to gender stereotypes regarding vocal style, rather than to the sex of the person with a voice disorder. A man may choose a feminine

14. Benign vocal fold lesions include nodules, polyps, contact ulcers, and contact granulomas.

15. Phonotrauma is broadly defined as high impact forces on the vocal folds during phonation.

16. Laryngopharyngeal reflux (LPR) is a diagnosis linked to gastroesophageal reflux disease (GERD). In the case of GERD, stomach acid comes into the esophagus and remains there, causing the sensation of heartburn. In the case of LPR, the acid moves beyond the upper esophageal sphincter and spills onto the soft tissues lining the larynx. This type of reflux can result in the development of benign vocal fold lesions, such as a contact granuloma.

17. Glottal is the adjective for glottis, and glottis is the anatomical name for the space in between the vocal folds.

18. Hyperadduction occurs when the vocal folds press together too much, resulting in a loud, pressed quality.

19. Hypoadduction occurs when the vocal folds remain separated, resulting in a quiet, breathy quality.

20. Supraglottal literally means "above the glottis." Muscles there include the pharyngeal constrictors.

vocal style, and a woman may choose a masculine vocal style. Nevertheless, not every person who uses the vocal style ascribed to the other sex develops a voice disorder. Under what circumstances, then, do these disorders develop in the opposite sex?

Why would a man develop a functional voice disorder like PVD? Since PVDs indicate a stereotypically powerless, feminine, and introverted vocal style, a man with a PVD would most likely exhibit an introverted, neurotic personality (Roy, Bless, & Heisey 2000). Similarly, Satterfield (2001) found a link between PVDs and high interpersonal sensitivity[21] levels; therefore, it is likely that such a man would be highly susceptible to perceived threats to his well-being in his interactions with others. Moreover, he would probably find himself in a situation wherein he feels himself to be helpless, as in a futile combat situation or a job in which he feels powerless either to affect change or to leave (Baker 2002). The voice would sound breathy, with aspirate onsets.[22] Important to note, not all men who choose a feminine vocal style develop PVDs. Several men (e.g., a subset of homosexual men) choose a more feminine vocal style independent of feelings of helplessness; they prefer the feminine style, so it does not reflect underlying anxiety for these men. It is when the feminine style is unconsciously chosen in response to feelings of helplessness that a PVD can result.

Why would a woman develop vocal fold lesions like nodules? As we have seen, vocal fold lesions imply a stereotypically powerful, masculine, extraverted vocal style. Therefore, it is highly likely that a woman with vocal nodules would have an extraverted personality type. It is possible but not necessary that she is also highly neurotic, experiencing anxiety around the act of communication and managing others' impressions of her (Roy, Bless, & Heisey 2000). Additionally, Aronson (1990) found that people who develop vocal lesions tend to have "chronic interpersonal problems," excessive drive, impatience, and high levels of anxiety, anger, and aggressiveness (125). Therefore, it is likely that a woman with vocal nodules has developed hyperfunction at the glottal level, and she uses her voice more than average. The voice sounds pressed, and hard glottal attacks[23] are often discernable in her conversational speech.

Given gender stereotypes regarding masculine voice use (in the United States), masculine vocal quality is not typically perceived as deviant or even pathological. Men and women who choose a masculine voice may seek treatment less often for voice patterns that are vocally abusive but socially rewarded. Since individuals judge voice problems based on their habitual voice use patterns and others' evaluations of their vocal production, neither men nor women are likely to seek help for habitual hyperadduction or voice overuse until they perceive a great enough change in vocal quality to suspect a medical (i.e., organic) problem.

It is telling that vocal fold lesions are most common in male children and female adults (Aronson 1990). Significantly, the higher average fundamental frequency in women's speaking voices means the vocal folds come together more times per second than those in men. If a man and a woman both used a pressed vocal style (i.e., glottal hyperfunction) and spoke the same amount, the woman would probably develop vocal fold lesions first, given that her

21. Interpersonal sensitivity is defined here as feelings of being easily hurt by others.

22. Aspirate onsets are the acoustic correlate of airflow through the glottis starting before the vocal folds come together for phonation. These result in the perception of an "h" sound or sigh at the start of words. These occur frequently when a person is devoicing. They have also been referred to as breathy onsets.

23. Hard glottal attacks are the acoustic correlate of the onset of sound after the vocal folds have been pressed together before airflow for phonation is begun. When voicing begins, air flows through the glottis at a relatively high rate, and is accompanied by an abrupt and rough bursting sound. They typically occur in vowel-initial words when speech sounds are choppy.

Voice and Speech Science, Vocal Health

Psychogenic Voice Disorders and Gender: An Interdisciplinary Look at Prevention, Identification, and Treatment of the Voice in Disequilibrium by Amanda Loy-Jung (continued)

vocal folds come together more times per second. It is also possible that inherent structural differences (e.g., in vocal fold thickness) could account for women developing vocal fold lesions more often.

Let us take a subtler example. A father and a daughter are having a conversation. The father is a highly sensitive, introverted person. He has worked for the past five years in a job where his boss belittles him, but he feels powerless to change his work situation. The daughter is an extraverted cheerleader who is very popular at school and spends hours every evening talking to her many friends. The father is asking her to get off the phone and come to dinner in a soft, breathy voice. When she finally stops ignoring him, she yells at him using a pressed vocal style. She interrupts him frequently and berates him for "butting in" on her phone conversation. Her onsets are marked by hard glottal attacks, and her voice is overly loud for the situation at hand. Eventually, he backs down, feeling hurt by his daughter's verbal attacks. Since this conversation is representative of their habitual vocal styles, it is no surprise when, following the development of an upper respiratory tract infection the following winter, the father loses his voice, and the daughter is diagnosed with vocal fold nodules at the conclusion of the football season.

THE THREE LEVELS OF VOICE: VOCAL EQUILIBRIUM AND DISEQUILIBRIUM

Up to this point, both internal and external explanations for the diagnoses of PVDs and vocal lesions have been discussed. However, the moment when a patient is diagnosed with a voice disorder is not the moment when his/her story begins. Rather, he/she has been developing habitual patterns of voice use since childhood, and the present symptoms reveal both habits (i.e., personality, preference for either a more feminine or more masculine vocal style) and the current social context in which the person finds him/herself (i.e., gender stereotypes, interpersonal conflicts). In subtler forms, then, vocal disequilibrium can occur long before the development of a diagnosable voice disorder.

Rodenburg's Three Circles: Denial, Centeredness, and Bluff

Within the field of theater voice training, Rodenburg (1992) discusses hyperfunction within the framework of learned physiological habits. She talks about the socialization process for boys and girls, wherein girls lose their voices and boys lose relationship. As a result, she finds that in emotional release work with adult actors, women typically need to express rage and inner strength, and men typically need to show grief and vulnerability (Rodenburg 1992). She distinguishes the most common vocal pattern in women: "devoicing" (79). She notes that men, by contrast, tend to overuse their voices in public speaking contexts.

Rodenburg (2000) has suggested a framework for three circles of performance voice. The first circle is "denial"; the second is "centeredness"; the third is "bluff." In this framework, denial parallels movement and voice patterns associated with extreme femininity: shoulders hunched, weight off balance, looking down at the floor, speaking quietly and indistinctly, and back resonance[24] (31). In contrast, bluff serves as a caricature of extreme masculinity: shoulders pulled back, feet too set, eyes looking beyond the conversational partner, speaking loudly, and body too rigid (32). In sum, denial gives the impression

24. Back resonance is a vocal quality that sounds muffled. It produces vibrations in the back of the oral cavity, rather than in the mask. The voice sounds like it is trapped at the back of the mouth, as if one is simultaneously speaking and holding back the words. This could be a physiological correlate of "conflict over speaking out."

25. "Vocal efficiency is a quantitative measure of the ability of the larynx to convert subglottal power to acoustic power" (Jiang, Stern, Chen, & Solomon 2004, 277). Resonant voice is produced through efficient conversion of lung pressure into sound, so one produces the loudest sound possible for the minimal amount of muscle effort.

of no confidence, and bluff implies false confidence. Both denial and bluff are extreme vocal postures, neither of which communicates a state of relaxed readiness like that found in the second circle. From the second circle position, "an actor is so charged that she or he can shift in any direction at any moment" (37). Locating and maintaining this state of conscious energy and focus requires training.

Verdolini's Resonant Voice Therapy: Hypoadduction, Resonant Voice, and Hyperadduction

Based on extensive research in both the speech-language pathology and motor learning fields, Verdolini (2004) has developed Lessac-Madsen Resonant Voice Therapy (LMRVT) as a means of treating both hypoadduction and hyperadduction. Aerodynamic testing has revealed greater airflow through the glottis on hypoadduction, which is perceived as a breathy quality, and reduced airflow through the glottis on hyperadduction, which is perceived as pressed vocal quality (Peterson, Verdolini-Marston, Barkmeier, & Hoffman 1994).

Resonant voice, in contrast to either of these extremes, is produced with a *barely adducted, barely abducted vocal fold configuration*, which produces sympathetic vibrations in the front of the face, or "mask" (Verdolini, Druker, Palmer, & Samawi 1998), and maximizes vocal efficiency[25] (Berry, Verdolini, Montequin, Hess, Chan, & Titze 2001). If a patient responds with "yes" to each of the following questions: "Do you feel vibrations in the mask?" and "Is it easy?" then he/she is likely to be producing resonant voice (Verdolini 2004). LMRVT has been applied successfully to several voice therapy patient populations, including patients with vocal fold nodules (Verdolini-Marston, Burke, Lessac, Glaze, & Caldwell 1995). It is also possible that PVD sufferers would benefit from LMRVT, because they present with hypoadduction.

Taken as a whole, these findings provide physiological descriptions for the concepts of "feminine" and "masculine" voice, where hypoadduction/breathy vocal quality is considered feminine and hyperadduction/pressed vocal quality is considered masculine. Resonant voice is the more balanced form of voice use which, in terms of gender in this context, makes it the androgynous alternative.

Androgyny and Context-Dependent Voice Use

Gender orientation refers to the set of gender characteristics with which an individual identifies: primarily feminine, primarily masculine, or androgynous. Harter, Waters, Whitesell, and Kastelic (1998) found that adolescent girls who identified as feminine voiced their views primarily in private contexts (e.g., with close friends), whereas girls who identified as androgynous spoke up equally in private and public settings (e.g., in classrooms). This finding reflects the traditional division of private speaking as feminine and public speaking as masculine, with many girls choosing to take on a more masculine communication style (Tannen 1990). However, as we have seen, when women simply imitate masculine voicing patterns and hyperadduct, they run the risk of developing vocal fold lesions.

Rather than impersonating masculine or feminine voice, men and women alike could move toward a more androgynous way of voicing. This would be resonant voice, or second circle. If hypoadduction is viewed as feminine and hyperadduction as masculine, then resonant voice may be perceived as the vocal fold physiology equivalent of androgyny. Similarly, first circle represents femininity in performance, and third circle represents masculinity in performance. Therefore, a state of readiness (i.e., second circle) is somewhere in between, or androgynous. The fear people have in many situations (e.g., interviews, auditions, dates) that what they have to offer is not enough (see Berry's reference to "anxiety to please") leads to "false-self behavior" (Harter, Waters, & Whitesell 1997; Harter et al. 1998, 894), or not being true to oneself, which triggers laryngeal hyperfunction patterns that can be seen and heard. In these situations, if people train to release tension and cultivate a state of readiness, they free their voices to be resonant, and come into vocal equilibrium.

Vocal Equilibrium and Disequilibrium

In the field of theater voice training, working toward vocal equilibrium is nothing new (Berry 1973, 1992). Yet, patterns of voice and silence in plays reflect gender stereotypes about those in real life (Loy 2000); therefore, performers and nonperformers alike can benefit from becoming aware of vocal disequilibrium in their lives and the process of working toward vocal equilibrium. The points made in this article have highlighted the need to look at vocal disequilibrium from psychological, social, and vocal health perspectives, as well as from the performance perspective. Gender has been suggested as an organizing framework, whereby stereotypes of femininity, masculinity, and androgyny parallel observations, made in several fields (e.g., speech-language pathology, psychology, and theater), of the three levels of voice.

Aronson (1990) included "psychologic disequilibrium" within the definition of PVD, a diagnosis with a feminine gender bias (i.e., loss of "volitional control over phonation," 121). It is worthwhile to expand the concept of vocal disequilibrium to cover both the feminine and masculine deviations from centeredness. These have physiological correlates which, in their extreme, are diagnosable as PVDs and vocal fold lesions, respectively. Furthermore, vocal disequilibrium has direct

Voice and Speech Science, Vocal Health

Psychogenic Voice Disorders and Gender: An Interdisciplinary Look at Prevention, Identification,
and Treatment of the Voice in Disequilibrium by Amanda Loy-Jung (continued)

metaphorical connections to psychological disequilibrium, so that no one who is working with the voice can afford to ignore psychology entirely. Figure 1 visually represents the three levels of voice in terms of gender along a continuum.

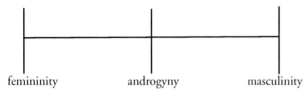

femininity   androgyny   masculinity

Figure 1. Three levels of voice in terms of gender.

Androgyny, then, is represented by the midpoint on the continuum. The midpoint corresponds to muscle use balance, psychological balance, and gender balance concurrently. In order to achieve balance, *the goal of voice work is to move a person's vocal patterns toward the midpoint.* The directionality of the movement toward the midpoint depends on the person's previous habitual vocal style.

Notably, deviations from center can be subtle or extreme, as illustrated in Figure 2. The more subtle form of PVDs is difficulty in asserting oneself in conversation (i.e., "denial"); the more subtle form of vocal fold lesions is difficulty in listening to others (i.e., "bluff"). These more subtle forms of vocal disequilibrium are commonplace and fit into social norms for gender-appropriate vocal behaviors; therefore, they are not considered pathological. However, commonplace vocal behavior is not optimal voice use; few people speak using resonant voice in most circumstances. The challenge for an actor is to represent common characters in extraordinary circumstances. Actors require resonant voice use for the stage so they can be heard, and so they have vocal stamina. In everyday life, there is no such necessity, and individuals often use their voices in imbalanced, but socially acceptable, ways. Still, voice professionals must be aware of the subtle physical manifestations of vocal disequilibrium, so these problems can be identified early on, before they become full-blown, diagnosable PVDs or vocal fold lesions.

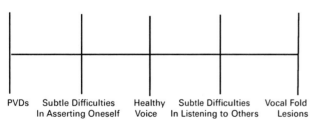

PVDs   Subtle Difficulties   Healthy   Subtle Difficulties   Vocal Fold
        In Asserting Oneself   Voice   In Listening to Others Lesions

Figure 2. Vocal equilibrium and disequilibrium.

It is possible that conversational partners tend to "meet each other where they are." This means if, in a particular interaction, one person demonstrates difficulty with self-assertion, then the other participant tends to over-exert his/her voice in order to "fill the gap" in the conversation. Over time, these patterns can become habitual or expected within particular conversational pairs. The imbalance may be prolonged into a long-term state of being with that person and perhaps in other conversational contexts, as well. Frequently, this internal state of imbalance is manifested in muscular hyperfunction, indicative of some form of anxiety; in other words, psychological disequilibrium is converted into physical symptoms. When a person is anxious specifically about the act of voicing, the muscular hyperfunction occurs in the area of throat. An antecedent event, such as an upper respiratory infection or a weekend of intense voice use, simply reveals the internal state of imbalance, rather than creating it from nothing. From this perspective, effective prevention, identification, and treatment of PVDs and vocal fold lesions depends on addressing this underlying state of anxiety attendant with both extremes of vocal use.

To review, Table 1 (on the facing page) summarizes the characteristics of the three levels of voice in chart form.

Based on these broadly defined criteria, it could be argued that the phenomenon of not being centered in oneself (i.e., psychological and vocal disequilibrium) occurs more commonly than one might expect, even among personality types and interpersonal contexts that are widely viewed as "normal." Working toward vocal equilibrium is a process of moving from imbalance to balance, and voice professionals can help with this process. While it is possible for an individual to be in first circle in some conversational contexts and in third circle in other conversational contexts, it is physiologically impossible to use both hypoadduction and hyperadduction at the same time. If aspects of both are attempted, then a barely abducted, barely adducted vocal fold configuration, or resonant voice, results.

Let us take a more ideal example. A man and a woman meet at a party. Each person is interested in the other person, and each listens to what the other person has to say, creating an environment in which the other person can feel free to assert his/her views without judgment. Each person feels a sense of ease in talking with the other person. As a result, each person feels comfortable speaking and releases any excessive tension that may have been present in and around the larynx. Given that the muscles in the throat are working in balance, neither too much or too little, there is a resonant quality in each voice. They both feel calm and relaxed, confident they are being heard, and so ready to hear what the other person has to say.

Psychogenic Voice Disorders	Healthy Vocal Production	Vocal Fold Lesions
Feminine	Androgynous	Masculine
Passive Aggressiveness	Appropriate Assertiveness	Aggressiveness
Powerlessness	Balance of Power	Overbearing Power
Silence/Devoicing	Expressing thoughts and feelings authentically	Loud Voice/Pushing the Voice Out
Hysteria/Conversion Reaction	Mental Health/Psychological Equilibrium	Borderline Personality Disorder
Supraglottal Hyperfunction	Effective Muscle Tone	Glottal Hyperfunction
Muscle Use Imbalance	Muscle Use Balance	Muscle Use Imbalance
Voice Underuse	Optimal Amount of Voice Use	Voice Overuse
Introversion	Being Present	Extraversion
Fear of not being enough/ "Anxiety to please"	Love and Acceptance of Self, "What you have to offer is good enough"	Fear of not being enough/ "Anxiety to please"
Feeling threatened	Feeling calm	Feeling threatened
First Circle	Second Circle	Third Circle
Denial	Centeredness	Bluff
Hypoadduction (incomplete vocal fold closure)	Resonant Voice (barely adducted, barely abducted vocal fold configuration)	Hyperadduction (pressed vocal fold closure for the majority of voicing)
Breathy Voice Quality	Clear Voice Quality	Pressed Vocal Quality
Inefficient Voice Use	Efficient Voice Use	Inefficient Voice Use
Lack of Confidence	Real Confidence	False Confidence
False Self-Behavior	Authenticity	False Self-Behavior
Vocal Disequilibrium	Vocal Equilibrium	Vocal Disequilibrium

Table 1. Summary of the three levels of voice.

INTERDISCIPLINARY PREVENTION, IDENTIFICATION, AND TREATMENT OF VOCAL DISEQUILIBRIUM

Traditional Approaches to Voice Work

Traditionally, the roles of theater voice and speech trainers, speech-language pathologists, and psychologists in treating vocal difficulties have been separate. Voice and speech trainers have focused on specific changes in breath, pitch, loudness, quality, vocal variation, articulation, and resonance, which communicate (to the audience) the inner lives of characters on stage. Speech-language pathologists have worked within the medical model, treating voice disorders (diagnosed by doctors) by using physiological and perceptual approaches, along with vocal health advice, to bring patients within normal limits of vocal usage consistent with their regular vocal demands.

Psychologists have delved into the impact of self-esteem on metaphorical voice use (and vice versa), as well as the effects of physical and emotional abuse on self-expression, interpersonal relationships, coping skills, and thought processes (conscious and unconscious) as they relate to self-expression. Often, voice and speech trainers and speech-language pathologists retreat too quickly from any psychological factors that might be involved in a voice problem. Conversely, psychologists rarely consider or understand the physical process of voicing.

Treatment Methods for Vocal Disequilibrium

It has been found that PVDs do not respond well to traditional treatment approaches (Butcher et al. 1987). Several alternative programs have been suggested for the treatment of PVDs. For the purposes of this discussion, these methods will be reviewed

Psychogenic Voice Disorders and Gender: An Interdisciplinary Look at Prevention, Identification,
and Treatment of the Voice in Disequilibrium by Amanda Loy-Jung (continued)

as a means of treating some form of vocal disequilibrium. These methods are creative and interdisciplinary in nature.

- *Cognitive Behavior Therapy* (CBT). This method is based on the notion that habitually negative thought patterns and ineffective interpersonal actions create negative emotions in a person, which in turn are reflected in abnormal vocal quality. Therefore, CBT practitioners seek to retrain negative thought and behavior patterns so a person can experience a greater sense of well-being, and vocal symptoms can subsequently resolve. In order to achieve these results, several methods are employed, including: uncovering negative thought patterns and ineffective interpersonal behaviors, changing negative self-talk into "positive self-instruction," breathing from the diaphragm, progressive muscle relaxation, anxiety control training, stress reduction, brainstorming alternative interpersonal behaviors, and role playing those alternative behaviors in therapy (Butcher et al. 1993). In their study on treatment efficacy for PVDs, Butcher et al. (1987) found that patients who were experiencing excessive laryngeal muscle contraction and CSO did not respond to voice therapy alone; rather, half of the study's participants (6/12) responded to a combination of voice therapy and psychological counseling.[26]
- *Tension Release Exercises.* Butcher et al. (1993) and Verdolini (2004) include tension release exercises, such as relaxation and stretches, in their treatment protocols. It is essential that tension release exercises focus on letting go of *excessive* muscle contraction, rather than relaxing to the point of muscle flaccidity. Ideally, the muscles should be activated and used in balance with one another, so that no one muscle group has to work harder than another.
- *Combination of Vocal Exercises, Communicative Exercises, and Psychological Counseling.* Andersson and Schalen (1998) suggested a combination of vocal exercises (i.e., relaxation exercises, diaphragmatic breathing, and the Accent Method[27]), communicative exercises (i.e., combination of expressive movements, phonation, and the corresponding emotional content), and psychological counseling (i.e., discussion of interpersonal conflicts and ways of dealing with it, expression of a variety of emotions, and CBT). In their follow-up study, they found that 12 of 30 subjects had maintained the vocal quality achieved during treatment. These authors pointed to congruence between movement, voice, and internal emotional state as healing for vocal symptoms.
- *Sensitive Psychosocial Interviewing.* Baker (1998) emphasized the importance of sensitive questioning of PVD clients and the establishment of an atmosphere of trust.
- *Exploration of Coping Mechanisms.* Andrews (2006) advocated exploration of coping mechanisms available to the patient, including the reasons why these coping mechanisms were chosen, alternative coping mechanisms, means to apply alternatives, and possible outcomes of alternative actions.
- *Telling a Personal Narrative.* Baker (2003) highlighted the process of telling a personal narrative as beneficial to the treatment process.
- *Vocal Play/Role Play with Alternative Voice and Movement Patterns.* Personality as a unitary construct is very limiting, because it allows an individual freedom to pursue only one set of voice and movement patterns: those they have habitually used since childhood. If we encourage our patients/clients/students to play with other ways of being in the world

26. The authors hypothesized that in the other 6/12 cases, where vocal symptoms did not respond to treatment, either noncompliance or ongoing significant life stress accounted for the lack of improvement in voice.

27. The Accent Method consists of rhythmic patterns of stressed and unstressed syllables on voiced continuants (e.g., /v/ and /z/), supported by diaphragmatic breath, swaying movements, and percussion (Kotby 1995).

(e.g., vocal archetype work), then we teach them that they are capable of transformation. Moreover, alternative means of voicing may help unlock habitual vocal patterns by opening new sensorimotor pathways through the periaqueductal grey (PAG), the convergence point for voluntary and involuntary control of phonation (Baker 2002, 88). Actors frequently demonstrate how, through voice and movement changes, the same person can take on a whole new "personality" of a character. This is part of the work that actors train to do, and it is work of which we are all capable.

• *Lessac-Madsen Resonant Voice Thearpy* (LMRVT). As stated above, LMRVT is an excellent treatment modality for all forms of vocal disequilibrium, given that it was designed to treat both hypoadduction and hyperadduction (Verdolini 2004).

• *Laryngeal Massage/Manual Circumlaryngeal Techniques* (MCTs). Roy (2004) advocated the use of MCTs in the treatment of functional voice disorders by trained speech-language pathologists. MCTs involve digital manipulation[28] of the larynx in order to help the client regain the normal phonation of which he/she is capable. Significantly, he noted a high rate of recurrence of symptoms, which could be attributed to continuing psychological issues not addressed directly by this treatment method.

• *Alba Emoting*. Dal Vera (2001) provided an excellent description of this method in which actors are taught combinations of breath, posture, and facial expression (and sometimes vocalization) that trigger corresponding emotional states. In Alba emoting, the process goes from the outside in. Because it targets a variety of emotional states (e.g., fear, anger, joy, tenderness), this work can be extremely helpful in getting clients or students to expand their "emotional palette" for performance (Janet Rodgers, personal communication).

Alternative Framework for Treating Vocal Disequilibrium

Undoubtedly, an interdisciplinary approach is required to treat vocal disequilibrium effectively. Vocal disequilibrium is a problem for the whole person, so no one discipline can successfully treat the problem alone. Voice professionals need to take courses in other voice disciplines so that we understand and appreciate a variety of different approaches to voice work (Elias, Raven, Butcher, & Littlejohns 1989). We also need to be aware of signs of both subtle and extreme forms of vocal disequilibrium so we can refer appropriately to other voice professionals. When any professional suspects a diagnosable voice disorder, a referral to a medical doctor (preferably a laryngologist[29]) is essential; only doctors can diagnose medical conditions.

One exciting alternative for treating vocal disequilibrium is the "co-therapist" format put forth by Butcher et al. (1987, 92). Within this framework, two voice professionals work with a patient/client/student in the same session, rather than referring the person for separate treatment sessions with another professional. In this model, "referral" means setting up a time when both professionals and the client can meet.

This approach could take on several variations. For example, if a theater voice trainer noticed that a particular actor had difficulty releasing laryngeal tension, then co-treatment sessions with a voice pathologist[30] could be set up, wherein the voice pathologist could train healthy voice production, and the

28. Digital manipulation is using the fingers (i.e., digits), placed in the space between the thyroid cartilage and the hyoid bone, to release muscle tension accompanying moving the larynx back, down, etc.

29. A laryngologist is an ear, nose, and throat doctor specializing in treating voice disorders.

30. A voice pathologist is a speech-language pathologist specializing in treating voice disorders.

Voice and Speech Science, Vocal Health

Psychogenic Voice Disorders and Gender: An Interdisciplinary Look at Prevention, Identification,
and Treatment of the Voice in Disequilibrium by Amanda Loy-Jung (continued)

theater voice trainer could apply that work directly to character work, in the moment. Alternatively, a voice pathologist could suspect that significant interpersonal problems are contributing to a functional voice disorder. A collaborative session could involve the retelling of one's personal narrative to a psychologist, who would train self-assertion techniques, while the voice pathologist would be present to train resonant voice use in emotionally-laden conversations. Finally, a psychologist working with an actor might suspect that she has trouble playing feminine characters because she habitually uses a masculine speaking style and is anxious about exposing her vulnerability in performance. Collaborative sessions could involve the psychologist discussing these issues with a client while a voice and speech trainer teaches expansion of the emotional palette for the stage.

Above all, effective treatment of vocal disequilibrium requires a holistic view of voice as it pertains to psychology, gender, interpersonal communication, and overall health and well-being. The ultimate goal of treating vocal disequilibrium is the release of the "anxiety to please" and with it, excessive laryngeal muscle tension, so that voice emerges authentically in the moment. This is an exciting challenge that voice professionals can face, working together as a community of healers.

❦

References

Andersson, K, & Schalen, L. "Etiology and treatment of psychogenic voice disorder: Results of a follow-up study of thirty patients." *Journal of Voice*, 12(1) (1998), 96-106.

Andrews, M. L. *Manual of voice treatment: Pediatrics through geriatrics* (3rd Edition). Clifton Park, NY: Thomson Delmar Learning, 2006.

Aronson, A. E. *Clinical voice disorders: An interdisciplinary approach* (3rd Edition). New York: Thieme, 1990.

Aston, E. "Finding a body, finding a voice." In *Feminist theatre practice: A handbook*. London: Routledge, (1999), 43-56.

Baker, J. "Psychogenic dysphonia: Peeling back the layers." *Journal of Voice*, 12(4) (1998), 527-535.

———. "Psychogenic voice disorders—heroes or hysterics? A brief overview with questions and discussion." *Log Phon Vocol*, 27, (2002), 84-91.

———. "Psychogenic voice disorders and traumatic stress experience: A discussion paper with two case reports." *Journal of Voice*, 17(3), (2003), 308-318.

Berry, C. *Voice and the actor*. New York: MacMillan, 1973.

———. *The actor and the text*. New York: Applause Books, 1992.

Berry, D., Verdolini, K., Montequin, D. W., Hess, M. M., Chan, R. W., & Titze, I. R. "A quantitative output-cost ratio in voice production." *Journal of Speech, Language, and Hearing Research*, 44, (2001), 29-37.

Butcher, P., Elias, A., & Raven, R. *Psychogenic voice disorders and cognitive behaviour therapy*. San Diego: Singular Publishing Group, Inc., 1993.

Butcher, P., Elias, A., Raven, R., Yeatman, J., & Littlejohns, D. "Psychogenic voice disorder unresponsive to speech therapy: Psychological characteristics and cognitive-behaviour therapy." *British Journal of Disorders of Communication*, 22, (1987), 81-92.

Dal Vera, R. "The voice in heightened affective states." In: Dal Vera, R. (Ed). *The Voice in Violence and other contemporary issues in professional voice and speech training*. The Voice and Speech Review, a publication of the Voice and Speech Trainers Association (VASTA), 2001.

Duffy, J. R. "Acquired psychogenic and related nonorganic speech disorders." In: *Motor speech disorders: Substrates, differential diagnosis, and management* (2nd Edition). Philadelphia: Mosby, a Division of Elsevier Publishing, (2005). 381-407.

Elias, A., Raven, R., Butcher, P., & Littlejohns, D. W. "Speech therapy for psychogenic voice disorder: A survey of current practice and training." *British Journal of Disorders of Communication*, 24, (1989), 61-76.

Freud, S. Beyond the pleasure principle. In: Stachey, J., Ed. *The Standard Edition of the Complete Works of Sigmund Freud*. London: Hogarth Press,1920.

Gilligan, C. "In a different voice: Women's conceptions of self and of morality." In: Eisenstein, H., & Jardine, A., Eds. *The Future of Difference*. New Brunswick, NJ: Rutgers University Press, 1985.

Harter, S., Waters, P. L., & Whitesell, N. R. "Lack of voice as a manifestation of false self-behavior among adolescents: The school setting as a stage upon which the drama of authenticity is enacted." *Educational Psychology*, 32(3), (1997), 153-173.

Harter, S., Waters, P. L., Whitesell, N. R., & Kastelic, D. "Level of voice among female and male high school students: Relational context, support, and gender orientation." *Developmental Psychology*, 34(5), (1998), 892-901.

House, A. O., & Andrews, H. B. "The psychiatric and social characteristics of patients with functional dysphonia." *Journal of Psychosomatic Research*, 31(4), (1987), 483-490.

———. "Life events and difficulties preceding the onset of functional dysphonia." *Journal of Psychosomatic Research*, 32(3), (1988), 311-319.

Janet, P. *The major symptoms of hysteria*. New York: Hafner, 1920.

Jiang, J., Stern, J., Chen, H. J., & Solomon, N. P. "Vocal efficiency measurements in subjects with vocal polyps and nodules: A preliminary report." *Ann Otol Rhinol Laryngol*, 113(4), (2004), 277-282.

Jimenez, M. A. "Gender and psychiatry: Psychiatric conceptions of mental disorders in women, 1960-1994." *Affilia: Journal of Women and Social Work*, 12(2), (1997). 154-176.

Kotby, M. N. *The accent method of voice therapy*. San Diego: Singular Publishing Group, Inc. 1995.

Loy, A. *Dialogue as discourse: Sex-appropriate conversational style in plays as a competence model for real world linguistic interaction*. Unpublished thesis with distinction for bachelor's degree at Kenyon College, 2000.

Maley, A. *The language teacher's voice*. Oxford: MacMillan Heinemann English Language Teaching, 2000.

Pemberton, C., McCormack, P., & Russell, A. "Have women's voices lowered across time? A cross-sectional study of Australian women's voices." *Journal of Voice*, 12(2), (1998), 208-213.

Peterson, K. L., Verdolini-Marston, K., Barkmeier, J. M., & Hoffman, H. T. "Comparison of aerodynamic and electroglottographic parameters in evaluating clinically relevant voicing patterns." *Ann Otol Rhinol Laryngol*, 103, (1994), 335-346.

Rodenburg, P. *The right to speak: Working with the voice*. New York: Routledge, 1992.

———. *The actor speaks: Voice and the performer*. New York: St. Martin's Press, 2000.

Roy, N. "Manual Circumlaryngeal Techniques", speech presented at the conference *Voice Therapy: A Comprehensive Approach*, University of Pittsburgh Voice Center, Pittsburgh, PA, October, 2004.

Roy, N., Bless, D. M., & Heisey, D. "Personality and voice disorders: A multitrait-multidisorder analysis." *Journal of Voice*, 14(4), (2000), 521-548.

Rubin, J. S., & Greenberg, M. "Psychogenic voice disorder in performers: A psychodynamic model." *Journal of Voice*, 16(4), (2002), 544-548.

Satterfield, K. "Patients with selected voice disorders are subject to psychiatric problems." 2001. Retrieved from: *http://www.newswise.com/articles/view/25781/*.

Six, B., & Eckes, T. "A closer look at the complex structure of gender stereotypes." *Sex Roles*, 24(1), (1991), 57-71.

Tannen, D. *You just don't understand: Women and men in conversation*. New York: HarperCollins Publishers, Inc., 1990.

Verdolini, K. "Lessac-Madsen Resonant Voice Therapy Training", speech presented at the conference *Voice Therapy: A Comprehensive Approach*, University of Pittsburgh Voice Center, Pittsburgh, PA October, 2004.

Verdolini, K., Druker, D. G., Palmer, P. M., & Samawi, H. "Laryngeal adduction in resonant voice." *Journal of Voice*, 12(3), (1998), 315-327.

Verdolini-Marston, K., Burke, M. K., Lessac, A., Glaze, L., & Caldwell, E. "Preliminary study of two methods of treatment for laryngeal nodules." *Journal of Voice*, 9(1), (1995), 74-85.

Peer Reviewed Article *by Marth Munro & Daan Wissing*

Testing the Use of Lessac's Tonal NRG as a Voice Building Tool for Female Students at a South African University—A Perceptual Study

INTRODUCTION

The voice of the actor is required to work optimally in the process of performance, and required to repeat vocal tasks on a regular basis. For this to occur, the voice needs to be built and strengthened (Barton & Dal Vera 1995, 79). "Voice building" might tentatively be defined as developing the voice to deal with the rigors of performance. Laukkanen (1995, 11) states that the muscular functions of voice production have to be strengthened and improved in such a way that it will result in an "improved voice and/or phonatory quality." Good voice quality (sustainable over periods of time and repeatable) for theatre specifically, may be "defined as a result of an optimal use of the vocal organ in order to establish the maximum possible acoustic output by minimal muscular effort" (Laukkanen 1995, 18), to which will be added the aesthetic dimension, which is culturally bound. To clarify then, voice quality is the component of voice that is not (but may be related to) loudness, duration, or pitch. In scientific research voice quality is measured, among other methods, by determining the acoustic spectrum of a sound. This acoustic spectrum obviously correlates with the muscular function of the vocal apparatus in the moment of voice production.

Lessac (1997, 9) claims that part of his Approach is the building of a good voice. Here he refers specifically to the Tonal NRG part of the work and states that it will enhance audibility (1997, 139; 1967, 20). In answers to a questionnaire filled in at the Lessac Swarthmore convention in 1998:[1]

- Respondents all reported that they believe the Lessac Approach to be an effective voice-building tool.
- They agreed that the Tonal NRG enhances projection of both the male and female voice.

The research to be presented here is motivated by the results of that questionnaire, as well as by the desire to determine if the Lessac Tonal NRG approach actually does contribute to students' voice building, and in particular, for female students.

Voice can be analysed in three ways: physiologically, perceptually, and acoustically (Laukkanen 1995, 13; Miller & Schutte 1999, 206). Verdolini and colleagues (Verdolini, Druker et al. 1998; Verdolini-Marston, Burke et al. 1995) did extensive research on the physiological impact of the Tonal NRG of the Lessac Approach. The most important findings from those research projects seem to be that the Lessac Approach leads to low impact stress between the vocal folds and minimum subglottal pressure. The study reported here focused on the perceptual and acoustical analysis of the Tonal NRG as a voice-building tool.

Research aim

The main aim of this investigation was to evaluate the perceptual and acoustic effects of Lessac's training approach on the voices of female student actors. This paper will report on the outcome of the *perceptual* evaluation. Perceptual evaluation is very important when evaluating voice. Voice forms the bedrock of most communicative acts in performance events. As such the subjective reaction to voice cannot be omitted from any voice evaluation process. A separate paper (in preparation) will deal with the outcome of the acoustic analyses.

Marth Munro specializes in performance voice building, body/voice integration and vocal pedagogy. She holds a PhD in which she investigated the acoustic properties of Lessac's Tonal NRG and the "Actor's formant" in the female voice. She has completed a team research project on computer-aided training of the singing voice. Munro has been recognised by the National Research Foundation (South Africa) as a rated researcher. She is a Certified Laban/Bartenieff Movement Analyst, serves on the Laban Institute of Movement Studies board, and is a Certified Lessac Voice and Movement Teacher. She teaches in the Department of Drama, Tshwane University of Technology, South Africa. She publishes in popular and scholarly journals; teaches workshops for actors, singers and musicians; and directs opera, musical theatre and theatre.

Prof. Daan Wissing earned a D. Litt. From the Rijksuniversiteit, Utrecht, The Netherlands (1971) on a theoretical phonology topic. He has ever since been involved in research concerning the acoustic phonetics and phonology of a variety of languages (Arabic, SeSotho, Setswana, English, Dutch and Afrikaans). As a senior researcher, he is currently involved in the field of speech technology. He actively plays a role as acoustic phonetics and phonology expert in various international trans-disciplinary research projects. He is one of the driving forces behind the "Centre for Text Technology" at the North-West University, Potcehfstroom campus.

Testing the Use of Lessac's Tonal NRG as a Voice Building Tool for Female Students at a South African University—A Perceptual Study by Marth Munro & Daan Wissing (continued)

By way of placing the perceptual analysis in context, however, in the sense that perceptual judgment is highly dependent upon the acoustic properties of the sound heard, an overview of the acoustic characteristics of the "projected voice" is presented. Projection, or more specifically "carrying power," is an acoustic characteristic of the performer's voice (Leino 1993, 209). Sundberg (1988, 12) states that this is determined by two factors. The first is the vibratory process of the vocal folds leading to the glottal flow, also known as the voice source, and the second is the shaping of the vocal tract in order to optimally resonate the sound that is produced by the larynx. The vocal tract acts as a filter, or a "frequency selective transmission system" as described by Kent and Read (1992, 13).

The fundamental frequency, F_0, determines the vocal pitch and is a direct result of the voice source function. There are generally five formants below 5000 Hz that are important for the analysis of the human voice (Leino 1993, 207; Stone et al. 1999, 161):
- F1 and F2 primarily determine vowel recognition and quality
- F3 influences vowel characteristics but, linked to F4 and F5, it also influences voice quality
- F4 and F5 are determined by the laryngeal tube that acts as "a separate resonator" to provide the resonance characteristics that lead to a well-projected voice (Sundberg 1974, 842).

When an LTAS (long term average spectrum taken over some time, usually many seconds) of the singing or speaking voice is obtained, it is difficult to pinpoint the various formants because they shift a great deal during the utterance, especially if the utterance contains various vowels. Therefore, references are often made to the intensity clusters around certain frequencies. The frequencies of the actual formant clusters in singing differ between voice types (Stone, Cleveland et al. 1999, 161). Titze (1994) mentions that the performer's *speaking* voice differs acoustically from the classical *singing* voice as far as formants are concerned, seeing that no prescribed F_0 frequency (pitch) is expected from the professional actor's voice. It is thus necessary to study the professional actor's speaking voice as an independent subject.

Marth Munro with Arthur Lessac

Fant (1970) observed earlier that F3 and F4 seemed to be closer in trained than in untrained speaking voices. Leino performed several studies on the quality of the professional actor's speaking voice. It is of importance for this paper to reflect on the results of two of the projects executed by Leino. He reported a "Long-Term Average Spectrum (LTAS) study on speaking voice quality in male actors" (Leino 1993). Expert listeners perceptually graded the recordings into categories of good, fairly good, rather poor, and poor voice quality. No definition (perceptual or acoustic) for good voice quality was provided. Results indicated that the voices *perceptually* defined as "poor" displayed *acoustically* a clearly steeper spectral slope than the voices defined as "good." Of greater importance, however, was the "most notable" peak near the region of 3500 Hz. The group that was perceptually defined as having "good quality" displayed a higher amplitude than the other voice groups in this frequency cluster.

From this study one can ascertain that what is classified as a good actor's voice is *reflected* in an LTAS analysis with a frequency cluster between 3-4 kHz, with increased amplitude and relatively deep valleys around this phenomenon. In the second study Leino and Kärkkäinen supported the previous study (1995).

In this study, the preferred voice quality perceptually determined by experts in the fields of theatre and speech, acoustically displayed a clearer peak at 3.5 kHz, and an overall spectrum with a less steep slope. It thus seems that the professional actor's voice, when it is perceived to project well and has a sonorous quality (Nawka et al. 1997, 422), has as its acoustic characteristics a less steep spectral slope and an enhanced peak in the frequency range between 3 and 4 kHz which seem to be related to F4 and F5 (Leino 1993, 209).

So far most of the findings reflect on the possible relationship between the perceptual and acoustic findings of the male voice. Relatively little is known about the characteristics of the *female* actor's voice. It is generally accepted that it is more difficult to investigate the acoustic properties of the female voice.[2] Leino (pevoc[3] poster 2001) reported on research done on the female Finnish voice. A perceptual panel subjectively differentiated between good and poor voice quality. An LTAS analysis of these voices indicated that both groups had the tendency to have a peak at 4300 Hz, but that the voices considered as good had a stronger peak (thus a higher amplitude). One can thus ascertain that what an expert panel perceptually defines as a good voice may be reflected in the acoustic profile of the male as well as the female voice, although the acoustic characteristics may somewhat differ.

The project reported on here examined the development of female actors' voice quality, as very little formal research has been done in this specific area. The trajectory of the research followed a procedure of training the female voice using the Lessac Approach and performing a pre-post perceptual panel analysis of voice quality. A pre-post comparative acoustic analysis of the voices was also performed, and will be reported in a subsequent article.

METHODS
Experimental design
A one-group before-after design was used in this experiment. Because participants served as their own controls in this type of design, additional participants as a control group were not required.

Participants
Fifteen female students of a voice building class were randomly chosen to serve as the experimental group. Such training is part of the curriculum of an actor-training programme at a tertiary institution in South Africa. Ages ranged between 18 and 23 years. Represented first languages were Afrikaans, 8; English, 2; Tsonga, 1; Tswana, 1; Southern Sotho, 1; Xhosa, 1; Zulu, 1. They all voluntarily agreed to participate in this research having been assured that their identities would be protected. One of the researchers was the responsible teacher for this group. The group had a total of 28 contact hours over a period of 14 weeks.

Training
In the training process the Lessac Approach was used. Initially three-dimensional breathing and optimal body integration were explored, followed by the introduction and exploration of Tonal NRG as defined and described in the Lessac Approach (1997). An organic developmental flow was crucial so as to follow the holistic nature of the Lessac Approach. The class was thus introduced to the Y-buzz and then proceeded through +Y-buzz to Calls and lastly to Call phrases and limited application.

2. "The woman's pitch has a higher frequency than the man's pitch..." (Mendoza, Valencia, Munoz & Trujillo 1996). This leads to the harmonics of the female voice being further apart.

3. Pan European Voice Conference.

Voice and Speech Science, Vocal Health

Testing the Use of Lessac's Tonal NRG as a Voice Building Tool for Female Students at a
South African University—A Perceptual Study by Marth Munro & Daan Wissing (continued)

The medium of instruction in the classes was English. The use of self-developed first language phrases as equivalents to the English modes was encouraged. Students were expected to work in "buddy groups"[4] (20 minutes daily) on the explorations introduced in class, as preparation for the next class.

Recordings

Pre- and post-training recordings were made under controlled circumstances:
- All recordings were made in a sound-treated room at the tertiary institute.
- Recordings were made onto a DAT recorder (Sony ZA5ES Super bit mapping). Rec. level: 5; mode rate of recording: 44.1kHz; Input: analogue microphone.
- Microphone used: Shure SM48. Dynamic LOZ Unidirectional.
- Microphone-to-mouth distance: 40 cm.
- A sound level meter showing SPL (sound pressure level) was used to prevent overloading the DAT recorder. Students were asked not to go lower than 65 dB nor higher than 75 dB. The distance between the sound level meter and the mouth was the same as the microphone-to-mouth distance, thus 40 cm. It seemed to be easy for the students to stay within these parameters during the pre-training recordings. They struggled to maintain this in the post-training recordings, even going as high as 90 dB. When this occurred, they were asked to repeat the recording within the requested limits.

In the pre-training recording students were asked to do an "uh-uh" sound.[5] This was used to determine the pitch given for the Y-buzz sound in pre- as well as post- training recordings.

The different modes that were named and/or demonstrated were:[6]
1. Y-buzz on the pitch determined for the subject. (The pitch was given using a keyboard.)
2. +Y-buzz.
3. Calls.
4. English phrases and Call words.
5. First language text readings of approximately one minute without the use of words containing an /s/ sound as a high frequency noise pattern.

The instructions given for modes 1-3: "Please do the (different sounds inserted—named and demonstrated) as long and loud as is comfortably possible while staying in the parameters 65-75 dB on the SPL meter." The instructions given for modes 4 and 5 were:[7] "Please read the following (either English Sentences and Call words or first language texts) in a comfortable volume for performers in a speaking voice."

Each mode was recorded three times and the recording that was subjectively perceived by the experimenters as the "best" was selected to be used in this study.

Perceptual evaluation

- The specific perceptual panel for this project was made up of five theatre experts. Three of the five had at least five years of training in performer's voice. The other two work fulltime with students in tertiary institutions, as well as working professionally as directors and performers. They had more than ten years experience each.

4. Buddy groups are used within the Lessac Workshop set-up where two students are responsible for each other and work together during their preparation times between classes. This is an excellent tool, which guides the students towards discussion about the work and provides ear training.

5. This was borrowed from Timo Leino, a Finnish researcher. He asks the participant to release the head forward and when as relaxed as possible, do an "uh-uh" sound. This sound often has an aspirate quality due to the relaxed vocalization. The onset is never glottal. This is a safe way to determine the optimal speaking voice pitch to start the vocal explorations from.

6. Seeing that the instruction indicates that the utterances were to be done as long as what is comfortably possible, the recordings had different lengths of time reflecting on the participants' levels of competence. The first language text readings were all more or less one minute.

7. Please note that mode 5 is the first language texts recorded.

8. Essentially then, pre and post samples from three different modes from each participant were used as tokens to be played to the perception panel. These tokens were played in a random order within each mode. See tables 6 and 7 in the addendum for a graphic presentation of this.

9. Technical specifications: Satellite: 4.5 watts. 12ms power per channel (2 channels); subwoofer power: 12 watts RMS; Freq. Response 42Hz-20kHz; SNR:>75dB; Dimensions: Satellites (LxWxH) –21.1 cm x 19.2 cm x 19.2 cm.

10. See addendum.

11. "When the body produces excellent tones, the voice is not throaty, nasal, or forced; it is produced and resonated effortlessly. It has stentorian, resonant qualities and projection, full pitch range, and rich, warm, colorful timbre" (Lessac 1997, 9).

12. Credit to the Department of Statistical Support of the (then) Pretoria Technikon for assistance and guidance in this matter.

- Nine randomly chosen samples from each of the different modes (from three different modes for each subject) were prepared in a listening file.[8] The modes were played from a CD through a PC using a high quality amplifier and stereo speakers: Creative Inspire 2.1 2400[9] in order to maintain good sound quality. There was approximately 3 seconds between each of the 90 utterances (tokens) for the listeners to mark their questionnaire forms.
- An evaluation questionnaire[10] was provided to the panellists with a definition of good voice quality. As indicated above, good voice quality was "defined as a result of an optimal use of the vocal organ in order to establish the maximum possible acoustic output by minimal muscular effort" (Laukkanen 1995, 18). This definition was discussed (and supported by a quote from Lessac himself[11]) with the perceptual panel in order to make sure that they all understood what they were listening for. The questionnaire was set up according to a 5 point rating scale: 1 = very poor, 2 = poor, 3 = average, 4 = good, 5 = very good.
- The 90 (18x5; or 45 pre and 45 post) pre- and post-training tokens were arranged in random order and played to the expert panelists. The randomized samples were again ordered according to the structured teaching progression; thus all randomized y-buzz samples were presented first, followed by all the randomized +Y-buzz samples, etc.
- Cross tabulation tables were used for descriptive statistics. These provided an indication of the preferences of the perception panel should they exist. These tables served as preparation for the inferential statistics.
- For triangulation more than one inferential statistics analysis were performed on the data. 1) Paired t-test: H_0: μ diff(pre-post) $\neq$ 0; H_A: μ diff(pre-post) $\neq$ 0; α = 0.01. H_0 accepted when the p-value > α; H_0 rejected in favour of H_A when the p-value < α. In this study H_0 implies that the scores given to the pre-training recordings and the scores given to the post training recordings were equal (null). Should this be true, it would indicate that there was no change, according to the perceptual panel, in the sound quality of the post-training recordings. But should H_0 be rejected in favour of H_A, especially if the pre-scores minus the post-scores provide a negative numerical, it would imply that the total of the post scores was higher than the total of the pre-scores. This would indicate that the utterances contained in the post-training recordings improved in voice quality according to the perceptual panel.
2) Chi-square: H_0: 2 variables (phase and score) are independent; H_A: 2 variables (phase and score) are dependent. α = 0.01. H_0 accepted when the p-value > α; H_0 rejected in favor of H_A when the p-value < α. In this study this H_0 means that the scores were randomly attributed to the phases (pre- and post- training recordings) and that there is no correlation between the scores given to the voice quality and whether it is a pre- or post-recording. H_A in this case means that the pre-recordings have lower scores attributed to them and the post-recordings have higher scores attributed to them. This would indicate that the training had a positive influence over the voice quality as perceived by the perception panel.

Data analysis and processing of the perceptual evaluation

The evaluation scores of the perception group were statistically processed through the use of SAS[12] (Statistical Analysis Software package, version 8). A paired t-test for independence was done to compare pre-score means with

Voice and Speech Science, Vocal Health

Testing the Use of Lessac's Tonal NRG as a Voice Building Tool for Female Students at a South African University—A Perceptual Study by Marth Munro & Daan Wissing (continued)

post-score means for all the sound modes combined. For this paired t-test, null hypothesis testing was done where the mean difference equals zero (H_0: $\mu_{\text{diff(pre-post)}} = 0$), against the alternative where the mean does not equal zero (H_A: $\mu_{\text{diff(pre-post)}} \neq 0$).

The paired t-test for all the sound modes combined had the null hypothesis (H_0) as: *There is no statistically significant difference between the pre- and post-training recordings (referred to as phase in the t-test) of Test Group S (H_0: $\mu_{\text{diff(pre-post)}} = 0$) as indicated by the scores allocated by the perception panelists*; and the alternative hypothesis (H_A) as: *There is a statistically significant difference between the pre- and post-training recordings (phase) of Test Group S (H_A: $\mu_{\text{diff(pre-post)}} \neq 0$) as indicated by the scores allocated by the perception panelists. For this study to indicate that the training did affect the voice quality positively, the post-training recordings' scores have to be higher than those of the pre-training recordings.*

Frequency procedures were carried out and cross-tabulation tables were made for the different variables of all the different sound modes. These procedures and tables provide a descriptive profile of the weighting of the scores in relation to the pre- and post-training recordings as phase.

For the sake of triangulation, chi-square tests were done on appropriate cross tabulations, but due to expected cell frequencies being less than 5, regroupings were done. Sound modes 1, 2 and 3 (being Y-buzz, +Y-buzz, and Calls) were grouped as "Lessac Tonal explorations," whilst sound modes 4 and 5 (being English Phrases and Call words as well as first language texts) were grouped as "applications," seeing that these modes represent the carry-over of the explorations into functional speech. In the H_0 (null hypothesis) of the Chi-square test, the two variables (phase and score in this study) were independent. The question to determine was whether this H_0 is accepted or rejected for the alternative where the two variables are dependent.

The chi-square test for the Lessac explorations as well as for the applications had the null hypothesis (H_0) as: *The scores (ratings 1-5) were assigned/attributed to the utterances of the pre- and post-training recordings (phase) of Test Group S at random, without any statistically significant relations between the ratings and the 2 phases (being pre- and post-recordings). This will be indicated as the p-value being > 0.01*; and the alternative hypothesis (H_A) as: *The scores (ratings 1-5) were assigned/attributed to the utterances of the pre- and post-training recordings (phase) of Test Group S according to a statistically relevant relationship between the ratings and the 2 phases (pre- and post-recordings). For this study to indicate an improvement of voice quality, the ratings allocated to the post-training recordings have to be higher than the ratings allocated for the pre-training recordings. This will be indicated as the p-value being < than 0.01.*

The different language groups were sometimes too small, and as such could not be used to provide any statistically significant indication. Descriptive statistical analyses were conducted for the different first language groups.

RESULTS
Perceptual evaluation results
As mentioned above, a t-test for independence[13] was done for all the sound modes combined. The rule used was that H_0 (H_0: $\mu_{\text{diff}} = 0$) will be rejected if

13. Paired data.

14. Alpha (α) = P(Type 1 error); Alpha = P(reject H_0 when H_0 true).

15. For example observe the mean in Table 1.

16. In the cross tabulation tables the pre-training recording is indicated as Pre and the post-training recording as Post.

17. In frequency of score per phase.

	Score					
Phase	1	2	3	4	5	Total
Pre	16	12	12	3	2	45
Post	1	8	11	19	6	45
Total	17	20	23	22	8	90

Table 2: Test Group S, Ybuzz: Table of phase by score.

18. The +Y-buzz, Calls, English phrases and Call words as well as first language texts all reflected the same pattern and are available upon request.

19. As previously mentioned, the cross tabulation tables are descriptive statistics and don't have a null-hypothesis. This profile thus does not feed directly into the acceptance or rejection of an H_0, but, seeing that these tables are used in preparation for the chi-square test, it is already obvious that a positive relationship exists between score and phase, seeing that the weighting of the scores for the post-recordings is higher than the weighting of the scores for the pre-recordings.

20. Please note that the numerical contributed to Alpha is only applicable for the perceptual evaluation. Should the p-value be < α in this case, it would be statistically very significant.

the p-value < α (alpha) with alpha =0.01. It was decided on alpha as 1% to make the Type 1 error small.[14] The results of this study lead to the rejection of the null-hypothesis (H_0) in favor of the alternative where the mean difference was significantly different from zero (H_A: $\mu_{diff} \neq 0$) seeing that the p-value was shown as <.0001 (see Table 1). Since the mean differences were negative[15], it indicates that the pre-scores were significantly less than the post-scores ($\mu_{diff} < 0$). The perceptual evaluators, in general, thus preferred the voice quality of the post-recordings of the Test Group.

Analysis Variable: DIFF						
N	Mean	Std Dev	Minimum	Maximum	t Value	Pr > /t/
225	-1.2755	1.2191	-4.0000	2.0000	-15.69	< .0001

Table 1: T test for independence, Test Group S.

The cross tabulation tables for *all* the different sound modes (Y-buzz, +Y-buzz, Calls, English Phrases, and Call words, as well as first language text readings) indicated a clear difference between the pre- and post-training recordings where the post-recordings[16] were reflective of the preferred voice quality. In Table 2 the cross tabulation table of the Y-buzz of the Test Group[17] is provided as an example.

Table 2 indicates that the perceptual evaluators rated the Y-buzz modes of the pre-training recording primarily as very poor—score 1 (16/45 divided by 100 = 35.56%), poor—score 2 (26.67%), and average—score 3 (26.67%). The weighting of the post-training recording perceptual evaluation leans strongly towards average—score 3 (24.44%), good—score 4 (42.22%), and very good—score 5 (13.33%). This pattern is basically followed in all four of the other sound mode groups[18] with the score weighting moving from being centered on scores 1 and 2 to scores 4 and 5.[19]

As mentioned under "Data analysis and processing of the perceptual evaluation," chi-square tests were done on appropriate cross tabulations. For chi-square the H_0 is that the two variables (phase and score) are independent. This was tested against the alternative (H_A), which indicates the two variables are dependent. Regrouping had to be done due to expected cell frequencies being less than five. Sound modes 1, 2, and 3 (Y-buzz, +Y-buzz, and Calls) were grouped as Lessac Tonal explorations, whilst sound modes 4 and 5 (English Phrases and Call words as well as first language texts) were grouped as applications. The score possibilities were also combined so that scores 1 and 2 on the perception panel questionnaire were in the chi-square test regrouped as score 1; score 3 on the perception panel questionnaire remained 3 in the chi-square test and scores 4 and 5 on the perception panel questionnaire were regrouped as score 5 in the chi-square tests.

For the chi-square, the H_0 (null hypothesis) states that the two variables (phase and score in this study) are independent. This would be accepted should the p-value be > α, and rejected should the p-value be < α. Alpha (α) was set to 0.01[20] in order to make the type 1 error very small. The alternative (H_A) is that the two variables (phase and score) are dependent. Should the null hypothesis be rejected, it would thus be an indication that a relationship existed between the rating received by the perception panel and the phase

Testing the Use of Lessac's Tonal NRG as a Voice Building Tool for Female Students at a
South African University—A Perceptual Study by Marth Munro & Daan Wissing (continued)

(pre- or post-training recording). This relationship is positive or negative depending on the outcome of the cross tabulation and the chi-square test.

Table 3a provides the cross tabulation (of phase by score) in preparation for the chi-square test. Table 3b provides the chi-square test results of the Lessac explorations—sound modes 1, 2, and 3.[21]

21. Y-buzz, +Y-buzz and Calls.

Frequency Expected Percent Row Pct Col Pct	Table of phase by nscore			
	phase	nscore		Total
		1	3	5	
	Pre	85 50.5 31.48 62.96 84.16	37 39.5 13.70 27.41 46.84	13 45 4.81 9.63 14.44	135 50.00
	Post	16 50.5 5.93 11.85 15.84	42 39.5 15.56 31.11 53.16	77 45 28.52 57.04 85.56	135 50.00
	Total	101 37.41	79 29.26	90 33.33	270 100.00

Table 3a: Cross Tabulation in preparation for chi-square of the Lessac explorations.

Statistic	DF	Value	Prob
Chi-Square	2	92.9662	<.0001

Table 3b: The chi-square results of the Lessac explorations.

Table 4a provides the cross tabulation (of phase by score) in preparation for the chi-square test. Table 4b provides the chi-square test results of the applications—sound modes 4 and 5.[22]

22. English Phrases and Call words and First language texts.

23. The null hypothesis is that the two variables are independent.

Frequency Expected Percent Row Pct Col Pct	Table of phase by nscore			
	phase	nscore		Total
		1	3	5	
	Pre	52 29.5 28.89 57.78 88.14	26 29 14.44 28.89 44.83	12 31.5 6.67 13.33 19.05	90 50.00
	Post	7 29.5 3.89 7.78 11.86	32 29 17.78 35.56 55.17	51 31.5 28.33 56.67 80.95	90 50.00
	Total	59 32.78	58 32.22	63 35.00	180 100.00

Table 4a: Cross Tabulation in preparation for chi-square of the applications.

Statistic	DF	Value	Prob
Chi-Square	2	59.0856	<.0001

Table 4b: The chi-square results of the applications.

The tables indicate a preference for the post-training recordings. The Lessac explorations pre-training recordings only have 9.63% of their total amount for scores allocated as score 5, but the post-training recordings have 57% of their total scores allocated to score 5. Similarly, the application modes only have 13.33% of the scores being 5 for the pre-training recordings but 56.67% of the scores being 5 in the post-training recordings. Since the p-value for both the Lessac explorations (Y-buzz, +Y-buzz and Calls—see Figure 3b) and the applications (English Phrases and Calls words and first language—see Figure 4b) is less than .0001, the p-value of both these cases is smaller than α (α=0.01). The null hypothesis[23] is therefore rejected. It is therefore evident that phase does affect score. The perception panelists rated the post-recordings in both cases (explorations and applications) significantly higher than the pre-recordings, indicating that the post-training recordings contained the preferred sounds and improved voice quality.

Cross tabulation tables were made for the scores of the three pre-training recordings, as well as three post-training recordings for each participant in Test Group S that were played to the perception panel. Table 5 depicts this cross tabulation for one of the participants (called AA in the table), selected at random.

Phase	Score 1	Score 2	Score 3	Score 4	Score 5	Row Totals
Pre	1	11	2	1	0	15
Post	0	0	3	11	1	15
Total	1	11	5	12	1	30

Table 5: Cross Tabulation Table: Group S, participant AA, all sound modes.

Seeing that this table is typical, it functions as an example to indicate that *each* participant's voice has, according to the perception panel, improved during the training process, as the post-training recordings ratings centre around the higher scores.

Although an indication of the profiles of the perception panelists has been provided before, it will contribute to the effectiveness of this study to reflect on their reliability as a group. Statistical analysis on the inter-reliability of the perception panel was done according to the information gathered. All the perception panelists (raters) separately indicated a significant improvement in the post-training recordings versus the pre-training recordings, with the results of the paired t-tests done for each rater indicating a p-value of <.0001. It is thus clear that the H_0 (μ_{diff} = 0) was rejected in favour of the H_A ($\mu_{diff} \neq 0$) with $\mu_{diff} < 0$ by each rater.

CONCLUSION

Perceptually it is strongly suggested from this study that the Tonal NRG of the Lessac Approach significantly contributes to voice quality improvement (and therefore to voice building) of female students at the South African University where the study was performed. There are strong indications that this improvement is not language specific. Further research needs to include the use of larger test groups as well as the inclusion of more language groups. It may also be of interest to use test groups taught by other independent Lessac Teachers.

References

Acker, B. "Vocal Tract Adjustments for the Projected Voice." *Journal of Voice* Vol. 1, No 1 (1987), 77-82.

Bartholomew, W.T. "A Physical Definition Of Good Voice Quality." *Journal of the Acoustical Society of America*. Vol. 6 (1934), 25-33.

Barrichello, O; Heuer, R.I; Dean, C.M & Sataloff, R.T. "Comparison of Singer's Formant, Speaker's Ring, and LTA spectrum Among Classical Singers and Untrained Normal Speakers." *Journal of Voice*. Vol.15, No 3 (2001), 344-350.

Barton, R. & Dal Vera, R. *Voice: Onstage and Off.* Fort Worth: Harcourt Brace College Publishers, 1995.

Dmitriev, L & Kiselev, A. "Relationship between the Formant Structure of Different Voice Types of Singing Voices and the Dimensions of Supraglottic Cavities." *Folia Phoniatrica*. 31 (1979), 238-241.

Fant, G. *Acoustic Theory of Speech Production.* Paris, France: Mouton, 1970.

Gauffin, J & Sundberg, J. "Spectral Correlates of Glottal Voice Source Waveform Characteristics." *Journal of Speech and Hearing Research.* Vol. 32 (September 1989), 556-565,

Kent, R.D. & Read, C. *The Acoustic Analysis of Speech.* San Diego: Singular Press, 1992.

Laukkanen, A-M. *On Speaking Voice Exercises.* Academic dissertation. ACTA Universitatis Tamperensis. Ser. A vol. 445. Tampere: University of Tampere, 1995.

Leino, T. "Long-term average spectrum study on speaking voice quality in male actors." *Proceedings of the Stockholm Music Acoustics Conference*, (Eds: A. Friberg, J.Iwarsson, E.Jansson & J. Sundberg), Jul.28 - Aug.1, 1993.

Leino, T. & Kärkkäinen, P. "On the effects of vocal training on the speaking voice quality of male student actors." *Proceedings of the XIIIth International Congress of Phonetic Sciences.* Stockholm, Sweden, (Eds: K. Elenius & P. Branderud), Aug. 13 – 19, 1995.

Leino, T. "Voice Quality Of Finnish Female Actors." Poster presented at PEVOC, Stockholm, 2001.

Lessac, A. *The Use and Training of the Human Voice*, 2nd edition, New York: Drama Book Publishers, 1967.

–––. *The Use and Training of the Human Voice: a Bio-Dynamic Approach to Vocal Life*, 3rd Edition. California: Mayfield, 1997.

Mendoza, E., Valencia, N., Munoz, J., & Trujillo, H. "Differences in Voice Quality Between Men and Women: Use of the Long-term Average Spectrum (LTAS)." *Journal of Voice*. Vol. 10. No. 1. (1996), 59-66.

Miller, D, & Schutte, H. "The Use of the spectrum analysis in the Voice Studio." In: *Voice-tradition and Technology*. Nair, G. (1999), 211-226.

Munro, M. *Lessac's Tonal Action in Women's Voices and the "Actor's Formant": A Comparative Study.* Unpublished PhD. Dissertation, North West University (formerly PU for CHE), 2002.

Munro, M., Leino, T., Wissing, D. "Lessac's Y buzz as a pedagogical tool in the teaching of the Projection of an Actor's Voice." *South African Journal of Linguistics.* Suppl.34, (Dec. 1996), 25 36.

Nair, G. *Voice Tradition and Technology.* New York: Singular Press, 1999.

Nawka, T., Anders, L.C., Cebulla, M., Zurakowski, D. "The Speaker's Formant in Male Voices." *Journal of Voice.* Vol 11. No. 4, (1997), 422-428.

Raphael, B. & Scherer, R.. "Voice modification for stage actors: Acoustic analysis." *Journal of Voice*, Vol. 1, No. 183-87, 1987.

Rietveld, AMC, & Van Heuven, V. *Algemene fonetiek.* Bussum: Coutinho, 1997.

Stone, R.E. (ed); Cleveland, T.F & Sundberg, J." Formant Frequencies in Country Singers' Speech and Singing." *Journal of Voice.* Vol. 13. No. 2, (1999), 161-167.

Sundberg, J. & Gauffin, J. "Waveform and Spectrum of the Glottal Voice Source." *Speech Transmission Laboratory, Quarterly status and progress report*, 2-3/1978. Stockholm: Royal Institute of Technology. (1978), 35-50.

Sundberg, J. "Articulatory Interpretation of the 'Singing Formant.'" *JASA.* Vol. 55, No. 4. April 1974.

–––. *The Science of the Singing Voice.* Dekalb: Northern Illinois Univ. Press, 1987.

–––. "Vocal Tract Resonance in Singing." In: *The NATS Journal* March/April 1988, 11-31.

Voice and Speech Science, Vocal Health

Testing the Use of Lessac's Tonal NRG as a Voice Building Tool for Female Students at a
South African University—A Perceptual Study by Marth Munro & Daan Wissing (continued)

Titze, I. *Principles on Voice Production.* New Jersey: Prentice Hall, 1994.

Vennard, W. *The Mechanism and Technique.* New York: Carl Fischer, 1967.

Verdolini-Marston, K., Burke, M.K., Lessac, A., Glaze, L. & Caldwell, E. A
  "Preliminary Study on two methods of treatment for Laryngeal Nodes."
  Journal of Voice. Vol. 9, (1995), 74-85.

Verdolini-Marston, K., Druker, D.G., Palmer, P.M. & Samawi, H.
  "Laryngeal adduction in resonant Voice." *Journal of Voice.* 1998.

Addendum

Perceptual evaluation sheet of Pre- and Post recordings.

"Good voice quality may be "defined as a result of an optimal use of the vocal organ in order to establish the maximum possible acoustic output by minimal muscular effort" (Laukkanen, 1995:18).

"When the body produces excellent tones, the voice is not throaty, nasal, or forced; it is produced and resonated effortlessly. It has stentorian, resonant qualities and projection, full pitch range, and rich, warm, colorful timbre" (Lessac, 1997:9).

Please evaluate the voice samples as either:
- Very poor
- Poor
- Average
- Good
- Very Good

1) Y-Buzz:

Sample Number	Very poor	Poor	Average	Good	Very good
1					
2					
3					
4					
5					
6					
7					
8					
9					
10					
11					
12					
13					
14					
15					
16					
17					
18					

The same type of grid was used for all the other modes: +Y-buzz; Calls; Sentences and Mother tongue. In total 5 separate grids were used, one for each mode.

Table 6: Example of randomized selection process of pre and post samples of each mode to be played as tokens to the perception panel

Participant	M1	M2	M3	M4	M5
1	x		x		x
2	x	x		x	
3			x	x	x
4	x		x		x
5	x	x		x	
6		x	x		x
7	x	x		x	
8		x	x		x
9	x			x	x
10		x	x		x
11	x	x		x	
12		x		x	x
13	x		x	x	
14		x	x		x
15	x		x	x	

M=mode. M1 will thus indicate y-buzz; M2 +Y-Buzz and so forth.

Table 7: An example of the randomized order of the tokens played to the perception panel

Participant	Mode 1: Y-buzz
1	Participant 1 pre
2	Participant 15 post
3	Participant 2 post
4	Participant 4 pre
5	Participant 1 post
6	Participant 4 post
7	Participant 7 pre
8	Participant 15 post
9	Participant 7 post
10	Participant 2 pre

Peer Reviewed Article *by Malin Abrahamsson & Johan Sundberg*

Subglottal Pressure Variation in Actors' Stage Speech

* This investigation was co-author MA's master thesis carried out during her speech and language pathologist and therapist education at the Sahlgrenska University Hospital, Gothenburg, Sweden. Co-author JS served as the supervisor. A more complete account of the research is under preparation.

Introduction

In training actors, many teachers pay attention to the breathing habits. Most voice teachers agree that the breathing habits are important to the voice, and that inappropriate breathing habits can damage the voice.

In *conversational speech* the typical breathing pattern is quite straightforward. We inhale a small quantity of air, perhaps half a liter. With that quantity of air in the lungs, the elasticity of the respiratory apparatus provides an over-pressure of air that is sufficient for this type of speech. But the expiratory elasticity forces decrease with decreasing lung volume. Therefore, as the person releases the air and the lung volume decreases while the utterance is produced, expiratory muscular effort is needed to maintain the necessary air pressure in the lung. Moreover, the lung pressure, the primary controlling factor for vocal loudness, is generally quite constant in neutral speech. Stress and phrasing are typically reflected in terms of variation of syllable duration and voice pitch. Thus, the breathing apparatus mostly has an easy job when we talk.

Things are more complex in *acting*. Acting is often performed in front of large audiences requiring a loud voice, and a loud voice requires high lung pressure and consumes a relatively large amount of air. This implies that large lung volumes are needed.

Some years ago, co-author JS and collaborators measured the lung pressure in a professional actor who recited a poem as if he were addressing a large audience (Sundberg et al. 1993). Lung pressure was about 10 cm H_2O, which is about twice as high as needed for conversational speech. But, more surprising, the pressure was far from constant. Instead, it showed a number of sudden increases and decreases. As this investigation was a single subject study, the question remained if this actor's pressure behavior was representative of actors in general.

Experiment

Three male and three female adult actors, all professionals, volunteered as subjects. They recited the same Swedish poem as if addressing a large audience. They also gave some samples of conversational speech. The speech was picked up by a head mounted microphone. Air pressure data were obtained by asking them to swallow a thin catheter inserted through the nose. At the tip of the catheter there was a pressure transducer, and the catheter was adjusted such that this transducer was located in the esophagus. Figure 1 (next page) shows a picture of one of the subjects during the experiment. This procedure was straightforward and was not much more dramatic than swallowing spaghetti. The esophageal pressure is lower than the subglottic pressure, since the lung elasticity contributes only to the latter. Nevertheless, pressure changes that take place in the trachea, e.g., changes of subglottic pressure during speech, are reflected as changes of the esophageal pressure.

Malin Abrahamsson. Born in Vänersborg, Sweden in 1974. Received a master's degree in Speech Therapy from the University of Gothenburg in 2002, and is currently working as a speech pathologist and therapist at the Department of Logopedics and Phoniatrics at Sahlgrenska University Hospital, in Gothenburg, Sweden. Within her own company Vocalization, Ms. Abrahamsson also works with voice development aimed at speech and singing voices. She has extensive practical experience in the art of music; both as choir director, background singer and as a soloist.

Johan Sundberg. Born in 1936. Received his PhD musicology, doctor HC University of York, UK, 1996. Professor of music acoustics at KTH (Royal Inst. Technology) Stockholm, founded and headed its music acoustics research group, retired 2001. Research particularly on singing voice and music performance. Written *The Science of the Singing Voice* (1987) and *The Science of Musical Sounds* (1991), edited or co-edited many proceedings of music acoustic meetings. He has practical experience in performing music (choir and solo singing). Member of Royal Swedish Academy of Music, Swedish Acoustical Society (President 1976-81) and fellow of the Acoustical Society of America, its Silver Medal in Musical Acoustics 2003.

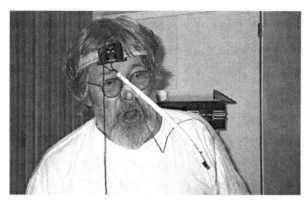

Figure 1. Photograph of one of the subjects during the recording session. The head mounted microphone was fastened to the end of a copper wire covered by white plastic tubing. The pressure transducer was inserted through the nose and fastened by means of a band aid. The subject gave his permission for use of the picture of himself for publication purposes.

The pressure and speech signals were recorded on separate tracks on a multichannel TEAC PCM DAT recorder. The audio signal was calibrated by recording a sustained vowel, the sound pressure level (SPL) of which was measured by means of a sound level meter that was held next to the recording microphone. The SPL value thus observed was announced on the recording. The pressure transducer was calibrated by recording its output signal in free air and while it was immersed into water. The distance between the transducer and the water surface was announced on the recording as the water column pressure.

Results

Figure 2 compares pressure curves recorded from two actors' conversational speech and from their reciting of the poem. The differences are striking. The pressures were much higher for the stage speech than for the conversational speech. One actor actually used pressures as high as 60 cm H_2O. This is

not unexpected in view of the degree of vocal loudness needed in stage speech when addressing a great audience.

More interesting is that the pressure curves for the performance recitation contains a number of more or less sharp peaks, while, as expected, the curves for neutral speech are quite smooth. The pressure peaks occurring in the performance recitation were mostly at least twice as high as the pressure peaks in the conversational speech.

The Swedish poem contained 52 syllables, so the entire recitation material consisted of 6 x 52 = 312 syllables. In this material we observed a total of 77 clear pressure pulses. Of these 43 appeared on stressed vowels, 17 on unstressed vowels, and 17 on consonants, nine of which were continuants such as /l, m, n/. These pulses were obviously produced by respiratory muscles. Pressure pulses of comparable amplitudes never occurred or occurred rarely in the recordings of the actors' conversational speech.

A careful analysis of the timing of these pulses showed quite interesting results. About half of the pulses were synchronous with stressed vowels, while the remainder appeared on certain categories of consonants, such as /m/, /n/, and /s/, i.e., on consonants which, unlike stop consonants, can be sustained, also called continuant consonants. The consonants produced with pressure pulses did not seem to be strategically chosen.

Figure 3 shows two examples of consonants produced with pressure pulses, one produced by a male actor (arrow in left panel) and the other by a female actor (arrow in right panel). The male subject increased his pressure by more than 50% during the vowel /o:/ such that the pressure peak occurred at the onset of the consonant /m/. During this pressure increase the sound level and F_0 also increased. The F_0 peak occurred slightly earlier than the pressure peak. Pressure, F_0 and sound level decreased after the pressure peak. The female subject synchronized a pressure peak with the nasal /n/ in the word /svenska/ (*Swedish*). The pressure pulse was accompanied by a marginal increase of the sound level and an F_0 decrease.

The relative amplitude of each pressure pulse observed in the entire material was measured as illustrated in Figure 4, by computing the ratio between the amplitude of the peak (P_{peak}) and the average of the pressure amplitudes that appeared just before (P_{before}) the pressure increase ending with the peak, and at the end of the pressure decrease that followed the peak (P_{after}). This *relative pulse amplitude*, henceforth

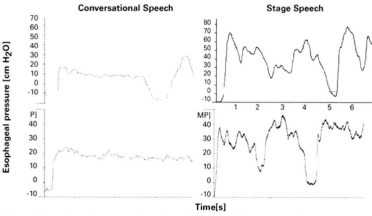

Figure 2. Examples of two actors' esophageal pressure during conversational speech and stage speech (left and right panels, respectively). Note the numerous pressure peaks in the stage speech.

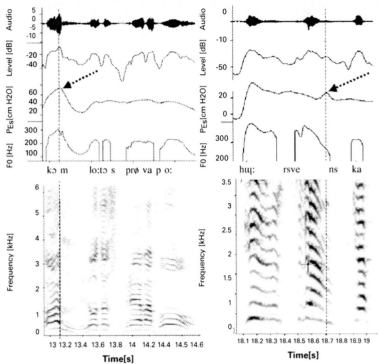

Figure 3. Examples of timing of the pressure pulses, marked by arrows, in two of the actors. In the upper part of the figure the curves show, from top: audio, sound level (L), pressure (P), and voice fundamental frequency (F0). The lower part of the figure shows the associated spectrogram. In the left panel the pressure pulse occurs at the onset of the consonant /m/, and in the right panel the pressure peak is synchronized with the consonant /n/.

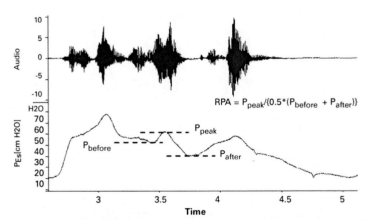

$$RPA = P_{peak}/\{0.5*(P_{before} + P_{after})\}$$

Figure 4. Illustration of the method used for measuring the relative pressure amplitudes PRA. The amplitude of the pressure peak (P_{peak}) is divided by average of the pressures occurring before (P_{before}) and after (P_{after}) the peak.

RPA, thus reflected the maximum relative pressure increase during the pulse.

The results revealed that the actors produced carefully timed pressure pulses when they recited the poem, and thus controlled their breathing apparatus quite accurately. To find an answer to the question whether or not these pressure pulses were performed to produce stress, we asked a panel of listeners to rate the degree of stress of each syllable in each of the six actors' renderings of the poem. The listeners gave their ratings by markings on visual analogue scales, one for each syllable.

We then examined the correlation between the median of the ratings of perceived syllable stress and all RPA values exceeding 1.25. Also obtained was the relation between the median of the ratings and (1) the sound level, (2) the mean F_0 during the syllable, and (3) the duration of the syllable.

Actor	RPA	N	SPL	F0	Dur
1F	0.066	7	0.477	0.177	**0.704**
2F	0.265	12	0.466	0.254	**0.658**
3F	0.368	9	0.512	0.389	**0.721**
1M	**0.673**	9	0.540	0.331	**0.688**
2M	0.570	16	0.403	0.299	**0.732**
3M	0.221	24	0.517	0.308	**0.662**

Table 1. **Correlation coefficients** (linear regression) between the median of the quantized rated syllable stress and the relative pulse amplitude (RPA), mean SPL during the syllable (SPL), mean F_0 during the syllable (F_0), and syllable duration (Dur). N represents the number of RPAs exceeding 1.25. The correlations with SPL, F_0 and Dur were based upon all 52 syllables in the poem. Correlation coefficients above 0.600 are bolded.

A quite unexpected and interesting result was obtained, as can be seen in Table 1. There was no clear relationship between the respiratory pressure pulses and the ratings of syllable stress. Rather, these *stress ratings seemed more related to syllable duration*. For the different actors, the correlation between the median of the ratings of stress and the RPA values varied between 0.066 and 0.673. The correlation between mean rated stress and sound level, mean F_0 and syllable duration was clearly higher, duration showing the highest correlations, between 0.658 and 0.732. This shows that our six actors used syllable duration as a main tool for signaling stress.

Discussion

The pressures measured in some of our actor subjects were quite extreme. While in conversational speech subglottal pressures normally are lower than 10 cm H_2O, pressures in the vicinity of 40 cm H_2O were not uncommon in the actors' stage speech. One actor even reached pressures near 80 cm H_2O, as was shown in Figure 2. There are, however, strong reasons for regarding these pressure readings as reliable. First, for each subject the pressure transducer was calibrated directly after the experiment. Second, the actors used normal pressures during conversational speech. Third, the stage speech was of course quite loud. It should also be mentioned that the actor who used the highest pressures had a harsh voice during the day of the recording, possibly because of some vocal fold disorder.

The results pose the question why the actors produced these carefully timed pressure pulses. Enhancing *text intelligibility* seems a likely answer, at least in some cases. In the total material consisting of 312 syllables, 77 relative pulse amplitude values exceeding 1.25 were observed. Of these, slightly less than half occurred on unstressed vowels or on consonants, and nine of the 17 pulses observed during consonants occurred during continuants such as /l, m, n/. This means that, on average, a pressure pulse was produced on every fourth syllable. Pulses of similar amplitudes were very rarely observed in the actors' conversational speech, so it seems quite likely that the production of *short pressure pulses belong to the characteristics of actors' stage speech.*

The pressure pulses appearing on consonants are crucial to text intelligibility. An increase of subglottal pressure enhances the higher overtones of the source spectrum more than the lower overtones, such that the higher overtones become more prominent in the spectrum. *As consonants are associated with characteristic patterns in the second and third formants, the amplitudes of partials in the higher part of the spectrum are relevant to the identification of consonants. At the same time consonants are not very loud, but their higher partials in particular will become louder if they are produced with a high lung pressure. In this sense, the consonantal pressure pulses would contribute to text intelligibility.*

We would also like to speculate that the key to the respiratory behavior that produces these pressure pulses is not so much awareness of breathing as the desire to communicate and the urge to reach distant listeners. Nevertheless, pedagogy tends to profit from the teachers' awareness of the physical realities underlying the skills being taught.

Our results show that in stage speech subglottal pressure is changed quickly and accurately dependent upon the text spoken. A need to change subglottal pressure quickly and accurately occurs also in singing and wind instrument playing, where this pressure must be adapted not only to loudness but also to pitch (Fuks and Sundberg 1999; Leanderson et al. 1987). It is thought-provoking that singers, wind instrumentalists, and actors tend to use the term "support" for an important aspect of their breathing technique, thus suggesting that "support" is related to the need to constantly change subglottal pressure.

In summary, this investigation has shown that actors performing recitation as if in front of a large audience:

1. change subglottal pressure quickly and accurately,
2. producing pressure pulses synchronized with not only stressed vowels but also consonants.
3. The pressure pulses did not increase the degree of perceived stress for the syllable where they appeared;
4. rather, stress was perceived when syllable duration was longer.
5. It seems likely that the pressure pulses increase text intelligibility.

References
Sundberg, J., N. Elliot, P. Gramming & L. Nord "Short-term variation of subglottal pressure for expressive purposes in singing and stage speech. A preliminary investigation", *Journal of Voice* 7, (1993), 227-234.
Fuks, L. & J. Sundberg "Blowing pressures in bassoon, clarinet, oboe and saxophone", *Acustica/Acta acustica* 85, (1999), 267-277.
Leanderson, R., J. Sundberg & C. von Euler. "Role of the diaphragmatic activity during singing: a study of transdiaphragmatic pressures", *J Appl Physiol* 62, (1987), 259-270.

Pronunciation, Phonetics, Linguistics, Dialect/Accent Coaching *Lynn Watson, Associate Editor*

Editorial Column *by Lynn Watson, Associate Editor*

Phonetics receives the focus of attention in this edition of *VSR*'s PPLDAS section, though pronunciation, linguistics and dialect/accent studies are crucial elements of the discussions to follow. Two articles address the teaching of IPA; both had their origins in a VASTA Focus Group panel titled "Why IPA" that was presented at the 2006 ATHE conference in Chicago. In the interest of full disclosure, I should add that I organized and was chair of that panel.

Paul Schierhorn offers practical and technical information to help streamline the process of typing IPA. He outlines freeware programs that allow the user to reconfigure a computer keyboard to make specific, personalized choices in layout. In other words, you can assign that [ə] symbol to whichever key you want on your keyboard. Keyboard mapping is described for both Mac and PC.

Ruth Childs makes a compelling case for teaching IPA in an introductory, general education college course in voice and speech. Part of Childs' rationale involves raising awareness in her students of language difference, allowing them to become curious and interested in the unique individual sounds and patterns of language, rather than becoming mired in unproductive, inhibiting judgments of "good" and "bad" relative to their own speech and the speech they encounter from others.

The case for teaching IPA is continued by Phil Thompson and located within the setting of training for actors. Thompson makes what he terms a "deep case" for teaching phonetics, including IPA, and for teaching it in a comprehensive and detailed manner. The article examines several factors that prevent actors from identifying and producing speech sounds accurately, and posits the teaching of phonetics as not only an effective way around those barriers, but as a path to expanding "imagination and flexibility" in an actor.

Taken together, the articles in this section point the way to methods of working with actors and voice users—both in training and in the professions—that incorporate in-depth, objective observation of the sounds of language and how they are formed. As two of the pieces suggest, teaching phonetics and IPA can be a pleasurable and intellectually stimulating investigation of language that builds awareness of an exciting range of linguistic choices. These choices are then subject to the unique and varied needs of the actor or voice user, rather than being limited to prescribed choices based on arbitrary ideas of "correctness." Given a variety of speech and pronunciation options, an actor or voice user can take into account the myriad of situational or dramatic circumstances before them, and select what seems most fitting. That ability to choose can lead to a stronger sense of individual ownership of language as opposed to reaction to external judgment, to a greater sense of joy in creation.

Lynn Watson has consulted extensively on voice, speech, text and dialects at leading regional theatres. Her credits include numerous productions at Arena Stage, Kennedy Center (*The Glass Menagerie* and *Cat on a Hot Tin Roof*), South Coast Repertory, Mark Taper Forum, ACT San Francisco and Maryland Stage Company. She has acted off-Broadway and in leading classical and Shakespearean roles regionally. She is an associate editor for the "International Dialects of English Archive" and is certified as an Associate Teacher of Fitzmaurice Voicework. She teaches voice, speech, and acting at the University of Maryland, Baltimore County.

Peer Reviewed Article *by Phil Thompson*

Phonetics and Perception: The Deep Case for Phonetics Training

Philip Thompson is the current president of VASTA. He is an Associate Professor at the University of California, Irvine where he heads the MFA program in Acting. He works frequently as a voice and dialect coach for theatres such as the Cincinnati Playhouse in the Park, South Coast Repertory, OperaPacific, Pasadena Playhouse and the Alabama Shakespeare Festival. He has been a resident vocal coach for 10 seasons at the Utah Shakespearean Festival. He is a master teacher of Fitzmaurice Voicework and teaches frequently in training workshops around the country.

The International Phonetic Alphabet has become an almost universally accepted tool in teaching speech to actors and is taught in one form or another in most actor training institutions in the United States. Even when there is disagreement about what pronunciation choices should be taught or the best methods for teaching, most speech teachers, and the people who hire them, agree the IPA is something an actor ought to learn. There are some very good, practical arguments to support this point of view. An actor who can read and write in the International Phonetic Alphabet can do a number of useful things. She can:

1) Read articles on the topic of speech and accent
2) Read pronunciations in pronouncing dictionaries given in IPA
3) Make her own notations of sounds she observes in accent source material
4) Read pronunciation notes given by a voice coach
5) Make note of pronunciations in an accurate and commonly understood form
6) Rely on the stability of that written record.

Certainly, a phonetic alphabet is a wonderful tool, and its practical value alone makes it worthy of study. I believe, however, there are two arguments for the value of phonetics *training* that are far more compelling, and my belief in their importance influences the way I teach the material.

I believe that studying phonetics helps us to untangle perceptual confusions that arise when we compare the sounds we hear and make to our internal model of language. I also believe that training in phonetics enriches an actor's linguistic inner life, providing useful contextual knowledge and developing skill in perceiving and performing. I'll even go so far as to say that an enriched perception of the variety of sounds in language builds an actor's imagination and flexibility. Finally, I feel that these benefits can be maximized in speech training and that improving an actor's understanding of language variation in general and their own perceptions specifically, should be a goal of speech training for actors.

At this point it would be useful to make a few distinctions. It is fairly common practice in writing and speaking about speech training to use the terms *phonetics* and *IPA* interchangeably and so far this essay has not distinguished clearly between the two. There are important differences however. Phonetics is the study of the description of speech sounds. The International Phonetic Alphabet (IPA)[1] is one means of describing those sounds but the science of Phonetics encompasses more than the IPA alone. It would be possible to study Phonetics without the IPA but it would not really be possible to study the IPA without studying Phonetics. For example, one could analyze a speech sound spectrographically or offer a physical description of the articulatory action that produced a sound. These are methods of describing the sounds of language without reference to an alphabet. The IPA is a concise symbolic means of referring to and describing those sounds. We could think of a phonetic symbol as a shorthand for the full description of the articulatory action which produces that sound. As a general principle, this alphabet represents each speech sound (called a *phone*) with a single distinct symbol. The addition of diacritics can further specify features of the sound being described. The entire alphabet and the principles upon which it is based provide a stable, widely accepted system of conventions for describing speech sounds very precisely

1. This acronym can also stand for the International Phonetic Association, the body responsible for defining the International Phonetic Alphabet. The Association's website is http://www.arts.gla.ac.uk/IPA/ipa.html.

and concisely. It is the IPA's precision in describing subtle variations in sound that is of particular value in clarifying students' understanding of the sounds they can make. The stability of the arbitrary conventions of the IPA and the lack of ambiguity in the direct correspondence of symbol to sound is extremely valuable in sorting out misunderstandings of listening and speech. Furthermore, the system of knowledge of phonetics as a whole provides a frame of reference that guards against confusion. This confusion is entirely natural and results from the way an untrained listener perceives and thinks about the sounds of language. I find it helpful to classify these confusions as *interference*.

The term *interference* was used by Uriel Weinreich in *Languages in Contact* (1953) to describe "instances of deviation from the norms of either language which occur in the speech of bilinguals as a result of their familiarity with more than one language."[2] More recently, the term *transfer* has been used and the distinction made between *positive transfer* of useful knowledge or skill from one's primary language and *negative transfer* in which some part of the primary language is used inappropriately in the secondary language. This is essentially the same as *interference*. I stick to the older word because I am more interested in addressing confusions that occur in the speech work of actors than I am in the larger field of Second Language Acquisition.

This essay is not intended to advance or to contradict Weinrich's arguments about the way languages change by coming into contact through the speakers of those languages. There is already a body of work discussing contact-induced language change and the role of interference. The term is introduced here in an attempt to clarify some issues encountered in speech training for actors.

Put simply, the interference I'm interested in is what happens when an actor mistakenly relies on a faulty idea about a pronunciation. For the most part, the challenges that face actors don't involve learning a second language. Actors, however, regularly deal with questions of pronunciation, whether on the large scale of performing an accent or on the small scale of a single word pronunciation. Actors should have access to a range of speech choices for vocal characterization or intelligibility. They need to perceive speech sounds accurately and be able to repeat, remember and notate them. In a way, actors are required to negotiate an *expanded* version of their own primary language.[3]

In tackling this difficult task, actors deal with two main forms of interference: orthographic interference and phonemic interference.[4] I'll begin by describing how this interference occurs and I'll make the case that when actors study the IPA they are inoculated against both.

Orthography refers to the system of writing with which a language is recorded. Every literate speaker of a language has internalized a set of rules for converting written words into speakable language. Orthographic interference occurs when the application of normal rules for turning written words into speech leads to errors in pronunciation. A common example of this would be an error made in reading unfamiliar word. A reader encountering the word "misled" never having heard it spoken, might very well read it [maɪzl̩d] Often speakers of a second language apply the reading rules of their first language to words they read in their second language. A native German speaker,

2. Weinreich, U. *Languages in Contact.* The Hague: Mouton, 1953, 1.

3. Obviously, there are actors who perform in a second, third or fourth language and genres of drama that take a bilingual approach. Although the particular challenges for these actors are interesting, they lie outside the scope of this essay.

4. Weinreich used the phrase *phonic interference* and the accepted term today is *phonetic interference.* I have again chosen to avoid the most current term of art, in part because I can't be certain that my understanding of the concept matches all that is implied by that term in the linguistics literature. I also feel that the word *phonemic* better expresses the problem I'm describing.

5. The correct pronunciation is [davɪð].

misapplying German rules to an English word, might read the word "vote" as [fot]. An English speaker might read the Welsh name "Dafydd" as [dæfɪd].[5] These errors are the source of some features of foreign accents.

But there is another way in which orthographic interference can cause problems when orthography stands in for phonetics. Because actors are preparing a learned, crafted performance they need a way to record pronunciations and represent them to others, in order to consider pronunciation choices and finally to memorize and perform them. To do this, an actor without phonetic training will frequently fall back on the phonetic features of spelling and that can be quite confusing.

I had a recent experience that demonstrates the problem. I was coaching *Hamlet* and I made the decision (a fairly arbitrary one) that we would pronounce the word "liege" as [liʤ] rather than [liʒ]. I informed the actors of this and other pronunciation choices before our first read-through. After a while I began to hear one actor pronouncing the word as [lig] At the intermission a few disconcerted actors came up to me to ask if they had misunderstood me. "No!" I said, "Stick with [liʤ]." Talking to the offending actor I noticed that he had spelled out on his page "L E E G." He had heard me say [ʤ] and this was his way of writing it. It made some sense: the letter "G" is sometimes pronounced [ʤ] in English words and by underlining the letter he emphasized that there was something particular about this "G." Unfortunately, letters can't be trusted to stand for a single sound and in the task of reading his note, he extracted another sound from the letter. What's so striking about an event like this is how quickly the actor got turned around and wandered off the path. He heard the sound, devised a method for representing it and less than 20 minutes later he read his own notation the wrong way. And this was an experienced professional actor, a PhD and a university professor. I think that demonstrates pretty clearly that spelling posing as phonetics can be spectacularly unhelpful. The problem isn't just that spelling isn't phonetics; it's that spelling is imperfectly phonetic.

6. It is worth noting that the Roman alphabet and its predecessors, the Greek and Phoenician alphabets, mark an extraordinary technological breakthrough in ancient societies in that they provide a means for recording the sounds of language. In this sense an alphabet is always phonetic.

The IPA, as discussed above, is designed to represent the sounds of language unambiguously. This is not the case with the Roman alphabet that we use, for example, to write English. The Roman alphabet does represent sounds.[6] The letter "b" can generally be relied on to represent a /b/ sound and we can be fairly certain how to pronounce most letters. For that reason, we can spell a completely invented word and expect most English speakers to read it the same way: "flimp" "shoobs" "vungacity." But there are some letters and letter combinations that can be interpreted in different ways. Could you be as confident of your pronunciation of "sprow" or "pough" or "thild"? As the story of "liege" demonstrates, we can't always rely on letters to stay put and only represent one sound.

7. By using the word "distinct" I intend to refer to the phonemes of English. An attempt to count of all the allophonic variations of these phonemes as pronounced in all varieties of English would end in frustration.

One reason is we don't have enough letters to go around. If we count up all the distinct[7] sounds used in English, we'll end up with a number in the low 40s. Any child, though, could tell us that there are only 26 letters. We combine some of them to describe more sounds (TH for example) but that still doesn't cover it. TH could stand for two different sounds in English. The sound [ʤ] can be represented by the letters "j" "g" or even by the combination of "dy" in "did you" or "di" in the Irish pronunciation of "idiot." But having chosen one representation of that sound ("g" for our actor) the letter "g" still holds the possibility of being read in a variety of ways.

This makes the Roman alphabet a fuzzy system, unsuited to exact recording of pronunciation. The alphabet is terrifically useful of course and this fuzziness doesn't seem to make it any less useful. In fact there is a marvelous convenience in a writing system that tolerates variety and error. We can pick up a text written by someone who speaks a very different dialect and still understand perfectly what was written. The Roman alphabet's fuzziness is, in fact, a benefit. As John Man writes in his book *Alpha Beta*, "the strength of the alphabet as an idea lies in its practical imperfection. Though it fits no language to perfection, it can, with some pushing and shoving, be adapted to all languages."[8] That very flexibility, though, can lead to confusion when we treat letters as stable records of speech sounds.

8. Man, J. *Alpha Beta: How 26 Letters Shaped the Western World.* New York: Wiley, 2000, 1.

This is a danger whenever we write down a representation of a pronunciation using the alphabet, but interference can also occur when we use our internal concept of a letter to think about sounds. Here's an example: My daughter is named "Maja." We pronounce it [maĭə]. Many people who encounter her name in print pronounce it [mɑʤə] or even [mɑha]. Those pronunciations reflect orthographic interference based on English or Spanish rules. But another confusion often occurs. When she has told someone her name it is quite common for that person, after some period of reflection to refer to her as [miə]. This indicates a kind of orthographic interference caused by an internal, alphabetic representation. The error occurs because the hearer has recorded the name in memory as a sequence of letters "M-I-A" and reconstructed the pronunciation [miə] as a plausible pronunciation of those letters.

That sort of internal orthographic interference occurs quite a bit because we need a way to think about and talk about the sounds of language, and the system we use to record our language is imperfectly adapted to that task. Throughout our speaking lives, we develop impressions and create narratives and form hypotheses about how our language works. When we learn to read and write, we fold that knowledge in with the rest, creating a big messy story for ourselves that partially explains what we know. Clearly there must be some rules about how to interpret the symbols of spelling or we wouldn't be able to read new words, but we aren't usually conscious of those rules. These cases of orthographic interference point us toward a recognition of the unreliability of our knowledge and perceptions. They remind us that when we think and talk about our own use of language, there is more going on than we may be aware of.

I would venture to assert that most people have a notion of perception that they develop in childhood and keep until challenged to investigate the matter more deeply. They imagine that hearing and seeing are a matter of the outside world entering the interior space of the self through the senses to be directly understood by the mind. That model works pretty well and matches most of our experiences. Every once in a while, though, we are presented with something (an optical illusion, perhaps) that makes us aware that there's something tricky going on in the path between outside and inside. There has been a great deal of research in the last half century investigating the mechanisms we use to turn sensory data into a sense of reality. Two things stand out as interesting when looking at this research:

First, our perceptual systems do a lot with very little data. In fact a big part of perceiving the world has to do with suppressing unnecessary input and finding the key pieces of information to track and interpret. Second, we are not generally aware of the process of cognition, and I think you may agree that that's a good thing. It cuts down on auto accidents and psychiatric hospitalization to be unaware of how we perceive the world. We just do it and get on with the complex job of living, but it's actually difficult to force our minds into contemplating the holes in our perception—to look behind the curtain, if you will.

These principles operate in our perception of the sounds of language. Earlier, I said the IPA describes speech sounds called *phones*. We can make a great variety of sounds that are discernibly different from one another. And with careful and experienced attention we can perceive all of those differences. But when we listen to speech we're listening not so much for phones but for phonemes. Phonemes are units of recognition. One way of describing a phoneme is as a speech sound that a listener recognizes as distinct from another—distinct enough that it would make the difference between one word and another. A phoneme is often described in terms of *minimal pairs*, that is, two words in a given language are recognized by speakers of that language as being different words because one speech sound is recognizably different. In English, "pat" and "bat" are different words because they have different initial sounds. In English then /p/ and /b/ are different phonemes. Likewise, in English, "hit" and "heat" are heard as different words because the second phoneme differs enough to count. A Russian speaker, hearing these two words might not hear that difference because in the phonemic system of Russian both of those sounds fall within the range of a single phoneme. When we hear a sound we determine the category for that sound and suppress any confusing detail about how close to the center of our expectations for that sound the actual sound came. Considering the blinding speed that speech comes at us, that's a necessity.

Our brains can only work so fast, so we use this method for capturing key data and ignoring the details. This is called *categorical perception*, a term introduced by Alvin Liberman.[9] Put simply, categorical perception is the process whereby we recognize things by the category they belong to. Furthermore, we tend to minimize variation within a category and emphasize those features that mark difference between categories. When we see coins scattered across a table top we see the things that make pennies different from nickels and quarters and we pay very little attention to the variation in color between the pennies.

Now we may reasonably ask, why we would do such a thing? Are we coin racists? Well, it makes a great deal of sense that we would have this ability to suppress information that isn't vital to decision making. Ignoring the rich array of penny varieties allows us to focus on the task of picking up quarters to pay the toll. If we couldn't do this sort of thing, life would move very slowly indeed. As Arthur Sullivan wrote in *The Gondoliers*, "When every one is somebodee, Then no one's anybody!" There must be distinctions between things and although this may be an unpalatable way of organizing society, it is a useful principle when we need to make quick decisions. Categorical perception helps us to deal with large amounts of information by discarding the unnecessary. When we hear someone say, "Watch out!" we don't want to be

9. Liberman, A. M., Harris, K. S., Hoffman, H. S. & Griffith, B. C. "The discrimination of speech sounds within and across phoneme boundaries." *Journal of Experimental Psychology* 54: 1957.

distracted by the details. And this makes for a very robust system of recognizing words. If I hear [xe ɸil vɑts aʊt fʊɚ dɛt bɑ̃s] I'm able to extract information enough to categorize the sounds into patterns I recognize, make a decision, and leap to safety. I don't stop processing just because the sound isn't exactly right. What's more, when I hear a sound that doesn't quite match my expectations for its phonemic category, I disregard the difference and actually perceive the sound as closer to my internal model of that phoneme. This effect is at the root of the problem of phonemic interference.

Just as in orthographic interference, errors in speaking a second language can be caused by the misapplication of phonological features from the speaker's first language. The French speaker, for example, lacking the phoneme /θ/ might use the closest candidate from their own phonology, /s/, and pronounce the word "think" as [sɪŋk] or the speaker might read the spelling of the word using French rules and pronounce it [tɪŋk]. In each case the speaker's first language knowledge interferes with their success in the second language. In the case of orthographic interference we saw that confusions happen because orthography is an unstable record of speech sounds. The same is true in phonemic interference. Categorical perception leads us to push unfamiliar sounds into the procrustean bed of our existing phonemic categories. The French speaker lacks the phoneme /θ/ and so it falls into the nearest phonemic category /s/. That speaker will tend to hear the sound as similar to /s/, suppressing their awareness of its difference.

The same thing can happen with speakers of the same language when we listen to someone with a different accent than ours. Our tendency is to hear that person's speech through the filter of our own. For example, many Americans believe that Canadians pronounce the phoneme /aʊ/ as /u/, rendering "out and about" as [ut n̩ əbut]. But this isn't really the case. Some Canadians pronounce the MOUTH[10] phoneme as /ɛ̈ʊ/. To an American ear this pronunciation seems so far out of the expected category that we reassign it to the GOOSE category. Many Americans pronounce their GOOSE phoneme with a tiny onglide from a fairly front and close position [ïu] and so the Canadian rendition of "out" seems to be a candidate for this phonemic category. When a Canadian says the word "out" the American listener not only assigns the word to the /u/ category but *hears* it as [ut].

This sort of confusion occurs because our cognitive perceptual system works, for the most part, outside of our awareness. This system automatically adjusts sounds to fit our pattern. We are not entirely conscious of the little adjustments we make to stretch these sounds to our purposes and, before long, we've strayed from the true path. I'm reminded of what can happen to a pilot flying through clouds. In the absence of the visual reminder of the horizon, a pilot can misinterpret the information from her own inner ear, make numerous, tiny overcorrections over time, and can reach a state of *spatial disorientation*[11] where she no longer believes her instruments. In this confusion the pilot "corrects" her position until she finally comes flying out of the cloudbank upside down.

This disorientation doesn't usually occur on a clear day with a visible horizon because there is a running comparison going on between what is felt and what is seen. It is this ability to coordinate these different sources of information that gives the pilot a more reliable sense of where she is. The absolute

10. MOUTH is one of J.C. Wells' lexical set words, used as a shorthand for a standard phonemic category in English.
Wells, John C. *Accents of English* (vol. 1). Cambridge: Cambridge University Press, 1982.

11. Spatial disorientation is the technical term for this effect. It can occur in a variety of situations but at the center of these cases of disorientation is some faulty perception at the level of the inner ear followed by a conscious but errant adjustment for perception.

position of the horizon allows the pilot to regularly test and realign the sense of balance provided by the inner ear. More experienced pilots also check their instruments more frequently and learn to trust what they see there. They become better at pinpointing their location on a map. They avoid disorientation by improving the quality and number of sources of information and they get better at coordinating that input. This is a useful idea for considering the way an actor is helped by phonetic study. When an actor has some understanding of how the sounds of speech are made, the natural tendency to conform the sounds we hear toward our own phonemic categories is counteracted by reference to the more stable landmarks in their phonetic map.

A map is a particularly apt image for thinking about speech sounds because these sounds are produced by the physical configuration of the articulators in space. When we talk about the distance between one sound and another we can refer to a literal distance between parts of the vocal tract. Our awareness of the position of our articulators can give us a vital, second source of stable information just as the horizon does for the pilot. That physical, proprioceptive awareness of the vocal tract developed in the study of phonetics gives actors better tools for counteracting the distorting influence of categorical perception. It is important for me, in my own teaching, to spend time and attention on feeling the physical actions that produce speech so that students can develop a sensitivity to these small movements and discover their relation to the sounds of speech. When we feel how and where we make speech sounds, then sounds falling in the border between phonemic categories can be located, perceived and reproduced. A detailed phonetic map with a direct correspondence to the physical topography of our own mouths helps us to keep track of the shifting landscape of phonemic categories.

In addition, in the process of filling in the details of our phonetic map we learn contextual information about language that can keep us oriented as we travel from accent to accent. We learn, for example about voiced/unvoiced distinctions and that gives us a way of describing what happens to some final consonants in German. We learn that the sound we think of as "r" may have different phonetic realizations in different languages or even in different places in a word. All of this information about how we speak is more than just entertaining. For an actor trying to reconfigure their automatic and unconscious language skill to create a characterization, this knowledge creates an objective framework from which to negotiate that transformation.

There is another kind of confusion that speech teachers and their students are faced with and it has less to do with the

peculiarities of our spelling or our perceptions and more to do with our attitudes. The field of linguistics underwent a profound change when it began to accept the concept, developed in anthropology, known as *cultural relativism*. This notion, that every culture is equally valid and must be studied objectively, overthrew a tradition which sought to classify cultures in terms of a hierarchy of value or arrange societies in terms of their "development." In the same way, languages had been thought of as more or less "primitive" or "advanced." The position of modern linguistics, and in particular the subfield of sociolinguistics, is to observe that language variation is natural and normal, and that patterns and structures are found across all varieties and are not limited to "standard" language varieties. These varieties may carry more or less prestige within a society and they are certainly all undergoing a process of change, but that change cannot be said to be toward or away from any right ideal of propriety. This point of view is widely accepted in the scientific community, but outside of the linguistics classroom, people generally have strong views about what they see as the good or bad in speech. The commonplace folk theory of language is that there is some ideal of correct language and that other varieties are distortions or deviations from that ideal.

I was asked to speak to a group of patrons of a regional theatre on my work as a dialect coach. I began the talk with a question, "who in the audience has an accent?" Not a hand was raised until a woman elbowed her husband and said, in an accent quite different from mine, "Charlie, for God's sake! *You* have an accent!" The truth is we *all* have accents and those accents all mean something in our society. The belief that accents are what other people have makes us deaf to our own. We see our pronunciation as neutral and all other varieties as carrying messages of difference. The difficulty for a student studying speech is that this false notion of neutrality in accents and the unexamined prejudice against some accents interferes with an objective assessment of the sounds of that accent. As with the cases of interference that have been discussed in this article, what we think we know can prevent us from perceiving what's in front of us.

I believe that actors benefit from a conscious and *objective* awareness of the formation of speech gestures so they can learn to make sounds that aren't in their phonetic inventory. In that process, they also benefit from reviewing their attitudes and associations with speech sounds. It is also useful for actors to have a sense of the "lay of the land" in the form of phonological rules. For example, when an actor knows that the words "pin" and "pen" are distinct in some folks' accents, he has a structure into which to place his observations of his own and others' speech. Let me be clear: I don't believe that an actor's speech should be self conscious. There is much in an actor's art that must remain in the realm of tacit knowledge, at least in the moment of performance, but in order to move beyond the narrow palette of his own voice and embody something else, an actor needs some explicit knowledge of what makes up the range of possible human expression and some experience consciously manipulating those sounds. Phonetics training can give students a perspective on the wide range of accent variety and help them to listen to the sounds of those accents (and their own) objectively. We need to be aware there is a potential for confusion when talking about and thinking about speech sounds and, at the minimum, warn our students about it. Any phonetics training gives students a useful frame of reference for sorting out these problems. It is possible, though, to adapt the way we teach phonetics in order to maximize this benefit. The following suggestions represent some steps I have taken to adapt my teaching to these ideas.[12]

1) *Begin actors' speech training with study of anatomy and exploration of the physical actions of articulation.*

> Little children delight to puzzle one another by assuming unusual positions of the tongue which others cannot imitate. They should be encouraged in this, for all exercises of that kind are of value as a preparation for speech. By such exercises they unconsciously gain control over the vocal organs and become better able to imitate positions of the mouth.
>
> Alexander Graham Bell, *The Mechanism of Speech* 1910[13]

Bell's main point here is absolutely true. Exercises of the tongue, even with no reference to speech help us to develop control of the vocal organs and improve our ability to imitate. But it is also true that such experiments in oral gymnastics can help establish a frame of reference that makes the student less prone to the problems of interference that they'll encounter in their speech training.

Let's look again at the example of the pilot becoming disoriented while flying through a cloud bank. Such spatial disorientation doesn't occur when the pilot has a clear view of the horizon. When the pilot can cross-reference this additional visual reference point with the sensations of the inner ear, confusing signals get sorted out. The presence of a second data stream of reliable information gives the pilot a much better ability to self correct. A student who takes the time at the beginning of a course of study in phonetics to become aware of the physical reality of the vocal tract will be able to call upon that knowledge to recover from confusing instances of interference. Familiarity with speech anatomy also prepares the student to conceptualize some of the information they will eventually learn, since phonetic charts are most often arranged in a layout that matches the position of each speech action in the mouth. Finally, by investigating possible articulatory actions apart from the labels for the sounds produced, a student has the opportunity to practice and experience a wide range of sounds that she might otherwise resist because those sounds fall outside of her linguistic identity. If she practices the action of nasal plosion without foreknowledge of its use in a particular accent, she avoids loading that action with a particular attitude. She may later discover that she or others have attitudes about the use of nasal plosion in the pronunciation of the word "didn't", but she will already have an experience of the action based solely on her objective experience. This is

12. I am unable to avoid repeating some recommendations already made by my colleague, Dudley Knight in his excellent article, "Standard Speech: The Ongoing Debate." That I haven't quoted him verbatim should not be taken to mean that I disagree with his suggestions in that article. If I'm lucky, the imperfect overlap of these lists will amplify rather than obscure what he has written.

Knight, D., "Standard Speech: The Ongoing Debate" in *The Vocal Vision*, Hampton M. (ed.), New York: Applause Theatre Books, 1997.

13. Bell, A.G., *The Mechanism of Speech*, New York & London: Funk & Wagnalls Company, 1910.

particularly important when working on articulatory settings that evoke strong attitudes. Nasality, for example, is a feature for which students and speech teachers seem to share an antipathy. In those instances when students practice increasing nasality, they may well add a variety of other features and extraneous muscular efforts as a commentary on the sound. Many American students attempting to reduce the degree of rhoticity in vowels may find themselves adopting unrelated features from non-rhotic accents such as Received Pronunciation. An experience of these adjustments as physical helps a student to isolate actions and to make much more refined adjustments to their speech.

2) *Be aware of developmental parallels in the acquisition of speech as well as reading and writing*
The observation that children acquire features of language in a predictable order, and that acquisition of a second language can often follow a similar pattern, has led to a great deal of discussion over the proper method of teaching languages. I do not intend to argue that phonetic training for actors should be organized in the order in which those features are first acquired by children but there are some helpful generalizations that can be made by comparing a speech student's experience to that of children.

In acquiring our primary language, exploration precedes explanation and this can be a useful model for the speech student. An adult learner is likely to be resistant to babbling like a baby but playing with sounds can sometimes yield experiences that would not be found by more somber exercise. The experience of performing the gestures of articulation improvisationally can be pleasant and a playful attitude often leads to surprising realizations. If nothing else, it makes phonetics class something to look forward to.

Although most people can't remember their early language acquisition, they may remember part of their experience of learning to read. Some students have unpleasant memories of reading before the class or of struggling to make the associations between spoken and written language. For these students, learning phonetics can feel like revisiting that experience and we will help their learning if we understand that discomfort. Try a little tenderness.

3) *Teach the IPA without any reference to a prescription for "correct speech"*
The International Phonetic Alphabet is a descriptive tool. It was designed to assist linguists in recording the rich variety of sounds found in the world's language. The IPA is neutral on the question of preference. If we use it to describe a narrow set of preferred sounds, we run the risk of presenting the IPA as

the mark of authority for those choices. That runs counter to the goals of the organization.

I have no difficulty in making prescriptions about speech. Artists are continually making choices and prescribing outcomes and when an actor is familiar with the IPA those choices can be efficiently communicated. However, to limit the IPA to describing only one set of choices is to make it nearly useless as a tool. There is no need to learn a new and complex system to describe a single set of outcomes. In such a situation it quickly becomes evident to a student that this new system of writing is not a tool for their own use, but the mechanism for delivering a program of speech correction.

No matter what the intentions and skills of the instructor, a student being asked to explore a sound while simultaneously being offered a single model of correctness is being placed in a bind which frustrates any true exploration. Mixed messages built into the teaching method only add to the confusion the student is prone to.

4) *Transcribe from speech*
When students write phonetic transcriptions, they should be describing speech that they hear rather than transcribing how written words might be pronounced. Transcriptions from texts imply a single correct pronunciation and unless that accent has been specified and carefully studied, students should first practice transcribing what they hear. It's certainly useful for actors to learn the patterns of an accent so that they might be able to look at a text and predict the pronunciation of a word, but phonetic transcription is a separate skill. By conflating the descriptive task of transcription with reading a script and applying knowledge of an accent, we invite orthographic interference.

5) *Cover all the sounds of the IPA*
If our goal is the expansion of a student's range of linguistic possibility, then this is a necessity. Not only will work on, say, nonpulmonic consonants be valuable if the actor is someday faced with the challenge of speaking Xhosa, the experience of exploring that consonant action will expand physical awareness. The practice of attempting outlying sounds that are not part of the student's current experience is more likely to give insight into well known sounds as the student compares and contrasts the experience.

It is a mistake to "streamline" a course by teaching a reduced and idealized inventory of "Good" or "American" speech sounds. First, when we call something "good" there is always an attendant context to that judgment, whether or not we're aware of it. Speech sounds can only be *good for* something or *a good example* of something. When we call things "good" with no reference to the context for that judgment, then we are making a moral judgment and that has no place in the teaching of speech. Producing a short list of "American" sounds is also problematic because there are so very many varieties of American English. By limiting the sounds we teach and claiming that they are the "American" sounds we imply that any deviation from that chosen sound is somehow "Un-American." The vowel in the word "dog" will most likely be pronounced differently in Brooklyn, Birmingham and Beloit. Which of those is the American vowel?

When we open up our teaching to the wide variety of sounds in human language we open our students to insights about their own speech by way of contrast and we prepare them for their job of transforming their speech to meet the demands of the character.

6) Avoid the use of keywords for memorizing sounds
Using keywords as tools for learning sounds is an invitation to phonemic interference. Writing down /ɔ/ = "law" won't help a student who pronounces that word with a different vowel. It will stand between the student and the experience of discovering the physical action represented by that symbol.

When pressed to give exemplary words to demonstrate the sound I may invent nonsense words that fit the bill. "/ɔ/ as in [sklɔdʒ] for example." This can be difficult for students to accept since they see keywords as a helpful shortcut. My intention, though, is to set up a roadblock to such shortcuts and to require the student to take a longer journey. Without recourse to spelling, they must remember the sound itself and associate it with an articulatory action rather than the vagaries of spelling.

7) Delay the introduction of symbols
Introducing phonetic symbols, which are for the most part identical to letters of the Roman alphabet, is an invitation to orthographic interference. Obviously, the symbols are a vital part of the students' study of phonetics, but work done before the introduction of symbols on anatomy and phonetic description provides a strong foundation of knowledge to counterbalance the pull of orthographic interference. The first phonetics quiz I give to my students is a test of their ability to describe sounds. I produce a sound, a [β] for example, and my students write down "voiced bilabial fricative." Then I hand each student a description of a sound and ask them to produce it. This is a slightly uncomfortable process for the students. They have, as I have described above, an imperfectly phonetic alphabet that they know very well. When I insist on "unvoiced alveolar plosive" when they know perfectly well that I mean "t" they wonder why they have to take the long road.

The answer, of course, is that there is nothing to be taught and nothing to be learned by cutting that corner and leaving that knowledge unexamined. An actor must be more interested in the action of /t/ and its allophones than they need be in the symbol that represents the sound. Fortunately, when the time comes for the symbols to reenter the equation, their familiarity with phonetic description gives them a context into which they can place the symbols. The symbols of the IPA including diacritics fit neatly and legibly on a single page and when the foundations are laid well the symbols can be learned quite quickly.

8) Invite interrogation
In the quizzes I describe above, I invite students to ask questions by modeling a distinction between sounds. If, for example, I ask students to transcribe [ʃubz]. I will encourage them to clarify any confusion by asking me, "Did you say [ʃubz] or [tʃubz]?" When students are given the opportunity to interrogate me during the quiz they gain confidence in their ability to hear distinctions and that what they are listening for is repeatable, open to reasoning and finally knowable. Most important, though, they develop a curiosity for sounds that carries them through the rest of their work on speech and dialects.

Every so often, when working with actors on their speech, I'm forced to take a step back and remember something I was once intimately aware of: Acting is hard. The work that actors do in adapting their speech to the needs of their art is only one part of the challenge of acting, and it is certainly a complex task. That task is made more difficult by problems of interference. Interference, as I've described it here is the misperception and resultant confusion that can occur when we rely on what we think we know. This can happen when we rely on spelling to behave in a strictly phonetic way or when our natural tendency to sort speech sounds into categories leads us to hear what we expect rather than what's before us. Interference, in this sense, can also occur when our attitudes and narratives about the value of accents prevents us from objectively perceiving the features of an accent.

Phonetics training of any sort can be extremely valuable in helping the actor avoid problems of interference because it offers a stable, systematic and physically perceivable frame of reference. It stands to reason, though, that we could teach more efficiently if we take interference into account. The eight points offered above are by no means a comprehensive account of my teaching practice. They represent some of the principles that guide me in teaching speech to actors, and I invite you to investigate these principles in your own classrooms.

Teaching the IPA

Ruth Childs is an Assistant Professor of Theatre at SUNY Brockport where she teaches voice, movement, and acting. Ruth holds an MFA in Acting from University of Minnesota in Minneapolis and is an associate teacher of Fitzmaurice Voicework. Ruth works extensively in the Rochester area as a voice and dialect coach, director, and actress. Recent projects include *King Lear*, *Faith Healer*, *The Lower Depths*, and *Machinal*.

I teach at SUNY Brockport in Western New York State. The theatre department has a BA program with approximately 60 majors. There is one voice class offered and it attracts primarily Theatre and Communications majors. The class traditionally has up to 24 students enrolled, and meets three times per week for an hour.

Evaluation is based on attendance and participation, three vocal evaluations throughout the semester (individual and group), regular reading assignments and quizzes, as well as attendance and participation. In addition, students attend the two mainstage performances scheduled during the semester and write critique papers on the vocal work done by the actors. I try to make class practical rather than theoretical, but I do use a textbook as the spine of the class. During each class session there is a warm up that focuses on what we are covering that day—anatomy, alignment, breath, support, articulation, etc. I also teach sections on voiceovers, special considerations for radio/TV/film, vocal health, and the IPA.

Most of the students enrolled in the class have had no vocal training other than perhaps some singing. Most are insecure about making any sound in front of a group of their peers, and they are also apprehensive about moving in front of their peers or coming into physical contact with each other. The majority have never done any acting or taken any theatre classes. Students appreciate the physical nature of the class—many sit in lecture classes all day—though they are not used to the non-traditional format of the class. Most find thorough and ongoing vocal and physical work very tough, and are quite resistant to the process. The class size and length is an obstacle to deep transformation and self-discovery, but I strive to allow all students to experience some change in their vocal and physical awareness.

What do the students want from the class? It is not a required class for the Theatre or Communication majors. Students take the class for many reasons: to modify their accent or the sound of their voice, an interest in a career in radio or TV, someone has advised them to get more voice training, or they are theatre majors with an acting emphasis.

Given the requirements of class, and my emphasis on vocal performance, there is one week (three class hours) for teaching and learning the IPA. So, why bother? There is so much to cover and so little time. I could focus the entire semester on body and breath, or support and articulation, or vocal evaluations. Including a section on the IPA seems like a waste of time. There are bigger issues! What can you do in just one week? Will they ever use it again? And, can I teach this?

So the first two years I taught the class I did not include the IPA. But I started using a new textbook (*The Voice Book* by Michael McCallion, Routledge, 1988) that had a chapter on the IPA, so I decided to teach a small unit. I was surprised by how much the students enjoyed it, and that they wanted to do more. I was also surprised by how much I enjoyed teaching the IPA!

My teaching/learning goals for the unit on the IPA are varied. They include:
  • Know what the IPA is—students are able to define the IPA and give some basic guidelines for use.

- Recognize, pronounce, and transcribe some of the symbols.
- Understand the various uses of the IPA, for example: analyze their own dialect; learn a dialect for a role; be able to be hired for better quality and more diverse work in radio, TV, film and theatre (this is very compelling to my students, many of whom complain about their western NY dialect and want to work in other markets); learn a language.
- Create interest in a subject that is completely new to most students.
- Continue to use terms/symbols/sounds in articulation work, warm-up, and performance throughout the semester, so that it is not an isolated week.
- Share the ideas that Dudley Knight advocates—that it is important to know how to make all sounds (so that the actor can then develop any dialect), that a richness of phonetic knowledge is desirable, that a diversity of dialect/sound is important and worth conserving.

Before the first class on the IPA, the students read the relevant chapter in the text book and are encouraged to do a little research on the internet. On the first day of IPA work, we discuss the reading, including the definition of the IPA. Most of the students are confused about what exactly the IPA is and why it was created. [Note: the IPA was created in 1886 to encourage the study of phonetics and to develop a standard for the phonetic notation of every sound in a language]. I also take some time to discuss the uses of the IPA and how it might impact their careers. We then review several of the vowels and consonants and practice sounding them, feeling them in the mouth, and transcribing them. The remainder of that first class is dedicated to playing with the IPA—writing out students names in the IPA, talking about the difference in pronunciation of a person's name and how that is transcribed, feeling the different sounds in the body, reviewing all aspects of the IPA chart: diacritics, suprasegmentals, vowels, and consonants. The end of that first class is dedicated to discussion of judgments based on how a person sounds. I have students from throughout New York State—New York City, Long Island, the Adirondack region, western New York, Syracuse. All of these students have stories of being perceived a certain way based on their speech, and the conversation is usually lively and personal.

During the following classes, my goal is increased precision of work such as heightening skills of articulation and the ability to hear and make subtle changes in sounds. Sample assignments and class work include: studying the phonetics charts in more detail, having students transcribe a short poem into their "home" dialect, deciphering and transcribing the speech of someone with a different dialect. We also talk about subtle shifts in pronunciation depending on the dialect, for example how people from Newcastle, England, North Boston, and Kenya pronounce certain words. During the final class we examine phonetics with a broader lens. I play a dialect tape in class so the students can hear how they might study a new dialect. We watch scenes from movies such as *Fargo*, *The Snapper*, or *Cry Freedom* and discuss the difference between primary and secondary sources for dialect study. I also show documentaries that focus on dialects and perception of dialects in the US, such as the excellent film *American Tongues*. My own experiences of how people perceive my dialect (I am from England) is also a topic for conversation, and provides an opening for us to discuss unconscious bias and perceived status based on the way a person sounds. My focus in this culminating discussion on the IPA is to connect it to the students' reality and goals, and to make the IPA relevant, interesting, and fun.

So what do the students think of the IPA? Much to my surprise, they love it! So much of the voice class is unlike any other class they have taken—it is personal, subjective, and difficult. But the unit on the IPA is technically precise and has an end product. There is a clear use for all the students in the class (they can use it for dialect work, learning a language, etc.), and it is a change in the routine.

My work in teaching the IPA is just beginning. There are several steps I need to take to make this unit more thorough. First, I need to increase my continued use of IPA throughout the remainder of the semester and beyond. For example, I do refer to the phonetic symbols/sounds when working on articulation, but I could do more. I can be more rigorous with my own teaching, but I must also manage the significant time constraints. I could also increase the amount of time dedicated to teaching the IPA. I plan on spending at least one class in the computer lab looking and listening to the wide variety of online resources, such as IDEA and the UCLA Phonetics Lab. We could actually learn a dialect in class, or at least research a particular dialect in depth. It has been sometime since I was in graduate school, so I should do more training in preparation to teach a more advanced unit.

Teaching the IPA has been a surprise to me. I was expecting the students to hate it, and that I would dread it. The opposite is true. I also discovered that my fundamental reason for teaching the IPA is to give my students tools to adapt when necessary, so that they have more choices to draw on from their voice and speech training.

Essay *by Paul Schierhorn*

IPA on a Word Processor: A Usable "Type"?

Paul Schierhorn has taught Voice, Speech, Acting, Performance, Dialects, Singing for the Stage, and Acting for the Microphone at Tulane since 1988. On Tulane's mainstage, he has directed Ionesco, Ibsen, Feydeau, Shakespeare, musicals, composed music, musical directed, acted. He co-founded the Shakespeare Festival at Tulane. A graduate of the Yale School of Drama, he also served on the faculty there and was an Associate Artist at the Yale Repertory Theatre. His work has appeared on Broadway (Tony Award nominee, *THE NEWS*, Best Original Score, Music/Lyrics), off-Broadway, many regional theatres, HBO and broadcast TV. He joined VASTA in 1997.

Once you teach your students the fifty-odd phonemes that make up "American English" in the International Phonetic Alphabet (IPA), the fun begins. They start linking the phonemes to each other. They become amused at some early short words ("of," in the rarely stressed position, looks amusing: ʌv). A new awareness of the IPA's possibilities dawns when I tell them, "Chart your full name exactly *as you wish it to be pronounced* and have somebody else read it." If they're like me (who's had my last name consistently mispronounced on first contact since the beginning of time), they get excited at this new possibility of clarity in communication.

Then they must learn to communicate in two directions: phonetic transcription and reading phonetic transcription. The former is clearly up to them; there's no substitute for writing, writing, writing and feedback, from me and from their peers. For the latter, they need an endless stream of phonetically charted text to improve their acquisition skills. Though they improve from reading each other's phonetic transcriptions, I provide a lot of material too, and as a left-handed writer whose handwriting has been rotten since grade school, I type it for them. New advances are being made in the field of keyboarding the IPA; the purpose of this article is to share them…and share more.

Let's go back now to the early 1990s, the Bronze Age of computers. I'm a very fast typist, and I got excited when I found IPA fonts that I could just add to my Mac Plus, with its giant 512k of RAM and its immense 10MB hard drive…but I got frustrated when I loaded fonts into my Mac and tried to type in IPA; I became a "hunt-and-peck" typist again because the keyboard layouts of the SILfonts seemed awkward and counterintuitive. I wanted the IPA phonemes to flow logically from under my fingers onto the screen. So I began designing a keyboard layout that I thought would make sense…and hoped that a way of implementing it would show up.

Hmm, where to begin designing the layout? With the *schwa*, obviously. There are many IPA symbols that look like orthographics, so I could leave much of the keyboard positions in place. But where did I put those DIFFERENT symbols like the schwa? I reasoned, "Well, let's take a key whose orthographic symbol *doesn't* appear in American phonetics and put the schwa there. And don't choose a weird place, because the schwa is the most frequently used sound in the language." So I chose the lower-case "y" as the schwa's new home; "y" isn't used as an IPA symbol in American English. Then I thought, well, why not put the "hooked schwa" (ɚ) as near as possible, to keep the "family" together? OK, how about SHIFT-y? Good, good…and I was off and running.

I put the voiceless theta (θ) as an upper-case T; the voiced theta (ð) as an upper-case D. Why? Well, in a lot of dialects, from most European languages to Brooklyn, the theta doesn't occur; the dental plosives "t" and "d" are used instead. So why not put them in the upper-case position of those orthographics on the keyboard, where the "T" and "D" would go unused? Hey, this was getting to be fun. I quickly laid out the rest of my keyboard:

q = q	W = W
w = w	W = ʍ
e = e	E = ɛ
r = r	R = ɝ
t = t	T = θ
y = ə	Y = ɚ
u = u	U = ʊ
i = i	I = ɪ
o = o	O = ɔ
p = p	P = P
a = a	A = æ
s = s	S = ʃ
d = d	D = ð
f = f	F = F
g = ɡ	G = G
h = h	H = H
j = j	J = J
k = k	K = K
l = l	L = L
z = z	Z = ʒ
x = x	X = X
c = c	C = C
v = v	V = ʌ
b = b	B = B
n = n	N = ŋ
m = m	M = M

for additional characters on a Mac keyboard:

option+d = ʤ
option+t = ʧ
option + o = ɒ
option+shift+ɑ = a
option+shift+R = ɜ

Obviously, this is not the ONLY way to lay out an IPA keyboard; but it seemed to make sense to me. I was happy with my newly-designed theoretical IPA keyboard universe…but how did I get it to WORK on my Mac keyboard?

Someplace I read about a software application called FontMixer, where you could grab symbols from any font you could (legally) use and place them wherever you wanted on your keyboard…Eureka! I bought the software, found it easy and intuitive to use, and designed my first keyboard layout, which had to be saved and named as a new font; so I called it *PaulPho*.

I happily used *PaulPho* for a decade or more, through Mac os7, os8, os9…even after Mac os x arrived, *PaulPho* worked just fine in Classic mode. But about two years ago, the party

ended; with the arrival of Mac os x.3 "Panther," (I think), *PaulPho* stopped working. NOW what?

Tulane University is blessed with a department called the Innovative Learning Center (ILC), which was begun by Professor Hugh Lester, the great former Chair of my Department of Theatre and Dance who was a staunch Mac advocate. I called over to ILC and explained my problem. I was hooked up with ILC 's Mac specialist Marie Carianna, who understood my need immediately. "It sounds like you want to use Unicode," she said. Unicode? Quest-que c'est Unicode?

She explained that the Unicode Standard was a decision by virtually all the big software giants (Microsoft, Apple, etc.) to agree on a unique identification code for every character, regardless of platform, code or language.

Once I understood what Unicode was, Marie cautioned, "Let's not re-invent the wheel if we don't have to; somebody's probably written an application that allows you to design a keyboard for Unicode. Let me nose around…" It was at that point she discovered Ukelele.

Ukelele is a small, brilliant, simple, free application for the Mac developed by John Brownie (*John_Brownie@sil.org*) that allows you to drag-and-drop a nearly infinite variety of Unicode characters already in your computer onto a template keyboard where you want them. It did the same thing that FontMixer did for me a decade ago, but even more easily and intuitively. To download Ukelele, go to:

http://mac.softpedia.com/get/System-Utilities/Ukelele.shtml

Windows Users: Microsoft makes a free application for this purpose too: the Microsoft Keyboard Layout Creator. To download it, go to:

http://www.microsoft.com/globaldev/tools/msklc.mspx

Now, a caveat about Ukelele: RTFM (for the uninitiated, this is computerspeak for Read The F****** Manual; a manual comes with the Ukelele application download). Though the drag-and-drop aspect of Ukelele is easy as pie, installing your new keyboard layout *in the right place on your computer* is vital. And, of course, you have to restart your computer (or at least log out and log back in), for your System to recognize the changes. The Ukelele manual will guide you through all these procedures. Once you've done all this, voila! You're off and running, batting out page upon page of IPA text with great speed and uniform legibility.

But why is all this important?

I tell my students that the IPA is "an art struggling to be a science." Nearly everyone agrees the IPA is a profoundly useful tool in analyzing and reproducing speech sounds, whether it be for learning dialects or "reducing dialects"—learning pronunciation to improve intelligibility. As our society becomes more global, more and more English-as-a-Second-Language (ESL) people are seeking out Speech Trainers to help them make their spoken English more immediately understandable. To me, the IPA is an essential tool for dialect learning and "reduction." I give my students pages upon pages of IPA transcription with which to practice, until they begin to think in IPA.

But once you learn the 50-odd phonemes of American English, you quickly discover that not everyone charts the IPA the same way. Some of the varieties are profound—Edith Skinner used a cursive style of phonetics notation! Some differences are smaller—the Kenyon and Knott *Pronouncing Dictionary of American English* uses the consonant "r" phoneme in many more places than I do. IPA transcription comes in many flavors. You might even say it comes in many dialects.

VASTA is all about sharing. If we could create a database where our IPA transcriptions can be shared with each other and our students are exposed to different "dialects" of the IPA, it could be a tremendous boon. So here's a humble beginning: I've placed a couple of .pdf files of my IPA transcriptions, along with .mp3 audio files of my reading the text, online at the following address:

http://homepage.mac.com/iachimo

Go into the folder labeled "IPA Transcriptions." Click on the DOWNLOAD arrow of the files you want and have a look and listen. As we get going, I invite others to upload their IPA transcriptions to the site in .pdf (Portable Document Format).

My estimable editor, Lynn Watson, suggested that a linked .mp3 file should be uploaded along with the phonetic transcription, so that a comparison could be made between the source recording and the IPA transcription. It's a brilliant idea down the road; but I don't want to scare anybody away by thinking they need too much technical know-how. My purpose here is to get us all typing and comparing our IPA. Let's start with that. Use Ukelele or Microsoft Keyboard Layout Editor to map your own IPA keyboard. Type a short passage in IPA. Convert your document into a .pdf file and upload it to my above site. Let's begin.

Paul Meier created the brilliant IDEA (International Dialects of English Archive). Perhaps an online database of IPA transcriptions will become a useful cousin of IDEA. I hope so.

Singing *Wendy DeLeo LeBorgne, Associate Editor*

Singing *Wendy DeLeo LeBorgne, Associate Editor*

As the theme of this edition is gender and voice, there is no better expert in my opinion, than Dr. Jean Abitbol. Dr. Jean Abitbol's approach to the human voice and the impact gender plays is best described in his own words:

> Does voice have a sex? If it does, is its character hormonal or chromosomal? Our voice changes over the years, it changes with our life story, with our appearance, and with our physique. It also changes as a function of our emotional environment. Where our fingerprint identifies a physical part of our anatomy, specific to us, unique to us, that has no duplicate, our voiceprint reveals our personality, our innermost self, our sensibility. It betrays our thoughts, reveals our sexuality…How does our voice, impregnated with hormones and programmed by chromosomes, transform itself, construct itself, and create an identity for itself? (*Odyssey of the Voice* 2006, 205)

From a vocal pedagogy standpoint, history provides an interesting perspective on men, women, and the role of gender throughout the centuries. Castrati (boys who were castrated before puberty in order to preserve their child-like vocal quality and range) were extremely popular from the 16th to 18th centuries in both the sacred and secular realms of vocal performance. Interestingly, during this time, women's opera roles were often played by castrati, while men's roles were given to women, who then dressed as men. Subsequently, the terms *breeches, trouser, pants,* and *skirt roles* have been used to describe characters which are cast to portray the opposite sex (man playing a woman or a woman playing a man). Historically, the pants roles (women playing men) came into existence for several reasons: end of the castrato era, humor, and the use of a woman as a potential sexual object. There are at least twenty-five operas which contain pants roles from Bellini's *I Capuleti e i Montecchi* (Romeo) to Mozart's *The Marriage of Figaro* (Cherubino). Musical theater performances also provide some roles which are either written for the opposite sex to play or who are purposely cast in a counter-gender role. Singing pedagogy does not generally train gender-opposite technique, with the exception of the counter-tenor.

The authors who have submitted articles for the singing column provide VASTA readers with quality pedagogical information on the singing voice. Betty Moulton's article, "International Performers and Voice Teachers Speak: Diverse Methods for Integrating the Disciplines of the Spoken and the Singing Voice," provides a series of interviews with international teachers of voice conducted at the Giving Voice Festival in Aberystwyth and Cardiff in Wales. This article examines perspectives on various training techniques and philosophies used by these expert voice trainers. The second article by Fredrick Willard, "A Missing Link Between Vocalise and Repertoire," gives VASTA readers specific vocal exercises to facilitate carry-over from traditional vocal exercises using standard Italian vowels to American vowels used in contemporary singing styles.

Wendy DeLeo LeBorgne, Ph.D. CCC-SLP is a voice pathologist, singing voice specialist and the director of the Blaine Block Institute for Voice Analysis and Rehabilitation and The Professional Voice Center of Greater Cincinnati. Dr. LeBorgne holds a BFA in Musical Theater from Shenandoah Conservatory and a MA and PhD from the University of Cincinnati in Communication Sciences and Disorders with a specialty in voice disorders. Her research has focused primarily on the professional singing voice and has been published in the *Journal of Voice*. She is a contributing author to *Voice Therapy: Clinical Studies* (2000).

International Performers and Voice Teachers Speak: Diverse Methods for Integrating the Disciplines of the Spoken and Singing Voice

Betty Moulton has worked with the spoken and sung voice as a professional actor, teacher and coach for over 30 years. Currently she is a Professor and Coordinator of the new MFA in Theatre Voice Pedagogy at the University of Alberta. Her work in professional theatre companies and actor training programs includes 10 seasons at the Colorado Shakespeare Festival, SMU (Dallas) University of Washington, Seattle Rep, the Citadel Theatre. She also coaches professional actors and business clients. Betty is a past board member of the Voice and Speech Trainers Association (VASTA), and a member of the Canadian Voice Care Foundation (CVCF).

Interviewees

Frankie Armstrong (UK)
Frankie has been singing professionally since 1964, initially alongside working as a social worker and trainer for 20 years. In 1975 she pioneered Voice Workshops based on ethnic vocal styles and songs. Since then, she has taught in most European countries, the US and Canada, India and Australia. She passionately believes that singing is our birthright. She is well known for using chants and songs from around the world to help create singers' own improvisations and compositions.

Anne-Marie Blink (Netherlands)
Anne-Marie trained as a Primary School teacher at the Conservatorium of Groningen for singing and school music. She now conducts choirs and gives lectures, workshops, private lessons and performances; always searching for different forms of playing and singing with the voice as well as with the body. She has worked closely with Jean-Rene Toussaint within the Foundation Stichting Rondom Stemwerk and by integrating his work she has developed a unique method for singing. She has worked very successfully with children on aggression and communication problems and gives them an opportunity to be heard. Website is: <www.andereklank.nl>.

Introduction

In April 2004 I took the opportunity to interview international teachers of voice at the Giving Voice Festival in Aberystwyth and Cardiff in Wales. "The philosophy and psychology of the voice" was the theme of the Festival/Conference.

In my position as Voice, Speech and Text Specialist in the Drama Department of the University of Alberta, I work with actors and other professionals who primarily use their speaking voices. For the six years previous to 2004, I had also focused strongly on exploring and adapting the use of actor training techniques for singers who have primarily lived with the classical tradition in their approach to the singing voice.

I therefore decided to use these interviews to discover each presenter's philosophy and psychology of the voice, as it relates to their work with singers who have trained classically. I wanted to further the dialogue between the two "disciplines"; to hear how these international teachers find similar connections between the seemingly separate approaches to speaking and singing voice training.

Background

The incredible passion that singers feel and express in the sustained nature of their sounding, I feel is closely allied with the sustained passion excited by heightened text. Shakespeare's texts especially seek to capture and illuminate the human spirit through the heightened form of rhythm and poetry. Shakespeare's characters seem to experience the same heights of love, hate, revenge, jealousy, and nobility as those in opera. What I have learned from working with actors on breath freedom and text specificity for Shakespeare text, has positively informed my work with classically trained singers. Many of the methods I have adapted from this kind of text work have been the foundation of my research with singers in Edmonton's Opera NUOVA program (NUOVA: Newly United Opera Vocalists Association).

Opera NUOVA conducts a five-week summer program in Edmonton, Alberta, Canada "that offers singers and pianists intensive training and a professional experience of preparing and performing a fully produced, operatic work with orchestra under the guidance of a distinguished faculty."[1] These are mature and trained singers, just graduated from music programs or with even more experience, who come for more training in performance. Since Kim Mattice-Wanat, the Artistic Director, started the program in 1999, I have been teaching, researching and strengthening the connection between theatre voice exercises and practice, (voice, speech and text work) and the singer's art and craft.

From these explorations every summer, I have found singers need a better guide to awakening their imagination and involving their whole body in the process of developing a song for performance, whether it be for a recital or a role in an opera. The classical training they receive does not seem to put enough focus on imagination and inspiration sprung from the text, and whole body engagement, even in "performance" programs.

Singing

International Performers and Voice Teachers Speak: Diverse Methods for Integrating the Disciplines of the
Spoken and Singing Voice by Betty Moulton (continued)

I was anxious to hear if other international teachers and coaches had found a similar lack of connection between teaching approaches for the speaking and singing voice. Did they experience the same challenges as I had to awakening imagination and encouraging full body response to text in singers?

In the formal interviews, the master teachers at Giving Voice responded to specific questions to reveal the philosophies and psychologies they have developed through experience and that guide their practice. They all had exciting approaches for encouraging this imaginative and physical journey in the singers they teach and coach.

1. Are there Two Voices?
Because of this separation of the singing and speaking voice that is so prevalent in our western society, and which still exists in many current vocal training methods, I posed the question: In the artists you work with, do you feel there are two voices: one that speaks and one that sings?

Agnes Pollner (AP): I would say there are millions more! [laughter]

Frankie Armstrong (FA): Yes and no I think is the answer to that, particularly when I'm trying to encourage people who think they can't sing. What I'm trying to do is get away from this notion that there are those who can sing and those who can't. This is why I first move back and forth between spoken and sung tones in order to encourage people to see that singing and speaking are on a continuum: that there isn't a cut off point saying "Oh everybody can speak, but only this number of people can sing." So for me it's a very important, educative, philosophic point to say singing and speaking are on a continuum.

Joan Mills (JM): Somehow I always thought of the voice as a continuum. My feeling is that the speaking voice should be expressive as it can be, and it should contain the full range of the voice—the same with the singing voice. In my work, I often slide, I slither around between the spoken and sung constantly.

Tara McAllister-Viel (TM-V): I think traditionally that's been the held belief. I think there are some techniques that are specifically designed for singing voice that would be inappropriate for speaking voice, and vice versa. However, the work that I do integrates sung voice and spoken voice. In fact, I shy away from saying the words *singing*, and I choose instead *sung voice*, because I feel, within the English language, *singing* has come to mean such a specific art form, that I find even those definitions make it difficult for me to do integration.

…My inspiration is coming from certain storytelling techniques, like P'ansori, in which there are ch'ang (or sung passages) and aniri (spoken passages). And the way in which the sung passages and spoken passages are interconnected depends on not separating the categories. When an academic scholar might write about P'ansori as having sung and spoken passages, I think the tendency is for the readership then to think about them in two different categories. But for a performer, you really need to see that as a continuum. For instance if #1 would be the sung voice and #10 would be the

Joan Mills (UK)
Joan is a theatre director, voice practitioner, the Centre for Performance Research's Voice Director and Fellow in Voice and Performance at the Department of Theatre Film and Television Studies, University of Wales, Aberystwyth. She has directed a wide range of theatre over the past thirty years, from new writing to TIE, classical text to visual performance, and has created a number of original theatre pieces focused on the voice. Her work is influenced by her understanding of voice practice from wide range of cultures, developed through her curation of the Giving Voice project which she has directed since 1990.

Agnes Pollner (Germany)
Agnes trained as an actress at the Mozarteum, Salzburg. She worked in that profession for over 10 years in German theatres, while also training as a classical singer. For a number of years she worked with John Costopoulos, method-acting trainer from New York. He encouraged her to take up teaching herself. Her interest for the voice led her to the Roy Hart Theatre, where she learned from several members, most intensively from Paul and Clara Silber. Currently she is working as a voice and acting teacher, helping professionals to realize their talent to full extent.

Dr. Ralf Peters (Germany)
(PhD Philosophy 1998). He continues studies in anthropology and the relation between voice, culture and psyche. Ralf has worked with the Roy Hart Theatre in Malérargues, France and is co-editor of some Roy-Hart-Archives CDs (www.roy-hart.com). He performs public readings, solo programmes with literature and songs (Goethe, Heine, Rilke), experimental voice performances (ImproVoice, Mass for voice solo, The Passions of the Soul (for voice and stethoscope)) and projects with the American performance artist and sculpturist Terry Fox. A recognized Roy Hart Teacher since 2006, he gives voice lessons and workshops in the tradition of Alfred Wolfsohn and Roy Hart. Website: www.stimm-feld.de

Judith Shahn (USA)
Judith is in her 17th year as a Voice, Dialects and Shakespeare teacher at The University of Washington. She is a leading vocal/dialect coach in the Northwest and has coached dozens of productions at The Seattle Rep, Intiman Theatre and ACT among others. Judith has taught at The Giving Voice in Wales and has coached at The Oregon Shakespeare Festival and Utah Shakespearean Festival. She is a director and a performer and has a CD called "Sing Together", an instructional CD for those who love to sing acapella songs in parts and harmony.

Jean-René Toussaint (France)
French theatre director, actor and voice teacher/therapist, Jean-Rene is founder and director of Stichting Rondom Stemwerk (Foundation Around Voice Work) in Rotterdam, The Netherlands. He works intensively with the voice in the artistic, educational and pedagogical fields. Jean-Rene studied Drama at the University of Paris, and did work placements with Jerzy Grotowski, Annick Nozati, Bob Wilson, the Living Theatre and the Roy Hart Theatre. Through his work with deaf children, he developed Stemwerk. He leads voice workshops and individual sessions for doctors, therapists, speech therapists, singers, actors, private individuals and companies.

Tara McAllister-Viel (USA)
Dr. Tara McAllister-Viel (PhD-Performance Practice (Voice) University of Exeter; MFA (Acting) University of Wisconsin-Madison, Asian/Experimental Theatre programme. Currently teaches Voice at The Central School of Speech and Drama, London. An actress, voice-over specialist, voice coach and director, she has worked in the US and abroad for 17 years. She was a Visiting Professor-Voice at The Korean National University of Arts, School of Drama, Seoul, Korea. She studied the traditional Korean vocal art form p'ansori from Human Cultural Treasures Han Nong Son and Song Uhyang. Tara combines both Western and p'ansori singing and spoken voice training techniques.

Kim Mattice-Wanat (Canada)
Kim is a performer, teacher, and director. She is the founding Artistic Director of Opera NUOVA, a summer intensive program for emerging opera professionals in Edmonton, Alberta. She has over 20 years' experience in roles for musical theatre, oratorio and operatic productions. She is presently the singing instructor at the University of Alberta BFA acting program and regularly works as a musical director and director of opera and music theatre productions. In 2001, she was honoured with the Edmonton YWCA—Woman of Distinction in Arts and Culture Award and in 2003 was awarded "Woman of Vision" recognition from Global Television.

Linda Wise (Kenya/France)
Linda was a founding member of the Roy Hart Centre and performed in most of the major productions of the company from 1974 until 1989. In 1985 she joined the research programmes of Enrique Pardo and Pantheatre as an actress and later as co-director of the Myth and Theatre Festival and the Paris professional training programme. She continues to work as a freelance actress and director most often in the domain of music theatre, recital or inter-disciplinary experimental work—collaborating with jazz musicians, choreographers, circus performers, painters etc. She has taught extensively throughout Europe, South America and Australia.

spoken voice, the way in which you tell a story will somehow land somewhere in that continuum. Either you can land on a 5 or 6 let's say, or you can move around. By switching your thought process in that way can help to integrate the two.

Linda Wise (LW): I used to think it's the same voice, but I'm beginning to think it is the same voice—but it's informed differently according to the material you're using. And so it's hard to keep that contact with yourself and your immediate spontaneous feeling, and have this thing of singing where you don't lose the sound, which you can't afford to do when you're singing opera.

Kim Mattice-Wanat (KM-W): I think it's yes, because we've created a separation, not because it exists as that. I think that it should be one voice, whether or not you're speaking or singing, that it's coming from the same root. Because when you're speaking and when you're singing, it should be an extension of what it is you wish to say as an artist, as a person, as a human being.

2. Impediments from Previous Training
I then asked about difficulties that seem to stem from the singer's previous training. I have found, in a variety of singers over the past six years, many common issues that seemed to prevent flexible physical engagement and specific text connection. These include set or historical perceptions of the correct way to "present" the song which can lead to just skimming the surface of the meaning the words represent in favour of the correct "sound," or standing without movement the way they have been told to stand for a supposed "maximum benefit to breathing," for example. So I asked the presenters at Giving Voice: **What have you encountered that seems to spring from a singer's previous training, that hampers freer expression?**

FA: I think it comes down to, in a simple formulation, they're working from the outside-in rather than the inside-out. They're trying at some level to meet an external expectation as to how they should sound. I think that's the wrong place to start. I think if you start off finding your own sounds, be they highly unmelodic from time to time, then you can move into whichever direction you want to take the voice, be it spoken text, purely improvised and experimental, be it art music or folk music, because you've got the natural physical body/breath bedrock. But the whole training of most, particularly the old fashioned classical singers, is so based on the right/wrong, correct/incorrect notions both about tone and accuracy of pitching and intonation. It seems to me such a stultifying place to start.

LW: One of the things is very simply, when you're going for opera training, there is an expectation of a sound. And when that sound doesn't come, you have to try to restructure something in order for that sound to come. If you're working with voices of actors, and the way I work, you're accepting what comes and building from there. Whatever comes is legitimate, and it can be augmented. But you don't put yourself into an attitude or a structure. I think that's what makes it so difficult for a lot people, why people have rejected classical training in singing. Very often there are teachers—you go to make the sound [sounds one note] and they respond, "No" [sounds the note

Singing

*International Performers and Voice Teachers Speak: Diverse Methods for Integrating the Disciplines of the
Spoken and Singing Voice* by Betty Moulton (continued)

again], "No." And you're against this constantly. It's a "No." So you never get to that feeling of just being able to let go. You don't ever get to the moment of trusting your body. I believe, let the voice go, let it go in all directions. Open the spaces, and then you can channel. Let your material out first.

JM: I think that they're too focused on technique, perhaps. This has certainly been during the past, although people are moving away from this. If you've been taught in some way which has given you the impression that there must be a very particular body set from which you're going to sing, I find immediately that makes you less flexible, less coordinated. It shouldn't do, but that's not the way they've been taught. So they'll often fix in a position, for example, and be unable to move from that. That's the first thing that might be difficult. If you asked them to move, they're very surprised and almost aggressive. "How can one possibly do that *and* this?" Also certain things to do with pronunciation—the vowel sounds. Personally I can't see the point of singing anything if you can't understand what's said. It doesn't make sense. Having said that, of course I'll go and thoroughly enjoy an Italian opera sung in Italian. But what I mean is, if it happens to be in English but actually sounds less understandable than the Italian, that worries me. Those issues come into it.

KM-W: There are lots of things that have been part of a singer's previous training. I guess the number one thing is that singers at a very young age are taught about "posture." But instead of becoming something to have freedom from (where the Alexander technique will teach you how to be free in many different physical states) singers will be taught to stand in their "singer's stance" and that is "correct posture." But what it does is begin to limit them from feeling energy move through their body and feeling the freedom to move onstage. Even something as simple as a gesture becomes a dilemma; taking two steps forward can become a dilemma because they've grounded themselves into a place that is impacted with tension, instead of the ability to be free…

Betty Moulton (BM): This lack of freedom, does it have anything to do with the fact that they go to a little studio, or someone's living room and stand there beside a piano and sing?

KM-W: Absolutely. The other thing that I always say is that our vocabulary of movement, our vocabulary of sound is limited to our experience. If you are with a number of people as you are learning and you are watching them, you start to see how they physicalize a tiny motif and you say, "Oh yeah, that's good" and you put it into your body through modelling, "Oh I can feel that" and it expands our vocabulary of physicality and our vocabulary of vibration.

The second major impediment is the preconceived notion of right and wrong sound; anything to do with setting the sound. "This is what I want the sound to sound like." So they start to cut off, first of all their own instinctive response to sound.

TM-V: I think the more exposure you have as a singer to other cultures and the way in which sound is used in other cultures—the way in which the body and anatomy is used to produce sound, and how those sounds can be thought of as beautiful within another discipline or culture that you haven't been trained in—it really challenges certain assumptions that you make about the voice. You may have categorized the voice in such a certain limited way in order to live up to the audience's expectations or the teacher's expectations, or personal expectations about what you feel is a beauty aesthetic, or what you feel is proper technique.

If your ear is constantly fed very good examples of what you're training in, you tend to mimic or emulate them. Take that same principle and expose that student to a variety of different kinds of sounds. As long as there is an informed relationship happening instead of a mystification or exotification of sound—"Oh, isn't it weird, isn't it a freakish sound, what is that?"—if it comes from an informed place, you can begin to emulate that as a training methodology.

AP: In the first place, you have to connect to the need to utter. Somehow you need to get to this need. If it's an artistic need to express yourself, or a personal need—without this curiosity, this energy coming up—I need to know what this is.

But it's not where they start. Because when they come, mostly they have a problem. For instance with auditioning or with getting a job, or "I don't like what I'm doing, I feel insecure." On the surface this seems to be a problem, and most of the problem has to do with people when they are not successful enough. But when you go on to work, you can sort some of these problems out. But you can't really get to the source of creativity if there is no curiosity. I find this interesting, because Einstein calls it the divine curiosity of the human being. If it's not there, it may be fine, and you can show some progress, but for me it's not really interesting.

Dr. Ralf Peters (RP): The first answer I would've given—I agree absolutely with what you say—is the answer of Alfred Wolfson who said when asked nearly the same question, "It's just about fear. It's always about fear." The only reason why people can't get enough of one note or why men normally don't sing high soprano or women don't sing tenor or bass is because they're afraid of doing these sounds. Because if they would be able to do it, they're afraid they would lose their self understanding. They lose their idea about themselves. This is a great part of the work, to encourage people to lose themselves, to find a bigger [idea].

Certain fears are, "I was taught to sing in this way and everything else is unhealthy. So I'm going to hurt my voice if I start to do what you asked me to do." That's a very strong argument.

For me there are two possible beginnings. The one is, singers have a voice and they were told that that's the voice they should sing with. Everything else is bad, is ugly, is not what they should show because this one is the beautiful one if they are opera singers or folk singers or rock singers, whatever. There's the idea, this must be the voice; everything else is bad. And so they start to get problems of course because if you work so much with your voice, then the other part of your voice just says "hello, we are also here…we would like to be included." The first thing you can do is try to find out what the voice these people work with really tells. What part of their personality is in this part of the voice? What does it show, what does it express, and what does it hide?

AP: Preconceived concepts about what their voice should be. For instance, modeling their voice after something they've heard or something they have been told. But also, I've worked with people who had so much emotion, so much feeling, that they did not know how to express it, because it would overwhelm them. So they put themselves in a safe structure, and would be very careful not to surpass it. They would need a very careful coaching to trust their emotion, and find ways how to express this. I find it has a lot to do with personality. Sometimes the gift of the voice is so big that the personality is not yet there.

RP: The whole problem with an opera singer and classical singing nowadays, most people who do it are only taught to be technically perfect. But this has nothing to do with the meaning of what they come to sing. I don't think they even ask this question. Quite rarely they do, at least in the music schools.

AP: For instance, "I can't do this movement because if I do I will lose the placement of my voice." Or, mostly with women who sing soprano, "I need to be in such and such a position for the high notes." They have a very specific notion about how the high notes should be produced and how they should sound.

People tend to hold onto their bodies. But this comes also out of the circumstances where you normally sing. When you go

371

to an audition, you go onto the stage and stand beside the piano and sing. Even for jazz singers, everybody else has their instrument and you stand in front of your microphone and sing. So it's not a place where you go and move and do something. So the whole circumstances have this kind of body impediment in it. You have to feel very secure of yourself to do something else.

Judith Shahn (JS): I think the women (sopranos) are disconnected completely from the bottom octave of their speaking voice. Part of it is a mythology that they were told by their singing teacher (what I believe is a mythology) saying it's not healthy for your voice to speak down there. So for a "healthy voice," you want everything forward placed, everything coming forward [demonstrates as she speaks] all up in here, in the mask of face, for speaking, because they are sopranos. So the speaking voice becomes limited to "up here" and it has this placed feeling about it. And it sounds pretty but it is devoid of that impulse that is so necessary in a speaking voice. The other thing in my approach to the breath that I got from my training with Kristin Linklater[2], is the breath should not be structured or controlled or sustained in any way, artificially. If the breath is free, then that can connect so the thought can be free and the emotions can be free. So the breath being more "released" is the more useful word then, not controlled and sustained which classical singers are almost always taught…there is still this sense of letting go through it rather than controlling.

Jean-René Toussaint (JRT): In singing there is what I call the fascism of expressing. We are busy to "express," we are busy to show, we are busy to be concurrent, we are busy to be the best, better. For me singing is listening. Because when you listen, the word, the sounds are crossing you, and all of what you are built with—memories, emotion, events past—all the memories are awakened. It's not a matter of hearing in the ears and feeling in the stomach. It's really crossing your flesh, your body, your sense. In a way you express like a pregnancy and a birth because it's coming on a natural way, it has to come out. I think it is a mistake to show to impress, to prove, to manipulate. [You have to rebalance the focus of the person. Listen first and the technique comes after.]

Anne-Marie Blink (AMB): And I try as much as possible to get everybody singing from where they are, who they are, how they are. And in a way there is an incredible respect from pupil to pupil. The people who come to listen, they are really sitting there and judging because sometimes somebody is not in tune, or somebody is moving too much, or making a primitive sound. But there is really something to do about listening

Singing

International Performers and Voice Teachers Speak: Diverse Methods for Integrating the Disciplines of the
Spoken and Singing Voice by Betty Moulton (continued)

and changing the attitude of listening which doesn't have to weigh the product but to receive the person.

JRT: Is a performer a mirror of the society, with all his imperfections and emotion, or a kind of example threatening society's stability? Edith Piaf—she was sometimes false—but she brought an emotion…to dare to die, to confront ourselves with the death, with the limits. This is what I mean about rituals, what I mean about the sound which starts from you and you don't know where it is finishing. For me it is the art of the singer. Of course to please the specificity of certain aesthetics, [to achieve] a certain result, is completely something different. Perhaps we have to discover something in between but it is very paradoxical, because the society is growing because people are thinking differently, painting differently, dancing differently. This is a paradox; we are asked to perform perfectly, to please, at the same time the society can only grow if we step out of it.

3. Awakening Imagination
As defined by the teachers at Giving Voice, the job of the voice teacher is to hear potential in the person and in the material, to guide the singer to fully explore their whole voice. I asked each master teacher, **"What specific strategies do you use to help awaken the imagination of the performer?"**

FA: The most useful of the things I have to offer are the voices—the archetypes of myth which are heavily dependent upon physicality and imagination—the body and imagination, and story telling. It is what I use to free up a whole range of vocal colours, qualities, impulses. But I'm not often directly involved with text. We have little mantras to help people to get into the quality of the archetypes and I say to people if words come to you and you really feel the need to say them, fine, but otherwise I work just with sounds or even made up language.

I've discovered in the process, if I make up a language so that it's content free, but it's still communicative (has all the elements of language but doesn't get people caught up in the content) and if I start off with heavily pitched but nevertheless spoken tone, then everybody follows, pitch perfect. Shall I just give you a demonstration? [she proceeds to do so] and then they echo it back. And then gradually without people even being consciously aware of it I bring in sung tones, maybe just at the end of the line [demonstrates] and they just work from the spoken into the sung tone, and then from the sung to the spoken tone. So as a number of people have said, "Frankie I was convinced I couldn't sing and you snuck singing up on me." [laughter] I just find the sounds take me into quite distinct moods and emotional territories. I don't ladle them on but they happen in the process of just opening my mouth and

trying to keep my body and my mind as free as possible. So that's one area where although I'm not using text, I'm certainly using communicative language. It just happens to be a made up language.

The other thing I do is hold workshops that approach performance skills and song interpretation. Some people come from a classical background and sing Art songs. That's so interesting to work on with people who have classical training because as you say, often they haven't actually explored the text. They haven't thought about the phrasing of the text, and the meaning of the text and how that therefore needs to inform the way the melody works and the way the tonal quality of the voice works. Similarly if people want to sing traditional songs, folk songs, but come from a trained background it's like there's all kinds of layers you have to get through. It's like peeling off the layers in an onion to get to the natural vocal quality and the natural phrasing that's absolutely essential for traditional singing.

JM: For me, when I'm working with actors and with imagining the situation or character or whatever, I work very physically. So the imagination has a physical response. The questions I ask them are nearly always physical questions. "So if at this moment this happens, how fast is his heart beating? Is he sweating, is he cold? Is there a cold trickle down his back?" I don't think those questions get asked of classical singers very often. They may have considered similar questions, but it's still at a slightly cerebral level. I'm a bit more visceral than that. I tend to get down to the reality, as you say. To me an interesting question might be, "Why tonight?"

Often it won't be obviously going for the imagination first. I will try to make their breath become spontaneous. I work a lot with balls and balloons of all sizes. It's very important to the major center of my work and it works best with group work. It's about finding a listening, yielding, responsive way of being and breathing, so that the breath is not so active as responsive. If you throw the ball to me, I'd breathe out as I catch it, and the whole body will soften. Then as I throw it, I will really release the breath. This is an analogy for the speaking or for the song. Then it will happen with voice, with song, with calling, with text, and so on. Eventually it stops being just like an exercise and becomes a very complex improvisation. Eventually I will make suggestions about the quality of the balloon that is being worked with which requires them to connect this breath/emotional response to the imagination. But the important thing is, it isn't actually thought. It isn't thinking carefully about something…This is about what's in the unconscious, certainly the subconscious. This is about what happens when we're entirely spontaneous, and we really don't think, and we allow a river of emotion and response to run through us. With my choir…I'll do crazy games with them. I have this thing where I'll set up little cards of different colors with different words. You'll end up with a little sentence, and that's your text—by random choice. One is always a verb and the other one is a name or object, (also conjunctions etc.). You take one of each of the colors, there might be four of them, and you have this little phrase. You have to instantly sing it. I often give them a style. It might be operatic style. They find that very scary, because it is completely unknown what you're going to do. But the fascinating thing is, they're so imaginative about how that comes along. There's something about it that's so ridiculously demanding, that they'll quite often do it extremely well. It makes everyone laugh, so laughter is a great freer of the imagination.

One of the things again I do is deliberately teach songs that are in another language, particularly a language they don't know. I think it frees people up, because they don't know what the word is. Or in an invented language. It's interesting how successful Karl Jenkins[3] [of the ensemble] Adiemus is. He creates the language in all of those [pieces]. People are singing what people think is a beautiful African song in great harmony, but he's made it up. He likes the sounds in the mouth. Some other sections of Adiemus sound as if they are in Latin, but they are not. He invented it and used the sounds that he liked for the vocal orchestration.

RP: I would say it depends on who I work with. Sometimes it's very easy for them to find images, especially professional singers; maybe this is why they sing, very easy images, maybe memories or dreams. There's a lot of material you can work with which is the imagination, then you can really use that to go forward. But sometimes it frightens them. Sometimes if you ask them, do you have any images, do you have any feelings?—"no." They don't want to have any.

AP: But I think in a larger way to invite somebody to find other voices, to listen to themselves in another way, is already expanding the imagination. It takes it to other realms. You hear different things and see your personality from another angle. That's often the case when you work in a group. We do individual work, but with everybody else listening and watching and giving feedback. Not of what this person did, but what they felt when this person sang. So you get a feedback like a vocal portrait from the audience: what they felt, what images they had when you sang. There might be a whole world opening up of images that you had never dreamt of, provoking another person when you sang a simple song. Already this gives some people so much space.

JS: The actors (in the MFA at the University of Washington) are doing *King Lear* in the studio and I'm given the task of doing an ensemble rendering, somehow, of the "Blow winds" which is so full of image and imagination. We were playing with it in many different ways—one of them started off with some sound and movement work having to do with individual vowel sounds and individual consonant sounds and the idea that these sounds must move the body, activate the body. So at this point you cannot just speak sounds and be still. The premise is they have enough energy to move you so that *zzzz* is going to move you some way that's different from *ee* or *ah* or *b*. So we start with individual sounds, then we do an information sharing so that there are the vowel people over here, and the consonant people over here and they come together and they create new words. Then I feed in a word, a sound at a time (*b*, *l*, *oh*) and keep repeating that until they get that it is the elements of "blow" and then they put it together. Then, once the sounds are now a syllable or a word the image, the response to that word is then going to take over, and come through the body. It connects to a meaning. So I'll feed in all the key words of that speech, then I get them working in small groups to create those first two words, then, "crack your cheeks," and I say, "Keep finding what that is. Now we're going to put them together," [demonstrates the two phrases one after the other] and I divide it into two groups and get them working as a team to do this. Then I'll have them do it without any movement and just standing there with their eyes closed and listening. I love doing the text like that—good 'ole sound and movement work.

JRT: You have to feel the person, to bring the person in a kind of need, in a kind of perception of himself/herself that is like a pregnancy you know. You have to get as much food, as much influence, as much stimulation from outside, then your personal ritual is bringing you from the inside to the outside to sing. Then singing is an incident in a way. It is a need because you have so many influences, so much information, stimulation, experiences, events that somewhere there is a moment we have to scream out the result of it and it is your personal song. It is very interesting because in the spirituality of the new age we are completely out of it. People, they all want to go to their centre, and in fact what we are teaching people is "don't go to your centre—come from it." If you come from where you are coming from, your centre defines itself. But if you search to go to your centre, you will be always disappointed.

TM-V: I think information awakens the imagination. Skill development awakens the imagination. If your voice or ear is not trained to really examine something closely, you haven't developed the skills that allow you to imagine the possibilities.

Singing

International Performers and Voice Teachers Speak: Diverse Methods for Integrating the Disciplines of the Spoken and Singing Voice by Betty Moulton (continued)

So when we do our interviews, [she has the students interview speakers] we pick apart, for instance, a laugh. We look at the different (Rudolf) Laban[4] qualities within a laugh: punch, press, glide. And by breaking up that laugh within maybe three or four qualities and creating a stylized laugh, then they can take that laugh and morph it into something else, a bird call. That feeds the imagination. When you break apart that laugh, what else can it become? Very much in the same way that we do a prop improv, where you take a hat and use it traditionally as a hat or use it as this or that. That awakens students' imagination, simply because you're taking away the definition, the traditional way of viewing "hat." I try to take away the traditional way of viewing voice. Instead, I just feed them questions. "Do you think you could do this? Well what if you didn't think about this as a song? What if it instead was just a story? Now what do you do?"

LW: I work a lot with separating the two: language and music. It's a big problem. You can get someone to sing you a song and then you say, "What's your text talking about?" The reply is something very general. I do a lot of taking the words away from the tune. Of course memory goes, that's the first thing that goes. And then if you ask someone to speak the text, it will go into the rhythm of the song. I try to break those rhythms. It's all to do with deconstructing.

Changing phrasing, absolutely. Trying to find what the story of the song is. Then I work with the music, trying to find how the music is written. If you were singing the phrase without the song, how do you hear it, where do you hear the most important point of it? Is it support or the rhythm that you're working with in the melody? Then putting them together and see how have they been written…Do you go for the music or the words? Are they fighting each other?

I think there's a lot of work to be done there…I often ask people to improvise on the words of the song. Improvise with association, and then improvise with a totally different melody.

KMW: You have to say, "In this language, where is the noun, where is the verb? How does that connect to the musical line, and what is that telling you about the musical line?" It's an arduous task for singers. It's a tough, tough thing to be able to not only create the language so that it's stylistically correct and sounds like the language, but to do that expressively.

It's the same with Shakespeare, that whole sense of capitalizing on the rhythm of the text…suddenly for me as a listener, Shakespeare comes entirely to life. It's like you're not working against the fabric of what was given to you, you're buying in and you're being informed by it…Well that's what the composer's done. He's given you a palette of information and it's very detailed. So you're not supposed to deny it. Singers do that all the time! They stop looking at the score once they feel like they know the role, they know the music. Michael McMahon[5] kept saying "You have to keep looking at your score. You have to keep asking, 'Now why on earth is this written right there, and not three beats later?'" And lots of singers will say, "I don't care. It must have been a mistake. I feel it here." There are lots of coaches who will say, "No, you need to figure out why that's where it is. You're wrong to just impose your musical artistry onto that and think you know better than the composer. You've chosen the wrong intention, and that's why it's not working for you. Choose a different intention." The composer has tried very hard to answer the questions that would come up. So if you're a director who watches very carefully what that musical map is you don't deny the musical map…It doesn't mean that you can't have any ideas about the journey, it's just that there are a lot of road marks there that are supposed to be looked at and considered.

4. Methods from Spoken word

As I have found through my work with singers, the translation of "theatre exercises" into exercises for singing interpretation and expression seem a crucial element to opening up more creative expression in song. These help to anchor the singer into the imaginative situation from which the song flows. **What are some of your methods to illuminate the text of a song for yourself and/or for your students, that are directly from a theatre and spoken word approach taken with actors?**

FA: Of course I've prepared the voice through warm ups, collective singing, and getting a whole sense of trust in the group, but if we're working with a song with text, with any thought, then it's the text that has to inform the other things. You put the song into a kind of context: creating the conditions out of which the song might have come. Like the song about the famine, we might create an improvisation about "that point at which we can't stay;" we have to get on the immigrant boat and leave our land behind. We'd explore that and then the song would come out of that. Or sometimes we'd simply create a context such as that of a family around a fire in the evening when someone might sing this song when it was still an organic part of everybody's culture and life.

Speak the text, forget about singing it altogether. Just speak it as you would speak it. So I'll get somebody to say the lines however many times it takes till the penny drops. For example a classic one [she pronounces every syllable with the same length and weight throughout] *The water is wide I cannot get o'er* which is how so many people sing it. [sings it and second line *And neither have I wings to fly* the same even way] because that's how many of them have got it out of the book. But if you say it…[demonstrates phrasing the whole verse for sense, so it groups words together and varies the length and weight of syllables and words, hence makes sense, tells the story and varies the rhythm] then really get them to work that into the melody—it's almost as if you have to take the visual memory of the dots away from them, so they start to work in the body. And again I'll often get people moving, walking, imagining they're working in the fields, just something to break them from still seeing the notes and the text, until they feel that it's got an integrity. When they all come together—the meaning, the imagination, and the voice—then you can start with the tune.

JM: We do an interesting project in Aberystwyth with actors where we work on a whole set of monologues and duologues and directing pieces with our second year students. Then we go to a big house in the country, which the university owns, and we examine that work. We assess the work, site-specific. So an extra dimension comes in for the students. I will do the speech work in many places. But I'm going to be on the steps now, and I'd like to do it as the sun is going down on the steps. They therefore take that into account at the moment they play it. Even then, can the student take into account, whether they were speaking or singing, the fact that just as they begin to speak, birds decide to start circling over the tree and making a hell of a racket settling for the night? If the person just goes on talking straight through that, you know they're not in the present. They have identified where the speech or song is, but they haven't identified with this moment, with this audience, now. Because if they did, they would've stopped. The bird sound would've had to integrate with the song or speech.

RP: They need other people to listen. It can be helpful to have a teacher who can tell them something. But it's sometimes more helpful that other people in a group can tell them what they hear or what they feel. So they can get an absolutely new idea of what they do when they sing. It can be very helpful.

AP: What I try to do is engage the body and I try to do it in a way they wouldn't expect it. Like what Enrique Pardo[6] said the other night, to give the body something totally else to do. Something that distracts them, that takes their whole attention from their voice into this physical experience. This can be something very physically engaging, but it can be something also emotionally engaging. It can be something to do with another person, like some other person tries to fight with them or tries to tickle them. Or I give them a game to play, or something. That's one thing I do. The other thing is I try to find a personal hook for the story. First of all I try to find out what they think the story is about. For instance, if it's the

Jewel aria from *Faust*, then I try to find out what is it all about, who is this girl, and how can you connect to the story. What does it tell you? Maybe people find one image or one remembrance of an image from their life. Or I often say, sing this to a person from your life. Is there somebody you would like to know about this? Is there somebody you would like to sing this to? If it's a group, I put another person on the other side of the hall and say, sing to this person over there.

AP: Sometimes we tell people to sing a song very slowly, dead slow [demonstrates with Ave Maria]. You real feel how the vowels connect. Then often it's the case people start to cry. If you really give the voice and the vowels the space, the time, to really connect, often tears will come.

JS: My singing mentor would often talk about how jazz was like speaking and she would try to get us to speak the text, just speak the text. Or we would do the text on "Bah"—take the words away totally, but you're still thinking the words. Then you go back and put the words in. I use devices like that when working on text to get people more connected to the thought because it's so easy to go into a set pattern. So that's one way to break up the pattern. I try to get singers to do more of speak singing, so rather than sustaining the notes right away, it's coming off the pitch, maybe it's a little more like recitative. When I'm working on trying to get people connected to language, it's always trying to get the words to come through the body. So much of speaking in the Western world has come from the neck up, so it's going to this extreme of getting the whole body involved. I love Kristin's (Linklater) work with the vowel ladder which is based on the bel canto scale—the "zoo woah, shaw" that travels up through the body so the idea is that the lower pitches are lower in the body and the higher pitches are higher in the body and it matches the level of the intrinsic vowel pitches. So I would think that would be really useful for singers as well. It's like the whole body is speaking. It comes from somewhere other than just the vocal folds, or the diaphragm, it's more physical.

(JRT and AMB were less interested in talking about the actual methods, but kept returning to the philosophical underpinnings of their approach and its connection to the world in which we live.)

JRT: Each singer, each actor has something so pure and wonderful; the care of each teacher is to give a different education for each singer. We must give for each singer a different process. I used to work with people as a therapist for psychological, emotional or social problems, and I used to work with deaf children—it is even more clear. You take two deaf children the same age, perhaps the same sex, it doesn't matter.

Singing

International Performers and Voice Teachers Speak: Diverse Methods for Integrating the Disciplines of the
Spoken and Singing Voice by Betty Moulton (continued)

You cannot do the same work. You have to find the work which fits with the identity of each of them to get the best of them. They have to take this over. In fact I think the lessons and the teaching are too much similar for people who are too much different.

AMB: By singing with Jean-René, he taught me to go into my body. Not to dig in the form of the song but to dig in my sense, in my emotion. There are some songs of Piaf that are so strong that I really felt my resistance at first and thought "My God, what is this resistance?" By working with him about that, it really reached the level of craziness that's in the song. But you reach your own level of craziness because we all have that. This way of working has brought me to another way of thinking.

JRT: I don't teach people how to do something. I awake, unfold the unknown. I let free some channels. I try to stimulate what is there and not to let them imitate what is not yet there. It is very important to stimulate some functions, and not to fix some steps the person has to reach or prove or fit into a pretended progression.

TM-V: I start with ear training. I have the students go out and take recordings of various different situations. For instance, I just finished a project with my students called *High Street*. They started with soundscapes. They took their tape recorders and went to High Street and started taping children playing, an old couple fighting. We broke down those taped samples into melodic progression and rhythm. So already they were taking a look at the spoken voice, even in environmental sounds, like a bus or a car going by, and were looking at it as a piece of music. Much in the same way that John Cage[7] looks at environmental sounds as music. His audience members had the opportunity to realize that if you listen carefully, you can hear the buzzing of the florescent lights, or you can hear the building shift and creak; and that even those environmental sounds have tempo to them. They even have a melodic progression in a microtonal sort of way. Based on this understanding, my students collect soundscapes, but they also do interviews. This is very much based on some of the work that Anna Deveare-Smith has done or Studs Terkel's interviews in his book *Working*. We take those interviews, and we're looking at the way that the spoken voice inhabits melodic progression and rhythm. It's easy to hear melodic progression in a dialect or vocal inflection. But I think it's much more difficult, and you really have to train your ear, to hear melodic progression within the stop-start pattern of "*mm, er, ah*"...all those incidental sounds during the interview. And we keep those in with the interviews. So even though we do edit the interview down into maybe a five minute monologue, we try to keep as much as possible the rhythm of the language, the melody of

the way that speaker speaks. So when they're listening and creating an oral/aural relationship to either the environmental sounds or their interview, the students are beginning to pick up the way in which the sung voice and the spoken voice are closely related in patterning, specifically. I teach them if they want to stay within the genre of realism, they need to break up the pattern to help the listener understand that sense of spontaneity. But if they don't want to remain in the genre of realism and progress more towards the sung voice end of the spectrum, they set a pattern or they repeat a pattern. You can find that in poetry slams or in rap music. The moment that the pattern is established, for some reason, perhaps culturally, we begin to identify that as music or song. But in class we start to develop this out of the spoken voice, progressing maybe into chant, then to call and response, then eventually into sung voice.

LW: One opera singer came to work with me. Fabulous voice, perfect ear, brilliant musician. When someone like that comes to me I think, what am I going to do with her? The first thing, she couldn't allow her voice to slide. Consequently, she couldn't really improvise. That is a very basic exercise that I find a lot of singers can't do. They can't slide between sounds [demonstrates a simple slide up through a few pitches]. It's like the musical reference points get too lost in the sliding. She said, "I can't sing without thinking sol, mi, do." It's a refusal, because it's a change of mode. Not a refusal in this woman's case, because she wanted to explore. But simply that her training has trained her in one mode, one very wonderful placement of the voice. The breathing is structured, everything's structured. So to get out of it, she has to destructure herself and trust her body to go with the sounds that are in her body, and find what I call the modes, or channels. Everyone talks about the break point in their voice. In that one very extreme way we'd say, you're changing modes actually, and you can sing through those break points without changing modes. You can train yourself to marry them and bridge the spaces together.

In Stepanida's[8] class today, one of her first exercises is just holding a note. It's so fascinating because their singing is all about movement [demonstrates the "wavering" between two notes]. But the very basic exercise is just being able to hold a note very steady for a very long time. And it's on that steadiness that you develop. It's so fascinating hearing how difficult it was for everybody, even people I know who sing very well, how difficult it was just to hold that note in the way she was asking.

KMW: All of the Laban movement, that explorative movement work, I do with singing in warm-ups. I ask, "If you had to choose a Laban movement that coincided with this musical expression, what would you do?" And then I often get people to do an opposing Laban movement but they still have to sing the vocal line as if they're not opposing physically, so they can feel the resources they use to line up the sound, when physically they are challenged in a new way. That's a very "theatre" way of thinking about things.

With text work I always am saying, "You have to have a verb attached to this line of thought. Where does the line of thought end? How does the line of thought shift for this character? Why does it shift? How come you need to begin singing in the first place? Where are you, as a person, as this character that you absolutely need to start to express from a singing point of view, instead of simply a speaking point of view? When you are singing a high note, why is the high note there? What is the expressive reason for that high note?" Not that you're just singing a high note because it's at the arc of a phrase. "If there is a rhythmic pulse in the music, why is the rhythmic pulse there; does it have something to do with your own inner rhythm as a character or is it more about a physical world around you that the composer has tried to implement into the story?" Like Erlkonig in Shubert's lied piece—the music itself is the physical world of the horse galloping along through the night with this child and this father. So for me, every single aspect of the music—why do you get louder, why do you get softer— comes right back to the theatre world.

5. Imagery used to describe the Magic Moment
So often, voice teachers share vivid language when describing the magic of what we do, so I finally asked each teacher, **Can you provide any imagery-based quotes that you have used, to help describe the magic moment: the moment when a performer physically and emotionally completely transforms in performance; the moment when technique is no longer apparent and the performer becomes a new character?**

JM: It is difficult to describe, and you know it absolutely when you see it. In terms of song, it's when the material of the song has become absorbed. I talk to my choir about, "I don't want to just sing this or learn this. We will absorb it." So it's through the body. It really is as if it's soaked into us, so that now it's not a separate thing. We are embodying the song. That's one way I think of it. In terms of harmony, there's also a thing about the whole group becoming present, focused, and the song is alive. I always talk about it as being locked in. It's when the different voices completely lock. It happened on Saturday during the rehearsal with my 95 people for the Karl Jenkins piece, for a moment. Then suddenly—I had been talking to them about the wash of the sea and what kind of sea it was, and how there's a big swell. We were also using our arms and feeling this. Suddenly, this roll of the waves came in

and bang, we heard it. Locked in sound. That's with the harmony.

But I think with the performer, it is about presence of course. The person is entirely present in what they're doing. Their focus is in entirely the right place, and they're not outside themselves judging or thinking about it externally with their imagination dead, because their focus is on something technical. It's gone beyond that. The other words that sound it for me are integration, flexibility, coordination…It is where everything pulls together, whether it's the harmony or for the individual, and clicks into place and is one. That's why I think it's about absorption. You have to do the work, and when it's absorbed then there'll be this moment of absolutely being there. And you want to make that moment of "being there" be in each breath that follows. It's that being there, being there, over and over again.

AP: I find that every person does it so differently. Some people relax into it, that's often the case. For some people, it's more the quality that they come alive, and you feel everything in them is alive, and they're connected to an environment. It's not, "I'm here and the surroundings are there." It is, "I'm connected with what's going on, and with the space, and it's feeding me." Others are completely filled with something. The mind and the heart are full of something: the song, the partner.

RP: Sometimes I think it's tough to tell a story. This is very obvious for me. If something is going on, they're in the middle of something. But then they really start to tell a story.

AP: It's interesting, because when this special moment happens, it has a certain beauty. The beauty has nothing to do with it being in a conventional sense beautiful. It can be something very ugly in a conventional sense. But you feel its rightness because it has this beauty. You look at it and say, "Yep, this is right. It can happen in so many ways but you would know it wouldn't you?

RP: Sometimes it starts to become a Gestalt. This is very often the moment you get a meaning out of it. Or the [performers] really start to be a character. First they maybe try to do it. They're looking for it, and [snaps his fingers] then they are there. Sometimes it's only for a minute and then they'll have lost it again.

AP: For me, it has also to do with not trying to do so much, and more let it happen to you. But you have to prepare the ground, you have to find what it's all about. You have to open your imagery, you have to open your voice, you have to open

Singing

International Performers and Voice Teachers Speak: Diverse Methods for Integrating the Disciplines of the Spoken and Singing Voice by Betty Moulton (continued)

your perception. And you have to know what you're doing. Then you can relax into it and let it happen. Then mostly it happens. It goes away at the moment when you try to grasp it. "Ah, that's it!" And then it's crashed! Because it's alive and you can't grasp it. What Alice Lagaay[9] said yesterday, the voice is the immediate present and nothing else. But that's what every creative moment is. Every moment really, being creative or not. Life is only in the present, so you can't grasp it. But creating in this way is also balancing on this razorblade. You go this way and this way, and sort of play along.

RP: Sometimes "this moment" has to do with losing a kind of distance to what you do. For people who are not well trained and not advanced as singers or actors, this is sometimes much easier in the beginning. Advanced singers have so much training and techniques, and expectations and whatever. That's why it's very helpful for these people to work together with so-called beginners, because beginners are very often fast in this moment. They cannot really work with it.

AP: They can't repeat it.

RP: This is the problem with them. But at least professional actors and singers can see what it is about, the aim where they should come to again.

AP: They can feel inspiration.

KMW: A word that I use a lot is aligned. "You're completely aligned at that point." Because at that point you're aligned with the text, you're aligned with the music, you're aligned with the character, you're completely integrated into the artistic body at all times.

TM-V: I think a lot of that has to do with preparation. I think when preparation meets opportunity, that's when that happens. The studio is the preparation and the performance is the opportunity. If we have that moment in studio, it simply makes them more aware of what they're shooting for in front of an audience. But that is not the goal. Once they do get out on stage and the audience begins to teach them what pleases an audience, and they begin to fine tune everything we've been working on together in the studio, that preparation in studio is waiting for this opportunity when the audience and the performer finally touch, when they get in sync. A lot of that has to do with the energy of the space, and the energy of the people as well. I believe in *ki* energy, not simply as a concept, but as a real existing essence that lives within an individual's body and then lives within the distance between two bodies. It can be felt either as a by-product, like heat, or it can be felt as a vibration in song. It's a very physical, real thing. So when I talk about *ki* energy, I'm not simply talking about a

concept. I'm talking about a palpable, "you can feel it" kind of thing. For me, that moment of connection is in part about the physical properties of *ki* energy.

LW: "Now you've focused, now you've brought it all together." Connection, yes, "that's connected." I sometimes feel there are singers who are in the past, the present, or the future. It's like present, "okay now you've found—you're present." Everything that goes with presence. This moment, as opposed to being ahead of yourself or behind yourself.

JS: One thing that's clear, the class always knows when those moments happen. Sometimes I use the word extroverting but it really does feel to me like the whole body has coordinated, has kicked into gear and because of that the energy can just sail out. It's got a freedom that just opens up, sails out, extroverts, takes off. It's like that image from sonnet 29: *When to the lark at break of day arising from sullen earth sings hymns at heaven's gate.* It's like that.

I always say what excites me is when I can see people thinking, feeling and speaking all in the same moment. And when that happens, when it's not just emotion for its own sake, when all those things come together and get articulated, you see someone in that moment of revelation as if they've never said those words before. The need to communicate is so strong I would describe it as powerful; it could reach the back wall of any theatre and could reach into the bones of anybody in the audience. That's what does it for me.

AMB: You have to let it escape. It's very interesting to look at classical music from a point of "non-doing," because very often, the ornaments and the lines of the music, if you are really entering it from a physical level, are really coming from the body. It's not that often that you have to approach it in a mental way. A lot of music you can really approach also from a physical level and then reach the point where technique is needed.

FA: Well just thinking back to this lass who was doing *The trees they do grow high*, the penultimate verse is [demonstrates and after the last line]—now I've just given myself shivers with that line "o'er his grave the grass grew green"—I just got her to close her eyes and see the grave, really see the grave and then suddenly she had me in tears because this image just changed the quality of her voice.

Antony Ingle (musical director at the London Academy of Music and Dramatic Art) just kept saying [after one of Frankie's workshops], "Frankie, what I'm taking away from this is just the place to start. It's the imagination. If you're not harnessing the imagination, it'll never really come through." I met his wife later when I went to rehearse with him and she said, "He came back just buzzing. Now I know why you want to go to workshops!" Just the use of the imagination.

One of them said for the workshop I did with Opera Circus, when we finished doing the work in the fields, "Listen to all the different vocal qualities we've just made, but they were all natural, they were all free and natural. That's what we're looking for isn't it?"

Conclusion

The interviews at "Giving Voice" provided me with a clear sense of each master teacher's approach: how they encourage and promote deep and connected soulful sounding. Their philosophies reflect a great respect for all forms of expression, when the communication employs the full person, using the full range of voice, regardless of the label of speaking or singing.

They all practise imaginative exercises from both ends of the "continuum" between spoken and sung tones, and treat "voice work" as work on the whole expressive person, embracing all aspects of the human voice as valuable and rich. Imagination and strong connection to the ideas in the text are crucial components of the singer's art and craft as they teach and coach it.

I believe there is much more room in all our practices for more integration between speaking and singing methods in training the expressive performer. There were many common experiences noted by the presenters at Giving Voice that support this belief. If more singing and speaking teachers brought approaches that encouraged a stronger connection to the continuum of a whole voice sounding, then performance would surely be more powerful in connecting the performers and the listeners.

The notion of separation gives rise to the question of how we encourage vocal expression in the formative years: from an early age, through to the teen years. Do current activities to do with the voice in expression, at these early ages, encourage separation and categorization? Is it possible to encourage and practise the philosophy of one expressive voice, not separating so severely into spoken voice and sung voice? If this philosophy and practice was the norm in our school system and in private lessons for speakers and singers, would not the performers benefit tremendously? As they came into further training and performance later in life, they would have a well developed imagination and a stronger physical connection to their own vocal expression that would fire their performance.

There is more room for encouragement of the integration of the disciplines in our organizations, our memberships, our conferences, meetings, training schools and private practices.

From my experience, current training practised by the teachers at Opera NUOVA and at the Giving Voice Festival, is dedicated to this integration; paying attention to all aspects of the expressive and powerful performer.

Integrating the Disciplines: celebrating the whole performer, the whole voice.

❦

Endnotes
1. Quote from NUOVA 2004 brochure.
2. **Kristin Linklater** (USA) Kristin is the author of *Freeing the Natural Voice* (1976) and *Freeing Shakespeare's Voice* (1992). She has worked with the Open Theater; the Negro Ensemble Company; Stratford, Ontario; the Guthrie Theatre; and Broadway shows. She is cofounder of Shakespeare & Company, and a 1981 Guggenheim Fellow. She played the title role in *King Lear*, produced by The Company of Women, codirected with Carol Gilligan, She has taught at NYU and Columbia, Emerson College, Boston, and been awarded the ATHE and NETC Career Achievement Awards. In 2001, Kristin was inducted into the College of Fellows of the American Theatre.
3. **Karl Jenkins** (Wales) Karl did post graduate studies at the Royal Academy of Music, London, becoming increasingly interested in jazz (playing saxophone), which was to have a significant bearing on his compositional style in later years. Following his studies he won awards as a jazz oboist and multi-instrumentalist. He co-founded Nucleus in 1972, winning first prize at the Montreux Jazz Festival, before joining Soft Machine. Jenkins is probably best known for his Adiemus project. The first three albums—*Songs of Sanctuary*, *Cantata Mundi* and *Dances of Time*—have found enormous success worldwide, achieving silver, gold and platinum awards globally.
4. **Rudolf Laban** (Hungary/England) Laban was a dancer and dance theorist from central Europe, who developed Labanotation, a system of notating movement, still the foundation and primary system used to notate dance. Initially studying architecture, he moved into dance and the movement arts after being influenced by dancer/choreographer Heidi Dzinkowska. Later he established the Choreographic Institute in Zurich in 1915 to study movement. During and after the 2nd world war, he shifted his focus to workers in industry and their movement patterns. He published the book Effort in 1947, documenting the results of his research in the workplace.
5. **Michael McMahon** (Canada) A pianist and vocal coach Michael studied at McGill University, in Vienna at the Franz Schubert Institute, and in Salzburg at the International Summer Academy held at the Mozarteum. He has performed throughout Canada, Europe and the USA with a great variety of singers, earning him the reputation of being a "luxury partner." He has been a guest artist with such organizations as Les Violons du Roy, L'Opéra de Montréal, Société Pro Musica, the Wexford Festival, the André Turp Society and Debut Atlantic. At McGill, where he is currently an associate professor, Michael teaches in both the Voice and Piano areas.

Singing

International Performers and Voice Teachers Speak: Diverse Methods for Integrating the Disciplines of the
Spoken and Singing Voice by Betty Moulton (continued)

6. **Enrique Pardo** (Peru/France) Enrique is a theatre director, performer, and writer; he founded the company Pantheatre in 1981 with a now legendary solo performance on the god Pan: *Calling for Pan.*
He performed with the Roy Hart Theatre (until 1980) and taught voice within the "Roy Hart" model. He has pursued a career as a vocalist-performer in contemporary opera and his own theatre productions. The three main sources for the work of Pantheatre are the voice, choreographic theatre and myth. Enrique has performed and taught in Europe, North and South America, Australia and New Zealand, where he directed *Xenophoria,* in 1993, a performance by Bert van Dijk, now director of Pantheatre Poneke (New Zealand). During the last few years, Enrique has directed mainly performances by artists linked to PANTHEATRE ACTS Voice Performance School.

7. **John Cage** (USA) Cage was an experimental music composer, widely known for *4'33",* a three movement composition with no musical notes. He was the partner and long-term collaborator with choreographer/dancer Merce Cunningham. He practiced "chance music" (leaving some elements up to chance) and used musical instruments in non-standard ways, pioneering the use of electronic music. He is considered an important pioneer of 20th century music using his music as an "affirmation of life".

8. Female shaman from Siberia, presented singing master class at Giving Voice.

9. Researcher in the Collaborative Research Centre "Cultures of the Performative" at the Free University, Berlin. Presented talk "Towards a Philosophy of Voice" at Giving Voice.

Bibliography

Balk, H. Wesley, *Performing Power: A new approach for the Singer-Actor.*
  Minneapolis, University of Minnesota Press, 1985.
– – – *The Radiant Performer: The Spiral Path to Performing Power.*
  Minneapolis, University of Minnesota Press, 1991.
Clark, Mark Ross and Clark, Lynn V. *Singing, Acting and movement in*
  Opera: A guide to singer-getics. Bloomington: Indiana University Press,
  2002.
Fields, Victor Alexander. *Training the Singing Voice: An analysis of the*
  working concepts contained in recent contributions to vocal pedagogy.
  New York: Da Capo Press, 1947.
Melton, Joan, and Tom, Kenneth. *One Voice: integrating singing*
  technique and theatre voice training. Portsmouth, Heinemann, 2003.
Schiotz, Aksel. *The Singer and His Art.* New York, Harper and Row, 1970.

Essay *by Frederick Willard*

Hangin' With the Cousins:
A Missing Link Between Vocalise and Repertoire

After receiving a Master's degree in Musicology (Syracuse University) and the Choirmaster certificate (American Guild of Organists), he went on to work extensively in New York City, on and off Broadway as well as throughout the United States conducting and orchestrating Musical Theatre for over 20 years. Broadway: *Meet Me In St. Louis, Lend Me a Tenor, Anything Goes*. Off-Broadway: *Amphigorey, Pageant, Billy Bishop Goes to War*. Fred has written arrangements for the late Lionel Hampton, Melba Moore, American Movie Classics and the Hartford Symphony Orchestra. He has also taught at Tisch School of the Arts (NYC) and Syracuse University.

As with many teachers, coaches and conductors, if I had a nickel for every time I heard "it was perfect when I practiced it," I would be a millionaire. The reality is twofold: 1) the time in the practice room wasn't *really* so perfect or 2) it could not be repeated (especially in the instructor's presence) because the student didn't really understand *how* they achieved the desired result. The purpose of this article is to explore a frequently neglected connection between rehearsal and performance.

One reason for the gap between the vocalise and repertoire is the vowels on which we vocalize are NOT the vowels we really use in repertoire—at least songs and arias in English. Whether we use Marchesi, Vaccai or a pattern of our own choosing, we tend to favor the Italian vowels, since they represent the *bel canto* tradition of historical vocal pedagogy. However, this does not help the singer when the repertoire requires non-Italian vowels (found in much of the contemporary English-language based music) such as /I/, /U/, /ʌ/ and so forth, because the "memory" of effective production of these vowels has not been established. If these vowels are not imprinted in the vocal tract muscle memory, it is almost impossible to expect them to find their way into repertoire. This problem can be corrected by a simple adjustment: in any practice session, be sure to include at least one of the "American" vowels in your vocalises.

This simplistic solution begs a number of questions, one of which is "how do I bring the resonance of the Italian vowels into the American ones?" How many singers have cursed composers who make them sustain high notes on /æ/ or /ɝ/? The mechanism of bringing these families of vowels together lies in a relationship I call *concomitant resonance*, and joins the resonant properties of Italian vowels to a corresponding American vowel, or its American "cousin." By pairing the muscle memory established by singing Italian vowels, it provides the singer a basis for which to "match" the American vowel in terms of a similar vocal tract shape. Theoretically, the singer would maintain a larger vocal tract (stemming from the *bel canto* tradition) when singing the American vowels and thus produce a more aesthetically appealing (and appropriate) vowel.

We take five common Italian vowels: /i/, /ɑ/, /ɔ/, /ɛ/, /u/. (leaving out [e] and [o] for the moment.) and set up a "cousin" relationship with our often troublesome American vowels. It looks something like this:

Italian	American	
[i]	[ɪ]	(tongue)
[ɛ]	[æ]	
[ɑ]	[ʌ]	
[ɔ]	[ɝ]	
[u]	[ʊ]	(lip)

Exercises for *concomitant resonance*:

Exercise 1: Start by sustaining a single pitch on the Italian vowel with optimum breath and resonance on the tone. Make the smallest anatomical adjustment (tongue, lips, etc.) possible to maintain concomitant resonance with the American cousin. For example, with /i/ and /I/, lower the middle of the tongue ever so slowly and slightly while keeping a buzzy sensation and open throat as you migrate towards /ɪ/. Remember that feeling—now find that /ɪ/ vowel again without the /i/. The same principle works for all of the above pairings. In this exercise (and always), one needs to have a very specific sense of the anatomical reality of each vowel.

What typically occurs is the adjustment between Italian and American cousins is smaller than the singer envisions. A pair of outside ears is very helpful when initially implementing this new technique. Once you have mastered the initial transition to the American vowels, move up by semitones in order to create appropriate muscle memory throughout your range. If vowel modification is necessary as you increase frequency, you can use the same auxiliary vowel for both! Add crescendo and diminuendo to taste and skill level.

Exercise 2: Now you can put the cousins to work with any vocalise that pleases you. Here is a simple five-note exercise that starts with a speech-like quality and leads into sustained notes:

Zi   Zi   Zi   I   i   I   i   I   i

Exercise 3: As we know, exercises in velocity can help smooth over a *passagio*, so adapt your favorite scalar or arpeggiated pattern to include our cousins:

Zi---------- I---------- Zi---------- I---------- i

Hi   HI   Hε..Hε Hε Hæ Hæ Hæ Hε

After this, the sky's the limit. Use the cousins with any exercise in your book or with short phrases of actual repertoire repeated at different pitch levels.

So where does this procedure fit into the larger picture of finding a link between rehearsal and performance? Over the years, I've developed a five- step process for preparation of songs and arias (not unlike one described by Beverly Patton in the Nov-Dec. issue of *Journal of Singing*). Briefly described, they are:

1) The Lyric as monologue: Use of given circumstance, objectives, tactics and other standard tools of the actor.
2) The Lyric in the composer's rhythm: Issues of prosody, syntax and phrasing are considered. The singer weighs the literal values of notes against natural textual declamation and their own impulses as discovered in step one.
3) Melody on individual vowels: Exploration of the purely vocal/technical and musical considerations of the piece

at hand. Use of musical phrases as vocalises on different vowels.
4) Melody on appropriate vowels: Singing the song without ANY consonants to insure maximum resononance and tonal energy on each note. (I used to call this the "Patti LuPone" step, but she's a lot better these days….)
5) Sing the song!

Through this method we are able to isolate vocal problems with step 4, and as a result are able to find optimum resonance and appropriate vowel coloring for each note. When an American vowel proves to be less than stellar, students are able to find their way into the vowel by substituting the Italian cousin, until they become more proficient at the technique. Once they have mastered that, they are then able to adjust the tongue, lips, or other articulators to arrive at the actual vowel contained in the word. At this stage, we are completely flexible with regards to the genre, so the same basic procedure can be used if we are singing an Art Song, an Opera Aria, or a Show Tune.

Try this on the most common word in song: "love." Since the vowel is /ʌ/, start by sustaining on the Italian cousin, or /ɑ/. Once it feels right, lower the middle of the tongue slightly to accomplish a nice resonant /ʌ/; remember what that felt like. Now sing the /ʌ/ without using the Italian cousin first and notice the difference.

Using this procedure, you can work your way through an entire song or aria just on vowels. The key here is never speed, but finding optimum resonance for each vowel. Break the piece into the smallest units—two bars, four bars, and then the entire phrase. As you do this, you gradually establish this feeling in your muscles (i.e. muscle memory) and will eventually find it easy to carry over into repertoire without thinking about it!

Once the technical demands are attended to, we are able to return to our interpretive work with a new sense of freedom. The vowels will become habitual and we can begin to sing artistically as if the song was being written before our eyes, out of a need, and in the moment. When we use the cousins, we begin to delve into the magical synthesis of works, music and human emotion; the pay-off is enormous.

🍃

Endnotes

1. Patton, Beverly A. "Seven Ways to Practice a Song or Homage to Sergius Kagen" *Journal of Singing* Volume 59 (November, 2002):165. In that every moment of proscribed practice time must be spent wisely, the author has extracted Kagen's ideas from his chapter on vocal technique in *On Studying Singing* and reworked, paraphrased, adapted, and integrated them into a practice syllabus.

Reviews and Sources *Karen Ryker, Associate Editor*

Editorial Column *by Karen Ryker, Associate Editor*

It is a pleasure to introduce this collection of reviews, and to note that more than one half of the works reviewed include accompanying interactive electronic materials.

Leading with our Voice and Gender cover topic, Troy Dwyer introduces a pioneer publication *Voice and Communication Therapy for the Transgender/ Transsexual Client*, which will be of interest to voice and speech pathologists, clinicians, and specialists with interest in LGBTQ perspectives. Its accompanying CD offers recorded samples of some astounding transformations. Dr. Jean Abitbol's *Odyssey of the Voice*, described by reviewer Joanna Cazden as an "unabashedly poetic yet clinically reliable ode to the wonders of vocalization," delves into issues of gender and gender alteration as part of the larger "odyssey" of voice as an expressive organ. And Flloyd Kennedy introduces philosopher Adriana Cavarero's *For More Than One Voice* as an analysis of western civilization's attitude to the human voice, the silencing of the female voice, and the ultimate uniqueness and significance of the individual human voice.

Five new works represent the performer's voice and expression. Tara McAllister-Viel introduces Wlodzimierz Staniewski's *Hidden Territories: the theatre of gardzienice*, and lauds an accompanying CD which enables one to see and hear exercises described. Elizabeth Terrell reviews Michael Edgerton's, *The 21st Century Voice*, about the extreme potentials of the human voice accompanied by CD samples. Kate Ufema treats Donna Soto-Morettini's *Popular Singing*, whose CD demonstrates the techniques/styles discussed in the book. Kevin Otos reviews *The Expressive Actor*, in which author Michael Lugering makes a case for an integrated approach to actor training; Craig Tompkins introduces *The Performer's Voice*, a practical compendium for all types of voice users, by Meribeth Bunch Dayme.

It comes as no surprise that the works treating accent and dialect all include interactive materials. Eric Armstrong reviews the website which provides an interactive experience of material gathered for *The Atlas of North American English*. Krista Scott introduces readers to the 4th edition of Paul Meier's *Accents and Dialects for Stage and Screen* with its instructional CDs and link to the IDEA website. And Elizabeth van den Berg reviews Paul Meier's new e-book, *The Standard British English Dialect*. And the new DVD/video series, *Laryngeal Teaching Series* created by Starr Cookman and Kate DeVore, is reviewed by Claudia Anderson.

Books about performance of Shakespeare are always popular, and we offer reviews of several recent works: John Basil's *Will Power* reviewed by Judylee Vivier; Rhona Silverbush's *Speak the Speech* reviewed by Marlene Johnson; and David Carey reviews *Pronouncing Shakespeare* by David Crystal, which details his involvement with an "original pronunciation" production of *Romeo and Juliet* at Shakespeare's Globe. We follow this with complementary play reviews, by David Carey and Mary Howland, of the original pronunciation version of *Troilus and Cressida*, staged by Shakespeare's Globe in the 2005 season.

Finally, another round of thesis abstracts introduce the work of our up and coming voice trainers as they investigate intriguing issues having an impact in the contemporary field of voice and speech studies.

Karen Ryker, associate editor, teaches voice, text and acting in University of Connecticut's MFA and BFA programs, and was previously Head of MFA actor training at University of Wisconsin. Recent coaching credits include Connecticut Repertory Theatre, Berkshire Theatre Festival, Illinois Shakespeare Festival. She is a member of AEA and appears on stage, in industrials and commercials. A former board member of VASTA, she has written for *The Journal of Voice, The Voice and Speech Review,* and contributed to *The Complete Voice and Speech Workout Book* . MFA from Brandeis, MA from U of Michigan, BA from Clarke College.

Book Review *by Troy Dwyer*
Voice and Communication Therapy for the Transgender/Transsexual Client
edited by Richard K. Adler, Sandy Hirsch & Michelle Mordaunt

Troy Dwyer is an Assistant Professor in the Department of Theatre & Dance at Muhlenberg College in Allentown, Pennsylvania, where he teaches courses in voice & speech, realist acting, acting classical verse, and queer studies. A writer and performer, he has co-written several works for the stage, including the original musical *Lures & Snares* (with Beth Schachter and Mike Krisukas), *Journey/Cave* (with Tim Miller) and *Tar* (with Charles O. Anderson). He holds a BA from Oglethorpe University, an MFA in Acting from the University of Wisconsin—Madison, and is a proud member of VASTA.

To call *Voice and Communication Therapy for the Transgender/Transsexual Client* a pioneering publication in the world of speech-language pathology and voice training is no overstatement. Not only is it the first-ever clinical manual to address considerations of communication therapy for individuals transitioning between genders (a small but budding patient population for many clinicians), it also represents the foremost and earliest published indexical compendium of literature to-date related to gender-queerness and the voice. As such, this significant book (and accompanying CD) will not only prove useful to clinical professionals, but also may be heartily appreciated by any voice and speech specialist interested in LGBTQ perspectives within voice training.

The reader needn't be familiar with transgenderism/transsexuality (TG/TS) to find the book accessible. Early chapters use plain language to introduce a basic conceptual framework for understanding TG/TS from several perspectives, including the humanistic, psychosocial, psychotherapeutic and endocrinologic. Editor/contributors Adler, Hirsch and Mordaunt do not assume that the reader is either familiar or comfortable with the client population in question, and they wisely take time to make cordial acquaintances, contextualizing their introduction of TG/TS in terms of a pool of underserved patients with genuine therapeutic needs. This overview is merged with a multi-chapter discussion encompassing the ethical role of the clinician (highlighting the "team" approach to treatment management, a model that foregrounds communicative coalition between a single transitioning TG/TS patient's disparate care providers) alongside a concomitant assessment of the application of "evidence-based practice" in voice therapy for TG/TS clients. For the non-clinical trainer, "evidence-based practice" refers to a medical paradigm directing that course of therapy be dictated by up-to-date best evidence as derived from available experimental and observational research. Interestingly, contributor Jennifer Oates concludes her comprehensive analysis of the application of evidence-based practice by conceding a paucity of strong evidence for the effectiveness of voice therapy for TG/TS clients. (36) However, this may not be surprising, given the relative youth of speech-language pathology as a clinical discipline and the even younger TG/TS subspecialization. Indeed, any doubt about the potential efficacy of therapy will likely be dispelled upon listening to the twelve "before-and-after" recordings contained on the accompanying CD, in which the pre- and post-therapy voices of actual male-to-female TG/TS clients are juxtaposed, putting into relief rather astounding transformations of pitch-placement, resonance-placement, intonation, articulation and prosody. What is so striking about these recorded samples is the way in which the clients achieve "passing" feminine voices by successfully manipulating multiple factors simultaneously. That is, they're not just speaking at higher frequencies, they're engaging in a complex and multivariate feat of communicative recalibration. (The CD features only male-to-female speakers; the book as a whole favors this population, as it constitutes the bulk of TG/TS clients who seek treatment. However, editor Richard K. Adler and contributor John Van Borsel set aside an entire chapter to discuss considerations pertinent to the female-to-male client.)

The understanding that emerges, and that serves as the organizing principle for the ten chapters that constitute the second half of the book, is that no single vocal attribute alone genders a voice. Rather, the perception of vocal femininity or masculinity derives from the confluence of many characteristics. Chapters 10 through 17 each concentrate in turn on one of these characteristics in the form of a detailed instructive essay on focused therapeutic techniques for assisting the TG/TS client in manipulating a single variable. Variables considered include pitch, intonation, resonance, articulation, rate, loudness, linguistic syntax, situational discursiveness and nonverbal communication. Though these characteristics are addressed discretely, each contributor carefully points out important areas of intersection in which the variable at hand is either affected by or affects another variable in a way that substantially genders the voice.

San Diego, CA: Plural Publishing, Inc.

It may be no surprise that principal among these intersections is that of pitch and intonation, and editor/contributor Michelle Mordaunt provides a lengthy, well-written and detailed appraisal of techniques to safely and healthfully help the male-to-female TS/TG client adjust speaking fundamental frequency (sf$_0$) range, paying special attention to the intricacies of relocating new pitches within familiar standard intoning patterns. (It should be noted here that Mordaunt deals exclusively with American patterns, and indeed *Voice and Communication Therapy for the Transgender/Transsexual Client* does appear to presume its reader to be American). Perhaps unexpectedly, Mordaunt abjures the goal of relocating the TS/TG client's sf$_0$ to that of the average range for the client's new gender, citing risks to vocal health due to excess tension. (172) Instead, she advocates targeting a safer gender-ambiguous pitch range of 150 to 185 Hz, suggesting that the adjustment of other vocal variables (in addition to sf$_0$) do valuable work to persuade the listener's ear of the speaker's target gender. In other words, though the client's new sf$_0$ range may be gender-ambiguous, her gender-attribution won't be, as long as she works to develop other features of her voice in addition to her pitch.

Subsequent chapters contribute valuable elaboration upon the understanding of the multivariate composition of a voice's gender and to therapy models that incorporate work on multiple factors. Voice and speech trainers for theatre may particularly appreciate editor/contributor Sandy Hirsch's endorsement of techniques for altering resonance-placement predicated upon the work of Arthur Lessac, notably the Lessac Resonant Voice Therapy approach (LRVT) developed by Katherine Verdolini (213). (This reviewer found particularly enlightening Hirsch's discussion of effectively feminizing resonance placement by what she jokingly calls "[i]-fying" vowels, that is coloring all vowels with the [i] phoneme facial posture) (220). Additionally, Hirsch's later chapters (one of which is co-written with contributor John Van Borsel) on the gendered aspects of nonverbal cueing are superb, shedding detailed light on an aspect of communication which may largely pass under the radar of the average voice and speech specialist.

Though *Voice and Communication Therapy for the Transgender/Transsexual Client* is pitched to the clinician serving the TG/TS population, the book's usefulness and applicability reaches well past this audience. For instance, it may prove a helpful and accessible resource for certain TS/TG individuals, provided that they are not put-off by some clinical terminology. The book's straightforward writing, clear explanation of exercises, and exhaustive bibliographic suggestions will most certainly make it a welcome addition to the bookshelf of any voice trainer, teacher or coach seeking to make visible for herself—and her clients and students—the complex and secreted relationship between gender and communication.

🦡

Book Review *by Joanna Cazden*

Odyssey of the Voice
by Jean Abitbol
Translated by Patricia Crossley

Joanna Cazden, MFA, MS-CCC is a speech patholo-gist, voice therapist, singer, and intuitive healer in Southern California. She holds theater degrees from CalArts and the University of Washington, and she currently serves on VASTA's Board of Directors. She had an active career as a singer/songwriter in the women's music movement of the 1970s, releasing six solo albums and performing at major folk music, womens' music and womens' theater festivals. She has written on vocal health issues for *Electronic Musician, Onstage, Folkworks, Whole Life Times,* and the 2003 issue of VASTA's *Voice and Speech Review.*

Vocal artists and performance teachers who are interested in voice science and medicine, but who hesitate to plunge fully into the jargons of physics and clinical practice, now have an accessible option. Renowned otolaryngologist, phoniatrist, and surgeon Jean Abitbol, of the University of Paris, has united his expertise in voice physiology, psychology, and endocrinology with broad knowledge of speech-language development and his personal love for singers and singing.

The result is a highly readable, unabashedly poetic yet clinically reliable ode to the wonders of vocalization. First published in French in 2005, it became available in English early in 2006. The book is divided into three sections covering the evolution of voice as an expressive organ; vocal health, gender, and expressiveness; and vocal mysteries and fascinations.

Chapters in each section are further broken into subtitled "chunks" whose connections to each other are often more tangential than logical. This unclear organization—the book's greatest weakness—nevertheless allows easy browsing by the curious novice, and an extensive bibliography is provided to fill informational gaps.

Part 1: To the Roots of the Voice discusses the fossil record of laryngeal evolu-tion; brain regions involved in vocal expression; relationships among thought, voice, and language; principles of vocal fold vibration; and "virtual" (electronically synthesized) voices. Case studies from the author's medical practice add personality and context to descriptions of cells, measurements, and genetic codes.

Part 2: The Voice and Emotion emphasizes Dr. Abitbol's research specialty: the impact of gender hormones on the voice, including subtle changes due to the menstrual cycle, the variability of voice change after menopause, and laryn-geal options for male-to-female transgender change. This section also reviews vocal health, risk factors, the impact of common illnesses and physical trau-mas, nutritional guidelines, and performance concerns such as stage fright.

Part 3: The Mystery of Voice skims through vocal curiosities from ventriloquism and the Delphic oracle to songbirds and castrati.

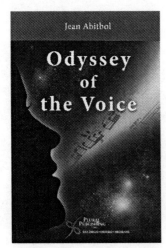

San Diego: Plural Publishing Inc. 2006 (French edition ©2005 E'ditions Robert Laffont)

Dr. Abitbol's constant interweaving of science and human interest creates less a comprehensive textbook than a wide-ranging conversation with a friendly expert.

> Between the cell and the larynx, the brain and language, hearing and giving voice, the vocal landscape of *Homo vocalis* takes shape...Its beauty, its weaknesses, its diversity, its charisma, its psychological impact are a reflection of the scars we carry...when all is said and done, is the vocal print not simply the imprint left by the breath of life?
> (Preface, page x)

Readers who seek strictly organized health information may find Abitbol's approach frustrating. *The Odyssey of Voice* will better please those vocal artists, teachers and students who prefer science to be liberally seasoned with poetic wonder.

Book Review *by Flloyd Kennedy*
For More Than One Voice: Towards a Philosophy of Vocal Expression
by Adriana Cavarero

There are studies galore investigating the science of voice and vocal expression, but to date there have been few, if any, creditably researched studies into how we think about the voice, and why. This book analyses western civilisation's attitude to the human voice since Plato, drawing specific attention to the silencing of the female voice.

Cavarero is an Italian feminist philosopher, and possibly the first scholar not primarily concerned with voice training or pathology to propose the voice as a serious object of study. She addresses Western Society's lack of recognition of the voice as an indicator of uniqueness, and proposes a public discourse which could bring the voice and voice studies into the public arena and public consciousness as something worthy of attention. The breadth and depth of Cavarero's research provides rich material for voice practitioners to enhance their armoury of mythic and cultural imagery.

Looking to Plato and his influence through subsequent millennia, Cavarero explores the relegation of the voice over time to a mere carrier of language. She takes exception to the privileging of *logos* over the voice which speaks it, pointing out that "[s]peech, understood as speech that emits from someone's mouth, is not simply the verbal sphere of expression; it is also the point of tension between the uniqueness of the voice and the system of language"(14). She reminds her reader that Socrates himself, "intends philosophizing as speaking, never as thinking or contemplating"(67).

Drawing upon Levinas, Kafka, Adorno, Cixious and Kristeva, she argues that the voice is primarily a device for invoking relationships; it "communicates uniqueness," since speech is a sonorous act and "to speak to one another is to communicate oneself to others"(13). This may be obvious to those who train performers; however, it is not so within other disciplines, or in the general community. Cavarero invokes Greek mythology and modern cinema to illustrate how we have been acculturated to deny the power, beauty and, even more important, the significance of the human voice. Long associated with the feminine, it has long been dismissed as either irrelevant or dangerous to the rational being.

Caverero illustrates how the voice has been reduced, renounced, even reviled as a result of its perceived transcendental nature. Her final chapter is a respectful but provocative critique of Derrida's attempt to reconstitute the voice, which he designates the indicator of presence, the necessary carrier of *logos*. In the process he inadvertently foregrounds *logos*, in its interior, unspoken or written form, as being the worthy focus of attention, while the actual voice remains inaccessible to research because of its uniqueness, which is reduced to insubstantiality.

This is a complex book with all its twists and turns of argument. Nevertheless, by addressing the path taken by western philosophy this book becomes a critique of western society and its assumption that the interior word can be examined with credibility in isolation. The metaphysical voice to which philosophy (and one might just as well say "society") ascribes presence is, first and foremost, a sonorous voice.

Flloyd Kennedy has worked in Australia, UK and USA as actor, director, folk singer, cabaret artist and street performer, and was artistic director of Golden Age Theatre, Scotland, 1991-96. Since returning to Brisbane in 1997, she has directed opera and theatre productions, (professional and student), performed in a number of independent theatre and film productions and currently provides vocal and acting training for professional, community and educational organisations, including QUT and UQ. She is presently undertaking research at UQ into the voice in performance (with particular reference to Shakespeare).

Stanford: Stanford University Press, 2005

Book Review *by Tara McAllister-Viel*

Hidden Territories: the theatre of gardzienice
by Wlodzimierz Staniewski with Alison Hodge

Tara McAllister-Viel received her PhD in Performance Practice-Voice from the University of Exeter, England and her Masters of Fine Arts—Acting from the University of Wisconsin—Madison, Asian/Experimental Theatre Program, USA. While a Visiting Professor of Voice at The Korean National University of Arts, School of Drama, Tara also studied a traditional Korean vocal art form. Tara's research and teaching focus is adapting p'ansori training techniques, Hatha yoga and tai chi chuan (Wu form) into an intercultural/interdisciplinary approach to training actors' voices. Currently, Tara is Voice lecturer at The Central School of Speech and Drama, London.

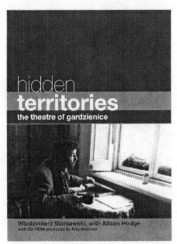

New York: Routledge, 2004.

Have you ever read a passage describing an acting exercise and wondered what it might look/sound like? This book doesn't keep you wondering—tucked into the back cover is a CD-ROM by Peter Hulton (Arts Archives) filled with video and audio samples. Together with pictures, an interview-style narrative with Artistic Director Wlodzimierz Staniewski and scholarly essays by Alison Hodge (Senior lecturer-Drama at Royal Holloway, University of London) this book provides a unique, in-depth look at one of the most well-respected experimental theatre companies in Poland.

Known by the shortened name "Gardzienice" (the Polish town in which it is located) the Centre for Theatre Practices was founded in 1977 by Wlodzimierz Staniewski. Clearly influenced by the work of Grotowski with whom Staniewski worked closely in the early 70s, Gardzienice has developed its own signature aesthetic. The company's ways of working and performing throughout a politically tumultuous 25 years of Polish history, have played an integral role in developing not only Polish theatre but also international theatre praxis. This book provides essential background information on Polish politics, religion, culture and art as the context from which to understand both the actor training and performances unique to Staniewski's work.

Section One, "Origins," maps out the key principles that underlie the practice. Section Two, "Practice," introduces the company's use of traditional cultural practices through planned "expeditions" or excursions into neighbouring Polish villages to collect folk songs. The resulting "gatherings" at the end of these expeditions are comprised of villagers and company members sharing performances. Within the accompanying CD-ROM, samples of the training exercises and performances that developed from these "gatherings" provide an important insight into one approach to intercultural practice.

Section Three, "Technique," introduces the way Staniewski and company work with "musicality" and "mutuality," which may be of particular interest to those who train actors' voices. The CD-ROM video sample of a chorus of women creating a "song" based on bird calls is a creative example of one way Staniewski and his company work with "musicality" and nature in vocal performance. I teach from this section of the book and my students find Gardzienice's "musicality" helps them devise performance ideas when we work with sung voice/spoken voice combinations in lamentation.

Section Four, "Performances" discusses a few of Gardzienice's most famous endeavours, *Avvvakum*, *Carmina Burana*, and *Metamorphosis*. Again, the performance samples in the CD-ROM will help the reader understand the written passages better. Section Five concludes the interview/discussion between Staniewski and Hodge with thoughts on the future of "home" theatre and theatre in a democratic Poland, touching on the larger notion of creating theatre in a true democracy.

This book is useful not only in providing one perspective of Polish experimental theatre but in offering an alternative perspective to creating theatre and training actors. There is no substitution for seeing a Gardzienice performance live, but this book comes close to giving readers the sense of intimacy, energy, power and innovation that defines their work.

Book Review *by Elizabeth Terrel*

The 21ˢᵗ Century Voice: Contemporary and Traditional Extra-Normal Voice
by Michael Edward Edgerton

The 21ˢᵗ Century Voice by Michael Edward Edgerton is an indispensable guide to vocal techniques and practices used in non-traditional voice work, focused on the singing voice. This is a book about the extreme potentials of the human voice, placed within the biomechanical framework of vocal technique with which we are all familiar. Its 200 pages are packed with illustrations, charts, graphs, and sheet music examples. An audio CD allows the reader to hear examples of the techniques discussed.

This book is a needed reference as extended voice work becomes more prevalent and moves into the mainstream. Edgerton does an admirable job of citing and reporting recent findings in voice research. Be warned: this book is not light reading by any stretch of the imagination. This is a technical manual of voice production that reads like a dissertation. While some of it seems to be more grammatically complex than necessary, it is admirable that Edgerton did not skimp on his explanations in order to make it accessible for all audiences.

As mentioned, Edgerton places non-traditional singing techniques within the traditional structure. He examines the processes of vocal production one section at a time and then ties them all together at the end. Part I deals with techniques involving Air Flow (egressive and ingressive breathing, and source and duration of airflow).

Part II deals with Source and issues related to vocal fold use. He covers techniques ranging from the familiar (vibrato) to the less familiar (including pressed voice, damped sound, laryngeal manipulation, glottal whistle, and sub- and supra-glottal sound production). He relates the technical aspects of gender related voice production and addresses issues related to controversial vocal registers, citing techniques used in Korean P'ansori singing, to which he refers several times throughout the book.

Part III covers issues of resonance and articulation, vocal tract mapping (notably the Edgerton Model of Filter Articulation, which he covers in great detail). This section includes IPA, language issues, and techniques involved in the modification of airflow.

Part IV on Heightened Potentials deals with issues such as multiphonic (more than one pitch at a time) sound; extreme vocal use (shouting, screaming, rasping, etc.); and the variety of ways in which the human voice can interface with other forms of media and instrumentation.

In Part V Edgerton discusses how the covered techniques are placed in the context of an artistic framework. Part VI is the Appendices, Glossary, and Index, which are comprehensive. Additionally, each chapter of the book has an extensive list of suggested readings and references.

One potentially problematic issue is the availability of replacement copies of the CD. The publisher states that it is not available separately. Also the book's print is quite small, particularly in some of the charts and music samples.

This book is a valuable addition to any voice trainer's library. It's thorough and provides concrete examples with a tremendous amount of information in one place. It is a much needed treatise on the power and potential of the human voice. ❦

Elizabeth Terrel teaches and resides in the Chicago area. She coaches voice and is currently training in Fitzmaurice Voicework. She also teaches acting, focusing on the Meisner Technique and the Stanislavski approach. She is a voice and movement coach for the Gately-Poole Acting Intensives. A professional actress with a background in straight and musical theatre, camera and voice-over work, she has performed cabaret individually and with jazz and standards bands. Her MFA in Acting is from Northern Illinois University.

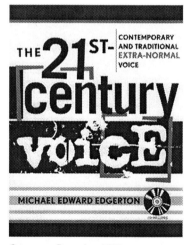

THE **21ˢᵀ-** CONTEMPORARY AND TRADITIONAL EXTRA-NORMAL VOICE

century

VOICE

MICHAEL EDWARD EDGERTON

Scarecrow Press, Inc. 2006

Book Review *by Kate Ufema*

Popular Singing
A Practical Guide to: Pop, Jazz, Blues, Rock, Country and Gospel
by Donna Soto-Morettini

Kate Ufema, Voice and Speech Specialist in the Professional Actor-Training Program at the University of Minnesota Duluth. An Equity actress, singer, director, musical director, voice/dialect coach, and professional voice consultant and trainer. Trains and coaches voices in all the performance media, including CNN, CBS, NBC, ABC, National Public Radio and American Public Radio. Has acted, directed, and coached in theatres across the country, and presented workshops and adjudicated theatre competitions and festivals from Colorado to the East Coast and abroad. A charter member of VASTA, holding BA, MA, and MFA degrees from Penn State University.

A & C Black Publishers Ltd (2006)

Donna Soto-Morettini is a ten-year professional pop-singer veteran who has dissected several popular singing styles (jazz, blues, rock, country and gospel specifically) in order to demystify their learning and practice. Ms. Morettini's book presents a wealth of information particularly useful for singers, singer wanna-be's, and singing teachers alike.

This unique book can be a very specific guide for any singer who wishes to increase his/her vocal art through the enhancement of stylistic nuance and experimentation. Its strength lies in the fact that Ms. Morettini has not only performed all these styles, but has also studied and taught the craft of pop singing to many for many years. Thus, her book not only imparts impeccable technique (in both word and recorded CD demonstration), but also profound wisdoms regarding vocal usage, stamina building, and care.

Ms. Morettini's apparently endless knowledge of her subject is shared, casually yet specifically, and without bias. Her approach to style is one of knowledgeable experimentation, always suggesting a means of approach—never a result. She stresses the importance of ear-training and mimicry—listening and mimicking the vocal nuance of different, carefully selected artists in order to build a vocal vocabulary from which to create one's own style.

The book is divided into six major sections:
1. Teaching and Learning Style—including a definition of style and addressing the pros, cons, and difficulties of style 'training'.
2. A Practical Guide for Exploring Your Own Voice—discusses some basic vocal anatomy and singing skills, while practically exploring certain voice qualities including: aspirate, elongated, twang, belt, and what Ms. Morettini labels as 'dangerous' qualities.
3. The Complementary Elements of Style—a detailed exploration of style ornamentation including: onset, decay, vibrato, phrase weight and placement, attack, breath, diction, and improvisation.
4. Hearing Voices—listening to and analyzing style using specific examples provided by Ms. Morettini.
5. The Interview: Paul McCartney—an interesting discussion with Sir McCartney about training, performing, stamina, and listening.
6. Resources for Listening and Reading—a wonderful listening list of songs and song artists organized by style, songs which are cheaply available through iTunes.

Beyond, Ms. Morettini includes a recorded CD of her own voice demonstrating all she discusses, encouraging the reader to listen and sing along for experimental purposes only. Unfortunately, the CD has no order list of its excerpts though they are referred to in the book. Thus, this reviewer found herself creating her own CD excerpt chart.

Also, it cannot be stated enough that Ms. Morettini has studied the work of Jo Estill. Ms. Morettini does mention Ms. Estill in her book, as it is quite clear that Ms. Morettini uses a great deal of the Estill 'voice quality' work as the foundation of her approach. *Popular Singing* is a gift to anyone who wishes to sing or teach popular singing. It is specific, wise, and true; written by a woman who knows her subject both academically and practically, and one who loves songs and singers of all types and styles.

Book Review *by Kevin Otos*
The Expressive Actor: Integrated Voice, Movement and Acting Training
by Michael Lugering

The case for an integrated approach to actor training receives articulate advocacy in Michael Lugering's *The Expressive Actor: Integrated Voice, Movement and Acting Training*. Here Lugering presents an innovative approach for training the actor, stating that "the study of acting should begin with human expression, rather than with scripts, character, language, style, or performance."

This book will interest those seeking both theoretical justification for an integrated approach to actor-training and practical ways to achieve this. This approach is ambitious, progressive, and requires patience. Lugering projects that it will take a student two to three years to reorganize her/his instrument as s/he explores the universal characteristics of how human beings express themselves before arriving at "…a rich, full bodied expressive action that is deeply rooted in sensation."

Central to his approach is what Lugering terms expressive action, which is "any physical action that simultaneously contains and reveals thought and feeling." Lugering explains that there are "five interrelated components—energy, orientation, size, progression, and flow—that unite to form the major properties of an expressive action." These components provide a methodical process for integrated investigations designed to increase each actor's expressive capabilities.

This text is divided into four well-written sections. In the first, he explains the nature of expressive action and provides evidence from numerous sources, including the somatic psychologists James Kepner and Edward Smith. This section is peppered with accessible exercises that easily illuminate these principles.

The other three sections—rich with clear and sequential exercises that seek to strengthen and integrate the elements of expression within the actor's body, voice, and acting—are devoted to awareness, centering, breathing, sounding and structured improvisations that investigate expressive action while encouraging creative agility. They are performed lying, sitting, and/or standing—either in stillness or in motion. The voice and speech work utilizes raw sounds and language, both dropped from the body and sustained, to expand the voice's expressive qualities. One of the values of Lugering's approach is that these exercises marry purposeful movement and purposeful sound in the service of an actable verb. Within the text the reader will also find adaptations of principles and exercises associated with pioneering teachers like F. Mathias Alexander, Erick Hawkins, Rudolf Laban and Kristin Linklater, whom Lugering openly credits in his writing and lists in the text's extensive bibliography.

This book is an excellent blueprint for instruction. It could be used as a text book, though the student will find it beneficial to have a background in basic acting technique. His approach could work well for professionals and students of all levels. Lugering's graphics and charts are also helpful.

This book challenges the way in which most actor training takes place in the United States. A discussion of the theoretical and practical applications implicit in his premise is merited but is beyond the scope of this review. Nonetheless, voice, movement and acting teachers alike will find his explanation of expressive action and the numerous exercises he presents useful in a variety of settings. They compliment and integrate well into a host of vocal and movement systems and, of critical importance, with any action-oriented acting system. This is an important work that deserves serious consideration.

Kevin Otos is an Assistant Professor at Elon University where he teaches acting. He has also taught at Whitman College and more recently at Oklahoma State University where he served as Head of Acting. His MFA was completed at Florida State University where he studied with outstanding teachers including José Quintero. His directing credits include *Measure for Measure* and *The Merchant of Venice* among others; and he recently assisted John Basil with his book on acting Shakespeare entitled *Will Power*. Kevin enjoys physical comedy and will train in the Commedia dell'Arte this summer.

Heinemann, 2007

Book Review *by Craig Tompkins*
The Performer's Voice: Realizing Your Vocal Potential
by Meribeth Bunch Dayme

Craig Tompkins, tenor, is the President of the Vancouver Chapter of the National Association of Teachers of Singing. He maintains busy studios at the Steveston Arts Connection and the Royal Oak Conservatory of Music in Burnaby. Craig is also a member of the Canadian Voice Care Foundation as well as VASTA and was on the host committee for the International Congress of Voice Teachers 6th Conference held in Vancouver in August 2005. He gives workshops on healthy voice use to groups ranging from swim instructors to NATS members and has sung with the renowned Vancouver Chamber Choir since 1979.

W. W. Norton & Co., 2005

This small book is a compendium of practical information for all types of voice users: singers, actors, speakers, lawyers, clergy, announcers etc. The author invites users to explore the book to meet their own requirements.

The book is divided into an introduction, three main sections (Making Sense of Vocal Mechanics, The Art of Vocal Expression and Presentation, and The Art of Performing) and ends with an epilogue. The chapters in each section include both activities for observing the body and the voice working together without interference, and exercises to incorporate this natural function into performance. The many illustrations and anatomical drawings that accompany the text are clear and uncluttered and serve to further illuminate Dayme's lucid writing.

In the first section, "Making Sense of Vocal Mechanics," Dayme leads us in a thorough investigation of the structures involved in producing the voice with simple but effective exercises for: improving posture and alignment, ease of inhalation and exhalation, connecting the breath to the sound, releasing tensions in the face and vocal tract, and freedom and flexibility of the articulators. Parallel with these exercises are suggested observations that serve to illustrate the points being made in the text.

In "The Art of Vocal Expression and Presentation," we are asked "to consider how effectively your message is being delivered and whether it is achieving its target." The same format is followed with exercises and observations suggested for exploring text and developing physical expression. The author explores ideas about structuring presentations and uncovers many of the pitfalls that can trap an inexperienced presenter.

In "The Art of Performing," Dayme offers a multitude of ideas for developing awareness and presence, for centering and focusing and for warming up the body and the voice. This section concludes with a chapter on vocal health that outlines a series of habits for a healthy voice and touches upon some of the most common vocal misuses and abuses.

Although small in size, this book is packed with common sense information that the reader is encouraged to explore by watching, listening, doing and feeling—thus appealing to not only the visual learner but also the aural and kinesthetic learner. No book could ever replace a teacher, but this little volume is a gold mine of material that complements any type of voice training.

Book Review *by Eric Armstrong*

The Atlas of North American English:
Phonetics, Phonology and Sound Change
by William Labov, Sharon Ash, & Charles Boberg

The Atlas of North American English (*ANAE*) provides an overall view of the dialects of the US and Canada. Authors William Labov, one of the world's leading sociolinguists, together with his colleagues Sharon Ash and Charles Boberg, redefine North American regional dialects based on sound changes active in the 1990s and draw the boundaries of those changes through colorful maps. Based on an exhaustive telephone survey of local speakers, it represents all the urbanized areas of North America. Published as a book and CD-ROM, with an accompanying website, this review is based upon the website demo (the publisher, Mouton de Gruyter, indicates that there are small differences between the final product and the demo). Exploring the website gives you an interactive experience of the material gathered for the study, including sound samples from 762 speakers from all over the continent and maps that reveal the different dialectal regions.

In typical hypertext fashion, you can work your way through the site in a logical, structured fashion following the sequence of headings on the left side of the screen, or you can jump around following your own whim. Either way works well, and novices to linguistics can learn a lot about the theory and methodology behind the survey by reading the content in the "Introductory Concepts" chapters on "the Study of Dialects" and "the Study of Sound." If you just want to hear the samples, a shortcut at the bottom of the screen to the "Sample Searcher" allows you to sort the 762 samples.

The site's main component is an atlas, linking the audio data and analysis with a map of North America. Clicking on one of the dots on the map brings up a new window featuring two or three screens of data, including the informant's personal information, sample keywords with audio, and optionally, an interview (which may or may not be transcribed into English). The transcribed interviews are particularly easy to follow as the text is highlighted as you hear the audio.

The survey (aka TELSUR) was done by telephone in the 1990s and sampled 297 urbanized areas representing 68% of the total 1997 North American population of 300,000,000. In major centers with population over one million, four speakers were interviewed, while in smaller centers only two were interviewed. The assumption that if someone was native to a region meant that her/his speech was representative occasionally led to some rather interesting data. Informants were selected based on their last names in telephone directories, focusing on Euro-Americans of German, English, and Irish ancestry. You won't find information on Hispanic, African-American-Vernacular-English, or other non-white, non-mainstream dialects in this research. Great care was taken that the speech gathered was spontaneous by eliciting pronunciations based upon questions of meaning.

Compared with the *International Dialects of English Archive*'s standard reading of *Comma Gets a Cure* along with its three minutes of spontaneous speech, the sampling used in *ANAE*'s survey was exhaustive, but contains more limited material. Many of the samples on the site are very short (often as short as 16 seconds), and at best about a minute. Many informants are represented online by their pronunciation of the fifteen TELSUR words alone, with no sample from their interview available at all.

Eric Armstrong is Acting Area Co-ordinator for the Department of Theatre at York University (Toronto), where he teaches voice, dialects and text. Apart from his busy family life, Eric works as a dialect coach for theatre, film and television, designs websites for theatre professionals, and continues to refine his phonetics workbook, *Introducing the IPA*. Recent VSR articles include: "R and its Articulation" (with Paul Meier), & "Hybrid Dialects," in *Shakespeare Around the Globe*, and "This is Normal?: A Theatre Coach Works in Film," in *Film, Broadcast and eMedia Coaching*. He received a *Leadership and Service Award* from VASTA in 2006.

The "Cross-Continental Word Comparison" map serves as a unique way to compare specific phonemes across North America. You can select a word from a menu, and the dots representing the informants change color to indicate whether the word is representative of the sound changes heard in their region. By clicking across the map you can quickly hear how a phoneme sounds in different parts of the continent. I suspect that a demonstration of this would be a delightful accompaniment to any class teaching phonetics. By following a link in the Regional Dialects section, you can read about the defining characteristics of each region. The "Mapping Dialect Features" section opens an interactive map that allows one to see the region impacted by each of the dialect-defining features, including features such as "the Low Back Merger, the Northern Cities Shift, Canadian Raising or vocalization of /r/." Though the survey helps to identify dialect regions in a new way for most voice and speech trainers, it does not provide enough information to teach each region's dialect. There just aren't enough "signature sounds"—to use terminology coined by IDEA founder Paul Meier—for some regions, though the information gleaned is certainly enough to give a "flavor" of a dialect.

book and CD-ROM with accompanying website
Mouton de Gruyter 2005

The biggest strike against the *Atlas of North American English* for the average private practice dialect coach/designer is its cost, at $620 USD; though the website is very informative and useful, this price could be prohibitive. This publication should be found in an academic library, and those trainers working in an academic setting should make sure that the book & CD-ROM is ordered, as it will make an excellent addition to any collection.

An aspect of the publication that takes some getting used to is the phonological use of IPA, rather than a phonetic usage. Lexical sets are defined not by Wells' lexical set words (FLEECE, KIT, DRESS, TRAP, etc.) but by phonological symbols. For example, the lexical set that Wells' defines with THOUGHT is here represented by /oh/, which seems rather counter-intuitive to those who are more familiar with a symbolic representation of /ɔ/. Unfortunately I found no centralized key to the phoneme symbols used in the site, an omission that could have very easily been remedied.

System Requirements for *ANAE* are remarkably low scale. Run with Macromedia's ubiquitous Flash Plug-in, almost all contemporary computers will run the software with ease. Though it does not work in the fairly standard Mac browser Safari, I managed to get it to work in both Firefox and Internet Explorer.

Book Review *by Krista Scott*

Accents and Dialects for Stage and Screen, 2007 Edition
by Paul Meier

Paul Meier, a leader in the field of dialects and accent training and the founder of the International Dialects of English Archive website (IDEA), brings dialect study into the 21st century with his practical training system, *Accents and Dialects for Stage and Screen, 2007 edition*. This IPA-based instructional text and CD compilation is a much-welcomed addition to the existing publications on dialect and accent training.

Accents and Dialects for Stage and Screen combines the best aspects of other popular dialect training methods into a succinct, comprehensive and affordable training tool. Sentence drilling similar to that in Jerry Blunt's *Stage Dialects*, modeling of the dialect in David Alan Stern's *Acting with an Accent* series, and authentic speaker samples similar to Gillian Lane-Plescia's compilations are all incorporated into Meier's "Seven Step Method" of learning an accent or dialect. Using John Wells' familiar lexical sets in each study, Meier lays out the phonetic "signature sounds" prior to the sentence drills, and the specific phonemic adjustments are adroitly described and modeled by Meier in the recording. Additional features (particularly unique linguistic characteristics) are described next, followed by an explanation of the rhythm, stress, intonation and tone. Coordination exercises and sample dramatic texts include full IPA narrow transcriptions and references to the sound change lessons.

Like Stern's recordings, Meier's is the only voice providing instruction on his CDs; however, he stresses that listening to authentic speakers on the related IDEA website is "central to the study," and provides concise descriptions of pertinent characteristics of the particular online samples. This combination of internet technology and phonetic drilling promotes authenticity and precision in pronunciation for actors and instructors, and increases awareness of the specific articulation adjustment needed for accuracy. In his footnotes, Meier also graciously references Lane-Plescia, Stern and other dialect specialists who suggest alternate pronunciations or approaches.

The compact disc compilation and accompanying manual are extremely user-friendly for a self-learner; since all of the instructional text is spoken on the discs, one could easily brush up a dialect in the car on the way to an audition or rehearsal. The length of each lesson is also well constructed, with ample pause time to mimic the sentence drills, coordination exercises and monologue lines. The sequence of twenty-three dialects and accents is particularly comprehensive in its survey of Anglo-European dialects of English, and also includes Indian, Spanish and Yiddish among the foreign language accents, which are absent from the 1967 Blunt publication.

The large pages and print, spiral binding and CD pouches make this a very attractive and practical instructional package. Having adopted this as the main training tool for my dialects course for the last three years, I couldn't be happier with the improvement it has made in the students' comprehension and accuracy, and in my own ease in class preparation and execution. My students also give this practical training manual and method an enthusiastic two thumbs up!

Krista Scott is an associate editor of the International Dialects of English Archive and a certified Associate Teacher of Fitzmaurice Voicework. She serves VASTA as its current treasurer, and was previously its membership director. Reviews of Shakespearean acting texts and Shakespeare pronunciation dictionaries have been published in the 2005 *Shakespeare Around the Globe* and the 2001 *The Voice in Violence* editions of *The Voice and Speech Review*, She received her MFA in Acting from the University of Minnesota and has held university teaching posts at Ithaca College, the University of Mississippi, and the American University in Cairo. Prior to her teaching career, Krista was Co-founder and Associate Director of The New Tradition Theatre Company in St. Cloud, MN.

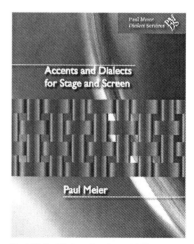

Paul Meier Dialect Services, 2007

eBook Review *by Elizabeth van den Berg*

Standard British English:
a Dialect Instruction System for Actors and Others
by Paul Meier

An eBook By Paul Meier
Paul Meier Dialect Services 2006

Elizabeth van den Berg has works as a dialect and vocal coach in the Washington DC Metropolitan area. Her work has recently been heard at the Olney Theatre, Signature Theatre, Studio Theatre, Kennedy Center, and Synetic Theatre. She is assistant professor of Theatre Arts at McDaniel College, where she recently directed *Urinetown: The Musical*. Over the summer she serves as Producing Artistic Director for Theatre on the Hill in Westminster, MD. She recently received a Kennedy Center Gold Medallion for her work with the American College Theatre Festival.

It's great that Paul Meier is bringing us into the 21st century with his use of the website IDEA (International Dialects of English Archives); his books that integrate the use of CDs, print, and IDEA; and now with this new e-book which makes it all accessible with just the click of a mouse. All you need is a computer with MP3 capability and a connection to the internet!

At my request, Meier sent me the book with download instructions provided and clearly laid out. It takes three downloads, unless you already have the International Phonetic Alphabet (IPA) fonts on your computer.

His introduction clarifies differences between "accent" and "dialect," and how the book uses the terms. He also nicely delineates the difference between foreigners speaking English with an accent, versus dialects of English. The subsequent chapter introduces the reader to Meier's "Seven Step Method" of learning Standard British English, giving the student a process for learning. Chapter Four explains the geographical, social, economic, and historical aspects of the dialect, giving the reader context for use on the stage.

Turning the "page" to the next chapter, I was delighted to find the playback device right at the top of the page. He reminds the reader that this is where you'd need to have the IPA fonts, and then delves right in to his "Signature Sounds," the first of his "Seven Steps." His voice is warm, friendly, and definitely accessible. He also addresses the fact that the actor's personal dialect may transform the way they hear/articulate the sound. In addition he mentions how a character's age or the time period in which the play is set may vary pronunciation. Chapter Six includes an examination of differences in tone, pitch and volume, pointing out characteristics of RP.

Mr. Meier leaves a very short pause after each practice sentence in Chapters Seven and Nine, but it's easy to hit the pause button at the top of the page. It becomes more difficult when the sentence is further down the page, as you have to scroll up to get to the button, and then you can't read the sentence. It's wonderful to be able to click directly to IDEA from the page, allowing for a variety of authentic speakers to listen to, although the transcription samples were not included in the eBook for ease of listening/reading.

I'm very impressed with this first eBook in what I hope will become a series. This will be extremely useful for the actor who finds out that she has an upcoming audition, because Meier can e-mail the book to you—even cheaper and faster than overnight mail! I was able to use it in a coaching session with an actor as I had it with me on my laptop—very convenient. I didn't have to find a CD player or dig to find the instructional pamphlet—it was all there with a click of the mouse.

DVD Review *by Claudia Anderson*

Laryngeal Teaching Series, Volume 4:
Compilation of Volumes 1, 2 and 3
created by Starr Cookman & Kate DeVore

The Laryngeal Teaching Series presents a view inside the throat, and shows speaking, screaming and singing as well as laughing, sobbing and noises a human being can make with the voice. Volume 4, a single DVD of 36 minutes, contains the three volumes, each of approximately 13 minutes, described below. In the first, *Inside the Voice*, a male voice takes on the character of the larynx and humorously demonstrates speaking, laughing, sobbing and animal noises. Volume 2, *Inside the Scream*, shows a voice trainer's larynx as she demonstrates the techniques she uses to scream in healthy and effective ways. Volume 3, *Inside the Singing Voice*, is devoted to different types of singers, and uses many different voices to demonstrate different "styles" of singing.

The Laryngeal Teaching Series is both informative and entertaining: excellent quality with clear video and audio. The style of presentation is upbeat and fast-moving, and never bogs down in excess explanation. The audience can learn a great deal about how the larynx produces sound by observing the actual physical actions of the larynx while the person/larynx is producing sound. The full series covers a great range of different sounds that the human voice is capable of producing. The section on screaming gives a useful amount of detail, pointing out the technical shifts the voice is making and the intent of the speaker. This section might serve as an introduction to screaming in a voice class, because the student hears the sounds and sees the throat respond to the speaker's intent. In Volume 3, the inclusion of different styles of throat singing as well as sounds from an operatic voice and a counter-tenor is important in demonstrating the extent of sounds the human voice can produce.

There are few weaknesses in the series, other than this viewer's desire for even more detail and definition. And since there is no agreement in the field as to what constitutes a "contemporary radio style," a "classical style," a "munchkin style," etc. perhaps each singer could describe his/her approach.

The series is very useful for acting students. Four classes of beginning acting students watched the entire 36 minutes of all three volumes with rapt attention and curiosity. They were entertained by its music and contemporary language, such as "cool" and "check it out," and after a momentary shock that they were looking inside a throat, they surrendered to its charm. The larynx is presented as a character in Volume 1, and the depth and amount of new information keeps their interest in Volumes 2 and 3. Besides giving them an anatomy lesson, the DVD sparked their interest in the variety and range of sounds their voices were capable of producing.

The Laryngeal Teaching Series is an outstanding tool for teaching voice and speech. It fulfills a need for technical information and audio-visual learning about the larynx in a unique and entertaining way. I would like to see many more volumes in the series.

Claudia Anderson teaches voice and speech at The Theatre School, DePaul University. She serves as production voice coach, helping students carry over their training into production. Coming to DePaul in 2000, she has been teaching in actor-training programs since 1984. A founding member of VASTA and past Board member, she is a designated Linklater teacher. She also studies with Richard Armstrong from the Roy Hart tradition. Current interests include singing and playing Irish/Scottish music, drumming and topics in teaching and learning.

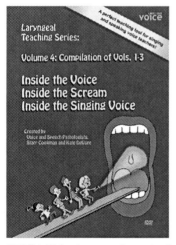

2006 Total Voice, Inc. www.loveyourvoice.com

Will Power: How to Act Shakespeare in 21 Days
by John Basil with Stephanie Gunning

Judylee Vivier heads the MFA acting program at Brooklyn College, teaching acting and voice to graduates and undergraduates. She received her MFA in acting from Tisch School of the Arts, New York University, as a Fulbright scholar, and an MA and BA Honors from the University of Natal, Durban, South Africa. In her native South Africa, Ms. Vivier worked as actress, educator, director, including work with Athol Fugard. She continues to perform in New York, most recently her original solo piece at the 78th Street Theatre Lab. Judylee has taught at many institutions including Rutgers, NYU, AMDA, and the Michael Howard Studios. She is member of the Board for the Voice and Speech Trainers' Association (VASTA).

Will Power is a useful guide for both professional actors and promising newcomers via a vigorous 21-day rehearsal process that culminates in the day of actual audition or performance. Very clear stepping-stones are laid out in the book that simply reveal Shakespeare's own directions. The book is practical, encouraging actors to get up on their feet in the first rehearsal, helping them to embody the text and acting clues from the start. Extensive hours sitting around the table analyzing the text can lead to intellectualizing the text which deadens the language as well as the actors' process of owning and speaking the text.

The undertaking to read this book was immediately met with a fleeting thought "…another book on how to act Shakespeare? What else can possibly be added to the library of books already covering the subject? What does John Basil have to add to that invaluable information?" And so I read on with a hint of misgiving since titles that include a time period "in 21 days," suggest a "quick fix" and fill me with apprehension. In the introduction, however, John Basil insists *Will Power* is not meant to be, "a Shake 'n Bake-style instant Shakespeare, nor is it easy Shakespeare."

Like a journey into a foreign land, John Basil structures this book as a very specific travel guide that leads the actor step-by-step through 21 sets of acting tasks. These tasks are divided into a detailed three-week daily rehearsal process that instructs and prepares the actor to uncover the distinctive layers of meaning in Shakespeare's language, to embody this information, and to use it in the process of acting Shakespeare. On day 22 the actual day of performance, he brings the book to a very sweet and neat close. Within this journey, John Basil introduces and reinforces the concept of the *7 Cs of acting*: commitment, concentration, conditioning, control, confidence, courage, and clarity while explaining how to perform these brilliantly crafted plays.

The first three phases of the book are separated as follows:
Phase 1 Map Reading: Secrets of Your Script Unfolded—leads the actor from day 1 through to day 8: each day covers an aspect of the written structure of the text such as punctuation, use of verbs, adjective/similes/ metaphors, and looks at a formula for persuasive rhetoric.
Phase 2 Scouting the Landscape: Going on Instinct, Getting Off Book—covers day 9 through day 12 offering the actor useful techniques for memorization.
Phase 3 Charting Your Course: Moments of Variety and Nuance—day 13 through to day 17, identifies Shakespeare's directions embedded in the text that demand the language/speeches to be spoken in a particular way that clearly illuminates the action and the intention.

Phase 4 Your Claim: Stanislavski's Approach is the treasure, the most unique and invaluable aspect of the book. Days 18 through 21 detail specific aspects of Stanislavski's method that allows the actor to fully own character and the need to speak. So often the actor becomes obsessed with the effort to make the language clear that they forget they are representing real human beings who experience strong desires and needs. In this chapter, Basil reminds the actor to "find and reveal the heart and soul" of the character and suggests ways to do that without falling prey to playing the emotion. A series of tasks establish the character's given circumstances. The language structures present discriminating information about the character, which encourages bold physical choices. He identifies five basic human needs: to survive, to love and to be loved, to seek validation, to seek happiness, and to win and be at the top of the heap. He highlights eight basic "doings" or pursuable goals that drive the character's emotional state and physical behavior and shows how to identify a goal(s) for a scene and select strong playable action verbs. Day 22 concludes the book by reminding the actor how to take care of himself on this high-pressured day.

Like Patrick Tucker and Neil Freeman, Basil works with the First Folio to highlight the acting clues and stage directions embedded in its idiosyncratic variations in the text, which are clearly defined and illustrated with text examples and activities related to the specific goals of that day's rehearsal.

This book is written from the perspective of a very experienced actor, director, and impassioned teacher; artful in the employment of his conversational but dynamic "voice," style, and obvious gift for teaching. Consequently the material is accessible, engaging, enlightening, and stimulating to actors of all levels of experience. And although much of the information is not new or surprising, what is unique is Basil's "director/teacher voice" that speaks clearly, persuasively, and passionately without the clamor of the ego. Very refreshing! The skills with which he equips actors are applicable to all heightened language, the Greeks, Restoration, Molière, Shaw, thus empowering actors to tackle any heightened text.

I started reading *Will Power* with some measure of qualm. In conclusion, I am completely persuaded and recommend this book highly as a refreshing read with a distinct "voice."

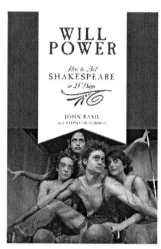

New York: Applause Theatre & Cinema Books, 2006

Book Review *by Marlene Johnson*
Speak the Speech! Shakespeare's Monologues Illuminated
by Rhona Silverbush & Sami Plotkin

Marlene Johnson directs, performs, and teaches acting and voice at University of Alabama Birmingham. She has vocal directed over 40 shows, including coaching at the Alliance Theatre, Theatre Virginia, and PA Stage. She has taught at Florida State, Virginia Commonwealth University, and a Shakespearean Acting class at the University of Westminster in London. She trained at American Repertory Theatre with Bonnie Raphael, Shakespeare and Company with Kristin Linklater, Canadian National Voice Intensive with David Smukler, National Theatre in London with Patsy Rodenburg, Terry Schreiber Studio with Terry Schreiber in NYC, and received an MFA from VCU and an MA from Miami University. She is Voice and Speech Chair for SETC and a past Board Member of VASTA.

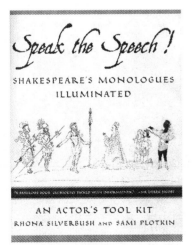

Faber and Faber, 2002

Speak the Speech is a comprehensive, actor-friendly book full of useful information. The authors have provided ample information in one text that combines monologues and historical, mythological, and literary background so the actor can make "confident, creative choices." The book, subtitled *Shakespeare's Monologues Illuminated: An Actor's Tool Kit*, elaborately fulfills its purpose to "illuminate acting options presented by Shakespeare's use of meter and other poetic and rhetorical devices."

Both Silverbush and Plotkin pay tribute to Alexander Schmidt's *Lexicon* (their "good friend") and other well-known works by C.T. Onions, Eric Partridge, Frankie Rubenstein, Caroline Spurgeon, and Dale F. Coye. They especially scoured the *Oxford English Dictionary* and studied numerous editions of every play. The result feels comprehensive and thorough while remaining focused on the actor, using a down-to-earth, humorous style.

The early portion of the book focuses on distinguishing features of Shakespeare's verse in such sections as "Cracking the Code," claiming scansion does not have to be academic or "scary" but is "just about noticing what Shakespeare did, and exploring how it benefits you as an actor." Silverbush and Plotkin include a discussion of metrical feet so that the actor can try to "make the shoe fit the foot." Rhetorical and sound devices are explained in the context of how they can inform acting choices. The authors frame potential options for the actor. It is like having a good director right in the room to suggest possibilities.

Finally, the "readiness is all" as the authors state "the tools explained here and applied throughout this book ready you for—and support—your basic acting work, rather than replacing it. Recognizing the elements contained in the text and knowing how to exploit them will heighten your ability to express your objectives and characterization, whatever method of acting you practice."

The book features 152 monologues each with extensive annotations and commentary. Each monologue contains a discussion of significant scans to help the actor with playing choices. The monologues are arranged by genre.

Other features include: a glossary of common archaic words, verb forms, elisions and contractions; handy charts including the genealogy of King John, a genealogy of the French monarchs and the English claim to the French throne; and a chart clarifying the War of the Roses. Humorous, informative side boxes appear such as "Aristocratic Self-Aggrandizement Run Amok" and "Dauphin, Dolphin, Same Thing." There is ample material on England and the theatre in Shakespeare's time. In future editions an index with terms used in the book would be helpful.

I found the book useful as I was coaching two Shakespeare productions. One of the book's side boxes explains, for example, four steps to marriage in Elizabethan times, including the custom of handfasting and how each "couple" in *Measure for Measure* is at a different level in the four steps, clarifying one of the sometimes puzzling problems of the play. The book is not a replacement for such standards as *Freeing Shakespeare's Verse* by Kristin Linklater and *Speaking Shakespeare* by Patsy Rodenburg, as well as works cited earlier in this review, but it is an important work and will be a useful addition to your libraries.

Book Review *by David Carey*

Pronouncing Shakespeare
by David Crystal

David Crystal is one of the most influential scholars of modern linguistics in the UK. The book under review is his personal account of his involvement in the Shakespeare's Globe production of *Romeo and Juliet* in the original pronunciation (OP), which was given three performances in June 2004.

In a very accessible way Crystal outlines the extent of our knowledge of Shakespearean English: on the evidence of the written form, the pronunciation of vowels and consonants and the rhythmic structure of words and lines have been largely established for some time; but it has been more difficult to establish intonation patterns or tones of voice. He observes that there can be no definitive OP because the historical linguist is forced to make many decisions, based on rhymes and puns for example, which might be challenged by other scholars. Crystal was asked to produce a partial phonetic transcription of the play, that is, only the words that differed in pronunciation from today were transcribed into OP. Even so, the transcription presented Crystal with a number of choices, and he discusses his reasons for choosing an informal and quick tempo style of pronunciation, and for representing generational and social differences between characters through differences in Elizabethan pronunciation of specific vowels, consonants and individual words.[1]

Crystal points out that OP is similar to modern accents such as American, Irish or Cornish, and he was concerned lest actors lapsed into an all-purpose stereotype. To accommodate this, a judgment was made at an early point in rehearsal "to let the actors colour the OP by their own natural accent (24)." He makes it clear that phonetic uniformity amongst the actors was never a goal of the production since this would not have been evident amongst Elizabethan actors either. But he accepted that there would be a need for "a kind of Elizabethan dialect coach (35)" who would breathe life into the phonetic transcription that he would provide. Consequently, the Globe contracted Charmian Hoare, a leading UK dialect coach, to work on the production.

The actors, who had already opened the modern version, were initially suspicious of the whole venture on the first day of rehearsal. Several reported various feelings of panic, but after Crystal provided a spoken example of the accent and talked through stylistic choices, they relaxed and were prepared to try it out. Charmian Hoare then took over the detailed coaching and, as a result of her work, the actors gained ownership of the accent and became a community of OP speakers. The process was like work on any accent, except that the actors only had three complete days as a company to bring it together—time for a read-through, a run-through on stage, and a final run-through in the rehearsal room before the first public performance.

Crystal describes this first performance as "electrifying" and "exhilarating." The audience reaction was very positive—OP seemed to be more accessible to many of them than modern RP. The actors, too, found a new accessibility: discovering fresh energies and interpretations, feeling earthed in the play more strongly and engaged in the characters' language more deeply.

Crystal's writing style is relaxed and informal, academic-lite but drawing on a deep knowledge of language. It is an entertaining piece of story-telling and provides fascinating insights into the Globe's artistic process. I can recommend it as a valuable addition to your Shakespearean shelves.

David Carey is Voice Tutor at the Royal Academy of Dramatic Art, London. He trained at the Royal Scottish Academy of Music and Drama, and has degrees from both Edinburgh and Reading Universities. David has worked nationally and internationally within higher education and the professional theatre, including 4 years as assistant to Cicely Berry at the Royal Shakespeare Company. As Course Leader of the Voice Studies course at the Central School of Speech and Drama he trained over 200 voice teachers from around the world. He recently coached at the RSC, the Oregon Shakespeare, and summer 2007 at the Stratford Ontario Festival.

1. A sample is available at www.shakespearswords.com. See also the Globe's own web site at www.shakespeares-globe.org/globelink.

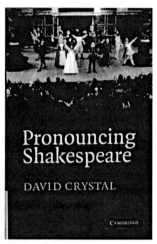

Cambridge University Press, 2005

2 Play Reviews *by David Carey & Mary Howland*
Troilus and Cressida by William Shakespeare
in Original Pronunciation
Directed by Giles Block, Shakespeare's Globe, London, 2005 Season

Review #1
By David Carey:

The OP experiment was repeated in 2005 when the Globe mounted an OP production of *Troilus and Cressida*, but this time the actors rehearsed in OP from the beginning—there was no modern English production of the play in repertoire as there had been with *R&J*—and they had a longer time to absorb the pronunciation. Crystal has written separately about this production in the Spring 2006 edition of the Globe's magazine *Around the Globe*, and I attended a performance of it in September 2005.

In his article, "Were you on your auditory mettle?," Crystal claims there are "three big pay-offs" to an OP performance. The first of these is what he calls the *frisson* of encountering the accent for the first time. I can certainly attest to this. As I sat on my rented cushion in one of the upper galleries of the theatre, my ears were already pricked at the anticipation of hearing something unusual if not unique, and when the Prologue to the play began I felt a shiver of delight as the language rang out across the wooden O. "In Troy there lies the scene. From Isles of Greece,/ the princes orgulous, their high blood chafed,/ have to the port of Athens sent their ships/ fraught with the ministers and instruments of cruel war…" It is a speech I know well, as it is an excellent piece of strong, muscular writing for students to work on; and it was thrilling to hear it in OP, which I would characterize as a tantalising mix of the wonderfully strange and oddly normal—unfamiliar pronunciations knocking up against almost contemporary sounds. At the end of the speech, the actor (Sam Alexander) had made a cheeky addition in iambic pentameter: "Attune your ears to Shakespeare's way of sounding." As we plunged into the play proper, my ears had to adjust to the quick delivery of less familiar language within an accent for which my brain had no strong reference point. Suddenly, it was like listening to an unusual dialect, or a foreign accent, or even an actor who isn't very secure in the accent of his character. Crystal describes this as the "auditory shock" at hearing the rapidity of OP for the first time. When listening to a well-known text, it's easy to tune in; but when the text is less familiar, you feel you have to really concentrate. Crystal observes that "one of the most noticeable things about an OP audience [is] the way they listen." While I wouldn't disagree with this, I would observe that concentrated listening can produce the contradictory result of not really absorbing the language of the play. You aren't drawn in if you are consciously listening all the time. But perhaps I was also distracted by *reading*—like many of the audience, I had brought a copy of the text to refer to, and found myself using it whenever I was thrown by an unfamiliar pronunciation. (Apparently, I was in good company.

Peter Forbes (Pandarus) and Juliet Rylance (Cressida) in *Troilus and Cressida* at Shakespeare's Globe, 2005. Photo by Stephen Vaughan.

John Lahr, in his review of this production for the September 10, 2005 edition of *The New Yorker* entitled "Talking the Talk," describes finding "only about thirty per cent of the production…comprehensible…I had to read along to get the full meaning…")

The second pay-off to an OP performance that Crystal identifies is "the way it can make you hear lines in fresh ways" because of the rhymes and word-play that become apparent in the accent. However, he admits that *Troilus* is not the best of plays for this aspect of OP—there are few rhymes and little word-play that are enhanced by OP—and suggests that the *Dream* would be a better example. I would positively agree, not just for this reason but because the *Dream* is a much more familiar play. The text of *Troilus* is challenging, some of the

Reviews and Source

2 Play Reviews of Troilus and Cressida *by William Shakespeare*
in Original Pronunciation, Shakespeare's Globe, London, 2005 Season by David Carey (continued)

scenes are particularly wordy and philosophical, and it is not regularly performed. It seemed a strange choice for an OP production, where the audience already has to attune themselves to a new way of listening before wrestling with a complex and cynical plot.

The third payoff that Crystal claims for an OP performance is "the way it makes the actors approach their characters." He cites the actor Philip Bird who, in playing both Hector and Calchas, found that the OP enabled him to differentiate the characters more strongly, as their characteristic OP vowel sounds took him to different places vocally. Crystal also quotes Penelope Beaumont, who played Ulysses and found that the OP "made [her] play him much more as 'one of the lads'" than she had expected. And Sam Alexander found that using OP liberated him from his "Shakespeare voice" and allowed him to feel the words as more alive in his mouth. I am sure all these discoveries are accurate reflections of the actors' processes, and I was impressed by Philip Bird's performances and Sam Alexander's vocal freedom, but the overall effect of the production was disappointing. According to Crystal, the reason that four women were given male roles in this production was that the director, Giles Block, "had to crowbar *The Winter's Tale* company into the very masculine *Troilus*." A similar ad hoc effect seemed to hang over the staging and some of the costumes, while some performances lacked emotional depth, suggesting that not enough time and money had been invested in the production. Crystal states that "*Troilus* produced some of the best OP I have ever heard," but as a theatregoer I wanted stronger production values to flesh out this particular version of the OP experiment. If the Globe were prepared to learn from both the *R&J* and *Troilus* processes and invest in a fully realised OP production of a play like the *Dream*, with time for both accent work and acting work, with a strong cast and effective direction, then an audience might find itself transported by a truly original theatrical experience.

Mary Howland studied English and Drama at Birmingham University, acted for a short while at the Birmingham Repertory Theatre, and then got her MA in Voice Studies in 2001 from the Central School of Speech and Drama. She has worked as a voice and accent coach for the BBC, Birmingham Rep, Nottingham Playhouse and other theatre companies, shows including *Glorious, On the Piste, Bill Hicks: a Slight Return* and *Volpone*. After five years as Head of Voice at the Birmingham School of Acting, she now works in London as an accent coach and voice tutor.

Review #2:
By Mary Howland:

The first thing I should probably get clear is that I have a huge admiration for the work the Globe has been doing, extending our understanding of how Shakespearean theatre works, and how that sublime space can inform performance styles of any age. I have been fascinated by the research into "Original Pronunciation"—at last there is a solid, academic and artistic rationale for not welding Shakespeare to RP.

I must also confess that my two fellow groundlings were somewhat tricked into hearing this show (at the Globe, one hears, rather than sees). A balmy evening of clear skies and a not-jam-packed courtyard lulled them into a false sense of security, producing a noticeably startled reaction, when the Prologue began "In Truy theer lays the sayne." Shakespeareswords.com, cited in the companion review, provides sound clips of Professor Crystal reading excerpts from *Romeo and Juliet* in this OP system. I hesitate to use the word "accent," because it was clear from the performance that the actors have found small variations of the patterns that allow for some regional variation—Irish, West Country, Yorkshire, etc. This is the first time a production will use this system for the whole of its run. Not that the Globe has ever insisted on "RSCRP" from its actors—at least not in the shows I have seen, with a Yorkshire Cassius, Welsh Mark Anthony, Scots Angelo, etc.—except where appropriate to the actor and character. The aim is to see what is gained or lost by performing Shakespeare in his own tongue, rather than that of 400 years later.

Of the overall production itself, there are a few things to note. The first is that a basic knowledge of the Trojan wars is useful, though the production in its story-telling is as simple and clear as the Globe does best—nothing added to the text, nothing taken away. The two warring sides are clearly denoted through costume, and while there is a lot of doubling up of smaller roles, characters remain defined through uniforms, the convention being set up by having the fight between Menelaus and Paris become a skilful piece of mimed self-assault. The blocking has the habitual fluidity that the Company has found works with those two great pillars, and scene changes are breathtakingly swift with minimal furniture, appropriate music and a change of energy being brought on with the new scene.

Another point should be noted before going on to the speaking. As most of us know, the Globe has a very open policy to gender casting, with all male and all female productions, as well as gender-appropriate. This production gives us something new. Aeneas, Agamemnon, Ulysses, Nestor are all played by women.

The thing I always love about watching shows at the Globe is how much even well known plays can still take audiences by surprise. I still remember the gasp in last year's *Measure for Measure* when Angelo says "Who will believe thee, Isabel?," and the spontaneous boo/hissing that accompanied his exit. Here, another gasp when Cressida brings out Troilus' sleeve as a token for Diomed, and various expressions of "just not cricket" outrage when

Reviews and Source

2 Play Reviews of Troilus and Cressida *by William Shakespeare*
in Original Pronunciation, Shakespeare's Globe, London, 2005 Season by Mary Howland (continued)

Achilles pulls a gun on the defenceless Hector (they're in modern dress, you see). It is a wonderful thing to be able to keep people on their toes who have been on their feet for two hours already!

So, on to the speaking. I must admit, it did take a little getting used to—professional habit getting the better of me, so I was slightly more absorbed in "Oh, so the fricative is made plosive, is it?" than fully following the story. And I will admit that it probably took till a good half hour in before I fully got into the patterns and, inevitably, some actors found a way of placing the sound changes to keep the speech clear. And when it was not clear, it did become difficult to understand—though that is surely as applicable to RP as to any accent or pronunciation. However, the reactions of the audience (not all of whom were native English speakers) showed that it was accessible; indeed, one friend said that he hadn't realised how many jokes were in the text.

What was supremely evident was that the actors were not imposing this speech system onto the text: there was no sense of awkwardness about it, or it holding any performance or characterisation back. I wouldn't go so far as to say that the OP became unnoticeable, but it rapidly became irrelevant, because we were too involved in the story and characters. My expectation before the performance was that it might come across as a historical experiment—clinical, academic, Shakespeare that you can't understand and therefore must be good for you. But the artistic team appears very wary of becoming Stratford on Thames, and therefore the opposite seems to be happening—they have as authentic a theatre as British Health and Safety laws will allow, their wardrobe department will never use Velcro when a few dozen laces will do, the music and dances are authentic, and now even the speaking is a replica of four hundred years ago—yet the plays are livelier, more robust and engaging than I have seen in a long time.

What is lost by using OP? Yes, a certain amount of understanding, but I do not think this is due to the OP itself, but to *how* it is used, otherwise all the characters would be unintelligible, and this was not the case. The OP is not preventing any character/actor from feeling the joy/pain/grief/terror of the situation they may be in.

Does one lose *poetry*? Here perhaps I might say yes, insofar as you could never imagine Gielgud speaking OP. But is that a bad thing? Perhaps we could look at this as a gain— something in the vowel sounds seems to put a hold on artful musicality. There is

something very *practical* about this way of speaking, which certainly helped Ulysses—those long speeches that could so easily become meandering rivers of voice beautiful, lulling one to sleep, here became business-like, rational, a means to an end—intention behind the words uppermost. And the inverted clauses and phrase structure somehow sound less contrived and "clever" and therefore less intimidating. The Anglo-Saxon elements of the language seem to be highlighted, creating a sense of something very grounded and secure, truthful and heartfelt. So often we are given a general sense of a rather wispy emotion on which floaty streams of words ride. Here, we receive the character's pain or joy through what they say, rather than how they say it. I couldn't honestly say that the sound of OP is beautiful, but it is certainly livelier than most RP Shakespeare I have heard—and how ironic is that!

So, is OP the way forward? Will it become the "Arrr–SC" as opposed to the "Ah–SC"? I doubt it, and personally I do not think it should be so. What the Globe has given us is the chance to experience not just the conventions, sights and surroundings of Shakespeare's plays but the sounds of them as well. Even a 400 year-old speech system can live when connected to *such* written words, especially when those words had that sound in the author's head. To be given the chance to *hear* what those original groundlings heard somehow closes that gap of time, and makes the play fresher and more immediate than trying to give it contemporary relevance by setting it on, say, a council estate. These actors at the Globe sounded like real people, even though the OP is a construct. They do not sound like actors wishing to be admired for their diction and ability to sustain the breath over four lines of verse; they sound like nervous lovers, dirty old men, devious politicians, anxious soldiers—and that surely is the most important thing?

David Sturzaker (Troilus), Peter Forbes (Pandarus) and Juliet Rylance (Cressida)in *Troilus and Cressida* at Shakespeare's Globe, 2005. Photo by Stephen Vaughan.

Selected Thesis and Dissertation Abstracts

Edited by Karen Ryker, Associate Editor

Editor's Note:
The following abstracts are provided as a service to help researchers and interested readers stay abreast of current thesis and dissertation work in the field of the voice and speech. The papers themselves have not been read or vetted by the Journal editors. Material submitted to this department may be edited for space and style

Title: **Singing My Story: The Roy Hart Theatre Work And The Fitzmaurice Voicework In Tandem**
Author: Elizabeth Allen
Type: Master's Performance Thesis
Year: December 2005
Institution: New York University's Gallatin School of Individualized Study
Faculty Advisor: Laurin Raiken

This Performance Thesis is comprised of four basic parts: a background history essay, a technical essay, an artistic aims essay and an appendix with two interviews.

The background essay looks at how I was personally introduced to the unique vocal pedagogies of Roy Hart Theatre Work and Fitzmaurice Voicework as well as how these two artists, Roy Hart and Catherine Fitzmaurice, both developed their groundbreaking techniques at the same time and in the same place—London, England in the 1960s. Both Catherine and Roy studied in traditional acting conservatories and then went on to perform and teach what they found there as well as push boundaries when they combined classical acting and voice techniques with the studies of the modern psychologists Wilhelm Reich and Carl Jung, respectively.

The artistic aims essay focuses specifically on the key concepts I have studied and then implemented as an actor, singer and voice coach. My own philosophy of voice has come into being with the creation of this text together with the essential concept of my emerging pedagogy, The Mother Tongue. This is not only a metaphor for the native language I speak but also a way to examine the flux and terrain of vocal improvisation.

The technical essay examines my personal practice of singing, writing and acting in performance as well as the preparation involved in mounting a creative work for the stage.

In the appendix I have included two interviews from 2005 with the teaching artists, Jonathan Hart Makwaia and Rosemary Quinn.

Title: **Fitzmaurice Voicework: Constructing the Holistic Actor**
Author: Michael Keith Morgan
Type: PhD Dissertation
Year: 2006
Institution: University of California at Santa Barbara
Faculty Advisors: Simon Williams, Judith Olauson, Leo Cabranes-Grant, Joanna Cazden

Traditionally, the actor's voice-training arena in the United States has been based largely in a preponderance of European and American theories. Many of the most prevalent approaches to voice for the actor have been examined in this western insularity. But, increasingly, the influences of other cultural traditions are gaining tenancy in many western venues, including university dramatic art departments. These cultural convergences offer opportunities for fertile dialogues that may generate new and expansive creative outcomes in the laboratory of the classroom and the playing field of the theater. These transactions, however, do not always occur without tensions, as diverse cultural disciplines seek balance between fluid intercourse and maintenance of traditional integrity.

This study examines how one relatively undocumented approach, which is gaining popularity in actor training venues across America—Fitzmaurice Voicework—addresses the tension of intercultural dialogue in dramatic art. The study will observe how Fitzmaurice Voicework provides theoretical and working interchange between Reichian therapy and bioenergetics from the West, along with yoga and shiatsu from the East. Through historical and theoretical documentation, the research will show that Fitzmaurice Voicework's innovative terminology—destructuring and restructuring—interfaces with the fundamental program of synthesis that provides foundation for bioenergetics, yoga, and shiatsu. The study looks at how the cultural tensions are resolved through incorporating an element of creative chaos in this psychophysical approach to voice that shifts structural and mental blockages via breath and energetic flow, pulling from both eastern and western disciplines.

The result of this research will demonstrate that Fitzmaurice Voicework is potentially poised in the vanguard of voice training to offer a solution to the East/West dichotomy encountered in theater pedagogy. The theory that it purports has global and holistic possibility for the actor, giving a wide palette for play and vocal expressiveness.

Title: **Training Actors with Speech Differences**
Authors: Irene Pauzer and Lori Holmes SLP
Type: Research Project
Year: 2005-6
Institution: Ryerson University, Toronto, Canada

How can voice and speech teachers in theatre programmes negotiate the time, expertise and money required for a student actor requiring speech language therapy?

This project has been a two-year and ongoing development of an investigation into an interdisciplinary model with a voice and speech teacher and a Speech Language Pathologist to aid students with speech differences. This model is being developed as a cost-effective and time-efficient way to facilitate teachers working with these students in a proficient manner and allowing these student actors to become the vocal athletes that the professional theatre and performance world require.

Title: **Lessons of Vocal Coaching Shakespeare in Hollywood: A Production Analysis**
Author: Deborah Thomas
Type: MFA
Year: 2006
Institution: Virginia Commonwealth University
Faculty Advisor: Janet B. Rodgers

This thesis is a personal narrative of my experience as vocal coach on a production of Ken Ludwig's *Shakespeare in Hollywood* directed by BT McNicholl and performed in the Raymond Hodges Theatre of Virginia Commonwealth University in November 2005. Chapter one covers my identification of the play's vocal and aural challenges; what I did to prepare for those challenges; the research I gathered on 1930s Hollywood prototypes for the play; an examination of Shakespearean verse, especially that in *A Midsummer Night's Dream* and how Ludwig synthesized Shakespeare's verse with that of his own. Chapter two is divided into an account of the rehearsal process; a description of my sessions with the individual actors and an exploration of the dynamics of the vocal coach-director relationship. Chapter three focuses on the finished production and summarizes my response to the experience.

Title: **Following the Fear: Developing Long Form Improv Techniques for the Teaching of Voice Work in Actor Training**
Author: Kara Tsiaperas
Type: MA Voice Studies
Year: 2006
Institution: Central School of Speech and Drama
Faculty Advisor: Joe Windley

This analytical enquiry examines the relationship between voice and improv, in order to investigate long form improv techniques in the voice training of the actor. Although various forms of improv has been incorporated into actor training programs, this research will specifically focus on the techniques of long form improv and its applications to voice training.

Grounded theory is being used in an art-based research context in order to allow a theory to emerge, as opposed to testing a theory. Both grounded theory and improv rely upon the similar principle of allowing, a theory or in the latter case a story, to emerge. Research conducted in New York and Chicago included: participating, performing, interviewing, observing and reading relevant literature. Participation included full-time improv training for two weeks, performing in two improv shows and a weekend's workshop with Chicago improvisers. Observations encompassed attending long form improv shows in both New York and Chicago. Interviews and reading relevant literature emerged from the fieldwork of interacting with the New York improv world, and to a lesser degree the improv world in Chicago.

There are three main aspects of improv that emerged that could be developed by the voice teacher. First, there is breathing through the uncertainty of non-scripted improvisations; second there is the use of patterns that tap into the subconscious; and third there is the opportunity for actors to expand upon their habitual vocal choices. The emerging theory is that these elements of improv could be taught in voice training in order to assist actors with breath work, text work and vocal exploration.

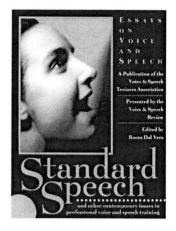

Title: Standard Speech and other contemporary issues in professional voice and speech training presented by the Voice and Speech Review
Editor: Dal Vera, Rocco
Date: 2000
ISBN: 1-55783-455-5
Publisher: Voice and Speech Trainers Association, Incorporated, Cincinnati, OH
Description: The official journal of the Voice and Speech Trainers Association containing 55 articles on a wide variety of issues in professional voice and speech use and training, many centered on the topic of standardized theatrical dialects. 332 pages, 8.5" x 11", paperback.

Title: The Voice in Violence and other contemporary issues in professional voice and speech training presented by the Voice and Speech Review
Editor: Dal Vera, Rocco
Date: 2001
ISBN: 1-55783-497-0
Publisher: Voice and Speech Trainers Association, Incorporated, Cincinnati, OH
Description: The official journal of the Voice and Speech Trainers Association containing 61 articles on a wide variety of issues in professional voice and speech use and training, many centered on the topic of vocal use in staged violence. 338 pages, 8.5" x 11", paperback.

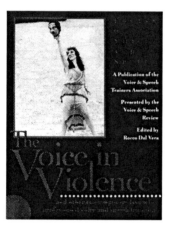

Title: Film, Broadcast and e-Media Coaching and other contemporary issues in professional voice and speech training presented by the Voice and Speech Review
Editor: Dal Vera, Rocco
Date: 2003
ISBN: 1-55783-522-5
Publisher: Voice and Speech Trainers Association, Incorporated, Cincinnati, OH
Description: The official journal of the Voice and Speech Trainers Association containing 67 articles on a wide variety of issues in professional voice and speech use and training, many centered on the topic of coaching actors for performances for the camera and microphone. 334 pages, 8.5" x 11", paperback.
Library of Congress Catalog Card Number: 00-106487

Title: Shakespeare Around the Globe and other contemporary issues in professional voice and speech training presented by the Voice and Speech Review
Editor: Rees, Mandy
Date: 2005
ISBN: 0-9773876-0-7
Publisher: Voice and Speech Trainers Association, Incorporated, Cincinnati, OH
Description: The official journal of the Voice and Speech Trainers Association containing 78 articles on a wide variety of issues in professional voice and speech use and training, many centered on the topic of coaching actors to speak Shakespeare. 397 pages, 8.5" x 11", paperback.

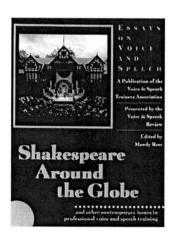

Breinigsville, PA USA
30 April 2010
237101BV00002B/4/A